PENGUIN ENGLISH LIBRARY

ENGLISH MYSTERY PLAYS

Peter Happé read English at Cambridge and afterwards took a Ph.D. at Birkbeck College, London, with a thesis on Tudor drama. He has published an edition of *The Winter's Tale*, and has edited *Tudor Interludes* and *Four Morality Plays* for the Penguin English Library. He is now Headmaster of the Rutland Sixth Form College.

English Mystery Plays

A SELECTION

*Edited with an
introduction and notes by*
PETER HAPPÉ

PENGUIN BOOKS

Penguin Books Ltd, Harmondsworth, Middlesex, England
Penguin Books, 40 West 23rd Street, New York, New York 10010, U.S.A.
Penguin Books Australia Ltd, Ringwood, Victoria, Australia
Penguin Books Canada Ltd, 2801 John Street, Markham, Ontario, Canada L3R 1B4
Penguin Books (N.Z.) Ltd, 182–190 Wairau Road, Auckland 10, New Zealand

First published by Penguin Books 1975
Reprinted 1980, 1984

Copyright © Peter Happé, 1975
All rights reserved

Set, printed and bound in Great Britain by
Cox & Wyman Ltd, Reading
Set in Monotype Fournier

Except in the United States of America,
this book is sold subject to the condition
that it shall not, by way of trade or otherwise,
be lent, re-sold, hired out, or otherwise circulated
without the publisher's prior consent in any form of
binding or cover other than that in which it is
published and without a similar condition
including this condition being imposed
on the subsequent purchaser

Contents

Introduction	9
A Note on Books	36
Acknowledgements	40
The Pre-Reformation Banns of the *Chester* Cycle	41

The Plays

1. The Fall of Lucifer [Chester 1] — 49
2. The Creation, and Adam and Eve [Ch.2] — 62
3. The Killing of Abel [Towneley 2] — 79
4. Noah [T.3] — 97
5. Noah [Ch.3] — 118
6. Abraham and Isaac [Ch.4] — 133
7. Abraham and Isaac [Brome] — 152
8. Moses [York 11] — 172
9. Balaam, Balak and the Prophets [Ch.5] — 188
10. The Parliament of Heaven, the Salutation and Conception [Ludus Coventriae 11] — 207
11. Joseph [L.C.12] — 221
12. The Nativity [L.C.15] — 230
13. The First Shepherds' Play [T.12] — 244
14. The Second Shepherds' Play [T.13] — 265
15. Introduction to The Three Kings [Y.16] — 295
16. The Adoration [Y.17] — 298
17. The Flight into Egypt [T.15] — 311
18. The Purification, and Christ with the Doctors [Ch.11] — 318
19. The Death of Herod [L.C.20] — 332
20. The Shearmen and Tailors' Play [Coventry] — 343
21. John the Baptist [Y.21] — 381
22. The Temptation of Christ, and the Woman Taken in Adultery [Ch.12] — 388
23. Lazarus [T.31] — 400

CONTENTS

The Passion Play I	409
24. The Council of the Jews [L.C.26]	411
25. The Last Supper [L.C.27]	432
26. The Betrayal [L.C.28]	456
27. The Buffeting [T.21]	465
28. The Dream of Pilate's Wife [Y.30]	484
29. The Scourging [T.22]	507
30. The Crucifixion [Y.35]	525
31. The Death and Burial [Y.36]	537
32. The Harrowing of Hell [Y.37]	552
33. The Resurrection [T.26]	567
34. Christ's Appearances to the Disciples [L.C.38]	592
35. The Ascension [Ch.20]	607
36. Pentecost [Y.44]	616
37. The Assumption and Coronation of the Virgin [Y.47]	625
38. Judgement Day [Y.48]	631
Notes	647
Glossary	695

Introduction

I

THE cycles of the English mystery plays which are represented in this anthology are one of the chief glories of late medieval literature. They are the most comprehensive achievement of dramatic inspiration in their times, successful in their dramatic effects, and powerful in their literary expression. To give a sample of them is to offer an insight into one of the great literary achievements of the past, and one which had immense formative influence on the work of later dramatists. However, they remain, for the modern reader, distinctively medieval, requiring an act of historical imagination to give them life, and to allow them to be fully appreciated.

Such an appreciation is complicated by the fact that the authors of these plays had for their primary objective not a literary intention so much as a religious and didactic one which they attempted to realize by means of dramatic expression. The real achievement of these authors could only be appreciated by experiencing a performance in medieval times, when it appears the efforts of whole cities were expended in their realization. Fortunately in modern times there have been attempts to revive the cycles in performance, and though these performances cannot recreate completely the original circumstances, much has been done to make the original achievement more accessible.

It needs to be stressed that the plays were, in their most successful periods, produced in the form of cycles. We know that a large number of medieval towns and cities possessed cycles and we know that in several of these there were performances of the whole cycles at regular intervals, besides performances of individual plays for special occasions. The survival even of records of performances, let alone of actual texts, is a matter of pure chance, but it is clear that for about two hundred years a very considerable amount of money and talent was employed in producing the cycles. Nothing survives of the plays of the following, though records indicate considerable

INTRODUCTION

activity: Aberdeen, Bath, Beverley (a full list survives), Bristol, Canterbury, Dublin, Ipswich, Leicester, Worcester, and possibly Lincoln and London[1]. Individual plays have been preserved from cycles at Norwich (one play in two versions), Northampton, and Newcastle upon Tyne. Two plays have survived from the Coventry cycle, and from Brome in Suffolk we have the *Abraham*, which may have been part of a cycle. How closely each of these presumed cycles resembled the texts of the surviving cycles is a matter of conjecture. The Beverley list, it is true, indicates a close resemblance to the two other Yorkshire cycles but the Cornish cycle (originally written in the fourteenth century, and preserved in a fifteenth-century manuscript) is either incomplete or atypical since it does not deal with the Nativity. The London plays also appear not to have followed the design of the cycles.

Our knowledge of the cycles, then, rests chiefly upon the four texts which have survived. These are virtually complete and are the main source from which the present selection is made[2]. Two of the four, those of York (forty-eight plays) and Chester (twenty-four plays), are well supported by other civic documents and must remain our best insight into the place of the cycles in the life of the medieval cities from which they come. There is less detail available for the *Towneley* cycle (thirty-two plays) which comes from Wakefield in Yorkshire. The fourth cycle is known as the *Ludus Coventriae* (forty-two plays) from an early attribution which has long been known to be false: the cycle does not belong to Coventry, the balance of the linguistic evidence being for an East Midlands origin. Thus what remains is a considerable bulk of plays, though there is good reason to suppose that very many more have been lost. The cycles we have show a remarkable and consistent similarity which leads to important conclusions about origins and interrelationships to which we shall return later.

II

Before considering each of the cycles in turn it is important to state that the similarities of general design are great indeed. The plays were

1. E. K. Chambers, *The Mediaeval Stage*, Oxford, 1903, Vol. II, Appendix W, pp. 329–460.
2. For editions of the texts see Note on Books, p. 36.

INTRODUCTION

written as part of a theological message, and were intended, no doubt, to be an act of teaching and worship combined. Such were the vigour with which they were executed, and the popularity which accrued to them that many other minor objectives grew up: but essentially the plays were meant to celebrate the Christian story from the Creation to Doomsday, with two central peaks in the Nativity and the Passion of Christ. All four of the cycles do this, and all four are arranged with roughly similar emphasis upon the great climaxes of the Christian story.

The *York* cycle is represented by one manuscript, British Museum Additional MS 35,290. This manuscript was written in the years 1430–40, and saw service as the official register of the plays for over a century. The origins of the plays at York, as in the case of the other cycles, are obscure. There is an early reference for 1378, and it is generally supposed that from this date a series of plays was in existence and was regularly performed. We may take *York* as typical of the other cycles in saying that the development is fascinatingly complex, and our information for judging the rate of growth of the cycles is tantalizingly sparse. The city of York is distinguished in having other dramatic activities at the end of the fourteenth century, for we know that there were plays dealing with the Creed and with the Pater Noster[3]. The cycle as we have it took several decades to grow; and no doubt it went on changing. The manuscript gives some evidence of this by the fact that some plays were copied into it after 1440, and is particularly interesting in that by the mid-sixteenth century changes stemming from the Reformation and the decline of the old religion led to alterations in the manuscript. Especially relevant to the rate of growth and the changes that were made are the lists of plays written by Richard Burton in 1415 and shortly afterwards. These lists contain over fifty plays, so that a process of combination and deletion had already begun by the time our copy of the plays was made.

One important aspect of the growth of the plays which must be touched on is the question of revision. Whatever the state of the cycle when it was first performed, it is clear that it could not exist indefinitely in that state. The most significant aspect of this is that the guilds who were responsible for the performances were not stable

3. Chambers, op. cit., pp. 403–6.

INTRODUCTION

institutions. New guilds came, others declined, amalgamations became necessary in a number of cases. Sometimes new versions of the plays had to be evolved because of these changes, so that the text is now uneven in its literary merits. There seems to have been one particularly effective writer who re-wrote the Crucifixion sequence with a realism and terror not found elsewhere in the cycle. The evidence of the metrical characteristics is a valuable indication of where revision has taken place, and so too is the presence of an alliterative style which is the work of a considerable poet.

The questions of growth and revision are equally complex in the *Towneley* cycle. It is written, like the *York* plays, in fifteenth-century Yorkshire dialect (many of the expressions are still astonishingly alive today) and its close affinity with the *York* cycle cannot be doubted since six of the plays are virtually the same in both cycles (Pharaoh, Christ before the Doctors, Christ Led up to Calvary, the Harrowing of Hell, the Resurrection, and the Last Judgement) and there are a significant number of other identical passages. The manuscript, HM1 in the Henry E. Huntington Library, California, is thought to have been written in about 1450. Its name derives from the Towneley family of Burnley in Lancashire who kept it for many years. The attribution to Wakefield, though not entirely free from objection, is fairly reliable in that the name Wakefield appears at two places in the manuscript. But the only references to performances at Wakefield are for 1554 and 1556: it is clear from these that the plays were indeed craft plays, and the manuscript itself mentions the names of several guilds.

If the manuscript is 1450, and the only known performances are 1554 and 1556, the date when the cycle first came into existence is obscure. It has been thought, from the correspondences with the *York* cycle, that originally the citizens of Wakefield must have borrowed that text and gradually made it their own. The complications to this view are that some plays in the *Towneley* cycle appear less sophisticated, more primitive than the *York* counterparts, and also that some *Towneley* plays are much more complex than those of York. The explanation is probably that after the borrowing of the text, the process of revision at York went on (before 1430–40?) whilst at Wakefield some revision was carried out, though the plays which were chosen for revision were not necessarily the same in

INTRODUCTION

both cycles. The principal reviser of the *Towneley* plays is the so-called Wakefield Master who worked on six plays, *Mactatio Abel, Processus Noe cum Filiis, Prima Pastorum, Secunda Pastorum, Magnus Herodes,* and *Coliphizacio*. His work is chiefly in a nine-line stanza, and exhibits a fine sense of dramatic effect, especially comedy. He is a poet in his use of language which is potent and subtle, and he is without doubt one of the most gifted of writers for the stage. His revisions have been dated in the first half of the fifteenth century, but there is no way of being more specific. His work, whilst it exhibits a sense of human comedy and pathos, shows much evidence of being that of a learned man – at least, one might say, a clerk who has been educated by the Church.

The *Chester* cycle was formerly thought to be the oldest of the four extant cycles, but this view cannot now be substantiated[4]. It seems likely that it first appeared around 1375, which corresponds roughly with what we know of the *York* plays. There is some evidence of relationships between the *Chester* and other known plays, but the manuscript position is very much more complicated. Five complete versions of the cycle exist[5], but they were all written very late, when the plays had ceased to be performed. The most reliable of these appears to be British Museum Harley MS 2124 of 1607, though two others were written a decade earlier. Two plays have survived independently: *Antichrist*, probably a prompter's copy from 1475–1500; and *The Trial and Flagellation*, copied in 1599[6].

The background information available from municipal records is perhaps more complete than at York and it is possible to reconstruct the development of the *Chester* cycle in more detail. We know that a play existed in about 1375, and that by 1422 plays were being performed by the guilds. Various references provide evidence that they continued to perform them throughout the fifteenth century. By 1467 eight guilds were certainly producing plays, and the early Banns which were first written at that date, and subsequently enlarged, give evidence of eighteen guilds. By 1500 the number of guilds had risen

4. F. M. Salter, *Mediaeval Drama in Chester*, Toronto, 1955, pp. 40–42.
5. Details in Chambers, op. cit., p. 407.
6. F. M. Salter, 'The "Trial and Flagellation": a new manuscript', in *Chester Play Studies*, ed. W. W. Greg (Malone Society Studies), 1935.

INTRODUCTION

to twenty-four, and the early Banns, enlarged by 1540, detail twenty-six. The Reformation produced some pressure on the production of plays, and the late Banns (1575) show that there were twenty-four plays. It is possible that the original author may have been Sir Henry Francis, but there is very little that can be adduced to make this certain. Various other writers no doubt contributed to the development of the cycle subsequently, but their work is not easy to isolate. There is no evidence of the work of able dramatists such as are found at York and Wakefield contributing a personal style. Indeed the cycle is characterized by few hints of individual genius.

The *Ludus Coventriae* (also known as the Hegge Plays, and the N-town Cycle) has survived in one manuscript, British Museum Cotton MS Vespasian D viii, written entirely by one scribe and dated 1468. It is distinct in having no evidence that it was performed by guilds. Nor has the place of its origin been discovered. The language is East Midlands, and though Lincoln has been suggested, some of the linguistic forms indicate that it must have been written south of Lincolnshire[7]. Some of the staging arrangements are so complex as to suggest that it must have been performed in one place rather than as a procession of pageants.

The text is prefaced by a Proclamation which gives details of what is to come, but when this is compared to the contents of the cycle, there appear a number of discrepancies. It looks as though the scribe was acting as a compiler, and that one of the materials he had before him was the Proclamation which he tried to fit in, but he found that a perfect match could not be made. Much of the material appears broadly similar to the other cycles, though one does not find close verbal correspondence with them.

Certain features are peculiar. The stage directions are very full. Some are in Latin, and the plays in which these appear have been held to be the oldest layer of composition, relics perhaps of an earlier cycle which the scribe incorporated. Besides this, three parts of the cycle have special features. The plays dealing with the Passion of Christ are grouped into two Passion Plays which were intended to be used as alternatives from year to year. Why this arrangement was devised remains a mystery. It does not seem to have been the idea

7. M. Eccles, '*Ludus Coventriae*: Lincoln or Norfolk?', *Medium Aevum* 60, 1971, pp. 135-41.

of the scribe: evidence suggests that the two Passion Plays had an independent existence, and that he incorporated them perhaps because they were the only material he had to hand. The stage directions are entirely in English in this part of the cycle, and there is a specially written Prologue. Another section of the cycle used apocryphal material which makes up a Saint Anne's Day play not found in the other cycles. The possibility is that this part was performed by a guild of Saint Anne. The Assumption of the Blessed Virgin Mary appears in the cycle as a separate item, distinguished from the rest in style, paper and handwriting. It bears corrections by the scribe who wrote the rest of the manuscript, and this too comes from an independent source. But the interest in Mary is echoed in other parts of the cycle, and it has been suggested that these too come from separate sources, probably two in number, and were incorporated by the scribe as he compiled the cycle.

Thus the *Ludus Coventriae* is of particular interest. In one sense it shows that the compiler was aware of a structure typified in other cycles, but that the material which he had available made it necessary for him to make special arrangements to combine the various items into a cycle which is not, in the end, as close to the other cycles as they are to each other. Special interests in the life of Mary may have dictated his arrangements, but we have no way of knowing whether this was a deliberate act of selection, or purely a matter of chance depending upon what material happened to be to hand.

All the cycles bear much evidence of theological learning – they were the products of the ecclesiastical *milieu* in which they were created – but the *Ludus Coventriae* is more learned, more consciously the work of a religious scholar, than the rest. This fact, together with the unusually full stage directions, has led some modern scholars to believe that the text of the cycle is really meant to be read rather than performed. This does not mean that it is not dramatic, but that the text as we have it has been presented in a literary form. The compiler, whoever he was, was not working with the same objectives as the scribes of the other cycles, who were probably, at some stage or other, working as the servants of the corporations and making a master copy for reference, and as a means of controlling the performances. Thus the *Ludus Coventriae* does not seem to have been subjected to pruning to meet the requirements of post-Reformation

INTRODUCTION

theologians and politicians. Nor was this scribe or compiler working purely as an antiquarian. The concern he feels for his material is that of a teacher: this accounts for the use of the *Contemplacio* figure, and perhaps too for the hint of morality play technique in the *Death of Herod*.

To complete this rather brief review of the texts of the cycles as they have come down to us, it is appropriate at this point to consider two other items for which a place has been found in the present selection: the Coventry *Shearmen and Tailors' Play* and the *Brome Abraham*.

The Coventry plays were perhaps the most famous in England in the fifteenth and sixteenth centuries. On several occasions in the fifteenth century there were royal visits to performances. The first mention of the plays is for 1392, and the songs were added to the manuscript as late as 1581. Only two play texts from the cycle have come down into modern times: the *Shearmen and Tailors' Play*, which was published by Thomas Sharp in 1817 and 1828, and was destroyed by a fire at the Birmingham Free Library in 1879; and the *Weavers' Play*, which Sharp published in 1836, and which then disappeared until Hardin Craig rediscovered and published it in 1902[8]. The manuscripts were written in 1534 by Robert Croo, who was paid for work on the texts of plays at various times over twenty years.

There is some further evidence about the nature and development of the cycle at Coventry to be found in municipal records. It appears that the cycle contained fewer plays than was generally the case. Although seventeen crafts are mentioned in the Leet Book in 1445, other records indicate that there were only ten pageants, and that the guilds combined regularly to perform them. It is not easy to show that any of these dealt with Old Testament subjects, though the probability is that some did. The number of stations for the performances was also unusually small, perhaps only four.

Both the existing plays are longer than plays in other cycles and they contain more incidents. The *Shearmen and Tailors' Play*, for example, combines two plays. The first deals with the Annunciation, the Nativity, and the Visit of the Shepherds. This is linked by a

8. H. Craig (ed.), *Two Coventry Corpus Christi Plays* (1902), 1957, Early English Text Society.

INTRODUCTION

dialogue between three Prophets to the second and longer sequence, which comprises the Visit of the Kings, the Flight into Egypt, and the Slaughter of the Innocents. The texts are very mixed as to metre, which suggests very considerable revision – not surprising if Croo was working on material going back at least one hundred and forty years. One of the metres is similar to that of most of the *Chester* cycle. It has been established that there is some close verbal similarity between the Doctors episode in the *Weavers' Play* and the same episode in the cycles. It is quite close to *Chester* but the nature of these similarities makes it impossible to establish which came first. It is likely that the *Towneley* version is older, and it may be that this goes back through the *York* play as it once existed to an older version from Northumberland. Such a link gives an important indication of the origin of the cycles, and we shall return to it later.

There is no certainty that the *Brome* Abraham is part of a cycle, and there are no indications in the text to suggest that it was eve performed by a craft guild. But it is similar in general terms to plays in the cycles, and the text is very close for some two hun lines to that of the *Chester* Abraham. These factors justify its in sion in the present selection.

The manuscript is part of a commonplace book, *The Book Brome*, which was started as a collection of moral and religious items and then passed to other scribes who added material of a quite different nature, some of it legal documents. The part of the book which contains the play has been dated 1450–75[9]. It originated at Brome in Suffolk and, until recent times when it went to the Yale University Library, it remained in the locality and for most of the time in the possession of a local family. The scribe had some difficulty with rimes and in several lines the word order has been changed. It is probable that he was attempting to restore the rimes of his exemplar, but that at times he was unable to do so, or was daunted by the complexity of his task. The similarity with the *Chester* play mentioned above has been much debated. The most convincing argument recognizes the superiority of the *Brome* version in general terms. It is likely that the writer of the *Brome* version (presumably not the scribe himself) used an original which

9. N. Davis (ed.), *Non-Cycle Plays and Fragments*, 1970, Early English Text Society, Supplementary Text No. 1, p. lxii.

INTRODUCTION

was also the original used by the writer of the *Chester* play. The latter author was, however, less careful and thorough in his work, or perhaps his version of the original was less reliable.

It will be seen that there is a considerable body of cyclic drama from which the editor may select. Though much has been lost, we are able to form an impression of this dramatic achievement which is based upon reliable data. Let us now look more closely at the origins and development of the cyclic drama.

III

The historical account of the mystery plays which follows makes no claim to be original. It is rather an attempt to survey the field of knowledge as it now stands and to put the many speculations which have arisen over the origins of the cycles into some sort of perspective. The question of origin is a thorny one because there are few [facts] to go on, and there is no convenient chronicler who thought [it worth] while to record the steps by which the cycles came into [existence]. Nevertheless the subject has great fascination, partly [because] of its complexity, and it is worth attempting to penetrate [the] obscurity, or at least to indicate where the obscurity lies.

In the survey of the existing manuscripts above, it has already been mentioned that there is a reference at York to the play in 1378, when a fine was levied on the Bakers. The Guild Book at Beverley refers to 'pagentes' in 1377, and it is thought that the *Chester* plays originated in about 1375. The *Coventry* plays are first mentioned in 1392. These dates indicate that plays were in existence: when they were composed is quite another matter. Before the last quarter of the century there are two significant factors which contributed to the development of the cycles. The first is the existence of liturgical plays in a number of ecclesiastical centres. These dramatic episodes were played as part of the liturgy of the Church and strictly related to the time in the Church's calendar when they were performed. They were enacted inside the Church building. The *Regularis Concordia* of St Ethelwold from the eleventh century shows how the coming of the three Marys to the sepulchre and their encounter with the Angel were to be represented at Mattins on Easter Day by four brothers suitably costumed. The words they were to use were in

INTRODUCTION

Latin. In the *Shrewsbury Fragments* of the early fifteenth century we find the same subject, *Officium Resurrectionis*, in a text which is in Latin and English. The first of these fragments, *Officium Pastorum*, containing the lines of the Third Shepherd and his cues, is very similar to the *York* play on the same subject and this probably indicates that there was a common source. Two points thus emerge. One of the sources of the *York* cycle lies within the liturgical drama and it is possible to suppose that this may be true of some other plays in this and other cycles. Secondly we do not know how widespread the liturgical drama was (much, though not all, of the available evidence comes from the Continent), nor whether it had any pretensions to being cyclic in form. It appears rather that the liturgical drama remained within the Church, and was maintained by the clergy, using Church music and perhaps vestments for its performance. We are probably right to look for other sources for the idea of cyclic form.

This brings us to the second important influence upon the formation of the cycles, the establishment of the Feast of Corpus Christi. This was established at the Council of Vienne in 1311, and by 1318 it was widespread in Europe and in Great Britain. The Feast was celebrated by a procession of religious organizations who visited churches and holy places. It occurred on the Thursday after Trinity Sunday, and quickly attracted the attention of craft guilds, as well as stimulating the establishment of Guilds of Corpus Christi. It is notable that the Feast had no specific reference to the calendar of the Church, unlike other Feasts which by tradition had their own liturgical offices with quotations from scripture, appropriate music and dramatic episodes. There was no story or episode associated with Corpus Christi. The fact that the Feast occurred in June meant that the day was long and it no doubt gave opportunity for elaboration of the public ceremonies, and there seems to have been something very deliberate about the establishment of the Feast which may have led to the concentration of dramatic episodes on that day. The Feast celebrated the completion of the sacrifice of Christ, which was reached annually on Trinity Sunday. In view of these factors it seems likely that it was decided to present the story of Christ from Adam and Eve to Judgement Day, but this is a supposition which can only be supported from probability. It is true that other cyclic

INTRODUCTION

performances have been discovered on the Continent, but what we have to suppose, without any proof, is that someone had the idea of concentrating various elements around the Corpus Christi procession. Whether this was the same person as the one who first actually composed a play is open to conjecture. Probably the growth was gradual from about 1318 through the middle years of the fourteenth century. Perhaps we are right to suppose that what happened is a kind of group invention whereby a number of people associated with the procession arrived, by experiment, at a workable arrangement.

Even more intriguing than the problem of who were the creators of the cycles is that of where it all happened for the first time. As it is unlikely that they were created in one blow, it is also unlikely that they were created in one place. Yet the surviving cycles do seem to suggest that the North of England is the more likely area, and the various exchanges of material which we have noticed so far seem to suggest a process whereby the successful achievements of one area were taken over by another, though such exchanges would not always be in one direction.

The nature of the earlier layers of the cycles may give us an important clue here. They were undoubtedly the work of writers working within the orbit of the Church. The close correspondence of *Shrewsbury Fragment I* and the *York* play shows that one writer at least was intimately connected with the Church. There is a tradition at Coventry that the authors were Friars. This is probably not very reliable, but it may help us to see that the Church must have influenced firmly though indirectly the nature of the material that went into the cycles. The earliest plays were not just invented, they were derived by a scholarly process from what was already well established and well known. They are also very concentrated: extraneous matter from other sources seems on the whole to come in later. Thus it is reasonable to suppose that the men who had the greatest formative influence might have been secular clergy, perhaps priests associated with guilds.

Indeed, it is the guilds which made the most practical contribution to the development of the cycles. They were often rich, and it seems that the fourteenth century was a time when they rose in civic importance. The organization of the cities depended largely upon the interrelationships of the guilds and the prosperity which they were

INTRODUCTION

able to achieve. The guilds no doubt strove with one another for a place of influence in order to protect their interests. Perhaps through the Corpus Christi processions it became necessary to assert importance by the carrying of banners and emblems, and the parading of liveried members in their groups. It seems likely that in this process is to be found the important change from clerical to lay actors. As soon as records of the cycles begin it becomes clear that the players were guild members, and that considerable obligations were laid upon the guilds by the corporation to ensure that their members took an active part in the plays. There is even a regulation at York which restrains actors from playing in more than two plays.

As time went on the corporation and the guilds retained their authority. They made arrangements for performances, arranged for storage of carts and their good order. Changes in status of individual guilds required official adjustment so that guilds could amalgamate or separate. Rehearsals and other preparations came under their control. Thus the cycles were essentially amateur productions, associated with the prestige of the city and calling upon vast resources of men and materials to maintain standards. Sometimes there were complaints about the burdens on guilds, and sanctions had to be applied to keep dilatory guilds up to the mark. But there seems little doubt that the intensity of the amateur commitment contributed to the popularity of the cycles and enabled them to grow and develop for perhaps two hundred years.

The guilds had to maintain the text of their plays, and it is here that one may suspect that the Church (and the State) maintained influence on the plays. There had been objections to religious drama for some time from within the Church, and some modern writers on the subject have felt that the movement from within the Church buildings to the streets of the town was partly a rejection by the Church authorities of a rather unruly offspring. This theory is now discredited as the main impulse leading to the development of the cycles, but the assumption of responsibility by the guilds was no doubt very convenient for the Church in as much as civic control was asserted over the crowds, and additional monies were made available, always provided that the resulting drama maintained and supported religious experience. This happened through the

21

INTRODUCTION

agency of the scribes and the writers who maintained the texts for the guilds. Many of the revisions of the cycles took place after the cyclic form had been evolved, and the revisers continued to use scriptural and homiletic material which was approved by the Church and available for their use. Though there may be a humanizing process discernible in the work of the revisers, there seems little doubt that, like Chaucer, they wished their work to remain in line with the teachings of the Church.

With amateur actors, a 'secretariat' in the hands of the minor clergy, and substantial financial backing, there was a basis for continuity in the presentation of the cycles. One further important formative influence was the use of the English language. The fourteenth century is the time of Chaucer, Langland, and the poetry of the north-west represented by *Sir Gawayne and the Grene Knight* and *Pearl*. For the first time, if one may be permitted a generalization, the English language was a means of literary expression of the first rank, even though it was still under the powerful influence of regional dialects. It was in this century, too, that John of Trevisa noticed that grammar schools were using English as a means of instruction. The fact that the performance of the mystery cycles was in the hands of common labouring men meant that English had to be used there too. The language acquired a new status in the community, and there seems little doubt that the development of the cycles was part of this process. Only in some stage directions, and in certain scriptural quotations which amplify the texts do we find Latin regularly used. If common men used the language, they would also invent, and so we may suggest that the common actors in this way were able to contribute directly to the texts as they evolved. This is not to overlook the contributions of the dramatic poets we have already mentioned: it is noticeable in the case of the Wakefield Master that the vigour of everyday language plays an important part in the effectiveness of what he writes.

To conclude this account of the origin and development of the cycles we must raise two issues which were important in their history. In general the cycles were referred to as Corpus Christi plays, and this is true even in the records of a number of towns whose plays have not been recovered. It appears that plays were usually performed on the Feast of Corpus Christi. This was certainly so

INTRODUCTION

at York, though there are records of attempts to move them to other days, perhaps because of the difficulty of mounting the whole cycle on a day when time had to be found for religious ceremonial. The same difficulty seems to have occurred at Chester. There the plays were performed at Corpus Christi until possibly 1447, when they are recorded at Whitsun. There is little to go on at Wakefield beyond a strong probability that they were given at Corpus Christi. We also know that there were performances on that day at Newcastle upon Tyne, Coventry, Dublin, and Hereford. Whatever the difficulties of presentation, it is certain that the cycles became generally known as Corpus Christi plays even when they were moved to other days. The reasons for this lie in the tradition which they established, and in the main religious objective, which was never forgotten, to celebrate the Eucharist.

The second issue is really a *caveat*. In considering the cycles we must beware of seeing them as ever being in a definitive state. Because they were always changing to meet changes in the community year by year, we may correctly say that the cycles never existed in a perfect form. The first contributors can have had no idea what their work was to become as it was used by later generations. Even in the case of the York manuscript, which was an attempt to produce a reliable register, we can see that changes were constantly being made, even in minor ways as new words and expressions are interlined. The provision of alternative versions of individual plays in the manuscripts is a further indication of this, as in the two Shepherds' plays of the *Towneley* cycle.

The cycles were finally suppressed because they were contrary to the new doctrines of the Reformation[10]. In the last years of Henry VIII and the reign of Edward VI we find revisions, particularly the omission of plays on the Assumption and Coronation of the Virgin. The reign of Queen Mary and the revival of Catholicism saw a return to the old ways for a time, but in the time of Elizabeth I there was a determined attempt by the ecclesiastical authorities to make it more difficult for the plays to appear. This was done at York and Chester by calling in the books for revision, and prolonging the examination until it was too late to put a performance in hand. That the suppression was in the hands of the Church itself is an indication

10. H. C. Gardiner, *Mysteries' End*, New Haven, 1946.

INTRODUCTION

that it was a political change working through the new Protestant hierarchy. It was a change not generally welcomed by the corporations of the North, but it was brought about in spite of them. The last recorded performance of a complete cycle seems to have been at Coventry in 1580. The *Chester* cycle was last performed in 1575, and the *York* in 1569. Subsequent attempts at revivals of the cycles were unsuccessful, and there is evidence of very considerable official criticism of those who promoted them. It is interesting to note that the *Mystères*, the medieval French plays which correspond in some ways to the English mystery cycles, were also suppressed at the Reformation, by an enactment of the Parlement de Paris in 1548, and that they too were destroyed whilst they were still enjoying great popularity[11].

IV

The subjects which are dealt with in the mystery cycles are an important factor in making a choice of them. In this section it is intended to look at the principles underlying their subject matter, and to consider briefly some of the sources which the compilers relied upon.

If the central assumption regarding the origins of the cycles is correct – that the establishment of the Feast of Corpus Christi gave both a religious and civic opportunity for their development – it follows that the celebration of the Passion of Christ is the chief object of these plays. Around the betrayal of Christ, his Death and Resurrection are centred the essential truths of Christianity. Upon this depends the Eucharist, and the possibility of man's redemption. Even the liturgical drama, which preceded the establishment of Corpus Christi, placed emphasis upon these episodes, and it is natural that the authors of the cycles adopted them. Most of the remaining items in the cycles can be related to the Passion, as foreshadowing it, or revealing its consequences.

The items which the authors chose to include show a remarkable

11. L. Petit de Julleville, *Histoire de la Langue et de la Littérature Française des Origines à 1900*, Paris, 1896, tome II, p. 420. The French plays were not connected with craft guilds, and the arrangements for performance were different.

INTRODUCTION

consistency in the four cycles and in the Beverley list[12]. These are

The Fall of Lucifer
The Creation and Fall of Man
Cain and Abel
Noah and the Flood
Abraham and Isaac
Moses (not Beverley)
The Prophets (not Beverley; Balaam at Chester)
The Nativity – Annunciation, Suspicion of Joseph, Shepherds, Purification, Magi, Flight into Egypt, Massacre of the Innocents
The Baptism (not Chester)
The Temptation (not Towneley)
Lazarus
The Passion – Conspiracy, Judas, Last Supper, Caiaphas, Condemnation, Crucifixion, Lament of Mary, Death
The Resurrection and Ascension
The Assumption and Coronation of the Virgin (not Towneley)
Doomsday

That the English mystery cycles are so consistent is particularly fascinating since we find that the French *Mystères* show a rather different choice, giving space to Joseph and Job from the Old Testament. This may cause us to suspect that the origins of the four cycles that we have (and of Beverley) may lie very close together. Be that as it may, the English selection is determined by the intention to represent the important episodes of scriptural history which prefigure the life of Christ. Much of what might have been included is omitted; what is there seems to be chosen to illustrate the central theme of Christ's sacrifice and the redemption of man. Thus the death of Abel and the sacrifice of Isaac foreshadow the Crucifixion. The Fall of Lucifer anticipates the Fall of Man, and this in turn is echoed by the Temptation of Christ. The Flood and Doomsday are related. God's Promises run through Noah, Moses, the Baptism and the Harrowing of Hell. The Prophets remind us of the Annunciation and the Nativity. The many correspondences of this type cannot

12. See Chambers, op. cit., pp. 321–3; V. A. Kolve, *The Play Called Corpus Christi*, 1966, pp. 33–100.

INTRODUCTION

here be followed in detail; indeed it is possible that the many complexities of cross-references are not fully accessible to modern scholarship. But this theory provides an insight into why the plays take the form that they do. The cycles depended for their structure on their capacity to suggest a totally organized cosmos in which the individual man might know his own salvation. To present a picture of such a universe required that the authors make a purposeful selection of the events in the Christian narrative rather than attempt to encompass its entirety. So powerful were the principles underlying the selection that we find very little deviation from it in the long period of time when the cycles were being actively enlarged and performed.

The sources of these principles lie in the homiletic literature which was the inheritance of the clerkly authors. There has been a good deal of work on individual authorities which appear to provide source material, in terms of the narratives themselves, the language which was used, and the theological implications of what was to be enacted. The main source for narrative is the Vulgate, but a wide variety of paraphrases and collections of apocryphal material was also available. Thus the *Gospel of Nicodemus* provides a good deal of material for the sequences about Pilate in the *York* cycle, particularly in the Trial, and in Pilate's Wife's Dream. There is also evidence that the Harrowing of Hell owes something to the same source. One of the most widely known collections was the *Northern Passion* which was translated from the French in the early fourteenth century and which was widely circulated. The Passion group of plays at York is partly based upon it. At Chester two possible sources are of particular interest. Manuscripts of the *Stanzaic Life of Christ* were copied at Chester in the fifteenth century, and the poem seems to have influenced plays dealing with the Purification and the Temptation, though the influence was felt in revision rather than in the original composition. There are also some close parallels with *Le Mistère du Viel Testament*. These have occupied scholars for some years[13]. The problem is partly that the French plays exist in a printed edition of 1500, which is too late for the original composition at Chester: but this does not exclude the possibility that the imitation or translation occurred earlier.

13. H. Craig, *English Religious Drama of the Middle Ages*, Oxford, 1955, pp. 171–8.

INTRODUCTION

The chief importance of the bulk of the source material, however, lies in the indications it gives of the purposes of the original compilers and of the revisers who sought to translate the teaching of the Church into a dramatic form which could be appreciated and performed by the laity. It is further evidence that the Church never lost its interest in the cycles.

V

Let us now look at some of the technical considerations which arose in the production of the cycles. This means that we shall have to deal in generalizations because of the long period during which the cycles were performed: what may have obtained at one point may not have been continuous throughout.

The civic records of York and Chester show that the plays were performed on pageant carts[14]. These were expensive to make and maintain, and special arrangements had to be made for their storage. The guilds bore the financial burden, but it was often so great that several guilds would share the same pageant cart, which would appear several times in the course of the performance. This happened at Chester, where the performance was spread over three days.

It must be admitted, however, that this would require a fair amount of organizing since the carts were decorated and elaborated to represent several places simultaneously. We are hampered as to the general appearance of the carts, and to their size. Some had six wheels, and at Coventry they were moved by horses. They almost certainly had a closed space which would be used as a dressing room[15].

The scenes which the plays demand must have presented a considerable challenge to the ingenuity of those building the carts. Several plays call for an upper layer from which angels might descend. The episode of the Last Supper implies an upper room and a council chamber simultaneously. Graves and tombs were sometimes asked for, as well as a multiplicity of courts and meeting places where two or more actions might go on at the same time. The records of

14. For a challenge to the accepted view that the York performance was processional, see A. H. Nelson, *The Medieval English Stage*, Chicago, 1974, pp. 15–81.

15. For a reconstruction of the pageants see G. Wickham, *Early English Stages, 1300–1660*, vol. 1, 1300–1576, 1959, pp. 172–3.

INTRODUCTION

scaffolds at York and Chester are an indication of a possible solution to these complex problems. In one case these had wheels and this means that they could be taken around the streets and set up close to the pageant carts themselves, so enlarging the acting area. Guild accounts show considerable expenditure on paint and carpentry, which suggests that the carts were adapted to provide various kinds of framework for the actors, perhaps not unlike the floats in a modern carnival or Lord Mayor's Show. Indeed the skills necessary for many types of civic procession in medieval cities could have benefited the presentation of plays.

The question of mobility is a very important one. We note that expenditure was often necessary on new axles for the carts, and there is also provision for soap to grease the wheels. At York and Chester we have lists of stations where the plays were performed. The routes can still be traced through the streets of these cities with reasonable accuracy. The number of stations varied from time to time, especially where they were in front of the private houses of important and ambitious citizens. We shall return later to the implications of the processional nature of the performances, but it is important to note here that one of the effects was that a very large number of people could see the plays as they waited at the stations while the pageants passed over the route. The audience was static and most people probably stood during the performance of the episodes. However, in the case of the stations which were established in front of the houses of citizens of repute, the upstairs windows would become a prized vantage point, and it appears that seats placed there could be used by important visitors such as the royal parties which viewed the performances from time to time.

Besides the furnishing of the carts, the accounts of the guilds list expenditure on clothing. Some of it appears to be ecclesiastical – copes (cloths of gold, red velvet), albs, stoles. There is also payment for masks – for devils presumably – and for gloves. Individual costumes, particularly Pilate's which was no doubt very expensive, were sometimes paid as a separate item. The splendour of this character, and perhaps of the important ecclesiastical figures like Annas and Caiaphas, who were probably mitred, may have made protection against the weather a necessity. The pageant carts were partly roofed, providing some shelter.

INTRODUCTION

The performances obviously required a good deal of preparation. Besides work on costumes and the pageant carts, and the rehearsing, there was an official statement of the intention of performance. At Chester there was both a Proclamation setting up the legal requirements of peace and good order, and Banns which described the contents of the plays, possibly for the benefit of the actors as well as the audience. The Riding of the Banns was a procession in itself, with representatives of the guilds in their costumes. The Banns were called through the city, perhaps establishing the route of the main procession and clearing the way for it. If one looks at some of the narrower places in the medieval streets of York and Chester, one gains the impression that to move large pageant carts through them might be a difficult operation: a preliminary check on the route might therefore be very functional, as well as having the effect of increasing expectation. Special payments were made to those who actually read out the Banns.

In conclusion, we must notice that the *Ludus Coventriae* is different from the other cycles in being arranged for a static performance. There is no evidence that it was processional. The idea of simultaneous action in a number of 'houses' or locations which was used to a limited extent on the pageant carts of York is extensively elaborated, particularly in the Passion Play. We should note that the French tradition with the *Mystères* in the fifteenth and sixteenth centuries calls for many locations arranged around the acting area: at Mons in 1501 there were as many as seventy locations. There is no doubt that although the processional performances of most of the cycles had distinct advantages, the extensive use of simultaneous staging in the *Ludus Coventriae* shows a movement towards a more complex kind of dramatic effect.

But whether the performances were processional or static, the length of cycles is astonishing. At Chester it took three days to perform the whole cycle. At York, where there were forty-eight plays, the cycle was performed on Corpus Christi day, sometimes displacing the procession. Because of the size it was necessary to assemble the actors at 4.30 in the morning so as to make the best use of the hours of daylight. It is small wonder that in both cities there are records of payment for food and drink for those taking part.

INTRODUCTION

VI

In attempting a critical evaluation of the cycles the modern reader faces two difficulties. The first is the length of time during which they were evolved and performed. With so many different authors or compilers, it becomes impossible to use the critical standards which might be applied to the coherent work of one dramatist. The process of composition was one of translation, accretion, adaptation, revision. With very few exceptions the plays lack the stamp of an individual creating mind. The second difficulty is that the works have no critical theory – no poetics. As far as we know none of the authors wrote anything about his work. There is no attempt to justify, explain, or theorize. The only early writings about the plays are the administrative documents of the corporations and guilds, and the notes of a few antiquarians at the end of the sixteenth century. The absence of contemporary criticism may be an accident of oblivion, but the plays themselves give us little evidence of literary theory. The emphasis in the Banns is rather didactic and expositional, and the authors would not have considered themselves as artists, or poets, or dramatists.

In spite of all this the modern reader has to consider the plays as literature, and indeed it is possible to do so, if one at first takes full account of the religious objectives of the authors.

As we have seen there is a strong possibility that those who worked on the texts were clerics. The sources which they used were the devotional literature which was available to them. Most of the source books which we know about formed part of the wealth of medieval literature which was devised to train and support the priesthood and others who lived a life of devotion. Some of the works were rather more popular or encyclopaedic in type, perhaps reflecting the need to cater for some whose educational standard was low. The outlook of the authors as far as we can determine it is conservative. There appears to be little attempt to break new ground, the intention being to present the essential truths of Christianity, with the implication that these were settled and apparent. A brief comparison with Chaucer is useful here, for he too is conservative as far as religious doctrine is concerned, though he is quick to seize upon abuses. But Chaucer shows us what the dramatists did not do. His sources were literary, and he ranged widely over secular and religious writings in English, French, Latin, and Italian, and though he was never wildly revolutionary his work breaks new cultural and intellectual ground, even to the extent that he occasionally seems to want to draw back.

If the truths are self-evident, then the purpose of the authors is to display them. Spokesmen like the Expositor and Contemplacio point out the significance of what is performed, and act as a link between episodes. The authors aim to reveal the Divine, and this involves worship, which the plays often are. They celebrate truths, and show how divine promises are made and kept. The action and speeches of characters in the Old Testament plays continually point to Christ who is yet to come.

The Redemption implies the corruption of man, a theme which is elaborated throughout, from the Fall of Adam to the wickedness of Herod. Indeed the corruption of man is much emphasized. We see jealousy, pride, wrath, ambition. Man appears ignorant, lost, wrong-headed. The divine figures, as well as the prophets, angels and disciples, are in contrast, and offer reassurance and hope. The plays raise the terror of sin and death, and in many places they show the sufferings of man. Even the personal sufferings of Christ at the Crucifixion are seen in human terms.

There are many hints that the authors intended to reach all ranks of society. One feels, and the evidence of the performances supports this, that the plays were written on the assumption that society was unified and hierarchical and that all men in their ranks should mark the message that was being sent. This affects the types of character which are included.

In stressing these religious objectives we have already begun to consider some of the literary aspects which are now as important. The overall structure supports and maintains the didactic elements. One of the most striking effects of seeing even a modern performance is the sense of purpose which is communicated. Because the cycles contain humour, pathos, suffering, as well as the culminating magnificence of the Crucifixion and Resurrection, one derives a sense of coherence. A comparison with the architecture of medieval cathedrals seems appropriate when we are considering overall design. For often we find in these buildings a sense of completeness, even though the chapter house is built in a different style from the

INTRODUCTION

west front, and the spire has been burned down twice. Perhaps the key to this comparison lies deep in the medieval ethos: the certainty that the individual and his particular and personal efforts are part of a whole. In the cycles the quasi-chronological sequence contributes to this, and one must remember that in composing the cycles the authors left out many biblical and legendary episodes which could not be fitted into their design.

Besides this structural power, one must also consider the dramatic strength of many of the episodes. One notices particularly the ability to centre a play on a striking episode which has a powerful visual impact. The dove that re-appears with the olive branch in its beak, the empty tomb, Christ walking with his disciples unbeknown to them: these are incidents which though traditional in story are given powerful visual emphasis. They are shown in spite of the technical difficulties they must have presented. The determination to do this is astonishing: how could the Red Sea be made to divide before the eyes of the spectators? Yet the story would not be dramatic without it happening, and such was the style of drama that the difficulty was solved. The solutions which were found for this kind of difficulty were not realistic: indeed there is a remarkable disregard for realistic enactments. The dramatic impulse of the cycles works in quite another manner. Just as ages pass in the twinkling of an eye, so the elements, the locations and the buildings are incorporated in the performances in a forthright and simple way.

Perhaps the easiest approach for the modern reader is through the psychological realism of many of the characters. Yet it is important to note that this comes about partly because the didactic impulse led the authors to devise ways by which the audience could identify with the characters. Many examples of the problems of everyday experience are to be found. Noah's wife is famous for her railing, but there are other places where the comedy which arises from tension in human relationships is used. Joseph's anxiety about his young wife is a case in point, and so too are the relationships between Cain and Abel and between Pilate and his wife. The social criticism presented by the poor shepherds gives vent to the resentment felt by the common man in hard times. The proud and ruthless tyrant, exemplified by Herod, is the object of bitter ridicule. In these characterizations the attitudes of the audience are directed and strengthened and the

INTRODUCTION

conflicts which surround the biblical stories are elaborated, sometimes from the merest hint in the source.

But this process is not confined to the comic. The wretchedness of Abraham, torn between his desire to serve God and his love for his son (a child in the *Brome* and *Chester* plays), has the beginnings of a tragic dilemma. Though the cycles never touch the matter of romantic love, there are many other occasions when human feelings are strongly aroused. The cruelty of the Tormentors in the Crucifixion is sharpened by their calculating skill, and their feeling of success when their work is effectively done. Often the destructive impulses which the action embodies are pointed by the savage enjoyment of it. Particularly effective here is the joke played on Christ in the Buffeting, and the soldiers' cruelty in the Slaughter of the Innocents. Even the fear of death is shown in the Death of Herod, where Mors carries off Herod in an incident reminiscent of the Dance of Death. Often, as in these episodes, the realism is related to an appreciation of the violence in man.

In characterization there are a number of important successes: Pilate, who is often viewed sympathetically, Mrs Noah, Mak and Gill, Cain, Annas and Caiaphas, and Herod whose ranting became proverbial. There are lively and cheeky servants like Jak Garcio, one of the character types who was to be elaborated in later drama. Particularly effective are the groups of characters who react to momentous events, the Shepherds, the Kings, the Torturers, the Devils. These are not always distinguished as to individual characteristics, but they provide an effective commentary, and are an important feature in the drama of display.

Much has been written of the work of the Wakefield Master. He is unquestionably the most able of the writers, and the most accessible for the modern reader because he offers an individual's view. His embittered social criticism and his dramatic use of symbols and parallels make him a powerful voice. In these and other respects he extends and enlarges the work of his predecessors. The mock nativity, the sheep in the cradle, which is a punning reference to the Lamb of God, and the scene in which the sheep is discovered are beautifully plotted, and written in a language which exploits the poetic possibilities of everyday speech. The speech is sharpened and concentrated by irony and proverb, and is essentially dramatic in its

INTRODUCTION

peculiar appositeness to the apparent and the symbolic meaning of what is enacted. Important too is his reliance upon material from the folk games. Here he brings into the religious drama an expression of reverence and vitality which is other than the purely Christian. In this respect we feel again that he was in close contact with the world of man.

But however important the Wakefield Master is, his work is but a small part of a rich achievement. His writings are very much within the orbit of his fellow authors. Though he may have seen the world more sharply and responded to it with greater literary subtlety, his world is the same as that of the other authors. The power of Christ's Incarnation is expressed in his work, and the vitality and variety of life are seen in the light of the Redemption.

VII

In making the present selection from the cyclic plays a number of considerations have been borne in mind. It seemed desirable to offer as full a collection as possible: there is one set of Banns and some thirty-eight plays. If, as was suggested above, it is possible to find common ground in the structure of the cycles, it seemed best to offer a selection here which would include all the incidents which are common to the extant cycles; and this, with a few minor exceptions, is what has been done in the composite cycle which follows. This is the only authority behind the selection, apart from the editor's personal preference for one version over another. No claim is made that the resulting collection is related to the protocycle which some critics have thought lies behind the original composition. Indeed it does not seem that there is a case for a protocycle: as we have seen, the process of composition probably operated quite differently.

It has been possible to select plays so as to give some other results. Some long sequences have been included from the individual cycles: the first five plays from *Chester* are here, and so is the Passion Play I from the *Ludus Coventriae*. The work of the Wakefield Master and the York poet are represented. Some parallel versions of the same episode may be compared: *Chester* and *Towneley* Noah, and *Chester* and *Brome* Abraham. It has been possible to include the Coventry *Shearmen and Tailors' Play*, which gives a strong contrast

INTRODUCTION

with Nativity sequences from *Towneley* and *York*. Again it is possible to see work from different dates: the earliest is probably part of the Coventry play.

Such a collection, then, is a personal choice, but there may be some justification for it when we remember that for all the cycles it is difficult to say what the definitive form was.

The texts which are printed here are treated conservatively. There is not much choice as to which to follow, except in the case of *Chester*. Where possible the texts have been collated with the manuscripts or with photocopies of them, and as few changes as possible have been made with regard to spelling. Indeed, a great deal of editorial conjecture has been disregarded. Brackets are used to indicate departures from the manuscripts. Modern punctuation and capital letters have been supplied, obsolete letters have been transliterated – with some odd-looking results in one or two places – and the modern conventions for 'u' and 'v' have been followed. All the original stage directions have been included, and some additional ones supplied in brackets. Each play is prefaced by a brief note giving details of the date of composition, where it can be supposed, and other general matters.

Difficult words are explained at the foot of the page on their first appearance, and sometimes I have repeated the explanations. A list of these explanations, arranged alphabetically, is at the end of the volume. Fuller explanations of individual phrases and other notes are numbered and printed after the last play.

A Note on Books

The bibliography of the mystery plays is a vast subject. The most comprehensive attempt is that by Stratman (revised in 1972). He tries to cover the very large amount of unpublished material on the plays, much of it being in the U.S.A. I give below a list of the works which have been of most help to me in preparing this selection. The place of publication is London, unless otherwise specified.

1. TEXTS

i. The Four Cycles

Chester

British Museum (B.M.) Additional MS 10,305.
B. M. Harley MS 2124 (generally regarded as the best text).
B. M. Harley MS 2013.
Bodley MS 175.
Devonshire MS.
The Chester Plays, ed. H. Diemling and Dr Matthews, Early English Text Society (E.E.T.S.) (2 vols.), e.s. 62, 1892, and e.s. 115, 1916.
The Chester Mystery Cycle, a facsimile of Bodley MS 175, ed. R. M. Lumiansky and David Mills, Leeds, 1973.
The Chester Mystery Cycle, ed. R. M. Lumiansky and David Mills, E.E.T.S., s.s. 3, 1974.

Ludus Coventriae

B. M. Cotton MS Vespasian D viii.
Ludus Coventriae, or The Plaie Called Corpus Christi, ed. K. S. Block, E.E.T.S., e.s. 120, 1922.
The Corpus Christi Play of the Middle Ages, ed. R. T. Davies, 1972.

Towneley

Huntington Library MS HM1.
The Towneley Plays, ed. G. England and A. W. Pollard, E.E.T.S., e.s. 71, 1897.

A NOTE ON BOOKS

The Wakefield Pageants in the Towneley Cycle, ed. A. C. Cawley, Manchester, 1958.

York

B. M. Additional MS 35,290.
The York Plays, ed. L. Toulmin Smith, Oxford, 1885 (repr. 1963).

ii. Collections

Chief Pre-Shakespearean Dramas, ed. J. Q. Adams, Boston, 1924.
Everyman and Mediaeval Miracle Plays, ed. A. C. Cawley, 1956.
Two Coventry Corpus Christi Plays, ed. H. Craig, E.E.T.S., e.s. 87 (1902), 1957.
Non-Cycle Plays and Fragments, ed. N. Davis, E.E.T.S., s.s.1, 1970 (contains the Shrewsbury Fragments, Norwich Grocers' Play of the Creation, Newcastle Play of Noah, Northampton and Brome Plays of Abraham).
Le Mistère du Viel Testament, ed. J. de Rothschild, Société des Anciens Textes Français (6 vols.), Paris, 1878.
The Macro Plays, ed. M. Eccles, E.E.T.S. 262, 1969.
Ancient Mysteries Described, W. Hone, 1823.
Specimens of the Pre-Shakespearean Drama, ed. J. M. Manly (2 vols.), Boston, 1897 (repr. London, 1967).
The Ancient Cornish Drama, ed. with translation, E. Norris, Oxford, 1859.
Fourteenth Century Verse and Prose, ed. K. Sisam, Oxford, 1921.
Ten Miracle Plays, ed. R. G. Thomas, 1966.

2. CRITICAL STUDIES

M. D. Anderson, *Drama and Imagery in English Mediaeval Churches*, Cambridge, 1963.
R. Axton, *European Drama of the Early Middle Ages*, 1974.
E. K. Chambers, *The Mediaeval Stage* (2 vols.), Oxford, 1903.
   English Literature at the Close of the Middle Ages, Oxford, 1945.
G. Cohen, *Le Théâtre en France au Moyen Age* (2 vols.), Paris, 1928.
H. Craig, *English Religious Drama of the Middle Ages*, Oxford, 1955.
N. Denny (ed.), *Mediaeval Drama* (Stratford-upon-Avon Studies 16), 1973.
M. Eccles, '*Ludus Coventriae*: Lincoln or Norfolk?', *Medium Aevum* 60, 1971, pp. 135–41.
G. Frank, *The Mediaeval French Drama*, Oxford, 1954.

A NOTE ON BOOKS

'On the Relation of the York and Towneley Plays', *PMLA* 44, 1929, pp. 313–19.

H. C. Gardiner, *Mysteries' End*, New Haven, 1946.

J. Gardner, 'Theme and Irony in the Wakefield *Mactatio Abel*', *PMLA* 80, 1965, pp. 515–21.

W. W. Greg, 'Bibliographical and Textual Problems of the English Miracle Cycles', *Library* 5, 1914 (four parts).

Chester Play Studies, Malone Society, 1935.

A. Harbage, *Annals of English Drama, 975–1700*, revised by S. Schoenbaum, 1962 (Supplements 1966 and 1970).

O. B. Hardison, Jr, *Christian Rite and Christian Drama in the Middle Ages*, Baltimore, 1965.

S. J. Kahrl, *Traditions of Medieval English Drama*, 1974.

A. M. Kinghorn, *Mediaeval Drama*, 1968.

V. A. Kolve, *The Play Called Corpus Christi*, 1966.

M. C. Lyle, *The Original Identity of the York and Towneley Cycles*, Minneapolis, 1919.

W. F. McNeir, 'The Corpus Christi Plays as Dramatic Art', *Studies in Philology* 48, 1951, pp. 601–28.

A. H. Nelson, *The Mediaeval English Stage*, Chicago, 1974.

R. E. Parker, 'The Reputation of Herod in Early English Literature', *Speculum* 8, 1933, pp. 59–67.

L. Petit de Julleville, *Les Mystères* (2 vols.), Paris, 1880.

E. Prosser, *Drama and Religion in the English Mystery Plays*, Stanford, 1961.

J. S. Purvis, *From Minster to Market Place*, York, 1969.

C. Ricks (ed.), *English Drama to 1710*, 1971.

J. W. Robinson, 'The Art of the York Realist', *Modern Philology* 60, 1963, pp. 241–51.

A. P. Rossiter, *English Drama from Early Times to the Elizabethans*, 1950.

F. M. Salter, *Mediaeval Drama in Chester*, Toronto, 1955, New York, 1968.

'The Banns of the *Chester Plays*', *Review of English Studies* 15, 1939, pp. 432–57; 16, pp. 1–17, 137–48.

J. B. Severs, 'The Relationship between the Brome and Chester Plays of *Abraham and Isaac*', *Modern Philology* 42, 1945, pp. 137–51.

T. Sharp, *Dissertation on the Pageants or Dramatic Mysteries Anciently Performed at Coventry*, Coventry, 1825.

R. Southern, *The Staging of Plays before Shakespeare*, 1973.

J. Speirs, 'The Towneley Shepherds' Plays', in *The Age of Chaucer*, ed. B. Ford (Penguin Books), 1954.

A NOTE ON BOOKS

C. J. Stratman, *A Bibliography of Mediaeval Drama*, Berkeley, 1954. Second edition 1972.

E. L. Swenson, *An Enquiry into the Composition and Structure of 'Ludus Coventriae'*, Minneapolis, 1914.

J. H. Taylor and A. H. Nelson (eds.), *Mediaeval English Drama*, Chicago, 1972.

M. P. Tilley, *A Dictionary of the Proverbs in England in the Sixteenth and Seventeenth Centuries*, Ann Arbor, 1950.

J. R. Wallis, 'The Miracle Play of *Crucifixio Christi* in the York Cycle', *Modern Language Review* 12, 1917, pp. 494–5.

H. A. Watt, 'The Dramatic Unity of the *Secunda Pastorum*', *Essays and Studies in Honor of Carleton Brown*, New York, 1940.

G. Wickham, *Early English Stages* (2 vols.), 1959–62.
    The Medieval Theatre, 1974.

A. Williams, *The Characterization of Pilate in the Towneley Plays*, East Lansing, 1950.

R. H. Wilson, '*The Stanzaic Life of Christ* and the Chester Plays', *Studies in Philology* 28, 1931, pp. 413–32.

R. Woolf, *The English Mystery Plays*, 1972.

K. Young, *The Drama of the Mediaeval Church* (2 vols.), Oxford, 1933.

Acknowledgements

Besides the debt which I owe to many of the authors named in the above list, I acknowledge permission to print given by the Huntington Library, San Marino, California, who supplied photocopies of the nine *Towneley Plays* (MS HM1); and by the Beinecke Rare Book and Manuscript Library of Yale University, who supplied microfilm of *Abraham and Isaac* from *The Book of Brome* (MS 365).

The Pre-Reformation Banns of the *Chester* Cycle

These Banns, intended to be read aloud at the beginning of performances of the Chester *cycle, have survived in a copy originating c.1540 (Harl. MS 2150). They mention twenty-six plays, of which all but two, the Assumption and the clerical play for the day of Corpus Christi, have survived in the manuscripts of the whole cycle which were copied at the end of the sixteenth century. It is thought that these Banns were originally composed as early as 1467, at a time when the plays were undergoing considerable revision, and when there were about eighteen plays in the cycle. The Banns themselves show evidence of revision in that the stanzas are sometimes irregular, and that there are two passages marked 'erazed in the booke'.*

These early Banns are much closer to the cycle in the years of its fullest development than are the later post-Reformation Banns which are part of the attempt to modify the plays to fit new Protestant requirements.

In this edition I have numbered the stanzas, and regrouped the lines into regular octaves where possible. The anomalies which remain are an indication of changes to take in new material from time to time.

∞

The Comen Bannes[1] to be proclaymed and ryddon with the Stewardys of every occupacion.

(1)
    Lordinges royall and reverentt,
    Lovely ladies that here be lentt,
    Sovereigne citizins, hether am I sent

Comen common   2 *be lentt* are present

ENGLISH MYSTERY PLAYS

A message for to say.
I pray you all that be present
That you will here with good intent,
And lett your eares to be lent
Hertffull, I you pray.

(2)

Our wurshipffull Mair of this Citie,
With all this royall cominaltie,
Solem pagens[2] ordent hath he
At the Fest of Whitsonday tyde.
How every craft in his decree
Bryng forth their playes solemplye
I shall declare you brefely,
Yf ye will a while abyde[3].

(3)

The worshipfull *Tanners* of thys towne
Bryng forth the hevenly mancion,
Thorders of angelles and theire creacion,
According done to the best;
And when thangelles be made so clere,
Then folowyth the falling of Lucifere.
To bryng forth this play with good chere
The Tanners be full prest.

(4)

You wurshipffull men of the *Draperye*,
Loke that Paradyce be all redye;
Prepare also the *Mappa Mundi*[4],
Adam and eke Eve.
The *Water-leders* and *Drawers* of Dee,
Loke that Noyes Shipp be sett on hie,
That you lett not the storye,
And then shall you well cheve.

6 *here* hear 8 *Hertffull* willingly 10 *cominaltie* commonalty (the self-governing community of Chester) 11 *ordent* ordained 13 *decree* rank, station 14 *solemplye* with ceremony 18 *mancion* dwelling-place 24 *prest* ready 31 *lett* hinder 32 *cheve* achieve

THE PRE-REFORMATION BANNS OF THE *CHESTER* CYCLE

(5)

The *Barbers* and *Wax-chaundlers* also that day
Of the Patriarche you shall play,
Abram that putt was to assay
To sley Isack his sonne.
The *Cappers* and *Pynners* forth shall bryng
Balack that fears and mightie kyng,
And Balam on an asse sytting;
Loke that this be done.   40

(6)

Youe *Wrightys* and *Slaters* wilbe fayne,
Bryng forth your cariage[5] of Marie myld quene,
And of Octavyan so cruell and kene,
And also of Sybell the sage;
For fynding of that royall thing
I graunt you all the blessing
Of the high imperiall king,
Both the maister and his page.

(7)

Paynters, *Glasiars*, and *Broderers* in fere
Have taken on theym with full good chere   50
That the Sheppardes play then shall appere,
And that with right good wyll[6].

(8)

The *Vynteners* then as doth befall
Bringe forth the three kings royall
Of Colyn[7] or pagent memoryall,
And worthy to appere.
There shall you see how thos kyngs all
Came bouldly into the hall

---

33 *Wax-chaundlers* makers of wax candles   35 *assay* test   37 *Cappers* makers of caps   *Pynners* makers of nails and pins   38 *fears* fierce   41 *Wrightys* carpenters   *fayne* willing   49 *Broderers* embroiderers   *fere* company

43

Before Herald, proude in paulle,
Of Crysts byrth to heare. 60

(9)

The *Mercers* worshipfull of degre
The Presentation[8] that have yee;
Hit fallyth best for your see
By right reason and skyle.

(10)

Of caryage I have no doubt,
Both within and also without,
It shall be deckyd, that all the rowte
Full gladly on it shall be to loke;
With sondry cullors it shall shine
Of velvit, satten and damaske fyne 70
Taffyta sersnett of poppyngee grene[9]
................................[10]

(11)

The *Gouldsmyths* then full soone will hye,
And *Massons* theyre craft to magnifye;
Theis two crafts will them applye,
Theyre worshipp for to wyne,
How Herode, King of Galalye,
For that intent Cryst to distrye,
Slew the Inosents most cruely
Of tow yers and within. 80

(12)

Semely *Smythis* also in syght
A lovely caryage the will dyght,
Candilmas Day for soth it hyght,
The find it with good will.
The *Butchers* pagend shall not be myst,

59 *Herald* Herod   *paulle* royal robe   63 *Hit* it   *see* position   64 *skyle* cause   67 *rowte* people (audience)   69 *cullors* colours   73 *hye* hasten   75 *Theis* these   77 *Galalye* Galilee   78 *distrye* destroy   80 *tow* two   81 *Semely* decorously   82 *the* they   83 *hyght* is called

How Satan temp[t]ed our Savyour Cryst;
It is an history of the best
As wittneseth the Gospell.

(13)

Nedys must I rehers the *Glover*[s] –
The give me gloves and gay gere – 90
The find the Toumbe of Lazarey,
That pagend cometh next:
Also the *Corvesers* with all their myght,
The fynde a full fayre syght;
Ierusalem their caryage hyght,
For so sayth the text.

(14)

And the *Bakers* also be-dene
The find the Maunday¹¹, as I wene;
It is a carriage full well besene,
As then it shall appeare. 100
Flechers, Bowyers, with great honors,
The *Cowpers* find the Tormentors,
That bobbyde God with gret horrors
As he sat in his chere.

(15)

The *Yron-mongers* find a caryage good:
How Iesu dyed on the rode
And shed for us his precyus blud,
The find it in fere.
Cryst after his passion
Brake hell for our redempcion; 110
That find the *Cookes* and *Hostelers* of this towne
And that with full good chere.

---

91 *Lazarey* Lazarus   93 *Corvesers* shoemakers   97 *be-dene* indeed
98 *wene* think   101 *Flechers, Bowyers* makers of arrows and bows
102 *Cowpers* makers of barrels and casks   103 *bobbyde* mocked   104 *chere*
chair   106 *rode* rood, cross   108 *The* they   111 *Hostelers* innkeepers

(16)

    Also the *Skynners*[12] they be bowne,
    With great worship and renowne,
    They find the Resurection:
    Fayre maye them befall.

(17)

    Sadlers and *Foysters* have the good grace,
    The find the Castell of Emawse,
    Where Cryst appered to Cleophas;
    A faire pagend you shall see.   120

(18)

    Also the *Taylers* with trew intent
    Have taken on them verament
    The Assencyon, by one assent,
    To bringe it forth full right.
    Fysshe-mongers, men of faith,
    As that day will doe thair slayth[13]
    To bringe there caryage furth in grayth:
    Wytsonday it hight.

(19)

    The wurshipffull *Wyffys*[14] of this towne
    Fynd of Our Lady Thassumpcion;   130
    It to bryng forth they be bowne
    And mey[n]tene with all theyre might.

(20)

    The *Shermen* will not behynd,
    Butt bryng theire cariage with good mynde;
    The pagent of Prophettys they do fynd,
    That prophecied full truly
    Of the comyng of Anticrist,

---

113 *bowne* ready   117 *Foysters* makers of saddle-trees   118 *Emawse* Emmaus   122 *verament* certainly   127 *there* their   *grayth* readiness   128 *hight* is called   132 *meyntene* persevere   133 *Shermen* cutters of cloth

That Goodys faith wold resist;
That cariage, I warrand, shall not myst,
Butt sett forth full dewly.   140

(21)

The *Hewsters*, that be men full sage,
They bryng forth a wurthy cariage,
That is a thing of grett costage;
Antycryst[15] hit hight.
They *Weyvers* in every dede
Fynd the Day of Dome: well may they spede.
I graunt theym holly to theire neede
The blysse of heven bright.

(22)

Sovereigne syrs, to you I say,
And to all this feyre cuntre,   150
That played shalbe this godely play
In the Whitson weke:
That is brefely for to sey
Uppon Monday, Tuysday, and Wennysday.
Whoo lust to see them he may,
And non of theym to seke.

(23)

erazed in   *Also maister Maire of this citie,*
the booke   *With all his bretheryn accordingly,*
            A solempne procession ordent hath he
            To be done to the best   160
            Appon the day of Corpus [Ch]r[ist]i[16]:
            The blessed sacrament caried shalbe,
            And a play sett forth by the clergye
            In honor of the fest.

138 *Goodys* God's   140 *dewly* duly   141 *Hewsters* dyers   143 *costage*
expense   147 *holly* wholly   150 *cuntre* district   155 *lust* wishes
156 *seke* seek   161 *Appon* upon

47

ENGLISH MYSTERY PLAYS

(24)

erazed in the booke
Many torches there may you see,
Marchaunty[s] and craftys of this citie,
By order passing in theire degree,
A goodly sight that day.
They come from Saynt Maries on the hill,
The churche of Saynt Iohns untill, 170
And there the sacrament leve they will,
The south as I you say.

(25)

Whoo so comyth these playes to see,
With good devocion merelye,
Hertely welcome shall he be,
And have right good chere.
Sur Iohn Aneway[17] was Maire of this citie
When these playes were begon truly.
God graunt us merely,
And see theym many a yere. 180

(26)

Now have I done that lyeth in me
To procure this solempnitie,
That these playes contynued may be
And well sett fourth alway.
Iesu Crist that syttys on hee,
erazed[18] *And his blessyd mother Marie,*
Save all this goodely company
And kepe you nyght and day.

170 *untill* unto   171 *leve* leave   172 *south* truth   174 *merelye* simply
185 *hee* high

1. The Fall of Lucifer

CHESTER 1: TANNERS

Though there is some evidence for the existence of liturgical plays dealing with Lucifer from the twelfth century in Germany, the subject probably reached the Chester cycle some time after the latter's inception. Salter has suggested that it entered the cycle after 1410 and before 1540, and that the style of the play indicates an author and reviser working between 1467 and 1488. Previously the Tanners had assisted the Skinners and Shoemakers, and the story of Lucifer was probably one with the Creation performed by the Drapers. The subject appears in the other three cycles, though at York the surviving text is a later revision.

The inclusion of the story in the cycles at a relatively late date may be accounted for by the fact that it is not Scriptural. Moreover it does not relate directly to the Church calendar. Its inclusion and development rest rather on its relevance to theological and figurative objectives. The Fall of Lucifer gives a cosmic reference to the Fall of Adam because it takes place before time begins. The one anticipates the other as a kind of double – a technique apparent in many aspects of medieval art – and it provides a motive which is superhuman. The possible dramatic weakness which a repetition of the fall plot might contain is offset by making Lucifer, in common with other devils elsewhere in the cycles, a grotesque and unrepentant villain who thoroughly deserves his fate. This impression is intensified by his boastful and witless companion Lightborne. In the long term the Falls of Lucifer and Adam became types for tragedy.

[Scene: Heaven.]

(1)

DEUS PATER[1]: *Ego sum alpha et ω,*
Primus et nobilissimus[2];
It is my will yt sholde be soe
Yt is, it was, yt shall be thus.

(2)

I am greate God gracious, which never had beginninge.
The holy foode of parentes is set in my [*essentia*[3];]
I am the tryall[4] of the Trynitie that never shall be twynninge;
Peareles patron imperiall, and *patris sapientia*[5].
My beames be all beatytude, all blisse is in my buyldinge;
All myrthe is in my mansuetude *cum dei potentia*[6]. 10
Bothe visible and eke invisible, all is my weldinge;
As God greatest and glorious, all lyeth *in mea licentia*[7].

(3)

For all the mighte of the maiestye is magnified in me,
Prince principall proved in my perpetuall prudens.
I was never but one and ever one in three,
Sett in substantiall sothenes[8] within celestiall sapience.
These three tryalls in a trone and [true] Trynitie
Be grounded in my godhead, exalted by my excellence;
The mighte of my making is marked all in [me],
Dissolved under a dyademe by my divyne experyence[9]. 20

(4)

Now sithe I am thus solemne and set in my solation,
A biglie blisse here will I builde, a heaven without ending,
And cast a comlye compasse by my comely creation:

3 *yt* it   7 *twynninge* dividing   8 *Peareles* without equal   10 *mansuetude* gentleness, mildness   11 *eke* also   *weldinge* making (by means of heat)   16 *sothenes* reality, truth   17 *trone* throne   21 *sithe* since   *solemne* ceremonial (adj.)   *solation* ?pleasure   22 *biglie* firm   23 *cast* set up   *comlye*, comely beautiful   *compasse* boundary

THE FALL OF LUCIFER

Neene orders of angells[10] be ever to one attending.
Doe your endeavour, and doubte ye not under my
    domynacion
To sitt in celestyall safetye, all solace to your sending,
For all the lyking in this lordshipp be laude to my
    lawdation[11];
Throughe the might of my most maiestye your mirth
    shall ever be mending.

(5)

LUCIFER: Lord, throughe thy grace and mighte thou hast
    us wrought:
Nyne orders of angelles here as you may see,   30
Cherubyn and Seraphyn throughe your thoughte,
Trones and Domynacions in blisse to bee,

(6)

With Principatus, that order brighte,
And Potestates in blissefull heighte,
Also Virtutes throughe your great mighte,
Angeli, also Archangeli.

(7)

Nyne orders here be full witterlye
That you have made here full brighte;
In thie blisse full righte [they] be,
And I the principall lord here in thie sighte.   40

(8)

DEUS: Here have I wrought with heavenlye might
Of angels nine orders of greate bewtye,
Eche one with other, as it is righte,
To walk about the Trynitie.

---

24 *Neene* nine 25 *endeavour* duty *doubte* fear 26 *solace* comfort
sending request 28 *mending* improving 37 *witterlye* surely

(9)

Now Lucifer and Lightburne[12], lookes lowlie you be attendinge[13]!
The blessing of my benignitie I geve to my first operacion:
For crafte ne for cunninge cast never comprehendinge[14],
Exalte you not to exellency in no heighe exaltation.
Loke that you tende righte wislye, for hense I wilbe wendinge.
The worlde that is both voyde and vayne, I forme in this formation, 50
With a dungeon of darkenes that never shall have endinge.
These workes now well be done by my devyne formation.

(10)

[This work is nowe well i-wrought
That is so cleane and cleare.
As I you made of noughte,
My blessing I geve you here.]

(11)

ANGELI: Wee thanke the, Lorde, full soverayntlie
That us hath formed so cleane and cleare,
And in this blisse to abyde thee bye;
Graunt us thy grace aye to abyde here. 60

(12)

ARCHANGELI: Here for to abyde God graunt us grace,
And please this prince withoutten peere;
Hym for to thanke with somp solace,
A songe now let us singe in feare.
    Tunc cantabunt[15].

---

46 *benignitie* meekness *geve* give *operacion* labour 49 *tende* behave *wendinge* going 50 *formation* act of creation 52 *devyne* divine 53 *i-wrought* completed 57 *the* thee *soverayntlie* in the manner for a king 60 *aye* ever 63 *somp* ceremony 64 *in feare* together

THE FALL OF LUCIFER

(13)

DEUS: Now sithe I have formed you so fayre,
And exalted yow so exellent,
And here I see you next my chayre,
My love to you is so fervent;
Looke ye fall not in no dispayre;
Touche not my trone by non assent.　　　　　　70
All your bewty I shall apayre
And pride fall ought in your intent.

(14)

LUCIFER: Nay, Lorde, that will not wee in dede,
For nothing trespas unto thee;
Thy great godhead ay will we dreade,
And never exalte ourselves so hye.
Thou hast marked us with great myrth and mayne
In thy blisse evermore to abyde and be,
In lasting life our life to leade,
And bearer of light thou hast made me.　　　　　　80

(15)

LIGHTBORNE: And I am marked of the same mowld;
Loving be to our Creator,
That us hath made gaier then gould,
Under his diademe aye to endure.

(16)

DEUS: I have forbyd that yow ne sholde
But kepe yow well in this stature[16];
The same covenant, I charge yow, hold,
In payne of heaven ever forfeyture.

(17)

For I will wend and take my trace,
And se this blisse in every towre.　　　　　　90

---

70 *assent* act of will　71 *apayre* spoil　72 *And if intent* will　77 *mayne* power　86 *stature* law　89 *wend* go　*trace* way　90 *towre* tower

53

Eche one of you kepe well his place,
And, Lucifer, I make the governour.
Now I charge here the ground of grace
That it be set in my order.
Behold the beames of my bright face[17],
Which ever was and shall endure.

(18)

This is your health in every case,
For to behold your Creator;
Was never non like me under lace,
Ne never shalbe as my figure.
Here will I abyde now in this place,
For to be Angels Comfortour;
To be revisible in shorte space,
Yt is my will in this same hower.
 Tunc cantabunt et recedet Deus[18].

(19)

LUCIFER: Ah! Ah! That I am wonderous bright
Among yow all shyning so cleare!
Of all heaven I beare the light,
Thoughe God himself and he were here.

(20)

All in this trone if that I were
Then sholde I be as wise as he.
What say yow, Angells all that be here?
Some comforte sone now let me see.

(21)

VIRTUTES: We will not [as]sent unto your pryde,
Ne in our hartes take such a thought,
But that our Lord shall be our guyde,
And kepe to us that he hath wrought.

103 *revisible* seen again 104 *hower* hour 112 *sone* soon 115 *But that* unless

THE FALL OF LUCIFER

(22)

CHERUBYN: Our Lord comaunded all that be here
    To kepe his hestes, both more and lesse;
    Therfore I warne the, Lucifere,
    This pride will turne to great distresse.   120

(23)

LUCIFERE: Distresse! I commaunde yow all to cease,
    And se the bewtye that I beare;
    All heaven shynes throughe my brightnes,
    For God him-selfe shynes not so cleare.

(24)

DOMINATIONS: Of all Angells yow beare the pryce,
    And most bewtye is yow befall.
    My counsell is that yow be wise,
    That yow bringe not your-selfe in thrall.

(25)

PRINCIPATUS: And if that yow in thrall yow bringe,
    Then shall yow have a wicked fall,   130
    And also all your ofspringe
    Away withe yow they shall all.

(26)

[CERAPHINE:] Our brethrens counsell is good to heare,
    To yow I say, Lucifer and Lightburne;
    Wherfore beware yow of that chayre[19],
    Lest that yow have a fowle spurne.

(27)

LIGHTBOURNE: In faithe, brother, but yet yow shall
    Sit in this trone, bothe cleane and cleare,
    That yow may be as wise withall
    As God him self if he were here.   140

---

118 *hestes* commands   125 *pryce* highest esteem   128 *thrall* slavery
136 *spurne* kick

(28)

    [Therefore ye shalbe sett here]
    That all heaven may yow behold.
    The brightnes of your body cleare
    Is brighter then God a thowsand fould.

(29)

THRONES: Alas, that bewty will yow spill,
    If yow kepe yt all in your thoughte;
    Then will pryde have all his will
    And bring your brightnes all to naught.

(30)

    Let yt passe out of your thoughte,
    And cast away all wicked pryde,   150
    And kepe your brightnes that to you is wrought,
    And let our Lord be all your guide.

(31)

POTESTATES: Alas, that pride is the wall of lewtye[20],
    That turnes your thought to great offence;
    The great brightnes of your [fayer] bodye
    Will make yow sone for to goe hence.

(32)

LUCIFER: Behould, seigniours, on every syde,
    And unto me cast your eyne:
    I charge yow, Angels, in this tyde,
    Behold and se what I doe meane.   160
    Above great God I will me guyde,
    And set my-self here, as I wene:
    I am pereles and prince of pryde,
    For God him self shynes not so sheene.

---

144 *then* than   145 *spill* ruin   158 *eyne* eyes   159 *tyde* time   160 *se* see
162 *wene* think   164 *sheene* bright

THE FALL OF LUCIFER

(33)

    Here will I sit now in this stid
    To exalt my-selfe in this same sea.
    Behold my body, both handes and head!
    The might of God is marked in me.
    All Angelles turne to me, I redd,
    And to your soveraigne knele on your knee!   170
    I am your comfort both lord and head,
    The myrth and the might of the maiesty.

(34)

LIGHTBURNE: And I am next of the same degree,
    Repleat all by experyence;
    Me thinke if I might sit by the
    All heaven shold doe me reverence.
    All orders are assent to the and me;
    Thou hast us turned by eloquence.
    And here were now the Trynitie,
    We sholde him pass by our fulgence.   180

(35)

DOMINATIONES: Alas! Why make yow this great offence?
    Bothe Lucifer and Lightburne, to yow I say:
    Our Soveraigne Lorde will have yow hence,
    And he fynd yow in this aray.
    Goe to your seates and wende hence!
    Yow have begun a parlous playe.
    Yow shall well wyt the subsequence;
    This daunce will turne yow to teene and traye.

(36)

LUCIFER: I redd yow all, doe me reverence,
    That am repleat with heavenly grace.   190

---

165 *stid* place   166 *sea* seat   169 *redd* command   174 *Repleat* full *experyence* knowledge   180 *fulgence* brightness   184 *aray* state 186 *parlous* perilous   *playe* game, risk   187 *wyt* know   *subsequence* consequence   188 *teene* pain   *traye* grief

Thoughe God come here, I will not hence,
But sit right here before his face.
    Et sedet[21].

(37)

DEUS: Say, what aray doe yow make here?
    Where is your prince and principall?
        Tunc quatiunt et tremescunt[22].
    I made thee Angell and Lucifer,
    And here thou would be lord over all!
    Therfore I charge this order cleare
    Fast from this place loke that ye fall.
    Full sone I shall doe change your cheare,
    For your foule pryde to hell yow shall.   200

(38)

Lucifer, who set thee here, when I was goe?
[What have I offended unto thee?]
I made thee my frende, thou arte my foe!
[Whie hast thou] trespassed thus to me?
Above all Angels there were no mo
That sate so nighe the maiestye.
I charge yow fall tyll I byd 'Noe!'
To the pitt of hell, evermore to be!
    Tunc cadent Lucifer et Lightburne[23].

(39)

I DEMON: Alas! That ever we were wrought!
    That we shold come into this place!   210
    We were in ioy, now we be nought.
    Alas, we have forfeyted our grace.
II DEMON: And even hither thou hast us brought,
    Into a dungeon to take our trace.
    All this sorrow thou hast yt sought;
    The devill may speede thy stinking face![24]

  199 *cheare* gladness   204 *Whie* why   205 *mo* more   206 *sate* sat
211 *ioy* joy   214 *trace* way

THE FALL OF LUCIFER

(40)

I DEMON: My face, false fayture, for thy fare!
Thou hast us brought to teene and tray.
I comber, I canker, I kindle in care,
I sinke in sorrow; what shall I saye? 220

(41)

II DEMON: Thou hast us brought this wicked way,
Thorough thy might all and thy pryde,
Out of ioy that lastethe aye,
In sorrow evermore for to abyde.

(42)

I DEMON: Thy wytt it was as well as myne,
Of that pride that we did showe,
And now lyethe here in hell pyne,
Till the day of Dome that beames shall blowe.

(43)

II DEMON: Then shall we never care for woe,
But lye here lyke two feendes blacke. 230
Alas, that we did forfayt soe
The Lordes love, that did us forsake.

(44)

I DEMON: And therfore I shall for his sake
Showe mankind great envie;
As sone as ever he can him make
I shall send him for to destroye.

(45)

Some of my order shall he be,
To make mankinde to do amisse;
Ruffian[25], my frend fayre and free,
Loke that thou kepe mankinde from bliss! 240

---

217 *fayture* impostor *fare* behaviour 219 *comber* become entangled
canker rust 227 *pyne* pain 228 *beames* trumpets 231 *forfayt* forfeit
234 *envie* malice 239 *free* noble

(46)

> That I and my fellowes fell downe for aye,
> He will ordayne mankind agayne,
> In bliss to be with great aray,
> And we evermore in hell pyne.

(47)

II DEMON: Out! Harrow! Where is our might,
> That wee were wont for to show,
> And in heaven bare so great light,
> And now lye in hell full lowe!

(48)

I DEMON: Out! Alas! for wo and wickednes!
> I am so fast bound in this cheare,   250
> And never away hence shall passe,
> But lye in hell all still here!

(49)

DEUS: Ah! Wicked pryde aye worth thee wo![26]
> My myrth hast thou made amisse.
> I may well suffer: my will is not soe
> That they shold part thus from my bliss.
> Ah! Pryde, when might thou burst in two?
> Why did they so? Why did they this?
> Behold, my Angels: pride is your foe,
> All sorrow shall shew wherever it is.   260

(50)

> And thoughe they have broken my commaundment,
> Me ruethe yt sore full soveraynelye;
> Never the less, I will have myne intent:
> What I first thought, yet so will I.
> I, and two parsons, are at one assent
> A solemne matter for to trye.

250 *cheare* state   262 *Me ruethe* I regret   *yt* it   *soveraynelye* greatly
265 *parsons* persons

THE FALL OF LUCIFER

A full fayre image now have I ment
That this same stydd shall multeply.

(51)

In my blessing here I begin,
The first thing that shall be to my pay[27]:
Lightenes, darkenes, I byd yow twyn,
The darke to the night, the light to the day[28].
Kepe yow this course for more [or] myn[29],
And suffer not – to yow I say –
But save your-self, both out and in!
That is my will, and will alway.

(52)

As I have made all thinges of nought,
After my will and my wishing,
My first day now have I wrought,
I geve yt fullie my blessing.

Finis primae paginae[30].

268 *stydd* place   271 *twyn* divide

2. The Creation, and Adam and Eve
De Creatione Mundi et Adami et Evae,
de Eorumque Tentatione

CHESTER 2: DRAPERS

This play is known to have been in the cycle before 1467. It was originally joined with what is now the first pageant (the Tanners). The earliest date for the Drapers is 1461, though they had a pageant cart some years before this. If, as seems possible, the Tanners had an interest in the play at an earlier time, they would be able to provide white leather costumes for Adam and Eve. The play is written in the Chester stanza, and is typical of the plain style of the earliest plays in this cycle.

The content follows Genesis 1–3, which provides much of the detail. God's initial speech is static, perhaps the only way to present an episode which was both solemn and of the highest theological importance.

Two locations are used: the place for God's act of creation, and Paradise itself with the tree. In these two places the dramatic style of the episodes is very different. The first part is more ritualistic, whereas the temptation itself involves an impression of human nature.

The story of Cain, which follows the expulsion from Paradise, is omitted from this edition.

፠

(1)
DEUS: I, God, most in maiestye,
    In whom beginning none may be,
    Endles as most of postye,
    I am and have bene ever.

    3 *postye* power   4 *bene* been

THE CREATION, AND ADAM AND EVE

Now heaven and earth is made through me:
The earthe is voyde onely I see,
Therefore light for more lee,
Through my crafte I will kever.

(2)

At my bydding now made be light! [1]
Light is good, I see in sighte;   10
Twynned shalbe throughe my mighte
The lighte from thesternes.
Light daye I will be called aye,
And thesternes night, as I say;
Thus morrow and even the first day
Is made full and expresse.

(3)

Now will I make the fyrmament
In myddes the waters to be lent,
For to be a divident,
To twyne the waters aye;   20
Above the welkin, benethe also,
And heaven yt shall be called oo;
Thus commen is even and morrow also
Of the seacond daye.

(4)

Now will I waters everichone,
That under heaven be great won,
That they [gather] into one,
And drynes sone him showe.
That drynes earth men shall call;
The gathering of the waters all,   30
Seas to name have the shall,
Thereby men shall [them] knowe.

---

7 *lee* brightness   8 *kever* gain   12 *thesternes* darkness   16 *expresse* complete   17 *fyrmament* sky   18 *myddes* midst   *lent* placed   19 *divident* dividing   21 *welkin* sky   22 *oo* always   23 *commen* come   26 *won* in existence

(5)

> I will on earth that hearbes springe,
> Each one in kinde seede gevinge,
> Trees dyvers fruytes forth bringe,
> After there kinde eache one,
> The seede of which for aye shall be
> Within the fruyte of each tree;
> Thus morrow and even of dayes three
> Is bothe comen and gone.   40

(6)

> Now will I make through my might
> Lightninge in the welken brighte,
> To twyn the day from the nighte,
> And lighten the earthe with lee.
> Greate lightes also I will make twoo,
> The sonne and eke the mone also;
> The sonne for daye to serve for oo,
> The mone for nighte to be.

(7)

> I will make on the fyrmament
> Starres also, throughe myne intent;   50
> The earth to lighten there they be sent,
> And knowne may be there-bye
> Cowrses of planetts nothing amisse.
> Now se I this worke good, i-wisse;
> Thus morrow and even both made is
> The fourthe daye fully.

(8)

> Now will I in waters fishe forth bringe,
> Fowles in the firmament flyinge,
> Great whalles in the sea swymminge;
> All make I with a thoughte.   60

33 *hearbes* plants 34 *kinde* nature 44 *lee* brightness 46 *sonne* sun *mone* moon 54 *i-wisse* indeed 59 *whalles* whales

THE CREATION, AND ADAM AND EVE

Beastes, fowles, stone and tree,
These workes are good, well I see,
Therfore to blesse all lykes me
These workes that I have wroughte.

(9)

All beastes I byd yow multeply
In earth, in water, by and bye,
And fowles in ayre for to flye
The earth to fulfill.
Thus morrow and even, through my might,
Of the fifte daye and the night 70
Is made and ended well arighte,
All at myne owne will.

(10)

Now will I on earth forth bringe anone
All kindes of beastes, everichon,
That creepen, flye, or els gone,
Each one in his kinde.
Now is done all my biddinge,
Beastes going, flyinge and creeping,
And all my workes at my lyking
Fully now I finde. 80
Tunc recedet de illo loco ad locum ubi creavit Adamum, et faciet signum, quasi faceret ipsum[2].

(11)

Now heaven and earth is made expresse,
Make we man to our lyckenes;
Fishe, foule, beastes, more and lesse
To maister he shall have might[3].
To our shape now make I thee;
Man and woman I will ther be.
Growe and multeply shall ye
And fulfill earth in height.

63 *lykes* pleases   75 *gone* move   82 *lyckenes* likeness   86 *ther* there

(12)

> To helpe thee, thou shalt have here
> Hearbes, trees, sede, fruite in feare;
> All shalbe put in thy power,
> And beastes eke also,
> All that in earth be sterring,
> Fowles in the ayer flying,
> And all that ghoste hath and lyking,
> To sustayne yow from woe.

(13)

> Now this is done, I see aright,
> And all thinges made through my might,
> The sixte daye here in my sight
> Is made all of the beste.
> Heaven and earth is wrought within,
> And all that needes to be therin;
> To-morrow, the seventh day, I will blyn,
> And of worke take my reste.

(14)

> But now this man that I have made
> With ghoste of life I will him glade;
> Ryse up, Adame, rise up rade,
> A man full of soule and life,
> *Et spiritum vitae efflavit in faciem eius*[4].
> And come with me to Paradise,
> A place of daynty and delice.
> But it is good that thou be wise;
> Bring not thy selfe in strife!

(15)

> Here, Adam, I geve thee this place,
> Thee to comforte and solace.
> Kepe to yt while thou yt hase,

---

93 *sterring* stirring 94 *ayer* air 95 *ghoste* spirit 103 *blyn* stop
106 *glade* enliven 107 *rade* ready 110 *daynty* pleasure *delice* delight

THE CREATION, AND ADAM AND EVE

Then doe as I thee saye.
   Tunc Creator adducet eum in Paradisum ante lignum[5].
Of all the trees that be here in
Thou shalt eate and nothing synne,
But of this tree for wayle or wynne
Thou eate not by no waye.   120

(16)

What tyme thou eats of this tree
Death thee behoves, leeve thou me[6].
Therfore this fruite I will [thou] flee,
And be thou not so boulde.
Beastes and fowles that yow may see,
To thee obedyent aye shall be;
What name they be geven by thee,
That name the shall hould.
   Tunc Creator capiens manum Adami et faciet ipsum iacere et capiet costam[7].

(17)

Hit is not good man onely to be;
Helpe to him now make wee[8].   130
But excite sleepe behoveth me
Anone in this man here.
   Dormit[9].
On sleape thou art now, well I see,
Therfore a bone I take of thee,
And fleshe also with hart free,
To make thee a feere.

(18)

ADAM: O Lorde, where have I longe bene?
For, sithe I slepte, much have I seene;
Wonders that withoutten wene
Hereafter shall be wiste.   140

---

119 *wayle* grief   *wynne* joy   127 *geven* given   129 *onely* alone   136 *feere* companion   139 *wene* belief   140 *wiste* known

ENGLISH MYSTERY PLAYS

DEUS: Rise up, Adam, and awake!
 Here have I formed thee a make.
 Here to the thou shalt take,
 And name her as thy list.
   Adam surgit.[10]

(19)

ADAM: I see well, Lord, through thy grace,
 Bone of my bone thou her mase,
 And fleshe of my flesh she hase,
 And my shape through thy saw.
 Therefore shall she be called, i-wis,
 Virago, nothing amisse,   150
 For out of man taken she is,
 And to man shall she draw.

(20)

 Of earthe first thou madest me
 Bothe bone and flesh, as nowe I see,
 Thou hast her geven through thy posty
 Of that I in me had.
 Therfore man kindely shall forsake
 Father and mother, and to wife take,
 Twoo in one fleshe as thou can make,
 Ether other for to glade.   160
   Tunc Adam et Eva stabunt nudi et non verecundabunt,
   et veniet Serpens ad paradisum positum in specie
   Demonis et ambulando dicat[11]

(21)

DEMON: Out, out! What sorow is this
 That I have lost so much blisse!
 For once I thoughte to doe amisse,

---

142 *make* mate   143 *Here* her   144 *list* pleasure   146 *mase* made
147 *hase* has   148 *saw* command   150 *Virago* woman made like man
(*Genesis* 2 23)   152 *draw* turn   157 *kindely* by nature   160 *Ether* each

THE CREATION, AND ADAM AND EVE

Out of heaven I fell.
The brightest angell I was ere this[12]
That ever was or yet is,
But pride cast me downe, i-wis,
From heaven right to hell.

(22)

Ghostelie paradice I was in,
But thence I fell through my sinne.
Of earthelie paradice now, as I myn,
A man is geven mastrye
By Belzabub[13], shall I never blyn
Tyll I may make him by some synne
From that place for to twyn
And trespace, as did I.

(23)

Shold suche a caytife made of claye
Have suche blisse? Nay be my laye![14]
For I shall teache his wife a playe;
And I maye have a while
For her deceave, I hope I maye,
And through her bringe them both awaye;
For she will doe as I her saye.
Her hope I to beguile.

(24)

That woman is forbyd to doe
For any thinge therto will shooe[15];
Therefore that tree shall shee come to,
And assaye which it is.
Disguise me I will anon tyte,
And profer her of that ilke fruit;
So shall they both for ther delight
Be banished from the blisse.

169 *Ghostelie* spiritual   171 *myn* remember   177 *caytife* wretch
181 *deceave* deception   186 *shooe* she   189 *tyte* quickly   190 *ilke* same

ENGLISH MYSTERY PLAYS

(25)

> A manner of an adder is in this place,
> That wynges like a byrd she hase,
> Feete as an adder, a maydens face[16];
> Her kindenes I will take.
> And of that tree of paradice
> She shall eate through my coyntice,
> For women are full liccoris,
> That she will not forsake. 200

(26)

> And eate she of it as witterly
> They shall fare bothe as did I –
> Be banished bouth of that baylie,
> And their offspring for aye[17].
> Therefore as brocke I my [pane[18]],
> My adders coate I will put on,
> And into Paradice will I gone
> As fast as ever I may.

Versus: Spinx volucris penna, serpens pede, fronte puella[19].

(27)

SERPENS: Woman, why was God so nyce
> To byd yow leve so your delyce, 210
> And of ech tre of Paradyce
> To forsake the meate?

EVA: Nay, of the fruite of ech tree
> For to eat good leave have we,
> Save the fruite of one we must flee;
> Of it we may not eate.

(28)

> This tree, that here in the middes is,
> Eate we of it we do amisse[20].

---

196 *kindenes* likeness   198 *coyntice* cunning   199 *liccoris* eager for dainties   201 *And if*   *witterly* knowingly   203 *baylie* castle, court   209 *nyce* foolish   210 *leve* leave   *delyce* pleasure

70

THE CREATION, AND ADAM AND EVE

God said we shold dye, i-wis,
And we touched that tree. 220
SERPENS: Woman, I say, leeve not this!
For yt shall not lose yow blisse,
Ne no ioy that is his,
But be as wise as he.

(29)

God is coynt and wyse of wytt,
And wottes well, when yow eate hit,
Then your eyes shalbe unknit;
Like goddes yow shall be
And knowe both good and evill also.
Therefore he counselled yow therfro, 230
Yow may well wyt he was your foe,
Therfore dose after me.

(30)

Take of this fruite and assaie.
It is good meate, I dare laye.
And but thou fynde yt to thy paye,
Say that I am false.
Eate thou on apple and no moe,
And yow shall knew both wayle and woe,
And be lyke to goddess, both twoo,
Thou and thy housband also. 240

(31)

EVA: Ah, lord, this tree is fayre and bright,
Greene and semelye in my sighte,
The fruyte swete and much of mighte,
That goddes it may us make.
An apple of it I will eate,
To assaye which is the meate;

225 *coynt* clever 226 *wottes* knows *hit* it 227 *unknit* untied, opened
232 *dose* do 234 *laye* bet 235 *but* unless *paye* advantage 237 *on* one
238 *wayle* grief 242 *semelye* beautiful

71

ENGLISH MYSTERY PLAYS

And my housband I will get
One morsell for to take.

(32)

Adam, husband, life and deere,
Eate some of this apple here –   250
It is fayre, my leeif fere,
It may thou not forsake.
ADAM: That is sooth, Eve, without weere.
The fruite is sweete and fayre in feere;
Therfore I will doe thy prayer,
One morsell I will take.
   *Tunc Adam comedit et statim nudi sunt, et lamentando
   dicat*[21]

(33)

Out! Alas! What eales me?
I am naked, well I see;
Woman, cursed must thou be
For bothe now we be shente.   260
I wotte not for shame whether to flee,
For this fruite was forbydden me;
Now have I broken, through red of the,
My Lordes commaundement.

(34)

EVA: Alas! This adder hath done me nye.
Alas! Her red why did I?
Naked we bene bothe for-thye,
And of our shape ashamed.
ADAM: Yea, soothe said I in prophesie,
When thou wast taken of my body,   270
Mans woe thou woldest be witlie;
Therefore thou wast so named[22].

249, 251 *life, leeif* dear   251 *fere* mate   253 *weere* doubt   257 *eales* ails
260 *shente* destroyed   263 *red* advice   265 *nye* harm   267 *for-thye*
therefore   271 *witlie* knowingly

THE CREATION, AND ADAM AND EVE

(35)

EVA: Adam, husband, I red we take
   Thes figg-leaves, for shame sake,
   And to our members a hillinge make
   Of them for thee and me.
ADAM: Therewith my members I will hyde,
   And under this tre I will abyde;
   For sickerlie come God us beside
   Owt of this place shall we[23].   280
   *Tunc Adam et Eva cooperiant genitalia sua cum foliis et
   stabunt sub arbore, et venit Deus clamans cum alta voce*[24]

(36)

DEUS: Adam, Adam, where art thou?
ADAM: Ah, Lord, I hard thy voyce right now;
   I am naked, I make a vowe,
   Therfore nowe I hyde me.
DEUS: Whoe tolde the, Adam, thou naked was,
   Save onelie thyne owne trespasse,
   That of the tree thou eaten hase
   That I forbad thee?

(37)

ADAM: Lord, this woman that is here,
   That thou gave me to my fere,   290
   Gave me part: I did [att] her prayer;
   Of it I did eate[25].
DEUS: Woman, why hast thou done soe?
EVA: This adder, Lorde, shee was my foe,
   And sothelie deceaved me thoe,
   And made me to eate that meate.

(38)

DEUS: Adder, for that thou hast done this noye,
   Among all beastes on earth the bye,

275 *hillinge* covering   279 *sickerlie* certainly   280 *Owt* out   295 *sothelie*
certainly   *thoe* then   297 *noye* harm   298 *the* thee   *bye* near

73

Cursed shalt thou be for thye,
For this womans sake.   300
Upon thy breast thou shalt goe[26],
And eate the earth to and froe;
And enmytie betwixt yow twoo
Hence forth I will make.

(39)

Betwixt thy seade and hers also,
I shall excyte sorrow and woe;
To breake thy heade and be thy foe
She shall have maystry aye.
No beast on earth, I the behet,
That man so lyttle shall of let,   310
And troden be fowle under his feete,
For thy misdeede to-daye.
  Tunc recedet serpens, vocem serpentinam faciens[27].

(40)

And, woman, I warne thee wytterlie,
Thy mischeife I shall multeply;
With pennaunce, sorrow and great anoye
Thy children shalt thou beare.
And for thou hast done so to-daye[28],
The man shall mayster thee alwaye,
And under his power thou shalt be aye,
Thee for to drive and deere.   320

(41)

And man, also, I say to the,
For thou hast not done after me,
Thy wifes counsell for to flee,
But done so her bydding,
To eate the fruite of this tree,
In thy worke waryed the earth shalbe,

308 *maystry* power   309 *behet* command   310 *of let* leave off
315 *anoye* grief   320 *drive* go *deere* suffer   326 *waryed* cursed

THE CREATION, AND ADAM AND EVE

And in great traveyle behoveth the
On earth to get thy lyving.

(42)

When on the earthe traveyled thou hase,
Fruite shall not grow on that place,   330
But thornes and bryers for thy trespace
To the on earth shall spring.
Hearbes and rootes thou shalt eate,
And for thy sustenance sore sweate
With great mischeife to wyn thy meat,
Nothing to thy lyking.

(43)

Thus shalt thou lyve, soth to sayne,
For thou hast bene to me unbeyne,
Ever till tyme thou turne againe
To earthe there thou came froe.   340
For earth thou art, as well is seene,
And after this world wo and tene
To earth thou shalt, withoutten wene,
And all thy kinde also.

(44)

ADAM: Alas! In languor now I am lent!
Alas, now shamfullie I am shente!
For I was inobedyente,
Of wayle now I am wayved[29].
Now all my kinde by me is kent
To flee womans intisement;   350
That trustes them in anye intent
Truly he is decayved.

(45)

My licorous wife hath bene my foe,
The devilles envye shent me also,

---

327 *traveyle* labour   338 *unbeyne* unkind   342 *tene* suffering   343 *wene* doubt   345 *lent* placed   349 *kent* advised   350 *intisement* enticement

They twayne together well may goe,
The sister and the brother.
His wrath hath done me much woe,
Her glottony[30] greved me alsoe;
God let never man trust them twoo
The one more than the other!   360

(46)

DEUS: Now shall ye parte from this lee.
Hilled yow behoves to be;
Dead beastes skinnes, as thinketh me,
Is best yow on yow beare.
For deadlie[31] bothe now bene yee,
And death no way may you flee;
Such clothes are best for your degree,
And such now ye shall weare.
  Tunc Deus induet Adam et Eva tunicis pelliciis[32].

(47)

Adam, now hast thou thy willing,
For thou desiredst over all thinge   370
Of good and evill to have knowing;
Now wrought is all thy will.
Thou woldest knowe bothe wayle and woe:
Now is yt fallen to thee soe.
Therefore hence thou must goe
And thy desire fulfill.

(48)

Now, lest thou covet [eate more],
And doe as thou hast done before,
Eate of this fruite, to lief evermore,
Here may thou not be.   380
To earth [theider] thou must gone,
With traveyle leade thy life thereon;

---

358 *greved* harmed   359 *let* allow   361 *lee* protection   362 *Hilled* covered   379 *lief* live   381 *theider* thither

THE CREATION, AND ADAM AND EVE

For sicker ther is non other wone.
Goe forth, take Eve with thee!
 Tunc Deus emittet eos de Paradiso[33].

(49)

Now will I that there lenge within
The angells order Cherubyn,
To kepe this place of wayle and wyn[34]
That Adame lorne thus hase;
With sharpe sworde on everye side
And flame of fyre here to abyde, 390
That never a earthlie man in glide,
For gright they bene that grace.

(50)

I ANGELUS: Lord, that order, as is righte,
Is ready set here in thy sight,
With flame of fyre ready to fight
Against mankinde, thy foe.
To whom grace cleane is gright
Shall none of them lenge in my sight,
Till wisdome, right, mercy, and might
By them and other moe. 400

(51)

II ANGELUS: I, Cherubyn, most here by choice,
To kepe this place of great price;
Sith that man was so unwise,
This woning I must weare,
That he by crafte ne no coyntice
Shall not come in that was his,
[But deprived be of Paradice],
No more for to come there.

---

383 *sicker* certainly *wone* dwelling place   385 *lenge* linger, stay
388 *lorne* lost 391 *glide* go 392 *gright* forfeited 404 *woning* place *weare* guard

ENGLISH MYSTERY PLAYS

(52)

III ANGELUS: And in this heritage I will be,
　　Sleelie for to oversee,　　　　　　　　　　　　　410
　　That no man come in this cyttie,
　　As God hath me beheighte.
　　Swordes of fyre have all we
　　To make man from this place to flee,
　　From his dwelling of great dayntie,
　　That to him first was dighte.

(53)

IV ANGELUS: Of this order I am made one,
　　From mankind to weare this won
　　That throughe his guilt he hath forgone,
　　For gright they bene that grace.　　　　　　　　420
　　Therfore eschue they must ech one,
　　Or els sword shall be there bone,
　　And my-self, also there fone,
　　To flame them in the face.

[*With Adam and Eve banished from Paradise, the play continues with the story of Cain and Abel.*]

410 *Sleelie* carefully　　411 *cyttie* city　　412 *beheighte* commanded
415 *dayntie* pleasure　416 *dighte* ordained　418 *won* place　419 *forgone* lost
422 *bone* payment　　423 *fone* foes

3. The Killing of Abel
Mactatio Abel

TOWNELEY 2: GLOVERS (?)

The story of Cain is a completion of the Fall. It shows how the corruption of man intensifies following the expulsion from Paradise. The character of Cain is developed beyond the account in Genesis *to make him blasphemous and self-interested. His abuse of God is vigorous and obscene. The picture of human corruption is intensified by the introduction of Cain's servant, Pikeharnes, who follows the characterization of a number of other irreverent servants and boys (see Jak Garcio in No. 13, and Froward in No. 27). By contrast Abel is shown as a type of obedience, perhaps foreshadowing Isaac and Christ as victims.*

Part of the play is thought to be the work of the Wakefield Master. If he was responsible for a revision, however, his work is difficult to identify specifically. One stanza (No. 35) could be taken as an example of his favourite metre, and the vigorous language of Cain and Pikeharnes is very similar to other work by him, particularly in its use of irony and proverb.

The words 'Glover pac...' have been added to the MS by a sixteenth-century scribe in the margin by the title.

ଅଧ

[*Enter Garcio.*]
(1)
GARCIO: All hayll, all hayll, both blithe and glad,
    For here com I, a mery lad!
    Be peasse youre dyn, my master bad,

3 *peasse* silent   *dyn* noise   *bad* commanded

ENGLISH MYSTERY PLAYS

Or els the dwill you spede.
Wote ye not I com before?
Bot who that ianglis any more
He must blaw my blak hoill bore[1],
Both behynd and before,
Till his tethe blede.
Felows, here I you forbede   10
To make nother nose ne cry;
Who so is so hardy to do that dede
The dwill hang hym up to dry.

(2)

Gedlyngis, I am a full grete wat.
A good yoman my master hat.
Full well ye all hym ken.
Begyn he with you for to stryfe,
Certis, then mon ye never thryfe;
Bot I trow, bi God on life,
Som of you ar his men.   20
Bot let youre lippis cover youre ten[2],
Harlottys everichon!
For if my master com, welcom hym then.
Farewell, for I am gone.
    [*Exit.*]

(3)

    [*Enter Cain, ploughing.*]
CAYN: Io furth, Greynhorne! and war oute, Gryme![3]
Drawes on! God gif you ill to tyme!
Ye stand as ye were fallen in swyme.
What, will ye no forther, mare?
War! Let me se how Down will draw;
Yit, shrew, yit, pull on a thraw.   30
What! It semys for me ye stand none aw.

---

4 *dwill* devil 6 *ianglis* chatters 11 *nose* noise 14 *Gedlyngis* fellows *wat* chap 15 *hat* is called 18 *mon* shall *thryfe* prosper 25 *Io furth* gee up! *war oute* wake up! 27 *swyme* swoon 30 *thraw* time 31 *aw* fear

THE KILLING OF ABEL

I say, Donnyng, go fare!
Aha, God gif the soro and care!
Lo, now hard she what I saide;
Now yit art thou the warst mare
In plogh that ever I haide.

(4)

How, Pikeharnes[4], how! Com heder belife!
  [*Enter Garcio.*]
GARCIO: I fend, Godys forbot, that ever thou thrife!
CAYN: What, boy, shal I both hold and drife?
  Heris thou not how I cry?
GARCIO: Say, Mall and Stott, will ye not go?
  Lemyng, Morell, Whitehorn, io!
  Now will ye not se how thay hy?

(5)

CAYN: Gog gif the sorow, boy; want of mete it gars.
GARCIO: Thare provand, sir, forthi, I lay behynd thare ars,
  And tyes them fast bi the nekys,
  With many stanys in thare hekys[5].
CAYN: That shall bi thi fals chekys.

(6)

GARCIO: And have agane as right.
CAYN: I am thi master; wilt thou fight?
GARCIO: Yai, with the same mesure and weght
  That I boro will I qwite.
CAYN: We! Now no thyng bot call on tyte,
  That we had ployde this land.
GARCIO: Harrer, Morell! io furth, hyte!
  And let the plogh stand.

---

36 *haide* had   37 *belife* quickly   38 *fend* prohibit   39 *drife* drive
44 *gif* give   *mete* meat   *gars* causes   45 *provand* food   *forthi* therefore
47 *stanys* stones   *hekys* rack   48 *chekys* cheeks   52 *qwite* give back
53 *tyte* soon   54 *ployde* ploughed   55 *hyte* go on

81

(7)

[*Enter Abel.*]

ABELL: God, as he both may and can,
    Spede the, brother, and thi man.
CAYN: Com kis myne ars! Me list not ban,
    As welcom standys ther oute.   60
    Thou shuld have bide til thou were cald;
    Com nar, and other drife or hald,
    And kys the dwillis toute.
    Go grese thi shepe under the toute,
    For that is the moste lefe.
ABELL: Broder, ther is none here aboute
    That wold the any grefe.

(8)

Bot, leif brother, here my sawe:
It is the custom of oure law,
All that wyrk as the wise   70
Shall worship God with sacrifice.
Oure fader us bad, oure fader us kend,
That oure tend shuld be brend.
Com furth, brothere, and let us gang
To worship God; we dwell full lang;
Gif we hym parte of oure fee,
Corne or catall, wheder it be.

(9)

And therfor, brother, let us weynd,
And first clens us from the feynd
Or we make sacrifice;   80
Then blis withoutten end
Get we for oure servyce,

(10)

Of hym that is oure saulis leche.

---

59 *ban* curse   63 *toute* backside   65 *lefe* dear   70 *wyrk* act   72 *kend* taught   73 *tend* tithe   *brend* burned   80 *Or* before   83 *saulis* soul's *leche* healer

82

THE KILLING OF ABEL

CAYN: How! Let furth youre geyse, the fox will preche.
    How long wilt thou me appech
    With thi sermonyng?
    Hold thi tong, yit I say,
    Even ther the good wife strokid the hay[6];
    Or sit downe in the dwill way,
    With thi vayn carpyng.   90

(11)

    Shuld I leife my plogh and all thyng
    And go with the to make offeryng?
    Nay, thou fyndys me not so mad!
    Go to the dwill, and say I bad!
    What gifys God the, to rose hym so?
    Me gifys he noght bot soro and wo.

(12)

ABELL: Caym, leife this vayn carpyng,
    For God giffys the all thi lifyng.
CAYN: Yit boroed I never a farthyng
    Of hym – here my hend.   100
ABELL: Brother, as elders have us kend,
    First shuld we tend with oure hend,
    And to his lofyng sithen be brend[7].

(13)

CAYN: My farthyng is in the preest hand
    Syn last tyme I offyrd.
ABELL: Leif brother, let us be walkand;
    I wold oure tend were profyrd.

(14)

CAYN: We! Wherof shuld I tend, leif brothere?
    For I am ich yere wars then othere;

---

84 *geyse* geese   85 *appech* delay   90 *carpyng* criticizing   95 *rose* praise
98 *lifyng* living   100 *hend* hand   102 *tend* pay tithe   103 *lofyng* praise

ENGLISH MYSTERY PLAYS

Here my trouth, it is none othere.   110
My wynnyngys ar bot meyn,
No wonder if that I be leyn;
Full long till hym I may me meyn,
For bi hym that me dere boght,
I traw that he will leyn me noght.

(15)
ABELL: Yis, all the good thou has in wone
   Of Godys grace is bot a lone[8].
CAYN: Lenys he me? As com thrift apon the so!
   For he has ever yit beyn my fo;
   For had he my freynd beyn,   120
   Other-gatys it had beyn seyn.
   When all mens corn was fayre in feld
   Then was myne not worth a neld.
   When I shuld saw, and wantyd seyde,
   And of corn had full grete neyde,
   Then gaf he me none of his,
   No more will I gif hym of this.
   Hardely hold me to blame
   Bot if I serve hym of the same.
ABELL: Leif brother, say not so,   130
   Bot let us furth togeder go;
   Good brother, let us weynd sone,
   No longer here I rede we hone.
CAYN: Yei, yei, thou iangyls waste!
   The dwill me spede if I have hast,
   As long as I may lif,
   To dele my good or gif[9],
   Ather to God or yit to man,
   Of any good that ever I wan.
   For had I giffen away my goode,   140
   Then myght I go with a ryffen hood,

---

111 *meyn* small   112 *leyn* lean   113 *meyn* complain   115 *leyn* give
117 *lone* gift   118 *Lenys* gives   121 *Other-gatys* otherwise   123 *neld*
needle   124 *seyde* seed   133 *hone* delay   134 *waste* in vain   139 *wan* won
141 *ryffen* torn

THE KILLING OF ABEL

And it is better hold that I have,
Then go from doore to doore and crave.

ABELL: Brother, com furth in Godys name,
I am full ferd that we get blame;
Hy we fast that we were thore.

CAYN: We! Ryn on, in the dwills nayme, before!
Wemay, man, I hold the mad!
Wenys thou now that I list gad
To gif away my warldys aght?
The dwill hym spede that me so taght!
What nede had I my travell to lose,
To were my shoyn and ryfe my hose?

ABELL: Dere brother, hit were grete wonder
That I and thou shuld go in sonder,
Then wold oure fader have grete ferly;
Ar we not brether, thou and I?

CAYN: No, bot cry on, cry, whyls the thynk good!
Here my trowth, I hold the woode.
Wheder that he be blithe or wroth
To dele my good is me full lothe.
I have gone oft on softer wise
Ther I trowed som prow wold rise.
Bot well I se go must I nede;
Now weynd before, ill myght thou spede!
Syn that we shall algatys go.

ABELL: Leif brother, whi sais thou so?
Bot go we furth both togeder.
Blissid be God we have fare weder.

[*They go to an altar.*]

CAYN: Lay downe thi trussell apon this hill.

ABELL: Forsoth, broder, so I will;
Gog of heven take it to good.

CAYN: Thou shall tend first if thou were wood.

---

146 *thore* there   147 *Ryn* run   148 *Wemay* hurry!   149 *Wenys* do you think? *gad* go   150 *warldys* worldly   *aght* possessions   152 *travell* labour   153 *shoyn* shoes   *ryfe* tear   156 *ferly* wonder   159 *woode* mad   163 *prow* profit   165 *weynd* go   166 *algatys* always   170 *trussell* bundle

ABELL: God that shope both erth and heven,
  I pray to the thou here my steven,
  And take in thank, if thi will be,
  The tend that I offre here to the;
  For I gif it in good entent
  To the, my Lord, that all has sent.
  I bren it now, with stedfast thoght,   180
  In worship of hym that all has wroght.
CAYN: Ryse! Let me now, syn thou has done;
  Lord of heven, thou here my boyne!
  And over Godys forbot be to the
  Thank or thew to kun me[10];
  For, as browke I thise two shankys
  It is full sore, myne unthankys,
  The teynd that I here gif to the,
  Of corn or thyng that newys me;
  Bot now begyn will I then,   190
  Syn I must nede my tend to bren.
  Oone shefe, oone, and this makys two,
  Bot nawder of thise may I forgo[11].
  Two, two, now this is thre,
  Yei, this also shall leif with me:
  For I will chose and best have –
  This hold I thrift – of all this thrafe.
  Wemo, wemo, foure, lo, here!
  Better groved me no this yere.
  At yere tyme I sew fayre corn,   200
  Yit was it sich when it was shorne,
  Thystyls and brerys, yei grete plente
  And all kyn wedys that myght be.
  Foure shefys, foure, lo, this makys fyfe –
  Deyll I fast thus long or I thrife[12] –
  Fyfe and sex, now this is sevyn,
  Bot this gettys never God of heven.

174 *shope* made   175 *steven* voice   183 *boyne* prayer   185 *thew* courtesy
186 *browke* use   *shankys* legs   189 *newys me* grows for me   195 *leif*
stay   197 *thrafe* measure   198 *wemo* well!   199 *groved* grew
203 *wedys* weeds   204 *shefys* sheaves

THE KILLING OF ABEL

Nor none of thise foure, at my myght,
Shall never com in Godys sight.
Sevyn, sevyn, now this is aght – 210
ABELL: Cain, brother, thou art not God betaght.
CAYN: We! Therfor is it that I say,
For I will not deyle my good away:
Bot had I gyffen hym this to teynd
Then wold thou say he were my freynd;
Bot I thynk not, bi my hode,
To departe so lightly fro my goode.
We! Aght, aght, and neyn, and ten is this,
We! This may we best mys.
Gif hym that that ligys thore? 220
It goyse agans myn hart full sore.

(16)

ABELL: Cam, teynd right of all bedeyn.
CAYN: We lo! Twelve, fyfteyn, sexteyn.
ABELL: Caym, thou tendys wrang, and of the warst.
CAYN: We! Com nar and hide myne een[13];
In the wenyand wist ye now at last.
Or els will thou that I wynk?
Then shall I doy no wrong, me thynk.

(17)

Let me se now how it is –
Lo, yit I hold me paide; 230
I teyndyd wonder well bi Ges,
And so even I laide.

(18)

ABELL: Came, of God me thynke thou has no drede.
CAME: Now and he get more, the dwill me spede!
As mych as oone reepe,
For that cam hym full light chepe;

---

210 *aght* eight 211 *betaght* devoted 213 *deyle* give 220 *ligys* lies
222 *bedeyn* at once 226 *wenyand* waning (of the moon) 228 *doy* do
231 *Ges* Jesus 235 *oone* one *reepe* handful 236 *chepe* cost

ENGLISH MYSTERY PLAYS

Not as mekill, grete ne small,
As he myght wipe his ars with all.
For that, and this that lyys here
Have cost me full dere;
Or it was shorne, and broght in stak,
Had I many a wery bak;
Therfor aske me no more of this,
For I have giffen that my will is.

ABELL: Cam, I rede thou tend right,
For drede of hym that sittys on hight.

CAYN: How that I tend, rek the never a deill,
Bot tend thi skabbid shepe wele;
For if thou to my teynd tent take[14],
It bese the wars for thi sake.
Thou wold I gaf hym this shefe? or this sheyfe?
Na, nawder of thise ij will I leife;
Bot take this, now had he two,
And for my saull now mot it go,
Bot it gos sore agans my will,
And shal he like full ill.

ABELL: Cam, I reyde thou so teynd
That God of heven be thi freynd.

CAYN: My freynd? Na, not bot if he will!
I did hym never yit bot skill.
If he be never so my fo,
I am avisid gif hym no mo;
Bot chaunge thi conscience, as I do myn,
Yit teynd thou not thi mesel swyne?

ABELL: If thou teynd right thou mon it fynde.

CAYN: Yei, kys the dwills ars behynde;
The dwill hang the bi the nek!
How that I teynd, never thou rek.
Will thou not yit hold thi peasse?
Of this ianglyng I reyde thou seasse.
And teynd I well, or tend I ill,

---

239 *lyys* lies 247 *rek* care *deill* scrap 248 *skabbid* scabby 254 *saull* soul 257 *reyde* advise 260 *skill* reason 264 *mesel* measly

THE KILLING OF ABEL

Bere the even and speke bot skill.
Bot now syn thou has teyndid thyne,
Now will I set fyr on myne.
We! Out! Haro! Help to blaw!
It will not bren for me, I traw;
Puf! This smoke dos me mych shame –
Now bren, in the dwillys name!
A! What dwill of hell is it?
Almost had myne breth beyn dit.
Had I blawen oone blast more
I had beyn choked right thore;
It stank like the dwill in hell,
That longer ther myght I not dwell.

ABELL: Cam, this is not worth oone leke;
Thy tend shuld bren withoutten smeke.

CAYM: Com kys the dwill right in the ars,
For the it brens bot the wars;
I wold that it were in thi throte,
Fyr, and shefe, and ich a sprote.

[*God speaks from above.*]

DEUS: Cam, whi art thou so rebell
Agans thi brother Abell?
Thar thou nowther flyte ne chyde[15];
If thou tend right thou gettys thi mede;
And be thou sekir, if thou teynd fals,
Thou bese alowed ther after als.

(19)

CAYM: Whi, who is that Hob-over-the-wall?
We! Who was that that piped so small?
Com, go we hens, for perels all;
God is out of hys wit.
Com furth, Abell, and let us weynd;

---

275 *blaw* blow   280 *dit* stopped   285 *leke* leek   286 *smeke* smoke
290 *ich a* every   *sprote* shoot   293 *flyte* quarrel   296 *alowed* praised
299 *perels* perils

Me thynk that God is not my freynd;
On land then will I flyt.

(20)

ABELL: A, Caym, brother, that is ill done.
CAYN: No, bot go we hens sone;
　　And if I may, I shall be
　　Ther as God shall not me see.
ABELL: Dere brother, I will fayre
　　On feld ther oure bestys ar
　　To looke if thay be holgh or full.
CAYM: Na, na, abide, we have a craw to pull[16];
　　Hark, speke with me or thou go;
　　What, wenys thou to skape so?
　　We! Na! I aght the a fowll dispyte,
　　And now is tyme that I hit qwite.
ABELL: Brother, whi art thou so to me in ire?
CAYM: We! Theyf, whi brend thi tend so shyre?
　　Ther myne did bot smoked
　　Right as it wold us both have choked.
ABELL: Godys will I trow it were
　　That myn brened so clere;
　　If thyne smoked am I to wite?
CAYM: We! Yei! That shal thou sore abite;
　　With cheke bon[17], or that I blyn,
　　Shal I the and thi life twyn;
　　　[*Cain kills Abel.*]
　　So lig down ther and take thi rest,
　　Thus shall shrewes be chastysed best.

(21)

ABELL: Veniance, veniance, Lord, I cry!
　　For I am slayn, and not gilty.
CAYN: Yei, ly ther, old shrew, ly ther, ly!

---

310 *holgh* empty　314 *aght* owe　315 *qwite* repay　317 *shyre* brightly
322 *wite* blame　323 *abite* pay for　326 *lig* lie

THE KILLING OF ABEL

(22)

And if any of you thynk I did amys
I shal it amend wars then it is,
That all men may it se:
Well wars then it is
Right so shall it be.

(23)

Bot now, syn he is broght on slepe,
Into som hole fayn wold I crepe;
For ferd I qwake and can no rede[18];
For be I taken, I be bot dede.
Here will I lig thise fourty dayes, 340
And I shrew hym that me fyrst rayse.

DEUS: Caym, Caym!
CAYM: Who is that that callis me?
I am yonder, may thou not se?
DEUS: Caym, where is thi brother Abell?
CAYM: What askys thou me? I trow at hell:
At hell I trow he be –
Who so were ther then myght he se –
Or somwhere fallen on slepyng;
When was he in my kepyng?
DEUS: Caym, Caym, thou was wode; 350
The voyce of thi brotherys blode
That thou has slayn, on fals wise,
From erth to heven venyance cryse.
And, for thou has broght thi brother downe,
Here I gif the my malison.
CAYM: Yei, dele aboute the, for I will none,
Or take it the when I am gone[19].
Syn I have done so mekill syn,
That I may not thi mercy wyn,
And thou thus dos me fro thi grace; 360
I shall hyde me fro thi face.
And where so any man may fynd me,

338 *ferd* fear   341 *shrew* (v) curse   355 *malison* curse

Let hym slo me hardely;
And where so any man may me meyte,
Ayther bi sty, or yit by strete;
And hardely, when I am dede,
Bery me in Gudeboure at the quarell hede[20],
For, may I pas this place in quarte,
Bi all men set I not a fart.

DEUS: Nay, Caym, it bese not so; 370
I will that no man other slo,
For he that sloys yong or old
It shall be punyshid sevenfold.
[*Exit Deus.*]

CAYM: No force, I wote wheder I shall;
In hell I wote mon be my stall.
It is no boyte mercy to crave,
For if I do I mon none have;
Bot this cors I wold were hid,
For som man myght com at ungayn;
'Fle, fals shrew!' wold he bid, 380
And weyn I had my brother slayn.
Bot were Pikeharnes, my knafe, here,
We shuld bery hum both in fere.
How, Pykeharnes! Scape-thryft! How, Pikeharnes, how!
[*Enter Garcio.*]

GARCIO: Master, master!

CAYN: Harstow, boy? Ther is a podyng in the pot[21];
Take the that, boy, tak the that!
[*Strikes him.*]

GARCIO: I shrew thi ball under thi hode,
If thou were my syre of flesh and blode;
All the day to ryn and trott, 390
And ever amang thou strykeand,
Thus am I comen bofettys to fott.

CAYN: Peas, man, I did it bot to use my hand;

363 *slo* slay *hardely* certainly   365 *sty* path   368 *quarte* good health
370 *bese* is   372 *sloys* slays   376 *boyte* use   378 *cors* corpse   379 *at ungayn* awkwardly   384 *Scape-thryft* spendthrift   388 *ball* head
390 *trott* hurry   391 *strykeand* striking   392 *bofettys* blows   *fott* get

THE KILLING OF ABEL

(24)

    Bot harke, boy, I have a counsell to the to say —
    I slogh my brother this same day;
    I pray the, good boy, and thou may,
    To ryn away with the bayn.
GARCIO: We! Out apon the, there!
    Has thou thi brother slayn?
CAYM: Peasse, man, for Godys payn!   400

(25)

    I saide it for a skaunce.
GARCIO: Yey, bot for ferde of grevance
    Here I the forsake;
    We mon have a mekill myschaunce
    And the bayles us take.

(26)

CAYM: A, syr, I cry you marcy! Seasse!
    And I shall make you a releasse.
GARCIO: What, wilt thou cry my peasse

(27)

    Thrughout this land?
CAYN: Yey, that I gif God a vow, belife
GARCIO: How will thou do long or thou thrife —   410
CAYM: Stand up, my good boy, belife,
    And thaym peasse both man and wife;

(28)

    And who so will do after me
    Full slape of thrift then shal he be.
    Bot thou must be my good boy,
    And cry 'Oyes, oyes, oy[22]!'
GARCIO: Browes, browes to thi boy[23].

---

397 *bayn* bone   401 *skaunce* joke   405 *bayles* bailiffs   409 *belife* quickly
414 *slape of thrift* cunning with regard to self-preservation   417 *Browes* broth

(29)

CAYM: I commaund you in the kyngys nayme –
GARCIO: And in my masteres, fals Cayme –
CAYM: That no man at thame fynd fawt ne blame –
GARCIO: Yey, cold rost is at my masteres hame.

(30)

CAYM: Nowther with hym nor with his knafe –
GARCIO: What, I hope my master rafe.
CAYM: For thay ar trew, full many fold –
GARCIO: My master suppys no coyle bot cold.
CAYM: The kyng wrytys you untill.
GARCIO: Yit ete I never half my fill.

(31)

CAYM: The kyng will that thay be safe –
CARCIO: Yey, a draght of drynke fayne wold I hayfe.
CAYM: At thare awne will let tham wafe –
GARCIO: My stomak is redy to receyfe.

(32)

CAYM: Loke no man say to theym, on nor other –
GARCIO: This same is he that slo his brother.
CAYM: Byd every man thaym luf and lowt –
GARCIO: Yey, ill spon weft ay comes foule out[24].
CAYM: Long or thou get thi hoyse and thou go thus aboute.

(33)

Byd every man theym pleasse to pay.
GARCIO: Yey, gif Don, thyne hors, a wisp of hay!
   [*Climbs out of reach*[25].]
CAYM: We! Com downe in twenty dwill way,
   The dwill I betake;

421 *rost* roast   423 *rafe* raves   424 *fold* times   425 *coyle* cabbage
429 *hayfe* have   430 *wafe* wander   434 *lowt* revere   436 *hoyse* hose
439 *dwill* devils'   440 *betake* give

THE KILLING OF ABEL

For bot it were Abell, my brothere,
Yit knew I never thi make.

(34)

GARCIO: Now old and yong, or that ye weynd,
The same blissyng withoutten end
All sam then shall ye have
That God of heven my master has giffen;
Browke it well, whils that ye liffen,
He vowche it full well safe.

(35)

CAYM: Com downe yit in the dwillys way,
And angre me no more; 450
And take yond plogh, I say,
And weynd the furth fast before;
And I shall, if I may,
Tech the another lore;
I warn the, lad, for ay,
Fro now furth, evermore,
That thou greve me noght;
For, bi Godys sydys, if thou do,
I shall hang the apon this plo,
With this rope, lo, lad, lo! 460
By hym that me dere boght[26].

(36)

Now fayre well, felows all,
For I must nedys weynd,
And to the dwill be thrall,
Warld withoutten end.
Ordand ther is my stall,
With Sathanas the feynd[27];
Ever ill myght hym befall
That theder me commend
This tyde. 470

442 *make* mate, equal   447 *Browke* enjoy

Fare well les, and fare well more,
For now and ever more
I will go me to hyde.

Explicit Mactacio Abell. Sequitur Noe [28].

4. Noah
Processus Noe cum Filiis. Wakefeld

TOWNELEY 3

The Wakefield Master's revision of the Noah play took place after the division of York and Towneley. The word 'Wakefeld' appears in the title of the play in the manuscript. The play emphasizes the corruption of man, as in the Scriptural account (Genesis 6–9). The symbolism of the play is seen in terms of the Creation and of the Judgement Day. Perhaps the most important theme is Noah's obedience to the will of God. Noah's wife is the strongest challenge to this. Indeed the action of the play places great emphasis upon the conflict between them. This antagonism is characteristic of most of the English versions of the story, and the dramatist makes much of it here. It is notable, however, that after three challenges, Mrs Noah becomes acquiescent as she enters the Ark, even to the point of offering help and advice. Theologically her rebelliousness is an example of the inferiority and corruptibility of woman (cf. Eve in Paradise Lost*), but the subject was widespread in medieval literature and art. It offered much scope for comedy and the lively dialogue in which this dramatist excels.*

∞

[*Enter Noah.*]

(1)

NOE[1]: Myghtfull God veray,   maker of all that is,
    Thre persons withoutten nay,   oone God in endles blis,
    Thou maide both nyght and day,   beest, fowle, and fysh,
    All creatures that lif may   wroght thou at thi wish,
    As thou wel myght;

ENGLISH MYSTERY PLAYS

The son, the moyne, verament,
Thou maide; the firmament,
The sternes also full fervent,
To shyne thou maide ful bright.

(2)

Angels thou maide ful even,   all orders that is,
To have the blis in heven: this did thou more and les,
Full mervelus to neven.   Yit was ther unkyndnes
More bi foldis seven   then I can well expres[2];
Forwhi
Of all angels in brightnes
God gaf Lucifer most lightnes,
Yit prowdly he flyt his des,
And set hym even hym by.

(3)

He thoght hymself as worthi   as hym that hym made,
In brightnes, in bewty;   therfor he hym degrade;
Put hym in a low degre   soyn after, in a brade,
Hym and all his menye,   wher he may be unglad
For ever.
Shall thay never wyn away
Hence unto domysday,
Bot burne in bayle for ay,
Shall thay never dyssever[3].

(4)

Soyne after that gracyous Lord   to his liknes maide man,
That place to be restord,   even as he began,
Of the Trinite bi accord,   Adam, and Eve that woman
To multiplie without discord,   in Paradise put he thaym,
And sithen to both
Gaf in commaundement
On the tre of life to lay no hend;

6 *moyne* moon   8 *sternes* stars   *fervent* glowing   12 *neven* mention
17 *flyt* moved   *des* seat   21 *soyn* soon   *brade* moment   27 *dyssever*
depart   32 *sithen* then

NOAH

Bot yit the fals feynd
Made hym with man wroth,

(5)

Entysyd man to glotony,   styrd him to syn in pride;
Bot in Paradise, securly,   myght no syn abide,
And therfor man full hastely   was put out in that tyde,
In wo and wandreth for to be,   in paynes full unrid   40
To knowe[4]:
Fyrst in erth, [and] sythen in hell
With feyndis for to dwell,
Bot he his mercy mell
To those that will hym trawe[5].

(6)

Oyle of mercy he hus hight[6]   as I have hard red,
To every lifyng wight   that wold luf hym and dred;
Bot now before his sight   every liffyng leyde,
Most party day and night[7],   syn in word and dede
Full bold;   50
Som in pride, ire and envy,
Som in covetous and glotyny,
Som in sloth and lechery,
And other wise many fold.

(7)

Therfor I drede lest God   on us will take veniance,
For syn is now alod   without any repentance;
Sex hundreth yeris and od   have I, without distance,
In erth, as any sod,   liffyd with grete grevance
All way;
And now I wax old,   60
Seke, sory, and cold,
As muk apon mold
I widder away;

---

40 *wandreth* misery   42 *sythen* then   45 *trawe* trust   48 *leyde* man
56 *alod* ?lost   62 *muk* muck   *mold* ground

(8)

> Bot yit will I cry   for mercy and call;
> Noe thi servant am I,   Lord, over all!
> Therfor me and my fry   shal with me fall;
> Save from velany   and bryng to thi hall
> In heven;
> And kepe me from syn,
> This warld within;
> Comly kyng of mankyn,
> I pray the, here my stevyn.

70

(9)

> [*God appears.*]
> DEUS: Syn I have maide all thyng   that is liffand,
> Duke, emperour, and kyng,   with myne awne hand,
> For to have thare likyng   bi see and bi sand,
> Every man to my bydyng   shuld be bowand
> Full fervent;
> That maide man sich a creatoure,
> Farest of favoure,
> Man must luf me paramoure,
> By reson, and repent.

80

(10)

> Me thoght I shewed man luf   when I made hym to be
> All angels abuf,   like to the Trynyte;
> And now in grete reprufe   full low ligis he,
> In erth hymself to stuf   with syn that displeasse me
> Most of all;
> Veniance will I take
> In erth for syn sake,
> My grame thus will I wake,
> Both of grete and small.

90

---

66 *fry* children   72 *stevyn* voice   75 *see* sea   80 *paramoure* with devotion   84 *ligis* lies   85 *stuf* gorge   89 *grame* anger

NOAH

(11)

    I repente full sore   that ever maide I man;
Bi me he settis no store   and I am his soferan;
I will distroy therfor   both beest, man, and woman,
All shall perish, les and more,   that bargan may thay ban,
That ill has done[8].
In erth I se right noght
Bot syn that is unsoght[9];
Of those that well has wroght
Fynd I bot a fone.

(12)

    Therfor shall I fordo   all this medill-erd
With floodis that shall flo   and ryn with hidous rerd;
I have good cause therto   for me no man is ferd.
As I say, shal I do,   of veniance draw my swerd,
And make end
Of all that beris life,
Sayf Noe and his wife,
For thay wold never stryfe
With me then me offend.

(13)

    Hym to mekill wyn   hastly will I go[10],
To Noe my servand, or I blyn,   to warn hym of his wo.
In erth I se bot syn   reynand to and fro,
Emang both more and myn,   ichon other fo[11]
With all thare entent.
All shall I fordo
With floodis that shall floo;
Wirk shall I thaym wo
That will not repent.

---

99 *fone* few   100 *fordo* destroy   101 *rerd* roar   108 *then* nor
111 *reynand* ruling

ENGLISH MYSTERY PLAYS

(14)

Noe, my freend, I thee commaund,   from cares the to keyle,
A ship that thou ordand   of nayle and bord ful wele.
Thou was alway well wirkand,   to me trew as stele,   120
To my bydyng obediand;   frendship shal thou fele
To mede;
Of lennthe thi ship be
Thre hundreth cubettis, warn I the,
Of heght even thrirte,
Of fyfty als in brede.

(15)

Anoynt thi ship with pik and tar   without and als within,
The water out to spar[12]   this is a noble gyn;
Look no man the mar.   Thre chese[13] chambres begyn;
Thou must spend many a spar   this wark or thou wyn   130
To end fully.
Make in thi ship also
Parloures oone or two,
And houses of offyce mo
For beestis that ther must be.

(16)

Oone cubite on hight   a wyndo shal thou make;
On the syde a doore with slyght   be-neyth shal thou take;
With the shal no man fyght,   nor do the no kyn wrake.
When all is doyne thus right   thi wife, that is thi make,
Take in to the;   140
Thi sonnes of good fame,
Sem, Iaphet, and Came,
Take in also hame,
Thare wifis also thre.

---

118 *keyle* cool, relieve   122 *mede* reward   125 *thrirte* thirty   126 *brede* breadth   127 *pik* pitch   128 *gyn* plan   133 *Parloures* rooms   137 *slyght* craft   143 *hame* them

NOAH

(17)

    For all shal be fordone   that lif in land bot ye,
    With floodis that from abone   shal fall, and that plente;
    It shall begyn full sone   to rayn uncessantle,
    After dayes seven be done,   and induyr dayes fourty,
    Withoutten fayll.
    Take to thi ship also   150
    Of ich kynd beestis two,
    Mayll and femayll, bot no mo,
    Or thou pull up thi sayll.

(18)

    For thay may the avayll   when al this thyng is wroght;
    Stuf thi ship with vitayll,   for hungre that ye perish noght;
    Of beestis, foull, and catayll   for thaym have thou in thoght;
    For thaym is my counsayll   that som socour be soght
    In hast;
    Thay must have corn and hay,
    And oder mete alway;   160
    Do now as I the say,
    In the name of the Holy Gast.

(19)

NOE: A, *benedicite!* What art thou that thus
    Tellys afore that shall be?   Thou art full mervelus!
    Tell me, for charite,   thi name so gracius.
DEUS: My name is of dignyte,   and also full glorius
    To knowe.
    I am God most myghty,
    Oone God in Trynyty,
    Made the and ich man to be;   170
    To luf me well thou awe.

(20)

NOE: I thank the, Lord, so dere,   that wold vowch-sayf
    Thus low to appere   to a symple knafe;

---

146 *abone* above   148 *induyr* last   160 *oder* other   173 *knafe* man

Blis us, Lord, here, for charite I hit crafe,
The better may we stere the ship that we shall hafe,
Certayn.
DEUS: Noe, to the and to thi fry
My blyssyng graunt I;
Ye shall wax and multiply,
And fill the erth agane,

(21)

When all thise floodis ar past and fully gone away.
NOE: Lord, homward will I hast as fast as that I may;
My [wife] will I frast what she will say, *Exit Deus.*
And I am agast that we get som fray
Betwixt us both[14];
For she is full tethee,
For litill oft angre,
If any thyng wrang be,
Soyne is she wroth.
Tunc perget ad uxorem[15].

(22)

God spede, dere wife! How fayre ye?
UXOR: Now, as ever myght I thryfe the wars I the see;
Do tell me, belife, where has thou thus long be?
To dede may we dryfe, or lif, for the,
For want[16].
When we swete or swynk,
Thou dos what thou thynk,
Yit of mete and of drynk
Have we veray skant.

(23)

NOE: Wife, we ar hard sted with tythyngis new.
UXOR: Bot thou were worthi be cled in Stafford blew[17];
For thou art alway adred, be it fals or trew;

---

174 *crafe* crave, beg 183 *frast* ask 186 *tethee* bad-tempered 189 *Soyne* soon 191 *wars* worse 193 *dryfe* rush 195 *swynk* toil 198 *skant* shortage 199 *sted* pressed *tythyngis* news 201 *adred* afraid

Bot God knowes I am led,   and that may I rew,
Full ill;
For I dar be thi borow,
From even unto morow
Thou spekis ever of sorrow;
God send the onys thi fill!

(24)

We women may wary   all ill husbandis;
I have oone, bi Mary   that lowsyd me of my bandis[18];
If he teyn, I must tary,   how so ever it standis,
With seymland full sory[19],   wryngand both my handis
For drede.
Bot yit other while,
What with gam and with gyle,
I shall smyte and smyle,
And qwite hym his mede.

(25)

NOE: We! Hold thi tong, ramskyt,   or I shall the still.
UXOR: By my thryft, if thou smyte   I shal turne the untill.
NOE: We shall assay as tyte.   Have at the, Gill!
Apon the bone shal it byte. [*Strikes her.*]
UXOR: A, so! Mary, thou smytis ill!
Bot I suppose
I shal not in thi det,
Flyt of this flett!
Take the ther a langett
To tye up thi hose! [*Strikes him.*]

(26)

NOE: A, wilt thou so?   Mary, that is myne.
UXOR: Thou shal thre for two,   I swere bi Godis pyne.
NOE: And I shall qwyte the tho,   in fayth or syne.
UXOR: Out apon the, ho!

---

204 *borow* guarantee   209 *lowsyd* loosened   210 *teyn* rage   217 *ramskyt* ram shit   219 *tyte* quickly   223 *Flyt* go   *flett* flood   224 *langett* thong   227 *pyne* pain

NOE: Thou can both byte and whyne
  With a rerd;   230
  For all if she stryke
  Yit fast will she skryke;
  In fayth I hold none slyke
  In all medill-erd.

(27)

  Bot I will kepe charyte,   for I have at do[20].
UXOR: Here shal no man tary the;   I pray the go to!
  Full well may we mys the,   as ever have I ro[21].
  To spyn will I dres me.
NOE: We! Fare well, lo;
  Bot, wife,
  Pray for me besele,   240
  To eft I com unto the.
UXOR: Even as thou prays for me,
  As ever myght I thrife.   [*Exit Uxor.*]

(28)

NOE: I tary full lang   fro my warke, I traw;
  Now my gere will I fang,   and thederward draw;
  I may full ill gang,   the soth for to knaw,
  Bot if God help amang,   I may sit downe daw
  To ken[22].
  Now assay will I
  How I can of wrightry,   250
  In nomine patris, et filii,
  Et spiritus sancti[23], *Amen.*

(29)

  To begyn[24] of this tree   my bonys will I bend;
  I traw from the Trynyte   socoure will be send;
  It fayres full fayre, thynk me,   this wark to my hend;
  Now blissid be he   that this can amend.

230 *rerd* roar   232 *skryke* shriek   233 *slyke* similar   240 *besele* busily
241 *eft* again   245 *gere* tools   *fang* fetch   247 *daw* fool   250 *wrightry*
carpentry

Lo, here the lenght,
Thre hundreth cubettis evenly;
Of breed, lo, is it fyfty;
The heght is even thyrty   260
Cubettis full strenght.

(30)

Now my gowne will I cast   and wyrk in my cote.
Make will I the mast   or I flyt oone foote.
A, my bak, I traw, will brast!   This is a sory note!
Hit is wonder that I last,   sich an old dote,
All dold,
To begyn sich a wark!
My bonys ar so stark,
No wonder if thay wark,
For I am full old.   270

(31)

The top and the sayll   both will I make,
The helme and the castell   also will I take,
To drife ich a nayll   will I not forsake.
This gere may never fayll,   that dar I undertake
Onone.
This is a nobull gyn,
Thise nayles so thay ryn,
Thoro more and myn[25],
Thise bordis ichon;

(32)

Wyndow and doore   even as he saide;   280
Thre ches chambre,   thay ar well maide,
Pyk and tar full sure   ther-apon laide,
This will ever endure,   therof am I paide,
For why
It is better wroght
Then I coude haif thoght;

---

260 *heght* height   264 *brast* break   265 *dote* dotard   266 *dold* old
268 *stark* stiff   274 *gere* equipment   275 *Onone* at once   281 *ches* tiers

Hym that maide all of noght
I thank oonly.

(33)

Now will I hy me,   and no-thyng be leder,
My wife and my meneye   to bryng even heder.   290
  [*Goes to his family.*]
Tent hedir tydely,   wife, and consider,
Hens must us fle,   all sam togeder,
In hast.
UXOR: Whi, syr, what alis you?
Who is that asalis you?
To fle it avalis you,
And ye be agast.

(34)

NOE: Ther is garn on the reyll   other, my dame[26].
UXOR: Tell me that ich a deyll[27],   els get ye blame.
NOE: He that cares may keill,   blissid be his name,   300
He has [het], for oure seyll,   to sheld us fro shame,
And sayd,
All this warld aboute
With floodis so stoute,
That shall ryn on a route,
Shall be overlaide.

(35)

He saide all shall be slayn,   bot oonely we,
Oure barnes that ar bayn,   and thare wifis thre;
A ship he bad me ordayn,   to safe us and oure fee.
Therfor with all oure mayn   thank we that fre   310
Beytter of bayll[28];
Hy us fast, go we thedir.

---

289 *leder* lazy   290 *meneye* company   291 *tydely* quickly   296 *it avalis you* it is to your advantage   298 *garn* yarn   *reyll* reel   300 *keill* cool, relieve   301 *seyll* happiness   305 *on a route* in a mass   308 *barnes* children   *bayn* obedient

NOAH

UXOR: I wote never whedir:
   I dase and I dedir
   For ferd of that tayll[29].

(36)

NOE: Be not aferd. Have done;   trus sam oure gere,
   That we be ther or none   without more dere.
I FILIUS: It shall be done full sone.   Brether, help to bere.
II FILIUS: Full long shall I not hoyne   to do my devere,
   Brether sam.
III FILIUS: Without any yelp
   At my myght shall I help.
UXOR: Yit for drede of a skelp
   Help well thi dam.

(37)

NOE [*approaches the Ark*]: Now ar we there   as we shuld be;
   Do get in oure gere,   oure catall and fe,
   In-to this vessell here,   my chylder fre.
UXOR: I was never bard ere,   as ever myght I the,
   In sich an oostre as this.
   In fath, I can not fynd
   Which is before, which is behynd;
   Bot shall we here be pynd,
   Noe, as have thou blis?[30]

(38)

NOE: Dame, as it is skill,   here must us abide grace;
   Therfor, wife, with good will,   com into this place.
UXOR: Sir, for Iak nor for Gill   will I turne my face
   Till I have on this hill   spon a space
   On my rok.
   Well were he myght get me;
   Now will I downe set me,

---

316 *trus sam* pack   317 *dere* harm   319 *hoyne* delay   *devere* duty
320 *sam* together   321 *yelp* boast   323 *skelp* blow   328 *bard* shut in
the thrive   329 *oostre* inn   337 *spon* spun   338 *rok* distaff

Yit reede I no man let me,
For drede of a knok.

(39)

NOE: Behold to the heven!   The cateractes all,
That are open full even,   grete and small,
And the planettis seven   left has thare stall;
Thise thoners and levyn   downe gar fall
Full stout,
Both halles and bowers,
Castels and towres;
Full sharp ar thise showers, 350
That renys aboute.

(40)

Therfor, wife, have done;   com into ship fast.
UXOR: Yei, Noe, go cloute thi shone!   The better will thai last.
I MULIER: Good moder, com in sone,   for all is over cast,
Both the sone and the mone.
II MULIER: And many wynd blast
Full sharp;
Thise floodis so thay ryn,
Therfor, moder, come in.
UXOR: In fayth yit will I spyn;
All in vayn ye carp. 360

(41)

III MULIER: If ye like ye may spyn,   moder, in the ship.
NOE: Now is this twyys com in,   dame, on my frenship.
UXOR: Wheder I lose or I wyn,   in fayth, thi felowship
Set I not at a pyn.   This spyndill will I slip
Apon this hill,
Or I styr oone fote.
NOE: Peter! I traw we dote;

341 *reede* advise   *let* hinder   346 *thoners* thunders   *levyn* lightning
gar begin to   353 *cloute* mend   *shone* shoes   360 *carp* complain
362 *twyys* twice   364 *spyndill* spindle

NOAH

Without any more note
Come in if ye will.

(42)

UXOR: Yei, water nyghys so nere   that I sit not dry.   370
Into ship with a byr,   therfor will I hy
For drede that I drone here. [*Rushes into Ark.*]
NOE: Dame, securly,
It bees boght full dere   ye abode so long by
Out of ship.
UXOR: I will not, for thi bydyng,
Go from doore to mydyng.
NOE: In fayth, and for youre long taryyng
Ye shal lik on the whyp.

(43)

UXOR: Spare me not, I pray the,   bot even as thou thynk,
Thise grete wordis shall not flay me.
NOE: Abide, dame, and   380
    drynk,
For betyn shall thou be   with this staf to thou stynk.
Ar strokis good? Say me.
UXOR: What say ye, Wat Wynk?
NOE: Speke!
Cry me mercy, I say!
UXOR: Therto say I nay.
NOE: Bot thou do, bi this day,
Thi hede shall I breke.

(44)

UXOR: Lord, I were at ese,   and hertely full hoylle[31],
Might I onys have a measse   of wedows coyll;
For thi saull, without lese,   shuld I dele penny doyll[32];   390
So wold mo, no frese,   that I se on this sole
Of wifis that ar here,
For the life that thay leyd,

---

371 *byr* rush   376 *mydyng* midden   378 *lik* lick, taste   380 *flay* scare
381 *to* till   389 *measse* dish   *coyll* cabbage   390 *lese* loss   391 *frese*
doubt   *sole* place

III

Wold thare husbandis were dede,
For, as ever ete I brede,
So wold I oure syre were.

(45)
NOE: Yee men that has wifis, whyls they ar yong,
If ye luf youre lifis, chastice thare tong:
Me thynk my hert ryfis, both levyr and long,
To se sich stryfis wedmen emong[33];   400
Bot I,
As have I blys,
Shall chastyse this.
UXOR: Yit may ye mys,
Nicholl Nedy!

(46)
NOE: I shall make the still as stone, begynnar of blunder!
I shall bete the bak and bone, and breke all in sonder.
  [*They fight.*]
UXOR: Out, alas, I am gone! Oute apon the, mans wonder!
NOE: Se how she can grone, and I lig under;
Bot, wife,   410
In this hast let us ho,
For my bak is nere in two.
UXOR: And I am bet so blo
That I may not thryfe.
  [*They enter the Ark.*]

(47)
I FILIUS: A, whi fare ye thus, fader and moder both?
II FILIUS: Ye shuld not be so spitus, standyng in sich a woth.
III FILIUS: Thise [weders] ar so hidus, with many a cold
  coth.
NOE: We will do as ye bid us; we will no more be wroth,
Dere barnes!
Now to the helme will I hent,   420
And to my ship tent.

398 *chastice* chastise 399 *ryfis* breaks *levyr* liver *long* lung 409 *lig*
(v) lie 416 *spitus* spiteful *woth* danger 417 *hidus* frightful *coth* illness

UXOR: I se on the firmament,
  Me thynk, the seven starnes[34].

(48)

NOE: This is a grete flood,   wife, take hede.
UXOR: So me thoght, as I stode,   we ar in grete drede;
  Thise wawghes ar so wode.
NOE: Help, God, in this nede!
  As thou art stere-man good,   and best, as I rede,
  Of all;
  Thou rewle us in this rase,
  As thou me behete hase.   430
UXOR: This is a perlous case:
  Help, God, when we call!

(49)

NOE: Wife, tent the stere-tre,   and I shall asay
  The depnes of the see   that we bere, if I may.
UXOR: That shall I do ful wysely.   Now go thi way,
  For apon this flood have we   flett many a day,
  With pyne.
NOE: Now the water will I fownd:
  A, it is far to the grownd;
  This travell I expownd   440
  Had I to tyne[35].

(50)

  Above all hillys bedeyn   the water is rysen late
  Cubettis xv.   Bot in a highter state
  It may not be, I weyn,   for this well I wate,
  This fourty dayes has rayn beyn;   it will therfor abate
  Full lele.
  This water in hast,
  Eft will I tast;
  Now am I agast,
  It is wanyd a grete dele.   450

---

426 *wawghes* waves   427 *stere-man* steersman   429 *rase* rush, current
433 *stere-tre* tiller   444 *wate* know   446 *lele* truly   450 *wanyd* waned

(51)

Now are the weders cest, and cateractes knyt,
Both the most and the leest.
UXOR: Me thynk, bi my wit,
The son shynes in the eest. Lo, is not yond it?
We shuld have a good feest, were thise floodis flyt
So spytus.
NOE: We have been here, all we,
CCC dayes and fyfty.
UXOR: Yei, now wanys the see;
Lord, well is us!

(52)

NOE: The thryd tyme will I prufe what depnes we bere. 460
UXOR: How long shall thou hufe? Lay in thy lyne there.
NOE: I may towch with my lufe the grownd evyn here.
UXOR: Then begynnys to grufe to us mery chere;
Bot, husband,
What grownd may this be?
NOE: The hyllys of Armonye[36].
UXOR: Now blissid be he
That thus for us can ordand!

(53)

NOE: I see toppys of hyllys he, many at a syght;
No thyng to let me, the wedir is so bright. 470
UXOR: Thise ar of mercy tokyns full right.
NOE: Dame, thi counsell me what fowll best myght,
And cowth,
With flight of wyng
Bryng, without taryyng,
Of mercy som tokynyng
Ayther bi north or southe?

---

451 *cest* ceased 461 *hufe* wait 462 *lufe* palm 463 *grufe* grow 469 *he* high 473 *cowth* can

NOAH

(54)
For this is the fyrst day   of the tent moyne.
UXOR: The ravyn, durst I lay,   will com agane sone;
As fast as thou may   cast hum furth – have done!   480
  [Noah releases the raven.]
He may happyn to day   com agane or none
With grath.
NOE: I will cast out also
Dowfys oone or two:
Go youre way, go;
God send you som wathe!
  [Releases doves.]

(55)
Now ar thise fowles flone   into seyr countre;
Pray we fast ichon,   kneland on our kne,
To hym that is alone   worthiest of degre,
That he wold send anone   oure fowles som fee   490
To glad us.
UXOR: Thai may not fayll of land,
The water is so wanand.
NOE: Thank we God all weldand,
That Lord that made us.

(56)
It is a wonder thyng,   me thynk, sothle,
Thai ar so long taryyng,   the fowles that we
Cast out in the mornyng.
UXOR: Syr, it may be
Thai tary to thay bryng.
NOE: The ravyn is a-hungrye
All way;   500
He is without any reson;
And he fynd any caryon,
As peraventure may be fon,
He will not away.

---

478 *tent* tenth   482 *grath* speed   486 *wathe* prey   487 *seyr* various
494 *weldand* making   499 *to thay bryng* till they bring (something)
503 *fon* found

(57)

    The dowfe is more gentill: her trust I untew,
    Like unto the turtill,   for she is ay trew.
UXOR: Hence bot a litill   she commys, lew, lew!
    She bryngys in her bill   som novels new;
    Behald!
    It is of an olif tre   510
    A branch, thynkys me.
NOE: It is soth, perde,
    Right so is it cald.

(58)

    Doufe, byrd full blist,   fayre myght the befall!
    Thou art trew for to trist   as ston in the wall;
    Full well I it wist   thou wold com to thi hall.
UXOR: A trew tokyn ist   we shall be savyd all,
    Forwhi
    The water, syn she com,
    Of depnes plom,   520
    Is fallen a fathom,
    And more hardely.

(59)

I FILIUS: Thise floodis ar gone,   fader, behold.
II FILIUS: Ther is left right none,   and that be ye bold.
III FILIUS: As still as a stone   oure ship is stold.
NOE: Apon land here anone   that we were, fayn I wold;
    My childer dere,
    Sem, Iaphet, and Cam,
    With gle and with gam,
    Com go we all sam;   530
    We will no longer abide here.

505, 514 *dowfe, doufe* dove   505 *untew* unto   506 *turtill* turtle dove   518 *Forwhi* because   520 *plom* plumb   525 *stold* stuck   529 *gle* mirth *gam* delight   530 *sam* together

(60)

UXOR: Here have we beyn,   Noy, long enogh,
   With tray and with teyn,   and dreed mekill wogh.
NOE: Behald on this greyn!   Nowder cart ne plogh
   Is left, as I weyn,   nowder tre then bogh,
   Ne other thyng,
   Bot all is away;
   Many castels, I say,
   Grete townes of aray,
   Flitt has this flowyng.   540

(61)

UXOR: Thise floodis not afright   all this warld so wide
   Has mevid with myght   on se and bi side.
NOE: To dede ar thai dyght,   prowdist of pryde,
   Ever ich a wyght   that ever was spyde,
   With syn,
   All ar thai slayn,
   And put unto payn.
UXOR: From thens agayn
   May thai never wyn?

(62)

NOE: Wyn? No, i-wis,   bot he that myght hase   550
   Wold myn of thare mys,   and admytte thaym to grace;
   As he in bayll is blis,   I pray hym in this space,
   In heven hye with his   to purvaye us a place,
   That we,
   With his santis in sight,
   And his angels bright,
   May com to his light:
   Amen, for charite.

   Explicit processus Noe, sequitur Abraham.

533 *tray* misery   *teyn* suffering   *wogh* harm   534 *greyn* grass
540 *flowyng* flood   542 *mevid* shifted   *side* shore   549 *wyn* escape
551 *myn* remember   *mys* loss   555 *santis* saints

5. Noah
De Deluvio Noe

CHESTER 3: WATERLEADERS AND DRAWERS OF DEE

The play was in the cycle before 1467, and the text itself is probably somewhat older. The manuscripts show some discrepancy: Harley 2124, which is somewhat fuller, is followed here.

The conflict between Noah and his wife is given its due place and comic overtones are suggested, but the dramatist is clearly concerned with a wider range of symbolic ideas. He gives much attention to the details of building the Ark, and to the procession of animals. Noah himself is a strong figure whose virtues are apparent, and whose persistence is rewarded. He shows more authority than the Towneley Noah, and is given a much more powerful part. He draws attention to the significance of the dove as the bringer of peace.

A comparison with the Towneley Noah suggests that the Chester dramatist was more orthodox and comprehensive in his approach to the story. The comedy here is kept under strict control, and there is room to introduce the more touching aspects of Noah's devotion to God.

༄༅

Et primo in aliquo supremo loco sive in nubibus, si fieri poterit, loquatur Deus ad Noe extra Archam existentem cum tota familia sua[1].

(1)

DEUS: I, God, that all the world have wrought,
    Heaven and earth, and all of nought,
    I see my people, in deede and thought,
    Are fowle sotted in synne.

NOAH

My ghost shall not lenge in man
That through fleshlie liking is my fone,
But till VI skore yeares be gone,
To loke if they will blynne².

(2)

Manne that I made I will destroy,
Beast, worme, and fowle to flie;
For on earthe they doe me nye,
The folke that is theron.
Hit harmes me so hartfullie,
The malyce now that can multeply,
That sore it greves [me] inwardlie
That ever I made manne.

(3)

Therfore, Noe, my servant free,
That righteous man art as I see,
A shipp sone thou shalt make the
Of trees drye and lighte.
Little chambers therein thou make
And bynding slich also thou take,
With-in and out thou ne slake
To anoynte it through all thy mighte.

(4)

300 cubytes it shall be long,
And 50 of breadeth, to mak it stronge,
Of heighte 50³: the [mete] thou fonge;
Thus measure it about⁴.
One wyndow worch through thy [wytte],
One cubyte of length and breadeth make it;
Upon the side a dore shall sit
For to come in and out.

---

5 *ghost* spirit   *lenge* stay   8 *blynne* cease   10 *worme* worm, serpent
11 *nye* annoy   22 *slich* mud (for caulking)   23 *slake* neglect   27 *mete*
measure   *fonge* catch, seize   29 *worch* make

(5)

    Eating places thou make also,
    Three roofed chambers, one or two;
    For with water I thinke to slowe
    Man that I can make.
    Destroyed all the world shalbe,
    Save thou; thy wife, thy sonnes three,
    And all there wives also with thee
    Shall saved be for thy sake.   40

(6)

NOE: Ah, Lord, I thanke the lowd and still
    That to me art in such will,
    And spares me and my house to spill[5],
    As now I sothlie fynde.
    Thy bydding, Lord, I shall fulfill,
    And never more the greeve ne grill,
    That suche grace hast sent me till
    Among all mankinde.

(7)

    Have done, yow men and women all!
    Helpe for ought that may befall   50
    To worke this shipp, chamber and hall,
    As God hath bydden us doe.
SEM: Father, I am already bowne;
    Anne axe I have, by my crowne,
    As sharpe as any in all this towne,
    For to goe there-to.

(8)

HAM: I have a hatchet wonder-kene
    To byte well, as may be seene;
    A better grownden, as I wene,
    Is not in all this towne.   60

---

35 *slowe* slay   41 *still* constantly   46 *grill* vex   47 *till* towards
53 *bowne* prepared   59 *grownden* ground, sharpened

NOAH

IAPHET: And I can well make a pyn,
   And with this hammer knocke yt in;
   Goe and worche without more dynne,
   And I am ready bowne.

(9)

UXOR NOE: And we shall bring tymber to,
   For wee mon nothing els doe;
   Women be weake to underfoe
   Any great travayle.
UXOR SEM: Here is a good hackstock;
   On this yow maye hew and knock;   70
   Shall non be idle in this flocke,
   Ne now may no man fayle.

(10)

UXOR HAM: And I will goe to gather sliche,
   The ship for to cleane and piche;
   Anoynted yt must be every stich,
   Board, tree, and pyn.
UXOR IAPHET: And I will gather chippes here
   To make a fire for yow in feere,
   And for to dight your dynner,
   Against yow come in.   80
   Tunc faciunt signa, quasi laborarent cum diversis instrumentis[6].

(11)

NOE: Now in the name of God I will begin
   To make the shippe that we shall in,
   That we be ready for to swym
   At the cominge of the flood.
   These bordes I ioyne here together,
   To keepe us safe from the wedder,
   That we may rowe both hither and thider,
   And safe be from this floode.

---

61 *pyn* wooden bolt   67 *underfoe* undergo   69 *hackstock* chopping block
79 *dight* prepare

ENGLISH MYSTERY PLAYS

(12)
    Of this tree will I [make] the mast
    Tyde with gables that will last,   90
    With a sayle-yarde for each blast,
    And each thinge in the[r] kinde.
    With topcastle[7] and bewsprytt,
    With coardes and ropes I hold all meete
    To sayle forth at the next weete;
    This shipp is at an ende.
        Tunc Noe iterum cum tota familia faciunt signa laborandi cum diversis instrumentis[8].

(13)
    Wife, in this castle we shall be keped,
    My childer and thou, I wold, in leaped.
UXOR NOE: In faith, Noe, I had as lief thou slepped
    For all thy frankish fare;   100
    For I will not doe after thy red.
NOE: Good wife, doe now as I the bydd.
UXOR NOE: By Christ, not or I see more neede,
    Though thou stand all the day and stare.

(14)
NOE: Lord, that women be crabbed aye,
    And never are meke, that dare I saye.
    This is well sene by me to-daye,
    In witnes of yow each one.
    Good wife, let be all this beere
    That thou makes in this place here;   110
    For all they wene thou art master[9],
    And so thou art by St John.

(15)
DEUS: Noe, take thou thy meanye,
    And in the shippe hye that yow be:

90 *Tyde* tied   *gables* ropes   93 *bewsprytt* bowsprit   95 *weete* rainstorm   97 *castle* cabin   100 *frankish* fancy   *fare* behaviour   105 *crabbed* bad-tempered   109 *beere* tumult   113 *meanye* company   114 *hye* hurry

NOAH

For none so righteous man to me
Is now on earth lyvinge.
Of cleane beastes with thee thou take
Seaven and seaven[10], or thou slake;
Hee and shee, make to make,
Be-lyve in that thou bringe[11],   120

(16)

Of beastes uncleane two and two
Male and female, without moe;
Of cleane fowles seaven alsoe
The hee and shee together,
Of fowles uncleane two and no more
[As I of beastes saide before;]
That shalbe saved throughe my lore
Against I send the wedder.

(17)

Of all meates that must be eaten
Into the ship loke there be getten;   130
For that no way man be foryeten,
And doe all this bydeene,
To sustayne man and beastes therein,
Aye till the water cease and blyn.
This world is filled full of synne,
And that is now well sene.

(18)

Seaven dayes be yet coming
You shall have space them into bringe,
After that is my lyking
Mankinde for to nye.   140
40 dayes and 40 nightes
Rayne shall fall for ther unrightes;

---

118 *or* before   *slake* stop   127 *lore* advice   128 *wedder* weather
131 *foryeten* forgotten   132 *bydeene* at once   142 *unrightes* wrongs

123

And that I have[12] made through my mightes
Now think I to destroye.

(19)

NOE: Lord, at your byddinge I am bayne,
Sith non other grace will gayne,
Hit will I fulfill fayne,
For gratious I thee fynde.
A 100 wynters and 20
This shipp making taried have I,   150
If through amendment any mercye
Wolde fall unto mankinde.

(20)

Have done, you men and women all!
Hye you lest this water fall,
That each beast were in his stall,
And into the ship broughte.
Of cleane beastes seaven shalbe,
Of uncleane two, this God bade me;
This floode is nye, well may we see,
Therfore tary you noughte.   160
> *Tunc Noe introibit archam et familia sua dabit et recitabit omnia animalia depicta in cartis et, postquam unusquisque suam locutus est partem, ibit in Archam, uxore Noe excepta, et animalia depicta cum verbis concordare debent, et sic incipiet Primus Filius*[13]

(21)

SEM: Syr, here are lyons, libardes in,
Horses, mares, oxen, and swyne,
Geates, calves, sheepe and kine,
Here sitten thou may see.
HAM: Camels, asses, men may finde,
Bucke, doe, harte, and hynde,

---

145 *bayne* obedient   151 *If* to see if   161 *libardes* leopards   163 *Geates* goats   *kine* cattle

NOAH

And beastes of all manner kinde
Here bene, as thinckes mee.

(22)

IAPHET: Take here cattes and dogges to,
Otter, fox, fulmart also,
Hares hopping gaylie can goe
Have cowle here for to eate.
UXOR NOE: And here are beares, wolfes sett,
Apes, owles, marmoset,
Weesells, squirrels and firret;
Here they eaten their meate.

(23)

UXOR SEM: Yet more beastes are in this howse:
Here cattis maken it full crowse[14];
Here a rotten, here a mowse,
They stand nye together.
UXOR HAM: And here are fowles, les and more:
Hearnes, cranes, and byttour,
Swans, peacockes, and them before
Meate for this wedder.

(24)

UXOR IAPHET: Here are cockes, kites, crowes,
Rookes, ravens, many rowes,
Duckes, curlewes, who ever knowes
Eache one in his kinde?
And here are doves, digges, drakes,
Redshankes runninge through the lakes,
And each fowle that ledden makes
In this shipp men may finde.

(25)

NOE: Wife, come in! Why standes thou there
Thou art ever froward, that dare I sweare.

170 *fulmart* polecat 172 *cowle* turnip 173 *sett* in a group 178 *cattis* cats 179 *rotten* rats 182 *Hearnes* herons *byttour* bitterns 186 *rowes* groups 189 *digges* ducks 191 *ledden* song 194 *froward* perverse

Come in, on Gods half![15] Tyme yt were,
For feare lest that we drowne.
UXOR NOE: Yea, sir, set up your sayle
And rowe forth with evill heale!
For, without any fayle,
I will not out of this towne.   200

(26)

But I have my gossips everichon
One foote further I will not gone;
They shall not drowne, by St John,
And I may save their lyfe.
They loved me full well, by Christ;
But thou wilt let them in thy chist,
Els rowe forth, Noe, whether thou list,
And get thee a new wife[16].

(27)

NOE: Sem, sonne, loe, thy mother is wraw.
For sooth such another I do not know.   210
SEM: Father, I shall fett her in, I trow,
Without any fayle.
Mother, my father after thee send,
And bydds the into yonder ship wend.
Loke up and se the wynde,
For we be readye to sayle.

(28)

UXOR NOE: Sonne, goe again to him and say:
I will not come therein to-daye.
NOE: Come in, wife, in 20 devills waye,
Or els stand there without.   220
HAM: Shall wee all fet her in?
NOE: Yea, sonnes, in Christs blessinge and myne:
I would yow hyde yow betyme,
For of this flood I am in doubte.

198 *heale* health, condition   206 *chist* ark   209 *wraw* angry   211 *fett* fetch   223 *hyde* hurried   *betyme* in good time   224 *doubte* fear

NOAH

(29)

THE GOOD GOSSOPES: The flood comes in full fleetinge fast[17],
On every side it spredeth full fare;
For feare of drowning I am agast,
Good gossip, let us draw neare.

(30)

And let us drinke or we depart
For often tymes we have done soe;
For at a draught thou drinkes a quarte
And so will I doe, or I goe.
    Here is a pottell of malmesy[18] good and stronge,
It will reioye both hart and tong;
Thou Noy thinke us never so long
Yet wee will drinke alyke[19].

(31)

IAPHET: Mother, we praye you altogether —
For we are here your [owne] childer —
Come into the ship for feare of the wedder,
For his love that you boughte[20].
UXOR NOE: That will I not for all your call,
But I have my gossopes all.
SAM: In feyth, mother, yet you shall
Whether you will or not.
    Tunc ibit[21].

(32)

NOE: Welcome, wife, into this boate.
UXOR NOE: And have thou that for thy mote!
    Et dat alapam vita[22].
NOE: A! Ha! Mary, this is hote,
It is good to be still.
A, childer, me thinkes my boate remeves,
Our tarying here hugelie me greves.
Over the lande the water spredes:
God doe as he will.

227 *agast* afraid   246 *mote* arguing   247 *hote* hot

(33)

Ah, great God that art so good!
[That worchis not thie will is wood.]
Now all this world is on a flood
As I see well in sighte.
This window will I steake anon,
And into my chamber will I gone,
Till this water, so great one,
Be slaked through thy mighte.   260

> *Tunc Noe claudet fenestram Archae et per modicum spatium infra tectum cantent psalmum 'Save mee, O God,' et aperiens fenestram et respiciens*[23].

(34)

Now 40 dayes are fullie gone.
Send a raven I will anone
If ought-where earth, tree, or stone
Be drye in any place.
And if this foule come not againe,
It is a signe, soth to sayne,
That drye it is on hill or playne,
And God hath done some grace.

> *Tunc dimittet corvum et capiens columbam in manibus dicat*[24].

(35)

Ah, Lord, wherever this raven be,
Somewhere is drye, well I see;   270
But yet a dove, by my lewtye,
After I will sende.
Thou wilt turne againe to me

. . . .

For of all fowles that may flye
Thou art most meke and hend.

---

254 *wood* mad   263 *ought-where* anywhere   271 *lewtye* faith   276 *hend* gentle

NOAH

Tunc emittet columbam et erit in nave alia columba ferens olivam in ore, quam dimittet ex malo per funem in manus Noe, et postea dicat Noe[25]

(36)
Ah, Lord, blessed be thou aye,
That me hast comfort thus to-day;
By this sight I may well saye
This flood beginnes to cease. 280
My sweete dove to me brought hase
A branch of olyve from some place
This betokeneth God has done us some grace,
And is a signe of peace.

(37)
Ah, Lord, honoured most thou be,
All earthe dryes now I see,
But yet tyll thou comaunde me,
Hence will I not hye.
All this water is awaye
Therfore as sone as I maye 290
Sacrifice I shall doe in faye
To thee devoutlye.

(38)
DEUS: Noe, take thy wife anone
And thy children every one;
Out of the shippe thou shalt gone,
And they all with thee.
Beastes and all that can flie
Out anone they shall hye,
On earth to grow and multeplye.
I will that yt be soe. 300

(39)
NOE: Lord, I thanke the through thy mighte,
Thy bidding shall be done in height,

291 *faye* faith

And as fast as I may dighte
I will doe the honoure,
And to thee offer sacrifice;
Therfore comes in all wise[26],
For of these beastes that bene hise
Offer I will this stower.

> *Tunc egrediens Archam cum tota familia sua accipiet animalia sua et volucres et offeret ea et mactabit*[27].

(40)

Lord God in maiestye,
That such grace hast graunted me,
Where all was lorne, safe to be,
Therfore now I am bowne,
My wife, my childer, my meanye
With sacrifice to honoure thee
With beastes, fowles, as thou may see,
I offer here right sone.

(41)

DEUS: Noe, to me thou arte full able,
And thy sacrifice acceptable;
For I have fownd thee trew and stable
On the now must I myn.
Warry Earth will I no more
For mans synne that greves [me] sore;
For of youth man full yore
Has byn enclyned to syne[28].

(42)

You shall now grow and multeply,
And earth againe you edefie;
Each beast and fowle that may flie,
Shall be afrayd of you.
And fishe in sea that may flytte

303 *dighte* prepare   307 *hise* his   308 *stower* hour   311 *lorne* lost
317 *able* empowered   320 *myn* remember   321 *Warry* trouble
323 *yore* for a long time   326 *edefie* establish

NOAH

Shall susteyne yow, I yow behite;   330
To eate of them yow ne lett
That cleane bene you may knowe[29].

(43)

Thereas you have eaten before
Grasse and rootes, sith you were bore,
Of cleane beastes now, les and more,
I geve you leave to eate,
Safe bloode and flesh bothe in feare[30]
Of wrong dead carren that is here,
Eates not of that in no manere;
For that aye you shall let.   340

(44)

Manslaughter also you shall flee;
For that is not pleasant to me:
That shedes bloode, he or shee,
Ought-where amonge mankinde,
That sheedes blood, his blood shed shall be[31],
And vengence have, that men shall se;
Therfore beware now all yee,
You fall not in that synne.

(45)

And forwarde now with yow I make,
And all thy seede for thy sake   350
Of suche vengeance for to slake,
For now I have my will.
Here I behet the a heaste
That man, woman, fowle ne beaste
With water, while the world shall last,
I will no more spill.

---

331 *lett* refrain   338 *carren* carrion   349 *forwarde* promise   351 *slake* stop

(46)

> My Bowe[32] betwene you and me
> In the firmament shall bee,
> By verey token that you may see
> That such vengeance shall cease, 360
> That man ne woman shall never more
> Be wasted by water as is before,
> But for syn that greveth me sore,
> Therfore this vengeance was.

(47)

> Where cloudes in the welkin bene,
> That ilke bowe shall be sene
> In tokeninge that my wrath and tene
> Shall never thus wroken be.
> The stringe is turned toward you
> And toward me is bend the bowe, 370
> That such wedder shall never showe,
> And this behet I thee.

(48)

> My blessing now I geve the here
> To thee, Noe, my servant dere,
> For vengeance shall no more appeare;
> And now fare well, my darling deere.

Finis paginae tertiae.

359 *verey* true   366 *ilke* same   367 *tene* anger   372 *behet* promise

6. Abraham and Isaac
De Abrahamo et Melchisedech et Loth

CHESTER 4: BARBERS (AND PAINTERS)

This play, which was in the cycle by 1467, begins with the episode of Melchisadech. The incident is not found elsewhere in the English mystery plays, though there is a separate play devoted to it in Le Mistère du Viel Testament (Play 15). *There are hints in other* Chester *plays that there was some influence from the French cycle. The importance of the incident here lies in its foreshadowing of the bread and wine. There is no doubt that the Chester dramatist was particularly interested in the presentation of themes of symbolic importance.*

This tendency is also evident in the main episode, the sacrifice of Isaac. Here the figure presented is that Abraham stands for God the Father, and Isaac for Christ who must be sacrificed. These associations are made clear in the play. Isaac is a willing victim of divine necessity, and it has been suggested that his carrying of the wood to the place of sacrifice is linked with Christ's carrying of the Cross.

The dramatist is restrained as to style, but the emotional states of both father and son are clearly shown. Isaac is portrayed as a child, and much is made of his pathetic obedience, and his concern for his father and his mother. In the York *cycle he appears as a man of thirty: the effect there being to intensify the link with Christ at the Crucifixion, but at the expense of pathos. There is no doubt that in spite of the firm theological basis for the play the Chester dramatist gives a hint of tragedy in the reaction to suffering.*

One of the most interesting aspects of this play is the close similarity of part of it to the Brome *Abraham and Isaac: this is discussed in the Introduction to the next play.*

[*Enter Nuntius.*]

(1)

NUNTIUS: All peace, lordinges, that be present
And herken now with good intent,
Now Noe away from us is went
And all his companye;
And Abraham through Gods grace
He is comen into this place,
And yow will geve him rowme and space
[To tell you of storye.]

(2)

This playe, forsooth, begin shall he
In worship of the Trynitie 10
That yee may all here and see
That shall be done to-daye.
My name is Gobet-on-the-Grene[1].
With yow no longer I maye bene;
Farewell, my lordinges, all by-dene,
For letting of your playe.
Et exit.
[*Enter Abraham, with Lot.*]

(3)

ABRAHAM: A, thou high God, graunter of grace,
That ending ne beginning hase,
I thank thee, lord, that to me hase
To-daye geven victorye. 20
Lothe[2], my brother, that taken was,
I have restored him in this case
And brought him home into this place,
Through thy might and mastrye.

---

15 *by-dene* withal, indeed (primarily a rime-word) 16 *For letting* for fear of preventing

134

ABRAHAM AND ISAAC

(4)

>To worship the I will not wond,
>That 4 kinges of uncouth land
>To-daye hast sent into my hand,
>And of riches great araye.
>Therefore of all that I can wyn
>To geve thee tyth I will begin, 30
>The cyttie sone when I come in
>And part with the my praye.

(5)

>Melchisadech[3], that here kinge is
>And Gods preist also, I wis,
>The tyth I will geve him of this
>As skill is that I doe.
>God that hase send me victorye
>Of 4 kinges graciouslie,
>With him my praye departe will I
>The cittye when I come to. 40

(6)

LOTHE: Abraham, brother, I thank it thee,
>That this daye hast delyvered me
>Of enemyes handes and there postye
>And saved me from woe.
>Therefore I will geve tithinge
>Of my good whyle I am lyvinge,
>And now also of his sendinge
>Tythe I will geve also.
>>*Tunc venit Armiger ad Melchisadech*[4].

(7)

ARMIGER: My lord, the kings tydinges arighte,
>Your harte for to glade and lighte, 50
>Abraham hath slayne in fighte
>4 kinges sith he went.

25 *wond* omit   26 *uncouth* unknown   30 *tyth* tithe   36 *skill* proper

Here he will be this ilke nighte
And riches with hym enough dight.
I hard him thank God almight,
Of grace he had hym sent.
    Melchisedech extendens manus ad Caelum[5]

(8)

MELCHISEDECH: Ah, blessed be God that is but one!
Against Abraham I will gone,
Worshipfullie and that anone,
My office to fulfill,   60
And present hym with bread and wyne[6]
For grace of God is him withine;
Speedes fast for love myne!
For this is Godes will.

(9)

ARMIGER [*cum cuppa*]: Syr, here is wyne, withouten were,
And [therto] bread, both white and cleere,
To present him in good manere
That so [us] holpen hase.
MELCHISADECH: To God, I wot, he is full deere,
For of all thinges his prayer,   70
He hath without danger[7],
And speciallie great grace.

(10)

    *Tunc Melchisadeck equitabit versus Abraham, offerens
    calicem cum vino et panem super patinam.*[8]
Abraham, welcome must thou be;
Gods grace is fullie in the;
Blessed ever [must thou] be
That enemyes so can meke.
I have brought, as you may see,
Bread and wyne for thy degree

54 *dight* ready   55 *hard* heard   63 *Speedes* be quick   65 *were* doubt
76 *meke* (v) humble

ABRAHAM AND ISAAC

Receave this present now at me,
And that I thee beseke.   80

(11)

ABRAHAM: Syr kinge, welcome in good faye,
Thy present is welcome to my paye.
God hase holpen me to-daye,
Unworthy though I were.
He shall have parte of my praye
That I wan, sith I went awaye.
Therfore to thee thou take it maye,
The tenth I offer here.
  Tunc tradet equum oneratum sibi[9].

(12)

MELCHISADECH: And your present, sir, take I,
And honour yt devoutelye   90
For much good yt may signefie
In tyme that is cominge.
Therfore horse, harnes, and perye,
As falles for your dignitie,
The tythe of yt [I] take of thee,
And receave thy offringe.
  *Tunc Abraham recipiet panem et vinum, et Melchisedech
  equum oneratum Loth Decimae*[10].

(13)

LOTHE: And I will offer with good intent
Of such good [as] God hath me sent
To Melchisadech here present,
As Godis will [is to] be.   100
Abraham, my brother, offred hase,
And so will I through Gods grace,
This royall cupp before your face;
Receave yt now at mee.
  *Tunc Loth offeret cuppam cum vino et pane et recipiet
  Melchisadech*[11].

80 *beseke* beseech   93 *perye* jewellery

ENGLISH MYSTERY PLAYS

(14)

MELCHISADECH: Syr, your offringe welcome is
 And well I wot forsoth, I wis,
 That fullie Gods will yt is
 That is now done to-daye.
 Goe wee together to my cyttie,
 And now God hartelie thank we
 That helpes us aye through his postye;
 For so we full well maye.

(15)

EXPOSITOR [*equitando*]: Lordinges, what this may signifie
 I will expound apertlie,
 That lewed standing hereby
 May knowe that this may be.
 This offring, I saie verament,
 Signifieth the new testament,
 That now is used with good intent
 Througheout all Christianitye.

(16)

 In the old lawe, without leasing,
 When these two good men were lyving,
 Of beastes was all their offring,
 And [eck] their sacramente.
 But sith Christ dyed on the roode tree
 With bread and wyne him worship we;
 And on Sherthursday, in his maundye[12],
 Was his comaundment.

(17)

 But for this thinge used shold be
 Afterward as now done wee,
 In signification, [as] leve you me,
 Melchisedech did soe;

114 *apertlie* openly   115 *lewed* ignorant people   117 *verament* truly
121 *leasing* lying   124 *eck* also   127 *Sherthursday* Holy (Maundy)
Thursday   131 *leve* believe

ABRAHAM AND ISAAC

And tythes-makinge, as you se here,
Of Abraham begunnen were,
Therfore he was to God full deare,
And so were they both twoo.

(18)

By Abraham understand I may
The Father of heaven[13] in good faye,
Melchisadech a preist to his paye
To minister that sacrament,
That Christ ordayned on Sherethursday
In bread and wyne to honour him aye –
[This signifieth the south to saye]
Melchisadechs present.

(19)

DEUS: Abraham, my servant, I saie to thee
Thy helpe and succour I will be,
For thy good deed much pleaseth me,
I tell thee wytterlie.
ABRAHAM: Lord, one thing that thou wilt see
That I praie after with hart free:
Graunt me, Lord, through thy postye,
Some fruyte of my bodye!

(20)

I have no childe, fowle ne fayre,
Safe my Nurry[14] to be my heyre;
That makes me greatlie to apayre,
On me, Lord, have mercye!
DEUS: My frend, Abraham, leve thou me,
Thy Nurry thyne heyre shall not bee,
But one sonne I shall send the,
[Be]gotten of thy bodye.

---

148 *wytterlie* surely   154 *Safe* except   155 *apayre* decay

ENGLISH MYSTERY PLAYS

(21)

>Abraham, doe as I thee saye:
>Looke up and tell me, if thou maye,
>Starres standing on the straye –
>That unpossible were.
>No more shalt thou for thy meede,
>Nomber of thy bodye the seede,
>That thou shalt have for thy good deede,
>Thou art to me so deere.

(22)

>Wherfore, Abraham, servant free,
>Loke that thou be trewe to me,
>And forward here I make with the
>Thy seede to multeplie.
>[So much more further shalt thou be
>Kingis of thie seed men shall see]
>And one Child of great degree
>All mankind shall forbye.

(23)

>I will that from henceforth alwaie
>Ech knaveschild [one] the eight daye
>Be cyrcumcised[15], as I saye,
>And thou thy-self full sone;
>And who circumcised ne is
>Forsaken [shalbe with me,] i-wis;
>For inobedyent that man is.
>Therfore looke that this be done.

(24)

>ABRAHAM: Lord, already, in good faye,
>Blessed be thou, ever and aye;
>For that men verey knowe may
>Thy folke from other men,

163 *straye* ?open sky   169 *free* noble   171 *forward* bargain   176 *forbye* redeem   178 *knaveschild* boy   *one* on   187 *verey* truly

ABRAHAM AND ISAAC

Cyrcumcised they shall be all,
Anon for ought that may befall.
[I thank thie,] lord, thy owne thrall,
Kneling on my knen.

(25)

EXPOSITOR: Lordinges all, takes good intent
What betokens this comaundment;
This was sometyme a sacrament
In thould lawe truely tane.
As followeth now verament
So was this in the Old Testament;
But when Christ dyed, away yt went,
And Baptisme then began.

(26)

Also God behetes here
To Abraham, his servant deere,
So much seede that in no manere
Nombred might not be;
And one seede, mankinde to forby,
That was Ihesus Christ witterlye,
For of his kinde was our Lady,
And so also was he.

(27)

DEUS: Abraham, my servant Abraham!
ABRAHAM: Loe, Lord, already here I am.
DEUS: Take Isaack, thy sonne by name
That thou lovest best of all,
And in sacrafice offer him to me
Upon that hill, besyde thee.
Abraham, I will that yt be so
For ought that may befall.

---

191 *thrall* servant   192 *knen* knees   196 *thould* the old   *tane* taken
201 *behetes* (v) promises   205 *forby* redeem

(28)

ABRAHAM: My Lord, to thee is my entent
   Ever to be obedyent;
   That sonne that thou to me hast sent
   Offer I will to thee,   220
   And fulfill thy comaundment
   With harty will, as I am kent.
   High God, Lord omnipotent,
   Thy bydding done shall be.

(29)

   My meany and my childer ech one
   Lenges at home, both all and one,
   Safe Isaak shall with me gone
   To an hill here besyde.
   Make thee ready, my derling[16],
   For we must doe a lyttle thing.   230
   This wood upon thy back it bring.
   We must not long abyde.

(30)

   A sword and fire I will take
   For sacrifice I must make;
   [Godis] bydding will I not forsake,
   But aye obedyent bee.
ISAAK: Father, I am all readye
   To doe your bydding mekelie,
   To beare this wood [full] bowne am I,
   As you comaund me.   240

(31)

ABRAHAM: O Isaak, Isaak, my derling deere,
   My blessing [now] I geve the here.
   Take up this fagot with good cheare,
   And on thy backe yt bringe,

---

222 *kent* instructed   225 *meany* followers   226 *Lenges* remain
239 *bowne* ready

ABRAHAM AND ISAAC

And fire with me I will take.
ISAAK: Your bydding I will not forsake;
    Father, I will never slake
    To fulfill your byddinge.
    Tunc Isaak accipiet lignum super tergum et ad montem pariter ibunt[17].

(32)

ABRAHAM: Now Isaake, sonne, goe we our waye,
    To yonder mowntayne, if that we maye.   250
ISAAK: My deere father, I will assaye
    To follow you full fayne.
ABRAHAM: O! My hart will break in three,
    To heare thy wordes I have pyttie.
    As thou wilt, lord, so must yt be:
    To thee I will be bayne.

(33)

    Lay downe thy fagot, my owne sonne deere.
ISAAK: All ready, father, loe yt is here.
    But why make you so heavie cheare?
    Are you any thing adred?   260
    Father, if it be your will,
    Where is the beast that we shall kill?
ABRAHAM: Therof, sonne, is none upon this hill,
    That I see here in this steed.

(34)

ISAAK: Father, I am full sore afraide
    To see you beare this drawen sworde.
    I hope for all middle-yorde,
    You will not slaye your childe[18].
ABRAHAM: Dread not thou, my childe, I red.
    Our lord will send of his godhead,   270
    Some maner beast into this stydd,
    Ether tayme or wylde.

---

256 *bayne* obedient   264, 271 *steed, stydd* place   267 *middle-yorde* world

(35)

ISAAK: Father, tell me, or I goe,
  Whether I shall have harme or noe.
ABRAHAM: Ah dere God, that me is woe!
  Thou burstes my hart in sunder.
ISAAK: Father, tell me of this case
  Why you your sword drawen hase
  And beare yt naked in this place;
  Thereof I have great wonder.   280

(36)

ABRAHAM: Isaac, sonne, peace! I pray thee,
  Thou breakes my harte even in three.
ISAAC: I praye you, father, leane nothing from me,
  But tell me what you thinke.
ABRAHAM: O Isaac, Isaac, I must thee kill.
ISAAC: Alas! Father, is that your will,
  Your owne childe here for to spill,
  Upon this hilles brynke?

(37)

  If I have trespassed in any degree,
  With a yard you maye beate me;   290
  Put up your sword if your will be,
  For I am but a childe.
ABRAHAM: O my sonne, I am sory
  To doe to thie this great anye;
  Gods comaundment do must I;
  His workes are ay full mylde.

(38)

ISAAC: Wold God my mother were here with me!
  She wolde knele upon her knee,
  Praying you, father, if it might be,
  For to save my life.   300

283 *leane* hide   294 *anye* harm

ABRAHAM AND ISAAC

(39)

ABRAHAM: O comelie creature, but I thee kill,
I greeve my God, and that full ill:
I may not worke against his will
But ever obedyent be.
O Isaac, sonne, to thee I saye:
God has comaunded me this daye
Sacrifice — this is no naye —
To make of thy [boddye.]

(40)

ISAAC: Is it Gods will I shold be slayne?
ABRAHAM: Yea, sonne, it is not for to layne;   310
To his bydding I will be bayne,
Ever to his pleasinge.
But that I doe this dolefull deede,
My lord will not quyte me my meede.
ISAAC: Mary, father, God forbydd
But you doe your offringe.

(41)

Father, at home your sonnes you shall finde
That you must love by course of kinde.
Be I out once of your mynde
Your sorrow may sone cease;   320
But you must doe Gods bydding.
Father, tell my mother for nothing.
ABRAHAM: For sorrow I may my handes wring,
Thy mother I cannot please.

(42)

O Isaac, Isaac, blessed mot thou be!
Almost my wyt I lose for thee,
The blood of thy bodye so free
Me think full loth to sheed.
ISAAC: Father, sith you must needs doe soe,
Let it passe lightlie and overgoe;   330

301 *but* unless   307 *naye* denying   310 *layne* hide   314 *quyte* repay
meede desert   330 *overgoe* pass by

Kneling on my knees twoo
Your blessing on me spreade!

(43)

ABRAHAM: My blessing, deere sonne, give I the
And thy mothers with hart so free;
The blessing of the Trynitie,
My deare sonne, on the lighte!
ISAAC: Father, I pray you, hyde myne eyne,
That I se not your sword so kene;
Your stroke, father, wold I not seene,
Lest I against yt grill. 340

(44)

ABRAHAM: My deere sonne Isaac, speak no more,
Thy wordes make my hart full sore.
ISAAC: O deere father, wherfore? Wherfore?
Syth I must nedes be dead.
Of one thing I wold you praye,
[Since I must die the death this daye,]
As few strokes as you maye,
When you smyte of my heade.

(45)

ABRAHAM: Thy mekenes, childe, makes me afray;
My song may be 'well awaye!' 350
ISAAC: O deare father, doe awaye, doe awaye,
Your making so mickle mone!
Now truly, father, this talking
Doth but make long tarying.
I praye you, come and make ending,
And let me hence gone!

(46)

ABRAHAM: Come hither, my child, that art so sweete:
Thou must be bounden, hand and feete.
  Tunc colliget eum, et liga[b]it[19].

340 *grill* complain   352 *mickle* great

ABRAHAM AND ISAAC

ISAAC: A, father, we must no more mete
    By ought that I can see,   360
    But doe with me right as you will;
    I must obay, and that is skill,
    Gods comaundment to fulfill,
    [For needis so must it be.]

(47)

    Upon the purpose that you have set you,
    For sooth, father, I will not let you[20],
    But evermore unto you bowe
    Whyle that I maye.
    Father, greete well my brethren yonge,
    And praye my mother of her blessinge,   370
    I come no more under her winge.
    Farewell for ever and aye!

(48)

    But, father, I crye you mercye.
    Of that I have trespassed to thee,
    Forgeven, father, that yt may be
    Untill Domes-daye.

(49)

ABRAHAM: My deare sonne, let be thy mones;
    My child, thou greaved me but ones.
    Blessed by thou, bodye and bones,
    And I forgeve thee here.   380
    Loe, my deare sonne, here shalt thou lye;
    Unto my worke now must I hye,
    I had as leefe myselfe to dye
    As thou my darling dere.

---

359 *mete* meet   362 *skill* right   383 *leefe* rather

ENGLISH MYSTERY PLAYS

(50)

ISAAC: Father, if you be to me kinde,
About my heade a kercher bynde,
And let me lightlie out of your mynde,
And sone that I were spedd.
ABRAHAM: Farewell, my sweete sonne of grace!
ISAAC: I praye you, father, turne downe my face 390
A lyttle whyle, whyle you have space,
For I am full sore adred.

(51)

ABRAHAM: To doe this deede I am sorye.
ISAAC: Yea, lord, to thee I call and crye:
On my soule thou have mercye,
Hartelie I the praye.
ABRAHAM: Lord, I wold fayne worke thy will —
This yonge inocent that lyes so still
Full loth were me hym to kill,
By any manner of waye. 400

(52)

ISAAC: My deare father, I you praye,
Let me take my clothes awaye,
For sheeding blood[21] on them to-daie
At my last endinge.

(53)

ABRAHAM: Harte, if thou wolde breake in three,
Thou shalte never master me[22].
I will no lenger let for thee,
My God I may not greeve.
ISAAC: A mercye, father! Why tary you so?
Smyte of my head, and let me goe! 410
I praie you, rydd me of my woe;
For now I take my leave.

386 *kercher* kerchief, cloth   407 *let* refrain

ABRAHAM AND ISAAC

(54)

ABRAHAM: Ah, sonne, my harte will breake in three
   To heare thee speake such wordes to me.
   Ihesu, on me thou have pittie,
   That I have most in mynde!
ISAAC: Nowe, father, I se that I shall die,
   Almightie God in maiestie,
   My soule I offer unto thee:
   Lord, to yt be kinde.   420

Tunc accipiet gladium, faciens occidendi signum, et Angelus veniens capiet punctum gladii illius, ac postea dicat Angelus[23]

(55)

ANGELUS: Abraham, my servant deere!
ABRAHAM: Loe, lord! I am alreadye here.
ANGELUS I: Laie not thy sword in no maner
   On Isaac, thy deare derling!
   Naie, do thou hym no anoy.
   For thou dreades God, well se I,
   That of thy sonne hast no mercy
   To fulfill his byddinge.

(56)

ANGELUS II: And for his bydding thou doest aye,
   And spares nether for feare nor fraie   430
   To doe thy sonne to death to-daye,
   Isaac to thee full deere;
   Therefore God hase sent by me, in faye,
   A lambe[24] that is both good and gaie
   Into this place, as thou se maye.
   Loe, it is right here!

(57)

ABRAHAM: Ah, lord of heaven and king of blise,
   Thy bydding shall I doe, I wis.

---

430 *fraie* strife

Sacrifice here to me sent is
And all, lord, throughe thy grace.
A horned wedder here I se,
Among the breeres tyed is he,
To the offred it shall be
Anone right in this place.
Tunc Abraham mactabit arietem[25].

(58)

DEUS: Abraham, by my selfe I sweare,
For thou hast bene obedyent ever,
And spared not thy sonne so deare,
To fulfill my bydding,
Thou shalt be blessed, thou art worthy,
Thy seede I shall multeplye,
As starrs and sand, so many het I,
Of thy bodie cominge.

(59)

Of enemyes thou shalt have power,
And thy bloode also in feare[26],
For thou hast bene meke and boneere,
To doe as I the bade.
And all nations, leeve thou me,
Blessed evermore shal be
Through fruyt that shall come of thee,
And saved throughe thy seede.

(60)

EXPOSITOR: Lordinges, this significacion
Of this deed of devotion,
And you will, you wit mon,
May turne you to much good[27].
This deed you se done in this place,
In example of Ihesu[28] done yt was,

---

441 *wedder* wether   442 *breeres* briars   451 *het* promise   455 *boneere* willing, courteous

That for to wyn mankinde grace
Was sacrifised on the [rode.]

(61)

By Abraham I may understand
The Father of heaven that can fand
With his sonnes blood to breake that band
The Devil had brought us too.
By Isaac understand I may
Ihesu that was obedyent aye,
His fathers will to worke alway,
His death to underfonge.

Finis paginae quartae.

470 *fand* try   476 *underfonge* receive, endure

7. Abraham and Isaac

BROME, SUFFOLK

There is no record of a performance of this play which has survived in a manuscript of the second half of the fifteenth century. It was written into a kind of commonplace book which was later used for some accounts. The language is consistent with that of Suffolk in the fifteenth century, and there is no reason to suppose that its survival at Brome is anything other than a fortunate chance whereby it remained close to the place where it was written down. The scribe was not the author, and he had considerable trouble with the rimes. The original was probably not earlier than 1400. Brome is, and was, a very small community and there is no likelihood that there was ever a cyclic performance in the locality.

Nevertheless the play has many similarities with the genuine cycle plays. Not the least of these is the close correspondence between ll. 105– 315 of the Brome play and ll. 229–420 of Chester 4 (Play 6 in this selection). Though the two plays are not as close as the parallels which appear between York and Towneley in half a dozen plays, it is not doubted that there was some interrelationship, and there are several places where the words are the same. But the stanza forms are different, and from a dramatic point of view there are variations of pace and emphasis. There is no consensus as to which came first, though the article by J. B. Severs (see Note on Books, p. 38) has received strong support. He sought to show that the Brome play was coherent in places where the Chester was corrupt, and thus to establish that the Brome was nearer to being the original version.

Critics are also divided as to the merits of the two: such judgements are often made on modern aesthetic considerations, and the division of feeling is such that each play has been found to be both splendid and dull. Here it is perhaps sufficient to say that the Chester often seems the more restrained of the two. Where the plays divide, after the release of Isaac by the Angel, the Brome version adds much personal and emotional detail which perhaps weakens the impact of the main conflict. As in the

ABRAHAM AND ISAAC

Chester *play, Isaac is a boy, and much is made of the pathetic circumstances of the divine command.*

৩০

[*Enter Abraham, accompanied by Isaac.*]

(1)

ABRAHAM: Fader of Hevyn Omnipotent,
    Wyth all my hart to the I call;
    Thow hast goffe me both lond and rent,
    And my lyvelod thow hast me sent:
    I thanke the heyly evermore of all[1].

(2)

    Fyrst off the erth thou madyst Adam,
    And Eve also to be ys wyffe;
    All other creaturys of them too cam;
    And now thow hast grant to me, Abraham,
    Her in thys lond to lede my lyffe.   10

(3)

    In my age[2] thou hast grantyd me thys,
    That thys yowng chyld wyth me schall won;
    I love no thyng so myche, iwysse,
    Excepe thin owyn selffe, der Fader of blysse,
    As Ysaac her, my owyn swete son.

(4)

    I have dyverse chyldryn moo,
    The wych I love not halffe so wyll;
    Thys fayer swet chyld, he schereys me soo,
    In every place wer that I goo,
    That noo dessece her may I fell.   20

---

3 *goffe* given   4 *lyvelod* living   5 *heyly* greatly   12 *won* live   15 *her* here   17 *wyll* well   18 *swet* sweet   *schereys* cheers   20 *dessece* harm *fell* feel

ENGLISH MYSTERY PLAYS

(5)

    And ther-for, Fadyr of Hevyn, I the prey,
    For hys helth and also for hys grace;
    Now, Lord, kepe hym both nygth and day,
    That never dessese nor noo fray
    Cume to my chyld in noo place.

(6)

    Now cum on, Ysaac, my owyn swet chyld;
    Goo we hom and take owre rest.
YSAAC: Abraham, myn owyn fader so myld,
    To folowe yow I am full glad[3],
    Bothe erly and late.   30
ABRAHAM: Cume on, swete chyld, I love the best
    Off all the chyldryn that ever I begat.
    [*As they go their way, God sends the Angel.*]

(7)

DEUS: Myn Angell, fast hey the thy wey,
    And on-to medyll-erth anon thou goo;
    Abrams hart now wyll I asay,
    Wethere that he be stedfast or noo.

(8)

    Sey I commaw[n]dyd hym for to take
    Ysaac, hys yowng sonne, that he love so wyll,
    And wyth hys blood sacryfyce he make,
    Yffe ony off my freynchepe he wyll fell.   40

(9)

    Schow hym the wey on-to the hylle
    Wer that hys sacryffyce schall be;
    I schall asay now hys good wyll,
    Whether he lovy[th] better hys chyld or me.
    All men schall take exampyll be hym
    My commawmentys how they schall kepe[4].

24 *fray* fear   33 *hey the* go   34 *medyll-erth* earth   40 *freynchepe* friendship, affection

ABRAHAM AND ISAAC

(10)

ABRAHAM: Now, Fader of Hevyn, that formyd all thyng,
    My preyerys I make to the ageyn,
    For thys day my tender offryng
    Here must I geve to the, certeyn.   50
    A! Lord God, Allmyty Kyng,
    Wat maner best woll make the most fayn?
    Yff I had therof very knoyng,
    Yt schuld be don wyth all my mayn
    Full sone anon.
    To don thy plesyng on an hyll,
    Verely yt ys my wyll,
    Dere Fader God in Trenyte.

(11)

THE ANGELL: Abraham, Abraham, wyll thou rest!
    Owre Lord comandyth the for to take   60
    Ysaac, thy yowng son that thow lovyst best,
    And wyth hys blod sacryfyce that thow make.

(12)

    Into the lond of V[y]syon[5] thow goo,
    And offer thy chyld on-to thy Lord;
    I schall the lede: and schow all-soo
    Unto Goddys hest, Abraham, acord,
    And folow me up-on thys gren.
ABRAHAM: Wolle-com to me be my Lordys sond,
    And hys hest I wyll not wythstond;
    Yyt Ysaac, my yowng sonne in lond,   70
    A full dere chyld to me have byn.

(13)

    I had lever, yf God had be plesyd,
    For to a forbore all the good that I have[6],
    Than Ysaac my son schuld a be desessyd,
    So God in Hevyn my sowll mot save!

---

48 *the* thee   52 *fayn* pleased   53 *very* true   *knoyng* knowledge   54 *mayn* strength   67 *gren* grass   68 *sond* messenger   70 *Yyt* yet   *in lond* on earth

(14)

I lovyd never thyng soo mych in erthe,
And now I must the chyld goo kyll.
A! Lord God, my conseons ys stronly steryd,
And yyt, my dere Lord, I am sore aferd
To groche ony thyng agens yowre wyll.   80

(15)

I love my chyld as my lyffe,
But yyt I love my God myche more,
For thow my hart woold make ony stryffe,
Yyt wyll I not spare for chyld nor wyffe,
But don after my Lordys lore.

(16)

Thow I love my sonne never so wyll,
Yyt smyth of hys hed sone I schall.
A! Fader of Hevyn, to the I knell,
An hard deth my son schall fell
For to honore the, Lord, wythall.   90

(17)

THE ANGELL: Abraham, Abraham, thys ys wyll seyd,
And all thys comamentys loke that thou kepe;
But in thy hart be no-thyng dysmayd.
ABRAHAM: Nay, nay, forsoth, I hold me wyll plesyd,
To plesse my God wyth the best that I have;

(18)

For thow my hart be hevely sett
To see the blood of my owyn dere son,
Yyt for all thys I wyll not lett;
   [*Exit Angel.*]
But Ysaac, my son, I wyll goo fett,
And cum asse fast as ever we can.   100

---

78 *conseons* conscience   80 *groche* complain of   87 *smyth* smite
92 *comamentys* commandments   98 *lett* make difficulties

ABRAHAM AND ISAAC

(19)

Now, Ysaac, my owyn son dere,
Wer art thow, chyld? Speke to me.
YSAAC: My fayer swet fader, I am here,
And make my preyrys to the Trenyte.

(20)

ABRAHAM: Rysse up, my chlyd, and fast cum heder[7],
My gentyll barn that art so wysse,
For we to, chyld, must goo to-geder,
And onto my Lord make sacryffyce.

(21)

YSAAC: I am full redy, my fader, loo!
[Evyn] at yowr handys I stand rygth here,   110
And wat-so-ever ye byd me doo,
Yt schall be don with glad chere,
Full wyll and fyne.
ABRAHAM: A! Ysaac, my owyn son soo dere,
Godys blyssyng I gyffe the, and myn.

(22)

Hold thys fagot upon thi bake,
And her my-selffe fyere schall bryng.
YSAAC: Fader, all thys her wyll I packe[8];
I am full fayn to do yowre bedyng.
ABRAHAM: A! Lord of Hevyn, my handys I wryng;   120
Thys chyldys wordys all to-wond my harte.

(23)

Now, Ysaac, son, goo we owr wey
On-to yon mownte, wyth all owr mayn.
YSAAC: Gowe, my dere fader, as fast as I may
To folow yow I am full fayn,
All-thow I be slendyr.

106 *barn* child   119 *bedyng* bidding   121 *to-wond* wound deeply

157

ABRAHAM: A! Lord, my hart brekyth on tweyn,
Thys chyldys wordys, they be so tender.

(24)

[*They reach the mountain.*]
A! Ysaac, son, anon ley yt down,
No lenger upon thi backe yt bere;
For I must make me redy bon
To honowre my Lord God as I schuld.

(25)

YSAAC: Loo, my dere fader, wer yt ys!
To cher yow all-wey I draw me nere;
But, fader, I mervell sore of thys,
Wy that ye make thys hevy chere;

(26)

And also, fader, evermore dred I:
Wer ys yowr qweke best that ye schuld kyll?
Both fyer and wood we have redy,
But queke best have we non on this hyll.

(27)

A qwyke best, I wot wyll, must be ded,
Yowr sacryfyce for to make.
ABRAHAM: Dred the nowgth, my chyld, I the red,
Owre Lord wyll send me onto thys sted
Summ maner a best for to take,
Throw his swet sond.
YSAAC: Ya, fader, but my hart begynnyth to quake,
To se that scharpe sword in yowre hond.

(28)

Wy bere ye yowre sword drawyn soo?
Off youre [contenaunce] I have mych wonder.

127 *tweyn* twain   131 *redy bon* quite ready   138 *qweke* living   *best* animal   141 *wot* know   143 *nowgth* not   *red* tell   144 *sted* place

ABRAHAM AND ISAAC

ABRAHAM: A! Fader of Hevyn, so I am woo!
Thys chyld her brekyth my harte on too.

(29)

YSAAC: Tell me, my dere fader, or that ye ses,
Bere ye yowr sword draw for me?
ABRAHAM: A! Ysaac, swet son, pes! pes!
For i-wys thow breke my harte on thre.

(30)

YSAAC: Now trewly, sumwhat, fader, ye thynke
That ye morne thus more and more.
ABRAHAM: A! Lord of Hevyn, thy grace let synke[10],
For my hart wos never halffe so sore.   160

(31)

YSAAC: I preye yow, fader, that ye wyll let me yt wyt,
Wyther schall I have ony harme or noo?
ABRAHAM: I-wys, swet son, I may not tell the yyt[11],
My hart ys now soo full of woo.

(32)

YSAAC: Dere fader, I prey yow, hydygth not fro me,
But sum of yowr thowt that ye tell me.
ABRAHAM: A! Ysaac! Ysaac! I must kyll the.
YSAAC: Kyll me, fader? Alasse! Wat have I don?

(33)

Yff I have trespassyd agens yow owt,
With a yard ye may make me full myld;   170
And wyth yowre scharp sword kyll me nogth,
For i-wys, fader, I am but a chyld.

(34)

ABRAHAM: I am full sory, son, thy blood for to spyll,
But truly, my chyld, I may not chese.

153 *or that* before   161 *wyt* know   165 *hydygth* hide (it)   174 *chese* chose

159

YSAAC: Now I wold to God my moder were her on this hyll!
Sche woold knele for me on both hyre kneys
To save my lyffe.
And sythyn that my moder ys not here,
I prey yow, fader, schonge yowr chere,
And kyll me not wyth yowyre knyffe.   180

(35)
ABRAHAM: Forsothe, son, but gyf I the kyll[12],
I schuld greve God rygth sore, I drede;
Yt ys hys commawment and also hys wyll
That I schuld do thys same dede.

(36)
He commawndyd me, son, for serteyn,
To make my sacryfyce wyth thy blood.
YSAAC: And ys yt Goddys wyll that I schuld be slayn?
ABRAHAM: Ya, truly, Ysaac, my son soo good,
And ther-for my handys I wryng.
YSAAC: Now, fader, agens my Lordys wyll   190
I wyll never groche, lowd nor styll[13];
He mygth a sent me a better desteny
Yf yt had a be hys plecer.

(37)
ABRAHAM: For-sothe, son, but yf I ded this dede,
Grevously dysplessyd owre Lord wyll be.
YSAAC: Nay, nay, fader. God forbede
That ever ye schuld greve hym for me.

(38)
Ye have other chyldryn, on or too,
The wyche ye schuld love wyll be kynd;
I prey yow, fader, make ye no woo,   200
For, be I onys ded and fro yow goo,
I schall be sone owt of yowre mynd[14].

179 *schonge* change   181 *but gyf* unless   191 *styll* persistently   192 *a* have   193 *plecer* pleasure   194 *ded* did   199 *be kynd* by nature

ABRAHAM AND ISAAC

(39)

Therfor doo owre Lordys byddyng,
And wan I am ded, than prey for me;
But, good fader, tell ye my moder no-thyng;
Sey that I am in another cuntre dwellyng.

ABRAHAM: A! Ysaac, Ysaac, blyssyd mot thow be!

(40)

My hart begynnyth stronly to rysse,
To see the blood off thy blyssyd body.

YSAAC: Fadyr, syn yt may be noo other wysse,   210
Let yt passe over as wyll as I[15].

(41)

But, fader, or I goo onto my deth,
I prey yow blysse me wyth yowre hand.

ABRAHAM: Now, Ysaac, wyth all my breth,
My blyssyng I geve the upon thys lond,
And Godys also ther-to, i-wys.
A, Ysaac, Ysaac, son, up thow stond,
Thy fayere swete mowthe that I may kys.

(42)

YSAAC: Now, forwyll, my owyn fader so fyn,
And grete wyll my moder in erthe.   220
But I prey yow, fader, to hyd my eyne,
That I se not the stroke of yowr scharpe sword,
That my fleysse schall defyle.

ABRAHAM: Son, thy wordys make me to wepe full sore
Now, my dere son Ysaac, speke no more.

YSAAC: A, my owyn dere fader, were-fore?
We schall speke to-gedyr her but a wylle.

(43)

And sythyn that I must nedysse be ded,
Yyt, my dere fader, to yow I prey,
Smyth but fewe strokys at my hed,   230

---

219 *fyn* noble   220 *grete* greet   221 *eyne* eyes

> And make an end as sone as ye may,
> And tery not to longe.
>
> ABRAHAM: Thy meke wordys, chyld, make me afrayed;
> So welawey may be my songe[16],

(44)

> Excepe alonly Godys wyll[17].
> A! Ysaac, my owyn swete chyld,
> Yyt kysse me agen upon thys hyll!
> In all thys ward ys non soo myld.

(45)

> YSAAC: Now, truly, fader, all thys teryyng,
> Yt doth my hart but harme;
> I prey yow, fader, make an enddyng.
> ABRAHAM: Cume up, swet son, on-to my arme.

(46)

> I must bynd thy handys too,
> All-thow thow be never soo myld.
> YSAAC: A, mercy, fader! Wy schuld ye do soo?
> ABRAHAM: That thow schuldyst not let, my chyld.

(47)

> YSAAC: Nay, i-wysse, fader, I wyll not let yow;
> Do on for yowre wyll,
> And on the purpos that ye have set yow,
> For Godys love kepe yt forthe styll.

(48)

> I am full sory thys day to dey,
> But yyt I kepe not my God to greve;
> Do on yowre lyst for me hardly[18],
> My fayer swete fader, I geffe yow leve.

---

232 *tery* delay   235 *alonly* alone   238 *ward* world   239 *teryyng* delay
246 *let* hinder   251 *dey* die   252 *kepe* wish   254 *leve* leave

ABRAHAM AND ISAAC

(49)

But fader, I prey yow evermore,
Tell ye my moder no dell;
Yffe sche wost yt, sche wold wepe full sore,
For i-wysse, fader, sche lovyt me full wyll;
Goddys blyssyng mot sche have!
Now forwyll, my moder so swete, 260
We too be leke no mor to mete.

ABRAHAM: A, Ysaac, Ysaac! son, thou makyst me to gret,
And wyth thy wordys thow dystempurst me.

(50)

YSAAC: I-wysse, swete fader, I am sory to greve yow;
I cry yow mercy of that I have donne,
And of all trespasse that ever I ded meve yow;
Now, dere fader, forgyffe me that I have donne.
God of Hevyn be wyth me!

(51)

ABRAHAM: A, dere chyld, lefe of thy monys;
In all thy lyffe thow grevyd me never onys; 270
Now blyssyd be thow, body and bonys,
That ever thow were bred and born.

(52)

Thow hast be to me chyld full good;
But i-wysse, chyld, thow I morne never so fast,
Yyt must I nedys here at the last
In thys place sched all thy blood.

(53)

Therfor, my dere son, here schall thou lye,
On-to my warke I must me stede,
I-wysse I had as leve myselffe to dey,
Yffe God wyll be plecyd wyth my dede, 280

256 *no dell* nothing   257 *wost* knew   261 *leke* likely   262 *gret* weep
263 *dystempurst* sadden   266 *meve* move   269 *monys* complaints
278 *stede* set to

163

And myn owyn body for to offere.
YSAAC: A, mercy, fader, morne ye no more;
Yowr wepyng make my hart sore
As my owyn deth that I schall suffere.

(54)

Yowre kerche, fader, abowt my eyn ye wynd!
ABRAHAM: So I schall, my swettest chyld in erthe.
YSAAC: Now yyt, good fader, have thys in mynd,
And smyth me not oftyn wyth yowr scharp sword,
But hastely that yt be sped.
Here Abraham leyd a cloth over Ysaacys face, thus seyyng
ABRAHAM: Now forewyll, my chyld, so full of grace. 290
YSAAC: A, fader, fader, torne downgward my face,
For of yowre scharpe sword I am ever adred.

(55)

ABRAHAM: To don thys dede I am full sory,
But, Lord, thyn hest I wyll not wythstond.
YSAAC: A, Fader of Hevyn, to the I crye,
Lord, reseyve me in-to thy hand!

(56)

ABRAHAM: Loo, now ys the tyme cum, certeyn,
That my sword in hys necke schall synke.
A! Lord, my hart reysyth therageyn[19],
I may not fyndygth in my harte to smygth; 300
My hart wyll not now ther-too,
Yyt fayn I woold warke my Lordys wyll;
But thys yowng innosent lygth so styll,
I may not fyndygth in my hart hym to kyll.
O, Fader of Hevyn! What schall I doo?

(57)

YSAAC: A, mercy, fader, wy tery ye so,
And let me ley thus longe on this heth?

285 *kerche* kerchief   290 *forewyll* farewell   294 *hest* command
303 *lygth* lies   307 *heth* heath

ABRAHAM AND ISAAC

Now I wold to God the stroke were doo.
Fader, I prey yow hartely, schorte me of my woo,
And let me not loke thus after my degth.

(58)

ABRAHAM: Now, hart, wy wolddyst not thow breke on thre?
Yyt schall thou not make me to my God on-myld.
I wyll no lenger let for the,
For that my God agrevyd wold be.
Now hoold the stroke, my owyn dere chyld[20].
Her Abraham drew hys stroke and the Angell toke the sword in hys hond soddenly.

(59)

THE ANGELL: I am an angell, thow mayist be blythe,
That fro hevyn to the ys senth;
Owre Lord thanke the an C sythe[21]
For the kepyng of hys commawment.

(60)

He knowyt thi wyll and also thy harte,
That thow dredyst hym above all thyng,
And sum of thy hevynes for to departe
A fayer ram[22] yynder I gan brynge;

(61)

He standyth teyed, loo, among the brerys.
Now, Abraham, amend thy mood,
For Ysaac, thy yowng son that her ys,
Thys day schall not sched hys blood;

(62)

Goo, make thy sacryfece wyth yon rame,
For on-to hevyn I goo now hom.

---

309 *schorte me of* shorten for me 310 *loke ... after* anticipate *degth* death 312 *on-myld* rebellious 322 *departe* relieve 323 *yynder* yonder 324 *teyed* tied *brerys* briars

Now forwyll, blyssyd Abraham, 330
The wey ys full gayn.
Take up thy son soo free.
[Exit Angel.]
ABRAHAM: A! Lord, I thanke the of thy gret grace;
Now am I yethed on dyvers wysse.
A-rysse up, Ysaac, my dere sunne, a-rysse,
A-rysse up, swete chyld, and cum to me.

(63)

YSAAC: A, mercy, fader, wy smygth ye nowt yyt?
A, smygth on, fader, onys wyth yowre knyffe!
ABRAHAM: Pesse, my swet sun, and take no thowt,
For owre Lord of Hevyn hath grant thi lyffe, 340
Be hys Angell now,

(64)

That thou schalt not dey this day, sunne, truly.
YSAAC: A, fader, full glad than wer I,
I-wys, fader, I sey i-wys,
Yf thys tall wer trew!
ABRAHAM: An hundyrd tymys, my son fayer of hew,
For joy thi mowth now wyll I kys.

(65)

YSAAC: A! my dere fader, Abraham,
Wyll not God be wroth that we do thus?
ABRAHAM: Noo, noo! harly, my swyt son, 350
For yyn same rame he hath us sent,
Hethyr down to us.

(66)

Yyn best schall dey here in thi sted,
In the worthchup of owr Lord alon;
Goo fet hym hethyre, my chyld, inded.

---

334 *yethed* comforted, eased 339 *thowt* thought 345 *tall* tale 350 *harly* certainly 351 *yyn* yon 353 *best* beast 354 *worthchup* worship

ABRAHAM AND ISAAC

YSAAC: Fader, I wyll goo hent hym be the hed,
And bryng yon best wyth me a-non.

(67)

A, scheppe, scheppe, blyssyd mot thou be
That ever thow were sent down heder!
Thow schall thys day dey for me, 360
In the worchup of the Holy Trynyte.
Now cum fast and goo we togeder
To my fader [in hy²³].
Thow thou be never so jentyll and good,
Yyt had I lever thow schedyst thi blood,
I-wysse, scheppe, than I.

(68)

Loo, fader, I have browt here full smerte
Thys jentyll scheppe, and hym to yow I gyffe:
But, Lord God, I thank the with all my hart,
For I am glad that I schall leve, 370
And kys onys my dere moder.
ABRAHAM: Now be rygth myry, my swete chylld,
For thys qwyke best that ys so myld,
Here I schall present be-fore all othere.

(69)

YSAAC: And I wyll fast begynne to blowe,
Thys fyere schall brene a full good spyd.
But, fader, wyll I stowppe down lowe,
Ye wyll not kyll me with yowre sword, I trowe?²⁴
ABRAHAM: Noo, harly, swet son, have no dred,
My mornyng ys past. 380
YSAAC: Ya! but I woold that sword were in a glad,
For i-wys, fader, yt make me full yll agast.
*Here Abraham mad hys offryng, knelyng and seyyng
thus*

---

356 *hent* take, seize   372 *myry* merry   373 *qwyke* living   376 *brene* burn
377 *stowppe* stoop   380 *mornyng* grieving   381 *glad* sheath

(70)

ABRAHAM: Now, Lord God of Hevyn, in Trynyte,
All-myty God Omnipotent,
Myn offeryng I make in the worchope of the,
And wyth thys qweke best I the present.
Lord, reseyve thow myn intent,
As [thow] art God and grownd of owr grace.

(71)

DEUS: Abraham, Abraham, wyll mot thow sped,
And Ysaac, thi yowng son, the by![25] 390
Truly, Abraham, for thys dede
I schall multyplye yowrys botherys sede[26]
As thyke as sterrys be in the skye,
Bothe more and lesse;
And as thyke as gravell in the see,
So thyke multyplyed yowre sede schall be;
Thys grant I yow for yowre goodnesse.

(72)

Off yow schall cume frewte gret[27],
And ever be in blysse wythowt yynd,
For ye drede me as God a-lon 400
And kepe my commawmentys everyschon.
My blyssyng I geffe, wer-so-ever ye goo.

(73)

ABRAHAM: Loo! Ysaac, my son, how thynke ye
Be thys warke that we have wrogth?
Full glad and blythe we may be,
Agens the wyll of God that we grucched nott,
Upon thys fayere hetth.
YSAAC: A, fader, I thanke owre Lord every dell,
That my wyt servyd me so wyll,
For to drede God more than my detth. 410

387 *reseyve* receive   393 *sterrys* stars   395 *gravell* stones   399 *yynd* end
404 *wrogth* done   406 *grucched* complained   408 *dell* part, scrap

ABRAHAM AND ISAAC

(74)

ABRAHAM: Why! dere-wordy son, wer thow adred?
  Hardely, chyld, tell me thy lore.
YSAAC: Ya! be my feyth, fader, now [have[28]] I red,
  I wos never soo afrayd be-fore
  As I have byn at yyn hyll.
  But, be my feyth, I swere
  I wyll nevermore cume there
  But yt be agens my wyll.

(75)

ABRAHAM: Ya, cum on wyth me, my owyn swet son,
  And hom-ward fast now let us goon.   420
YSAAC: Be my feyth, fader, ther-to I grant;
  I had never so good wyll to gon hom,
  And to speke wyth my dere moder.
ABRAHAM: A! Lord of Hevyn, I thanke the,
  For now may I led hom wyth me
  Ysaac, my yownge son soo fre,
  The gentyllest chyld above all erthe:
  Thys may I wyll a-voee[29].

(76)

  Now goo we forthe, my blyssyd son.
YSAAC: I grant, fader, and let us gon,   430
  For be my trowthe, were I at home
  I wold never gon owt under that forme.
  I pray God geffe us grace evermo,
  And all thow that we be holdyng to[30].
    [*Exeunt Abraham and Isaac. Enter the Doctor.*]

(77)

DOCTOR: Lo, sovereyns and sorys, now have we schowyd
  Thys solom story[31] to gret a[nd] smale;

---

411 *dere-wordy* beloved   426 *fre* noble   428 *a-voee* declare, proclaim
432 *forme* way   435 *sorys* sirs   436 *solom* serious, weighty

It ys good lernyng to lernd and lewyd,
And the wysest of us all,
Wyth-owtyn ony berryng.
For thys story schoyt yowe [her]   440
How we schuld kepe to owr po[we]re
Goddy s commawmentys wyth-owt grochyng.

(78)

Trowe ye, sorys, and God sent an angell
And commawndyd yow [yowre chyld to slayn[32]],
Be yowre trowthe ys ther ony of yow
That eyther wold groche or stryve therageyn?

(79)

How thyngke ye now, sorys, therby?
I trow ther be iij ore iiij or moo;
And thys women that wepe so sorowfully
Whan that hyr chyldryn dey them froo,   450
As nater woll, and kynd![33]
Yt ys but folly, I may wyll awooe,
To groche a-gens God or to greve yow,
For ye schall never se hym meschevyd, wyll I know,
Be lond nor watyr; have thys in mynd.

(80)

And groche not a-gens awre Lord God,
In welthe or woo, wether that he yow send,
Thow ye be never so hard be-stad,
For whan he wyll, he may yt a-mend.
Hys comawmentys trewly yf ye kepe wyth goo[d] hart,   460
As thys story hath now scho[w]yd yow befor[n]e,
And feytheffully serve hym qwyll ye be quart,

---

437 *lewyd* ignorant   439 *berryng* exception   440 *schoyt* shows
442 *grochyng* complaint   451 *nater* nature   452 *awooe* declare, assert
454 *meschevyd* harmed   457 *wether* whichever   458 *be-stad* beset
462 *quart* alive

ABRAHAM AND ISAAC

That ye may plece God bothe evyn and morne.
Now Jhesu, that weryt the crown of thorne,
Bryng us all to hevyn-blysse!

464 *weryt* wore

8. Moses

YORK 11: HOSEERS (AND DRAPERS)

Moses has three functions in the mystery cycles: he presents the Ten Commandments; he appears as one of the prophets of the Nativity; and he acts as a focus for a number of figurative parallels. The York dramatists dealt with the first two aspects in other plays; in this pageant the attention is concentrated upon the third, which is approached through the episodes of the Burning Bush, the Plagues, and the Red Sea. The Burning Bush is a manifestation of God's miraculous power and his particular concern for the Jews and their descendants. As with Abraham and Jacob, God is concerned to show his intention that the Jews survive and multiply; and, of course, one may substitute Christians for the Jews. Moreover the episode suggests the important later incidents enacted in the Transfiguration and the Pentecost. Pharaoh's persecution of the Jews prefigures the Massacre of the Innocents: indeed, the ranting of Pharaoh is close to that of Herod, and there are hints of similar physical cruelties. At the same time the Egyptians subjected to the Plagues are like mankind punished by the Flood. Their final destruction by water is a parallel to the fate of Noah's contemporaries. The echoes of this continue through to Judgement Day. The episode of the Red Sea, with Moses as the quasi-divine saviour of the Chosen People, anticipates the Harrowing of Hell. Thus the play is a good example of the extensive use of 'figures'.

In Burton's list of 1415 there is mention only of the episode of the serpent: one may suppose that the other episodes were not present at that time. The amalgamation of the efforts of the Hosiers with the Drapers for a short time may be a further indication that the early years of the fifteenth century saw considerable modification and development in this play. As Towneley 8 *is virtually the same play, the revision must have occurred before the cycles diverged.*

MOSES

[*Scene: Egypt. The action takes place in three locations: Pharaoh's court, near Mount Sinai where the Jews live, and at the crossing of the Red Sea.*]

[*Pharaoh's court.*]

(1)

REX: O pees, I bidde that noman passe,
   But kepe the cours that I comaunde,
   And takes gud heede to hym that hasse
   Youre liff all haly in his hande.
   Kyng Pharo my fadir was,
   And led the lordshippe of this lande;
   I am hys hayre, as elde will asse[1],
   Evere in his steede to styrre and stande.
   All Egippe is myne awne,
   To lede aftir my lawe;   10
   I will my myght be knawen
   And honnoured als it awe.

(2)

   Ther-fore als Kyng I commaunde pees
   To all the pepill of this Empire,
   That noman putte hym fourthe in prees,
   But that will do als we desire.
   And of youre sawes I rede you sees,
   And sesse to me, youre sufferayne sire,
   That most youre comforte may encrese
   And at my liste lose liffe and lyre.   20
1 CONSULTOR: My lorde, yf any were
   That walde not wirke youre will,
   And we wist whilke thay were,
   Ful sone we sall thaym spill.

---

3 *hasse* has   4 *haly* wholly   8 *steede* place   *styrre* move   9 *awne* own
11 *knawen* known   12 *als* as   *awe* ought   15 *prees* crowd   17 *sawes*
words   *sees* cease   20 *liste* will   *lyre* flesh   22 *walde* would   23 *whilke*
which   24 *spill* destroy

ENGLISH MYSTERY PLAYS

(3)

REX: Thurgh-oute my kyngdome wolde I kenn,
And konne tham thanke that couthe me telle,
If any wer so weryd then
That wolde aught fande owre forse to fell.
II CON: My lorde, thar are a maner of men
That mustirs grete maistris tham emell,   30
The Jewes that wonnes here in Jessen
And er named the childir of Israell.
They multyplye so faste
That suthly we suppose
Thay are like, and they laste,
Yowre lordshippe for to lose.

(4)

REX: Why, devill, what gawdes have they begonne?
Er thai of myght to make a frayse?
I CON: Tho felons folke, sir, first was fonn
In kyng Pharo youre fadyr dayse;   40
Thay come of Joseph, Jacob sonn,
That was a prince worthy to prayse,
And sithen in ryste furthe are they run,
Now ar they like to lose our layse[2].
Thay sall confounde us clene,
Bot if thai sonner sese.
REX: What devill ever may it mene,
That they so fast encrese?

(5)

II CON: Howe they encrese, full wele we kenn,
Als oure elders be-fore us fande;   50
Thay were talde but sexty and ten

---

25 *kenn* know   26 *konne* give   *couthe* could   27 *weryd* cursed
28 *aught* anything   *fande* try   29 *maner* type   30 *mustirs* shows   *grete*
great   *maistris* powers   *emell* among   31 *wonnes* live   32 *er* are
34 *suthly* truly   36 *lose* destroy   37 *gawdes* tricks   38 *frayse* stir
39 *felons* wicked   *fonn* found   43 *sithen* then   *ryste* increase   46 *sonner*
sooner   50 *fande* discovered   51 *talde* counted

174

MOSES

Whan thei enterd in-to this lande.
Sithen have they soionerd here in Jessen
Foure houndereth yere, this we warande;
Now are they noumbered of myghty men,
Wele more than thre hundereth thowsande,
With-owten wiffe and childe,
And herdes that kepes ther fee[3].

REX: So myght we be bygillid
But certis that sall noght be,   60

(6)

For with qwantile[4] we sall tham qwelle,
That thei sall no farrar sprede.
I CON: Lorde, we have herde oure fadres telle
Howe clerkis that ful wele couthe rede
Saide a man shulde wax tham emell
That suld for-do us and owre dede.
REX: Fy on tham! to the devell of helle!
Swilke destanye sall we noght drede.
We sall make mydwayes[5] to spille tham,
Whenne oure Ebrewes are borne,   70
All that are mankynde to kille tham,
So sall they sone be lorne.

(7)

For of the other have I non awe;
Swilke bondage sall we to tham bede,
To dyke and delfe, beere and drawe,
And do all swilke un-honest dede.
Thus sall the laddis be holden lawe,
Als losellis ever thaire lyff to leede.
II CON: Certis, lorde, this is a sotell sawe,
So sall the folke no farrar sprede.   80

---

59 *bygillid* deceived   60 *sall* shall   61 *qwantile* cunning   *qwelle* kill
62 *farrar* further   65 *wax* grow   66 *suld* should   *for-do* ruin   *dede*
deed   69 *mydwayes* midwives   72 *lorne* destroyed   74 *bede* offer
75 *dyke* dig   *delfe* delve   *beere* carry   *drawe* pull   77 *lawe* low
78 *losellis* wretches   79 *sotell* clever

REX: Yaa! helpes to halde tham doune,
   That we no fant[n]yse fynde[6].
1 CON: Lorde, we sall ever be bowne
   In bondage tham to bynde.

(8)

MOYSES [*near Sinai*]: Grete God, that all this grounde be-gan,
   And governes evere in gud degree,
   That made me Moyses un-to man,
   And saved me sythen out of the see[7].
   Kyng Pharo he comaunded than
   So that no sonnes shulde saved be;   90
   Agayns his wille away I wan;
   Thus has God shewed his myght in me.
   Nowe am I here to kepe,
   Sett undir Synay syde,
   The bisshoppe Jetro[8] schepe,
   So bettir bute to bide[9].

(9)

   A, mercy, God! Mekill is thy myght.
   What man may of thy mervayles mene?
   I se yondyr a ful selcouth syght,
   Wher-of be-for no synge was seene.   100
   A busk I se yondir brennand bright,
   And the leves last ay in like grene.
   If it be werke of worldly wight
   I will go witte with-owten wene.
DEUS: Moyses, come noght to nere,
   Bot stille in that stede dwelle,
   And take hede to me here,
   And tente what I the telle.

---

81 *helpes* help (imperative)   *halde* hold   83 *bowne* ready   91 *wan* went
94 *Sett* placed   95 *schepe* sheep   97 *Mekill* great   98 *mervayles* wonders
mene speak   99 *selcouth* wonderful   100 *synge* sign   101 *busk* bush
brennand burning   102 *leves* leaves   103 *wight* man   104 *witte* find out
wene doubt   108 *tente* notice

(10)

> I am thy lorde, with-outyn lak,
> To lengh thi liffe even as me list,
> And the same God that som tyme spak
> Un-to thyne elders als thei wiste;
> But Abraham and Ysaac,
> And Jacob, saide I, suld be bliste,
> And multyplye and tham to mak,
> So that ther seede shulde noght be myste.
> And nowe kyng Pharo
> Fuls thare childir ful faste;
> If I suffir hym soo,
> Thare seede shulde sone be past.

(11)

> Go, make the message have I mende
> To hym that tham so harmed hase;
> Go, warne hym with wordes hende,
> So that he lette my pepull passe,
> That they to wildirnesse may wende,
> And wirshippe me als whilom was.
> And yf he lenger gar them lende,
> His sange ful sone sall be, 'allas!'

MOYSES: A, lord, syth with thy leve
That lynage loves me noght,
Gladly they walde me greve,
And I slyke boodword brought.

(12)

Ther-fore, Lord, late sum othir fraste
That hase more forse tham for to feere.

---

109 *lak* fail 110 *lengh* prolong 115 *mak* ?increase 116 *myste* lost
118 *Fuls* harms 121 *mende* spoken 123 *hende* polite 125 *wende* go
126 *whilom* formerly 127 *gar* causes *lende* to delay 128 *sange* song
131 *greve* afflict 132 *slyke* such *boodword* command 133 *fraste* attempt

DEUS: Moyses, be noght a-baste,
  My bidding baldely to bere;
  If thai with wrang ought walde the wrayste[10]
  Owte of all wothis I sall the were.
MOYSES: We! Lord, thai wil noght to me trayste
  For al the othes that I may swere.
  To neven slyke note of newe
  To folke of wykkyd will,
  With-outen taken trewe,
  They will noght take tente ther-till.

(13)

DEUS: And if they will noght undirstande
  Ne take heede how I have the sente,
  Before the kyng cast downe thy wande,
  And it sall seme as a serpent[11].
  Sithen take the tayle in thy hande,
  And hardely uppe thou itt hente,
  In the first state als thou it fande.
  So sall it turne be myn entent.
  Hyde thy hande in thy barme,
  And serpent it sall be like,
  Sithen hale with-outen harme,
  Thi syngnes sall be slyke.

(14)

  And if he wil not suffre than
  My pepull for to passe in pees,
  I sall send vengeaunce ix or x,
  To sewe hym sararre, or I sesse.
  Bot the Jewes that wonnes in Jessen
  Sall noght be merked with that messe;
  Als lange als thai my lawes will kenne
  Ther comfort sal I evere encresse.

---

135 *a-baste* downcast   136 *baldely* boldly   138 *wothis* dangers   *were* protect   139 *trayste* trust   141 *neven* proclaim   *of newe* anew   143 *taken* token, sign   153 *barme* bosom   155 *hale* whole   160 *sewe* pursue   *sararre* worse   162 *messe* measure

MOSES

MOYSES: A, Lorde, lovyd be thy wille
  That makes thy folke so free;
  I sall tell tham un-till
  Als thou telles un-to me.

(15)

  But to the kyng, Lorde, whan I come,
  And he ask me what is thy name,   170
  And I stande stille than, defe and dum,
  How sal I be withouten blame?
DEUS: I saie thus, *ego sum qui sum*[12],
  I am he that I am the same,
  And if thou myght not meke[13] ne mum,
  I sall the saffe fro synne and shame.
MOYSES: I undirstande this thyng
  With all the myght in me.
DEUS: Be bolde in my blissyng;
  Thy belde ay sall I be.   180

(16)

MOYSES: A, lorde of lyffe, lere me my layre,
  That I there tales may trewly tell;
  Un-to my frendis nowe will I fayre,
  The chosen childre of Israell,
  To telle tham comforte of ther care,
  And of there daunger that thei in dwell.
    [*He approaches the Jews.*]
  God mayntayne you and me evermare,
  And mekill myrthe be you emell.
I PUER: A, Moyses, maistir dere,
  Oure myrthe is al mornyng;   190
  We are harde halden here
  Als carls undir the kyng.

---

175 *mum* mutter   180 *belde* protection   181 *lere* teach   *layre* lesson
192 *carls* slaves

ENGLISH MYSTERY PLAYS

(17)

II PUER: Moyses, we may morne and myne[14];
Ther is no man us myrthes mase;
And sen we come al of a kynne,
Ken us som comforte in this case.

MOYSES: Beeths of youre mornyng blyne[15];
God wil defende you of your fays;
Oute of this woo he will you wynne,
To plese hym in more plener place.   200
I sall carpe to the kyng,
And fande to make you free.

III PUER: God sende us gud tythyngis,
And all may with you be.

[*Moses goes to Pharaoh's court*[16].]

(18)

MOYSES: Kyng Pharo! to me take tent!
REX: Why, what tydyngis can thou tell?
MOYSES: Fro God of heven thus am I sente,
To fecche his folke of Israell,
To wildirnesse he walde thei wente.
REX: Yaa, wende thou to the devell of hell;   210
I make no force howe thou has mente,
For in my daunger sall thei dwelle.
And, faytour, for thy sake,
Thei sall be putte to pyne.
MOYSES: Thanne will God vengeaunce take
On the and on al thyne.

(19)

REX: Fy on the, ladde! Oute of my lande!
Wenes thou with wiles to lose oure laye?[17]
[Who] is this warlowe with his wande,
That wolde thus wynne oure folke away?   220

---

194 *mase* makes   195 *kynne* kin   196 *Ken* teach   198 *fays* foes
201 *carpe* speak   202 *fande* try   212 *daunger* power   213 *faytour* trickster   214 *pyne* suffering   218 *laye* law   219 *warlowe* wizard

MOSES

II CON: It is Moyses, we wele warrand;
Agayne al Egipte is he ay.
Youre fadir grete faute in hym fande;
Nowe will he marre you if he may.
REX: Nay, nay, that daunce is done,
That lordan leryd overe late.
MOYSES: God biddis the graunte my bone,
And late me go my gate.

(20)

REX: Biddis God me? Fals lurdayne, thou lyes;
What takyn talde he, toke thou tent? 230
MOYSES: Yaa, sir, he saide thou suld despise
Botht me and all his comaundement.
In thy presence kast on this wise
My wande he bad by his assent,
And that thou shulde the wele avise
Howe it shulde turne to a serpent.
And in his haly name
Here sal I ley it downe.
Loo, ser, se her the same.
REX: A! Dogg! The devyll the drowne! 240

(21)

MOYSES: He saide that I shulde take the tayle,
So for to prove his poure playne,
And sone he saide it shuld not fayle
For to turne a wande agayne.
Loo, sir, be-halde!
REX: Hopp illa hayle![18]
Now certis this is a sotill swayne.
But this boyes sall byde here in oure bayle;
For all thair gaudis sall noght tham gayne,
Bot warse, both morne and none,

226, 229 *lordan, lurdayne* fool   226 *leryd* learned   *overe* too   227 *bone* request   228 *gate* way   230 *takyn* sign   247 *bayle* power

ENGLISH MYSTERY PLAYS

Sall thei fare for thy sake. 250
MOYSES: God sende sum vengeaunce sone,
And on thi werke take wrake.
[*Moses returns to the Jews: the Egyptians approach Pharaoh.*]

(22)

I EGIPTUS: Allas! Allas! This lande is lorne;
On lif we may no lenger lende.
II EGIP: So grete myscheffe is made sen morne,
Ther may no medycyne us amende.
I CON: Sir kyng, we banne that we wer borne;
Oure blisse is all with bales blende.
REX: Why crys you swa, laddis? Liste you scorne?
I EGIP: Sir kyng, slyk care was nevere kende. 260
Oure watir, that was ordand
To men and beestis fudde,
Thurghoute al Egipte lande
Is turned to rede blude;

(23)

Full ugly and full ill is it,
That was ful faire and fresshe before.
REX: This is grete wondir for to witt,
Of all the werkis that ever wore.
II EGIP: Nay, lorde, ther is anothir yitt,
That sodenly sewes us ful sore: 270
For tadys[19] and frosshis we may not flitte;
Thare venym loses lesse and more.
I EGIP: Lorde, grete myses[20] bothe morn and none
Bytis us full bittirlye,
And we hope al by done[21]
By Moyses, oure enemye.

252 *wrake* revenge 253 *lorne* lost 254 *lende* stay 257 *banne* curse
258 *bales* sorrows 270 *sewes* pursues 271 *frosshis* frogs *flitte* escape
272 *loses* kills 273 *myses* maggots

MOSES

(24)

1 CON: Lord, whills we with this menyhe meve,
  Mon never myrthe be us emange.
REX: Go, saie we salle no lenger greve,
  But thai sall nevere the tytar gang.   280
  [*II Egyptus goes to Moses.*]
II EGIP: Moyses, my lord has grauntyd leve
  At lede thy folk to likyng lande,
  So that we mende of oure myscheve.
  [*Returns.*]
MOYSES: I wate ful wele thar wordes er wrang,
  That sall ful sone be sene,
  For hardely I hym heete
  And he of malice mene.
  Mo mervaylles mon he mett.

(25)

1 EGIP [*at court*]: Lorde, allas! For dule we dye;
  We dar not loke oute at no dore.   290
REX: What devyll ayles yow so to crye?
II EGIP: We fare nowe werre than evere we fare.
  Grete loppis[22] overe all this lande thei flye
  That with bytyng makis mekill blure.
I EGIP: Lorde, oure beestis lyes dede and dry,
  Als wele on myddyng als on more;
  Both oxe, horse, and asse
  Fallis dede doune sodanly.
REX: Ther-of nc man harme has
  Halfe so mekill as I.   300

(26)

II CON: Yis, lorde, poure men has mekill woo
  To see ther catell be out cast;

---

277 *menyhe* company   280 *tytar* sooner   282 *At lede* to lead   *likyng* pleasant   284 *er* are   286 *heete* promise   288 *mett* meet   289 *dule* grief   294 *blure* noise, buzzing   296 *myddyng* dung hill   *more* moor

The Jews in Jessen faren noght soo:
They have al likyng in to last²³.
REX: Go saie we giffe tham lève to goo
To tyme there parellis be over past;
But, or thay flitte over farre us froo,
We sall garre feste tham foure so fast.
II EGIP [*goes to Jews*]: Moyses, my lord giffis leve
Thy men for to remewe.   310
[*Returns.*]
MOYSES: He mon have more mischeff
But if his tales be trewe.

(27)

I EGIP [*at court*]: We! lorde, we may not lede this liffe.
REX: Why, is ther grevaunce growen agayne?
II EGIP: Swilke pou[d]re²⁴, lord, a-pon us dryffe
That whare it bettis it makis a blayne.
I EGIP: Like mesellis makis it man and wyffe;
Sythen ar they hurte with hayle and rayne,
Oure wynes in mountaynes may not thryve,
So ar they threst and thondour slayne.   320
REX: How do thay in Jessen;
The Jewes, can ye aught say?
II EGIP: This care nothyng they ken;
Thay fele no such affray.

(28)

REX: No! Devill! And sitte they so in pees?
And we ilke day in doute and drede.
I EGIP: My lorde, this care will evere encrese
Tille Moyses have leve tham to lede.
I CON: Lorde, war they wente than walde it sese,
So shuld we save us and oure seede,   330
Eellis be we lorne; this is no lese²⁵.

306 *To tyme* until   *parellis* dangers   308 *garre feste* cause to be bound
foure ?feel   315 *dryffe* drifts   316 *bettis* falls   *blayne* sore   317 *mesellis*
lepers   320 *threst* beaten   *thondour* (by) thunder

MOSES

REX: Late hym do fourth! The devill hym spede!
    For his folke sall no ferre
    Yf he go welland woode.
II CON: Than will itt sone be warre,
    Yit war bettir thai yoode.

(29)

II EGIP: We! Lorde, new harme is comon to hande.
REX: No! Devill! Will itt no bettir be?
I EGIP: Wilde wormes[26] is laide overe al this lande;
    Thai leve no frute ne floure on tree;   340
    Agayne that storme may no thyng stande.
II EGIP: Lord, ther is more myscheff, thynke me,
    And thre daies hase itt bene durand,
    So myrke that non myght othir see.
I EGIP: My lorde, grete pestelence
    Is like ful lange to last.
REX: Owe! Come that in oure presence?
    Than is oure pride al past.

(30)

II EGIP: My lorde, this vengeaunce lastis lange,
    And mon till Moyses have his bone.   350
I CON: Lorde, late tham wende, els wirke [we] wrang;
    It may not helpe to hover na hone.
REX: Go, saie we graunte tham leve to gange,
    In the devill way, sen itt bus be done,
    For so may fall we sall tham fang,
    And marre tham or to-morne at none.
    [*I Egyptus goes to Moses.*]
I EGIP : Moyses, my lorde has saide,
    Thou sall have passage playne.
    [*Returns.*]

---

334 *welland* wildly, boilingly *woode* mad 336 *yoode* went 343 *durand* lasting 344 *myrke* dark 350 *bone* request 352 *hover* delay *hone* wait 354 *bus* must 355 *fang* catch 356 *or* before

MOYSES: And to passe am I paied,
    My frendes, bees nowe fayne;

(31)

    For at oure will now sall we wende,
    In lande of lykyng[27] for to lende.
I PUER: Kyng Pharo, that felowns fende,
    Will have grete care fro this be kende;
    Than will he schappe hym us to shende.
    And sone his ooste aftir us sende.
MOYSES: Beis noght aferde; God is youre frende;
    Fro alle oure fooes he will us fende.
    Tharfore comes furthe with me,
    Haves done, and drede yow noght.
II PUER: My lorde, loved mott thou bee,
    That thus fro bale has brought.

(32)

III PUER: Swilke frenshippe never before we fande.
    But in this faire defautys may fall;
    The Rede See is ryght nere at hande;
    Ther bus us bide to we be thrall[28].
MOYSES: I sall make us way with my wande,
    For God hase sayde he save us sall;
    On aythir syde the see sall stande,
    Tille we be wente, right as a wall.
    Therfore have ye no drede,
    But faynde ay God to plese.
I PUER: That lorde to lande us lede,
    Now wende we all at esse.
    [*Moses leads the Jews across the Red Sea.*]

(33)

I EGIP [*at court*]: Kyng Pharro, ther folke er gane.
REX: Howe nowe! Es ther any noyes of newe?

---

362 *lende* stay   363 *felowns* wicked   *fende* fiend   365 *shende* destroy
366 *ooste* host   382 *faynde* try

MOSES

II EGIP: The Ebrowes er wente ilkone.
REX: Now sais thou that?
I EGIP: Ther talis er trewe.
REX: Horse harneys tyte[29], that thei be tane;
   This ryott radly sall tham rewe.   390
   We sall not sese or they be slone,
   For to these we sall tham sew.
   Do charge oure charyottis swithe,
   And frekly folowes me.
II EGIP: My lorde, we are full blithe
   At youre biddyng to be.

(34)

II CON: Lorde, to youre biddyng we er boune,
   Owre bodies baldely for to bede,
   We sall noght byde, but dyng tham doune,
   Tylle all be dede, with-outen drede.   400
REX: Hefe uppe youre hartis ay to Mahownde;
   He will be nere us in oure nede.
   [*The Egyptians follow the Jews to the Red Sea and are overwhelmed[30].*]
   Owte! Ay herrowe! Devill, I drowne!
I EGIP: Allas! We dye for alle our dede.
I PUER: Now are we wonne fra waa, and saved oute of the see.
   Cantemus domino, to God a sange synge wee.

390 *radly* quickly   394 *frekly* hastily   398 *bede* offer   399 *dyng* strike

9. Balaam, Balak and the Prophets
De Mose et Rege Balaak et Balaam Propheta

CHESTER 5: CAPPERS

This play was introduced by the Cappers in 1521. It appears to be a transitional text. The story of Balaam and his ass is developed with a sense of comedy, and some kindly feeling towards the ass. This gives way to a procession of prophets introduced by the Expositor, an episode which is descended from the procession of prophets in the liturgical drama, and which here retains its very undramatic character. The Moses episode at the beginning is another point where the influence of Le Mistère du Viel Testament *has been detected.*

The text here is a somewhat complex one. MS Harley 2124 is the only one to retain the relic of the procession of prophets, whilst the other manuscripts enlarge the Balaam episode. It seemed desirable to print a full version here containing both these expansions. But it must be admitted that the result is not very coherent, and the following text is an interesting example of what the producers may have had to choose from as they prepared their performance.

The Balaam episode, from Numbers 22 23–30, was a very popular one in early times. It may have been a counter, in its liturgical form, to the Feast of Fools. On the Continent, the Prophets' Play was referred to as Processio Asinorum. *It is extraordinary that the ambivalence in the treatment of Balaam on the one hand and the Prophets on the other should have survived long enough to be apparent in the work of the* Chester *compilers.*

[*Godspeaks to Moses*]

(1)

DEUS: Moyses, my servaunte life and dere,
    And all the people that be here,
    Ye wott in Egipte when you were
    Out of thralldome I you broughte.
    I wyll[1] you honour no God save me;
    Ne mawmentrye none make yee;
    My name in vayne nam not yee,
    For that me lykes naughte.

(2)

    I will you hold your holy daye;
    And worshipp also by all waye
    Father and mother, all that you maye;
    And slaye no man no-where.
    Fornication you shall flee;
    No mens goods steale yee;
    Ne in no place abyde ne bee
    Falce wytnes for to beare.

(3)

    Your neighboures wyves covettes noughte,
    Servant ne good that he hath boughte,
    Oxe ne asse in deede ne thoughte,
    Nor any thinge that is his;
    Ne wrongefullie to have his thinge
    Agayne his will and his lykinge;
    In all these doe my byddinge
    That you doe not amisse.
      Tunc princeps Sinagogae statuet eum in loco quasi pro populo loquatur ad Dominum et Moysen[2].

---

1 *life* beloved   6 *mawmentrye* idols   7 *nam* take

(4)

PRINCEPS SINAGOGAE: Ah, good Lord, much of mighte,
    Thou comes with so great lighte;
    We bene so afraide of this sighte
    No man dare speak ne looke.
    God is so grym with us to deale,
    But Moyses, master, with us thou mele;   30
    Els we dyen many and feele,
    So afrayde bene all weel.
    Tunc Moyses stans super montem loquatur ad populum[3].

(5)

MOYSES: Gods folke, drede you noughte;
    To prove you with, God hath this wrought
    To make you afrayd in deede and thoughte
    Aye for to avoyde synne[4].
    By this sight you may now see
    That he is pereles of postye;
    Therfore his teaching looke done yee,
    Thereof that you not blyn.   40

(6)

PRINCEPS SINAGOGAE: Ah, highe Lord, God almighte,
    That Moyses shynes wondrous bright!
    I may no way for great lighte
    Now looke upon hym.
    And horned[5] he semes in our sighte
    Sith he came to the hyll; dight
    Our lawe he hase I hope aright,
    For was he never so grym.

(7)

MOYSES: You, Gods folke of Israell,
    Harkens to me that loven heale;   50

---

30 *mele* talk   31 *feele* many times   39 *done* do   40 *blyn* stop, cease
46 *dight* prepared   50 *heale* prosperity

God bade you sholde doe everye deale
As that I shall saye.
Six dayes boldelye worches all,
The seaventh Sabaoth you shall call;
That daye for ought that may befall
Hallowed shalbe aye.

(8)

That doth not this deede deade shall be;
In houses fire shall no man see.
First fruytes to God offer yee,
For so hym-selfe bade. 60
Gould and silver offers also,
Purple, bisse, and other moe,
To hym that shall save you from woe
And helpe you in your neede.

(9)

EXPOSITOR: Lordinges, this comaundment
Was of the Old Testamente,
And yet is used with good entent
With all that good bene.
This storye all if we shold fong,
To playe this moneth it were to longe; 70
Wherfore most frutefull there amonge
We taken, as shall be sene[6].

(10)

Also we read in this storie,
God in the Mownt of Synai
Toke Moises these comaundmentis verelye,
Wrytten with his owne hande
In tables of ston, as reade I;
But when men honoured mawmentry
He brake them in anger hastelye,
For that he wold not wonde. 80

62 *bisse* fine linen   69 *fong* undertake   75 *Toke* gave   80 *wonde* turn aside

(11)

But afterward sone, leeve ye me,
Other tables of stone made he
In which God bade wrytten shold be
His wordes that were before;
The which tables shryned were
After as God can Moyses leare;
And that shryne to them was deare
Thereafter evermore.

*Tunc Moyses descendet de monte et ex altera parte montis
dicet Rex Balaac equitando*[7].

(12)

BALAACK REX: I, Balaack, king of Moab land,
All Israell I had it in my hand; 90
I am so wroth I wold not wond
To slaye them, ech wighte.
For their God helpes them stiflye
Of other landes to have mastrye,
That it is bootles witterlie
Against them for to fighte.

(13)

What nation soever dose them noye,
Moyses prayes anone in hye.
Therefore have they sone the victorie
And other men they have the worse. 100
Therfore how will I wroken be
I am bethought, as mot I the!
Balaam, I will, shall come to me,
That people for to curse.

(14)

For sworde ne knife may not avayle
These ilke shroes for to assaile;
That fowndes to fight he shall faile,

---

86 *leare* teach 93 *stiflye* courageously 95 *witterlie* certainly 102 *the* thrive 106 *ilke* same *shroes* evil doers 107 *fowndes* advances

For sicker is hym no boote.
All nations they doe any
And my-selfe they can destroie, 110
As ox that gnawes biselie
The grasse right to the roote.

(15)

Who so Balaam blesses, i-wis,
Blessed sickerlie that man is;
Who so he curses, fareth amisse,
Such loos over all hase he.
   (a[8])
[But yet I trust venged to be,
With dint of sword or polecy,
Of these false losells, leaves ye,
Leave this withouten dowte. 120
For to be wrocken is my desier;
My hart burnes as hott as fier,
For vervent anger and for ire,
That this be brought about.
   (b)
Therfore my god and godes all,
O mightie Mars, on thie I call;
With all the powers infernall,
Rise now and helpe at neede.
I am informed by true report
How the mediaters[9] do resort 130
To wine my land to ther comfort,
Descended of Iacobs seed.
   (c)
Now show your power, ye goddis mightie,
So that these catyffes I maye destroy;
Having of them full victory,
And them brought to mischaunce,
Beat them downe in plaine battell,

---

108 *sicker* truly   109 *any* harm   111 *biselie* busily   116 *loos* fame
118 *polecy* craft   119 *losells* idlers   *leaves* believe   121 *wrocken* avenged
123 *vervent* burning   131 *wine* win

ENGLISH MYSTERY PLAYS

These false lossells soe cruell,
That all the world may here tell
We take on them vengeaunce.   140
(d)
Out of Egipt fled they be,
And passed through the Rede Sea.
The Egiptians that pursued them, truly,
Were drowned in that same flood.
The[y] have [trusted] on God mickell of mighte,
Which them doth aide in wrong or right.
Who so ever with them foundeth to feight
He winneth littel good[10].
(e)
They have slaine – this wott I well –
Through helpe of God of Israell   150
Both Seon and Ogg[11], kingis so fell,
And plainely them destroyed.
Therefore ryse up, ye godes echone!
Ye be an hundred godis for one.
I would be wroken them upon
For all ther pomp and pride.]
Therfore go fetch hym, bachler,
That he may curse the people here;
For sicker on them, on no manner,
Mon we not wroken be[12].   160

(16)

MILES: Syr, on your errand I will gone;
Yt shall be well done, and that anone,
For he shall wreak you on your fone,
The people of Israell.
BALAACK: Yea, looke, thou het hym gold great wone,
And riches for to lyve upon,
To destroy them if he can,
The freakes that be so fell.
    Tunc ibit ad Balaam[13].

157 *bachler* knight, warrior   160 *Mon* must   163 *wreak* avenge   165 *het* promised   *wone* quantity   168 *freakes* men   *fell* cruel

194

BALAAM, BALAK AND THE PROPHETS

(17)

MILES: Balaam, my lorde greetes well thee,
    And prayes the right sone at hym to be, 170
    To curse the people of Iudy
    That do hym great anoye.
BALAAM: Forsooth, I tell the, bacheler,
    That I may have no power
    But if Gods will were;
    That shall I witt in hye.

(18)

DEUS *in supremo loco*[14]: Balaam, I comaund the
    King Balaak his bydding that thou flee;
    That people that is blessed of me
    Curse thou not by no waye. 180
BALAAM: Lord, I must doe thy byddinge,
    Thoughe it be to me unlykeing,
    For truly much wynninge
    I might have had to-daye.

(19)

DEUS: Thoughe the folke be my foe,
    Thou shalt have leave thydder to goe;
    But looke that thou doe right soe
    As I have thee taughte.
BALAAM: Lord, it shall be done in height;
    This asse shall beare me aright. 190
    Goe we together anone, sir knight,
    For now leave I have coughte.
    Tunc equitabunt versus regem, et eundo dicat Balaam[15]

(20)

Now by the law I leve upon,
Sith I have leave for to gone,
They shalbe cursed every one,
And I ought wyn maye[16].

---

182 *unlykeing* unfavourable   192 *coughte* obtained   193 *leve* believe

ENGLISH MYSTERY PLAYS

If Balaak hold that he has heighte,
Gods hest I set at light;
Warryed they shalbe this night,
Or that I wend awaye.   200
    *Tunc Angelus obviabit Balaam cum gladio extracto in manu,
et stabit asina*[17].

(21)

Goe forth, Burnell! Goe forth, goe!
What the dyvell! My asse will not goe;
Served me she never soe.
What sorrow so her dose nye?
Rise up, Burnell! Make thee bowne,
And helpe to beare me out thee towne;
Or as brok I my crowne[18],
Thou shalt full sore abye!
    Tunc percutiet asinam, et loquetur aliquis in asina[19].

(22)

ASINA: Maister, thou dost evell witterly,
So good an ass as me to nye.   210
Now hast thou beaten me thry,
That beare the thus aboute.
BALAAM: Burnell, whye begiles thou me
When I have most nede to the?
ASINA: That sight that I before me see
Makes me downe to lowte.

(23)

Am I not, master, thyne owne ass,
That ever before ready was
To beare the whether thou woldest pas?
To smyte me now yt is shame.   220
Thou wottest well, master, pardy,
Thou haddest never ass like to me,
Ne never yet thus served I thee;

211 *thry* thrice   216 *lowte* bow   219 *pas* go, travel

196

BALAAM, BALAK AND THE PROPHETS

Now I am not to blame.
Tunc Balaam videns Angelum evaginatum gladium habentem adorans dicat[20]

(24)

BALAAM: Ah, Lord, to thee I make a vowe,
I had no sight of thee erre now;
Lyttle wist I it was thou
That feared my asse soe.
ANGELUS: Why hast thou beaten thy ass thry?
Now am I comen thee to nye, 230
That changes thy purpose falcelye,
And woldest be my foe.

(25)

And the ass had not downe gone,
I wold have slayne the here anone.
BALAAM: Lord, have pittye me upon
For sinned have I sore.
Is it thy will that I forth goe?
ANGELUS: Yea, but looke thou doe this folk no woe
Otherwise then God bade thee tho,
And saide to thee before. 240
Tunc Balaam et Miles ibunt, Balaack venit in obviam[21].

(26)

BALAACK: Ah, welcome, Balaam, my frend!
For all myne anguish thou shalt end,
If that thy will be to wend,
And wreake me of my foe.
BALAAM: Nought may I speake, so have I win,
But as God puttes me in
To forby all and my kin[22];
Therfore sure me is woe.

---

226 *erre* before   239 *tho* then   245 *win* bliss

(27)

BALAACK: Come forth, Balaam, come with me!
   For on this hill, so mot I thee, 250
   The folke of Israell thou shalt see,
   And curse them, I thee praye.
   Thou shalt have riches, golde, and fee,
   And I shall advance thy dignytye,
   To curse men – cursed they may be –
   That thou shalt see to-day[23].
     Tunc adducens secum Balaam in montem et ad australem
     partem respiciens dicat ut sequitur[24].
     (f[25])
   Lo, Balaam, now thou seest here
   Godis people all in feare,
   Cittie, castell, and river;
   Looke now how likes thie; 260
   Curse them now at my prayer,
   As thou wilte be to me full dere,
   And in my realme most of power,
   And greatest under me.
     Tunc Balaam versus austrum dicat[26]

(28)

BALAAM: How may I curse them in this place,
   The people that God blessed hase?
   In them is both might and grace,
   And that is alwayes seene.
   Wytnes I may none beare
   Against God that this can were, 270
   His people that no man may deare,
   Ne troble with no teene.

(29)

   I saye these folkes shall have their will;
   That no nation shall them gryll.

---

253 *fee* property   270 *were* defend   271 *deare* injure   272 *teene* injury
274 *gryll* anger

BALAAM, BALAK AND THE PROPHETS

The goodnes that they shall fulfill
Nombred may not be.
Their God shall them kepe and save.
No other repreve may I not have,
But such death as they shall have,
I praye God send me. 280

(30)

BALAACK: What the devilles! Eyles the, poplart?[27]
Thy speach is not worth a fart!
Doted I wot well thou art,
For woodlie thou hast wrougt.
I bade thee curse them, every one,
And thou blest them, blood and bone.
To this North syde thou shalt anon,
For here thy deed is nought.
  Tunc adducet eum ad borealem partem[28].

(31)

BALAAM: Herken, Balaack, what I say.
God may not gibb by no waye; 290
That he saith is veray,
For he may not lye.
To bless his folk he me sent,
Therfore I saie, as I am kent,
That in this land verament
Is used no mawmentry[29].

(32)

To Iacobs blood and Israell
God shall send ioy and heale;
And as a lyon[30] in his weale,
Christ shalbe haunsed hye 300
And rise also, in noble araye,
As a prynce to wyn great paye,

---

278 *repreve* reproof   283 *Doted* mad   284 *woodlie* madly   290 *gibb* waver   294 *kent* instructed, taught   300 *haunsed* exalted   *hye* high

Overcome his enemyes, as I say,
And them bowndly bye.

(33)

BALAACK: What the devill is this! Thou cursest them naught,
Nor blessest them nether as me thought?
BALAAM: Syr kinge, this I thee beheight
Or that I come here.
BALAACK: Yet shalt thou to an-other place
Ther Gods power for to embrace;
The dyvell geve the hard grace
But thou doe my prayer.
Ad occidentalem partem[31].

(34)

BALAAM: Ah, Lord, that here is fayre wonning,
Halls, chambers of great lyking,
Valleyes, woodes, grass springing,
Fayre yordes and eke rivers.
I wot well God made all this,
His folke to lyve in joye and blisse;
That warryeth them warried is[32].
That blessest them to God is deare.

(35)

BALAACK: Popelard! Thou preachest as a pie.
The devill of hell thee destroy!
I bade thee curse myne enemye;
Therfore thou came me to.
Now hast thou blessed them here thry,
For thou meanes me to nye.
BALAAM: So tould I the before twye,
I might none other doe.

---

304 *bowndly* readily 307 *beheight* promised 313 *wonning* dwelling-place
316 *yordes* fields 321 *Popelard* hypocrite *pie* magpie 325 *thry* thrice
327 *twye* twice

BALAAM, BALAK AND THE PROPHETS

(36)

BALAACK: Out, alas! What dyvell ayles thee?
  I have het thee gold and fee
  To speake but wordes two or three,
  And thou makes much distance.
  Yet once I will assay thee,
  If any boote of bale will be,
  And if thou falcely now faile me,
  Mahound geve thee mischance!
    Tunc Balaam ad caelum respiciens prophetando[33]

(37)

BALAAM: Now one thinge I will tell you all
  Hereafter what shall befall:
  A starre of Iacob springe shall,
  A man of Israell.
  He shall overcome and have in band
  All kinges, dukes of strang land,
  And all the world have in his hand,
  As lord to dight and deale[34].

(38)

ESAYAS[35]: I say a mayden meeke and mylde
  Shall conceave and beare a childe,
  Cleane without workes wilde,
  To wyne mankinde to wayle[36].
  Butter and hony shall be his meate,
  That he may all evill forgeat
  Our soules out of hell to get,
  And called Emanuell.

(39)

EXPOSITOR: Lordinges, these wordes are so veray
  That exposition in good faye
  None needes, but you know may

---

332 *distance* disagreement   334 *bale* suffering   350 *forgeat* forget, overcome

> This word Emanuell.
> Emanuell is as much to saye
> As 'God with us night and day,'
> Therfore that name for ever and aye
> To his sonne cordes wondrous well. 360

(40)

EZECHIELL[37]: I, Ezechiell, sothlie see
> A gate in Gods house on hye.
> Closed it was; no man came nye.
> Then told an angell me
> This gate shall no man open, i-wis,
> For God will come and goe by this,
> For him-self it reserved is,
> None shall come there but hee.

(41)

EXPOSITOR: By this gate, lords, verament,
> I understand in my intent 370
> That way the Holy Ghost in went,
> When God tooke flesh and bloode
> In that sweet mayden Mary;
> Shee was that gate, wytterly,
> For in her he light graciouslie,
> Mankind to doe good.

(42)

IHEREMIA [38]: My eyes must run and sorrow aye,
> Without ceasing, night and daye,
> For my daughter, soth to saye,
> Shall suffer great anye. 380
> And my folke shall doe, in faye,
> Thinges that they ne know may
> To that mayden, by many waye,
> And her sonne, sickerlie.

360 *cordes* accords   363 *nye* near

BALAAM, BALAK AND THE PROPHETS

(43)

EXPOSITOR: Lordinges, this prophesie, i-wis,
  Touches the passion nothing amisse,
  For the prophet see well this,
  What shall come, as I reade,
  That a childe borne of a maye
  Shall suffer death, sooth to saye, 390
  And they that mayden shall afray
  Have vengeance for that deede.

(44)

IONAS[39]: I, Ionas, in full great any[40]
  To God I prayed inwardlie,
  And he me hard through his mercy
  And on me did his grace.
  In myddes the sea cast was I,
  For I wrought inobedyentlie,
  But in a whalles bellye
  Three dayes saved I was. 400

(45)

EXPOSITOR: Lordinges, what this may signifie
  Christ expoundes apertlie,
  As we reade in the Evangely,
  That Christ him-self can saie.
  Right as Ionas was dayes three
  In wombe of whall, so shall he be
  In earth lyinge, as was he,
  And rise the third daye.

(46)

DAVID[41]: I, Davyd, saie that God almighte
  From the highest heaven to earth will light, 410
  And thidder againe with full might,
  Both God and man in feare,
  And after come to deeme the righte.

---

389 *maye* maid   391 *afray* disturb   399, 406 *whall(es)* whale('s)

May no man shape them of his sight,
Ne deeme that to mankind is dighte;
But all then must apeare[42].

(47)

EXPOSITOR: Lordes, this speach is so veray
That to expound it to your pay
It needes nothing, in good faye,
This speach is so expresse.
Each man by it knowe may
That of the Ascention, soth to saie,
David prophesied in his daye,
As yt rehearsed was.

(48)

IOELL[43]: I, Ioell, saie this sickerlye,
That my ghost send will I
Upon mankinde merciably
From heaven, sitting in see.
Then shold our childre prophesie,
Ould men meet swevens wytterly,
Yong se sightes, that therby
Many wise shall be.

(49)

EXPOSITOR: Lordinges, this prophet speakes here
In Gods person, as it were,
And prophesies that he will apeare,
Ghostlie, to mankinde;
This signes non other, in good faye,
But of his deede on Whitson-day,
Sending his ghost that we ever may
On hym have sadlie mynd[44].

---

427 *merciably* mercifully   430 *meet* (v) dream   *swevens* dreams
431 *sightes* visions

BALAAM, BALAK AND THE PROPHETS

(50)

MICHEAS[45]: I, Micheal, through my mynde,
Will saye that man shall sothlie finde
That a childe of kinges kinde
In Bethlem shall be borne,
That shall be duke to dight and deale,
And rule the folke of Israell,
Also wyn againe mankindes heale,
That through Adam was lorne.

(51)

EXPOSITOR: Lordinges, two thinges apertlie
You may see in this prophesie; 450
The place certefies thee sothlie
Where Christ borne will be;
And after his ending, sickerlie,
Of his deedes of great mercy,
That he shold sit soveraynly
In heaven thereas is he.

(52)

Moe prophetis, lordinges, we might play,
But yt wold tary much the daye;
Therfore six, sothe to say,
Are played in this place. 460
Twoo speakes of his Incarnation,
An other of Christe Passion,
The fourth of the Resurrection
In figure of Jonas[46].

(53)

The fifte speakes expreslie
How he from the highest heavenlye[47]
Light into earth us to forby,
And after thydder steigh
With oure kinde to heaven-blisse.

448 *lorne* lost   457 *Moe* more   467 *forby* redeem   468 *steigh* ascended

More love might he not shew, i-wis, 470
But right there as hym-selfe is,
He haunshed our kinde on high.

(54)

The sixt shewes, you may see,
His Goste to man send will he,
More stidfast that they shalbe
To love God evermore.
Thus that beleven, that leven we,
Of Gods deedes that had pittye
One man, when that he made them free,
Is prophesied here before[48]. 480

(55)

BALAACK[49]: Goe we forth! It is no boote
Longer with this man to moote,
For God of Iewes is crop and roote
And lord of heaven and hell.
Now see I well no man on lyve
Gaynes with him for to stryve,
Therefore here as mot I thryve
I will no longer dwell.

(56)

EXPOSITOR: Lordinges, much more matter
Is in this story then you see here[50], 490
But the substance without were
Is played you beforne;
And by these prophesies, leav you me,
Three kinges, as you shall played see,
Presented at his Nativitye
Christ when he was borne.

Finis paginae quintae.

472 *haunshed* exalted   477 *beleven* (n) belief   *leven* (v) believe
482 *moote* debate   491 *were* omission   493 *leav* believe

10. The Parliament of Heaven, the Salutation and Conception

LUDUS COVENTRIAE 11

Ludus Coventriae contains a series of plays about Mary. Its inclusion seems to have been the occasion of a number of changes in the order of the cycle, and to have been the work of a separate writer or writers. This is a special feature of the cycle and it appears that the sequence may have been intended as a separate St Anne's Day play. The present play has two episodes: the Parliament of Heaven, which was not in the cycle when the Proclamation was composed, but which is anticipated by a reference in Contemplatio's prologue to the tenth play of the cycle (The Betrothal); and the Annunciation, which differs from the version envisaged in the Proclamation. The first episode falls outside the general pattern of the cycles, but it is made relevant here by the dramatic emphasis upon divine justice and mercy. The second episode derives probably from Bonaventura's Meditationes Vitae Christi. *The two parts are undoubtedly conceived as a whole, and are striking in the distinctive and poetic celebration of the divine power. There is considerable reference to the liturgy.*

ರಿ‍ಖ

[*Enter Contemplatio and Virtues.*]

(1)

CONTEMPLACIO: Fowre thowsand sex undryd foure yere, I telle,
  Man for his offens and fowle foly
  Hath loyn yerys in the peynes of helle,

3 *loyn* lain

ENGLISH MYSTERY PLAYS

And were wurthy to ly ther-in endlesly;
But thanne xulde perysche your grete mercye –
Good Lord, have on man pyte;
Have mende of the prayour seyd by Ysaie[1];
Lete mercy meke thin hyest mageste.

(2)

Wolde God thou woldyst breke thin hefne myghtye
And com down here in to erth,
And levyn yerys thre and threttye,
Thyn famyt folke with thi fode to fede;
To staunche thi thryste lete thi syde blede,
For erste wole not be mad redempcion.
Cum vesyte us in this tyme of nede;
Of thi careful creaturys, Lord, have compassyon.

(3)

A, woo to us wrecchis, that wrecchis be,
For God hath addyd sorwe to sorwe.
I prey the, Lorde, thi sowlys com se,
How thei ly and sobbe bothe eve and morewe.
With thi blyssyd blood from balys hem borwe,
Thy careful creaturys cryenge in captyvyte[2],
And tary not, gracyous Lord, tyl it be to-morwe:
The devyl hath dysceyved hem be hys iniquite.

(4)

A, quod Jeremye[3], who xal gyf wellys to myn eynes,
That I may wepe bothe day and nyght
To se oure bretheryn in so longe peynes?
Here myschevys amende may thi mech myght;
As grett as the se, Lord, was Adamys contryssyon ryght;
From oure hed is falle the crowne;

---

5 *xulde* should   7 *mende* remembrance   8 *meke* (v) soften   *mageste* majesty   9 *hefne* heaven   12 *famyt* famished   *fode* food   13 *thryste* thirst   14 *erste* soon   17 *wrecchis* wretches   20 *morewe* morning   21 *balys* destruction   *borwe* save   24 *dysceyved* deceived   25 *quod* said   *xal* shall   *gyf* give   *wellys* wells   28 *Here* their   *mech* great

PARLIAMENT OF HEAVEN, SALUTATION AND CONCEPTION

Man is comeryd in synne, I crye to thi syght,
Gracyous Lord, gracyous Lord, gracyous Lord, come down!

(5)

VIRTUES: Lord, plesyth it thin hygh domynacion
On man that thou made to have pyte.
Patryarchys and prophetys han made supplycacion;
Oure offyse is to presente here prayerys to the.
Aungelys, Archaungelys, we thre
That ben in the fyrst ierarchie,
For man to thin hy mageste
Mercy, mercy, mercy, we crye.   40

(6)

The aungel, Lord, thou made so gloryous,
Whos synne hath mad hym a devyl in helle,
He mevyd man to be so contraryous;
Man repentyd and he in his obstynacye doth dwelle;
Hese grete males, good Lord, repelle
And take man on to thi grace;
Lete thi mercy make hym with aungelys dwelle,
Of Locyfere to restore the place[4].
   [*God appears.*]

(7)

PATER: *Propter miseriam inopum et gemitum pauperum nunc
      exurgam*[5]:
For the wretchydnes of the nedy
And the porys lamentacion,   50
Now xal I ryse that am Almyghty;
Tyme is come of reconsyliacion.
My prophetys with prayers have made supplicacion;
My contryte creaturys crye all for comforte;
All myn aungellys in hefne with-owte cessacion
They crye that grace to man myght exorte.

---

31 *comeryd* overcome   38 *ierarchie* hierarchy   43 *mevyd* moved
45 *Hese* his   *males* malice   50 *porys* of the poor   56 *exorte* arise

209

(8)

VERITAS[6]: Lord, I am thi dowtere Trewth;
  Thou wylt se I be not lore;
  Thyn unkynde creaturys to save were rewthe;
  The offens of man hath grevyd the sore.   60
  Whan Adam had synnyd thou seydest thore
  That he xulde deye and go to helle,
  And now to blysse hym to resstore,
  Twey contraryes mow not to-gedyr dwelle.

(9)

  Thy trewthe, Lord, xal leste withowtyn ende;
  I may in no wyse from the go.
  That wretche that was to the so unkende,
  He may not have to meche wo;
  He dyspysyd the and plesyd thi fo;
  Thou art his creatour and he is thi creature,   70
  Thou hast lovyd trewthe, it is seyd, evyr mo;
  Therfore in peynes lete hym evyr more endure.

(10)

MISERICORDIA: O Fadyr of mercy and God of comforte,
  That counsell us in eche trybulacion,
  Lete yowr dowtere Mercy to yow resorte,
  And on man that is myschevyd have compassyon.
  Hym grevyth ful gretly his transgressyon;
  All hefne and erthe crye for mercy;
  Me semyth ther xuld be non excepcion,
  Ther prayers ben offeryd so specyally.   80

(11)

  Trewth seyth she hath evyr be than;
  I graunt it wel she hath be so;
  And thou seyst endlesly that mercy thou hast kept for man,
  Than, mercyabyl Lorde, kepe us bothe to.

57 *dowtere* daughter   58 *lore* learned   59 *rewthe* pity   61 *thore* there
64 *Twey* two   *mow* may   67 *unkende* unnatural   68 *meche* much
84 *mercyabyl* merciful

210

PARLIAMENT OF HEAVEN, SALUTATION AND CONCEPTION

Thu seyst *Veritas mea et misericordia mea cum ipso*[7];
Suffyr not thi sowlys than in sorwe to slepe;
That helle hownde that hatyth the, byddyth hym ho;
Thi love man no lengere lete hym kepe[8].

(12)

JUSTICIA: Mercy, me merveylyth what yow movyth.
Ye know wel I am your systere Ryghtwysnes.
God is ryghtful and ryghtffulnes lovyth;
Man offendyd hym that is endles;
Therfore his endles punchement may nevyr sees.
Also he forsoke his makere that made hym of clay,
And the devyl to his mayster he ches;
Wulde he be savyd? Nay, nay, nay!

(13)

As wyse as is God he wolde a be[9];
This was the abhomynabyl presumpcion.
It is seyd ye know wel this of me
That the ryghtwysnes of God hath no diffynicion;
Therfore late this be oure conclusyon:
He that sore synnyd ly stylle in sorwe;
He may nevyr make a seyth[10] be reson
Whoo myght thanne thens hym borwe.

(14)

MISERICORDIA: Systyr Ryghtwysnes, ye are to vengeabyl:
Endles synne God endles may restore[11].
Above all hese werkys God is mercyabyl;
Thow he for-sook God by synne, be feyth he for-sook hym
      never the more;
And thow he presumyd nevyr so sore,
Ye must consyder the frelnes of mankende.
Lerne and ye lyst this is Goddys lore –
The mercy of God is with-owtyn ende.

---

87 *the* thee   *ho* stop   93 *punchement* punishment   95 *ches* chose
97 *a* have   100 *diffynicion* limitation   105 *vengeabyl* revengeful
110 *frelnes* frailty

(15)

PAX: To spare your speches, systerys, it syt.
It is not onest in vertuys to ben dyscencion,
The pes of God ovyr-comyth all wytt.
Thow Trewth and Ryght sey grett reson,
Yett Mercy seyth best to my pleson;
For yf mannys sowle xulde abyde in helle,
Be-twen God and man evyr xulde be dyvysyon,
And than myght not I, Pes, dwelle. 120

(16)

Therefore me semyth best ye thus acorde,
Than hefne and erthe ye xul qweme.
Putt bothe your sentens in oure Lorde,
And in his hygh wysdam lete hym deme.
This is most fyttynge, me xulde seme,
And lete se how we fowre may all a-byde;
That mannys sowle it xulde perysche it wore sweme,
Or that ony of us fro othere xulde dyvyde.

(17)

VERITAS: In trowthe, here-to I consente;
I wole prey oure Lord it may so be. 130
JUSTICIA: I, Ryghtwysnes, am wele contente,
For in hym is very equyte.
MISERICORDIA: And I, Mercy, fro this counsel wole not fle
Tyl wysdam hath seyd I xal ses.
PAX: Here is God now; here is unyte.
Hefne and erth is plesyd with pes.

(18)

FILIUS: I thynke the thoughtys of Pes, and nowth of wykkydnes.
This I deme to ses your contraversy:
If Adam had not deyd, peryschyd had Ryghtwysnes,

113 *syt* is fitting   114 *onest* honest   115 *pes* peace   117 *pleson* pleasure
122 *qweme* unite   123 *sentens* belief   127 *sweme* pity   134 *ses* cease
139 *deyd* died

And also Trewth had be lost ther-by; 140
Trewth and Ryght wolde chastyse foly.
Gif a-nother deth come not, Mercy xulde perysch;
Than Pes were exyled fynyaly;
So tweyn dethis[12] must be yow fowre to cherysch.

(19)

But he that xal deye, ye must knawe
That in hym may ben non iniquyte,
That helle may holde hym be no lawe,
But that he may pas at hese lyberte;
Qwere swyche on his, prevyde and se[13],
And hese deth for mannys deth xal be redempcion. 150
All hefne and erth seke now ye,
Plesyth it yow this conclusyon.

(20)

VERITAS: I, Trowthe, have sowte the erthe with-owt and with-
    inne,
And in sothe ther kan non be fownde
That is of o day byrth with-owte synne,
Nor to that deth wole be bownde.
MISERICORDIA: I, Mercy, have ronne the hevynly regyon
    rownde,
And ther is non of that charyte
That for man wole suffre a deddly wounde.
I, I can nott wete how this xal be. 160

(21)

JUSTICIA: Sure I can fynde non sufficyent,
For servauntys un-profytable we be ech on.
Hes love nedyth to be ful ardent
That for man to helle wolde gon.
PAX: That God may do is non but on;
Ther-fore this is Pesys a-vyse:

---

142 *Gif* if   145 *knawe* know   149 *Qwere* where   *swyche* such   *prevyde*
look   153 *sowte* sought   155 *o* one   157 *ronne* run   160 *wete* know

He that gaff this counsell, lete hym geve the comforte a-lon,
For the conclusyon in hym of all these lyse.

(22)

FILIUS: It peyneth me that man I mad,
  That is to seyn peyne I must suffre fore. 170
  A counsel of the Trinite must be had
  Whiche of us xal man restore.
PATER: In your wysdam, Son, man was made thore
  And in wysdam was his temptacion.
  Therfor, Sone, sapyens ye must ordeyn here-fore
  And se how of man may be salvacion.

(23)

FILIUS: Fadyr, he that xal do this must be both God and man;
  Lete me se how I may were that wede;
  And syth in my wysdam he be-gan,
  I am redy to do this dede. 180
SPIRITUS SANCTUS: I, the Holy Gost, of yow tweyn do procede.
  This charge I wole take on me;
  I, love, to your lover xal yow lede,
  This is the assent of oure unyte.
MISERICORDIA: Now is the loveday mad of us fowre fynialy;
  Now may we leve in pes, as we were wonte:
  Misericordia et Veritas obviaverunt sibi;
  Justicia et Pax osculatae sunt[14].

Et hic osculabunt pariter omnes[15].

(24)

PATER: From us, God, aungel Gabryel thou xalt be sende.
  In-to the countre of Galyle. 190
  The name of the cyte Nazareth is kende,

---

168 *lyse* lies 169 *peyneth* pains *mad* made 175 *sapyens* wisdom
178 *were* wear *wede* garment 180 *dede* deed 183 *lede* lead
185 *loveday* day of reconciliation 191 *kende* known

PARLIAMENT OF HEAVEN, SALUTATION AND CONCEPTION

  To a mayd, w[e]ddyd to a man is she
  Of whom the name is Joseph, se,
  Of the hous of Davyd bore;
  The name of the mayd fre
  Is Mary, that xal al restore.

(25)

FILIUS: Say that she is with-owte wo and ful of grace,
  And that I, the son of the godhead, of here xal be bore.
  Hye the thou were there a pace,
  Ellys we xal be there the be-fore.   200
  I have so grett hast to be man thore
  In that mekest and purest virgyne.
  Sey here[16] she xal restore
  Of yow aungellys the grett ruyne.

(26)

SPIRITUS SANCTUS: And if she aske the how it myth be,
  Telle here I the Holy Gost xal werke al this;
  Sche xal be savyd thorwe oure unyte.
  In tokyn here bareyn cosyn Elyzabeth is
  Qwyk with childe in here grett age i-wys.
  Sey here to us is no thynge impossyble;   210
  Here body xal be so ful-fylt with blys,
  That she xal sone thynke this sownde credyble.

(27)

GABRIEL: In thyn hey inbassett, Lord, I xal go;
  It xal be do with a thought.
  Be-holde now, Lord, I go here to;
  I take my flyth and byde nowth.
      [*He appears to Mary.*]
  Ave Maria, gratia plena, Dominus tecum[17].
  Heyl, ful of grace! God is with the;

---

195 *fre* noble   205 *myth* might   207 *thorwe* through   211 *ful-fylt* fulfilled   212 *sone* soon   *sownde* message   213 *hey* high   *inbassett* embassy   216 *flyth* flight

215

Amonge all women blyssyd art thu!
Here this name *Eva* is turnyd *Ave*, 220
That is to say with-owte sorwe are ye now.

(28)

Thow sorwe in yow hath no place,
Yett of joy, lady, ye nede more;
Therfore I adde and sey ful of grace,
For so ful of grace was nevyr non bore.
Yet who hath grace he nedyth kepyng sore,
Therfore I sey God is with the,
Whiche xal kepe yow endlesly thore;
So amonge all women blyssyd are ye.

(29)

MARIA: A, mercy, God! This is a mervelyous herynge. 230
In the aungelys wordys I am trobelyd her.
I thynk how may be this gretynge;
Aungelys dayly to me doth aper,
But not in the lyknes of man that is my fer;
And also thus hyghly to comendyd be,
And am most un-wurthy I can-not answere;
Grett shamfastnes and grett dred is in me.

(30)

GABRYEL: Mary, in this take ye no drede,
For at God grace fownde have ye;
Ye xal conceyve in your wombe in dede 240
A childe, the sone of the Trynyte.
His name of yow Jhesu clepyd xal be[18],
He xal be grett, the son of the hyest, clepyd of kende,
And of his fadyr David the Lord xal geve hym the se,
Reynyng in the hous of Jacob, of which regne xal be no ende.

---

230 *herynge* sound   231 *trobelyd* troubled   233 *aper* appear   234 *fer* companion   237 *shamfastnes* shyness   242 *clepyd* called   243 *kende* nature   244 *se* seat, throne

216

PARLIAMENT OF HEAVEN, SALUTATION AND CONCEPTION

(31)

MARIA: Aungel, I sey to yow
 In what manere of wyse xal this be?
 For knowyng of man I have non now,
 I have evyr more kept and xal my virginyte.
 I dowte not the wordys ye han seyd to me, 250
 But I aske how it xal be do.
GABRYEL: The Holy Gost xal come fro a-bove to the,
 And the vertu of hym hyest xal schadu the so.

(32)

Ther-fore that Holy Gost of the xal be bore;
He xal be clepyd the Son of God sage;
And se Elyzabeth your cosyn thore,
She hath conseyvid a son in hyre age.
This is the sexte monyth of here passage,
Of here that clepyd was bareyn.
No thynge is impossyble to Goddys usage; 260
They thynkyth longe to here what ye wyl seyn.
 Here the Aungel makyth a lytyl restynge and Mary be-
 holdyth hym, and the Aungel seyeth

(33)

[GABRIEL[19]:] Mary, come of and haste the,
 And take hede in thyn entent
 Whow the Holy Gost, blyssyd he be,
 A-bydyth thin answere and thin assent.
 Thorwe wyse werke of dyvinyte
 The secunde persone verament
 Is mad man by fraternyte,
 With-inne thi-self in place present.

(34)

Ferther-more take hede this space 270
Whow all the blyssyd spyrytys of vertu
That are in hefne by-fore Goddys face,

253 *schadu* overshadow   261 *seyn* say   266 *Thorwe* through

And all the gode levers and trew
That are here in this erthely place,
Thyn owyn kynrede the sothe ho knew,
And the chosyn sowlys this tyme of grace
That are in helle and byde rescu;

(35)

As Adam, Abraham, and Davyd in fere,
And many othere of good reputacion,
That thin answere desyre to here   280
And thin assent to the incarnacion,
In which thou standyst as persevere[20]
Of all man-kende sa[l]vacion;
Gyff me myn answere now, lady dere,
To all these creaturys comfortacion.

(36)

MARIA: With all mekenes I clyne to this a-corde,
Bowynge down my face with all benyngnyte;
Se here the hand-mayden of oure Lorde,
Aftyr thi worde be it don to me.
GABRYEL: Gramercy, my lady fre,   290
Gramercy of your answere on hyght,
Gramercy of your grett humylyte,
Gramercy, ye lanterne of lyght.
*Here the Holy Gost discendit with iij bemys to our lady,
the Sone of the Godhed nest with iij bemys to the Holy Gost,
the Fadyr godly with iij bemys to the Sone: and so entre all
thre to here bosom, and Mary seyth*

(37)

MARIA: A, now I fele in my body be
Parfyte God and parfyte man,
Havyng al schappe of chyldly carnalyte,
Evyn al at onys thus God be-gan.

---

273 *levers* livers, people alive   275 *ho* who   285 *comfortacion* comfort
286 *clyne* incline   295 *Parfyte* perfect   296 *carnalyte* incarnation

218

PARLIAMENT OF HEAVEN, SALUTATION AND CONCEPTION

(38)

    Nott takynge fyrst o membyr and sythe a-nother,
    But parfyte childhod ye have a-non,
    Of your hand-mayden now ye have mad your modyr   300
    With-owte peyne in flesche and bon.
    Thus conceyved nevyr woman non
    That evyr was beynge in this lyf.
    O myn hyest Fadyr in your tron,
    It is worthy your Son, now my Son, have a prerogatyf.

(39)

    I can not telle what joy, what blysse,
    Now I fele in my body.
    Aungel Gabryel, I thank yow for thys;
    Most mekely recomende me to my Faderys mercy;
    To have be the modyr of God ful lytyl wend I.   310
    Now myn cosyn Elyzabeth fayn wold I se,
    How sche hath conseyvid as ye dede specyfy;
    Now blyssyd be the hygh Trynyte.

(40)

GABRYEL: Fare weyl, turtyl, Goddys dowtere dere,
    Fare wel, Goddys modyr, I the honowre;
    Fare wel, Goddys sustyr, and his pleynge fere,
    Fare wel, Goddys chawmere and his bowre.

(41)

MARIA: Fare wel, Gabryel specyalye,
    Fare wel, Goddys masangere expresse;
    I thank yow for your traveyl hye;   320
    Gramercy of your grett goodnes,

(42)

    And namely of your comfortabyl massage,
    For I undyrstande by inspyracion;

---

305 *prerogatyf* sole right   310 *wend* thought   314 *turtyl* turtle dove, beloved   316 *pleynge fere* playfellow   317 *chawmere* chamber   *bowre* bower   320 *traveyl* labour

That ye knowe by syngulere prevylage
Most of my Sonys incarnacion.
I pray yow take it in to usage,
Be a custom ocupacion,
To vesyte me ofte be mene passage[21];
Your presence is my comfortacion.

(43)

GABRIEL: At your wyl, lady, so xal it be, 330
Ye gentyllest of blood and hyest of kynrede,
That reynyth in erth in ony degre,
Be pryncypal incheson of the God-hede.

(44)

I comende me on to yow, thou trone of the Trinyte,
O mekest mayde, now the modyr of Jhesu,
Qwen of hefne, lady of erth, and empres of helle be ye,
Socour to all synful that wole to yow sew,
Tho[rwe] your body beryth the babe oure blysse xal renew[22];
To yow, modyr of mercy, most mekely I recomende.
And as I began I ende with an *Ave* new 340
Enjonyd hefne and erth, with that I ascende.

Angeli cantando istam sequenciam
Ave Maria, gratia plena,
Dominus tecum, virgo se[r]ena[23].

327 *custom ocupacion* customary act   333 *incheson* cause   337 *wole* will
sew sue

11. Joseph

LUDUS COVENTRIAE 12

This play – or a version of it – was in the cycle when the Proclamation was written, though the MS shows that it was number eleven originally. Probably the part of the cycle concerned with Mary was re-worked, new material being added. But this play does not bear the marks of others in the group, and it may have been revised at a different time. It is clear that it is an interpolation at number twelve, between two plays which are the work of one writer.

It derives from Matthew 1 18–25, but the subject was much elaborated in the medieval versions of the Gospel. Several sources have been suggested, one of the most important being Bonaventura's Meditationes Vitae Christi. *It is notable that the other cycles all include the incident (York 13, Chester 6, Towneley 10), as does the* Coventry Shearmen and Tailors' Play. *The play is striking in the comic and ridiculous view it takes of Joseph's doubts – there is no justification for this in the Gospel – and the picture of an old cuckold is one that is shared by the other dramatic versions. Joseph radically misunderstands what has happened, and, thinking that Mary has played him false, he turns to the audience for sympathy. His picture of faithless and irritating wives is perhaps an echo of Mrs Noah. The placing of such an earthy episode in the story of Mary was a reminder of the corruption of man.*

ಜಣ

[*Joseph's house: Mary and Susanna within; Joseph knocks.*]

(1)

JOSEPH: How, dame, how! Un-do youre dore, un-do.
    Are ye at hom? Why speke ye notht?

  2 *hom* home   *notht* not

ENGLISH MYSTERY PLAYS

SUSANNA: Who is ther? Why cry ye so?
Telle us your herand! Wyl ye ought?
JOSEPH: Un-do your dore, I sey yow to,
For to com in is all my thought.
MARIA: It is my spowse that spekyth us to;
On-do the dore, his wyl were wrought[1].
[*Mary admits him.*]

(2)

Well-come hom, myn husbond dere.
How have ye ferd in fer countre?   10
JOSEPH: To gete oure levynge, with-owtyn dwere,
I have sore laboryd for the and me.
MARIA: Husbond, ryght gracyously now come be ye;
It solacyth me sore, sothly to se yow in syth.
JOSEPH: Me merveylyth, wyf, surely, your face I can not se,
But as the sonne with his bemys quan he is most bryth[2].

(3)

MARIA: Husbond, it is as it plesyth oure Lord; that grace of hym grew;
Who that evyr be-holdyth me veryly,
They xal be grettly steryed to vertu;
For his gyfte and many moo, good Lord, gramercy.   20

(4)

JOSEPH: How hast thou ferde, jentyl mayde,
Whyl I have be out of londe?
MARIA: Sekyr, sere, beth nowth dysmayde,
Ryth aftyr the wyl of Goddys sonde.
JOSEPH: That semyth evyl, I am afrayd;
Thi wombe to hyghe doth stonde:
I drede me sore I am be-trayd.
Sum other man the had in honde
Hens sythe that I went[3].
Thy wombe is gret; it gynnyth to ryse;   30

4 *herand* errand   9 *dere* dear   11 *dwere* fear   14 *syth* sight   16 *quan* when   19 *steryed* stirred   23 *Sekyr* certainly   *sere* sir   24 *sonde* message   26 *hyghe* high

JOSEPH

Than hast thou be-gownne a synfull gyse.
Telle me now in what wyse
Thy-self thou ast thus schent.

(5)

Ow, dame, what thinge menyth this?
With childe thou gynnyst ryth gret to gon.
Sey me, Mary, this childys fadyr ho is;
I pray the telle me and that anon.
MARIA: The Fadyr of hevyn and ye, it is –
Other fadyr hath he non.
I dede nevyr forfete with man i-wys, 40
Wher-fore I pray yow amende your mon;
This childe is Goddys and your.
JOSEPH: Goddys childe! Thou lyist, in fay!
God dede nevyr jape so with may,
And I cam nevyr ther, I dare wel say,
Yitt so nyh thi boure;
But yit I sey, Mary, whoos childe is this?
MARIA: Goddys and youre, I sey, i-wys.

(6)

JOSEPH: Ya, ya! all olde men to me take tent[4],
And weddyth no wyf in no kynnys wyse 50
That is a yonge wench, be myn a-sent.
For doute and drede and swyche servyse,
Alas, alas! my name is shent.
All men may me now dyspyse
And seyn 'Olde cokwold, thi bow is bent
Newly now, after the Frensche gyse.'[5]
Alas and welaway!
Alas, dame, why dedyst thou so?
For this synne that thou hast do
I the for-sake, and from the go 60
For onys evyr and ay.

---

31 *be-gownne* begun *gyse* way of life 33 *ast* hast *schent* disgraced
36 *ho* who 40 *forfete* wrong 41 *mon* complaint 44 *may* maid 46 *Yitt* yet *nyh* near 49 *tent* notice 50 *kynnys* kind (of) 55 *cokwold* cuckold

(7)

MARIA: Alas, gode spowse, why sey ye thus?
Alas, dere hosbund, a-mende your mod.
It is no man but swete Jhesus.
He wyll be clad in flesch and blood
And of your wyf be born.
SEPHOR[6]: For sothe the aungel thus seyd he:
That Goddys sone in trynite,
For mannys sake, a man wolde be,
To save that is for-lorn. 70

(8)

JOSEPH: An aungel! Allas! Alas! Fy for schame!
Ye syn now in that ye to say
To puttyn an aungel in so gret blame.
Alas, alas! Let be, do way!
It was sum boy be-gan this game,
That clothyd was clene and gay,
And ye geve hym now an aungel name.
Alas, alas, and wel-away,
That evyr this game be-tydde!
A, dame, what thought haddyst thou? 80
Here may all men this proverbe trow,
That many a man doth bete the bow,
Another man hath the brydde[7].

(9)

MARIA: A, gracyous God in hefne trone,
Comforte my spowse in this hard cas.
Mercyful God, a-mend his mone,
As I dede nevyr so gret trespas.

(10)

JOSEPH: Lo, lo, serys! What told I yow?
That it was not for my prow

63 *mod* mood 70 *for-lorn* lost 72 *to* two 79 *be-tydde* happened
83 *brydde* bird 89 *prow* advantage

JOSEPH

A wyf to take me to,   90
An that is wel sene now.
For Mary, I make God a vow,
Is grett with childe, lo!
Alas, why is it so?
To the busshop I wole it telle,
That he the law may here do,
With stonys[8] here to qwelle.

(11)

Nay, nay, yet God for-bede
That I xuld do that ve[n]geabyl dede
But if I wyst wel qwy[9].   100
I knew never with here, so God me spede,
Tokyn of thynge in word nor dede
That towchyd velany.
Nevyr the les, what for thy,
Thow she be meke and mylde,
With-owth mannys company
She myght not be with childe.

(12)

But I ensure myn was it nevyr;
Thow that she hath not don here devyr,
Rather than I xuld pleynyn opynly,   110
Serteynly yitt had I levyr
For-sake the countre for evyr
And nevyr come in here company.
For and men knew this velany,
In repreff thei wolde me holde;
And yett many bettyr than I,
Ya, hath ben made cokolde.

(13)

Now, alas, whedyr xal I gone?
I wot nevyr whedyr nor to what place,

---

97 *qwelle* kill   99 *vengeabyl* full of revenge   100 *qwy* why   102 *Tokyn* sign   108 *ensure* am sure   109 *devyr* duty   110 *pleynyn* complain
111 *levyr* rather

T–H   225

For oftyn tyme sorwe comyth sone,
And longe it is or it pace.
No comforte may I have here.
I-wys, wyf, thou dedyst me wronge;
Alas, I taryed from the to longe.
All men have pety on me amonge,
For to my sorwe is no chere.

(14)

MARIA: God, that in my body art sesyd,
Thou knowist myn husbond is dysplesyd
To se me in this plight.
For unknowlage he is desesyd,
And therfore help that he were esyd,
That he myght knowe the ful perfyght.
For I have levyr abyde respyt[10]
To kepe thi Sone in privite,
Grauntyd by the holy spyryt,
Than that it xulde be opynd by me.
  [*God sends the Angel.*]

(15)

DEUS: Descende, I sey, myn aungelle,
On to Joseph for to telle –
Such as my wyl is –
Byd hym with Mary a-byde and dwelle,
For it is my Sone ful snelle
That she is with i-wys.
ANGELUS: Almyghty God of blys,
I am redy for to wende,
Wedyr as thi wyl is,
To go bothe fer and hynde.
  [*Appears to Joseph.*]

---

121 *or* before *pace* passes   127 *sesyd* placed   130 *unknowlage* ignorance *desesyd* unhappy   132 *the* thee *perfyght* perfectly   141 *snelle* quick, alive   145 *Wedyr* whither   146 *fer* far *hynde* near

JOSEPH

(16)

Joseph, Joseph, thou wepyst shyrle;
Fro thi wyff why comyst thou owte?
JOSEPH: Good sere, lete me wepe my fylle;
Go forthe thi wey and lett me nowght. 150
ANGELUS: In thi wepynge thou dost ryght ylle;
A-gens God thou hast mys-wrought.
Go chere thi wyf with herty wylle,
And chawnge thi chere, amende thi thought;
Sche is a ful clene may.
I telle the God wyl of here be born,
And sche clene mayd as she was be-forn,
To save mankynd that is for-lorn.
Go chere hyre therfore I say.

(17)

JOSEPH: A, lord God, *benedicite!* 160
Of thi gret comforte I thank the
That thou sent me this space.
I myght wel a wyst, parde,
So good a creature as she
Wold nevyr a done trespace,
For sche is ful of grace.
I know wel I have myswrought.
I walk to my pore place
And aske for-gyfnes; I have mys-thought.

(18)

Now is the tyme sen at eye 170
That the childe is now to veryfye,
Which xal save mankende,
As it was spoke be prophesye.
I thank the God that syttys on hye,
With hert wyl and mende,

---

147 *shyrle* shrill   150 *lett* hinder   156 *wyl* will   159 *hyre* her   163 *a* have   *wyst* known   *parde* by God   170 *sen* seen   *at eye* at hand
171 *veryfye* prove to be true

ENGLISH MYSTERY PLAYS

    That evyr thou woldyst me bynde
    To wedde Mary to my wyff,
    Thi blysful Sone so nere to fynde,
    In his presens to lede my lyff.

(19)

    Alas, for joy I qwedyr and qwake!   180
    Alas, what hap now was this?
    A, mercy, mercy, my jentyl make,
    Mercy: I have seyd al amys.
    All that I have seyd here I for-sake;
    Your swete fete now lete me kys.
MARY: Nay, lett be my fete, not tho ye take,
    My mowthe ye may kys i-wys,
    And welcom on-to me.
JOSEPH: Gramercy, myn owyn swete wyf!
    Gramercy, myn hert, my love, my lyf!   190
    Xal I nevyr more make suche stryf
    Be-twyx me and the.

(20)

    A, Mary, Mary, wel thou be,
    And blyssyd be the frewte in the,
    Goddys Sone of myght.
    Now, good wyf, ful of pyte,
    As be not evyl payd with me,
    Thow that thou have good ryght.
    As for my wronge in syght
    To wyte the with ony synne[11].   200
    Had thou not be a vertuous wythe,
    God wold not a be the with-inne.

(21)

    I knowlage I have don a-mys;
    I was never wurthy, i-wys,

---

180 *qwedyr* quiver   *qwake* quake   182 *make* mate   194 *frewte* fruit
197 *evyl payd* ill-pleased   201 *wythe* person   203 *knowlage* acknowledge

JOSEPH

> For to be thin husbonde.
> I xal amende aftere thys,
> Ryght as thin owyn wyl is,
> To serve the at foot and honde,
> And thi chylde bothe to undyr-stonde,
> To wurchep hym with good affeccion;   210
> And therfore telle me, and nothynge whonde,
> The holy matere of your concepcion.

(22)

> MARIA: At yowre owyn wyll as ye bydde me –
> Ther cam an aunge[l] hyght Gabryell
> And gret me fayr and seyd *Ave*,
> And ferther more to me gan tell
> God xulde be borne of my bode,
> The fendys pouste for to felle,
> Thorwe the Holy Gost as I wel se;
> Thus God in me wyl byde and dwelle.   220

(23)

> JOSEPH: Now I thank God, with spech and spelle,
> That evyr, Mary, I was weddyd to the.
> MARY: It was the werk of God, as I yow telle;
> Now blyssyd be that Lord so purveyd for me.

[The visit to Elizabeth follows.]

211 *whonde* hesitate   218 *fendys* fiend's   *pouste* power   *felle* destroy
221 *spelle* words   224 *purveyd* provided

❧ ❧ ❧

12. The Nativity

LUDUS COVENTRIAE 15

The revision mentioned in the two previous notes probably affected this play; in the manuscript of the Proclamation its number was corrected from 13 to 15. It contributes to the sequence considerable emphasis upon the purity of Mary, and some indications of the folly of the aged Joseph. It incorporates two miracles designed to increase the faith: the Cherry Tree miracle and the story of the midwives, whose doubts about Mary are firmly overcome. The midwives represent a very old tradition which found its way early into the liturgical drama (see note 5, p. 664). This tradition was clearly a very strong one, and it is perhaps surprising to the modern reader that this rather crude miracle should be used in connection with such an important climax. The explanation for this may lie in the fact that the Passion had greater theological significance than the Nativity for the compilers. The play does not offer the poetic strength which is shown elsewhere. One feels that the dramatist is making theological points rather than expressing the richer complex of human experience which appears in other places.

※

[*Enter Joseph and Mary.*]

(1)

JOSEPH: Lord, what travayl to man is wrought!
  Rest in this werd be-hovyth hym non.
  Octavyan, oure Emperour, sadly hath be-sought
  Oure trybute hym to bere; folk must forth ichon;
  It is cryed in every bourgh and cety be name.

2 *werd* world   5 *bourgh* town, borough

THE NATIVITY

I that am a pore tymbre-wryth, born of the blood of Davyd,
The emperorys comawndement I must holde with,
And ellys I were to blame.

(2)

Now, my wyf, Mary, what sey ye to this?
For sekyr nedys I must forth wende
On to the cyte of Bedleem, fer hens i-wys;
Thus to labore I must my body bende.
MARIA: Myn husbond and my spowse, with yow wyl I wende;
A syght of that cyte fayn wolde I se;
If I myght of myn alye ony ther fynde
It wolde be grett joye on-to me.

(3)

JOSEPH: My spowse, ye be with childe; I fere yow to kary,
For me semyth it were werkys wylde,
But yow to plese ryght fayn wold I;
Yitt women ben ethe to greve whan thei be with childe.
Now latt us forth wende as fast as we may,
And al-myghty God spede us in oure jurnay.

(4)

MARIA: A, my swete husbond, wolde ye telle to me
What tre is yon standynge upon yon hylle?
JOSEPH: For sothe, Mary, it is clepyd a chery tre;
In tyme of yere ye myght fede yow theron your fylle.

(5)

MARIA: Turne a-geyn, husbonde, and beholde yon tre,
How that it blomyght[1] now so swetly.
JOSEPH: Cum on, Mary, that we worn at yon cyte;
Or ellys we may be blamyd, I telle yow lythly.

---

6 *tymbre-wryth* carpenter   15 *alye* relatives   18 *werkys* actions, business   20 *ethe* easy   25 *clepyd* called   29 *worn* were   30 *lythly* swiftly, quickly

(6)

MARIA: Now, my spowse, I pray yow to be-hold
　　How the cheryes growyn upon yon tre,
　　For to have ther-of ryght fayn I wold,
　　And it plesyd yow to labore so mech for me.

(7)

JOSEPH: Your desyre to fulfylle I xal assay sekyrly.
　　Ow! To plucke yow of these cheries it is a werk wylde,
　　For the tre is so hygh it wol not be lyghtly;
　　Therfore lete hym pluk yow cheryes be-gatt yow with
　　　　childe[2].

(8)

MARIA: Now, good Lord, I pray the, graunt me this boun,
　　To have of these cheries and it be your wylle.　　　　40
　　　　[*The tree bends down.*]
　　Now I thank it God this tre bowyth to me down;
　　I may now gaderyn a-nowe and etyn my fylle.

(9)

JOSEPH: Ow, I know weyl I have offendyd my God in
　　　　trinyte,
　　Spekyng to my spowse these unkynde wurdys;
　　For now I beleve wel it may non other be
　　But that my spowse beryght the kyngys son of blys;
　　He help us now at oure nede.
　　Of the kynrede of Jesse worthely were ye bore,
　　Kyngys and patryarkys yow be-fore,
　　All these wurthy of your kynred wore,　　　　50
　　As clerkys in story rede.

(10)

MARIA: Now gramercy, husbond, for your report.
　　In oure weys wysely late us forth wende;

34 *mech* much　　46 *beryght* bears

THE NATIVITY

The Fadyr all-myghty he be oure comfort;
The Holy Gost gloryous he be oure frende.
  [*They travel to Bethlehem.*]

(11)
JOSEPH: Heyl, wurchepful sere, and good day.
  A ceteceyn of this cyte ye seme to be.
  Of herborwe for spowse and me I yow pray,
  For trewly this woman is ful were,
  And fayn at reste, sere, wold she be.   60
  We wolde fulfylle the byddynge of oure emperour,
  For to pay trybute as ryght is oure,
  And to kepe oure-self from dolowre,
  We are come to this cyte.

(12)
CIVES: Sere, ostage in this town know I non,
  Thin wyf and thou in for to slepe.
  This cete is be-sett with pepyl every won,
  And yett thei ly with-owte ful every strete.

(13)
  With-inne no wall, man, comyst thou nowth,
  Be thou onys with-inne the cyte gate;   70
  On-ethys in the strete a place may be sowth,
  Ther on to rest with-owte debate.

(14)
JOSEPH: Nay, sere, debate that wyl I nowth –
  All such thyngys passyn my powere –
  But yitt my care and all my thought
  Is for Mary, my derlynge dere.

(15)
  A, swete wyf, what xal we do?
  Wher xal we logge this nyght?

---

57 *ceteceyn* citizen 58 *herborwe* shelter inn 59 *were* weary 65 *ostage* inn 68 *with-owte* outside, in the open 71 *On-ethys* with difficulty *sowth* sought 78 *logge* lodge

233

ENGLISH MYSTERY PLAYS

On to the Fadyr of hefne pray we so,
Us to kepe from every wykkyd whyt.   80

(16)

CIVES: Good man, o word I wyl the sey;
If thou wylt do by the counsel of me,
Yondyr is an hous of haras³ that stant be the wey;
Amonge the bestys herboryd may ye be.

(17)

MARIA: Now the Fadyr of hefne he mut yow yelde,
His Sone in my wombe forsothe he is,
He kepe the and thi good be fryth and felde.
Go we hens, husbond, for now tyme it is.

(18)

But herk now, good husbond, a new relacyon,
Which in my-self I know ryght well,   90
Cryst in me hath take in-carnacion,
Sone wele be borne the trowth I fele.
   [*They enter the stable.*]

(19)

In this pore logge my chawmere I take,
Here for to a-byde the blyssyd byrth
Of Hym that all this werd dude make;
Be-twyn myn sydys I fele he styrth.

(20)

JOSEPH: God be thin help, spowse: it swemyth me sore,
Thus febyly loggyd and in so pore degre,
Goddys Sone amonge bestys to be bore;
His woundyr werkys fulfyllyd must be.   100

---

81 *o* one   85 *mut* may   *yelde* reward   87 *fryth* wood   *felde* field
89 *relacyon* indication   92 *Sone* soon   93 *logge* lodging   95 *dude* did
96 *styrth* stirs   97 *swemyth* grieves   98 *febyly* poorly

THE NATIVITY

(21)

In an hous that is desolat with-owty any wall,
Fyer nor wood non here is.
MARIA: Joseph, myn husbond, a-bydyn here I xal,
For here wyl be born the Kyngys Sone of blys.

(22)

JOSEPH: Now, jentyll wyf, be of good myrth,
And if ye wyl owght have, telle me what ye thynk.
I xal not spare for schep nor derth;
Now telle me your lust of mete and drynk.

(23)

MARIA: For mete and drynk lust I right nowth;
All-myghty God my fode xal be. 110
Now that I am in chawmere brought,
I hope ryght wel my chylde to se.
Therfore, husbond, of your honeste,
A-voyd yow hens out of this place,
And I a-lone with humylite
Here xal abyde Goddys hygh grace.

(24)

JOSEPH: All redy, wyf, yow for to plese,
I wyl go hens out of your way,
And seke sum mydwyvys yow for to ese,
Whan that ye travayle of childe this day. 120
Fare well, trewe wyf, and also clene may!
God be your comforte in trinyte.
MARIA: To God in hevyn for yow I pray,
He yow preserve wher so ye be.
   Hic dum Joseph est absens parit Maria filium unigenitum[4].

---

102 *Fyer* fire   106 *wyl* desire   107 *schep* plenty   *derth* dearth

(25)

JOSEPH: Now God of whom comyth all releffe,
    And as all grace in the is grownde,
    So save my wyff from hurt and greffe,
    Tyl I sum mydwyvys for here have fownde.
    Travelynge women in care be bownde
    With grete throwys whan thei do grone;   130
    God helpe my wyf that sche not swownde;
    I am ful sory sche is a-lone.

(26)

    It is not convenyent a man to be
    Ther women gon in travalynge,
    Wher-fore sum mydwyff fayn wold I se,
    My wyff to helpe that is so yenge.

(27)

ZELOMY[5]: Why makyst thou, man, suche mornyng?
    Tell me sum dele of your gret mone.
JOSEPH: My wyf is now in gret longynge,
    Travelyng of chylde, and is a-lone.   140
    For Godys love that sytt in trone,
    As ye myd-wyvys that kan your good,
    Help my yonge spowse in hast a-none.
    I drede me sore of that fayr food.
SALOME: Be of good chere and of glad mood;
    We ij mydwyvys with the wyll go.
    Ther was nevyr woman in such plyght stood
    But we were redy here help to do.

(28)

    My name is Salomee: all men me knowe
    For a mydwyff of wurthy fame.   150
    Whan women travayl grace doth growe;
    Ther as I come I had nevyr shame.

---

126 *grownde* founded   130 *throwys* throes   131 *swownde* faint
136 *yenge* young   138 *dele* part   144 *food* offspring, person

THE NATIVITY

ZELOMYE: And I am Zelomye; men knowe my name.
    We tweyn with the wyl go togedyr
    And help thi wyff fro hurt and grame.
    Com forth, Joseph, go we streyth thedyr.

(29)

JOSEPH: I thank yow, damys, ye comforte my lyff;
    Streyte to my spowse walke we the way.
    In this pore logge lyght Mary my wyff.
    Hyre for to comforte, gode frendys, a-say.   160
SALOME: We dare not entre this logge, in fay –
    Ther is ther-in so gret bryghtnes;
    Mone be nyght nor sunne be day
    Shone nevyr so clere in ther lyghtnesse.

(30)

ZELOMYE: In to this hous dare I not gon;
    The woundyrffull lyght doth me affray.
JOSEPH: Than wyl my-self gon in alon,
    And chere my wyff if that I may.
      [Enters.]
    All heyl, maydon and wyff, I say.
    How dost thou fare? Telle me thi chere.   170
    The for to comforte in gesyne this day,
    Tweyn gode mydwyvis I have brought here.

(31)

    The for to helpe that art in harde bonde,
    Zelomye and Salomee be com with me.
    For dowte of drede with-owte thei do stond,
    And dare not come in for lyght that they se.
      Hic Maria subridendo dicat[6]
MARIA: The myght of the Godhede in his mageste
    Wyl not be hyd now at this whyle.

---

155 *grame* sorrow, harm   156 *streyth* straight   159 *lyght* lies   160 *gode* good   163 *Mone* moon   171 *gesyne* childbed

ENGLISH MYSTERY PLAYS

The chylde that is born wyl preve his modyr fre,
A very clene mayde, and therfore I smyle. 180

(32)

JOSEPH: Why do ye lawghe, wyff? Ye be to blame.
I pray yow, spowse, do no more so;
In happ the mydwyvys wyl take it to grame,
And at your nede helpe wele non do.
If ye have nede of mydwyvys, lo,
Per aventure thei wyl gon hens.
Therfor be sad and ye may so,
And wynnyth all the mydwyvis good diligens.

(33)

MARIA: Husbond, I pray yow dysplese yow nowth,
Thow that I lawghe and gret joye have. 190
Here is the chylde this werde hath wrought,
Born now of me, that all thynge xal save.
JOSEPH: I aske yow grace, for I dyde rave[7].
O gracyous childe, I aske mercy;
As thou art Lord, and I but knave,
For-geve me now my gret foly.

(34)

Alas, mydwyvis, what have I seyd?
I pray yow com to us more nere,
For here I fynde my wyff a mayd,
And in here arme a chyld hath here. 200
Bothe mayd and modyr sch[e] is in fere;
That God wole have may nevyr more fayle.
Modyr on erth was nevyr non clere,
With-owth sche had in byrth travayle.

(35)

ZELOMY: In byrth travayle muste sche nedys have,
Or ellys no chylde of here is born.

179 *fre* noble, pure   183 *grame* anger   191 *werde* world   195 *knave* common man   201 *in fere* together   203 *clere* pure

238

THE NATIVITY

JOSEPH: I pray yow, dame, and ye vowch-save,
    Com se the chylde my wyff be-forn.
SALOME: Grete God be in this place!
    Swete systyr, how fare ye?   210
MARIA: I thank the Fadyr of his hygh grace.
    His owyn Son and my chylde here ye may se.

(36)

ZELOMYE: All heyl, Mary, and ryght good morn!
    Who was mydwyfe of this fayr chyld?
MARIA: He that no thynge wyl have for-lorn
    Sent me this babe and I mayd mylde.

(37)

ZELOMYE: With honde lete me now towch and fele
    Yf ye have nede of medycyn;
    I xal yow comforte and helpe ryght wele
    As other women yf ye have pyn.   220
MARIA: Of this fayr byrth that here is myn,
    Peyne nere grevynge fele I ryght non.
    I am clene mayde and pure virgyn;
    Tast with your hand your-self a-lon.
        Hic palpat Zelomye beatam virginem dicens[8]

(38)

ZELOMY[E]: O myghtfull God, have mercy on me!
    A merveyle that nevyr was herd be-forn!
    Here opynly I fele and se
    A fayr chylde of a maydon is born,
    And nedyth no waschynge as other don;
    Ful clene and pure for soth is he,   230
    With-outyn spot or ony polucyon;
    His modyr nott hurte of virgynite.

(39)

Coom nere, gode systyr Salome;
Be-holde the brestys of this clene mayd,

220 *pyn* suffering   224 *Tast* test, examine

239

ENGLISH MYSTERY PLAYS

Ful of fayr mylke how that thei be;
And hyre chylde clene as I fyrst sayd,
As other ben nowth fowle arayd[9],
But clene and pure, bothe modyr and chylde.
Of this matyr I am dysmayd,
To se them both thus undefyled. 240

(40)

SALOME: It is not trewe; it may nevyr be;
That bothe be clene I can not be-leve.
A mayde mylke have, never man dyde se,
Ne woman bere chylde with-owte grett greve.
I xal nevyr trowe it but I it preve;
With hand towchynge[10] but I assay,
In my conscience it may nevyr cleve
That sche hath chylde and is a may.

(41)

MARIA: Yow for to putt clene out of dowth,
Towch with your hand and wele a-say, 250
Wysely ransake and trye the trewthe owth,
Whethyr I be fowlyd or a clene may.
*Hic tangit Salomee Marie et cum arescerit manus eius
ululando et quasi flendo dicit* [11]
SALOMEE: Alas, alas, and wele a-waye!
For my grett dowth and fals beleve
Myne hand is ded and drye as claye;
My fals untrost hath wrought myscheve.

(42)

Alas the tyme that I was born,
Thus to offende a-gens Goddys myght!
Myn handys power is now all lorn,
Styff as a stykke, and may nowth plyght. 260
For I dede tempte this mayde so bryght,

---

247 *cleve* stick   251 *ransake* search   256 *untrost* mistrust   260 *plyght* bend

240

THE NATIVITY

And helde a-gens here pure clennes,
In grett myscheff now am I pyght.
Alas, alas for my lewdnes!

(43)

O Lord of myght, thou knowyst the trowth,
That I have evyr had dred of the,
On every power whyght evyr I have rowthe,
And gove hem almes for love of the;
Bothe wyf and wedowe that askyght for the,
And frendles chylderyn that haddyn grett nede,   270
I dude them cure and all for the,
And toke no rewarde of them nor mede.

(44)

Now as a wrecch for fals be-leve,
That I shewyd in temptynge this mayde,
My hand is ded and doth me greve.
Alas that evyr I here assayde!
ANGELUS: Woman, thi sorwe to have de-layde,
Wurchep that childe that ther is born.
Towch the clothis ther he is layde,
For he xal save all that is lorn.   280

(45)

SALOMEE: O gloryous chylde and kynge of blysse!
I aske yow mercy for my trespace.
I knowlege my synne I demyd a-mys.
O blyssyd babe, grawnt me sum grace!
Of yow, mayde, also here in this place,
I aske mercy, knelynge on kne.
Moste holy mayde, grawnt me solace;
Sum wurde of comforte sey now to me.

---

263 *pyght* placed   264 *lewdnes* ignorance   267 *power* poor   *whyght* man
rowthe pity   268 *gove* gave   *hem* them   269 *askyght* asks   272 *mede*
reward   283 *knowlege* acknowledge

241

(46)

MARIA: As Goddys aungel to yow dede telle,
  My chyld is medycyn for every sor. 290
  Towch his clothis, be my cowncelle;
  Yowre hand ful sone he wyl restore.
  Hic Salomee tangit fimbriam Christi dicens[12]
SALOMEE: A, now blyssyd be this chylde ever more!
  The Sone of God – for sothe he is –
  Hath helyd myn hand, that was for-lore
  Thorwe fals be-leve and demynge a-mys.

(47)

In every place I xal telle this,
  Of a clene mayd that God is born,
  And in oure lyknes God now clad is,
  Mankend to save that was for-lorn; 300
  His modyr a mayde as sche was be-forn,
  Natt fowle polutyd as other women be,
  But fayr and fresch as rose on thorn,
  Lely-wyte clene with pure virginyte.

(48)

Of this blyssyd babe my leve now do I take,
  And also of yow, hygh modyr of blysse.
  Of this grett meracle more knowlege to make,
  I xal go telle it in iche place i-wys.
MARIA: Fare wel, good dame, and God your wey wysse;
  In all your jurnay God be your spede; 310
  And of his hygh mercy that Lord so yow blysse
  That ye nevyr offende more in word, thought nore dede.

(49)

ZELOMY: And I also do take my leve here,
  Of all this blyssyd good company,

290 *sor* harm, injury   296 *demynge* judging   308 *iche* each, every
309 *wysse* direct, show

THE NATIVITY

Praynge your grace bothe fere and nere,
On us to spede your endles mercy.

(50)

JOSEPH: The blyssyng of that Lord that is most myghty
Mote sprede on yow in every place,
Of all your enmyes to have the victory;
God that best may grawnt yow his grace. Amen.

13. The First Shepherds' Play
Incipit Pagina Pastorum

TOWNELEY 12

The two Shepherds' plays in the Towneley *cycle are the work of the Wakefield Master, who wrote in the first half of the fifteenth century, possibly under the influence of the* York *reviser of about 1415. There is no discernible reason to account for the two versions of the Nativity. The similarities between them are considerable. Both show a close and detailed appreciation of contemporary Yorkshire. They concentrate – in a satirical mode – upon the hardship and suffering of the Shepherds, their difficulties with landlords, the plague, and the weather. The Scriptural account of the Shepherds (Luke 2 8–20) is closely followed, but in both cases the author shows a remarkable capacity to graft on to the original story richly suggestive folk stories which illuminate the religious interpretation of events.*

Such an act of literary creation involves a number of important attitudes. The author sympathizes with the difficulties of the Shepherds, but at the same time he shows them as harsh, contentious, greedy and selfish. In doing so he gives a sharp and significant picture of the corruption of man. The language he uses is the local dialect of South Yorkshire, which even today is rich in proverbial expressions and pithy brevity. On the whole this impression is concentrated in the first part of both plays; the second part brings the Shepherds to Bethlehem, where their coarseness is transformed into humility. This structural feature is important in that it shows the contrast brought by the Nativity into the world of man. The turning point in both cases is the Angel's announcement, when the comedy of the first part is put aside. The comedy itself illuminates the world of suffering. The author shows, in the First Shepherds' Play, *the folly of the Shepherds in their quarrels about non-existent sheep. Here he relies upon two folk-tales, both of which demonstrate the stupidity of day-dreaming: the Fools of Gotham and Moll are all wishing for something they will never have, and in doing so their human short-*

THE FIRST SHEPHERDS' PLAY

sightedness is revealed. The paradox – and it is a doctrinal point of great importance – is that a miracle does occur, the miracle which was to end all follies, the Nativity.

One of the most striking things about the Wakefield Master is his learning. He carries it gracefully, but clearly he is well taught and sets out to establish important religious truths in traditional terms. Even though his characters are earthy and speak coarsely, he transmits through them the learning of the medieval Church. Besides this, he is sensitive to folk-tales, to the partly non-Christian religion of the people, and to classical learning. There is also evidence, in his choice of incident, that he knew something of French farce, and something of other treatments of the Nativity, particularly in the Chester *plays.*

೧೧

[*Scene: field near Bethlehem.*]

(1)

1 PASTOR: Lord, what thay ar weyll[1]   that hens ar past,
For thay noght feyll   theym to downe cast.
Here is mekyll unceyll,   and long has it last.
Now in hart, now in heyll,   now in weytt, now in blast[2],
Now in care,
Now in comforth agane,
Now is fayre, now is rane,
Now in hart full fane,
And after full sare.

(2)

Thus this warld, as I say,   farys on ylk syde,   10
For after oure play   com sorows unryde;
For he that most may   when he syttys in pryde,
When it comys on assay   is kesten downe wyde,
This is seyn.

1 *weyll* happy   2 *feyll* feel   3 *unceyll* misery   4 *heyll* health   *weytt* wet   8 *fane* joyful   9 *sare* sore   11 *unryde* hard   13 *assay* test   *kesten* cast

When ryches[t] is he,
Then comys poverte;
Hors-man Iak Cope
Walkys then, I weyn³.

(3)

I thank it God, hark ye what I mene,
For even or for od I have mekyll tene;
As hevy as a sod I grete with myn eene
When I nap on my cod, for care that has bene
And sorow.
All my shepe ar gone;
I am not left oone;
The rott has theym slone;
Now beg I and borow.

(4)

My handys may I wryng and mowrnyng make;
Bot if good will spryng the countre forsake⁴;
Fermes thyk ar comyng; my purs is bot wake;
I have nerehand nothyng to pay nor to take.
I may syng
With purs penneles
That makys this hevynes;
Wo is me this dystres
And has no helpyng.

(5)

Thus sett I my mynde truly to neven
By my wytt to fynde to cast the warld in seven⁵.
My shepe have I tynde by the moren full even;
Now if hap will grynde, God from his heven
Send grace.
To the fare will I me,

21 *grete* weep 22 *cod* pillow 26 *rott* liver-disease 30 *Fermes* rents *wake* weak 37 *neven* say 39 *tynde* lost *moren* plague *full even* indeed

246

THE FIRST SHEPHERDS' PLAY

To by shepe, perde,
And yit may I multyple
For all this hard case[6].

(6)

II PASTOR: Benste, benste   be us emang,
And save all that I se   here in this thrang!
He save you and me   overtwhart and endlang,
That hang on a tre,   I say you no wrang.
Cryst save us   50
From all myschefys,
From robers and thefys,
From those mens grefys
That oft ar agans us.

(7)

Both bosters[7] and bragers   God kepe us fro,
That with thare long dagers   dos mekyll wo:
From all byll hagers   with colknyfys that go.
Sich wryers and wragers   gose to and fro
For to crak.
Who so says hym agane   60
Were better be slane;
Both ploghe and wane
Amendys will not make.

(8)

He will make it as prowde   a lord as he were;
With a hede lyke a clowde   felterd his here;
He spekys on lowde   with a grym bere;
I wold not have trowde   so galy in gere
As he glydys.

---

46 *Benste* benedicite (blessing)   *emang* among   48 *overtwhart* across
endlang along   53 *grefys* sorrows   57 *byll hagers* men with bill hooks
colknyfys cabbage knives   58 *wryers* quarrellers   *wragers* arguers
60 *says hym agane* speaks against him   62 *ploghe* plough   *wane* wagon
65 *felterd* tangled   *here* hair   66 *bere* noise   67 *trowde* believed   *galy*
brightly

247

I wote not the better,
Nor wheder is gretter,   70
The lad or the master,
So stowtly he strydys.

(9)

If he hask me oght   that he wold to his pay,
Full dere bese it boght   if I say nay;
Bot God that all wroght,   to the now I say,
Help that thay were broght,   to a better way
For thare sawlys;
And send theym good mendyng
With a short endyng,
And with the to be lendyng   80
When that thou callys.

(10)

How, Gyb[8], goode morne!   Wheder goys thou?
Thou goys over the corne,   Gyb, I say, how!
I PASTOR: Who is that? John Horne,   I make God a vowe!
I say not in skorne,   [John,] how farys thou?
II PASTOR: Hay, ha!
Ar ye in this towne?
I PASTOR: Yey, by my crowne.
II PASTOR: I thoght by youre gowne
This was youre aray.   90

(11)

I PASTOR: I am ever elyke,   wote I never what it gars;
Is none in this ryke   a shephard farys wars[9].
II PASTOR: Poore men ar in the dyke   and oft tyme mars;
The warld is slyke;   also helpars
Is none here.
I PASTOR: It is sayde full ryfe,
'A man may not wyfe

---

91 *elyke* alike *gars* causes   92 *ryke* kingdom   94 *slyke* such   96 *ryfe* often

THE FIRST SHEPHERDS' PLAY

And also thryfe,
And all in a yere.'

(12)

II PASTOR: Fyrst must us crepe   and sythen go.
I PASTOR: I go to by shepe.
II PASTOR: Nay, not so!
What, dreme ye or slepe?   Where shuld thay go?
Here shall thou none kepe[10].
I PASTOR: A, good syr, ho!
Who am I?
I wyll pasture my fe
Where so ever lykys me;
Here shall thou theym se.
II PASTOR: Not so hardy!

(13)

Not oone shepe tayll   shall thou bryng hedyr.
I PASTOR: I shall bryng, no fayll,   a hundreth togedyr.
II PASTOR: What, art thou in ayll?   Longys thou oght whedir?[11]
I PASTOR: Thay shall go, saunce fayll.   Go now, bell-weder!
II PASTOR: I say, tyr!
I PASTOR: I say, tyr, now agane!
I say skyp over the plane.
II PASTOR: Wold thou never so fane,
Tup, I say, whyr!

(14)

I PASTOR: What, wyll thou not yit,   I say, let the shepe go?
Whop!
II PASTOR: Abyde yit!
I PASTOR: Will thou bot so?
Knafe, hens I byd flytt.   As good that thou do,

105 *fe* flock   109 *tayll* tail   111 *ayll* ale   112 *saunce* without   *bell-weder* bell-wether   113, 116, 118 *tyr, whyr, Whop* (shouts to drive sheep)   116 *fane* glad, eager   120 *Knafe* knave

ENGLISH MYSTERY PLAYS

    Or I shall the hytt   on thi pate – lo,
    Shall thou reyll!
    I say, gyf the shepe space.
II PASTOR: Syr, a letter of youre grace[12].
    Here comys Slaw-pase
    Fro the myln whele.
    [*Enter Third Shepherd.*]

(15)

III PASTOR: What a do, what a do   is this you betweyn?
    A good day, thou, and thou.
I PASTOR: Hark what I meyn
    You to say:
    I was bowne to by store,   130
    Drofe my shepe me before;
    He says not oone hore
    Shall pas by this way;

(16)

    Bot and he were wood   this way shall thay go.
III PASTOR: Yey, bot tell me, good,   where ar youre shepe,
        lo?
II PASTOR: Now, syr, by my hode,   yit se I no mo,
    Not syn I here stode.
III PASTOR: God gyf you wo
    And sorrow!
    Ye fysh before the nett,
    And stryfe on this bett[13];   140
    Sich folys never I mett
    Evyn or at morow.

(17)

    It is wonder to wyt   where wytt shuld be fownde;
    Here ar old knafys yit   standys on this grownde,
    These wold by thare wytt   make a shyp be drownde;
    He were well qwytt   had sold for a pownde

---

122 *reyll* stagger   126 *myln* mill   130 *bowne* ready   131 *Drofe* drove
132 *hore* hair   141 *folys* fools

THE FIRST SHEPHERDS' PLAY

Sich two.
Thay fyght and thay flyte
For that at comys not tyte;
It is far to byd hyte
To an eg or it go[14].

(18)

Tytter want ye sowll   then sorow, I pray![15]
Ye brayde of Mowll[16]   that went by the way —
Many shepe can she poll   bot oone had she ay —
Bot she happynyd full fowll: hyr pycher, I say,
Was broken.
'Ho, God!' she sayde;
Bot oone shepe yit she hade,
The mylk pycher was layde;
The skarthis was the tokyn.

(19)

Bot syn ye ar bare   of wysdom to knowe,
Take hede how I fare   and lere at my lawe;
Ye nede not to care,   if ye folow my sawe.
Hold ye my mare.   This sek[17] thou thrawe
On my bak,
Whylst I, with my hand,
Lawse the sek band;
Com nar and by stand,
Both Gyg and Iak.

(20)

Is not all shakyn owte,   and no meyll is therin?
I PASTOR: Yey, that is no dowte.
III PASTOR: So is youre wyttys thyn,
And ye look well abowte,   nawther more nor myn;

---

148 *flyte* quarrel   149 *tyte* soon   150 *hyte* go   152 *Tytter* more quickly
sowll sauce   153 *brayde of* resemble   154 *poll* shear   159 *pycher* pitcher
160 *skarthis* fragments   164 *sek* sack   *thrawe* throw   167 *Lawse* loosen
168 *nar* near   170 *meyll* meal   172 *myn* less

ENGLISH MYSTERY PLAYS

So gose youre wyttys owte,   evyn as it com in.
Geder up,
And seke it agane!
II PASTOR: May we not be fane,
He has told us full plane
Wysdom to sup.
   [*Enter Iak Garcio.*]

(21)

IAK GARCIO: Now God gyf you care,   foles all sam;
Sagh I never none so fare   bot the Foles of Gotham[18].   180
Wo is hir that yow bare!   Youre syre and youre dam,
Had she broght furth an hare,   a shepe, or a lam,
Had bene well.
Of all the foles I can tell,
From heven unto hell,
Ye thre bere the bell;
God gyf you unceyll!

(22)

I PASTOR: How pastures oure fee?[19]   Say me, good pen[20].
GARCIO: Thay ar gryssed to the kne.
II PASTOR: Fare fall the!
GARCIO: Amen.
   If ye will ye may se: youre bestes ye ken.   190
   [*Exit Garcio.*]
I PASTOR: Sytt we downe all thre,   and drynk shall we then.
III PASTOR: Yey, torde.
I am lever ete;
What is drynk withoute mete?
Gett mete, gett,
And sett us a borde,

(23)

Then may we go dyne,   oure bellys to fyll.
II PASTOR: Abyde unto syne.

174 *Geder* gather   187 *unceyll* unhappiness   188 *fee* flock   *pen* titch
189 *gryssed* in grass   192 *torde* turd   193 *am lever* had rather   196 *borde*
table   197 *bellys* bellies

252

THE FIRST SHEPHERDS' PLAY

III PASTOR: Be God, syr, I nyll!
I am worthy the wyne,   me thynk it good skyll.
My servyse I tyne;   I fare full yll
At youre mangere.
I PASTOR: Trus, go we to mete!
It is best that we trete;
I lyst not to plete
To stand in thi dangere.

(24)

Thou has ever bene curst   syn we met togeder[21].
III PASTOR: Now in fayth, if I durst,   ye ar even my broder.
II PASTOR: Syrs, let us cryb[22] furst   for oone thyng or oder,
That thise wordys be purst,   and let us go foder
Oure mompyns.
Lay furth of oure store[23]:
Lo, here browne of a bore.
I PASTOR: Set mustard afore;
Oure mete now begyns.

(25)

Here a foote of a cowe,   well sawsed, I wene,
The pestell of a sowe   that powderd has bene,
Two blodyngys, I trowe,   a leveryng betwene;
Do gladly, syrs, now,   my breder bedene,
With more –
Both befe, and moton
Of an ewe that was roton –
Good mete for a gloton –
Ete of this store.

---

198 *syne* later   *nyll* will not   200 *tyne* waste   201 *mangere* manger
203 *trete* negotiate   204 *plete* plead   209 *purst* put away   *foder* feed
210 *mompyns* teeth   212 *browne* brawn   *bore* boar   216 *pestell* leg
217 *blodyngys* blood-puddings   *leveryng* liver sausage   221 *roton* rotten

(26)

II PASTOR: I have here in my mayll   sothen and rost;
Even of an ox-tayll –   that wold not be lost.
Ha, ha, goderhayll!   I let for no cost;
A good py or we fayll –   this is good for the frost
In a mornyng –
And two swyne-gronys;
All a hare bot the lonys.   230
We myster no sponys
Here at oure mangyng.

(27)

III PASTOR: Here is to recorde   the leg of a goys,
With chekyns endorde,   pork, partryk to roys,
A tart for a lorde –   how thynk ye this doys?
A calf lyver skorde,   with the veryose:
Good sawse.
This is a restorete
To make a good appete.
I PASTOR: Yee speke all by clerge;   240
I here by your clause.

(28)

Cowth ye by youre gramery   reche us a drynk,
I shuld be more mery;   ye wote what I thynk.
II PASTOR: Have good ayll of Hely![24]   Bewar now, I wynk,
For and thou drynk drely   in thy poll wyll it synk.
I PASTOR: A, so!
This is boyte of oure bayll,
Good holsom ayll.

---

224 *mayll* pack   *sothen* boiled (meat)   226 *goderhayll* good luck
229 *swyne-gronys* swine-snouts   231 *myster* need   *sponys* spoons
232 *mangyng* eating   233 *goys* goose   234 *chekyns* chickens   *endorde*
covered with egg-yolk   *partryk* partridge   *roys* praise   236 *skorde*
scored, cut   *veryose* verjuice   238 *restorete* restorative   240 *clerge*
learning   242 *Cowth* if you could   *gramery* learning   245 *drely* heavily
poll head   247 *boyte* cure   *bayll* sorrow

THE FIRST SHEPHERDS' PLAY

III PASTOR: Ye hold long the skayll;
    Now lett me go to. 250

(29)

II PASTOR: I shrew those lyppys   bot thou leyff me som parte.
I PASTOR: Be God, he bot syppys;   begylde thou art.
    Behold how he kyppys![25]
II PASTOR: I shrew you so smart,
    And me on my hyppys   bot if I gart
    Abate.
    Be thou wyne, be thou ayll,
    Bot if my brethe fayll,
    I shall sett the on sayll;
    God send the good gayte.

(30)

III PASTOR: Be my dam saull, Alyce[26], it was sadly dronken. 260
I PASTOR: Now, as ever have I blys,   to the bothom it is sonken.
II PASTOR: Yit a botell here is.
III PASTOR: That is well spoken!
    By my thryft we must kys.
II PASTOR: That had I forgoten.
    Bot hark!
    Who so can best syng
    Shall have the begynnyng.
I PASTOR: Now prays at the partyng;
    I shall sett you on warke.
    [They sing.]

(31)

    We have done oure parte   and songyn right weyll;
    I drynk for my parte.
II PASTOR: Abyde, lett cop reyll! 270

---

249 *skayll* cup   253 *kyppys* snatches   254 *gart* cause it to   258 *sayll* sail
270 *cop* cup   *reyll* circulate

I PASTOR: Godys forbot, thou spart   and thou drynk every
    deyll.
III PASTOR: Thou has dronken a quart,   therfor choke the
    the deyll.
I PASTOR: Thou rafys;
    And it were for a sogh
    Ther is drynk enogh.
III PASTOR: I shrew the handys it drogh!
    Ye be both knafys.

(32)

I PASTOR: Nay, we knaves all,   thus thynk me best;
    So, sir, shuld ye call.
II PASTOR: Furth let it rest;
    We will not brall.
I PASTOR: Then wold I we fest   280
    This mete who shall   into panyere kest[27].
III PASTOR: Syrs, herys;
    For oure saules lett us do
    Poore men gyf it to.
I PASTOR: Geder up, lo, lo,
    Ye hungre begers frerys![28]

(33)

II PASTOR: It draes nere nyght.   Trus, go we to rest.
    I am even redy dyght;   I thynk it the best.
III PASTOR: For ferde we be fryght   a crosse lett us kest –
    Cryst crosse, benedyght   eest and west –   290
    For drede.
    Ihesus onazorus,
    Crucyefixus,
    Morcus, Andreus[29],
    God be oure spede!
        [*They sleep.*]

271 *spart* spare it   *deyll* drop   273 *rafys* ravest   274 *sogh* saw   280 *brall*
brawl   281 *panyere* pannier   *kest* throw   282 *herys* listen   286 *frerys*
friars   287 *draes* draws   290 *benedyght* blessed

256

THE FIRST SHEPHERDS' PLAY

(34)

ANGELUS: Herkyn, hyrdes, awake! Gyf lovyng ye shall;
He is borne for [y]oure sake, Lorde perpetuall.
He is comen to take and rawnson you all,
Youre sorowe to slake, kyng emperiall,
He behestys; 300
That chyld is borne
At Bethelem this morne;
Ye shall fynde hym beforne
Betwix two bestys.

(35)

I PASTOR: A, Godys dere Dominus! What was that sang?
It was wonder curiose, with small noytys emang[30];
I pray to God, save us now in this thrang;
I am ferd, by Ihesus, somewhat be wrang;
Me thoght
Oone scremyd on lowde; 310
I suppose it was a clowde;
In myn erys it sowde,
By hym that me boght!

(36)

II PASTOR: Nay, that may not be, I say you certan,
For he spake to us thre as he had bene a man;
When he lemyd on this lee my hart shakyd than;
An angell was he, tell you I can,
No dowte.
He spake of a barne;
We must seke hym, I you warne; 320
That betokyns yond starne,
That standys yonder owte[31].

(37)

III PASTOR: It was mervell to se, so bright as it shone;
I wold have trowyd, veraly, it had bene thoner-flone,

296 *hyrdes* shepherds   298 *rawnson* ransome   299 *slake* ease   306 *noytys* notes   307 *thrang* gathering   312 *sowde* sighed   316 *lemyd* shone   *lee* meadow   319 *barne* child   324 *trowyd* believed   *thonerflone* lightning

257

Bot I sagh with myn ee   as I lenyd to this stone.
It was a mery gle: sich hard I never none,
I recorde.
As he sayde in a skreme,
Or els that I dreme,
We shuld go to Bedleme,   330
To wyrship that lorde.

(38)

I PASTOR: That same childe is he   that prophetys of told,
    Shuld make them fre   that Adam had sold.
II PASTOR: Take tent unto me!   This is inrold
    By the wordys of Isae: a prynce most bold
Shall he be,
And kyng with crowne,
Sett on David trone;
Sich was never none
Seyn with oure ee.   340

(39)

III PASTOR: Also Isay says —   oure faders us told —
    That a vyrgyn shuld pas   of Iesse, that wold
    Bryng furth, by grace,   a floure so bold;
    That a vyrgyn now has,   these wordys uphold,
As ye se;
Trust it now we may,
He is borne this day;
*Exiet virga
De radice Iesse*[32].

(40)

I PASTOR: Of hym spake more: Sybyll[33], as I weyn;   350
    And Nabugodhonosor[34],   from oure faythe alyene,
    In the fornace where thay wore   thre childre sene,
    The fourt stode before,   Godys son lyke to bene.

325 *sagh* saw *lenyd* leaned 326 *gle* song 328 *skreme* scream 340 *Seyn* seen 350 *weyn* think 351 *alyene* alien 352 *fornace* furnace *wore* were

II PASTOR: That fygure
Was gyffen by revelacyon
That God wold have a son;
This is a good lesson
Us to consydure.

(41)

III PASTOR: Of hym spake Ieromy,   and Moyses also[35],
Where he sagh hym by   a bushe burnand, lo!   360
When he cam to aspy   if it were so,
Unburnyd was it truly   at commyng therto,
A wonder.
I PASTOR: That was for to se
Hir holy vyrgynyte,
That she unfylyd shuld be,
Thus can I ponder,

(42)

And shuld have a chyld   sich was never sene.
II PASTOR: Pese, man, thou art begyld!   Thou shall se hym with eene,
Of a madyn so myld,   greatt mervell I mene,   370
Yee, and she unfyld,   a virgyn clene,
So soyne[36].
I PASTOR: Nothyng is inpossybyll,
Sothly, that God wyll;
It shalbe stabyll
That God wyll have done.

(43)

II PASTOR: Abacuc and Ely   prophesyde so,
Elezabeth and Zachare[37],   and many other mo,
And David as veraly   is witnes therto,
Iohn Baptyste sewrly,   and Daniel also.   380

---

354 *fygure* symbol   360 *burnand* burning   366 *unfylyd* pure   375 *stabyll* certain   380 *sewrly* surely

ENGLISH MYSTERY PLAYS

III PASTOR: So sayng,
    He is Godys son alon,
    Without hym shalbe none,
    His sete and his trone
    Shall ever be lastyng.

(44)

I PASTOR: Virgill in his poetre   sayde in his verse,
    Even thus by gramere,   as I shall rehearse:
    '*Iam nova progenies celo demittitur alto,*
    Iam rediet virgo, redeunt saturnia regna[38].'
II PASTOR: Weme! Tord! What speke ye   here in myn eeres?   390
    Tell us no clerge.   I hold you of the freres;
    Ye preche.
    It semys by youre Laton
    Ye have lerd youre Caton[39].
I PASTOR: Herk, syrs, ye fon.
    I shall you teche:

(45)

    He sayde from heven   a new kynde is send,
    Whom a vyrgyn to neven,   oure mys to amend,
    Shall conceyve full even;   thus make I an end;
    And yit more to neven,   that Saturne shall bend   400
    Unto us,
    With peasse and plente,
    With ryches and menee,
    Good luf and charyte
    Blendyd amanges us.

(46)

III PASTOR: And I hold it trew,   for ther shuld be,
    When that kyng commys new,   peasse by land and se.
II PASTOR: Now, brethere, adew!   Take tent unto me;
    I wold that we knew   of this song so fre
    Of the angell;   410

384 *sete* seat   390 *Weme* stop   391 *clerge* learning   394 *lerd* learned
395 *fon* jest   397 *kynde* race   403 *menee* company   405 *amanges* amongst

THE FIRST SHEPHERDS' PLAY

I hard by hys steven
He was send downe fro heven.
I PASTOR: It is trouth that ye neven,
I hard hym well spell.

(47)

II PASTOR: Now, by God that me boght   it was a mery song;
I dar say that he broght   foure and twenty to a long[40].
III PASTOR: I wold it were soght,   that same, us emong.
I PASTOR: In fayth, I trow noght   so many he throng
On a heppe;
Thay were gentyll and small,   420
And well tonyd with all.
III PASTOR: Yee, bot I can thaym all,
Now lyst I lepe.

(48)

I PASTOR: Breke outt youre voce!   Let se as ye yelp.
III PASTOR: I may not, for the pose,   bot I have help.
II PASTOR: A, thy hart is in thy hose!
I PASTOR: Now, in payn of a skelp
This sang thou not lose[41].
III PASTOR: Thou art an yll qwelp
For angre.
II PASTOR: Go to now, begyn!
I PASTOR: He lyst not well ryn.   430
III PASTOR: God lett us never blyn;
Take at my sangre.
  [*He leads the song.*]

(49)

I PASTOR: Now an ende have we doyn   of oure song this tyde.
II PASTOR: Fayr fall thi growne!   Well has thou hyde.

---

414 *spell* speak, describe   418 *throng* thrust together   419 *heppe* heap
421 *tonyd* intoned   423 *lepe* leap   424 *yelp* sing loudly   425 *pose* head-
cold   426 *skelp* blow   427 *qwelp* whelp   431 *blyn* cease   432 *sangre*
song   433 *doyn* done   434 *growne* snout   *hyde* gone

261

ENGLISH MYSTERY PLAYS

III PASTOR: Then furth lett us ron; I wyll not abyde.
I PASTOR: No lyght makethe mone, that have I asspyde.
Never the les,
Lett us hold oure beheste.
II PASTOR: That hold I best.
III PASTOR: Then must we go eest, 440
After my ges.
[*They go to Bethlehem.*]

(50)

I PASTOR: Wold God that we myght this yong bab see!
II PASTOR: Many prophetys that syght desyryd veralee,
To have seen that bright.
III PASTOR: And God so hee
Wold shew us that wyght, we myght say, perde,
We had sene
That many sant desyryd,
With prophetys inspyryd,
If thay hym requyryd,
Yit i-closyd ar thare eene. 450

(51)

II PASTOR: God graunt us that grace.
III PASTOR: God so do.
I PASTOR: Abyde, syrs, a space. Lo, yonder, lo!
It commys on a rase, yond sterne us to.
II PASTOR: It is a grete blase! Oure gate let us go.
Here he is!
[*They approach the stable.*]
III PASTOR: Who shall go in before?
I PASTOR: I ne rek, by my hore.
II PASTOR: Ye ar of the old store;
It semys you, iwys.
[*They enter the stable.*]

---

441 *ges* guess 444 *bright* brightness 453 *rase* rush, flood 457 *hore* hair

THE FIRST SHEPHERDS' PLAY

(52)

I PASTOR: Hayll, kyng I the call!   Hayll, most of myght!   460
Hayll, worthyst of all!   Hayll, duke! Hayll, knyght!
Of greatt and small   thou art lorde by right;
Hayll, perpetuall!   Hayll, faryst wyght!
Here I offer,
I pray the to take –
If thou wold, for my sake,
With this may thou lake –
This lytyll spruse cofer[42].

(53)

II PASTOR: Hayll, lytyll tyn mop,   rewarder of mede!
Hayll! Bot oone drop   of grace at my nede;   470
Hayll, lytyll mylk-sop!   Hayll, David sede!
Of oure crede thou art crop: hayll, in God-hede!
This ball
That thou wold resave –
Lytyll is that I have;
This wyll I vowche-save –
To play the with all.

(54)

III PASTOR: Hayll, maker of man!   Hayll, swetyng!
Hayll, so as I can!   Hayll, praty mytyng!
I cowche to the than,   for fayn nere gretyng;   480
Hayll, Lord! Here I ordan,   now at oure metyng,
This botell –
It is an old by-worde,
It is a good bowrde,
For to drynk of a gowrde –
It holdys a mett potell.

---

468 *spruse* spruce wood   *coffer* box   469 *tyn* tiny   *mop* babe   *mede* virtue   471 *mylk-sop* babe   472 *crop* head   474 *resave* receive   479 *praty* pretty   *mytyng* small child   480 *cowche* bow   *nere* never   *gretyng* weeping   483 *by-worde* proverb   484 *bowrde* game   485 *gowrde* gourd   486 *mett* measured   *potell* two quarts

263

(55)

MARIA: He that all myghtys may,   the makere of heven,
  That is for to say,   my son that I neven,
  Rewarde you this day,   as he sett all on seven[43];
  He graunt you for ay   his blys full even   490
  Contynuyng;
  He gyf you good grace;
  Tell furth of this case;
  He spede youre pase,
  And graunt you good endyng.

(56)

I PASTOR: Fare well, fare Lorde,   with thy moder also.
II PASTOR: We shall this recorde   where as we go.
III PASTOR: We mon all be restorde: God graunt it be so!
I PASTOR: Amen, to that worde!   Syng we therto
  On hight: 500
  To ioy all sam,
  With myrth and gam,
  To the lawde of this lam
  Syng we in syght.

  Explicit Una pagina pastorum.

487 *may* can   501 *sam* together   502 *gam* delight   503 *lawde* praise
lam lamb

14. The Second Shepherds' Play
Incipit Alia Eorundem

TOWNELEY 13

[See the Note to the previous play, pp. 244-5.]

The specific qualities of this play centre upon the remarkable parallel between Mak's stolen sheep, which becomes a baby in a crib, and the Nativity. Mak and his wife are partly an imitation of the somewhat difficult relationship between Joseph and Mary in other mystery plays. The story of the sheep-stealing is made to prefigure the Nativity in a number of ways. The dead sheep anticipates the live Christ-Child (the Lamb of God). Perhaps drawing upon fertility rituals, the author incorporates the ritual of the death and re-birth which was celebrated at the winter solstice. This seems to be quite specific: at one point Mak is about to be executed for his crime, but instead the Shepherds toss him in a blanket, an act which can be interpreted as a symbolic death similar to the forming of the knot in the sword-dance. But these details are not a contradiction of orthodoxy so much as a wider dimension in which the coming of Christ can be truly interpreted. Even the comedy of the conflict between husband and wife is incorporated as a reflection of true harmony: the comedy is not blasphemy but a skilful dramatic device. This dramatic skill shows itself in other ways – particularly in the craft of keeping the audience in doubt as to whether Mak will give himself away at various crises. His final discovery is the result of unexpected generosity towards the 'child' on the part of the Shepherds.

[*Scene: field near Bethlehem.*]

(1)

1 PASTOR: Lord, what these weders ar cold! And I am yll happyd.
  I am nere hande dold, so long have I nappyd;
  My legys thay fold, my fyngers ar chappyd.
  It is not as I wold, for I am al lappyd
  In sorow.
  In stormes and tempest,
  Now in the eest, now in the west,
  Wo is hym has never rest
  Myd day nor morow!

(2)

  Bot we sely shepardes[1] that walkys on the moore,
  In fayth we ar nere handys outt of the doore.
  No wonder, as it standys, if we be poore,
  For the tylthe of oure landys lyys falow as the floore,
  As ye ken.
  We are so hamyd,
  For-taxed and ramyd,
  We are mayde hand tamyd
  With thys gentlery men[2].

(3)

  Thus thay refe us oure rest, oure Lady theym wary!
  These men that ar lord-fest, thay cause the ploghe tary.
  That men say is for the best, we fynde it contrary.
  Thus ar husbandys opprest, in po[i]nte to myscary
  On lyfe.

---

1 *happyd* covered   2, 11 *nere hande, nere handys* near, nearby   2 *dold* stupid   *nappyd* slept   4 *lappyd* entangled   10 *sely* wretched   13 *tylthe* tilth   *lyys* lies   *floore* floor   15 *hamyd* hamstrung   16 *For-taxed* overtaxed   *ramyd* oppressed   17 *hand tamyd* tame   18 *gentlery men* gentry   19 *refe* take away   *wary* curse   20 *lord-fest* bound to a lord

THE SECOND SHEPHERDS' PLAY

Thus hold thay us hunder;
Thus thay bryng us in blonder;
It were greatte wonder
And ever shuld we thryfe.

(4)

For may he gett a paynt slefe   or a broche now on dayes,
Wo is hym that hym grefe   or onys agane says!
Dar noman hym reprefe,   what mastry he mays[3],   30
And yit may noman lefe   oone word that he says,
No letter.
He can make purveance
With boste and bragance,
And all is thrugh mantenance
Of men that are gretter.

(5)

Ther shall com a swane   as prowde as a po,
He must borow my wane,   my ploghe also[4],
Then I am full fane   to graunt or he go.
Thus lyf we in payne,   anger, and wo,   40
By nyght and day.
He must have if he langyd,
If I shuld forgang it;
I were better be hangyd[5]
Then oones say hym nay.

(6)

It dos me good, as I walk   thus by myn oone,
Of this warld for to talk   in maner of mone.
To my shepe wyll I stalk,   and herkyn anone,
Ther abyde on a balk,   or sytt on a stone,
Full soyne.   50

---

24 *hunder* under   25 *blonder* trouble   28 *paynt* painted   *slefe* sleeve
broche brooch   30 *reprefe* reprove   31 *lefe* believe   33 *purveance* provision   34 *bragrance* bragging   35 *mantenance* maintenance   37 *swane*
serving-man   *po* peacock   42 *langyd* longed   43 *forgang* go without
47 *mone* moan   48 *stalk* stride   49 *balk* ridge   50 *soyne* soon

For I trowe, perde,
Trew men if thay be,
We gett more compane
Or it be noyne.

(7)

[*The Second Shepherd enters without noticing the First.*]

II PASTOR: Benste and Dominus! What may this bemeyne?
Why fares this warld thus? Oft have we not sene?
Lord, thyse weders ar spytus, and the [wyndys⁶] full kene,
And the frostys so hydus thay water myn eeyne –
No ly.
Now in dry, now in wete, 60
Now in snaw, now in slete;
When my shone freys to my fete,
It is not all esy.

(8)

Bot as far as I ken, or yit as I go,
We sely wedmen dre mekyll wo;
We have sorow then and then: it fallys oft so.
Sely Copyle⁷, oure hen, both to and fro
She kakyls;
Bot begyn she to crok,
To groyne or [to clo]k, 70
Wo is hym is of oure cok,
For he is in the shakyls.

(9)

These men that ar wed have not all thare wyll;
When thay ar full hard sted, thay sygh full styll;
God wayte thay ar led full hard and full yll;
In bower nor in bed thay say noght ther tyll,
This tyde.
My parte have I fun;

54 *noyne* noon 55 *bemeyne* mean 62 *shone* shoes *freys* freeze
65 *wedmen* married men *dre* suffer 69 *crok* croak 70 *groyne* groan
clok cluck 72 *shakyls* shackles 74 *sted* placed 75 *wayte* knows
78 *fun* found

THE SECOND SHEPHERDS' PLAY

I know my lesson.
Wo is hym that is bun,
For he must abyde.

(10)

Bot now late in oure lyfys   a mervell to me,
That I thynk my hart ryfys   sich wonders to see.
What that destany dryfys   it shuld so be;
Som men wyll have two wyfys   and som men thre,
In store;
Som ar wo that has any,
Bot so far can I,
Wo is hym that has many,
For he felys sore.

(11)

Bot yong men of wowyng,   for God that you boght,
Be well war of wedyng,   and thynk in youre thoght,
'Had I wyst'[8] is a thyng   it servys of noght;
Mekyll styll mowrnyng   has wedyng home broght,
And grefys,
With many a sharp showre;
For thou may cach in an owre
That shall [savour] fulle sowre
As long as thou lyffys[9].

(12)

For, as ever rede I pystyll   I have oone to my fere,
As sharp as a thystyll,   as rugh as a brere;
She is browyd lyke a brystyll   with a sowre-loten chere;
Had she oones wett hyr whystyll   she couth syng full clere
Hyr *Paternoster*.
She is as greatt as a whall;

---

80 *bun* bound   83 *ryfys* splits   90 *felys* feels, suffers   91 *wowyng* wooing   94 *styll* continuous   97 *owre* hour   100 *pystyll* Epistle   101 *brere* briar   102 *browyd* browed   *brystyll* bristle   *sowre-loten* sour-looking   105 *whall* whale

269

ENGLISH MYSTERY PLAYS

She has a galon of gall.
By hym that dyed for us all,
I wald I had ryn to I had lost hir[10].

(13)

I PASTOR: God looke over the raw![11]   Full defly ye stand.
II PASTOR: Yee, the dewill in thi maw,   so tariand.
Sagh thou awre of Daw?[12]
I PASTOR: Yee, on a ley land
Hard I hym blaw.   He commys here at hand,
Not far.
Stand styll.
II PASTOR: Qwhy?
I PASTOR: For he commys, hope I.
II PASTOR: He wyll make us both a ly
Bot if we be war.

(14)

[*Enter Third Shepherd.*]

III PASTOR: Crystys crosse me spede,   and Sant Nycholas!
Ther of had I nede;   it is wars then it was.
Whoso couthe take hede   and lett the warld pas,
It is ever in drede   and brekyll as glas,
And slythys.
This warld fowre never so,
With mervels mo and mo,
Now in weyll, now in wo,
And all thyng wrythys.

(15)

Was never syn Noe floode   sich floodys seyn;
Wyndys and ranys so rude,   and stormes so keyn[13];
Som stamerd, som stod   in dowte, as I weyn;

---

106 *gall* ill-temper   108 *ryn* run   109 *defly* as though deaf   111 *awre* anywhere   *ley* fallow   112 *blaw* blow   116 *ly* lie   121 *brekyll* brittle   122 *slythys* slips   123 *fowre* fared   126 *wrythys* twists

THE SECOND SHEPHERDS' PLAY

Now God turne all to good! I say as I mene,   130
For ponder.
These floodys so thay drowne,
Both feyldys and in towne,
And berys all downe,
And that is a wonder.

(16)

We that walk on the nyghtys, oure catell to kepe,
We se sodan syghtys when othere men slepe.
Yit me thynk my hart lyghtys; I se shrewys pepe[14];
Ye ar two all-wyghtys[15]. I wyll gyf my shepe
A turne.   140
Bot full yll have I ment;
As I walk on this bent,
I may lyghtly repent,
My toes if I spurne.

(17)

A, syr, God you save, and master myne!
A drynk fayn wold I have, and somwhat to dyne.
I PASTOR: Crystys curs, my knave, thou art a ledyr hyne!
II PASTOR: What, the boy lyst rave! Abyde unto syne;
We have mayde it[16].
Yll thryft on thy pate!   150
Though the shrew cam late,
Yit is he in state
To dyne, if he had it.

(18)

III PASTOR: Sich servandys as I, that swettys and swynkys,
Etys oure brede full dry, and that me forthynkys;
We ar oft weytt and wery when master-men wynkys;
Yit commys full lately both dyners and drynkys,
Bot nately.

138 *shrewys* villains *pepe* peer   142 *bent* field   144 *spurne* strike
147 *ledyr* lazy *hyne* servant   154 *swettys* sweat *swynkys* labour
155 *forthynkys* displeases   156 *wynkys* sleep   158 *nately* thoroughly

271

Both oure dame and oure syre,
When we have ryn in the myre, 160
Thay can nyp at oure hyre,
And pay us full lately.

(19)

Bot here my trouth, master: for the fayr that ye make,
I shall do therafter, wyrk as I take;
I shall do a lytyll, syr, and emang ever lake,
For yit lay my soper never on my stomake
In feyldys.
Wherto shuld I threpe?
With my staf can I lepe,
And men say 'Lyght chepe 170
Letherly for-yeldys.'

(20)

I PASTOR: Thou were an yll lad to ryde on wowyng[17]
With a man that had bot lytyll of spendyng.
II PASTOR: Peasse, boy, I bad. No more iangling,
Or I shall make the full rad, by the hevens kyng!
With thy gawdys –
Wher ar oure shepe, boy? – we skorne.
III PASTOR: Sir, this same day at morne
I thaym left in the corne,
When they rang lawdys. 180

(21)

Thay have pasture good, thay can not go wrong.
I PASTOR: That is right, by the roode! thyse nyghtys ar long,
Yit I wold, or we yode, oone gaf us a song.
II PASTOR: So I thoght as I stode, to myrth us emong.
III PASTOR: I grauntt.
I PASTOR: Lett me syng the tenory.

161 *nyp* trim 165 *lake* (v) play 168 *threpe* wrangle 171 *Letherly* badly *for-yeldys* repays 175 *rad* quickly 176 *gawdys* tricks 177 *skorne* despise (the 'tricks' in line 176) 180 *lawdys* first canonical hour or service 183 *yode* went 186 *tenory* tenor

THE SECOND SHEPHERDS' PLAY

II PASTOR: And I tryble so hye.
III PASTOR: Then the meyne fallys to me:
Lett se how ye chauntt.
   [They sing.]
   Tunc intrat Mak in clamide se super togam vestitus[18].

(22)

MAK: Now, Lord, for thy naymes vij,   that made both moyn
      and starnes   190
Well mo then can I neven   thi will, Lorde, of me tharnys;
I am all uneven,   that moves oft my harnes.
Now wold God I were in heven,   for the[re] wepe no barnes
So styll.
I PASTOR: Who is that pypys so poore?
MAK: Wold God ye wyst how I foore!
   Lo, a man that walkys on the moore,
   And has not all his wyll!

(23)

II PASTOR: Mak, where has thou gone?   Tell us tythyng.
III PASTOR: Is he commen? Then ylkon   take hede to his
      thyng.   200
   Et accipit clamidem ab ipso[19].
MAK: What! Ich be a yoman,   I tell you, of the king;
The self and the some,   sond from a greatt lordyng,
And sich.
Fy on you! Goyth hence
Out of my presence!
I must have reverence;
Why, who be ich?

(24)

I PASTOR: Why make ye it so qwaynt?   Mak, ye do wrang.
II PASTOR: Bot, Mak, lyst ye saynt?   I trow that ye lang.
III PASTOR: I trow the shrew can paynt,   the dewyll myght
      hym hang!   210

187 *tryble* treble   188 *meyne* middle   191 *tharnys* is lacking   192 *harnes* brains   195 *pypys* squeaks   196 *foore* fared   199 *tythyng* news   200 *ylkon* everyone   202 *some* same   *sond* messenger   208 *qwaynt* superior   209 *saynt* appear saintly   *lang* (v) wish (to)

ENGLISH MYSTERY PLAYS

MAK: Ich shall make complaynt,   and make you all to thwang
  At a worde,
  And tell evyn how ye doth.
I PASTOR: Bot, Mak, is that sothe?
  Now take outt that sothren tothe[20],
  And sett in a torde!

(25)

II PASTOR: Mak, the dewill in youre ee! A stroke wold I leyne you.
III PASTOR: Mak, know ye not me? By God, I couthe teyn you.
MAK: God looke you all thre! Me thoght I had sene you;
  Ye ar a fare compane.
I PASTOR: Can ye now mene you?   220
II PASTOR: Shrew, pepe![21]
  Thus late as thou goys,
  What wyll men suppos?
  And thou has an yll noys
  Of stelyng of shepe.

(26)

MAK: And I am trew as steyll,   all men waytt,
  Bot a sekenes I feyll   that haldys me full haytt;
  My belly farys not weyll;   it is out of astate.
III PASTOR: Seldom lyys the dewyll   dede by the gate[22].
MAK: Therfor   230
  Full sore am I and yll,
  If I stande stone styll;
  I ete not an nedyll
  Thys moneth and more.

(27)

I PASTOR: How farys thi wyff? By my hoode, how farys sho?[23]
MAK: Lyys walteryng, by the roode, by the fyere, lo!

---

211 *thwang* be beaten   217 *ee* eye   *leyne* give   224 *noys* reputation
226 *steyll* steel   *waytt* know   227 *haytt* hot   233 *nedyll* scrap
236 *walteryng* sprawling

THE SECOND SHEPHERDS' PLAY

And a howse full of brude. She drynkys well, to;
Yll spede othere good that she wyll do!
Bot s[h]o
Etys as fast as she can, 240
And ilk yere that commys to man
She bryngys furth a lakan,
And some yeres two.

(28)

Bot were I not more gracyus and rychere befar,
I were eten outt of howse and of harbar;
Yit is she a fowll dowse, if ye com nar;
Ther is none that trowse nor knowys a war
Then ken I.
Now wyll ye se what I profer,
To gyf all in my cofer 250
To morne at next to offer
Hyr hed mas-penny.

(29)

II PASTOR: I wote so forwakyd is none in this shyre:
I wold slepe if I takyd les to my hyere.
III PASTOR: I am cold and nakyd, and wold have a fyere.
I PASTOR: I am wery, for-rakyd, and run in the myre.
Wake thou!
II PASTOR: Nay, I wyll lyg downe by,
For I must slepe truly.
III PASTOR: As good a mans son was I 260
As any of you.

(30)

Bot, Mak, com heder! Betwene shall thou lyg downe.
[*Mak lies down with the Shepherds.*]
MAK: Then myght I lett you bedene of that ye wold rowne[24],

237 *brude* children 239 *sho* she 242 *lakan* baby 246 *dowse* wench
247 *war* worse 252 *hed mas-penny* penny for mass of the dead
253 *forwakyd* tired 254 *les* less 256 *for-rakyd* exhausted 263 *lett*
hinder *bedene* at once *rowne* whisper

No drede.
Fro my top to my too,
Manus tuas commendo,
Poncio Pilato[25];
Cryst crosse me spede!
   Tunc surgit, pastoribus dormientibus, et dicit[26]

(31)

Now were tyme for a man that lakkys what he wold
To stalk prevely than unto a fold,   270
And neemly to wyrk than, and be not to bold,
For he might aby the bargan, if it were told
   At the endyng.
Now were tyme for to reyll;
Bot he nedys good counsell
That fayn wold fare weyll,
   And has bot lytyll spendyng.

(32)

Bot abowte you a serkyll[27], as rownde as a moyn,
To I have done that I wyll, tyll that it be noyn,
That ye lyg stone styll to that I have doyne,   280
And I shall say thertyll of good wordys a foyne.
   'On hight
Over youre hedys my hand I lyft;
Outt go youre een! Fordo your syght!'
Bot yit I must make better shyft,
   And it be right.

(33)

Lord, what thay slepe hard! That may ye all here;
Was I never a shephard, bot now wyll I lere[28].
If the flok be skard, yit shall I nyp nere.
How, drawes hederward! Now mendys oure chere   290

271 *neemly* nimbly 272 *aby* buy 274 *reyll* revel 278 *serkyll* circle
279 *noyn* noon 281 *foyne* few 284 *Fordo* destroy 289 *skard* scared
290 *drawes* come

THE SECOND SHEPHERDS' PLAY

From sorow:
A fatt shepe, I dar say,
A good flese, dar I lay,
Eft-whyte when I may[29],
Bot this will I borow.
 [*Mak goes home to his wife.*]

(34)

How, Gyll, art thou in?   Gett us som lyght.
UXOR EIUS: Who makys sich dyn   this tyme of the nyght?
I am sett for to spyn;   I hope not I myght
Ryse a penny to wyn,   I shrew them on hight![30]
So farys   300
A huswyff that has bene
To be rasyd thus betwene:
Here may no note be sene
For sich small charys.

(35)

MAK: Good wyff, open the hek!   Seys thou not what I bryng?
UXOR: I may thole the dray the snek.   A, com in, my swetyng!
MAK: Yee, thou thar not rek   of my long standyng.
UXOR: By the nakyd nek   art thou lyke for to hyng.
MAK: Do way:
I am worthy my mete,   310
For in a strate can I gett
More then thay that swynke and swette
All the long day.

(36)

Thus it fell to my lott,   Gyll, I had sich grace.
UXOR: It were a fowll blott   to be hanged for the case.
MAK: I have skapyd, Ielott,   oft as hard a glase.
UXOR: Bot so long goys the pott   to the water, men says,

293 *flese* fleece   302 *rasyd* disturbed   303 *note* scrap   304 *charys* chores
305 *hek* inner door   306 *thole* allow   *dray* pull   *snek* latch   307 *rek*
care   308 *hyng* hang   311 *strate* strait   316 *Ielott* Gill   *glase* blow
317 *goys* goes

277

> At last
> Comys it home broken[31].

MAK: Well knowe I the token,
> Bot let it never be spoken;
> Bot come and help fast.

(37)

> I wold he were flayn;   I lyst well ete:
> This twelmothe was I not so fayn of oone shepe mete.

UXOR: Com thay or he be slayn,   and here the shepe blete –

MAK: Then myght I be tane.   That were a cold swette!
> Go spar
> The gaytt-doore.

UXOR: Yis, Mak,
> For and thay com at thy bak –

MAK: Then myght I by, for all the pak[32],
> The dewill of the war.

(38)

UXOR: A good bowrde have I spied,   syn thou can none.
> Here shall we hym hyde   to thay be gone;
> In my credyll abyde.   Lett me alone,
> And I shall lyg besyde   in chylbed, and grone.

MAK: Thou red;
> And I shall say thou was lyght
> Of a knave childe this nyght.

UXOR: Now well is me day bright,
> That ever was I bred.

(39)

> This is a good gyse   and a far cast;
> Yit a woman avyse   helpys at the last.
> I wote never who spyse,   agane go thou fast.

MAK: Bot I come or thay ryse,   els blawes a cold blast![33]
> I wyll go slepe.

323 *flayn* skinned   325 *or* before   326 *swette* sweat   327 *spar* fasten
328 *gaytt-dore* outer door   331 *the* thee   *war* (v) care   332 *bowrde* trick
334 *credyll* cradle   336 *red* get ready   341 *gyse* way   343 *agane* back

THE SECOND SHEPHERDS' PLAY

[*Mak returns to the Shepherds and lies down.*]
Yit slepys all this meneye,
And I shall go stalk prevely
As it had never bene I
That caryed thare shepe.

(40)

I PASTOR: *Resurrex a mortruis!*[34] Have hald my hand.
Iudas carnas dominus![34] I may not well stand:
My foytt slepys, by Ihesus, and I water fastand.
I thoght that we had layd us full nere Yngland.
II PASTOR: A ye!
Lord, what I have slept weyll;
As fresh as an eyll,
As lyght I me feyll
As leyfe on a tre.

(41)

III PASTOR: Benste be here in! So my [hart] qwakys,
My hart is outt of skyn[35], what so it makys.
Who makys all this dyn? So my browes blakys
To the dowore wyll I wyn. Harke, felows, wakys!
We were fowre:
Se ye awre of Mak now?
I PASTOR: We were up or thou.
II PASTOR: Man, I gyf God a vowe,
Yit yede he nawre.

(42)

III PASTOR: Me thoght he was lapt in a wolfe skyn[36].
I PASTOR: So are many hapt now namely within.
II PASTOR[37]: When we had long napt, me thoght with a gyn
A fatt shepe he trapt, bot he mayde no dyn.
III PASTOR[37]: Be styll:

352 *foytt* foot *water* stagger *fastand* fasting 356 *eyll* eel 358 *leyfe* leaf 361 *blakys* darkens 362 *dowore* door 367 *yede* went *nawre* nowhere 368 *lapt* wrapped 369 *hapt* covered 370 *gyn* trap

Thi dreme makys the woode:
It is bot fantom, by the roode.
I PASTOR: Now God turne all to good,
If it be his wyll.

(43)

II PASTOR: Ryse, Mak, for shame! Thou lygys right lang.
MAK: Now Crystys holy name   be us emang!
What is this? For Sant Iame,   I may not well gang!
I trow I be the same.   A, my nek has lygen wrang   380
Enoghe.
Mekill thanks syn yister even,
Now, by Sant S[t]evyn,
I was flayd with a swevyn,
My hart out of sloghe.

(44)

I thoght Gyll began to crok   and travell full sad,
Welner at the fyrst cok,   of a yong lad
For to mend our flok.   Then be I never glad;
I have tow on my rok   more then ever I had.
A, my heede!   390
A house full of yong tharmes;
The dewill knok outt thare harnes!
Wo is hym has many barnes,
And therto lytyll brede!

(45)

I must go home, by youre lefe,   to Gyll, as I thoght.
I pray you looke my slefe[38]   that I steyll noght:
I am loth you to grefe,   or from you take oght.
III PASTOR: Go furth, yll might thou chefe!   Now wold I we soght,
This morne,
That we had all oure store.   400

380 *lygen* lain   384 *flayd* frightened   *swevyn* dream   385 *sloghe* skin
387 *Welner* well nigh   389 *tow* flax   *rok* distaff   391 *tharmes* children
392 *harnes* brains   394 *brede* bread   396 *slefe* sleeve   398 *chefe* fare

THE SECOND SHEPHERDS' PLAY

I PASTOR: Bot I will go before;
Let us mete.
II PASTOR: Whore?
III PASTOR: At the crokyd thorne.
[*The Shepherds leave. Mak knocks at his door.*]

(46)

MAK: Undo this doore! Who is here? How long shall I stand?
UXOR EIUS: Who makys sich a bere? Now walk in the wenyand.
MAK: A, Gyll, what chere? It is I, Mak, youre husbande.
UXOR: Then may we be here the dewill in a bande,
Syr Gyle[39]:
Lo, he commys with a lote
As he were holden in the throte.   410
I may not syt at my note,
A hand-lang while.

(47)

MAK: Wyll ye here what fare she makys to gett hir a glose?
And dos noght bot lakys and clowse hir toose.
UXOR: Why, who wanders, who wakys? Who commys, who gose?
Who brewys, who bakys? What makys me thus hose?
And than,
It is rewthe to beholde,
Now in hote, now in colde,
Full wofull is the householde   420
That wantys a woman.

(48)

Bot what ende has thou mayde with the hyrdys, Mak?
MAK: The last worde that thay sayde when I turnyd my bak,
Thay wold looke that thay hade thare shepe, all the pak.

---

402 *Whore* where   405 *bere* noise   *wenyand* time of ill luck   409 *lote* noise   411 *note* work   412 *hand-lang* little   413 *gett hir a glose* make up an excuse   414 *lakys* plays about   *clowse* scratches   *toose* toes   416 *hose* hoarse

281

ENGLISH MYSTERY PLAYS

I hope thay wyll nott be well payde   when thay thare shepe lak[40],
Perde!
Bot how so the gam gose,
To me thay wyll suppose,
And make a fowll noyse,
And cry outt apon me.   430

(49)

Bot thou must do as thou hyght.
UXOR: I accorde me thertyll.
I shall swedyll hym right   in my credyll;
If it were a gretter slyght,   yit couthe I help tyll.
I wyll lyg downe stright.   Com hap me.
MAK: I wyll.
UXOR: Behynde!
Com Coll[41] and his maroo,
Thay will nyp us full naroo.
MAK: Bot I may cry out 'Haroo!'
The shepe if thay fynde.

(50)

UXOR: Harken ay when thay call;   thay will com onone.   440
Com and make redy all   and syng by thyn oone;
Syng 'lullay' thou shall,   for I must grone,
And cry outt by the wall   on Mary and Iohn[42],
For sore.
Syng 'lullay' on fast
When thou heris at the last;
And bot I play a fals cast,
Trust me no more.

(51)

[At the crooked thorn.]
III PASTOR: A, Coll, goode morne.   Why slepys thou nott?

431 *thertyll* to that   432 *swedyll* wrap   433 *slyght* trick   434 *hap* cover
436 *maroo* mate   437 *nyp* pinch   *naroo* hard   440 *onone* soon
446 *heris* hear   447 *cast* trick

282

THE SECOND SHEPHERDS' PLAY

I PASTOR: Alas, that ever was I borne!   We have a fowll blott.   450
A fat wedir have we lorne.
III PASTOR: Mary, Godys forbott!
II PASTOR: Who shuld do us that skorne?   That were a fowll spott.
I PASTOR: Som shrewe.
I have soght with my dogys
All Horbery[43] shrogys,
And of xv hogys
Fond I bot oone ewe.

(52)

III PASTOR: Now trow me, if ye will,   by Sant Thomas of Kent,
Ayther Mak or Gyll   was at that assent.
I PASTOR: Peasse, man, be still!   I sagh when he went;   460
Thou sklanders hym yll;   thou aght to repent,
Goode spede.
II PASTOR: Now as ever mygth I the,
If I shuld evyn here de,
I wold say it were he,
That dyd that same dede.

(53)

III PASTOR: Go we theder, I rede,   and ryn on oure feete.
Shall I never ete brede   the sothe to I wytt.
I PASTOR: Nor drynk in my heede   with hym tyll I mete.
II PASTOR: I wyll rest in no stede   tyll that I hym grete,   470
My brothere.
Oone I will hight:
Tyll I se hym in sight
Shall I never slepe one nyght
Ther I do anothere.

---

451 *lorne* lost   *forbott* forbid   455 *shrogys* bushes   459 *assent* affair
461 *sklanders* slanders   463 *the* thrive   464 *de* die   472 *Oone* one
hight promise

ENGLISH MYSTERY PLAYS

(54)

[*They approach Mak's house.*]

III PASTOR: Will ye here how thay hak?[44]   Oure syre lyst croyne.
I PASTOR: Hard I never none crak   so clere out of toyne;
Call on hym.
II PASTOR: Mak, undo youre doore soyne.
MAK: Who is that spak,   as it were noyne
On loft?   480
Who is that, I say?
III PASTOR: Goode felowse, were it day.
MAK: As far as ye may,
Good, spekys soft,

(55)

Over a seke womans heede   that is at mayll-easse;
I had lever be dede   or she had any dyseasse.
UXOR: Go to an-othere stede!   I may not well qweasse.
Ich fote that ye trede   goys thorow my nese,
So hee!
I PASTOR: Tell us, Mak, if ye may,   490
How fare ye, I say?
MAK: Bot ar ye in this towne to-day?
Now how fare ye?

(56)

Ye have ryn in the myre,   and ar weytt yit:
I shall make you a fyre,   if ye will syt.
A nores wold I hyre.   Thynk ye on yit,
Well qwytt is my hyre[45] —   my dreme this is itt —
A seson.
I have barnes, if ye knew,
Well mo then enewe,   500

---

476 *hak* sing   *lyst* wishes   *croyne* croon   477 *toyne* tune   479 *noyne* noon   480 *On loft* on high   485 *mayll-ease* sickness   487 *qweasse* breathe   488 *fote* step   *nese* nose   489 *hee* loudly   496 *nores* nurse   500 *enewe* enough

284

THE SECOND SHEPHERDS' PLAY

Bot we must drynk as we brew,
And that is bot reson.

(57)

I wold ye dynyd or ye yode. Me thynk that ye swette.
II PASTOR: Nay, nawther mendys oure mode   drynke nor mette.
MAK: Why, syr, alys you oght bot goode?
III PASTOR: Yee, oure shepe that we gett,
Ar stollyn as thay yode.   Oure los is grette.
MAK: Syrs, drynkys!
Had I bene thore,
Som shuld have boght it full sore.
I PASTOR: Mary, som men trowes that ye wore,   510
And that us forthynkys[46].

(58)

II PASTOR: Mak, some men trowys   that it shuld be ye.
III PASTOR: Ayther ye or youre spouse,   so say we.
MAK: Now if ye have suspowse   to Gill or to me,
Com and rype oure howse,   and then may ye se
Who had hir;
If I any shepe fott,
Ayther cow or stott;
And Gyll, my wife, rose nott
Here syn she lade hir.   520

(59)

As I am true and lele,   to God here I pray,
That this be the fyrst mele   that I shall ete this day.
I PASTOR: Mak, as have I ceyll,   avyse the, I say;
He lernyd tymely[47] to steyll   that couth not say nay.
UXOR: I swelt!
Outt, thefys, fro my wonys!

504 *mendys* soothes *mode* temper 505 *alys* ails 515 *rype* search
517 *fott* brought 518 *stott* heifer 523 *ceyll* happiness 525 *swelt* die
526 *wonys* home

ENGLISH MYSTERY PLAYS

Ye com to rob us for the nonys.
MAK: Here ye not how she gronys?
Youre hartys shuld melt.

(60)

UXOR: Outt, thefys, fro my barne! Negh hym not thor! 530
MAK: Wyst ye how she had farne, youre hartys wold be sore.
Ye do wrang, I you warne, that thus commys before
To a woman that has farne – bot I say no more.
UXOR: A, my medyll!
I pray to God so mylde,
If ever I you begyld,
That I ete[48] this chylde
That lygys in this credyll.

(61)

MAK: Peasse, woman, for Godys payn, and cry not so:
Thou spyllys thy brane, and makys me full wo. 540
II PASTOR: I trow oure shepe be slayn. What fynde ye two?
III PASTOR: All wyrk we in vayn; as well may we go.
Bot hatters,
I can fynde no flesh,
Hard nor nesh,
Salt nor fresh,
Bot two tome platers.

(62)

Whik catell bot this, tame nor wylde,
None, as have I blys, as lowde as he smylde.
UXOR: No, so God me blys, and gyf me ioy of my chylde! 550
I PASTOR: We have merkyd amys; I hold us begyld.
II PASTOR: Syr, don,
Syr, oure Lady hym save,
Is youre chyld a knave?

530 *Negh* approach *thor* there   538 *lygys* lies   543 *hatters* (mild oath)
545 *nesh* soft   547 *tome* empty   548 *Whik* living   549 *smylde* smelt
552 *don* (it is) agreed

THE SECOND SHEPHERDS' PLAY

MAK: Any lord myght hym have
This chyld to his son.

(63)

When he wakyns he kyppys, that ioy is to se.
III PASTOR: In good tyme to hys hyppys, and in cele.
Bot who was his gossyppys, so sone rede?
MAK: So fare fall thare lyppys!
I PASTOR: Hark now, a le.   560
MAK: So God thaym thank,
Parkyn, and Gybon Waller, I say,
And gentill Iohn Horne[49], in good fay,
He made all the garray,
With the greatt shank.

(64)

II PASTOR: Mak, freyndys will we be, for we ar all oone.
MAK: We? Now I hald for me, for mendys gett I none.
Fare well all thre! All glad were ye gone.
[*The Shepherds depart.*]
III PASTOR: Fare wordys may ther be, bot luf is ther none
This yere.   570
I PASTOR: Gaf ye the chyld any thyng?
II PASTOR: I trow not oone farthyng.
III PASTOR: Fast agane will I flyng,
Abyde ye me there.
[*Returns to the house.*]

(65)

Mak, take it to no grefe if I come to thi barne.
MAK: Nay, thou dos me greatt reprefe, and fowll has thou farne.
III PASTOR: The child will it not grefe, that lytyll day-starne[50].
Mak, with youre leyfe, let me gyf youre barne

---

557 *kyppys* snatches   558 *hyppys* hips   *cele* good luck   559 *gossyppys* god-parents   *rede* ready   560 *le* lie   564 *garray* noise   565 *shank* leg   567 *mendys* profit   573 *flyng* run   577 *day-starne* day star

Bot vj pence.
MAK: Nay, do way: he slepys.   580
III PASTOR: Me thynk he pepys.
MAK: When he wakyns he wepys.
I pray you go hence.
[*The other Shepherds return.*]

(66)

III PASTOR: Gyf me lefe hym to kys,   and lyft up the clowtt.
What the dewill is this?   He has a long snowte.
I PASTOR: He is merkyd amys.   We wate ill abowte.
II PASTOR: Ill-spon weft, iwys,   ay commys foull owte.
Ay, so!
He is lyke to oure shepe!
III PASTOR: How, Gyb[51], may I pepe?   590
I PASTOR: I trow kynde will crepe
Where it may not go[52].

(67)

II PASTOR: This was a qwantt gawde,   and a far cast.
It was a hee frawde.
III PASTOR: Yee, syrs, wast[53].
Lett bren this bawde,   and bynd hir fast.
A fals skawde   hang at the last;
So shall thou.
Wyll ye see how thay swedyll
His foure feytt in the medyll?
Sagh I never in a credyll   600
A hornyd lad[54] or now.

(68)

MAK: Peasse byd I. What,   lett be youre fare;
I am he that hym gatt,   and yond woman hym bare.
I PASTOR: What dewill shall he hatt,   Mak? Lo, God, Makys ayre.

584 *clowtt* clothes   586 *wate* watch   587 *Ill-spon* badly spun
593 *qwantt* crafty   *gawde* trick   *cast* trick   595 *bren* burn   596 *skawde* scold   598 *swedyll* wrap   604 *hatt* be called   *ayre* heir

THE SECOND SHEPHERDS' PLAY

II PASTOR: Lett be all that.   Now God gyf hym care,
I sagh.
UXOR: A pratty child is he
As syttys on a wamans kne;
A dyllydowne, perde,
To gar a man laghe.   610

(69)

III PASTOR: I know hym by the eere marke: that is a good tokyn.
MAK: I tell you, syrs, hark! —   hys noyse was brokyn.
Sythen told me a clerk   that he was forspokyn.
I PASTOR: This is a fals wark;   I wold fayn be wrokyn.
Gett wepyn.
UXOR: He was takyn with an elfe;
I saw it myself.
When the clok stroke twelf
Was he forshapyn.

(70)

II PASTOR[55]: Ye two ar well feft   sam in a stede.   620
III PASTOR[55]: Syn thay manteyn thare theft,   let do thaym to dede.
MAK: If I trespas eft,   gyrd of my heede.
With you will I be left.
I PASTOR: Syrs, do my reede.
For this trespas,
We will nawther ban ne flyte,
Fyght nor chyte,
Bot have done as tyte,
And cast hym in canvas[56].
    [*They toss Mak in a sheet.*]

---

606 *sagh* saw   609 *dyllydowne* darling   610 *gar* make   613 *forspokyn* bewitched   614 *wrokyn* avenged   619 *forshapyn* changed   620 *feft* endowed   622 *eft* again   *gyrd* cut   625 *ban* curse   *flyte* quarrel   626 *chyte* chide

289

(71)
Lord, what I am sore,   in poynt for to bryst.
In fayth I may no more;   therfor wyll I ryst.   630
II PASTOR: As a shepe of vij skore[57]   he weyd in my fyst.
For to slepe ay-whore   me thynk that I lyst.
III PASTOR: Now I pray you,
Lyg downe on this grene.
I PASTOR: On these thefys yit I mene.
III PASTOR: Wherto shuld ye tene?
Do as I say you.
   [*The Shepherds sleep.*]
   Angelus cantat 'Gloria in excelsis'; postea dicat[58]

(72)
ANGELUS: Ryse, hyrd-men heynd!   For now is he borne
That shall take fro the feynd   that Adam had lorne;
That warloo to sheynd,   this nyght is he borne.   640
God is made youre freynd   now at this morne.
He behestys
At Bedlem go se:
Ther lygys that fre
In a cryb full poorely,
Betwyx two bestys.

(73)
I PASTOR: This was a qwant stevyn   that ever yit I hard.
It is a mervell to nevyn,   thus to be skard.
II PASTOR: Of Godys son of hevyn   he spak upward.
All the wod on a levyn   me thoght that he gard   650
Appere.
III PASTOR: He spake of a barne
In Bedlem, I you warne.
I PASTOR: That betokyns yond starne.
Let us seke hym there.

629 *in poynt* on the point of   *bryst* burst   630 *ryst* rest   632 *ay-whore* anywhere   636 *tene* be annoyed   638 *heynd* gentle   640 *warloo* devil *sheynd* destroy   644 *fre* lord   648 *nevyn* mention   *skard* scared 649 *upward* above   650 *wod* wood   *levyn* lightning   *gard* caused to

THE SECOND SHEPHERDS' PLAY

(74)

II PASTOR: Say, what was his song?   Hard ye not how he crakyd it?
Thre brefes to a long.
III PASTOR: Yee, mary, he hakt it.
Was no crochett wrong,   nor no thyng that lakt it.
I PASTOR: For to syng us emong   right as he knakt it,
I can.   660
II PASTOR: Let se how ye croyne.
Can ye bark at the mone?
III PASTOR: Hold youre tonges, have done!
I PASTOR: Hark after than.
   [*Sings.*]

(75)

II PASTOR: To Bedlem he bad   that we shuld gang:
I am full fard   that we tary to lang.
III PASTOR: Be mery and not sad;   of myrth is oure sang;
Ever-lastyng glad   to mede may we fang,
Withoutt noyse.
I PASTOR: Hy we theder for-thy;   670
If we be wete and wery,
To that chyld and that lady,
We have it not to lose.

(76)

II PASTOR: We fynde by the prophecy –   let be youre dyn[59] –
Of David and Isay,   and mo then I myn,
Thay prophecyed by clergy   that in a vyrgyn
Shuld he lyght and ly,   to slokyn oure syn
And slake it,
Oure kynde from wo;
For Isay sayd so,   680

---

656 *crakyd* roared   657 *brefes* short notes   *long* long note   *hakt* sang
659 *knakt* sang   668 *fang* get   669 *noyse* harm   670 *for-thy* therefore
671 *wete* wet   675 *myn* remember   677 *lyght* descend   *ly* lie   *slokyn*
suppress   678 *slake* remove

*Ecce virgo
Concipiet*[60] a chylde that is nakyd.

(77)

III PASTOR: Full glad may we be, and abyde that day
That lufly to se, that all myghtys may.
Lord, well were me, for ones and for ay,
Myght I knele on my kne, som word for to say
To that chylde.
Bot the angell sayd
In a cryb was he layde;
He was poorly arayd, 690
Both mener and mylde.

(78)

I PASTOR: Patryarkes that has bene, and prophetys beforne,
Thay desyryd to have sene this chylde that is borne.
Thay ar gone full clene, that have thay lorne.
We shall se hym, I weyn, or it be morne,
To tokyn.
When I se hym and fele,
Then wote I full weyll
It is true as steyll
That prophetys have spokyn: 700

(79)

To so poore as we ar that he wold appere,
Fyrst fynd, and declare by his messyngere.
II PASTOR: Go we now, let us fare; the place is us nere.
III PASTOR: I am redy and yare; go we in fere
To that bright.
Lord, if thi wylles be,
We are lewde all thre,
Thou grauntt us somkyns gle
To comforth thi wight.
   [*They enter the stable.*]

684 *lufly* beautiful person   691 *mener* poor   696 *tokyn* proof   704 *yare* prepared   707 *lewde* ignorant   708 *somkyns* some kind of   *gle* joy

THE SECOND SHEPHERDS' PLAY

(80)

I PASTOR: Hayll, comly and clene! Hayll, yong child! 710
Hayll, maker, as I meyne, of a madyn so mylde!
Thou has waryd, I weyne, the warlo so wylde;
The fals gyler of teyn[61] now goys he begylde.
Lo, he mérys!
Lo, he laghys, my swetyng!
A wel fare metyng!
I have holden my hetyng;
Have a bob of cherys[62].

(81)

II PASTOR: Hayll, sufferan savyoure, for thou has us soght!
Hayll, frely foyde and floure, that all thyng has wroght! 720
Hayll, full of favoure, that made all of noght!
Hayll! I kneyll and I cowre. A byrd have I broght
To my barne.
Hayll, lytyll tyne mop!
Of oure crede thou art crop:
I wold drynk on thy cop,
Lytyll day starne.

(82)

III PASTOR: Hayll, derlyng dere, full of Godhede!
I pray the be nere when that I have nede.
Hayll, swete is thy chere! My hart wold blede 730
To se the sytt here in so poore wede,
With no pennys.
Hayll, put furth thy dall!
I bryng the bot a ball:
Have and play the with all,
And go to the tenys.

---

712 *waryd* cursed   717 *hetyng* promise   718 *bob* bunch   *cherys* cherries
720 *frely* noble   *foyde* child   *floure* flower   724 *tyne* tiny   *mop* baby
726 *cop* cup   731 *wede* clothing   733 *dall* hand   736 *tenys* tennis

(83)

MARIA: The fader of heven,   God omnypotent,
　　That sett all on seven[63],   his son has he sent.
　　My name couth he neven,   and lyght or he went.
　　I conceyvyd hym full even   thrugh myght, as he ment,　　　　740
　　And now is he borne.
　　He kepe you fro wo!
　　I shall pray hym so.
　　Tell furth as ye go,
　　And myn on this morne.

(84)

I PASTOR: Fare well, lady,   so fare to beholde,
　　With thy childe on thi kne.
II PASTOR: 　　　　-　　　　Bot he lygys full cold.
　　Lord, well is me!   Now we go, thou behold.
III PASTOR: For sothe all redy   it semys to be told
　　Full oft.　　　　　　　　　　　　　　　　　　　　　　　750
I PASTOR: What grace we have fun!
II PASTOR: Com furth: now ar we won.
III PASTOR: To syng ar we bun:
　　Let take on loft!
　　　[*They go out singing.*]

　　　Explicit pagina Pastorum.

740 *ment* intended   751 *fun* found   752 *won* saved

15. Introduction to The Three Kings

YORK 16: MASONS (later MINSTRELS)

The lines printed here are the beginning of a play assigned to the Masons in the York manuscript. The rest of the Masons' play is identical with ll.73–216 of the following play, the Adoration (Goldsmiths). Burton's list shows that in 1415 the Goldsmiths performed the incident here, followed by the incident which begins at l.73 of their own play, but, alterations to the list indicate that the Masons were afterwards allocated the episode. Perhaps for a time the versions were alternatives. Eventually, by 1561, the Musicians took over the play about Herod's inquiry; it appears that the Masons had some difficulty in preparation. It is also noticeable that the episode which is peculiarly theirs is alliterative, a possible indication that it is the work of a late alliterative reviser.

※

[*Scene: Herod's court.*]

(1)

HEROD: The clowdes clapped in clerenes that ther clematis in-closis,
   Jubiter and Jovis, Martis and Mercury emyde,
   Raykand overe my rialte on rawe me reioyses,
   Blonderande ther blastis, to blaw when I bidde.
   Saturne my subgett, that sotilly is hidde,
   I list at my likyng and laies hym full lowe;
   The rakke of the rede skye full rappely I ridde;

1 *clapped* surrounded *clematis* climates *in-closis* encloses 2 *emyde* amidst 3 *Raykand* wandering *rialte* royalty *on rawe* together 4 *Blonderande* stirring up 7 *rakke* clouds *rede* red *rappely* quickly *ridde* ride

ENGLISH MYSTERY PLAYS

    Thondres full thrallye by thousandes I thrawe
    When me likis;
    Venus his voice to me awe   10
    That princes to play in hym pikis[1].

(2)

    The prince of planetis that proudely is pight
    Sall brace furth his bemes that oure belde blithes;
    The mone at my myght he mosteres his myght;
    And kayssaris in castellis grete kyndynes me kythes;
    Lordis and ladis loo luffely me lithes,
    For I am fairer of face and fressher on folde –
    The soth yf I saie sall – sevene and sexti sithis
    Than glorius gulles that gayer is than golde
    In price[2];   20
    How thynke ye ther tales that I talde,
    I am worthy, witty, and wyse.

(3)

I MILES: All kynges to youre croune may clerly comende
    Youre lawe and youre lordshippe as lodsterne on hight;
    What traytoure un-trewe that will not attende,
    Ye sall lay thaim full lowe, fro leeme and fro light.
II MILES: What faitoure, in faithe, that dose you offende,
    We sall sette hym full sore, that sotte, in youre sight.
HERODES: In welthe sall I wisse you to wonne or I wende,
    For ye are wightis ful worthy, both witty and wighte.   30
    But ye knawe wele, ser knyghtis, in counsaill full conande,
    That my regioun so riall is ruled her be rest;
    For I wate of no wighte in this worlde that is wonnande
    That in forges any feloune, with force sall be fest;
    Arest ye tho rebaldes that unrewly are rownand;

---

8 *thrallye* eagerly   10 *awe* owes   11 *pikis* chooses   12 *pight* set   13 *brace* press   *belde* comfort   *blithes* cheers   15 *kayssaris* emperors   *kythes* show   16 *lithes* listen   17 *folde* land   18 *sithis* times   19 *gulles* heraldic red   23 *comende* praise   24 *lodsterne* guiding star   26 *leeme* beam 28 *sotte* fool   29 *wisse* lead   31 *conande* learned   32 *rest* quietness 33 *wate* know   *wonnande* dwelling   34 *forges* counterfeits   *fest* fast, bound   35 *rownand* whispering

INTRODUCTION TO THE THREE KINGS

    Be they kyngis or knyghtis, in care ye thaim cast;
    Yaa, and welde tham in woo to wonne, in the wanyand;
    What browle that is brawlyng his brayne loke ye brest,
    And dynge ye hym doune.
I MILES: Sir, what foode in faith will you feese,   40
    That sott full sone my-selfe sall hym sesse.
II MILES: We sall noght here doute to do hym disesse,
    But with countenaunce full cruell
    We sall crake her his croune.

(4)

HEROD: My sone that is semely, howe semes the ther sawes?
    Howe comely ther knyghtis, thei carpe in this case.
FILIUS: Fadir, if thai like noght to listyn youre lawes
    As traytoures on-trewe the sall teche them a trace,
    For, fadir, unkyndnes ye kythe them no cause.
HEROD: Faire falle the, my faire sone, so fettis of face!   50
    And knyghtis, I comaunde, who to dule drawes,
    Thas churles as cheveleres ye chastise and chase,
    And drede ye no doute.
FILIUS: Fadir, I sall fell tham in fight,
    What renke that reves you youre right.
I MILES: With dyntes to dede bes he dight
    That liste not youre lawes for to lowte
    His wille.
    [*Enter Nuntius.*]
NUNCIUS: My lorde, ser Herowde, king with croune![3]

    37 *welde* force   *wanyand* vengeance   38 *browle* brat   *brest* burst   40 *foode* person   *feese* punish   46 *carpe* speak   48 *the* they   *trace* way   50 *fettis* fair   51 *dule* grief   52 *Thas* those   *cheveleres* knights   53 *doute* fear   55 *renke* man   *reves* takes   56 *dyntes* blows   57 *lowte* revere

🐾 🐾 🐾

16. The Adoration

YORK 17: GOLDSMITHS
(ORFEVERS, GOLDBETERS, MONEMAKERS)

The Visit of the Kings appeared very early in the development of the liturgical drama in association with the Feast of the Epiphany. It is based upon Matthew *2 1–12. The* York *version here has obviously suffered from considerable development. The first incident is the Meeting of the Kings, which performs part of the function of the Prophets' Play. The liturgical version in England and on the Continent dealt with the second and third incidents, the Visit to Herod and the Presentation of Gifts. It is not difficult to see that these could be presented in spectacular ways. There are records of a moving star even in the liturgical versions, and it is not surprising that the Guild which performed the play at York was the Goldsmiths (at Chester it was given by the Mercers).*

๛

[*Scene: near Jerusalem. The Three Kings meet.*]

(1)

1 REX: Lorde, that levis evere-lastande lyff,
  I love the evir with harte and hande,
  That me has made to se this sight
  Whilke my kynrede was coveytande[1].
  Thay saide a sterne, with lemys bright,
  Owte of the Eest shulde stabely stande,
  And that it shulde meffe mekill myght
  Of I that shulde be lorde in lande,
  That men of synne shulde saff;

1 *levis* lives 4 *coveytande* desiring 5 *lemys* beams 6 *stabely* firmly
7 *meffe* move

THE ADORATION

And certis I sall saye, 10
God graunte me happe to have
Wissyng of redy waye.

(2)

II REX: All weldand God, that all has wroght,
I worshippe the als is worthye,
That with thy brightnes has me broght
Owte of my reame, riche Arabie.
I shall [noght] seys tille I have sought
What selcouth thyng it sall syngnyfie;
God graunte me happe so that I myght
Have grace to gete goode companye; 20
And my comforte encrese
With thy sterne schynyng schene,
For certis I sall noght cesse
Tille I witte what it mene.

(3)

III REX: Lorde God, that all goode has by-gonne
And all may ende both goode and evyll,
That made for man both mone and sonne
And stedde yone sterne to stande stone stille.
Tille I the cause may clerly knowe,
God wisse me with his worthy wille. 30
I hope I have her felaws fonde,
My yarnyng fayfully to full-fille.
Sirs, God yowe saffe ande see,
And were yow evere fro woo.
I REX: Amen! So myght it bee,
And saffe yow, sir, also.

(4)

III REX: Sirs, with youre wille, I wolde yow praye
To telle me some of youre entent,

12 *Wissyng* knowing   13 *All weldand* almighty   18 *selcouth* miraculous
22 *sterne* star   *schene* brightly   28 *stedde* placed   30 *wisse* guide
32 *yarnyng* desire   34 *were* defend

299

Whedir ye wende forthe in this way,
And fro what contre ye are wente?   40
II REX: Full gladly, sir, I shall you say.
A sodayne sight was till us sente,
A royall sterne that rose or day
Before us on the firmament,
That garte us fare fro home
Som poynte ther-of to presse.
III REX: Sertis, syrs, I sawe the same
That makis us thus to moyfe.

(5)

For, sirs, I have herde saye sertayne
Itt shulde be seyne of selcowthe seere,   50
And ferther ther-of I wolde freyne;
That makis me moffe in this manere.
I REX: Sir, of felashippe are we fayne;
Now sall we wende forth all in feere.
God graunte us or we come agayne
Som gode hartyng ther-of to here.
Sir, here is Jerusalem
To wisse us als we goo,
And be-yonde is Bedleem;
Ther schall we seke alsoo.   60

(6)

III REX: Sirs, ye schall wele undirstande,
For to be wise nowe were it nede;
Sir Herowde is kyng of this lande
And has his lawes her for to leede.
I REX: Sir, sen we neghe thus nerhand,
Un-till his helpe us muste take heede;
For have we his wille and his warande,
Than may we wende with-outen drede.

---

43 *or* before   45 *garte* caused   48 *moyfe* move, act   50 *seyne* sign   *seere* many   51 *freyne* ask   56 *hartyng* encouragement   65 *neghe* approach *nerhand* close

THE ADORATION

II REX: To have leve of the lorde,
   That is resoune and skyll.
III REX: And ther-to we all accorde,
   Wende we and witte his will.
   [*They journey to Herod's court.*]

(7)

NUNCIUS: Mi lorde, ser Herowde, kyng with croune![2]
HEROD: Pees, dastard, in the develes dispite!
NUN: Sire, new nott is full nere this towne.
HEROD: What, false losell, liste the flighte?
   Go, betis yone boy and dyngis hym downe.
II MILES: Lorde, messengers shulde no man wyte[3];
   It may be for youre awne rennowne.
HEROD: That wolde I here; do telle on tyte.
NUN: Mi lorde, I mette at morne
   iii kyngis carpand to-gedir
   Of One that is nowe borne,
   And thai hight to come hedir.

(8)

HEROD: Thre kyngis, forsothe!
NUN: Sir, so I saie,
   For I saughe them my-self all seere.
I CON: My lorde, appose hym, we yow praye.
HEROD: Say, felowe, ar they ferre or nere?
NUN: Mi lorde, thei will be here this day.
   That wotte I wele, withouten were.
HEROD: Have done; dresse us in riche array,
   And ilke man make tham mery chere,
   That no sembland be seene
   But frenshippe faire and stille
   Tille we wete what thei meene,
   Whedir it be gud or ill.
   [*Enter the Three Kings.*]

70 *skyll* good sense   75 *nott* affair   80 *tyte* quickly   86 *seere* many
90 *were* doubt

ENGLISH MYSTERY PLAYS

(9)

I REX: A, Lorde, that lenys this lastand light,
Whilke has us ledde oute of oure lande,
Kepe the, sir kyng, and comly knyght,
And all thi folke that we here fande.   100
HEROD: Mahounde, my god and most of myght,
That has myn hele all in his hande,
He saffe you, sirs, semely in sight;
And telle us nowe som new tythande.
II REX: Sum shall we saie you, sir;
A sterne stud us by-forne[4],
That makis us speke and spir
Of ane that is nowe borne.

(10)

HEROD: Nowe borne! That birthe halde I badde.
And certis, un-witty men ye werre   110
To lepe overe lande to late a ladde.
Say when lost ye hym? Ought lange be-fore?
All wyse men will wene ye madde,
And therfore moffis it nevere more.
III REX: Yis certis, such hartyng have we hadde,
We schall noght seys or we come thore.
HEROD: This were a wondir thyng!
Say, what barne shulde that be?
I REX: Sir, he shall be kyng
Of Jewes and of Jude.   120

(11)

HEROD: Kyng! In the devyl way, dogges, fy!
Now I se wele ye rothe and rave.
Be ony skymeryng of the skye
When ye shulde knawe owthir kyng or knave?[5]
Nay, I am kyng and non but I,

97 *lenys* gives   104 *tythande* tidings   107 *spir* ask   111 *late* seek
114 *moffis* moves   118 *barne* child   122 *rothe* boast   123 *skymeryng* skirmishing

302

THE ADORATION

> That shall ye kenne yff that ye crave;
> And I am juge of all Jury
> To speke or spille, to saie or saffe.
> Swilke gawdes may gretely greve,
> To wittenesse that nevere was. 130
>
> REX: Lorde, we aske noght but leve
> Be youre poure to passe.

(12)

> HEROD: Whedir, in the devyls name?
> To late a ladde here in my lande?
> Fals harlottis, but ye hye you hame
> Ye shall be bete and boune in bande.
> I I CON [*aside to Herod*]: My lorde, to felle this foule deffame,
> Lattis all such wondir folle on hande,
> And speres thaim sadly of the same;
> So shall ye stabely undirstande 140
> Ther mynde and ther menyng,
> And takis gud tente tham too.
> HEROD: I thanke the of this thyng,
> And certis so will I doo.

(13)

> [*To Kings*] Nowe, kyngis, to cache all care away,
> Sen ye ar comen oute of youre kytht,
> Loke noght ye legge agayne oure lay,
> Uppon peyne to lose both lyme and litht.
> And so that ye the soth will saye,
> To come and goo I graunte yow grith, 150
> And yf youre poynte be to my pay[6],
> May falle my-selfe shall wende you with.
> I REX: Sir kyng, we all accorde,
> And says a barne is borne
> That shall be kyng and lorde,
> And leche tham that ar lorne.

---

128 *spille* destroy   129 *gawdes* tricks   138 *Lattis* let   *folle* fall
139 *speres* ask   145 *cache* drive   146 *kytht* own people   147 *legge*
allege   *lay* law   148 *litht* joint   150 *grith* peace   156 *leche* heal

303

(14)

II REX: Sir, the thar mervayle no-thyng
　　　Of this ilke nott that thus-gate newes[7],
　　　For Balaham[8] saide a starne shulde spring
　　　Of Jacobe kynde, and that is Jewes.　　　　　　　　160
III REX: Sir, Isaie sais a mayden yenge
　　　Shall bere a sone amonge Ebrewes,
　　　That of all contrees shall be kyng,
　　　And governe all that on erthe grewes;
　　　Emanuell shalbe his name,
　　　To saie, 'God sone of heven',
　　　And certis this is the same,
　　　That we now to you neven.

(15)

I REX: Sirs, the proved prophete Osee[9]
　　　Full trulye talde, in towne and toure,　　　　　　　170
　　　That a mayden of Israell, sais he,
　　　Shall bere one like to the lely floure.
　　　He menys a barne consayved shulde be
　　　With-outen seede of man socour,
　　　And his modir a mayden free,
　　　And he both sone and saveour.
II REX: That fadirs has talde beforne
　　　Has noman myght to marre.
HEROD: Allas, than am I lorne;
　　　This waxith ay werre and werre.　　　　　　　　　180

(16)

I CON: My lorde, be ye no-thyng a-bast;
　　　This brygge shall well to ende be broght.
　　　Bidde tham go furthe and frendly frast
　　　The soth of this that thei have soght,
　　　And telle it you; so shall ye trast
　　　Whedir ther tales be trew or noght.

---

158 *thus-gate* in this way　168 *neven* proclaim　174 *socour* help　180 *werre* worse　181 *a-bast* cast down　182 *brygge* strife　183 *frast* try

THE ADORATION

    Than shall we wayte tham with a wrest,
    And make all wast that thei have wroght.
HEROD [*aside*]: Nowe, certis, this was wele saide;
    This matere makes me fayne.   190
    Sir kyngis, I halde me paide
    Of all youre purpose playne.

(17)

    Wendis furth, youre forward to fulfill,
    To Bedlem; it is but here at hande.
    And speris grathe, both goode and ill,
    Of hym that shulde be lorde in lande.
    And comes agayne than me untill,
    And telle me trulye youre tythande;
    To worshippe hym that is my will;
    Thus shall ye stabely undirstande.   200
II REX: Sertis, syr, we sall you say
    Alle the soth of that childe
    In alle the hast that we may.
II CON: Fares wele, ye be bygilid!
    [*Exeunt the Three Kings.*]

(18)

HEROD: Nowe certis, this is a sotille trayne;
    Nowe shall thei trewly take ther trace,
    And telle me of that litill swayne
    And ther counsaill in this case.
    If it be soth, thei shall be slayne.
    No golde shall gete tham bettir grace.   210
    Go we nowe, till thei come agayne,
    To playe us in som othir place.
    This halde I gud counsaill,
    Yitt wolde I no man wist;
    For sertis, we shall not faill
    To loyse tham as us list.

---

187 *wrest* trick   193 *forward* promise   195 *speris* ask   *grathe* directly   205 *trayne* device   216 *loyse* destroy

Nota[10], the Harrod passeth, and the iij kynges comyth agayn to make there offerynges.

(19)

I REX: A, sirs, for sight what shall I say?
Whare is oure syne? I se it not.
II REX: No more do I; nowe dar I lay
In oure wendyng som wrange is wroght.   220
III REX: Un-to that Prince I rede we praye,
That till us sente his syngne unsoght,
That he wysse us in redy way
So frendly that we fynde hym moght.
I REX: A, siris, I se it stande
A-boven where he is borne.
Lo! here is the house at hande;
We have noght myste this morne.

(20)

ANCILLA[11] [*opening door*]: Whame seke ye, syrs, be wayes wilde,
With talkyng, travelyng to and froo?   230
Her wonnes a woman with her childe,
And hir husband; her ar no moo.
II REX: We seke a barne that all shall bylde,
His sartayne syngne hath saide us soo;
And his modir, a mayden mylde.
Her hope we to fynde tham twoo.
ANC: Come nere, gud syrs, and see,
Youre way to ende is broght.
III REX: Behalde here, syyirs, her and se
The same that ye have soght.   240

(21)

I REX: Loved be that Lorde that lastis aye,
That us has kydde thus curtaysely,
To wende by many a wilsom way,
And come to this clene companye.

222 *syngne* sign   229 *Whame* whom   233 *bylde* protect   242 *kydde* shown   243 *wilsom* wild

THE ADORATION

II REX: Late us make nowe no more delay,
    But tyte take furth oure tresurry,
    And ordand giftis of gud aray
    To worshippe hym als is worthy.
III REX: He is worthy to welde
    All worshippe, welthe and wynne;   250
    And for honnoure and elde,
    Brother, ye shall begynne.

(22)

I REX: Hayle, the fairest of felde folke for to fynde,
    Fro the fende and his feeres faithefully us fende;
    Hayll, the best that shall be borne to unbynde
    All the barnes that are borne and in bale boune;
    Hayll, thou marc us thi men and make us in mynde,
    Sen thi myght is on molde misseis to amende;
    Hayll, clene that is comen of a kynges kynde,
    And shall be kyng of this kyth, all clergy has kende.   260
    And sith it shall worthe on this wise,
    Thy selffe have soght, sone, I say the,
    With golde that is grettest of price[12];
    Be paied of this present, I pray the.

(23)

II REX: Hayll, foode that thy folke fully may fede;
    Hayll, floure fairest, that never shall fade;
    Hayll, sone that is sente of this same sede,
    That shall save us of synne that oure syris had;
    Hayll, mylde, for thou mett to marke us to mede,
    Off a may makeles thi modir thou made,   270
    In that gude thurgh grace of thy godhede,
    Als the gleme in the glasse gladly thow glade;
    And sythyn yow shall sitte to be demand,
    To helle or to heven for to have us,

---

250 *wynne* pleasure   251 *elde* seniority   257 *marc* mark   258 *molde* earth   *misseis* evil   260 *kyth* people   269 *mett* measured   270 *may* maid   *makeles* without evil   272 *gleme* gleam   273 *demand* judging

ENGLISH MYSTERY PLAYS

In-sens to thi servis is semand.
Sone, se to thi suggettis and save us.

(24)

III REX: Hayll, barne that is best oure balys to bete,
For our boote shall thou be bounden and bett;
Hayll, frende faithfull, we fall to thy feete;
Thy fadiris folke fro the fende fals the to fette;   280
Hayll, man that is made to thi men meete,
Sen thou and thy modir with mirthis ar mette;
Hayll, duke that dryves dede undir fete,
But whan thy dedys ar done to dye is thi dette.
And sen thy body beryed shalbe
This mirre will I giffe to thi gravyng.
The gifte is not grete of degree;
Ressayve it, and se to oure savyng.

(25)

MARIA: Sir kyngis, ye travel not in vayne;
Als ye have ment, hyr may ye fynde;   290
For I consayved my sone sartayne
With-outen misse of man in mynde,
And bare hym here with-outen payne,
Where women are wonte to be pynyd.
Goddis aungell in his gretyng playne
Saide he shulde comforte al man kynde,
Thar-fore doute yow no dele
Here for to have youre bone;
I shall witnesse full wele
All that is saide and done.   300

(26)

I REX: For solas, ser, now may we synge.
All is parformed that we for prayde;

276 *suggettis* subjects 278 *bett* beaten 280 *fette* fetch 286 *gravyng* burial 298 *bone* good

THE ADORATION

But, gud barne, giffe us thy blissing,
For faire happe is be-fore the laide.
II REX: Wende we nowe to Herowde the kyng,
For of this poynte he will be paied,
And come hym-selffe and make offeryng
Un-to this same, for so he saide.
III REX: I rede we reste a thrawe,
For to maynteyne our myght, 310
And than do as we awe
Both un-to kyng and knyght.
[*Angel appears.*]

(27)

ANGELUS: Nowe, curtayse kynges, to me take tent,
And turne be-tyme or ye be tenyd;
Fro God hym-selfe thus am I sent
To warne yow, als youre faithfull frende.
Herowde the kyng has malise ment,
And shappis with shame yow for to shende;
And for that ye non harmes shulde hente,
Be othir waies God will ye wende 320
Even to youre awne contre.
And yf ye aske hym bone,
Youre beelde ay will he be,
For this that ye have done.

(28)

I REX: A, Lorde, I love the inwardly.
Sirs, God had gudly warned us thre;
His Aungell her now herde have I,
And how he saide.
II REX: Sir, so did we.
He saide Herowde is oure enmye,
And makis hym bowne oure bale to be 330
With feyned falsed, and for-thy
Farre fro his force I rede we flee.

---

306 *poynte* matter   309 *thrawe* while   314 *tenyd* harmed   318 *shende*
destroy   319 *hente* receive   323 *beelde* comfort   330 *bowne* ready

III REX: Syrs, faste I rede we flitte,
  Ilkone till oure contre.
  He that is welle of witte
  Us wisse – and with yow be.

335 *welle* source

17. The Flight into Egypt

TOWNELEY 15

This short play is notable for its quiet tone. It was written in an alliterative style, and may perhaps represent one of the older parts of the Towneley cycle; if it derives from the York cycle it is probably older than the existing York play (York 18). It lacks the imaginative power of many of the other plays in the Towneley cycle, but it gives a touching picture of the relationship between Mary and Joseph. The latter is partially a comic character, drawn in accordance with the tradition of the old and ill-tempered husband who is oppressed by the troubles of marriage. Yet the two characters do communicate with one another, and their reactions to the Angel's warning are properly motivated.

[The Angel appears to Joseph.]

(1)

ANGELUS: Awake, Ioseph, and take intent!
  Thou ryse and slepe nomare!
  If thou wyll save thy-self unshent,
  Fownde the fast to fare.
  I am an angell to the sent
  For thou shall no harmes hent,
  To cach the outt of care.
  If thou here longer lent,
  For rewth thou mon repent,
  And rew it wonder sare.   10

3 *unshent* unharmed   4 *Fownde* try   *the* thee   *fare* go   6 *hent* receive   7 *cach* take   8 *lent* remain   10 *rew* regret

ENGLISH MYSTERY PLAYS

IOSEPH: A, myghtfull God,
　What ever this ment,
　So swete of toyn?

(2)

ANGELUS: Lo, Ioseph, it is I,
　An angell send to the.
IOSEPH: We! Leyf, I pray the why?
　What is thy wyll with me?
ANGELUS: Hens behufys the hy,
　And take with the Mary,
　Also hir chyld so fre;
　For Herode dos to dy[1]
　All knave chyldren, securly,
　With-in two yere that be
　Of eld.
IOSEPH: Alas, full wo is me!
　Where may we beyld?

(3)

ANGELUS: Tyll Egypp shall thou fare
　With all the myght thou may;
　And, Ioseph, hold the thare,
　Tyll I wyll the at say.
IOSEPH: This is a febyll fare,
　A seke man and a sare
　To here of sich a fray;
　My bonys ar bursyd and bare
　For to do; I wold it ware
　Comen my last day
　Tyll ende;
　I ne wote which is the way;
　How shall we weynde?[2]

---

13 *toyn* tune　16 *Leyf* dear (one)　18 *behufys* it is fitting　*hy* go
26 *beyld* find safety　27 *Tyll* to　30 *at* there　31 *febyll* feeble, poor
32 *sare* wretched　33 *fray* attack　34 *bursyd* bruised　39 *weynde* go

THE FLIGHT INTO EGYPT

(4)

ANGELUS: Ther-of have thou no drede; 40
  Weynd furth and leyf thi dyn:
  The way he shall you lede,
  The kyng of all man-kyn.
  [*Exit.*]
IOSEPH: That heynd till us take hede,
  For I had lytyll nede
  Sich bargans to begyn;
  No wonder if I wede,
  I that may do no dede;
  How shuld I theder wyn
  For eld?
  I am full bare and thyn, 50
  And all unweld;

(5)

  My fors me falys to fare,
  And sight that I shuld se.
  [*Enter Mary.*]
  Mary, my darlyng dere,
  I am full wo for the!
MARIA: A, leyf Ioseph, what chere?
  Youre sorow on this manere
  It mekill mervels me.
IOSEPH: Oure noyes ar neghand nere 60
  If we dwell longer here;
  For-thi behofes us fle
  And flytt.
MARIA: Alas, how may this be?
  What ever menys it?

(6)

IOSEPH: It menys of sorow enoghe.
MARIA: A, dere Ioseph, how so?

---

41 *leyf* cease   44 *heynd* gracious person   47 *wede* am angry   52 *unweld* impotent   53 *fors* strength   *falys* fails   60 *noyes* harms   *neghand* approaching

IOSEPH: As I lay in a swogh,
Full sad slepand and thro,
An angell to me drogh,
As blossom bright on bogh,
And told betwix us two
That Herode wroght greatt wogh,
And all knave children slogh
In land that he myght to,
That feynd!
And he thy son wold slo
And shamely sheynd.

(7)

MARIA: My son? Alas, for care!
Who may my doyllys dyll?
Wo worth fals Herode are!
My son why shuld he spyll?
Alas, I lurk and dare!
To slo this barne I bare,
What wight in warld had wyll?
His hart shuld be full sare
Sichon for to fare,
That never yit dyd yll,
Ne thoght.
IOSEPH: Now leyfe Mary, be styll!
This helpys noght;

(8)

It is no boytt to grete,
Truly withoutten trayn;
Oure bayll it may not boytt,
Bot well more make oure payn.
MARIA: Alas, how shuld I lete?
My son that is so swete

68 *swogh* (n) faint   70 *drogh* came   73 *wogh* woe   74 *slogh* slew
78 *sheynd* destroy   80 *doyllys* griefs   *dyll* assuage   81 *are* anger
83 *lurk* stumble   *dare* tremble   92 *boytt* remedy   *grete* weep
93 *withoutten trayn* without cunning (used as an asseveration)   96 *lete* stop

THE FLIGHT INTO EGYPT

    Is soght for to be slayn;
    Full gryle may I grete
    My fomen and I mete;   100
    Tell me, Ioseph, with mayn,
    Youre red.
IOSEPH: Shortly swedyll us this swayn,
    And fle hys dede.

(9)

MARIA: His ded wold I not se,
    For all this warld to wyn;
    Alas, full wo were me,
    In two if we shuld twyn;
    My chyld so bright of ble,
    To slo hym were pyte,   110
    And a full hedus syn.
    Dere Ioseph, what red ye?
IOSEPH: Tyll Egypp weynd shall we;
    For-thi let be thi dyn
    And cry.
MARIA: How shall we theder wyn?
IOSEPH: Fulle well wote I;

(10)

    The best wyse that we may
    Hast us outt of this here.
    Ther is noght els to say   120
    Bot tytt pak up oure gere;
    For ferd of this affray,
    Lett us weynd hens away,
    Or any do us dere.
MARIA: Greatt God, as he well may,
    That shope both nyght and day,
    From wandreth he us were,
    And shame;

---

99 *gryle* shrilly   101 *with mayn* (an asseveration here)   108 *twyn* separate   109 *ble* face   110 *slo* slay   119 *here* place   121 *tytt* quickly   126 *shope* made   127 *wandreth* misfortune *were* protect

My chyld how shuld I bere
So far from hame? 130

(11)

Alas, I am full wo!
Was never wyght so wyll!
IOSEPH: God wote I may say so,
I have mater ther tyll;
For I may unyth go
To lede of land sich two;
No wonder if I be wyll,
And sythen has many a fo.
A, why wyll no ded me slo?
My lyfe I lyke yll 140
And sare;
He that all doyls may dyll,
He keyll my care!

(12)

So wyll as wyght as I
In warld was never man;
Howsehold and husbandry
Full sore I may it ban;
That bargan dere I by.
Yong men, bewar, red I:
Wedyng makys me all wan. 150
Take me thi brydyll, Mary;
Tent thou to that page grathly
With all the craft thou can;
And may
He that this warld began
Wysh us the way!

(13)

MARIA: Alas, full wo is me!
Is none so wyll as I!

132 *wyll* wild, bewildered   134 *ther tyll* concerned with that   135 *unyth* with difficulty   143 *keyll* cure   152 *Tent* take care   *grathly* readily

THE FLIGHT INTO EGYPT

    My hart wold breke in thre,
    My son to se hym dy. 160
IOSEPH: We! Leyf Mary, lett be,
    And nothyng drede thou the,
    Bot hard hens lett us hy;
    To save thi foode so fre,
    Fast furth now lett us fle,
    Dere leyf;
    To mete with his enmy,
    It were a greatt myschefe,

(14)

    And that wold I not wore,
    Away if we myght wyn; 170
    My hart wold be full sore
    In two to se you twyn.
    Tyll Egypp lett us fare;
    This pak, tyll I com thare,
    To bere I shall not blyn:
    For-thi have thou no care;
    If I may help the mare,
    Thou fyndys no fawte me in,
    I say.
    God blys you more and myn, 180
    And have now all good day!

   Explicit fugacio Iosep et Marie in Egiptum.

164 *foode* child   175 *blyn* stop   180 *myn* less

18. The Purification, and Christ with the Doctors
De Purificatione Beatae Virginis

CHESTER II: BLACKSMITHS

This play has a complicated history. The Purification, based on the Stanzaic Life of Christ, was in the cycle before 1467, performed by the Smiths. Shortly after this, during a series of revisions by which the Tanners were given a new play, the episode of the Doctors was added to the Smiths' pageant. This second part derives ultimately from York 20 and probably came by way of Towneley 18 and the Coventry Weavers' Pageant. It was in its present position by 1488. The two stories are close together in the Gospel; (Luke 2 22–38, and 41–51).

Both parts deal with the young Christ, but whilst he is an infant at the Purification, he is twelve years old when he disputes with the Doctors. The chief aspects of the Purification are that Mary, already pure, does not need to submit to the ritual, but willingly does so (as with Christ at the Baptism), and that Simon receives his Lord after long expectation. In the Doctors episode Christ merely recounts the Ten Commandments. Thus the two parts do not fit at all well. It may be that the reason for putting them together was a purely technical one: both plays needed a temple, and it may have been convenient to use the same cart (cf. F. M. Salter, Mediaeval Drama in Chester, p. 67). In general the writing is clumsy and in some places the writer has obscured the better sense of the York version.

Salter (op. cit., p. 76) prints the accounts for the 1554 performance, containing a payment of twelve pence for 'gelldinge Gods face', and payments for the actors (three shillings and fourpence for Simeon, and twelve pence for 'letall God'). He also shows (pp. 49–50) that the play was performed as a separate item for Prince Arthur in 1499.

THE PURIFICATION, AND CHRIST WITH THE DOCTORS

[*Scene: The Temple.*]

(1)

SIMEON: Mightie God, have mynd on me,
  That most are in maiesty,
  For many a wynter have I be
  Preist in Ierusalem.
  Much teene and incommodytye
  Followeth age, full well I see,
  And now that fitt may I not flee
  Think me never so swem.

(2)

  When I am dead and layd in clay,
  Wend I mott the same way   10
  That Abraham went, the sooth to say,
  And in his bosome be;
  But heaven-blisse after my day –
  Till Gods Sonne come, sooth to say,
  To ransome his folke in better aray
  To blisse come never we[1].

(3)

  That Christ shall come well I wott,
  But day ner tyme [may] no man wott;
  Therfore my books looke I mott
  My hart to glade and light.   20
  What Esay[2] sayeth I will see,
  For well I wott how it shall be;
  Or I dyed well were me
  Of hym to have a sight.

---

5 *incommodytye* trouble   7 *fitt* hardship   8 *swem* ?in grief   10 *Wend* go *mott* must   17 *wott* know   18 *ner* nor

ENGLISH MYSTERY PLAYS

(4)

> *Tunc librum respiciens legat prophetiam:* '*Ecce virgo conncipiet et pariet filium.*'[3]

A, Lord, much is thy power;
A wonder I fynd written here:
It sayeth a mayden cleane and cleer
Shall conceave and beare
A Sonne called Emanuell.
But of this leeve I never a deale; 30
It is wrong written, as have I heale,
Or ells wonder were.

(5)

He that wrott this was a fone
To wryte 'A virgin' here upon,
That shall conceave without helpe of man;
This writing marveyls me.
I will scrape this away anone,
Theras 'A virgin' is written on
I will wryte 'A good woman',
For so it should be. 40

> *Tunc librum fricabit quasi deleret hoc verbum 'Virgo'; et postea ponet librum super altare, et veniet Angelus et libro accepto faciet signum scribendi; et libro clauso recedet et dicat Anna vidua* [4]

(6)

[ANNA: Semion, father, south I see
That Christe shall come our boote to be
From the Father in magistie
On mankinde for to myne.
And when he cometh, leve thou me,
He will have mercye and pittie
On his folke to make them free,
And save them of their synne.

---

27 *cleer* pure 30 *deale* scrap 31 *heale* good fortune 33 *fone* fool
42 *boote* remedy 44 *myne* remember

THE PURIFICATION, AND CHRIST WITH THE DOCTORS

(7)

SIMEON: The tyme of his cominge knowe I nought,
   Yet manye bokes have I soughte.
   But wounderlye he that this wryttinge wroughte
   And marvaile thinketh me[5].
. . . .
   My boke to loke yf I fynde oughte
   What manner mankinde shalbe boughte
   And what tyme it shalbe.
     Tunc accipiet librum et admirando dicat [6]

(8)

O, Lorde, howe maie this be to-daie?
That I wrote laste, I fynde awaie,
And of redde letters in stowte araye,
'A virgine' wrytten theron.
May fay! After I will assaie
Wheither this mirackle be vereye,
And scrape this worde, written so gaye,
And wrytte 'a good woman'.
    Tunc iterum fabricat ut antea et dicat [7]

(9)

Dame Anne, thou maie see well heare
This is amended in good manere,
For a wounder thinge it were
To fall by anye waie.
Therfore, as it was a-misse,
I have written that souther is:
That 'a good woman' shall, I wisse,
Conseave and not 'a maye'.
    Tunc ponit librum super altare, et faciet Angellus ut antea[8].

---

51 *wounderlye* miraculously   52 *marvaile* marvel   58 *redde* red   *stowte* firm   69 *souther* more true   71 *maye* maid

(10)

ANNA: Sir, marvile you no thinge theiron,
　For God will take kinde in man[9];
　Through his godheade ordayne he can
　A mayde a childe to beare.
　For to that highe comlye kinge
　Impossible is no thinge;
　Therfore I leeve it no leasinge
　But south all that is heare.

(11)

SIMEON *accipiet librum*: By my faie! Yet will I see
　Whether my lettres chaunged be.
　A! Hie God in Trenitie,
　Honoured be thou aye!
　For goulden letters, by my lewty,
　Are wrytten through Godes postie
　Since I layde my boke from me
　And my wryttinge awaie.

(12)

　Ther as 'a good woman' written was,
　Righte now here before my face;
　Yet storred I not out of this place,
　And my lettre chaunged ys.
　This muste be needes by Godes grace,
　For an angell this wrytten hase.
　Nowe leeve I a mayden, in this case,
　Shall beare a baron of bliss[10].

(13)

　Nowe seith, Lorde, that it is so,
　That thou wilte be borne with blisse
　Of a mayden that never did amisse,
　On me, Lorde, thou have mynde!

73 *kinde* nature　76 *comlye* beautiful　78 *leasinge* lie　82 *Hie* high
85 *postie* power　90 *storred* stirred　96 *seith* since

THE PURIFICATION, AND CHRIST WITH THE DOCTORS

    Let me never death taste, Lorde, full of grace,   100
    Tell I have seene that Childes face,
    That prophescied is here in this place,
    To kever all mankinde.

(14)

ANGELLUS: Semeon, I tell thee sickerlye
    That Godes owne ghoste am I,
    Comen to warne thee witterlye:
    Death shalte thou never see,
    Tell thou have seen Christe vereye,
    That borne is of a mayden, Marye,
    And comen mankinde to forbye,   110
    From God in magistie.

(15)

SIMEON: A, Lorde, I thanke thee of thy grace
    That thy ghoste sente to me haste;
    Nowe hope I sickerlie in this place
    Thy Sonne for to see,
    That of a virgine muste be borne
    To save mankinde that was forlorne,
    As Esayes boke toulde me beforne.
    Lorde, blessed muste thou be!
      Tunc Simeon sedebit expectans consolationem de alio loco procull a templo, et dicat Maria[11]

(16)

MARIA: Iosephe, my trewe owine fere,   120
    Nowe rede I, if your will were,
    Seith fourtie daies are gone intier,
    The temple that we goe to,
    And Moyses lawe for to fulfill
    My sonne to offer Semion till;
    I wote well that it is Godes will
    That we now so doe.

---

103 *kever* recover   105 *ghoste* spirit   110 *forbye* redeem   120 *owine* own
fere mate   122 *intier* fully

(17)

IOSEPHE: Yea, Marye, though it be no nede
    Seith thou arte cleane in thoughte and deed,
    Yet it is good to do as God bade,   130
    And worcke after his lawe,
    And to the temple that we goe;
    And take we with us dove-byrdes towe,
    Or a turtell to offer also,
    And to fulfill Godes lawe.

(18)

MARIA: Rightewise, Semeon, God thee see!
    Here am I comen nowe to thee
    Purified for to be,
    With milde harte and meke.
    Receive my sonne nowe to me,   140
    And to my offeringe birdes three[12],
    As falles, sire, for your degree,
    And for your office eke.

(19)

IOSEPHE: A signe I offer here also
    Of virgine waxe, as other moe,
    In tockeninge shee hass lived oo
    In full devocion.
    And, sir Semion, leve well this,
    As cleane as this waxe nowe is,
    As cleane is my wife, I-wisse,   150
    From all corruptcion.
    Tunc Simeon accipiett puerum in ulnas[13].

(20)

SEMEON: Welckome, my Christe, my Savyour!
    Welkome, mankindes conqueroure!
    Welkome, of all frute the flower!
    Welkome with all my hart!

---

134 *turtell* turtle-dove   143 *eke* also   145 *waxe* wax   146 *oo* always

THE PURIFICATION, AND CHRIST WITH THE DOCTORS

> To thee worshipe, ioye, and honoure!
> For nowe I see my Savyour
> Is comen to leech my langoure,
> And bringe me unto blesse.

(21)

> Though I beare thee nowe, sweete wighte,
> Thou ruleste me as it is righte,
> For through thee I have mayne and mighte
> More then through waie of kinde.
> Therfore a songe as I have tighte,
> And laudes to thee with harte righte,
> I will shewe here in thy sighte.
> On me, Lorde, thou have mynde!
> > *Tunc cantabit 'Nunc dimitis servum tuum, Domine, in pace'*[14].

(22)

> Nowe, Lorde, let thy servante be
> After thy worde in peace and lee;
> For with my eyes nowe I see
> Thou arte mankindes heale.
> For thou haste ordeyned ther thy postie
> To people which thou haste pittie[15];
> Light is comen nowe through thee
> And ioye to Isarell.

(23)

> And Marye, mother, to thee I saie,
> Thy Sonne that I have seene to-daie
> Is comen, I tell thee, in good faye,
> For fallinge of manye fone,
> And to releave in good araye
> Manye a man as he well maie,
> In Isarell or he wende awaie,
> That shall leeve hym upon.

---

158 *leech* cure   159 *blesse* bliss   160 *wighte* man, person   164 *tighte* devised   169 *lee* shelter   179 *fallinge* destruction   182 *or* before

(24)
>Manye signes he shall shewe
>In which untrewe shall not trowe;
>And suffer thou shalte manye a harde thrawe,
>For sword of sorowe it shall goe
>Through thy harte – that men shall knowe
>Thoughtes in harte on a rowe
>Of men that shall contrarye you   190
>And founde to worke thee woo[16].

(25)
>ANNA VIDUA: And I acknowledge to thee, Lorde, heare,
>To leeve on thee through my power,
>That fower skore and fower yeaire
>Haste sente me mighte and grace,
>To leve in pennance and prayer;
>Nowe wote I well, withouten were,
>That thou arte Christe in godheade cleare,
>In thee whollye thou it haste.

(26)
>And openlye here south I saye   200
>To all thy people that I see maie,
>The which hath wayled manye a daie
>After thee our savyoure,
>That thou arte comen, Christe vereye;
>This wotte I well by manye a waie;
>Therfore I honoure thee for aye,
>My Christe, my creator.

(27)
>MARIA[17]: Iosephe, husbande leffe and deare,
>Our childe is gone upon his way.

---

185 *untrewe* (n) the faithless   *trowe* (v) believe   186 *thrawe* throe
190 *contrarye* oppose   191 *founde* try   193 *leeve* believe   197 *were* doubt
208 *leffe* beloved

THE PURIFICATION, AND CHRIST WITH THE DOCTORS

My harte were lighte and he were here — 210
Let us goe seeke hym, I thee praie.]
For suddaynly he went away
And left us both in Ierusalem,
Greatly in lyking many a day[18],
That will be lord over all the realme.

(28)

IOSEPH: Mary, of mirth we may us meane,
And trewly tell betwene us twooe
Of fearly sightes that we have sene,
Sith we came the citie froe.
[MARIA:] Deare Iosephe, you will not wene 220
Sith our childe has bene us with,
Homeward I red we hye,
He kept us both from grone and grith;

(29)

In all the might ever we may
For dread of wicked company,
Lest anie us mete upon the way,
Homeward therfore I red we hye[19].

(30)

[*Christ speaks to the Doctors in the Temple.*]

I DOCTOR: Heare our reason right on a row,
You clarkes that be of great coning;
Me [thinke] this child will learne our law, 230
He taketh great tent to our talking.

(31)

DEUS: You clarkes that be of great degree,
Unto my talke you take good heede!
My father that sitteth in maiesty,
He knowes your workes in thought and deede.
My Father and I together be

---

219 *froe* from   222 *hye* go   223 *grone* suffering   *grith* ?grief
229 *clarkes* learned men   *coning* (n) learning   231 *tent* notice

327

ENGLISH MYSTERY PLAYS

In one godhead withoutten dreed;
We bene both one in certayntie,
All these workes to rule and reade.

(32)

I DOCTOR: Harkes this childe in his bourding! 240
He wenes he kennes more then he knowes[20];
Certes, sonne, thou art over-yong
By clergie cleane to know our lawes.

(33)

Therfore, if thou wold never so fayne,
Further in age till thou have draw,
Yet art thou never of might nor mayne
To knowe it, as a clarke may know.
II DOCTOR: And thou will speake of Moses law,
Take good heede and thou may see,
In case be that thou can know, 250
Here in this booke they written be.

(34)

DEUS: The kingdome of heaven is in me light,
And hath me anoynted as a leach,
And geven me playne power and might
The kingdome of heaven to tell and teach.

(35)

II DOCTOR: Behold how he has [learned] our lawes,
And he learned never on booke to read;
Me thinke he saith suttle sawes
And very truth, if you take heede.
III DOCTOR: Let hym wend furth on his wayes, 260
For and he dwell, without dread,
The people will full sone hym praise
Well more then we for all our deede.

239 *reade* understand   240 *bourding* jesting   243 *clergie* learning
245 *draw* gone   253 *leach* healer   258 *sawes* sayings

328

THE PURIFICATION, AND CHRIST WITH THE DOCTORS

(36)

I DOCTOR: This is nothing to my intent;
   Such speach to spend I red we spare.
   As wyde in world as I have went,
   Yet found I never so ferly a fare.
II DOCTOR: By matters that this childe hath ment
   To knowe our lawes, both less and more,
   Out of heaven I hope hym sent 270
   Into the earth to salve our sore.

(37)

DEUS: You that be masters of Moises lawe,
   And worthy doctors of great degree,
   One comaundment to me you show
   That God on earth bad kept shold be[21].
I DOCTOR: I read this is the first bidding,
   And is the most in Moses lawe,
   To love our God above all thinges
   With all our might and all our sawe.

(38)

DEUS: That for to doe looke ye be bayne 280
   With all your hart in good intent.
   Take you not his name in vayne;
   This is my Fathers comaundment.

(39)

   Also you honour your holy daye;
   No workes save almes-deedes ye doe.
   These three, the certayne sooth to say,
   The first table belongen to.
   Also father and mother worship aye;
   Take no mans goodes without the right;
   All false witnesse you put away, 290
   And slay no man by day nor night.

---

267 *ferly* marvellous   *fare* display   268 *hath ment* has in mind
285 *almes-deedes* good deeds, charities

ENGLISH MYSTERY PLAYS

(40)
>   Envye doe by no woman,
>   To doe her shame by night or day.
>   Other mens wyves desire you not;
>   All such desires you put away.
>   Looke you ne steale by night nor day,
>   Whersoever that you be lent.
>   These wordes understand you may;
>   They are my Fathers commaundment.

(41)
> III DOCTOR: Sir, this childe of mickle price,　　　300
>   Which is yonge and tender of age,
>   I hould hym sent from the highe justice
>   To wyn againe our heritage.

(42)
> MARIA: Now blessed be he us hither brought,
>   In land there lyves none so light!
>   Se where he sitteth we have sought,
>   Amonge yonder masters, mickle of might!

(43)
>   Wend furth, Ioseph, upon your way
>   And fetch our sonne, and let us fare,
>   That sitteth with yonder Doctors gay;　　　310
>   For we have had of hym great care.

(44)
> IOSEPH: Mary, wife, thou wottes right well
>   That I must all my travayle teene[22];
>   With men of might I can not mell
>   That sittes so gay in furres fyne.

(45)
> MARIA: My worthy Sonne, to me so deare,
>   We have you sought full wonder-wyde.
>   I am right glad that you be here,
>   That we have found you in this tyde.

THE PURIFICATION, AND CHRIST WITH THE DOCTORS

(46)

DEUS: Mother, full oft I tould you till: 320
My Fathers workes for wayle or woe
Hether was I sent for to fulfill;
That must I needes doe, or I goe.

(47)

MARIA: Thy sawes, Sonne, as have I heale,
Can I nothing understand;
I shall think on them full well,
And found to do that they commaund.

(48)

ANGELUS: Now have you hard all in this place
That Christ is comen through his grace,
As holy Esaie prophesied hase, 330
And Symeon hath hym seene.
Leve you well this, lordes of might,
And kepe you all his lawes of right[23],
That you may in his blisse so bright
Evermore with hym to beene.

Finis paginae undecimae.

320 *you till* to you   321 *wayle* good   322 *Hether* hither   327 *found* try

19. The Death of Herod

LUDUS COVENTRIAE 20

The principal events here are common to the other cycles: the play presents Herod's ruthless intention to kill all the male children under two years old (Matthew 2 16) out of revenge for the challenge to his kingship. The cruelty of the Massacre of the Innocents is powerfully shown, and Herod is satisfied and pleased by what he hears. In some versions he dies immediately after this, and the writer here has turned this event into a striking scene. The Proclamation at the beginning of the cycle indicates that there were two plays on these events, and it is therefore reasonable to suppose that there has been a later revision. Certainly the appearance of Death at the feast is reminiscent of the morality plays, and has no parallel elsewhere in the cycles. The moralities frequently impressed upon their audiences the inevitability and suddenness of death. Though their structure was usually designed to show moral conflict, the warning about the necessity for virtue was sharpened and intensified by the idea that death could not be resisted by anyone of whatever rank. Herod's cruelty and arrogance, his blasphemy, and his triumphant self-indulgence at the feast mark him out for disaster. Death arrives and kills him with a spear, delivering to the audience his warning about the grave. It is a remarkable piece of writing, showing hints of tragedy in the morality idiom. One must recognize also that it is to some extent a departure from the idiom of the mystery plays.

୧୨

Tunc respiciens Senescallus vadyt ad Herodem dicens[1]

(1)

SENESCALLUS: Lord, I have walkyd be dale and hylle
And wayted as it is your wyll.

THE DEATH OF HEROD

The kyngys iii. stelyn awey full styll
Thorwe Bedleem londe.
They wyl nevyr, so moty the²,
Com in the lond of Galyle,
For to se your fay[r] cete,
Ne dedys of your honde.

(2)

HERODES REX: I ryde on my rowel ryche in my regne,
Rybbys ful reed with rape xal I rende,
Popetys and paphawkys I xal puttyn in peyne,
With my spere prevyn pychyn and to pende.
The gomys with gold crownys ne gete nevyr ageyn,
To seke tho sottys sondys xal I sende.
Do howlott howtyn, hoberd and heyn;
Whan here barnys blede undyr credyl bende,
Sharply I xal hem shende,
The knave childeryn that be
In all Israel countre;
Thei xul have blody ble
For on I calde unkende³.

(3)

It is tolde in grw
His name xulde be Jhesu.
I-fownde
To have hym ye gon,
Hewe the flesch with the bon,
And gyf hym wownde.
Now, kene knyghtys, kythe youre craftys,
And kyllyth knave chylderyn and castyth hem in clay,
Shewyth on your shulderys scheldys and schaftys,

---

9 *rowel* spur 10 *Rybbys* ribs *reed* red *rape* force 11 *Popetys* puppets *paphawkys* ?sucklings 12 *prevyn* test *pychyn* stab *pende* pinch 13 *gomys* men 14 *sottys* fools *sondys* messengers 15 *Do* make *howlott* owl (i.e. woman) *howtyn* hoot *hoberd* clown *heyn* villain 21 *unkende* unnatural 22 *grw* Greek 28 *kythe* make use of

ENGLISH MYSTERY PLAYS

Shapyht amonge [selcouthys[4]] ashyrlyng shray;
Doth rowncys rennyn with rakynge raftys
Tyl rybbys be to-rent with a reed ray[5].
Lete no barne beleve on bete baftys,
Tyl a beggere blede be bestys baye,
Mahound that best may[6].
I warne yow, my knyghtys,
A barn is born, I plyghtys,
Wolde clymbyn kynge and knytys,
And lett my lordly lay. 40

(4)

Knyghtys wyse,
Chosyn full chyse,
A-ryse, a-ryse,
And take youre tolle,
And every page
Of ii. yere age,
Or evyr ye swage,
Sleyth ilke a fool.

(5)

On of hem alle
Was born in stalle; 50
Folys hym calle
Kynge in crowne.
With byttyr galle
He xall down falle;
My myght in halle
Xal nevyr go down.

(6)

1 MILES: I xall sle scharlys,
And qwenys with therlys;

31 *ashyrlyng* shrilling *shray* clamour 32 *rowncys* horses *raftys* shafts 33 *ray* dance 34 *baftys* behind 35 *baye* stall 38 *plyghtys* promise 39 *clymbyn* (v) ?silence 40 *lett* hinder *lay* law 42 *chyse* choice 47 *swage* cease 57 *scharlys* churls 58 *qwenys* women *therlys* serfs

334

THE DEATH OF HEROD

Here knave gerlys
I xal steke. 60
Forth wyl I spede
To don hem blede;
Thow gerlys grede,
We xul be wreke.

(7)

11 MILES: For swerdys sharpe
 As an harpe,
 Quenys xul karpe
 And of sorwe synge.
 Barnys yonge,
 They xul be stunge 70
 Thurwe levyr and lunge;
 We xal hem stynge.
   [*The Angel appears to Joseph.*]

(8)

ANGELUS: A-wake, Joseph, and take thi wyff,
 Thy chylde also, ryd be-lyff 7,
 For Kynge Herowde with sharpe knyff
  His knyghtys he doth sende.
 The Fadyr of hevyn hath to the sent,
 In to Egypte that thou be bent,
 For cruel knyghtys thi childe have ment
  With swerde to sle and shende. 80

(9)

JOSEPH: Awake, good wyff, out of your slepe,
 And of your childe takyght good kepe,
 Whyl I your clothis ley on hepe
  And trus hem on the asse.
 Kynge Herowde the chylde wyl scloo;
 Therfore to Egypte muste we goo.

---

59 *gerlys* children   63 *grede* cry out   64 *wreke* avenged   67 *karpe* complain   79 *ment* threatened   85 *scloo* slay

335

An aungel of God seyd me soo,
   And ther-fore lete us passe.

(10)

> *Tunc ibunt milites ad pueros occidendos et dicat prima femina*[8]

I FEMINA: Longe lullynge have I lorn.
  Alas, qwhy was my baron born?   90
  With swappynge swerde how is he shorn,
    The heed ryght fro the nekke,
  Shanke and shulderyn is al to torn.
  Sorwyn I se be-hyndyn and be-forn,
  Both mydnyth, mydday, and at morn;
    Of my lyff I ne recke.

(11)

II FEMINA: Serteynly I sey the same.
  Gon is all my good game,
  My lytyll childe lyth all lame,
    That lullyd on my pappys.   100
  My fourty wekys gronynge
  Hath sent me sefne yere sorwynge;
  Mykyl is my mornynge,
    And ryght hard arne myn happys.

(12)

I MILES: Lorde in trone,
  Makyght no mone.
  Qwenys gyn grone
  In werdl aboute.
  Upon my spere
  A gerle I bere[9];   110
  I dare well swere,
  Lett moderys howte.

---

101 *wekys* weeks   102 *sefne* seven   104 *happys* fortune   108 *werdl* world   112 *howte* hoot

THE DEATH OF HEROD

(13)

II MILES: Lord, we han spad
  As ye bad,
  Barnis ben blad,
  And lyne in dych;
  Flesch and veyn
  Han tholyd peyn,
  And ye xul reyne
  Ever more rych.   120

(14)

HERODES REX: Ye xul have stedys
  To your medys,
  Londys and ledys,
  Fryth and fe.
  Wele have ye wrought;
  My fo is sought;
  To deth is he brought;
  Now come up to me.

(15)

In sete now am I sett as kynge of myghtys most;
All this werd for ther love to me xul thei lowt.   130
Both of hevyn and of erth and of helle cost,
For dygne of my dygnyte thei have of me dowt.
Ther is no lord lyke on lyve to me wurth a toost,
Nother kyng nor kayser in all this worlde abought.
If any brybour do bragge or blowe a-gens my bost,
I xal rappe tho rebawdys and rake them on rought,
With my bryght bronde.
Ther xal be neyther kayser nere k[yn]ge
But that I xal hem down dynge,
Lesse than he at my byddynge   140
    Be buxum to myn honde[10].

---

115 *blad* bled 118 *tholyd* suffered 123 *ledys* peoples 124 *Fryth* forest
fe property 130 *lowt* bow 131 *cost* region 132 *dowt* fear 133 *toost*
(piece of) toast 135 *brybour* scoundrel, thief 141 *buxum* obedient

ENGLISH MYSTERY PLAYS

(16)

Now, my jentyll and curteys knyghtys, herke to me this stownde.
Good tyme sone, me thynkygh, at dyner that we were;
Smertly therfore sett a tabyll a-non here full sownde,
Coverid with a coryous cloth and with rych wurthy fare,
Servyse for the lovelyest lorde that levynge is on grownde;
Beste metys and wurthyest wynes loke that ye non spare.
Thow that a lytyl pynt xulde coste a Ml. pownde,
Brynge alwey of the beste; for coste take ye no care,
Anon that it be done. 150

SENESCALLUS: My lorde, the tabyl is redy dyght.
Here is watyr; now wasch forthryght.
Now blowe up, mynstrall, with all your myght;
The servyse comyth in sone.

(17)

HERODES REX: Now am I sett at mete,
And wurthely servyd at my degre.
Com forth, knyghtys, sytt down and ete,
And be as mery as ye kan be.
I MILES: Lord, at yowre byddynge we take oure sete,
With herty wyl obey we the. 160
Ther is no lorde of myght so grett,
Thorwe all this werde in no countre,
In wurchepp to a-byde.
HERODES [REX]: I was nevyr meryer here be-forn,
Sythe that I was fyrst born,
Than I am now ryght in this morn;
In joy I gynne to glyde.

(18)

[*Enter Mors.*]

MORS: Ow! I herde a page make preysyng of pride;
All pryncys he passyth, he wenyth, of powste.
He wenyth to be the wurthyest of all this werde wyde; 170

142 *stownde* time 145 *coryous* fine, elaborate 163 *wurchepp* honour
167 *gynne* begin *glyde* go 168 *preysyng* praising 169 *wenyth* thinks
powste power

THE DEATH OF HEROD

Kynge ovyr all kyngys that page wenyth to be.
He sent into Bedlem to seke on every syde
Cryst for to qwelle yf thei myght hym se;
But of his wykkyd wyl lurdeyn yitt he lyede;
Goddys sone doth lyve. Ther is no lorde but he;
Over all lordys he is kynge.
I am Deth, Goddys masangere[11].
All-myghty God hath sent me here
Yon lordeyn to sle with-owtyn dwere,
    For his wykkyd werkynge.   180

(19)

I am sent fro God: Deth is my name.
All thynge that is on grownd I welde at my wylle,
Both man and beste and byrdys, wylde and tame,
Whan that I come them to with deth I do them kylle,
Erbe, gres and tres stronge take hem all in same,
Ya, the grete myghty okys with my dent I spylle.
What man that I wrastele with he xal ryght sone have schame.
I geve hym such a trepett, he xal evyr-more ly stylle,
For Deth kan no sporte.
Wher I smyte ther is no grace,   190
For aftere my strook man hath no space
To make amendys for his trespace
    But God hym graunt comforte.

(20)

Ow! se how prowdely yon kaytyff sytt at mete;
Of Deth hath he no dowte; he wenyth to leve evyr-more.
To hym wyl I go and geve hym such an hete
That all the lechis of the londe his lyf xul nevyr restore.
A-gens my dredful dentys it vaylyth nevyr to plete;
Or I hym part fro I xal make ful pore;
All the blood of his body I xal hym owt swete.   200

174, 179 *lurdeyn lordeyn* oaf   179 *dwere* fear   185 *Erbe* herb   *gres* grass   187 *wrastele* wrestle   188 *trepett* trip   196 *hete* blow   197 *lechis* doctors   198 *plete* plead   200 *owt swete* sweat out

For now I go to sle hym with strokys sad and sore,
　　This tyde.
Bothe hym and his knyghtys all,
I xal hem make to me but thrall;
With my spere sle hem I xall
　　And so cast down his pride.

(21)

HERODES REX: Now, kende knyghtys, be mery and glad;
　　With all good diligens shewe now sum myrth;
For be gracyous Mahound more myrth never I had,
　　Ne nevyr more joye was inne from tyme of my byrth, 210
For now my fo is ded and prendyd as a padde.
Above me is no kynge on grownd nere on gerth,
Merthis therfore make ye and be ryght no thynge sadde.
Spare nother mete nor drynke, and spare for no dyrthe
　　Of wyne nor of brede,
For now am I a kynge alone;
So wurthy as I may ther be none,
Therfore, knyghtys, be mery echone,
　　For now my fo is dede.

(22)

I MILES: Whan the boys sprawlyd at my sperys hende, 220
　　By Sathanas oure syre it was a goodly syght.
A good game it was that boy for to shende,
　　That wolde abene oure kynge and put yow from your ryght.
II MILES: Now trewly, my lorde the kynge, we had ben un-hende,
　　And nevyr non of us able for to be a knyght,
If that any of us to hem had ben a frende,
　　And asavyd any lyff a-gen thi mekyl myght,
　　From deth hem to flytt.
HERODES REX: Amonges all that grett rowthe,

---

207 *kende* proved　211 *prendyd* pinned, stuck　*padde* frog　212 *nere* nor *gerth* garth　214 *dyrthe* shortage　224 *un-hende* churlish, lacking in chivalry　228 *flytt* flee　229 *rowthe* company

THE DEATH OF HEROD

He is ded, I have no dowte; 230
Therfore, menstrell, rownd a-bowte
Blowe up a mery fytt.

*Hic dum buccinant Mors interficiat Herodem et duos
milites subito et diabolus recipiat eos*[12].

(23)

DIABOLUS: All oure! All oure! This catel is myn;
  I xall hem brynge on to my celle.
  I xal hem teche pleys fyn,
  And showe such myrthe as is in helle.
  It were more bettyr amonges swyn
  That evyr-more stynkyn ther be to dwelle,
  For in oure logge is so gret peyn
  That non erthely tonge can telle. 240
    With yow I go my way;
  I xal yow bere forth with me,
  And shewe yow sportys of oure gle;
  Of oure myrthis now xal ye se
    And evyr synge welawey.

(24)

MORS: Off Kynge Herowde all men beware,
  That hath rejoycyd in pompe and pryde;
  For all his boste of blysse ful bare,
  He lyth now ded here on his syde.
  For whan I come I can not spare; 250
  Fro me no whyht may hym hyde.
  Now is he ded and cast in care,
  In helle pytt evyr to a-byde;
    His lordchep is al lorn.
  Now is he as pore as I;
  Wormys mete is his body;
  His sowle in helle ful peynfully
    Of develis is al to-torn.

---

233 *oure* over *catel* property 235 *pleys* games *fyn* fine 243 *gle* delight 251 *whyht* man 258 *to-torn* torn to pieces

(25)

> All men dwellyng upon the grownde,
> Be-ware of me, be myn councel,
> For feynt felachep[13] in me is fownde.
> I kan no curtesy, as I yow tel;
> For be a man nevyr so sownde
> Of helth, in herte nevyr so wel,
> I come sodeynly with-in a stownde;
> Me with-stande may no castel.
> My jurnay wyl I spede;
> Of my comyng no man is ware;
> For when men make most mery fare,
> Than sodeynly I cast hem in care,
> And sle them evyn in dede.

(26)

> Thow I be nakyd and pore of array,
> And wurmys knawe me al a-bowte[14],
> Yit loke ye drede me nyth and day,
> For whan deth comyth ye stande in dowte.
> Evyn lyke to me, as I yow say,
> Shull all ye be here in this rowte.
> Whan I yow chalange at my day,
> I xal yow make ryght lowe to lowth,
> And nakyd for to be.
> Amonges wormes, as I yow telle,
> Undyr the erth xul ye dwelle,
> And thei xul etyn both flesch and felle
> As thei have don me.

265 *stownde* moment 279 *lowth* (v) bow 283 *felle* skin

20. The Shearmen and Tailors' Play

COVENTRY

The manuscript of this play was destroyed by fire at the Birmingham Free Library in 1879. It had been printed by Thomas Sharp in 1817 and 1825, and all modern editions derive from these. The most comprehensive edition is that by Hardin Craig, Two Coventry Corpus Christi Plays (E.E.T.S.), 1957 (second edition).

The play formed part of the Coventry cycle, and was probably written in the first quarter of the fifteenth century. The copy which Sharp used was made by Robert Croo in 1534. As far as can now be determined from other records there were only ten plays in the cycle, and there is little distinct evidence that there were any Old Testament subjects. Each was longer than was usual in other cycles, and we can assume that the Shearmen and Tailors' Play was typical in that it contained a number of elements normally separated. Broadly, it falls into two halves: the Annunciation, the Nativity, and the Shepherds; the Kings, the Flight, and the Slaughter of the Innocents. One Prophet speaks an introduction, and two more have a link passage (ll. 332–474).

The verse forms show considerable variety, which suggests that the play as we have it was put together from the work of several writers. There are a number of effective passages, amongst which must be mentioned the Herald's introduction for Herod in French, the raging of Herod, the determined struggle put up by the mothers of the Innocents, and Joseph's reaction to Mary's pregnancy. The tone is remarkable for its reverence throughout.

The reference to the pageant cart (stage direction, l. 784) makes it clear that the plays at Coventry were processional, and we know of four stations. Nevertheless there are difficulties in contemplating the production of such a wide variety of incidents for one cart. It is possible that each play used a more complex staging by introducing supplementary carts, but the play is written for one centre of action throughout. The words of the actors indicate the location, and there is some dialogue as they move on and off the stage. The stage direction which mentions that

ENGLISH MYSTERY PLAYS

Herod rages in the street may mean that such a move was exceptional, and that most of the action was confined to the cart (l.539). The Kings enter the stable at l.698 and speak to Mary, which suggests that she is placed on an inner stage. However it is clear that there is no attempt to present more than one group of actors before the audience at any given time.

※

[*Enter Isaiah.*]

(1)

ISAYE: The Sofferent thatt seithe evere seycrette[1],
    He save you all and make you parfett and stronge,
    And geven us grace with his marce forto mete!
    For now in grett mesere mankynd ys bownd,
    The sarpent hathe gevin us soo mortall a wonde
    That no creature ys abull us forto reyles
    Tyll thye right uncion[2] of Juda dothe seyse.

(2)

    Then schall moche myrthe and joie in-cresse;
    And the right rote in Isaraell sprynge,
    Thatt schall bryng forthe the greyne off whollenes;   10
    And owt of danger he schall us bryng
    In-to thatt reygeon where he ys kyng,
    Wyche above all othur far dothe a-bownde,
    And thatt cruell Sathan he schall confownde.

(3)

    Where-fore I cum here apon this grownde
    To comforde eyvere creature off birthe;
    For I, Isaye the profet, hathe fownde

1 *Sofferent* sovereign 3 *marce* mercy *mete* meet 6 *reyles* release
9 *rote* root 10 *greyne* grain *off* of

THE SHEARMEN AND TAILORS' PLAY

Many swete matters whereof we ma make myrth
On this same wyse;
For, thogh that Adam be demid to deythe
With all his childur, asse Abell and Seythe,
Yett *Ecce virgo consepeet*[3] –
Loo, where a reymede schall ryse!

(4)

Be-holde, a mayde schall consevye a childe
And gett us more grace then eyver men had,
And hir meydin-[h]od nothing defylid.
Sche ys deputyd to beare the Sun, Almyghte God.
Loo, sufferntis, now ma you be glad,
For of this meydin all we ma be fayne;
For Adam, that now lyis in sorrois full sade,
Hir gloreose birth schall reydeme hym ageyn
From bondage and thrall.
Now be myrre eyvere mon
For this dede bryffly in Isaraell schalbe done,
And before the Fathur in trone,
Thatt schall glade us all.

(5)

More of this matter fayne wolde I meve,
But lengur tyme I have not here for to dwell.
That Lorde that ys marcefull his marce soo in us ma preve
For to sawe owre sollis from the darknes of hell;
And to his blys
He us bryng,
Asse he ys
Bothe lord and kyng,
And shalbe eyverlastyng,
In secula seculorum[4], amen!
    [*Exit Isaiah. Gabriel speaks to Mary.*]

---

23 *reymede* remedy 28 *sufferntis* sovereigns 29 *meydin* maiden *fayne*
glad 33 *myrre* merry 40 *sawe* save

(6)

GABERELL: Hayle, Mare, full of grace!
   Owre Lord God ys with the;
   Above all wemen that eyver wasse,
   Lade, blesside mote thow be!   50

(7)

MARE: All-myght Fathur and King of blys,
   From all dysses thou save me now!
   For inwardely my spretis trubbuld ys,
   Thatt I am amacid and kno nott how.

(8)

GABERELL: Dred the nothyng, meydin, of this;
   From heyvin a-bowe hyddur am I sent
   Of ambassage from that Kyng of blys
   Unto the, lade and virgin reyverent!
   Salutyng the here asse most exselent,
   Whose virtu above all othur dothe abownde.   60
   Wherefore in the grace schalbe fownde;
   For thow schalt conseyve apon this grownd
   The Second Persone of God in trone;
   He wylbe borne of the alone;
   With-owt sin thou schalt hym see.
   Thy grace and thi goodnes wyl neyver be gone,
   But eyver to lyve in virgenete.

(9)

MARE: I marvell soore how thatt mabe.
   Manis cumpany knev I neyver yett
   Nor neyver to do, kast I me,   70
   Whyle thatt owre Lord sendith me my wytt.

(10)

GABERELL: The Wholle Gost in the schall lyght,
   And schado thy soll soo with virtu

---

50 *mote* must   52 *dysses* discomfort   53 *spretis* spirit   54 *amacid* amazed
63 *trone* throne   72 *Wholle* Holy   73 *schado* overshadow   *soll* soul

THE SHEARMEN AND TAILORS' PLAY

From the Fathur thatt ys on hyght.
These wordis, turtill, the[y] be full tru.

(11)

This chylde that of the schalbe borne
Ys the Second Persone in Trenete;
He schall save that wase forlorne
And the fyndis powar dystroie schall he.

(12)

These wordis, lade, full tru the[y] bene, 80
And furthur, lade, here in thy noone lenage
Be-holde Eylesabeth, thy cosyn clene,
The wyche wasse barren and past all age,

(13)

And now with chyld sche hath bene
Syx monethis and more, asse schalbe sene;
Where-for, discomforde the not, Mare,
For to God onpossibull nothyng mabe.

(14)

MARE: Now, and yt be thatt Lordis wyll
Of my bodde to be borne and forto be,
Hys hy pleysuris forto full-fyll 90
Asse his one hande-mayde I submyt me.

(15)

GABERELL: Now blessid be the tyme sett
That thou wast borne in thy degre!
For now ys the knott surely knytt
And God conseyvide in Trenete.

(16)

Now fare-well, lade off myghtis most!
Unto the God-hed I the be-teyche.

75 *turtill* turtle (dove)   81 *noone* own   *lenage* lineage   89 *bodde* body
97 *be-teyche* commit

ENGLISH MYSTERY PLAYS

MARE: Thatt Lorde the gyde in eyvere cost,
And looly he leyde me and be my leyche!
Here the Angell departyth, and Joseff cumyth in and seyth

(17)

JOSOFF: Mare, my wyff soo dere,
How doo ye, dame, and whatt chere
Ys with you this tyde?
MARE: Truly, husebonde, I am here
Owre Lordis wyll forto abyde.

(18)

JOSOFF: Whatt! I troo thatt we be all schent!
Sey, womon, who hath byn here sith I went,
To rage wyth thee?
MARE: Syr, here was nothur man nor mans eyvin,
But only the sond of owre Lorde God in heyvin.
JOSOFF: Sey not soo, womon; for schame, ley be![6]

(19)

Ye be with chyld soo wondurs grett,
Ye nede no more therof to tret
Agense all right.
Forsothe, this chylde, dame, ys not myne.
Alas, that eyver with my nynee
I suld see this syght!

(20)

Tell me, womon, whose ys this chyld?
MARE: Non but youris, husebond soo myld,
And thatt schalbe seyne, [ywis.]
JOSOFF: But myne? Alas, alas! Why sey ye soo?
Wele-awey! Womon, now may I goo,
Be-gyld as many a-nothur ys.

---

98 *cost* place   99 *looly* lowly   *leyche* leech, healer   108 *eyvin* (n) equal
109 *sond* messenger   115 *nynee* eye

THE SHEARMEN AND TAILORS' PLAY

(21)

MARE: Na, truly, sir, ye be not be-gylde,
  Not yet with spott of syn I am not defylde;
  Trust yt well, huse-bonde.
JOSOFF: Huse-bond, in feythe! and that acold![7]
  A! Weylle-awey, Josoff, as thow ar olde!
  Lyke a fole now ma I stand
  And truse[8].
  But, in feyth, Mare, thou art in syn, 130
  Soo moche ase I have cheyrischyd the, dame, and all thi kyn,
  Be-hynd my bake to serve me thus!

(22)

All olde men, insampull take be me –
How I am be-gylid here may you see –
To wed soo yong a chyld.
Now fare-well, Mare, I leyve the here alone –
[Wo] worthe the, dam, and thy warkis ycheone –
For I woll noo-more be [be-gylid]
For frynd nor fooe.
Now of this ded I am soo dull, 140
And off my lyff I am soo full
No farthur ma I goo.

[*He lies down to sleep: an Angel appears to him.*]

(23)

I ANGELL: Aryse up, Josoff, and goo whom ageyne
  Unto Mare, thy wyff, that is soo fre.
  To comford hir loke that thow be fayne,
  For, Josoff, a cleyne meydin ys schee:
  Sche hath conseyvid with-owt any trayne
  The Seycond Person in Trenete;
  Jhesu schalbe hys name, sarten,
  And all thys world sawe schall he; 150
  Be not agast.
JOSOFF: Now, Lorde, I thanke the with hart full sad,

137 *ycheone* every one 143 *whom* home 147 *trayne* deception 150 *sawe* save

349

For of these tythyngis I am soo glad
Thatt all my care awey ys cast;
Wherefore to Mare I woll in hast.
  [*He returns to Mary.*]

(24)

A, Mare, Mare, I knele full loo;
Forgeve me, swete wyff, here in this lond!
Marce, Mare! for now I kno
Of youre good governance and how yt doth stond.

(25)

Thogh that I dyd the mys-name, 160
Marcy, Mare! Whyle I leve
Wyll I neyver, swet wyff, the greve
In ernyst nor in game.
MARE: Now, thatt Lord in heyvin, sir, he you forgyve!
And I do for-geve yoe in hys name
For evermore.
JOSOFF: Now truly, swete wyff, to you I sey the same.

(26)

But now to Bedlem must I wynde
And scho[9] my-self, soo full of care;
And I to leyve you, this grett, behynd – 170
God wott the whyle, dame, how you schuld fare.

(27)

MARE: Na, hardely, husebond, dred ye nothyng;
For I woll walke with you on the wey.
I trust in God, all-myghte Kyng,
To spede right well in owre jurney.

(28)

JOSOFF: Now I thanke you, Mare, of youre goodnes
Thatt ye my wordis woll nott blame;
And syth that to Bedlem we schall us dresse,
Goo we to-gedur in Goddis wholle name.

168 *wynde* go   179 *wholle* holy

THE SHEARMEN AND TAILORS' PLAY

(29)

[*They journey to Bethlehem.*]
Now to Bedlem have we leygis three;   180
The day ys ny spent, yt drawyth toward nyght;
Fayne at your es, dame, I wold that ye schulde be,
For you gro[w]e all werely, yt semyth in my syght.

(30)

MARE: God have marcy, Josoffe, my spowse soo dere;
All profettis herto dothe beyre wyttnes,
The were tyme[10] now draith nere
Thatt my chyld wolbe borne, wyche ys Kyng of blis.

(31)

Unto sum place, Josoff, hyndly me leyde,
Thatt I moght rest me with grace in this tyde.
The lyght of the Fathur over hus both spreyde,   190
And the grace of my Sun with us here a-byde!

(32)

JOSOFF: Loo! blessid Mare, here schall ye lend,
Cheff chosyn of owre Lorde and cleynist in degre;
And I for help to towne woll I wende.
Ys nott this the best, dame? Whatt sey ye?

(33)

MARE: God have marce, Josoff, my huse-bond soo meke!
And hartely I pra you, goo now fro me.
JOSOFF: Thatt schalbe done in hast, Mare soo swete!
The comford of the Wholle Gost leyve I with the.

(34)

Now to Bedlem streyght woll I wynd   200
To gett som helpe for Mare soo free.
Sum helpe of wemmen God may me send,
Thatt Mare, full off grace, pleysid ma be.
[*Elsewhere a Shepherd searches for his sheep.*]

180 *leygis* leagues   182 *es* ease   188 *hyndly* kindly   190 *hus* us   *spreyde* spread   192 *lend* stay   193 *Cheff* chief

(35)

1 PASTOR: Now God that art in Trenete,
 Thow sawe my fellois and me!
 For I kno nott wheyre my scheepe nor the[y] be,
 Thys nyght yt ys soo colde.
 Now ys yt nygh the myddis of the nyght;
 These wedurs ar darke and dym of lyght,
 Thatt of them can hy have noo syght,
 Standyng here on this wold.

(36)

 But now to make there hartis lyght,
 Now wyll I full right
 Stand apon this looe,
 And to them cry with all my myght –
 Full well my voise the[y] kno:
 What hoo! Fellois! Hoo! Hooe! Hoo!
 [*Two more Shepherds appear.*]

(37)

II PASTOR: Hark, Sym, harke! I here owre brother on the looe;
 This ys hys voise, right well I knoo;
 There-fore toward hym lett us goo,
 And follo his voise a-right.
 See, Sym, se, where he doth stond!
 I am ryght glad we have hym fond!
 Brothur, where hast thow byn soo long,
 [And hit ys soo cold this nyght?]

(38)

1 PASTOR: E! Fryndis, ther came a pyrie of wynd with a myst suddenly,
 Thatt forth off my weyis went I,
 And grett heyvenes then made I,
 And wase full sore [afryght].

209 *wedurs* weathers   210 *hy* I   211 *wold* hill   214 *looe* hill   226 *pyrie* gust

THE SHEARMEN AND TAILORS' PLAY

Then forto goo wyst I nott whyddur,   230
But travellid on this loo hyddur and thyddur;
I wasse so were of this cold weddur
That nere past wasse my might.

(39)

III PASTOR: Brethur, now we be past that fryght,
And hit ys far within the nyght,
Full sone woll spryng the day-lyght;
Hit drawith full nere the tyde.
Here awhyle lett us rest,
And repast owreself of the best;
Tyll thatt the sun ryse in the est,   240
Let us all here abyde.

There the Scheppardis drawys furth there meyte and doth eyte and drynk; and asse the[y] drynk, the[y] fynd the star, and sey thus

(40)

Brethur, loke up and behold!
Whatt thyng ys yondur thatt schynith soo bryght?
Asse long ase eyver I have wachid my fold,
Yett sawe I neyver soche a syght
In fyld.
A ha! Now ys cum the tyme that old fathurs hath told,
Thatt in the wyntburs nyght soo cold
A chyld of meydyn borne be he wold
In whom all profeciys schalbe fullfyld.   250

(41)

I PASTOR: Truth yt ys with-owt naye,
Soo seyd the profett Isaye,
Thatt a chylde schuld be borne of a made soo bryght
In wentur ny the schortist dey[11],
Or elis in the myddis of the nyght.

230 *wyst* knew   232 *were* weary

(42)

II PASTOR: Loovid be God, most off myght,
    That owre grace ys to see thatt syght;
    Pray we to hym, ase hit ys right,
    Yff thatt his wyll yt be,
    Thatt we ma have knoleyge of this syngnefocacion   260
    And why hit aperith on this fassion;
    And eyver to hym lett us geve lawdacion,
    In yerthe whyle thatt we be.
    There the Angelis syng 'Glorea in exselsis Deo'.

(43)

III PASTOR: Harke! The[y] synge abo[v]e in the clowdis clere!
    Hard I neyver of soo myrre a quere.
    Now, gentyll brethur, draw we nere
    To here there armonye.
I PASTOR: Brothur, myrth and solas ys cum hus among;
    For be the swettnes of ther songe,
    Goddis Sun ys cum, whom we have lokid for long,   270
    Asse syngnefyith thys star that we do see.
II PASTOR: 'Glore, glorea in exselsis,' that wase ther songe;
    How sey ye, fellois, seyd the[y] not thus?
I PASTOR: Thatt ys wel seyd; now goo we hence
    To worschipe thatt chyld of hy manyffecence,
    And that we ma syng in his presence
    '*Et in tarra pax omynibus*'[12].
    There the Scheppardis syngis 'Ase I owt rodde'[13], and Josoff seyth

(44)

JOSOFF: Now, Lorde, this noise that I do here,
    With this grett solemnete,
    Gretly amendid hath my chere;   280
    I trust hy nevis schortly wolbe.
    There the Angellis syng 'Gloria in exsellsis' ageyne.

260 *syngnefocacion* manifestation 262 *lawdacion* praise 263 *yerthe* earth 265 *myrre* merry *quere* choir 281 *nevis* news

THE SHEARMEN AND TAILORS' PLAY

(45)

MARE: A! Josoff, husebond, cum heddur anon;
My chylde ys borne that ys Kyng of blys.
JOSOFFE: Now welcum to me, the Makar of mon,
With all the omage thatt I con;
Thy swete mothe here woll I kys.

(46)

MARE: A! Josoff, husebond, my chyld waxith cold,
And we have noo fyre to warme hym with.
JOSOFF: Now in my narmys I schall hym fold,
Kyng of all kyngis be fyld and be fryth;   290
He myght have had bettur, and hymselfe wold,
Then the breythyng of these bestis to warme hym with.

(47)

MARE: Now, Josoff, my husbond, fet heddur my chyld,
The Maker off man, and hy Kyng of blys.
JOSOFF: That schalbe done anon, Mare soo myld,
For the brethyng of these bestis hath warmyd [hym] well,
    i-wys.
    [*Angels appear to the Shepherds.*]

(48)

I ANGELL: Hyrd-men hynd,
Drede ye nothyng
Off thys star thatt ye do se;
For thys same morne
Godis Sun ys borne   300
In Bedlem of a meydin fre.

(49)

II ANGELL: Hy you thyddur in hast;
Yt ys hys wyll ye schall hym see
Lyinge in a crybbe of pore reypaste[14],
Yett of Davithis lyne cumon ys hee.
    [*The Shepherds approach Mary and the Child.*]

---

286 *mothe* mouth   289 *narmys* arms   290 *fryth* woods   297 *hynd* gentle
306 *cumon* come

(50)

I PASTOR: Hayle, mayde-modur and wyff soo myld!
  Asse the Angell seyd, soo have we fonde.
  I have nothyng to present with thi chylde
  But my pype; hold, hold, take yt in thy hond; 310
  Where-in moche pleysure that I have fond;
  And now, to oonowre thy gloreose byrthe,
  Thow schallt yt have to make the myrthe.

(51)

II PASTOR: Now, hayle be thow, chyld, and thy dame!
  For in a pore loggyn here art thow leyde,
  Soo the Angell seyde and tolde us thy name;
  Holde, take thow here my hat on thy hedde!
  And now off won thyng thow art well sped,
  For weddur thow hast noo nede to complayne,
  For wynd, ne sun, hayle, snoo and rayne. 320

(52)

III PASTOR: Hayle be thow, Lorde, over watur and landis!
  For thy cumyng all we ma make myrthe.
  Have here my myttens to pytt on thi hondis;
  Othur treysure have I non to present the with.

(53)

MARE: Now, herdmen hynd,
  For youre comyng
  To my chyld schall I prae,
  Asse he ys heyvin Kyng,
  To grant you his blessyng,
  And to hys blys that ye may wynd 330
  At your last day.
    *There the Scheppardis syngith ageyne[15] and goth forthe of the
    place; and the ij Profettis cumyth in and seyth thus*

---

312 *oonowre* honour   315 *loggyn* lodging

THE SHEARMEN AND TAILORS' PLAY

(54)

1 PROFETA[16]: Novellis, novellis
Of wonderfull marvellys,
Were hy and defuce unto the heryng!
Asse scripture tellis,
These strange novellis
To you I bryng.

(55)

11 PROFETA: Now hartely, sir, I desyre to knoo,
Yff hytt wolde pleyse you forto schoo,
Of whatt maner a thyng.   340
1 PROFETA: Were mystecall unto youre heryng –
Of the natevete off a kyng.

(56)

11 PROFETA: Of a kyng? Whence chuld he cum?
1 PROFETA: From that reygend ryall and mighty mancion,
The sede seylesteall and heyvinly wysedome;
The Seycond Person and Godis one Sun
For owre sake now ys man be-cum.

(57)

This godly spere
Desendid here
In-to a virgin clere,   350
Sche on-defyld;
Be whose warke obskeure
Owre frayle nature
Ys now begilde.
11 PROFETA: Why, hathe sche a chyld?

(58)

1 PROFETA: E! Trust hyt well;
And never the las
Yet ys sche a mayde evin asse sche wasse,
And hir Sun the King of Isaraell.

₃₃₂ *Novellis* news   ₃₃₄ *Were* very, truly   *defuce* difficult   ₃₄₁ *mystecall*
mystical, ?mysterious   ₃₄₄ *reygend* region   ₃₄₅ *sede* seat   ₃₄₈ *spere* spear

(59)

II PROFETA: A wondur-full marvell
How thatt ma be,
And far dothe exsell
All owre capasete:
How thatt the Trenete
Of soo hy regallete,
Schuld jonyd be
Unto owre mortallete!

(60)

I PROFETA: Of his one grett marce,
As ye shall se the exposyssion,
Throgh whose umanyte
All Adamis progene
Reydemyd schalbe owt of perdyssion.

(61)

Syth man did offend
Who schuld amend
But the seyd mon and no nothur?
For the wyche cawse he
Incarnate wold be
And lyve in mesere asse manis one brothur[17].

(62)

II PROFETA: Syr, unto the Deyite,
I beleve parfettle,
Onpossibull to be there ys nothyng;
How be yt this warke
Unto me is darke
In the opperacion or wyrkyng.
I PROFETA: Whatt more reypriff
Ys unto belyff
Then to be dowtyng?

373 *Syth* since   385 *reypriff* reproof

THE SHEARMEN AND TAILORS' PLAY

(63)

II PROFETA: Yet dowtis oftymis hathe derevacion.
I PROFETA: Thatt ys be the meynes of comenecacion
  Of trawthis to have a deu probacion 390
  Be the same dowts reysoning.
II PROFETA: Then to you this won thyng:
  Of whatt nobull and hy lenage ys schee
  Thatt myght this verabull princis modur be?

(64)

I PROFETA: Ondowtid sche ys cum of hy parrage,
  Of the howse of Davith and Salamon the sage;
  And won off the same lyne joynid to hir be mareage;
  Of whose trybe
  We do subscrybe
  This chy[l]dis lenage. 400

(65)

II PROFETA: And why in thatt wysse?
I PROFETA: For yt wasse the gysse
  To conte the parant on the manys lyne,
  And not on the feymy[ny]ne,
  Amonst us here in Isaraell.
II PROFETA: Yett can I nott aspy be noo wysse
  How thys chylde borne schuldbe with-ow[t] naturis prejudyse.
I PROFETA: Nay, no prejudyse unto nature, I dare well sey;
  For the kyng of nature may
  Have all at his one wyll. 410
  Dyd not the powar of God
  Make Aronis rod[18]
  Beyre frute in on day?

(66)

II PROFETA: Truth yt ys in-ded.
I PROFETA: Then loke you and rede.

---

388 *derevacion* cause 389 *comenecacion* discussion 390 *deu* due *probacion* proof 395 *parrage* descent 399 *subscrybe* attribute 402 *gysse* custom 415 *rede* understand, mark

II PROFETA: A! I perseyve the sede
    Where apon thatt you spake.
    Yt wasse for owre nede
    That he frayle nature did take,
    And his blod he schuld schede   420
    Amens forto make
    For owre transegression;
    Ase yt ys seyd in profece
    That of the lyne of Jude
    Schuld spryng a right Messe
    Be whom all wee
    Schall have reydemcion.

(67)

I PROFETA: Sir, now ys the tyme cum
    And the date there-of run
    Off his Natevete.   430
II PROFETA: Yett I beseke you hartele
    That ye wold schoo me how
    Thatt this strange nowelte
    Were broght unto you.

(68)

I PROFETA: This othur nyght soo cold,
    Hereby apon a wolde,
    Scheppardis wachyng there fold
    In the nyght soo far,
    To them aperid a star
    And eyver yt drew them nar;   440
    Wyche star the[y] did behold
    Bryghter the[y] sey M folde
    Then the sun so clere
    In his mydday spere,
    And the[y] these tythyngis tolde.

---

425 *Messe* Messiah   433 *nowelte* news   440 *nar* near   444 *spere* sphere

THE SHEARMEN AND TAILORS' PLAY

(69)

II PROFETA: Whatt, seycretly?
I PROFETA: Na, na, hardely;
  The[y] made there-of no conseil,
  For the song ase lowde
  Ase eyver the[y] cowde   450
  Presyng the kyng of Isaraell.
II PROFETA: Yett do I marvell
  In whatt pallays[19] or castell
  These herdmen dyd hym see.

(70)

I PROFETA: Nothur in hallis nor yett in bowris
  Born wold he not be,
  Nother in castellis nor yet in towris
  That semly were to se;

(71)

  But att hys Fathurs wyll
  The profeci to full-fyll,   460
  Be-twyxt an ox and an as
  Jesus, this Kyng, borne he was.
  Heyvin he bryng us tyll!

(72)

II PROFETA: Sir, a! but when these scheppardis had seyne hym there,
  In-to whatt place did the[y] repeyre?
I PROFETA: Forthe the[y] went and glad the[y] were;
  Going the[y] did syng;
  With myrthe and solas the[y] made good chere
  For joie of that new tythyng;

(73)

  And aftur, asse I hard the[m] tell,   470
  He reywardid them full well:

453 *pallays* palace

361

He graunt them hevyn ther-in to dwell;
In are the[y] gon with joie and myrthe,
And there songe hit ys 'Neowell.'
> *There the Profettis gothe furthe and Erod cumyth in, and the Messenger.*

(74)

NONCEOSE: Faytes[20] pais, dnyis, baronys de grande reynowne!
Payis, seneoris, schevaleris de nooble posance!
Pays, gentis homos, companeonys petis egrance!
Je vos command dugard treytus sylance.
Payis, tanque vottur nooble Roie syre ese presance!
Que nollis persone ese non fawis perwynt dedfferance, 480
Nese harde de frappas; mayis gardus toto paceance –
Mayis gardus voter seneor to cor reyverance;
Car elat vottur Roie toto puysance.
Anon de leo, pase tos! je vose cummande;
E lay Roie Erott: la grandeaboly vos umport.

(75)

ERODE: *Qui statis in Jude et Rex Iseraell*[21],
And the myghttyst conquerowre that eyver walkid on grownd;
For I am evyn he thatt made bothe hevin and hell[22],
And of my myghte powar holdith up this world rownd.
Magog and Madroke[23], bothe the[m] did I confownde, 490
And with this bryght bronde there bonis I brak onsunder,
Thatt all the wyde worlde on those rappis did wonder.

(76)

I am the cawse of this grett lyght and thunder;
Ytt ys throgh my fure that the[y] soche noyse dothe make.
My feyrefull contenance the clowdis so doth incumbur
That oftymis for drede ther-of the verre yerth doth quake.
Loke, when I with males this bryght brond doth schake,

491 *bronde* sword   492 *rappis* blows   494 *fure* fury   497 *males* malice

THE SHEARMEN AND TAILORS' PLAY

All the whole world from the north to the sowthe
I ma them dystroie with won worde of my mowthe!

(77)

> To reycownt unto you myn inneumerabull substance – 500
> Thatt were to moche for any tong to tell;
> For the whole Orent ys under myn obbeydeance,
> And prynce am I of purgatorre and cheff capten of hell;
> And those tyraneos trayturs be force ma I compell.
> Myne enmyis to vanquese and evyn to dust them dryve,
> And with a twynke of myn iee not won to be lafte alyve.

(78)

> Behold my contenance and my colur,
> Bryghtur then the sun in the meddis of the dey.
> Where can you have a more grettur succur
> Then to behold my person that ys soo gaye? 510
> My fawcun and my fassion, with my gorgis araye –
> He thatt had the grace all-wey ther-on to thynke,
> Lyve the[y] myght all-wey with-owt othur meyte or drynke.

(79)

> And thys my tryomfande fame most hylist dothe a-bownde
> Throgh-owt this world in all reygeons abrod,
> Reysemelyng the faver of thatt most myght Mahownd;
> From Jubytor be desent and cosyn to the grett God,
> And namyd the most reydowndid kyng Eyrodde,
> Wyche thatt all pryncis hath under subjeccion
> And all there whole powar undur my proteccion. 520

(80)

> And therefore, my hareode here, callid Calcas,
> Warne thow eyvere porte thatt noo schyppis a-ryve,
> Nor also aleond stranger throg[h] my realme pas,

506 *twynke* blink   511 *fawcun* sword   *gorgis* gorgeous   514 *hylist*
?mighty   516 *Reysemelyng* resembling   *faver* appearance   521 *hareode*
herald   523 *aleond* alien

But the[y] for there truage do pay markis fyve.
Now spede the forth hastele,
For the[y] thatt wyll the contrare
Apon a galowse hangid schalbe,
And, be Mahownde, of me the[y] gett noo grace!

(81)

NONCIOS: Now, lord and mastur, in all the hast
Thy worethe wyll ytt schall be wroght,
And thy ryall cuntreyis schalbe past
In asse schort tyme ase can be thoght.

(82)

ERODE: Now schall owre regeons throgh-owt be soght
In eyvere place bothe est and west;
Yff any katyffis to me be broght,
Yt schalbe nothyng for there best.
And the whyle thatt I do resst,
Trompettis, viallis, and othur armone
Schall bles the wakyng of my maieste.
Here Erod goth awey and the iij Kyngis speykyth in the strete.

(83)

I REX: Now blessid be God of his swet sonde,
For yondur a feyre bryght star I do see!
Now ys he comon, us a-monge,
Asse the profettis seyd thatt yt schuld be.

(84)

A seyd there schuld a babe be borne,
Comyng of the rote of Jesse,
To sawe mankynd that wasse for-lorne;
And truly comen now ys he.

---

524 *truage* tribute   530 *worethe* worthy   535 *katyffis* wretches
538 *viallis* viols   *armone* harmony   540 *sonde* message   544 *A* he

THE SHEARMEN AND TAILORS' PLAY

(85)

    Reyverence and worschip to hym woll I do
    Asse God and man, thatt all made of noght.
    All the profettis acordid and seyd evyn soo,   550
    That with hys presseos blod mankynd schuld be boght.

(86)

    He grant me grace,
    Be yonder star that I see,
    And in-to thatt place
    Bryng me,
    Thatt I ma hym worschipe with umellete
    And se hys gloreose face.

(87)

II REX: Owt of my wey I deme thatt I am,
    For toocuns of thys cuntrey can I non see;
    Now, God, thatt on yorth madist man,   560
    Send me sum knoleyge where thatt I be!

(88)

    Yondur, me thynke, a feyre, bryght star I see,
    The wyche be-tocunyth the byrth of a chyld
    Thatt hedur ys cum to make man fre;
    He borne of a mayde, and sche nothyng defyld.

(89)

    To worschip thatt chyld ys myn in-tent;
    Forth now wyll I take my wey.
    I trust sum cumpany God hathe me sent,
    For yonder I se a kyng labur on the wey;

(90)

    To-warde hym now woll I ryde.   570
    Harke! Cumly kyng, I you pray,
    In-to whatt cost wyll ye thys tyde[24],
    Or weddur lyis youre jurney?

---

556 *umellete* humility   559 *toocuns* landmarks   560 *yorth* earth

(91)

I REX: To seke a chylde ys myne in-tent
Of whom the profetis hathe ment;
The tyme ys cum, now ys he sent,
Be yondur star here ma [you] see.

II REX: Sir, I prey you, with your lysence,
To ryde with you unto his presence;
To hym wyll I offur frank-in-sence, 580
For the hed of all Whole Churche schall he be.

(92)

III REX: I ryde wanderyng in weyis wyde,
Over montens and dalis; I wot not where I am.
Now, Kyng of all kyngis, send me soche gyde
Thatt I myght have knoleyge of thys cuntreys name.

(93)

A! yondur I se a syght, be-semyng all afar[25],
The wyche be-tocuns sum nevis, ase I troo;
Asse me thynke, a chyld peryng in a stare.
I trust he be cum that schall defend us from woo.

(94)

To kyngis yondur I see, 590
And to them woll I ryde
Forto have there cumpane;
I trust the[y] wyll me abyde.

(95)

Hayle, cumly kyngis augent!
Good surs, I pray you, whedder ar ye ment?

I REX: To seke a chylde ys owre in-tent,
Wyche be-tocuns yonder star, asse ye ma see.

II REX: To hym I purpose thys present.

III REX: Surs, I pray you, and thatt ryght umblee,
With you thatt I ma ryde in cumpane. 600

581 *Whole* Holy 583 *dalis* dales 587 *nevis* news 588 *peryng* appearing
594 *augent* ?white

THE SHEARMEN AND TAILORS' PLAY

[ALL:] To all-myghte God now prey we
    Thatt hys pressiose persone we ma se.
    Here Erode cumyth in ageyne and the Messengere seyth

(96)

NUNCIOS: Hayle, lorde most off myght!
    Thy commandement ys right;
    In-to thy land ys comyn this nyght
    iij kyngis and with them a grett cumpany.
EROD: Whatt make those kyngis in this cuntrey?
NONCIOS: To seke a kyng and a chyld, the[y] sey.
ERODE: Of whatt age schuld he bee?
NONCIOS: Skant twellve deyis old fulle[26].   610

(97)

EROD: And wasse he soo late borne?
NONCIOS: E! syr, soo the[y] schode me, thys same dey in the morne.
EROD: Now, in payne of deyth, bryng them me beforne.
    And there-fore, harrode, now hy the in hast,
    In all spede thatt thow were dyght,
    Or thatt those kyngis the cuntrey be past;
    Loke thow bryng them all iij before my syght;

(98)

    And in Jerusalem inquere more of that chyld.
    But I warne the that thy wordis be mylde,
    For there must thow hede and crafte wey[lde][27]   620
    How to for-do his powere; and those iij kyngis shalbe begild.

(99)

NONCIOS: Lorde, I am redde att youre byddyng
    To sarve the ase my lord and kyng;
    For joye there-of, loo, how I spryng
    With lyght hart and fresche gamboldyng
    Alofte here on this molde!

614 *harrode* herald   620 *weylde* use   626 *molde* earth

ERODE: Then sped the forthe hastely
And loke that thow beyre the eyvinly;
And also I pray the hartely
Thatt thow doo comand me 630
Bothe to yong and olde.
[*The Messenger goes to the Kings.*]

(100)

NUNCIOS: Hayle, syr kyngis, in youre degre;
Erood, kyng of these cuntreyis wyde,
Desyrith to speyke with you all thre,
And for youre comyng he dothe abyde.

(101)

1 REX: Syr, att his wyll we be ryght bayne.
Hy us, brethur, unto thatt lordis place;
To speyke with hym we wold be fayne;
Thatt chyld thatt we seke, he grant us of his grace!
[*They go to Herod.*]

(102)

NUNCIOS: Hayle, lorde with-owt pere! 640
These iij kyngis here have we broght.
ERODE: Now welcum, syr kyngis, all in fere;
But of my bryght ble, surs, bassche ye noght!

(103)

Sir kyngis, ase I undurstand,
A star hathe gydid you into my land,
Where-in grett harie ye have fonde
Be reysun of hir beymis bryght.
Wherefore I pray you hartely
The vere truthe thatt ye wold sertefy,
How long yt ys surely 650
Syn of that star you had furst syght.

630 *comand* commend   643 *ble* complexion   *bassche* be abashed
646 *harie* distress

THE SHEARMEN AND TAILORS' PLAY

(104)

I REX: Sir kynge, the vere truthe to sey
And forto schoo you ase hit ys best,
This same ys evin the xijth dey
Syth yt aperid to us be west.

(105)

ERODE: Brethur, then ys there no more to sey,
But with hart and wyll kepe ye your jurney
And cum whom by me this same wey[28],
Of your nevis thatt I myght knoo.
You schall tryomfe in this cuntre   660
And with grett conquorde bankett with me,
And thatt chyld myself then woll I see,
And honor hym also.

(106)

II REX: Sir, youre commandement we woll fullfyll,
And humbly abaye owreself there-tyll.
He thatt weldith all thyng at wyll
The redde way hus teyche,
Sir kyng, thatt we ma passe your land in pes!
ERODE: Yes, and walke softely eyvin at your one es;

(107)

Youre pase-porte for a C deyis   670
Here schall you have of clere cummand;
Owre reme to labur any weyis
Here schall you have be spesschall grante.

(108)

III REX: Now fare-well, kyng of hy degre,
Humbly of you owre leyve we take.

---

661 *conquorde* concord *bankett* (v) feast 665 *abaye* obey 667 *redde* wisest 672 *reme* realm

369

ERODE: Then ad[i]eu, sir kyngis all thre;
    And whyle I lyve, be bold of me!
    There ys nothyng in this cuntre
    But for youre one ye schall yt take.
       [*Exeunt the three Kings.*]

(109)

    Now these iij kyngis are gon on ther wey;   680
    On-wysely and on-wyttely have the[y] all wroghte.
    When the[y] cum ageyne, the[y] schall dy that same dey,
    And thus these vyle wreychis to deyth the[y] schalbe broght –
    Soche ys my lykyng.
    He that agenst my lawis wyll hold,
    Be he kyng or keysar neyver soo bold,
    I schall them cast in-to caris cold,
    And to deyth I schall them bryng.
       There Erode goth his weyis and the iij Kyngis cum in ageyne.

(110)

I REX: O blessid God, moche ys thy myght!
    Where ys this star thatt gave us lyght?   690

(111)

II REX: Now knele we downe here in this presence,
    Be-sekyng that Lord of hy mangnefecens
    That we ma see his hy exsellence,
    Yff thatt his swet wyll be.

(112)

III REX: Yondur, brothur, I see the star,
    Where-by I kno he ys nott far;
    Therefore, lordis, goo we nar
    Into this pore place.
       There the iij Kyngis gois in-to the jesen, to Mare and hir child.

692 *Be-sekyng* beseeching   697 *nar* near   698 (SD) *jesen* childbed

THE SHEARMEN AND TAILORS' PLAY

(113)

I REX: Hayle, Lorde thatt all this worlde hathe wroght!
Hale, God and man to-gedur in fere! 700
For thow hast made all thyng of noght,
Albe-yt thatt thow lyist porely here;
A cupe-full [of] golde here I have the broght,
In toconyng thow art with-out pere.

II REX: Hayle be thow, Lorde of hy mangnyffecens!
In toconyng of preste[h]od and dyngnete of offece,
To the I offur a cupe-full off in-sence,
For yt be-hovith the to have soche sacrefyce.

(114)

III REX: Hayle be thow, Lorde longe lokid fore!
I have broght the myre for mortalete, 710
In to-cunyng thow schalt mankynd restore
To lyff be thy deyth apon a tre.

(115)

MARE: God have marce, kyngis, of yowre goodnes;
Be the gydyng of the godhed hidder ar ye sent;
The provyssion off my swete Sun your weyis whom reydres,
And gostely reywarde you for youre present!
    [*Leaving the Child, they lie down to rest.*]

(116)

I REX: Syr kyngis, aftur owre promes
Whome be Erode I must nedis goo.
II REX: Now truly, brethur, we can noo las,
But I am soo for-wachid I wott not wat to do. 720

(117)

III REX: Ryght soo am I; where-fore, I you pray,
Lett all us rest us awhyle upon this grownd.
I REX: Brethur, your seying ys right well unto my pay.
The grace of thatt swet chylde save us all sownde!
    [*As they sleep the Angel appears.*]

---

710 *myre* myrrh   715 *whom* home *reydres* direct   720 *for-wachid* exhausted   723 *pay* (n) content

371

(118)

ANGELLUS: Kyng of Tawrus, Sir Jespar,
Kyng of Arraby, Sir Balthasar,
Melchor, Kyng of Aginare[29],
To you now am I sent.
For drede of Eyrode, goo you west whom;
In-to those parties when ye cum downe, 730
Ye schalbe byrrid with gret reynownne;
The Wholle Gost thys knoleyge hath sent.
[*Exit.*]

(119)

I REX: Awake, sir kyngis, I you praye,
For the voise of an angell I hard in my dreyme.
II REX: Thatt ys full tru thatt ye do sey,
For he reyherssid owre names playne.

(120)

III REX: He bad thatt we schuld goo downe be west
For drede of Eyrodis fawls be-traye.
I REX: Soo forto do, yt ys the best;
The Child that we have soght, gyde us the wey! 740

(121)

Now fare-well, the feyrist of schapp so swete!
And thankid be Jhesu of his sonde,
Thatt we iij to-geder soo suddenly schuld mete,
That dwell soo wyde and in straunge lond,

(122)

And here make owre presentacion
Unto this kyngis son, clensid soo cleyne,
And to his moder for owre salvacion;
Of moche myrth now ma we meyne,
Thatt we soo well hath done this obblacion.

731 *byrrid* buried   741 *feyrist* fairest   *schapp* form   748 *meyne* enjoy

THE SHEARMEN AND TAILORS' PLAY

(123)

II REX: Now farewell, Sir Jaspar, brothur, to you,   750
Kyng of Tawrus the most worthe;
Sir Balthasar, also to you I bow;
And I thanke you bothe of youre good cumpany
Thatt we togeddur have had.
He thatt made us to mete on hyll,
I thanke hym now and eyver I wyll;
For now may we goo with-owt yll,
And off owre offerynge be full [glad].

(124)

III REX: Now syth thatt we must nedly goo
For drede of Erode thatt ys soo wrothe,   760
Now fare-well, brothur, and brothur also,
I take my leve here at you bothe
This dey on fete.
Now he thatt made us to mete on playne
And offur to Mare in hir jeseyne,
He geve us grace in heyvin agayne
All to-geyder to mete!

[*Exeunt. Herod and his Court re-appear.*]

(125)

NUNCIOS: Hayle, kynge, most worthist in wede!
Hayle, manteinar of curtese throgh all this world wyde!
Hayle, the most myghtyst that eyver bestrod a stede!   770
Ha[y]ll, most monfullist mon in armor man to abyde!
Hayle, in thyne hoonowre!
Thesse iij kyngis that forthe were sent
And schuld have cum ageyne before the here present,
Another wey, lorde, whom the[y] went,
Contrare to thyn honowre.

(126)

ERODE: A-nothur wey? owt! owt! owtt!
Hath those fawls trayturs done me this ded?

763 *fete* feet   768 *wede* clothing   771 *monfullist* most manly   778 *ded* deed

I stampe! I stare! I loke all abowtt!
Myght I them take, I schuld them bren at a glede! 780
I rent! I rawe! and now run I wode!
A, thatt these velen trayturs hath mard this my mode!
The[y] schalbe hangid yf I ma cum them to!
  Here Erode ragis in the pagond and in the strete also[30].
E! and thatt kerne of Bedlem, he schalbe ded,
And thus schall I for-do his profece.
How sey you, sir knyghtis? ys not this the best red,
Thatt all yong chyldur for this schuld be dede,
Wyth sworde to be slayne?
Then schall I, Erod, lyve in lede,
And all folke me dowt and drede, 790
And offur to me bothe gold, rychesse, and mede;
Thereto wyll the[y] be full fayne.

(127)

I MYLES: My lorde, kyng Erode be name,
Thy wordis agenst my wyll schalbe;
To see soo many yong chylder dy ys schame;
Therefore consell ther-to gettis thou non of me.

(128)

II MYLES: Well seyd, fello, my trawth I plyght.
Sir kyng, perseyve right well you may,
Soo grett a morder to see of yong frute
Wyll make a rysyng in thi noone cuntrey. 800

(129)

ERODE: A rysyng! Owt! owt! owt!
  There Erode ragis ageyne and then seyth thus
Owt! velen wrychis, har apon you I cry!
My wyll utturly loke that yt be wroght,
Or apon a gallowse bothe you schall dy,
Be Mahownde most myghtyste, that me dere hath boght!

---

780 *bren* burn   *glede* fire   781 *rawe* rave   782 *velen* villainous
784 *kerne* wretch   789 *lede* kingdom   800 *noone* own   802 *har* ruin

THE SHEARMEN AND TAILORS' PLAY

(130)

I MYLES: Now, cruell Erode, syth we schall do this dede!
Your wyll nedefully in this realme muste be wroght;
All the chylder of that age dy the[y] must nede;
Now with all my myght the[y] schall be upsoght.

(131)

II MYLES: And I woll sweyre here apon your bryght sworde,   810
All the chylder thatt I fynd, sclayne the[y] schalbe;
Thatt make many a moder to wepe and be full sore aferde
In owre armor bryght when the[y] hus see.

(132)

ERODE: Now you have sworne, forth that ye goo,
And my wyll thatt ye wyrke bothe be dey and nyght,
And then wyll I for fayne trypp lyke a doo.
But whan the[y] be ded I warne you bryng ham be-fore my
  syght.
  [*Exeunt Herod and Soldiers. The Angel appears to Mary
  and Joseph.*]

(133)

ANGELLUS: Mare and Josoff[31], to you I sey,
Swete word from the Fathur I bryng you full ryght:
Owt of Bedlem in-to Eygype forth goo ye the wey   820
And with you take the King, full of myght,
For drede of Eroddis rede!
JOSOFF: A-ryse up, Mare, hastely and sone;
Owre Lordis wyll nedys must be done,
Lyke ase the Angell us bad.

(134)

MARE: Mekely, Josoff, my none spowse,
Towarde that cuntrey let us reypeyre;
Att Eygyp [to sum cun off[32]] howse,
God grant hus grace saff to cum there!
  Here the Wemen cum in wythe there chyldur, syngyng[33]
  them; and Mare and Josoff goth awey cleyne.

809 *upsoght* searched out   816 *doo* doe   826 *none* own

(135)

I WOMAN: I lolle my chylde wondursly swete, 830
 And in my narmis I do hyt kepe,
 Be-cawse thatt yt schuld not crye.
II WOMAN: Thatt babe thatt ys borne in Bedlem, so meke,
 He save my chyld and me from velany!

(136)

III WOMAN: Be styll, be styll, my lyttull chylde!
 That Lorde of lordis save bothe the and me!
 For Erode hath sworne with wordis wyld
 Thatt all yong chyldur sclayne the[y] schalbe.

(137)

I MYLES: Sey ye, wyddurde wyvis, whydder ar ye a-wey?
 What beyre you in youre armis nedis must we se. 840
 Yff the[y] be man-chyldur, dy the[y] must this dey,
 For at Eroddis wyll all thyng must be.

(138)

II MYLES: And I in handis wonys them hent,
 Them forto sley noght woll I spare;
 We must full-fyll Erodis commandement,
 Elis be we asse trayturs and cast all in care.

(139)

I WOMAN: Sir knyghtis, of youre curtessee,
 Thys dey schame not youre chevaldre,
 But on my child have pytte
 For my sake in this styde; 850
 For a sympull sclaghtur yt were to sloo
 Or to wyrke soche a chyld woo,
 That can noder speyke nor goo,
 Nor never harme did.

---

830 *lolle* lull   839 *wyddurde* ?withered, ?widowed   843 *wonys* once *hent* seize   848 *chevaldre* chivalry

THE SHEARMEN AND TAILORS' PLAY

(140)

II WOMAN: He thatt sleyis my chyld in syght,
Yff thatt my strokis on hym ma lyght,
Be he skwyar or knyght,
I hold hym but lost.
Se, thow fawls losyngere,
A stroke schalt thow beyre me here[34]   860
And spare for no cost.

(141)

III WOMAN: Sytt he neyver soo hy in saddull,
But I schall make his braynis addull,
And here with my pott-ladull
With hym woll I fyght.
I schall ley on hym a[s] thogh I wode were,
With thys same womanly geyre;
There schall noo man steyre,
Wheddur thatt he be kyng or knyght.
[They kill the boys.]

(142)

I MYLES: Who hard eyver soche a cry   870
Of wemen thatt there chyldur have lost
And grettly reybukyng chewaldry
Throgh-owt this reme in eyvere cost,
Wyche many a mans lyff ys lyke to cost?
For thys grett wreyche that here ys done
I feyre moche wengance ther-off woll cum.

(143)

II MYLES: E! brothur, soche talis may we not tell;
Where-fore to the kyng lett us goo,
For he ys lyke to beyre the perell,
Wyche wasse the cawser that we did soo.   880

---

857 *skwyar* squire   859 *losyngere* flatterer   867 *geyre* gear   868 *steyre* stir   875 *wreyche* evil   879 *perell* peril

Yett must the[y] all be broght hym to
With waynis and waggyns fully fryght;
I tro there wolbe a carefull syght.
   [*They go to Herod.*]

(144)

I MYLES: Loo, Eyrode, kyng, here mast thow see
How many M thatt we have slayne.
II MYLES: And nedis thy wyll full-fyllid must be;
There ma no mon sey there-ageyne.
   [*Enter Messenger.*]

(145)

NUNCIOS: Eyrode, kyng, I schall the tell,
All thy dedis ys cum to noght;
This chyld ys gone in-to Eygipte to dwell.   890
Loo, sir, in thy none land what wondurs byn wroght!

(146)

EROD: Into Eygipte? Alas, for woo!
Lengur in lande here I canot abyde;
Saddull my palfrey, for in hast wyll I goo.
Aftur yondur trayturs now wyll I ryde,
Them for to sloo.
Now all men hy fast
In-to Eygipte in hast!
All thatt cuntrey woll I tast,
Tyll I ma cum them to.   900

   Fynes lude de taylars and scharmen[35].

882 *waynis* carts *fryght* loaded 883 *carefull* full of care 896 *sloo* slay
899 *tast* search

THE SHEARMEN AND TAILORS' PLAY

Theise songes belonge to the Taylors and Shearemens Pagant. The first and the laste the Shepheards singe, and the second or middlemost the Women singe.

Song I

As I out rode this enderes night,
Of thre ioli sheppardes I saw a sight,
And all a-bowte there fold a star shone bright;
   They sange terli terlow;
   So mereli the sheppards ther pipes can blow.

Song II

Lully lulla, thow littell tine child,
By, by, lully lullay, thow littell tyne child,
   By, by, lully lullay!

O sisters too,
How may we do
   For to preserve this day
This pore yongling,
For whom we do singe
   By, by, lully lullay?

Herod, the king,
In his raging,
   Chargid he hath this day
His men of might
In his owne sight
   All yonge children to slay –

That wo is me,
Pore child, for thee,
   And ever morne and [may]
For thi parting
Nether say nor singe,
   By, by, lully lullay.

1 *enderes* just past

Song III

Doune from heaven, from heaven so hie,
Of angeles ther came a great companie;
With mirthe and ioy and great solemnitye
   The[y] sange terly terlow;
   So mereli the sheppards ther pipes can blow.

21. John the Baptist

YORK 21: BARBOURS

The text of this play corresponds to Burton's list. It appears to be one of the older elements. There are signs in marginal notes that some parts were revised, but in substance the play is simple. It relies upon Matthew 3 1–17, particularly in relation to John's reluctance to baptize Christ because Christ was not in need of it. Thus it expresses the need for Christ to present himself as human. It also seeks to justify baptism as a feature of the life of the Church.

ಐಐ

[*Scene: by the River Jordan.*]

(1)

JOHANNES: Almighty God and Lord verray,
   Full woundyrfull is mannys lesyng,
For yf I preche tham day be day,
   And telle tham, Lorde, of thy comyng,
     That all has wrought,
Men are so dull that my preching
     Serves of noght.

(2)

   When I have, Lord, in the name of the
Baptiste the folke in watir clere,
Than have I saide that aftir me
Shall he come that has more powere
     Than I to taste;
He schall giffe baptyme more entire
     In fire and gaste.

1 *verray* true   2 *lesyng* lying   12 *taste* test, feel   14 *gaste* spirit

ENGLISH MYSTERY PLAYS

(3)

> Thus am I comen in message right,
> And be fore-reyner in certayne
> In witnesse-bering of that light,
> The wiche schall light in ilka a man
>   That is comand
> In-to this worlde[1]; nowe whoso can
>   May undirstande.

(4)

> Thegh folke had farly of my fare
> And what I was full faste thei spied;
> They askid yf I a prophete ware
> And I saide 'nay': but sone I wreyede
>   High aperte[2].
> I saide I was a voyce that cryede
>   Here in deserte.

(5)

> 'Loke thou make the redy,' ay saide I,
> 'Un-to oure lord God most of myght,
> That is that thou be clene haly,
> In worde, in werke, ay redy dight
>   Agayns oure Lord,
> With parfitte liffe that ilke a wight
>   Be well restored.

(6)

> For if we be clene in levyng,
> Oure bodis are Goddis tempyll than,
> In the whilke he will make his dwellyng;
> Ther-fore be clene, bothe wiffe and man.
>   This is my reed;
> God will make in yowe haly than
>   His wonnyng-steed.

---

16 *fore-reyner* fore-runner   22 *Thegh* those   *farly* wonder   *fare* doings   25 *wreyede* showed forth, revealed   26 *aperte* openly   32 *dight* prepared   38 *whilke* which   40 *reed* advice   42 *wonnyng-steed* dwelling-place

JOHN THE BAPTIST

(7)

And if ye sette all youre delyte
In luste and lykyng of this liff,
Than will he turne fro yow als tyte
By-cause of synne, boyth of man and wiffe,
    And fro you flee,
For with whome that synne is riffe
    Will God noght be'.

(8)

    [*Two Angels appear.*]
I ANGELUS: Thou, John, take tente what I schall saye;   50
I brynge the tythandis wondir gode.
My lorde Jesus schall come this day
Fro Galylee un-to this flode
    Ye Jourdane call;
Baptyme to take myldely with mode,
    This day he schall.

(9)

John, of his sande ther-fore be gladde,
And thanke hym hartely, both lowde and still.
JOH: I thanke hym evere, but I am radde!
I am noght abill to full-fill   60
    This dede certayne.
II ANG: John, the aught with harte and will
    To be full bayne

(10)

To do his bidding, all by-dene.
Bot in his baptyme, John, take tente,
The hevenes schalle be oppen sene,
The Holy Gost schalle doune be sente
    To se in sight,
The Fadirs voyce with grete talent
    Be herde full right,   70

---

45 *tyte* quickly   48 *riffe* rife   55 *mode* mood   57 *sande* message
59 *radde* afraid   63 *bayne* obedient   64 *by-dene* at once   69 *talent* pleasure

(11)

That schall saie thus to hym for-thy[4]

. . . .

(12)

JOH: With wordes fewne
  I will be subgett nyght and day
    As me well awe,
  To serve my lord Jesu to paye
    In dede and sawe.

(13)

  Bot wele I wot, baptyme is tane
  To wasshe and clense man of synne,
  And wele I wotte that synne is none
  In hym, with-oute ne with-inne.   80
    What nedis hym than
  For to be baptiste more or myne[5]
    Als synfull man?

(14)

JESUS: John, kynde of man is freele
  To the whilke that I have me knytte,
  But I shall shewe the skyllis twa[6],
  That thou schallt knawe by kyndly witte
  By-cause why I have ordand swa;
    And ane is this,
  Mankynde may noght un-baptymde go   90
    To endless blys.

(15)

  And sithen my-selffe have taken mankynde
  For men schall me ther myrroure make
  I have my doyng in ther mynde,
  And also I do the baptyme take.
    I will for-thy

72 *fewne* few   74 *awe* ought   77 *tane* taken   84 *kynde* nature   *freele* frail   87 *kyndly* natural   92 *mankynde* man's nature

JOHN THE BAPTIST

My-selfe be baptiste, for ther sake,
   Full oppynly.

(16)
   Anodir skill I schall the tell:
   My wille is this, that fro this day
   The vertue of my baptyme dwelle
   In baptyme-watir evere and ay,
      Mankynde to taste,
   Thurgh my grace therto to take alway
      The Haly Gaste.

(17)
JOH: All myghtfull Lorde, grete is thi grace;
   I thanke the of thi grete fordede.
JESUS: Cum, baptise me, John, in this place.
JOH: Lorde, save thy grace that I for-bede
      That itt soo be;
   For, Lorde, me thynketh it wer more nede
      Thou baptised me.

(18)
   That place⁷ that I yarne moste of all,
   Fro thens come thou, Lorde, as I gesse;
   How schulde I than, that is a thrall,
   Giffe the baptyme, that rightwis is,
      And has ben evere?
   For thou arte roote of rightwissenesse,
      That forfette nevere.

(19)
   What riche man gose from dore to dore
   To begge at hym that has right noght?
   Lorde, thou arte riche and I am full poure;
   Thou may blisse all, sen thou all wrought.
      Fro heven come all
   That helpes in erthe, yf soth be sought;
      Fro erthe but small.

---

107 *fordede* preparation   113 *yarne* desire   119 *forfette* sinned   123 *sen* since

(20)

JESUS: Thou sais full wele, John, certaynly,
　　But suffre nowe, for hevenly mede,
　　That rightwisnesse, be noght oonlye
　　Fullfillid in worde, but also in dede, 130
　　　Thrughe baptyme clere.
　　Cum, baptise me in my manhed
　　　Appertly here.

(21)

　　Fyrst schall I take, sen schall I preche,
　　For so be-hovis mankynde fulfille
　　All right-wissenesse, als werray leche[8].
JOH: Lord, I am redy at thi will,
　　　And will be ay
　　Thy subgett, Lord, both lowde and still,
　　　In that I may. 140

(22)

　　A, Lorde, I trymble ther I stande,
　　So am I arow to do that dede,
　　But save me, Lorde, that all ordand,
　　For the to touche have I grete drede,
　　　For doyngs dark.
　　Now helpe me, Lorde, thurgh thi godhede,
　　　To do this werke.

(23)

　　Jesu, my Lord of myghtis most,
　　I baptise the here in the name
　　Of the Fadir, and of the Sone, and Holy Gost. 150
　　But in this dede, Lorde, right no blame
　　　This day by me.
　　And bryngis all thase to thy home
　　　That trowes in the.
　　　Tunc cantabunt duo angeli 'Veni creator spiritus'[9].

128 *mede* reward　133 *Appertly* openly　134 *sen* then　135 *be-hovis* must　136 *werray* true　142 *arow* reluctant

JOHN THE BAPTIST

(24)

JESUS: John, for mannys prophyte, wit thou wele,
  Take I this baptyme, certaynely.
  The dragons poure ilk a dele
  Thurgh my baptyme distroyed have I[10] –
    This is certayne –
  And saved mankynde, saule and body,
    Fro endles payne.

160

(25)

What man that trowis and baptised be
Schall saved be and come to blisse;
Who-so trowes noght, to payne endles
He schalbe dampned sone, trowe wele this.
  But wende we nowe
Wher most is nede the folke to wisse,
  Both I and you.

(26)

JOH: I love the, Lorde, as sovereyne leche,
  That come to salve men of thare sore.
  As thou comaundis I schall gar preche,
  And lere to every man that lare
    That are was thrall[11].
  Now, sirs, that barne that Marie bare
    Be with you all.

170

157 *ilk a dele* every bit   162 *trowis* believes   172 *lere* teach   *lare* lore
173 *are* before

🙵 🙵 🙵

22. The Temptation of Christ, and the Woman Taken in Adultery
De Tentatione Salvatoris

CHESTER 12: BUTCHERS

The play, performed by the Butchers, was in the cycle by 1467. It depends in part upon the Stanzaic Life of Christ *and upon the Gospels. The action is divided into two parts: the temptations of Christ by Satan (Matthew 4 1–11); and Christ's treatment of the woman taken in adultery (John 8 1–11). This combination is not found in any other cycle, though both incidents are common enough as examples of Christ's work. Indeed they here represent a process of testing (as the Chester title indicates) and are linked together thematically. As Christ is caught by Satan between human nature and divinity, so he is caught by the Jews between the old law and the new. The Expositor is introduced to comment upon the incidents – he is used not for narrative purposes but solely to support the homiletic points made by the narratives.*

Satan appears in the first episode, and connects Christ's predicament with Adam's, as well as looking forward with horror to his own defeat and loss of authority after the Passion.

∞

[*Enter Satan.*]

(1)

SATHANAS: Now by my soverayntie, I sweare,
And principalitie that I beare,
In hell payne when I am there
    A gammon I will assay.
There is a Doseberd[1] I wolde dear

4 *gammon* jest   5 *dear* damage

THE TEMPTATION OF CHRIST

That walkes about wyde-where;
Who is his father I wot nere,
The sooth if I shold say.

(2)

What master man ever be this
That in the world thus comen is?
His mother I wot did never amisse,
And that now marvayles me.
His father can I not finde, I-wisse,
For all my craft ne my quaintyce;
It seemes he thought heaven were his,
So stout a syre is he.

(3)

He is a man from foote to crowne[2],
And gotten without corruption;
So cleane of conversacion
Knew I never none before.
All men of hym marvayle mon,
For as man he goeth up and downe,
But as God with devocion
He has bene honoured yore.

(4)

Sith the world first began,
Knew I never such a man,
Borne of a deadlish woman,
And yet she is wemlesse.
Among the sinfull synne doth he none,
And cleaner then ever was any one;
He seemes to be of bloud and bone[3],
And wiser then ever man was.

(5)

Avaryce ne no envye
In hym cold I never espy;

---

6 *wyde-where* everywhere 13 *I-wisse* indeed 14 *quaintyce* cunning
24 *yore* for a long time 27 *deadlish* mortal 28 *wemlesse* without blemish

389

He hath no gold in treasury,
Ne tempted is he by no sight.
Pryde has he none ne glotony
Ne no lyking of lechery;
His mouth hard I never lye,
Nother day nor night. 40

(6)
My highnes aye he putis behynde,
For in hym falte can I none finde;
If he be God in mans kinde,
My craft then fully fayles.
For more then man I wot he is,
Ells somewhat he did amisse[4];
Saffe he is hungrie, I-wisse,
Ells I wot not what him ayles.

(7)
And this thing dare I soothly say:
If that he were God veray, 50
Hunger shold greeve hym by no way[5];
That were against reason.
Therfore now I will assay
With speach of bread hym to betray,
For he hath fasted many a day,
Now meat were in season.

(8)
[*He approaches Christ in the wilderness.*]
Thou man, abyde and speak with me:
Gods sonne if that thou be,
Make of these stones that thou may see
Bread through thy blessing. 60
IESUS: Satan, I tell thee sickerly:
Man lyves not by bread onely,
But through Gods word, verely,
Of his mouth coming.

39 *hard* heard   42 *falte* fault   47 *Saffe* unless   48 *ayles* troubles
49 *soothly* truly

THE TEMPTATION OF CHRIST

(9)

 Therfore thou pynes thee, Satanas,
To supplant me of my place
By meat, as Adam sometyme was[6],
Of blisse when he was brought.
Deceyved he was that tyme through thee,
But now must fayle thy posty;   70
Therfore to move that thing to me,
Yt shall serve the of naught.

(10)

 Sathan, through thy entycement,
Hunger shall not turne my entent;
For Gods will omnipotent
Is my meat without fayle,
And His word perfecte sustenance
To me alway, without distance,
For thou shalt fynde no varyance
In me that shall avayle.   80

(11)

SATHANAS: Out! Alas! What is this?
This matter fares all amisse:
For hongry I see that he is,
As man sholde kindly bee.
But through no craft ne no quoyntice
I may not turne his will, I-wis;
Ne neede of meate ne worldly blisse
In hym nothing hath he.

(12)

 For he may suffer all manner nye,
As man shold well and stiffly,   90
But ever he wynnes the victory,
As godhead in hym weare.

---

65 *pynes thee* strivest 74 *entent* intention 84 *kindly* naturally 89 *nye* harm 90 *stiffly* steadfastly

ENGLISH MYSTERY PLAYS

Some other sleight I must espie
This Dosaberd for to destroy,
For of me he hath the mastry
Unhappely now here.

(13)

Adam, that God hym-selfe wrought,
Through my deceipt in bale I brought;
But this syre that I have sought,
Borne of one woman,   100
For ne neede that hym-selfe hase
[With] no counsaile in this case,
To greeve hym I may have no grace,
For no craft that I can[7].

(14)

But I will seeke some subtilty:
Come furth, thou, Ihesu, come with me
Unto the holy citye;
I have an arrand to say.
Very God if that thou be
Now I shall full sone see,   110
For I shall ordayne honor for thee,
Or that thou wend away.

Tunc statuet Iesum super pinnaculum templi[8].

(15)

Say, thou that sittes there so hye,
If thou be Gods Sonne, be slye,
Come downe and I will say I see
Thee doe a fayre mastry.
Thyne owne Angell mon keepe thee,
That thou hurt nether foot nor knee;
Shew thy power, now lett see,
Thou may have honour therby.   120

---

96 *Unhappely* unfortunately   98 *bale* torment   109 *Very* true
116 *mastry* feat

392

THE TEMPTATION OF CHRIST

(16)

IESUS: Sathan, sickerly I thee say:
   It is written that thou ne may
   Tempt God thy Lord, by no way,
   What matter so ever be mooved.
      Descendet de pinnaclo[9].
SATHANAS: Alas! Woe is me to-day!
   Twise have I fayled of my pray,
   Was I never rowted in such aray,
   Ne so fowle reproved.

(17)

   Tunc Sathan adducet Iesum super montem et dicit Diabolus[10]
   But yet if it be thy will,
   Goe we play us upon this hill;   130
   An other point thou must fulfill,
   For ought that may befall.
   Looke about thee now and see
   Of all these realmes the royalty;
   For to kneele downe and honour me
   Thou shalte be lord of all.

(18)

IESUS: Goe furth, Satan! Goe furth, goe!
   It is wrytten and shall be soe,
   God, thy Lord, thou shalt honour oo
   And serve hym though it thee noye.   140
SATHANAS: Out! Alas! Now me is woe,
   For found I never so mickle a foe;
   Though I to threpe be never so thro,
   I am overcome thrye.

(19)

   Alas! my sleight now am I quitt;
   Adam I founded with a fitt,

---

124 *mooved* raised   127 *rowted* routed   143 *threpe* dispute   *thro* eager
144 *thrye* thrice   145 *sleight* trick   *quitt* paid back   146 *founded* tried, inflicted   *fitt* hardship, suffering

393

And hym in combrance sone I knitte
Throughe quayntice of my crafte.
Nowe sone out of sorrow he must be shut,
And I pyned in hell pitt;   150
Knew I never none of such a witt
As hym that I have lafte.

(20)

Alas! For shame! I am shent;
With helhoundes when I am hent
I must be ragged and all to-rent
And dryven all to dyrt.
Therfore is nowe myne intent,
Or I goe, to make my testament[11]:
To all that in this place be lent,
I bequeath the shitte.   160
   Exit.
   [*Enter Expositor.*]

(21)

EXPOSITOR: Loe! Lordinges, Gods righteousnes,
As St Gregorie[12] makes mynde expresse,
Since our forefather overcomen was
By three thinges to doe evill:
Gluttony, vayne glorye, there be twooe,
Covetuousnes of highnes alsoe,
By these three thinges, without moe,
Christ hath overcome the Devill.

(22)

That Adam was tempted in Glotony,
I may well prove apertly,   170
When of the frute falsly
The Devill made hym to eate.
And tempted he was in Vayne-glorye,

---

147 *combrance* harassment   *knitte* entrapped   153 *shent* ruined
154 *hent* seized   155 *to-rent* torn to pieces   160 *shitte* excrement

THE TEMPTATION OF CHRIST

 When he height hym great mastery,
 To have godhead, unworthely,
 Through eating of that meate.

(23)

 Also he was tempted in Avaryce,
 When he het hym to be wise,
 Knowe good and evill at his device,
 More then he was worthy.   180
 For Covetous, Gregory saieth expresse,
 Synnes not onely in riches,
 But in willing of highnes
 And state, unskilfully.

(24)

 Also Christ in these synnes three
 Was tempted, you might well see,
 For in Glotony, leave you me,
 He moved hym, you saw here,
 When he entyced hym through his red
 To turnes stones into bread,   190
 And so to prove his godhead,
 Which he was in weere.

(25)

 In Vayne-glory he tempted him also,
 When he excited hym downe to goe
 The pynacle of the temple froe,
 An unskilfull gate.
 And in Covetous he tempted was,
 When he shewed hym such riches
 And het hym landes, both more and lesse,
 And there-through greate estate.   200

(26)

 Thus overcome Christe in this case
 The Devill, as played was in this place,

192 *weere* doubt   196 *gate* way   199 *het* promised

ENGLISH MYSTERY PLAYS

With those three synnes that Adam was
Of wayle into woe wayved.
But Adam fell through his trespas,
And Iesu withstood hym through his grace,
For of his godhead Sathanas
That tyme was cleane deceyved.

Tunc venient duo Iudeorum cum muliere deprehensa in adulterio, ut Iesum tentarent: quare dicat Primus[13]

(27)

PRIMUS IUDEUS: Master, I redd us by God almight
    That we lead this wretched wight,   210
    That was taken thus to-night
    In fowle adultery,
    Before Iesus in his sight;
    For to tempte him I have tight,
    To witt whether he will deme the right
    Or ells unlawfully.

(28)

SECUNDUS IUDEUS: Hit is good redd, by my fay,
    So we may catch him by some way,
    For if he doe her grace to-day,
    He dothe against the law[14].   220
    And if he bydd punishe her sore,
    He dothe against his owne lore,
    That he hath preached here before:
    To mercy man shall draw.

Tunc venient ad Iesum[15].

(29)

Master, this woman that is heer
Is a weddit wyfe, without weer;
But with an-other man then her fere

---

204 *wayle* prosperity   *wayved* moved   214 *tight* intended, planned
215 *deme* judge   217 *Hit* it   *redd* counsel   226 *weer* doubt   227 *fere* companion (husband)

THE TEMPTATION OF CHRIST

Was found here doe amysse,
And Moyses law byddes us stone
All such women as be uncleane.   230
Therfore to thee we can us meane
To geve a dome of this.

(30)

IESUS: Now which of you everychon
Is without synne, buske him anon,
And cast at her the first stonne,
Be-lyve, or that you blynne!
   Tunc Iesus scribit super ter[r]am[16].
PRIMUS IEW: Speak on, master, somewhat to say:
Shall she be stoned or ells nay?
Or doe her mercy here to-day,
To forgeve her this synne?   240

(31)

SECUNDUS IEW: Master, why art thou so still?
What wrytes thou, master? If it be thy will,
Whether shall we save or spill
This woman found in blame?
   Tunc inspiciunt scripsionem[17].
What wrytes thou, master? Now lett see!
Out! Alas! That wo is me!
Here no longer dare I be –
I see my synnes so clearly –
For dread of worlds shame.
   Et fugiett: et postea dicat[18]

(32)

PRIMUS PHARASEUS: Why fleest thou, fellow? By my fay,   250
I will see sone and assay.
Alas! That I were away,
Farr behynde Fraunce![19]
Stand thou, Sibbel, him besyde!

---

231 *meane* refer   232 *dome* judgement   234 *buske* prepare   236 *Be-lyve*
at once   *blynne* hesitate

No longer here I darr abyde
Against thee now for to chyde,
As I have good chaunce.
  Et fugiet; et dicat Iesus ad Mulierem[20]

(33)

IESUS: Woman, wher be those men echon
 That putt this guilt thee uppon?
 To damne thee is ther none
 Of those that were before?
MULIER: Lord, to damne me ther is none,
 For all they beene away gone.
IESUS: Neither do I damne thee; thow, woman,
 Goe forth, and synne no more!

(34)

MULIER: A! Lord, blessed must thou be,
 That of mischefe hath holpen me!
 From hence-forth synne I will flee,
 And serve thee, in good fay.
 For godhead fully in thee I see,
 That knoweth all workes that done be;
 I honour thee, knelinge on my knee,
 And so I will doe aye.
  [*Exeunt Jesus and the Woman. Enter Expositor.*]

(35)

EXPOSITOR: Now, lordings, I pray you take hede
 Of the great goodnes of Gods deede;
 I will declare as it is nede,
 This thing that played was.
 As Augustyne sayeth expressely
 Of it in his Homely
 Uppon St Iohn Evangely,
 This he sayeth in this case:

258 *echon* each one

THE TEMPTATION OF CHRIST

(36)

> Two wayes they casten him to anoy,
> Sith he hadd preached much of mercy,
> And the law commaunded expresly
> Such women for to stone,
> That trespassed in adultery;
> Therfore they hoped witterly
> Variance in him to espye,
> Or blemishe the law clean.

(37)

> Then wist Iesus well ther thought
> And all ther witts sett at nought,
> But bade which no synne hadd wrought,
> Cast first at her a stone;
> And wrott in clay – leeve you me –
> Ther owne sinnes that they might see,
> That eche one fayne was to flee,
> And ther lafte never one.

(38)

> For eche one of them had grace
> To see theyr synnes in that place;
> Yet none of other wyser was,
> But his owne eche man knew[21].
> And fayne [they] were to take their way,
> Lest they had damned beene that day.
> Thus holpe the Woman, in good fay,
> Our sweet Lord Iesu.

Finis paginae duodecimae.

282 *casten* tried   288 *Variance* inconsistency   290 *wist* knew   294 *wrott* wrote

🙒 🙒 🙒

23. Lazarus

TOWNELEY 31

The story of Lazarus appears in all four cycles. Its importance lay in being a figure of the Resurrection. The Towneley *version differs from the* York *and is thought to have been included after the separation. It falls into two parts: a presentation of the story of Christ's actions up to the Raising of Lazarus, closely based on* John 11 1–44; *a long monologue by Lazarus, lyrical in nature, addressed to all men – to the extent that the rest of the characters are simply ignored. Whilst the first part is written in couplets, the monologue by Lazarus is written in stanzaic verse. It envisages with grim intensity the decay of the body and the inevitability of death.*

The play was included near the end of the cycle; there is no clear reason for this. It would normally appear immediately before the Passion as one of the miracles of the Ministry, and as an anticipation of the Resurrection.

෴

[*Scene: the road to Bethany.*]

(1)

IHESUS: Commes now, brethere, and go with me;
    We will pas furth untill Iude[1];
    To Betany will we weynde,
    To vyset Lazare that is oure freynde[2].
    Gladly I wold we with hym speke;
    I tell you sothely he is seke.
PETRUS: I red not that ye thider go;
    The Iues halden you for thare fo;

3 *weynde* go   4 *vyset* visit   6 *seke* sick

LAZARUS

I red ye com not in that stede,
For if ye do then be ye dede³.

IOHANNES: Master, trist thou [not] on the Iue,
For many day sen thou thaym knewe,
And last tyme that we were thore
We wenyd till have bene ded therfor.

THOMAS: When we were last in that contre,
This othere day, both thou and we,
We wenyd that thou ther shuld have bene slayn;
Will thou now go thider agane?

IHESUS: Herkyn, breder, and takys kepe;
Lazare oure freynde is fallyn on slepe⁴;
The way till hym now will we take,
To styr that knyght and gar hym wake.

PETRUS: Sir, me thynke it were the best
To let hym slepe and take his rest;
And kepe that no man com hym hend,
For if he slepe then mon he mend.

IHESUS: I say to you, with-outten fayll,
No kepyng may till hym availl,
Ne slepe may stand hym in no stede.
I say you sekerly he is dede;
Therfor I say you now at last
Leyfe this speche and go we fast.

THOMAS: Sir, what so ever ye bid us do
We assent us well ther to;
I hope to God ye shall not fynde
None of us shall lefe behynde;
For any parell that may befall
Weynde we with oure master all.

MARTHA: Help me, Lorde, and gif me red!
Lazare my broder now is dede,
That was to the both lefe and dere;
He had not dyed had thou bene here.

---

11 *trist* trust   12 *sen* since   13 *thore* there   14 *wenyd* thought
15 *contre* country   19 *kepe* heed   22 *gar* cause   25 *hend* near
30 *sekerly* surely   32 *Leyfe* leave   37 *parell* peril   39 *red* advice

IHESUS: Martha, Martha, thou may be fayn,
   Thi brothere shall rise and lif agayn.
MARTHA: Lorde, I wote that he shall ryse
   And com before the good iustyce;
   For at the dredfull day of dome
   There mon ye kepe hym at his come,
   To loke what dome ye will hym gif;
   Then mon he rise, then mon he lyf.
IHESUS: I warne you, both man and wyfe,
   That I am rysyng, and I am life;
   And whoso truly trowys in me,
   That I was ever and ay shall be,
   Oone thyng I shall hym gif,
   Though he be dede yit shall he lif.
   Say thou, woman, trowys thou this?
MARTHA: Yee, for sothe, my Lorde of blys,
   Ellys were I greatly to mysprase,
   For all is sothe-fast that thou says.
IHESUS: Go tell thi sister Mawdlayn
   That I com, ye may be fayn.
   [*Martha goes to Mary Magdalene.*]
MARTHA: Sister, lefe this sorowful bande;
   Oure Lorde commys here at hand,
   And his apostyls with hym also.
MARIA: A, for Godys luf let me go!
   Blissid be he that sende me grace,
   That I may se the in this place.
   Lorde, mekill sorow may men se
   Of my sister here and me;
   We are hevy as any lede,
   For our broder that thus is dede.
   Had thou bene here and on hym sene,
   Dede for sothe had he not bene.
IHESUS: Hider to you commen we ar
   To make you comforth of youre care,

---

43 *fayn* joyful   48 *come* coming   53 *trowys* trusts   59 *mysprase* blame
60 *sothe-fast* true   71 *lede* lead   73 *sene* looked

LAZARUS

    Bot loke no fayntyse ne no slawth
    Bryng you oute of stedfast trawthe,
    Then shall I hold you that I saide.
    Lo, where have ye his body laide?   80
MARIA: Lorde, if it be thi will,
    I hope be this he savers ill,
    For it is now the iiij day gone
    Sen he was laide under yonde stone.
IHESUS: I told the right now ther thou stode
    That thi trawth shuld ay be goode,
    And if thou may that fulfill
    All bees done right at thi will.
      Et lacrimatus est Ihesus dicens[6]

(2)

    Fader, I pray the that thou rase
    Lazare that was thi hyne,   90
    And bryng hym oute of his mysese
    And out of hell[7] pyne.
    When I the pray thou says all wayse
    Mi will is sich as thyne,
    Therfor will we now eke his dayse[8],
    To me thou will inclyne.

(3)

    Com furth, Lazare, and stand us by;
    In erth shall thou no langere ly;
    Take and lawse hym foote and hande,
    And from his throte take the bande,   100
    And the sudary take hym fro,
    And all that gere, and let hym go.

---

77 *fayntyse* cowardice   *slawth* sloth   78 *trawthe* belief   82 *hope* think   *savers ill* stinks   85 *stode* stood   89 *rase* raise   90 *hyne* servant   91 *mysese* suffering   98 *langere* longer   99 *lawse* untie   101 *sudary* shroud   102 *gere* wrapping

ENGLISH MYSTERY PLAYS

(4)

LAZARUS[9]: Lorde, that all thyng maide of noght,
Lovyng be to thee,
That sich wonder here has wroght;
Gretter may none be.
When I was dede to hell I soght,
And thou, thrugh thi pauste,
Rasid me up and thens me broght,
Behold and ye may se.   110

(5)

Ther is none so styf on stede,
Ne none so prowde in prese,
Ne none so dughty in his dede,
Ne none so dere on deese,
No kyng, no knyght, no wight in wede,
From dede have maide hym seese,
Ne flesh he was wonte to fede,
It shall be wormes mese[10].

(6)

Youre dede is wormes coke,
Youre myrroure here ye loke,   120
And let me be youre boke,
Youre sampill take by me;
Fro dede you cleke in cloke,
Sich shall ye all be.

(7)

Ilkon in sich aray   with dede thai shall be dight,
And closid colde in clay   wheder he be kyng or knyght;
For all his garmentes gay   that semely were in sight,
His flesh shall frete away   with many a wofull wight.
Then wofully sich wightys

---

108 *pauste* power 111 *styf* upright *stede* horse 112 *prese* crowd
113 *dughty* brave 114 *deese* dais 115 *wede* clothes 118 *mese* food
119 *coke* cook 122 *sampill* example 123 *cleke* ?seize *cloke* ?claw
125 *Ilkon* everyone 128 *frete* wear, waste

LAZARUS

Shall gnawe thise gay knyghtys, 130
Thare lunges and thare lightys,
Thare harte shall frete in sonder;
Thise masters most of myghtys
Thus shall thai be broght under.

(8)

Under the erthe ye shall   thus carefully then cowche;
The royfe of youre hall   youre nakyd nose shall towche[11];
Nawther great ne small   to you will knele ne crowche;
A shete shall be youre pall;   sich todys shall be youre nowche;
Todys shall you dere[12];
Feyndys will you fere; 140
Youre flesh that fare was here
Thus rufully shall rote;
In stede of fare colore
Sich bandys shall bynde youre throte.

(9)

Youre rud that was so red,   youre lyre the lylly lyke,
Then shall be wan as led   and stynke as dog in dyke;
Wormes shall in you brede   as bees dos in the byke,
And ees out of youre hede   thus-gate shall paddokys pyke;
To pike you ar preste
Many uncomly beest, 150
Thus thai shall make a feste
Of youre flesh and of youre blode.
For you then sorows leste
The moste has of youre goode[13].

(10)

Youre goodys ye shall forsake   if ye be never so lothe,
And nothing with you take   bot sich a wyndyng clothe;

---

131 *lightys* lights 136 *royfe* roof 138 *todys* toads *nowche* jewel
139 *dere* hurt 140 *fere* terrify 142 *rote* rot 145 *rud* flesh colour
lyre face 147 *byke* hive 148 *ees* eyes *thus-gate* in this way *paddokys* toads *pyke* (v) pick 149 *pike* peck *preste* ready

405

ENGLISH MYSTERY PLAYS

Youre wife sorow shall slake, youre chylder also both[14],
Unnes youre mynnyng make if ye be never so wrothe;
Thai myn you with nothyng
That may be youre helpyng,   160
Nawther in mes syngyng,
Ne yit with almus dede;
Therfor in youre levyng
Be wise and take good hede.

(11)

Take hede for you to dele whils ye ar on life;
Trust never freyndys frele nawthere of childe then wife;
For sectures ar not lele; then for youre good will stryfe;
To by youre saules hele there may no man thaym shrife.
To shrife no man thaym may,
After youre endyng day,   170
Youre saull for to glad;
Youre sectures will swere nay,
And say ye aght more then ye had.

(12)

Amende the, man, whils thou may;
Let never no myrthe fordo thi mynde;
Thynke thou on the dredefull day
When God shall deme all mankynde.
Thynke thou farys as dothe the wynde;
This warlde is wast and will away;
Man, have this in thi mynde,   180
And amende the whils that thou may.

(13)

Amende the, man, whils thou art here,
Agane thou go an othere gate[15];

157 *slake* humble   158 *Unnes* scarcely   *mynnyng* remembrance
159 *myn* remember   161 *mes* mass   162 *almus dede* almsgiving   165 *dele*
share   166 *frele* frail   167 *sectures* executors   *lele* loyal   168 *by* buy
saules soul's   *hele* health, salvation   *shrife* shrive   173 *aght* owed
175 *fordo* destroy   177 *deme* judge   178 *farys* farest   179 *wast* waste

406

When thou art dede and laide on bere,
Wyt thou well thou bees to late;
For if all the goode that ever thou gate
Were delt for the after thi day,
In heven it wolde not mende thi state.
Forthi amende the whils thou may.

(14)

If thou be right ryall in rente,
As is the stede standyng in stall,
In thi harte knowe and thynke
That thai ar Goddys goodys all.
He myght have maide the poore and small
As he that beggys fro day to day;
Wit thou well acountys gif thou shall;
Therfore amende the whils thou may.

(15)

And if I myght with you dwell
To tell you all my tyme,
Full mekill cowthe I tell
That I have harde and sene,
Of many a great mervell,
Sich as ye wolde not wene,
In the paynes of hell
There as I have bene.

(16)

Bene I have in wo;
Therfor kepe you ther fro;
Whilst ye lif do so
If ye will dwell with hym
That can gar you thus go,
And hele you lith and lym.

---

184 *bere* bier   186 *gate* got   187 *delt* shared   190 *ryall* royal   *rente* rent, income   196 *Wit* know   *acountys* accounts   200 *cowthe* could   211 *hele* heal   *lith* joint

(17)
    He is a lorde of grace;
    Umthynke you in this case,
    And pray hym, full of myght,
    He kepe you in this place
    And have you in his sight.
               Amen.

  Explicit Lazarus.

213 *Umthynke* meditate

THE PASSION PLAY I

24. The Council of the Jews
25. The Last Supper
26. The Betrayal

LUDUS COVENTRIAE 26, 27, 28

The first play is given a special heading in the manuscript: Passion
Play I. *Together with the two which follow, it appears to have had a
separate existence. The first leaf is marked and dirtied as though the
three plays had been used for some other purpose before they were incorporated
here. If they were, the circumstance throws useful light on the
process of compilation of the cycle. It appears that the compiler incorporated
this part of his material as a whole. He did not revise the
Proclamation to indicate this: indeed the numbering is inconsistent, for
the Proclamation gives the numbers 23, 24, and 25, whilst the plays
bear the numbers 26, 27, and 28. Moreover the next five plays are called*
Passion Play II, *and they also appear to have been separated at some
point. Before this second group, there is a prologue by Contemplatio
which includes the words 'the matere that we lefte the last yere', implying
the two Passion Plays were at some time alternatives.*

*It should be noted that the stage directions are in English whereas in
other parts of the cycle (though not everywhere) they are in Latin.*

The textual evidence for the separate existence of the Passion Play I
*is supported by two other general features: the staging, and the literary
characteristics.*

*The three plays cannot really be separated with regard to staging.
The action is continuous, and the audience's attention is directed to a
flow of incidents: Prologues by Demon and John the Baptist; Conspiracy
by Annas and Caiaphas, and others; the fetching of the ass, and
Palm Sunday; the arrival at the House of Simon the Leper; further
Conspiracy; Mary Magdalene; the Disciples and the threatened
Betrayal; Judas's bargain with the Jews; the Last Supper, with the*

departure of Judas, and the triumph of the Demon; the completion of the Last Supper; the journey to Bethany; the Agony in the Garden; the Arrest; Mary Magdalene reports the Arrest to Mary the Virgin. The acting area was adapted to make this flow possible. There were two separate stages, one for the Council of the Jews, and one for the Last Supper, each having a curtain, as well as two scaffolds for Annas and Caiaphas. The action revolves around these for most of the time, but the Agony in the Garden (Bethany) also requires a separate playing space. It may be that we should suppose some complex arrangement of stages and acting spaces like that depicted in the manuscript of the Castle of Perseverance. The advantages of this kind of staging are considerable, the chief being that attention can be switched dramatically from one group of players to another. The writer shows a fine sense of dramatic effect in his use of these features, though at one point (l.342) he changes his mind. It is plain, too, that a very large cast would be required for this trilogy, and it is legitimate to suppose that some of the larger parts might be played by professionals, especially as some aspects are strongly reminiscent of the morality plays, where a professional style developed early. It should be remembered that this cycle was not written for production by Guilds.

Not only does the dramatist show stage sense, he also works his subject matter towards clear literary objectives. He uses several short soliloquies which are really sermons; he develops the character of Judas so as to give him a new motive for the Betrayal; he extends the presence of Mary Magdalene. These latter are related to his intention of emphasizing Christ's love for man as a main theme. Christ, too, is given a very human reaction to the impending disaster.

The author's theological intentions are distinct. He shows little interest in the liturgy, unlike the authors of the other cycles. He relies upon the Bible and the commentators. His attitude to the Last Supper is made clear: it is an act of love, and to emphasize it he removes Judas after the incident of the bread, and he makes Christ partake of the body and blood during the Agony. None of these things can be regarded as profound departures from received doctrine, but they are signs that the Passion Play *is the work of an author with an independent and original approach to his material.*

24. The Council of the Jews

[*Prologues.*]

   [*Enter Demon.*]

(1)

DEMON[1]: I am your lord Lucifer that out of helle cam,
   Prince of this werd, and gret duke of helle;
   Wherefore my name is clepyd Sere Satan,
   Whech aperyth among yow, a matere to spelle.

(2)

   I am norsshere of synne to the confusyon of man,
   To bryng hym to my dongeon, ther in fyre to dwelle.
   Ho-so-evyr serve me so reward hym I kan
   That he xal syng wellaway ever in peynes felle.

(3)

   Lo thus bounteuous a lord than now am I
   To reward so synners as my kend is.   10
   Who so wole folwe my lore and serve me dayly,
   Of sorwe and peyne a-now he xal nevyr mys.

(4)

   For I began in hefne synne for to sowe
   Among all the angellys that weryn there so bryth,
   And ther-fore was I cast out[2] in to helle ful lowe,
   Not withstandyng I was the fayrest and berere of lyth.

(5)

   Yet I drowe in my tayle of tho angelys bryth
   With me in-to helle – takyth good hed what I say –

2 *werd* world 3 *clepyd* called 4 *spelle* relate 5 *norsshere* nourisher
6 *dongeon* dungeon 8 *felle* many 10 *kend* nature 16 *lyth* light
17 *drowe* drew

411

I lefte but tweyn a-gens on to abyde there in lyth,
But the iij^de part come with me: this may not be seyd nay.   20

(6)

Takyth hed to your prince than, my pepyl every-chon,
And seyth what maystryes in hefne I gan ther do play.
To gete a thowsand sowlys in an houre me thynkyth it but
    skorn
Syth I wan Adam and Eve on the fyrst day.

(7)

But now mervelous mendys rennyn in myn rememberawns
Of on Cryst wiche is clepyd Joseph and Maryes sone.
Thryes I tempte hym be ryth sotylle instawnce:
Aftyr he fast fourty days ageyns sensual myth or reson
For of the stonys to a mad bred, but sone I had conclusyon;
Than upon a pynnacle but angelys were to hym assystent;   30
His answerys were mervelous, I knew not his intencion;
And at the last to veyn glory, but nevyr I had myn intent.

(8)

And now hath he xij dysypulys to his attendauns;
To eche town and cety he sendyth hem as bedellys,
In dyverce place to make for hym purvyauns.
The pepyl of hese werkys ful grettly merveyllys:
To the crokyd, blynd and dowm his werkys provaylys;
Lazare that foure days lay ded his lyff recuryd.
And where I purpose me to tempt anon he me asaylys –
Mawdelyn playne remyssyon also he hath ensuryd³.   40

(9)

Goddys son he pretendyth, and to be born of a mayde,
And seyth he xal dey for mannys salvacion.
Than xal the trewth be tryed and no fordere be delayd

---

22 *maystryes* dominion, power *do play* bring about 24 *wan* conquered
25 *mendys* thoughts *rennyn* run 27 *ryth* right, very 28 *myth* power
34 *bedellys* messengers 36 *merveyllys* (v) wonder 37 *crokyd* lame
dowm dumb *provaylys* (v) benefit 42 *dey* die

THE COUNCIL OF THE JEWS

Whan the soule fro the body xal make separacion.
And as for hem that be undre my grett domynacion,
He xal fayle of hese intent and purpose also;
Be this tyxt of holde remembryd to myn intencion,
Quia in inferno nulla est redempcio[4].

(10)

But whan the tyme xal neyth of his persecucion,
I xal arere new engynes of malycious conspiracy;   50
Plente of reprevys I xal provide to his confusyon.
Thus xal I false the wordys that his pepyl doth testefy;
His discipulis xal for-sake hym and here mayster denye;
In-noumberabyl xal his woundys be of woful grevauns;
A tretowre xal countyrfe his deth to fortyfye;
The rebukys that he gyf me xal turne to his displesauns.

(11)

Some of hese dyscypulys xal be chef of this ordenawns,
That xal fortefye this term that in trost is treson.
Thus xal I venge be sotylte al my malycious grevauns
For no thyng may excede my prudens and dyscrecion.   60

(12)

Gyff me your love, grawnt me myn affeccion,
And I wyl inclose the tresour of lovys alyawns[5]
And gyff yow youre desyrys aftere youre intencion;
No poverte xal aproche yow fro plenteuous abundauns.

(13)

By-holde the dyvercyte of my dysgysyd varyauns[6],
Eche thyng sett of dewe naterall dysposycion,
And eche parte acordynge to his resemblauns
Fro the sool of the foot to the hyest asencion:

---

47 *tyxt* text *holde* old   49 *neyth* approach   50 *arere* raise   51 *reprevys* charges, reproofs   55 *tretowre* traitor   *countyrfe* contrive   *fortyfye* ensure   59 *sotylte* subtlety   62 *alyawns* bond   65 *varyauns* divergence, variety   66 *dewe* due, proper

413

(14)

Off fyne cordewan[7] a goodly peyre of long pekyd schon,
Hosyn enclosyd of the most costyous cloth of crenseyn –
Thus a bey to a jentylman to make comparycion –
With two doseyn poyntys of cheverelle, the aglottys of sylver feyn[8],

(15)

A shert of feyn holond[9], but care not for the payment,
A stomachere of clere reynes[10], the best may be bowth –
Thow poverte be chef lete pride ther be present,
And all tho that repreff pride thou sett hem at nowth[11];

(16)

Cadace wolle[12] or flokkys where it may be sowth
To stuffe with-al thi dobbelet and make the of proporcyon,
Two smale legges and a gret body thow it ryme nowth –
Yet loke that thou desyre to an the newe faccion –

(17)

A gowne of thre yerdys loke thou make comparison
Un-to all degrees dayly that passe thin astat,
A purse with-outyn mony, a daggere for devoscyon,
And there repref is of synne loke thu make debat[13].

(18)

With syde lokkys I schrewe thin here to thi colere hangyng down
To herborwe qweke bestys that tekele men onyth;
An hey smal bonet for curyng of the crowne.
And all beggerys and pore pepyll have hem on dyspyte.
On to the grete othys and lycherye gyf thi delyte.
To mayntein thin astate lete brybory be present,
And yf the lawe repreve the say thou wylt ffyth,
And gadere the a felachep after thin entent[14].

---

69 *pekyd* pointed 70 *crenseyn* crimson 71 *bey* boy 74 *bowth* bought
76 *nowth* nought 79 *ryme* match 80 *an* have 84 *there* where
85 *schrewe* curse 86 *herborwe* shelter *qweke* live *bestys* creatures
(?fleas) *tekele* tickle *onyth* at night 87 *hey* high 91 *ffyth* fight

THE COUNCIL OF THE JEWS

(19)

Loke thou sett not be precept nor be comawndement,
Both sevyle and canone sett thou at nowth[15].
Lette no membre of God but with othys be rent.
Lo thus this werd at this tyme to myn intent is browth!
I, Sathan, with my felawus this werd hath sowth.
And now we han it at houre plesawns,
For synne is not shamfast but boldnes hath bowth
That xal cause hem in helle to han inerytawns.   100

(20)

A beggerys dowtere to make gret purvyauns
To cownterfete a jentyl woman dysgeysyd as she can;
And yf mony lakke this is the newe chevesauns,
With here prevy plesawns to gett it of sum man.
Here colere splayed and furryd with ermyn calabere or satan[16],
A seyn to selle lechory to hem that wyl bey.
And thei that wyl not by it yet i-now xal thei han,
And telle hem it is for love she may it not deney.

(21)

I have browth yow newe namys[17], and wyl ye se why,
For synne is so plesaunt to ech mannys intent: 110
Ye xal kalle Pride Oneste, and Naterall Kend Lechory,
And Covetyse Wysdam – there tresure is present –

(22)

Wreth Manhod, and Envye callyd Chastement;
Seyse nere sessyon lete Perjery be chef[18];
Glotonye rest, let Abstynawnce beyn absent,
And he that wole exorte the to vertu put hem to repreff.

---

95 *membre* limb 98 *han* have 99 *shamfast* shy 100 *inerytawns* inheritance 103 *chevesauns* trick 106 *seyn* sign 108 *deney* deny 111 *Naterall Kend* natural love 113 *Wreth* anger *Chastement* chastisement

ENGLISH MYSTERY PLAYS

(23)
    To rehers al my servauntys my matere is to breff
    But all these xal eneryth the dyvicion eternal.
    Thow Cryst be his sotylte many materys meef,
    In evyr-lastynge peyne with me dwellyn thei xal.   120

(24)
    Remembre oure servauntys whoys sowlys ben mortall,
    For I must remeffe for more materys to provyde.
    I am with yow at all tymes whan ye to councel me call,
    But for a short tyme my-self I devoyde.
    [*Exit Demon. Enter John the Baptist.*]

(25)
JOHANNES BAPTISTA: I, Johan Baptyst, to yow thus prophesye
    That on xal come aftyr me and not tary longe,
    In many folde more strengere than I,
    Of whose shon I am not worthy to lose the thonge[19];
    Where-fore I councel the ye reforme all wronge
    In your concyens of the mortall dedys sevyn,   130
    And for to do penawns loke that ye ffonge,
    For now xal come the kyngdham of hevyn.

(26)
    The weys of oure Lord cast yow to aray[20],
    And ther-in to walk loke ye be applyande,
    And make his pathys as ryth as ye may,
    Kepyng ryth forth and be not declinande,
    Neyther to fele on ryth nor on lefte hande,
    But in the myddys purpose yow to holde;
    For that in all wyse is most plesande,
    As ye xal here whan I have tolde.   140

(27)
    Of this wey for to make moralysacyon:
    Be the ryth syde ye xal undyrstonde mercy,

118 *eneryth* inherit   119 *meef* move   124 *devoyde* take away   128 *shon* shoes   131 *ffonge* begin   133 *aray* ?follow, ?prepare for (cf. l. 163)

THE COUNCIL OF THE JEWS

And on the lefte syde lykkenyd dysperacion,
And the patthe be-twyn bothyn that may not wry
Schal be hope and drede to walke in perfectly,
Declynyng not to fele for no maner nede.
Grete cawsys I xal shoue yow why
That ye xal sewe the patthe of hope and drede.

(28)

On the mercy of God to meche ye xal not holde,
As in this wyse behold what I mene: 150
For to do synne be thou no more bolde
In trost that God wole mercyful bene,
And yf be sensualyte as it is ofte sene
Synnyst dedly thou xalt not therfore dyspeyre,
But therfore do penawns and confesse the clene
And of hevyn thou mayst trost to ben eyre.

(29)

The pathe that lyth to this blyssyd enherytawns
Is hope and drede copelyd be conjunccyon.
Be-twyx these tweyn may be no dysseverawns,
For hope with-outyn drede is maner of presumpcion, 160
And drede with-owtyn hope is maner of dysperacion;
So these tweyn must be knyt be on acorde.
How ye xal aray the wey I have made declararacion,
Also the ryth patthis agens the comyng of oure Lord.

[*Exit John the Baptist.*
With the Prologues completed, the action begins.]

Here xal Annas shewyn hym-self in his stage[21], *be-seyn
after a busshop of the hoold lawe in a skarlet gowne and over
that a blew tabbard furryd with whyte, and a mytere on his hed
after the hoold lawe: ij Doctorys stondyng by hym in furryd
hodys, and on be-forn hem with his staff of a-stat, and eche of
hem on here hedys a furryd cappe with a gret knop in the*

---

144 *wry* twist   147 *shoue* show   148 *sewe* follow   149 *meche* much
156 *eyre* heir

*crowne, and on stondyng be-forn as a Sarazyn[22], the wich xal
be his Masangere: Annas thus seyng*

(30)

ANNAS: As a prelat am I properyd, to provyde pes
And of Jewys jewge, the lawe to fortefye.
I, Annas, be my powere xal comawnde dowteles
The lawys of Moyses no man xal denye.
Hoo excede my comawndement anon ye certefye;
Yf any eretyk here reyn to me ye compleyn; 170
For in me lyth the powere all trewthis to trye,
And pryncypaly oure lawys tho must I susteyn.

(31)

Yef I may aspey the contrary no wheyle xal thei reyn,
But a-non to me be browth and stonde present,
Be-fore here jewge wich xal not feyn
But aftere here trespace to gef hem jugement.
Now, serys, for a prose heryth myn intent,
There is on Jhesus of Nazareth that oure lawys doth excede.
Yf he procede thus we xal us all repent,
For oure lawys he dystroyt dayly with his dede. 180

(32)

There-fore be your cowncel we must take hede
What is be[st] to provyde or do in this case.
For yf we let hym thus go and ferdere prosede,
Ageyn Sesare and oure lawe we do trespace.

(33)

1 DOCTOR: Sere, this is myn avyse that ye xal do:
Send to Cayphas for cowncel, knowe his intent.
For yf Jhesu proce[de] and thus forth go,
Oure lawys xal be dystroyd, thes se we present.

---

165 *properyd* empowered   173 *Yef* if   *aspey* perceive   175 *feyn* hesitate
177 *prose* story

THE COUNCIL OF THE JEWS

(34)

II DOCTOR: Sere, remember the gret charge that on yow is leyd
The lawe to ke[pe] which may not fayle. 190
Yf any defawth prevyd of yow be seyd,
The Jewys with trewth wyl yow a-sayl.
Tak hed whath cownsayl may best provayl.
After Rewfyn and Leyon I rede that ye sende;
They arn temperal jewgys, that knowyth the parayl
With youre cosyn Cayphas this matere to amende.

(35)

ANNAS: Now surely this cowncel revyfe myn herte.
Youre cowncel is best as I can se.
Arfexe, in hast loke that thou styrte,
And pray Cayphas my cosyn come speke with me. 200

(36)

To Rewfyn and Leon thu go also
And pray hem thei speke with me in hast,
For a prynclpal matere that have to do,
Wich must be knowe or this day be past.

(37)

ARFEXE: My sovereyn, at your intent I xal gon,
In al the hast that I kan hy,
On to Cayphas, Rewfyn, and Lyon,
And charge youre intent that thei xal ply.

Here goth the Masangere forth, and in the mene tyme Cayphas shewyth him-self in his skafhald arayd lych to Annas savyng his tabbard xal be red furryd with white; ij Doctorys with hym arayd with pellys[23] aftyr the old gyse and furryd cappys on here hedys: Cayphas thus seyng

191 *defawth* fault   195 *parayl* way   197 *revyfe* revives   199 *styrte* go

419

ENGLISH MYSTERY PLAYS

(38)

CAYPHAS: As a primat most preudent, I present here sensyble
    Buschopys of the lawe with al the cyrcumstawns.　　210
    I, Cayphas, am jewge with powerys possyble
    To distroye all errouris that in oure lawys make varyawns.
    All thyngys I convey be reson and temperawnce,
    And all materis possyble to me ben palpable.
    Of the lawe of Moyses I have a chef governawns;
    To severe ryth and wrong in me is termynable[24].

(39)

    But ther is on Cryst that oure lawys is varyable;
    He perverte the pepyl with his prechyng ill.
    We must seke a mene on to hym reprevable[25],
    For yf he procede oure lawys he wyl spyll.　　220

(40)

    We must take good cowncel in this case
    Of the wysest of the lawe that kan the trewthe telle,
    Of the jewgys[26] of Pharasy, and of my cosyn Annas,
    For yf he procede be prossesse, oure lawys he wyl felle.

(41)

I DOCT[OR]: Myn lord, plesyt yow to pardon me for to say
    The blame in yow is as we fynde,
    To lete Cryst contenue thus day be day
    With his fals wichcraft the pepyl to blynde.

(42)

    He werkyth fals meraclis ageyns all kende,
    And makyth oure pepyl to leve hem in.　　230
    It is your part to take hym and do hym bynde
    And gyf hym jugement for his gret syn.

(43)

II DOCTOR: For-sothe, sere, of trewth this is the case;
    On to our lawe ye don oppressyon

    209 *sensyble* to be seen   214 *palpable* apparent, obvious

THE COUNCIL OF THE JEWS

That ye let Cryst from you pace
And wyl not don on hym correxion.
Let Annas knowe your intencion,
With prestys and jewgys of the lawe,
And do Cryst forsake his fals oppynyon
Or in-to a preson lete hem be thrawe. 240

(44)

CAYPHAS: Wel, serys, ye xal se with-inne short whyle
I xal correcte hym for his trespas.
He xal no lenger oure pepyl be-gyle;
Out of myn dawngere he xal not pas.
Here comyth the Masangere to Cayphas; and in the mene tyme Rewfyn and Lyon schewyn hem in the place in ray tabardys furryd and ray hodys a-bouth here neckys furryd, the Masangere seyng

(45)

MASANGERE: Myn reverent sovereyn, and it do yow plese,
Sere Annas, my lord, hath to you sent.
He prayt you that ye xal not sese
Tyl that ye ben with hym present.

(46)

CAYPHAS: Sere, telle myn cosyn I xal not fayl.
It was my purpose hym for to se, 250
For serteyn materys that wyl provayle,
Thow he had notwth a sent to me.

(47)

MASA[N]GER: I recomende me to your hey degre,
On more massagys I must wende.
CAYPHAS: Fare wel, sere, and wel ye be!
Gret wel my cosyn and my fre[n]de.

239 *do* cause to   244 *dawngere* power   244 (SD) *ray* striped   252 *a* have

(48)

Here the Masager metyth with the Jewgys, sayng

MASA[N]GER: Heyl, jewgys of Jewry, of reson most prudent:
Of my massage to you I make relacion.
My lord, sere Annas, hath for you sent
To se his presens with-owth delacion.   260

(49)

REWFYN: Sere, we are redy at his comawndement
To se sere Annas in his place.
It was oure purpose and oure intent
To a be with hym with-inne short space.

(50)

LEYON: We are ful glad his presence to se,
Sere, telle hym we xal come in hast;
No declaracion ther-in xal be
But to his presens hye us fast.

(51)

MASA[N]GER: I xal telle my lord, seris, as ye say,
Ye wyl ful-fylle al his plesawns.   270
REWFYN: Sere, telle hym we xal make no delay
But come in hast at his instawns.

Here the Masangere comyth to Annas seyng

(52)

MASAN[GER]: My lord, and it plese you to have intellygens,
Ser Cayphas comyth to you in hast;
Rewfyn and Lyon wyl se your presens,
And se yow here or this day be past.

(53)

ANNAS: Sere, I kan the thank of thi dylygens[27].
Now ageyn my cosyn I wole walk.

260 *delacion* delay

Serys, folwyth me on to his presens,
For of these materys we must talk. 280
Here Annas goth down to mete with Cayphas, and in the mene tyme thus seyng

(54)

CAYPHAS: Now on to Annas let us wende
Ech of us to knowe otherys intent.
Many materys I have in mende
The wich to hym I xal present.

(55)

I DOCTOR: Sere, of all othere thyng remembre this case:
Loke that Ihesus be put to schame.
II DOCTOR: Whan we come present beforn Annas
Whe xal rehers all his gret blame.
Here the Buschopys with here Clerkys and the Pharaseus mett [at] the myd place, and ther xal be a lytil oratory with stolys and cusshonys clenly be-seyn lych as it were a cownsel hous; Annas thus seyng

(56)

ANNAS: Wel-come, ser Cayphas, and ye Jewgys alle!
Now xal ye knowe all myn entent. 290
A wondyr case, serys, here is be-falle
On wich we must gyf jewgement
Lyst that we aftyre the case repent
Of on Cryst that Goddys sone som doth hym calle.
He shewyth meraclys and sythe present[28]
That he is prynce of pryncys alle.

(57)

The pepyl so fast to hym doth falle,
Be prevy menys as we a-spye;
Gyf he procede son sen ye xalle
That oure lawys he wyl dystrye. 300

293 *Lyst* lest   295 *sythe* says   *present* here   299 *sen* see

(58)
>   It is oure part thus to deny.
>   What is your cowncell in this cas?
> CAYPHAS: Be reson the trewth here may we try.
>   I cannot dem hym with-outh trespace,
>   Be-cause he seyth in every a place
>   That he Kyng of Jewys in every degre,
>   Therfore he is fals, knowe wel the case:
>   Sesar is kyng and non but he.

(59)
> REWFYN: He is an eretyk and a tretour bolde
>   To Sesare and to oure lawe sertayn,   310
>   Bothe in word and in werke and ye be-holde;
>   He is worthy to dey with mekyl peyn.

(60)
> LEON: The cawse that we been here present
>   To fortefye the lawe and trewth to say.
>   Jhesus ful nere oure lawys hath shent,
>   Therfore he is worthy for to day.

(61)
> I DOCTOR AN[NAS]: Serys, ye that ben rewelerys of the lawe,
>   On Jhesu ye must gyf jugement.
>   Let hym fyrst be hangyn and drawe,
>   And thanne his body in fyre be brent.   320

(62)
> II DOCTOR AN[NAS]: Now xal ye here the intent of me:
>   Take Jhesu that werke us all gret schame,
>   Put hym to deth – let hym not fle –
>   For than the Comownys thei wyl yow blame.

(63)
> I DOCTOR CAYP[HAS]: He werke with weche-crafte in eche place,

304 *dem* judge 312, 316 *dey, day* die 317 *rewelerys* rulers
324 *Comownys* common people

THE COUNCIL OF THE JEWS

And drawyth the pepyl to hese intent.
Be whare, ye jewgys, let hym not passe,
Than be my trewthe ye xal repent.

(64)

11 DOCTOR CAYPHAS: Serys, takyth hede on to this case
And in your jewgement be not slawe. 330
Ther was nevyr man dyd so gret trespace
As Jhesu hath don ageyn oure lawe.

(65)

ANNAS: Now, bretheryn, than wyl ye here myn intent.
These ix days let us a-byde,
We may not gyf so hasty jugement,
But eche man inqwere on his syde,
Send spyes a-bouth the countre wyde
To se and recorde and testymonye;
And than hese werkys he xal not hyde
Nor have no power hem to denye. 340

(66)

CAYPHAS: This cowncell a-cordyth to my reson.
ANNAS: And we all to the same[29].

. . . . .

(67)

JHESUS: Frendys, be-holde the tyme of mercy
The whiche is come now with-owt dowth.
Mannys sowle in blys now xal edyfy,
And the prynce of the werd is cast owth.

(68)

Go to yon castel that standyth yow ageyn,
Sum of myn dyscyplis go forth ye to;
There xul ye fyndyn bestys tweyn,

330 *slawe* slow

An asse tyed and here fole also. 350
Un-losne that asse and brynge it to me pleyn.
If any ma[n] aske why that ye do so,
Sey that I have nede to this best certeyn,
And he xal not lett yow your weys for to go;
That best brynge ye to me.

I APOSTOLUS[30]: Holy prophete, we gon oure way –
We wyl not youre wourd de-lay –
Also sone as that we may,
We xal it brynge to the.

Here thei fecch the asse with the fole and the Burgeys[31] seyth

(69)

BURGENSIS: Herke, ye men, who gaf yow leve 360
Thus this best for to take away?
But only for pore men to releve
This asse is ordayned as I yow say.

PHILIPPUS: Good sere, take this at no greff;
Oure mayster us sent hedyr this day.
He hath grett nede with-owt repreff;
Therfore not lett us, I the pray,
This best for to lede.

BURGENSIS: Sethyn that it is so, that he hath yow sent,
Werkyth his wyll and his intent, 370
Take the beste as ye be bent,
And evyr wel mote ye spede.

(70)

JACOBUS MINOR: This best is brought ryght now here, lo,
Holy prophete, at thin owyn wylle,
And with this cloth anon also
This bestys bak we xal sone hylle.

PHILIPPUS: Now mayst thou ryde whedyr thou wylt go,
Thyn holy purpos to fulfylle.
Thy best ful redy is dyth the to;

350 *fole* foal 351 *Un-losne* untie 353 *best* beast 371 *bent* decided, intent upon 376 *hylle* cover 379 *dyth* prepared

THE COUNCIL OF THE JEWS

 Bothe meke and tame the best is stylle,   380
And we be redy also.
If it be plesynge to thi syght,
The to helpe a-non forth ryght,
Upon this best that thou were dyght
Thi jurney for to do.
 Here Cryst rydyth out of the place and he wyl, and Petyr and Johan abydyn stylle, and at the last whan thei have don ther prechyng thei mete with Jhesu.

(71)

PETRUS: O ye pepyl dyspeyryng, be glad!
 A grett cawse ye have and ye kan se;
The Lord that all thynge of nought mad
Is comynge your comfort to be.
All your langoris salvyn xal he;   390
Your helthe is more than ye kan wete;
He xal cawse the blynde[32] that thei xal se,
The def to here, the dome for to speke.

(72)

 Thei that be crokyd, he xal cause hem to goo,
In the way that Johan Baptyst of prophecyed.
Sweche a leche kam yow nevyr non too.
Wher-fore what he comawndyth loke ye applyed.
That som of yow be blynd it may not be denyid,
For hym that is your makere with your gostly ey ye xal not knowe,
Of his comaundementys in yow gret necglygens is aspyed, 400
Where-fore def fro gostly heryng clepe yow I howe.

(73)

 And some of yow may not go, ye be so crokyd,
For of good werkyng in yow is lytyl habundawns.
Tweyn fete hevery man xuld have and it were lokyd,
Wyche xuld bere the body gostly most of substawns:

390 *langoris* diseases 391 *wete* know 393 *dome* dumb 399 *ey* eye
401 *clepe* call *howe* ought

427

ENGLISH MYSTERY PLAYS

Fyrst is to love God above all other plesawns;
The secunde is to love thi neybore as thin owyn persone;
And yf these tweyn be kepte in perseverawns
Into the celestyal habytacion ye arn habyl to gone.

(74)

Many of yow be dome, why, for ye wole not redresse 410
Be mowthe your dedys mortal, but ther-in don perdure;
Of the wych but ye have contrycyon and yow confesse
Ye may not in-heryte hevyn – this I yow ensure.
And of all these maladyes ye may have gostly cure,
For the hevynly leche is comyng yow for to vicyte,
And as for payment he wole shewe yow no redrure,
For with the love of yowre hertys he wole be aqwhyte.

(75)

APOSTOLUS JOHANNES: On to my brotherys for-seyd rehersall,
That ye xuld geve the more veray confydens,
I come with hym as testymonyall, 420
For to conferme and fortefye his sentens.
This Lord xal come with-out resystens;
On to the cety-ward[33] he is now comyng,
Where-fore dresse yow with all dew dylygens
To honowre hym as your makere and kyng.

(76)

And to fulfylle the prophetys prophese[34],
Up-on an asse he wole hedyr ryde,
Shewyng yow exawmple of humylyte,
Devoydyng the abhomynable synne of pryde,
Whech hath ny conqweryd all the werd wyde, 430
Grettest cause of all your trybulacyon.
Use it ho so wole, for it is the best gyde
That ye may have to the place of dampnacyon.

---

411 *don perdure* continue in 415 *vicyte* visit 416 *redrure* harshness
417 *aqwhyte* repaid

THE COUNCIL OF THE JEWS

(77)

Now, brothyr in God, syth we have intellygens
That oure Lord is ny come to this cete,
To attend up-on his precyous presens
It syttyth to us, as semyth me;
Wherfore to mete whit hym now go we.
I wold fore no thyng we where to late;
To the cete-ward fast drawyth he, 440
Me semyth he is ny at the gate.
Here spekyth the iiij ceteseynys, the Fyrst thus seyng

(78)

I CIVES DE IHERUSALEM: Neyborys, gret joye in oure herte we may make
That this hef[n]ly kyng wole vycyte this cyte.
II CIVES: Yf oure eerly kyng swech a jorne xuld take,
To don hym honour and worchepe besy xuld we be.
III CIVES: Meche more than to the hevynly kyng bownd are we
For to do that xuld be to his persone reverens.
IIII CIVES: Late us than welcome hym with flowrys and brawnchis of the tre,
For he wole take that to plesawns becawse of redolens.
Here the iiij ceteseynys makyn hem redy for to mete with oure Lord goyng barfot and barelegged and in here shyrtys savyng thei xal have here gownys cast a-bouth theme, and qwan thei seen oure Lorde thei xal sprede ther clothis be-forn hyme, and he xal lyth and go ther upone, and thei xal falle downe up-on ther knes alle atonys, the Fyrst thus seyng

(79)

I CIVES: Now blyssyd he be that in oure Lordys name 450
To us in any wyse wole resorte,
And we be-leve veryly that thou dost the same,
For be thi marcy xal spryng mannys comforte.

---

438 *whit* with   444 *eerly* earthly   449 *redolens* sweet perfume

429

Here Cryst passyth forth: ther metyth with hym a serteyn of chylderyn with flowrys, and cast be-forn hyme, and they synggyn Gloria Laus, and be-forn on seyt

[CHILD:]
Thow sone of Davyd, thou be oure supporte
At oure last day whan we xal dye,
Where-fore we all atonys to the exorte,
Cryeng mercy, mercy, mercye.

(80)

JHESU: Frendys be-holde the tyme of mercy
The wich is come now with-owtyn dowth.
Mannys sowle in blysse now xal edyfy, 460
And the prynce of the werd is cast owth[35].
As I have prechyd in placys a-bowth,
And shewyd experyence to man and wyf,
In-to this werd Goddys sone hath sowth
For veray love man to revyfe.

(81)

The trewthe of trewthis xal now be tryede,
And a perfyth of corde[36] be-twyx God and man,
Wich trewth xal nevyr be dyvide,
Confusyon on to the fynd Sathan.

(82)

I PAUPER HOMO: Thou sone of Davyd, on us have mercye! 470
As we must stedfast be-levyn in the,
Thi goodnesse, Lord, lete us be nye,
Whech lyth blynd here and may not se.

(83)

II PAUPER HOMO: Lord, lete thi mercy to us be sewre,
And restore to us oure bodyly syth.
We know thou may us wel recure
With the lest poynt of thi gret myth.

453 (SD) *serteyn* number, group   474 *sewre* sure

(84)

JHESU: Yowre be-leve hath mad you for to se,
 And delyveryd you fro all mortal peyn.
 Blyssyd be all tho that be-leve on me, 480
 And se me not with here bodyly eyn.
   Here Cryst blyssyth here eyn, and thei may se, the Fyrst seyng

(85)

I PAUPER HOMO: Gromercy, Lord, of thi gret grace:
 I that was blynd now may se.
II PAUPER HOMO: Here I for-sake al my trespace,
 And stedfastly wyl be-levyn on the.

481 *eyn* eyes

25. The Last Supper

Here Cryst procedyth on fote with his Dyscipulys after hym, Cryst wepyng[1] up-on the cyte, sayng thus

(86)

JHESU: O Jherusalem, woful is the ordenawnce
   Of the day of thi gret persecucyon!
   Thou xalt be dystroy with woful grevans
   And thi ryalte browth to trew confusyon.
   Ye that in the cete han habytacyon,
   Thei xal course the tyme that thei were born,
   So gret advercyte and trybulacion
   Xal falle on hem both evyn and morwyn.

(87)

   Thei that han most chylderyn sonest xal wayle
   And seyn 'Alas! What may this meen?'
   Both mete and drynk sodeynly xal fayle;
   The vengeance of God ther xal be seen.
   The tyme is comyng hes woo xal ben,
   The day of trobyl and gret grevauns,
   Bothe templys and towrys they xal down cleen:
   O cete, ful woful is thin ordenawns!

(88)

PETRUS: Lord, where wolte thou kepe thi Maunde[2]?
   I pray the now lete us have knowyng,
   That we may make redy for the,
   The to serve with-owte latyng.
JOHANNES: To provyde, Lord, for thi comyng
   With all the obedyens we kan a-tende,
   And make redy for the in al thyng
   In-to what place thou wy[lt] us send.

---

8 *evyn* evening   *morwyn* morning.   20 *latyng* hindrance

THE LAST SUPPER

(89)

JHESU: Serys, goth to Syon and ye xal mete
    A pore man in sympyl a-ray
    Beryng watyr in the strete.
    Telle hym I xal come that way,
    On-to hym mekely loke that ye say
    That hese house I wele come tylle.   30
    He wele not onys to yow sey nay,
    But sofre to have all your wylle.

(90)

PETRUS: At thi wyl, Lord, it xal be don:
    To seke that place we xal us hye.
JOHANNES: In all the hast that we may go
    Thin comaw[n]dement nevyr to denye.
    Here Petyr and Johan gon forth metyng with Symon
    Leprows beryng a kan with watyr: Petyr thus seyng

(91)

PETRUS: Good man, the prophete, oure Lord Jhesus,
    This nyth wyl rest wyth-in thin halle.
    On massage to the he hath sent us
    That for his sopere ordeyn thou xalle.   40
JOHANNES: Ya, for hym and his dyscipulys alle
    Ordeyn thu for his Maunde
    A paschall lomb[3], what so be-falle,
    For he wyl kepe his pasch with the.

(92)

SYMON: What, wyl my Lord vesyte my plase?
    Blyssyd be the tyme of his comyng.
    I xal ordeyn with-inne short space
    For my good Lordys wel-comyng.
    Serys, walkyth in at the begynnyng
    And se what vetaylys that I xal take.   50

31 *onys* once   32 *sofre* suffer, allow   40 *sopere* supper   44 *pasch* Passover   50 *vetaylys* food

I am so glad of this tydyng,
I wot nevyr what joye that I may make.
> *Here the Dyscypulys gon in with Symone to se the ordenawns; and Cryst comyng thedyr-ward thus seyng*

(93)

JHESUS: This path is cal Sydon be goostly ordenawns,
Wech xal convey us wher we xal be.
I knowe ful redy is the purvyaunce
Of my frendys that lovyn me.
Contewnyng in pees now procede we:
For mannys love this wey I take;
With gostly ey I veryly se
That man for man an hende must make. 60
> *Here the Dyscipulys come a-geyn to Cryst, Petyr thus seyng*

(94)

PETRUS: All redy, Lord, is oure ordenawns,
As I hope to yow plesyng xal be.
Seymon hath don at youre instawns;
He is ful glad your presens to se.

(95)

JOHANNES: All thyng we have, Lord, at oure plesyng
That longyth to youre Mawnde with ful glad chere.
Whan he herd telle of your comyng
Gret joye in hym than dyd appere.
> *Here comyth Symon owt of his hous to welcome Cryst.*

(96)

SYMON: Gracyous Lord, wel-come thu be:
Reverens be to the, both God and man. 70
My poer hous that thou wylt se,
Weche am thi servaunt as I kan.

---

52 (SD) *ordenawns* arrangements   57 *Contewnyng* continuing   60 *hende* end   71 *poer* poor

THE LAST SUPPER

(97)

JHESU: There joye of all joyis to the is sewre.
　Symon, I knowe thi trewe intent;
　The blysse of hefne thou xalt recure:
　This rewarde I xal the grawnt present.

> *Here Cryst enteryth in-to the hous with his Disciplis and ete the paschal lomb, and in the mene tyme the cownsel hous beforn-seyd xal sodeynly*[4] *onclose schewyng the Buschopys, Prestys and Jewgys syttyng in here astat lyche as it were a Convocacyone: Annas seyng thus*

(98)

ANNAS: Be-hold, it is nowth al that we do,
　In alle houre materys we prophete nowth.
　Wole ye se wech peusawns of pepyl drawyth hym to,
　For the mervaylys that he hath wrowth?　　　　　　　80

(99)

　Some other sotylte must be sowth,
　For in no wyse we may not thus hym leve;
　Than to a schrewde conclusyon we xal be browth,
　For the Romaynes than wyl us myscheve,

(100)

　And take oure astat and put us to repreve,
　And convey all the pepyl at here owyn request,
　And thus all the pepyl in hym xal be-leve.
　Therfore I pray yow, cosyn, say what is the best.

(101)

CAYPHAS: Attende now, serys, to that I xal seye.
　On-to us all it is most expedyent　　　　　　　　　90
　That o man for the pepyl xuld deye
　Than all the pepyl xuld perysch and be shent.

---

75 *recure* obtain　　76 (SD) *onclose* open　　79 *peusawns* crowd
80 *wrowth* wrought　　81 *sowth* sought

(102)

> Therfor late us werk wysely that we us not repent.
> We must nedys put on hym som fals dede.
> I sey for me I had levyr he were brent
> Than he xuld us alle thus ovyr-lede.

(103)

> Ther-fore every man on his party help at this nede,
> And cowntyrfete all the sotyltes that ye kan.
> Now late se ho kan geve best rede,
> To ordeyn sum dystruccion for this man. 100

(104)

GAMALYEL: Late us no lenger make delacion,
> But do Jhesu be takyn in hondys fast⁵,
> And all here folwerys to here confusyon,
> And in-to a preson do hem be cast.
> Ley on hem yron that wol last,
> For he hath wrouth a-gens the ryth.
> And sythyn aftyr we xal in hast
> Jewge hym to deth with gret dyspyth.

(105)

REWFYN: For he hath trespacyd a-gens oure lawe,
> Me semyth this were best jewgement. 110
> With wyld hors lete hym be drawe,
> And afftyr in fyre he xal be brent.

(106)

LEYON: Serys, o thyng my self herd hym sey,
> That he was kyng of Jewys alle.
> That is a-now to do hym dey,
> For treson to Sezar we must it calle.

95 *brent* burnt   96 *ovyr-lede* ?overcome   99 *ho* who   102 *do* cause to
108 *dyspyth* cruelty   115 *a-now* enough

THE LAST SUPPER

(107)

He seyd also to personys that I know
That he xuld and myth serteyn
The gret tempyl mythtyly ovyr-throw,
And the thrydde day reysynt ageyn.   120

(108)

Seche materys the pepyl doth [constreyn[6]]
To geve credens to his werkys alle.
In hefne he seyth xal be his reyn;
Bothe God and man he doth hym calle.

(109)

REWFYN: And all this day we xuld contryve
What shameful deth Jhesu xuld have.
We may not do hym meche myscheve,
The worchep of oure lawe to save.

(110)

LEYON: Up-on a jebet lete hym hongyn be.
This jugement me semyth it is reson,   130
That all the countre may hym se,
And be ware be his gret treson.

(111)

REWFYN: Yet o thyng, serys, ye must a-spye,
And make a ryth sotyl ordenawns,
Be what menys ye may come hym bye,
For he hath many folwerys at his instawns[7].

(112)

ANNAS: Serys, ther-of we must have avysement,
And ben acordyd or than we go,
How we xal han hym at oure entent;
Som wey we xal fynd therto[8].   140

120 *reysynt* restore   129 *jebet* gibbet

437

(113)

[*The house of Simon.*]

MARIA MAGDALEN: As a cursyd creature closyd all in care,
And as a wyckyd wrecche all wrappyd in wo;
Of blysse was nevyr no berde so bare
As I my-self that here now go.
Alas! Alas! I xal for-fare
For tho grete synnys that I have do,
Lesse than my Lord God sum-del spare,
And his grett mercy receyve me to[9];
   Mary Maudelyn is my name.
Now wyl I go to Cryst Jhesu, 150
For he is lord of all vertu,
And for sum grace I thynke to sew,
   For of my-self I have grett shame.

(114)

A mercy, Lord, and salve my synne;
Maydenys floure, thou wasch me fre.
Ther was nevyr woman of mannys kynne
So ful of synne in no countre.
I have be-fowlyd be fryth and fenne,
And sowght synne in many a cete,
But thou me borwe, Lord, I xal brenne, 160
With blake fendys ay bowne to be.
   Where-fore, kyng of grace,
With this oynement that is so sote
Lete me a-noynte thin holy fote,
And for my balys thus wyn sum bote,
   And mercy, Lord, for my trespace!

(115)

JHESUS: Woman, for thi wepynge wylle,
Sum socowre God xal the sende.
The to save I have grett skylle,

---

143 *berde* woman   152 *sew* beg   158 *fryth* wood   *fenne* fen   160 *borwe* save   161 *bowne* bound   163 *sote* sweet

THE LAST SUPPER

For sorwefull hert may synne amende. 170
All thi prayour I xal fulfylle;
To thi good hert I wul attende,
And save the fro thi synne so hylle,
And fro vij develys I xal the fende.
    Fendys, fleth your weye!
Wyckyd spyritys, I yow conjowre,
Fleth out of hire bodyly bowre!
In my grace she xal evyr flowre,
    Tyl deth doth here to deye.

(116)

MARIA MAGDALENE: I thanke the, Lorde, of this grett grace. 180
Now these vij fendys be fro me flytt,
I xal nevyr forfett nor do trespace
In wurd nor dede, ne wyl nor wytt.
Now I am brought from the fendys brace,
In thi grett mercy closyd and shytt,
I xal nevyr returne to synful trace
That xulde me dampne to helle pytt.
I wurchep the on knes bare.
Blyssyd be the tyme that I hedyr sowth,
And this oynement that I hedyr brought. 190
For now myn hert is clensyd from thought
That fyrst was combryd with care.

(117)

JUDAS: Lord, me thynkyth thou dost ryght ylle
To lete this oynement so spylle.
To selle it yt were more skylle,
And bye mete to poer men.
The box was worth of good mone
iij C. pens fayr and fre.
This myght a bowht mete plente
To fede oure power ken[10]. 200

---

173 *hylle* ill   177 *bowre* bower   184 *brace* embrace   185 *shytt* shut
186 *trace* way   189 *sowth* sought   192 *combryd* encumbered

ENGLISH MYSTERY PLAYS

(118)

JHESUS: Pore men xul abyde[11].
    A-geyn the woman thou spekyst wronge,
    And I passe forth in a tyde;
    Of mercy is here mornyng songe.
        Here Cryst restyth and etyth a lytyl and seyth syttyng to his Disciplis and Mary Mawdelyn

(119)

JHESUS: Myn herte is ryght sory, and no wondyr is;
    Too deth I xal go and nevyr dyd trespas.
    But yitt most grevyth myn hert evyr of this:
    On of my bretheryn xal werke this manas;
    On of yow here syttynge my treson xal tras;
    On of yow is besy my deth here to dyth;   210
    And yitt was I nevyr in no synful plas,
    Where-fore my deth xuld so shamfully be pyght.

(120)

PETRUS: My dere Lord, I pray the the trewth for to telle
    Whiche of us ys he that treson xal do.
    Whatt traytour is he that his lord that wold selle?
    Expresse his name, Lord, that xal werke this woo.
JOHANNES: If that ther be on that wolde selle so,
    Good mayster, telle us now opynly his name.
    What traytour is hym that from the that wolde go,
    And with fals treson fulfylle his grett shame?   220

(121)

ANDREAS: It is right dredfull such tresson to thynke,
    And wel more dredful to werk that bad dede.
    For that fals treson to helle he xal synke,
    In endles peynes grett myscheff to lede.
JACOBUS MAIOR: It is not I, Lord, for dowte I have drede;
    This synne to fulfylle cam nevyr in my mende.

203 *tyde* time   208 *manas* threat   209 *tras* contrive   212 *pyght* fixed

440

THE LAST SUPPER

Iff that I solde the, thy blood for to blede,
In doyng that treson my sowle xulde I shende.

(122)

MATHEUS: Alas, my dere Lord, what man is so wood,
For gold or for sylvyr hym-self so to spylle?   230
He that the doth selle for gold or for other good,
With his grett covetyse hym-self he doth kylle.
BARTHOLOMEUS: What man so evyr he be, of so wyckyd wylle,
Dere Lord, among us tell us his name all owt.
He that to hym tendyth this dede to fulfille,
For his grett treson his sowle stondyth in dowt.

(123)

PHILIPPUS: Golde, sylver, and tresoour sone doth passe away,
But with-owtyn ende evyr doth laste thi grace.
A, Lorde, who is that wyll chaffare the for monay?
For he that sellyth his lord to grett is the trespace.   240
JACOBUS MINOR: That traytour that doth this orryble manace,
Bothe body and sowle I holde he be lorn,
Dampnyd to helle pytt fer from thi face,
Amonge all fowle fyndys to be rent and torn.

(124)

SYMON: To bad a marchawnt that traytour he is,
And for that monye he may mornyng make.
Alas, what cawsyth hym to selle the kyng of blys?
For his fals wynnynge the devyl hym xal take.
THOMAS: For his fals treson the fendys so blake
Xal bere his sowle depe down into helle pytt.   250
Resste xal he non have but evyr-more wake,
Brennyng in hoot fyre, in preson evyr shytt.

239 *chaffare* bargain for   243 *fer* far

(125)

THADEUS: I woundyr ryght sore who that he xuld be,
Amonges us all bretheryn, that xulde do this synne.
Alas, he is lorn! Ther may no grace be.
In depe helle donjeon his sowle he doth pynne.
JHESUS: In my dysche he etyht this treson xal be-gynne[12].
Wo xal be-tydyn hym for his werke of dred.
He may be ryght sory swych ryches to wynne,
A[n]d whysshe hymself un-born for that synful ded. 260

(126)

JUDAS: The trewth wolde I knowe as leff as ye,
And therfore, good sere, the trewth thou me telle
Whiche of us all here that traytour may be.
Am I that person that the now xal selle?
JHESUS: So seyst thi-self. Take hed att thi spelle.
Thou askyst me now here if thou xalt do that treson.
Remembyr thi-self – a-vyse the ryght welle –
Thou art of grett age[13], and wotysst what is reason.

(127)

Here Judas rysyth prevely and goth in the place and seyt[14]

JUDAS: Now cowntyrfetyd I have a prevy treson,
My masterys power for to felle. 270
I, Judas, xal a-say be some encheson
On-to the Jewys hym for to selle.
Som mony for hym yet wold I telle.
Be prevy menys I xal asay;
Myn intent I xal fulfylle;
No lenger I wole make delay.

(128)

The princys of prestys now be present,
Un-to hem now my way I take.
I wyl go tellyn hem myn entent.
I trow ful mery I xal hem make. 280

257 *etyht* eats   271 *encheson* reason   273 *telle* count, receive

THE LAST SUPPER

Mony I wyl non for-sake.
And thei profyr to my plesyng,
For covetyse I wyl with hem wake,
And on-to my maystyr I xal hem bryng.
  [*Goes to the Jews.*]

(129)

Heyl, prynsesse and prestys that ben present!
New tydyngys to yow I come to telle.
Gyf ye wole folwe myn intent,
My mayster Jhesu I wele yow selle,
Hese intent and purpose for to felle,
For I wole no lenger folwyn his lawe.   290
Late sen what mony that I xal telle,
And late Jhesu my maystyr ben hangyn and drawe.

(130)

GAMALYEL: Now welcome, Judas, oure owyn frende.
Take hym in, serys, be the honde.
We xal the both geve and lende,
And in every qwarel by the stonde.

(131)

REWFYN: Judas, what xal we for thi mayster pay?
Thi sylver is redy; and we a-corde[15],
The payment xal have no delay,
But be leyde down here at a worde.   300

(132)

JUDAS: Late the mony here down be layde,
And I xal telle yow as I kan,
In old termys I have herd seyde,
That mony makyth schapman.

---

283 *wake* watch   287 *Gyf* if   289 *felle* destroy   291 *Late sen* let me see
304 *schapman* merchant

(133)

REWFYN: Here is thretty platys of sylver bryth,
    Fast knyth withinne this glove;
    And we may have thi mayster this nyth,
    This xalt thou have and all oure love[16].

(134)

JUDAS: Ye are resonable chapmen to bye and selle.
    This bargany with yow now xal I make;   310
    Smyth up[17]; ye xal have al your wylle,
    For mony wyl I non for-sake.

(135)

LEYON: Now this bargany is mad ful and fast;
    Noyther part may it for-sake.
    But, Judas, thou must telle us in hast
    Be what menys we xal hym take.

(136)

REWFYN: Ya, ther be many that hym nevyr sowe
    Weche we wyl sende to hym in fere;
    Ther-for be a tokyn we must hym knowe,
    That must be prevy be-twyx us here.   320

(137)

LEYON: Ya, be ware of that for ony thynge,
    For o dyscypil is lyche thi mayster in al parayl,
    And ye go lyche in all clothyng;
    So myth we of oure purpose fayl.

(138)

JUDAS: As for that, serys, have ye no dowth:
    I xal ordeyn so ye xal not mysse;
    Whan that ye cum hym all a-bowth,
    Take the man that I xal kysse.

305 *platys* coins   306 *knyth* tied   311 *Smyth* smite   317 *sowe* saw
322 *parayl* apparel

THE LAST SUPPER

(139)

I must go to my maystyr a-geyn.
Dowth not, serys, this matere is sure i-now.   330

GAMALYEL: Fare wel, Judas, oure frend serteyn;
Thi labour we xal ryth wel a-low.

(140)

JUDAS: Now wyl I sotely go seke my mayster ageyn,
And make good face, as I nowth knew.
I have hym solde to wo and peyn;
I trowe ful sore he xal it rew.
Here Judas goth in sotylly wher-as he cam fro.

(141)

ANNAS: Lo, serys, a part we have of oure entent.
For to take Jhesu now we must provyde
A sotyl meny to be present,
That dare fyth and wele a-byde.   340

(142)

GAMALYEL: Ordeyn eche man on his party
Cressetys, lanternys and torchys lyth,
And this nyth to be ther redy,
With exys, gleyvis and swerdys bryth.

(143)

CAYPHAS: No lenger than make we teryeng,
But eche man to his place hym dyth,
And ordeyn prevely for this thyng,
That it be done this same nyth.
Here the Buschopys partyn in the place[18], and eche of hem takyn here leve be contenawns, resortyng eche man to his place with here meny to make redy to take Cryst; and than xal the place ther Cryst is in xal sodeynly un-close rownd abowtyn, shewyng Cryst syttyng at the table and hese Dyscypulys eche in ere degre, Cryst thus seyng

330 *Dowth* fear   334 *nowth* nothing   339 *meny* company   340 *fyth* fight
342 *Cressetys* lanterns   344 *exys* axes   *gleyvis* weapons

(144)
JHESU: Brederyn, this lambe that was set us beforn,
   That we alle have etyn in this nyth,   350
   It was comawndyd be my fadyr to Moyses and Aaron,
   Whan thei weryn with the chylderyn of Israel in Egythp.

(145)
   And as we with swete bredys have it ete,
   And also with the byttyr sokelyng,
   And as we take the hed with the fete,
   So dede thei in all maner thyng.

(146)
   And as we stodyn, so dede thei stond,
   And here reynes thei gyrdyn veryly,
   With schon on here fete and stavys in here hond,
   And as we ete it, so dede thei hastyly.   360
   This fygure xal sesse; a-nothyr xal folwe ther-by,
   Weche xal be of my body that am your hed,
   Weche xal be shewyd to yow be a mystery[19],
   Of my flesch and blood in forme of bred.

(147)
   And with fervent desyre of hertys affeccion,
   I have enterly desyryd to kepe my Mawnde
   A-mong yow er than I suffre my passyon.
   For of this no more to-gedyr suppe xal we.
   And as the paschal lomb etyn have we
   In the old lawe was usyd for a sacryfyce,   370
   So the newe lomb that xal be sacryd be me
   Xal be usyd for a sacryfyce most of price.
      *Here xal Jhesus take an oble[20] in his hand, lokyng upward
      in to hefne to the Fadyr, thus seyng*

(148)
   Where fore to the Fadyr of hefne that art eternall
   Thankyng and honor I yeld on to the,

---

354 *sokelyng* clover (also known as 'lamb-suckling')   358 *reynes* loins
359 *schon* shoes

THE LAST SUPPER

To whom be the godhed I am eqwall,
But be my manhod I am of less degre;
Where fore I as man worchep the deyte,
Thankyng the, Fadyr, that thou wylt shew this mystery;
And thus thurwe thi myth, Fadyr, and blyssyng of me,
Of this that was bred is mad my body. 380

Here xal he spekyn ageyn to his Dyscipulys thus seyng

(149)

Bretheryn, be the [vertu] of these wordys that[re]hercyd be,
This, that shewyth as bred to your apparens[21],
Is mad the very flesche and blod of me,
To the weche thei that wole be savyd must geve credens.

(150)

And as in the olde lawe it was comawndyd and precepte
To ete this lomb to the dystruccyon of Pharao un-kende,
So to dystroy your gostly enmye this xal be kepte
For your paschal lombe in-to the werdys ende.

(151)

For this is the very lombe with-owte spot of synne
Of weche Johan the Baptyst dede prophesy, 390
Whan this prophesye he dede be-gynne,
Seyng *Ecce agnus dey*.

(152)

And how ye xal ete this lombe I xal geve informacion
In the same forme as the eld lawe doth specyfye,
As I shewe be gostly interpretacyon;
Ther-fore to that I xal sey your wyllys loke ye replye.

(153)

With no byttyr bred this bred ete xal be,
That is to say with no byttyrnesse of hate and envye,
But with the suete bred of love and charyte[22],
Weche fortefyet the soule gretlye. 400

375 *be* by   378 *the* thee   384 *credens* belief   400 *fortefyet* defend

ENGLISH MYSTERY PLAYS

(154)

> And it schuld ben etyn with the byttyr sokelyng,
> That is to mene gyf a man be of synful dyspocycion,
> Hath led his lyff here with mys-levyng,
> Therfore in his hert he xal have byttyr contrycion.

(155)

> Also the hed with the feet ete xal ye:
> Be the hed ye xal undyr-stand my godhed,
> And be the feet ye xal take myn humanyte.
> These tweyn ye xal receyve to-gedyr in dede.

(156)

> This immaculat lombe that I xal yow geve
> Is not only the godhed a-lone,   410
> But bothe God and man, thus must ye beleve;
> Thus the hed with the feet ye xal receyve ech-on.

(157)

> Of this lombe un-ete yf owth be levyth[23] i-wys,
> Yt xuld be cast in the clere fyre and brent,
> Weche is to mene, yf thou undyrstande nowth al this,
> Put thi feyth in God and than thou xalt not be shent.

(158)

> The gyrdyl, that was comawndyd here reynes to sprede,
> Xal be the gyrdyl of clennes and chastyte,
> That is to sayn to be contynent in word, thought and dede,
> And all leccherous levyng cast yow for to fle.   420

(159)

> And the schon that xal be your feet up-on
> Is not ellys but exawnpyl of vertuis levyng
> Of your form faderys you be-forn;
> With these schon my steppys ye xal be sewyng.

---

403 *mys-levyng* wrong-doing   419 *contynent* continent   422 *levyng* living   423 *form* former (i.e. ancestors)

448

THE LAST SUPPER

(160)

    And the staf that in your handys ye xal holde
    Is not ellys but the exawmplys to other men teche;
    Hold fast your stavys in your handys and beth bolde
    To every creature myn precepttys for to preche.

(161)

    Also ye must ete this paschall lombe hastyly,
    Of weche sentens this is the very entent: 430
    At every oure and tyme ye xal be redy
    For to fulfylle my cowmawndement.

(162)

    For thow ye leve this day, ye are not sure
    Whedyr ye xal leve to-morwe or nowth;
    Ther-for hastyly every oure do youre besy cure
    To kepe my preceptys and than thar ye not dowth.

(163)

    Now have I lernyd yow how ye xal ete
    Your paschal lombe that is my precyous body.
    Now I wyl fede yow all with awngellys mete,
    Wherfore to reseyve it come forth seryattly.   440

(164)

PETRUS: Lord, for to receyve this gostly sustenawns
    In dewe forme it excedyth myn intellygens,
    For no man of hym-self may have substawns
    To receyve it with to meche reverens.

(165)

    For with more delycyous mete, Lord, thou may us not fede
    Than with thin owyn precyous body;
    Wherfore what I have trespacyd in word, thought or dede,
    With byttyr contrycion, Lord, I haske the mercy.

---

431 *oure* hour   440 *seryattly* in succession

Whan oure Lord gyvyth his body to his Dyscypulys he xal sey to eche of hem, except to Judas

(166)

JESUS: This is my body, flesch and blode,
    That for the xal dey up-on the rode. 450
    And whan Judas comyth last, oure Lord xal sey to hym

(167)

    Judas, art thou avysyd what thou xalt take?
JUDAS: Lord, thi body I wyl not for-sake.
    And sythyn oure Lord xal sey on-to Judas

(168)

JHESU: Myn body to the I wole not denye,
    Sythyn thou wylt presume ther-upon;
    Yt xal be thi dampnacyon verylye,
    I geve the warnyng now be-forn.
    And aftyr that Judas hath reseyvyd he xal syt ther he was, Cryst seyng

(169)

    On of yow hath be-trayd me,
    That at my borde with me hath ete[24];
    Bettyr it hadde hym for to a be
    Bothe un-born and un-begete. 460
    Than eche Dyscypyl xal loke on other and Petyr xal sey

(170)

PETRUS: Lord, it is not I.
    And so alle xul seyn tyl thei comyn at Judas, weche xal sey
JUDAS: Is it owth I, Lord?[25]
    Than Jhesus xal sey
JHESU: Judas, thou seyst that word.
    Me thou ast solde that was thi frend.
    That thou hast be-gonne, brenge to an ende.

THE LAST SUPPER

Than Judas xal gon a-geyn to the Jewys, and yf men wolne xal mete with hym and sey this spech folwyng, or levynt whether thei wyl, the Devyl thus seyng

(171)

DEMON: A, A, Judas, derlyng myn!
Thou art the best to me that evyr was bore;
Thou xalt be crownyd in helle peyn,
And ther-of thou xalt be sekyr for evyr-more.

(172)

Thow hast solde thi maystyr and etyn hym also;   470
I wolde thou kowdyst bryngyn hym to helle every del.
But yet I fere he xuld do ther sum sorwe and wo[26],
That all helle xal crye out on me that sel.

(173)

Sped up thi matere that thou hast be-gonne;
I xal to helle for the to mak redy.
Anon thou xalt come wher thou xalt wonne;
In fyre and stynk thou xalt sytt me by.

(174)

JHESU: Now the sone of God claryfyed is,
And God in hym is claryfyed also.
I am sory that Judas hath lost his blysse   480
Weche xal turne hym to sorwe and wo.

(175)

But now in the memory of my passyon,
To ben partabyl with me in my reyn above,
Ye xal drynk myn blood with gret devocyon,
Wheche xal be xad for mannys love.

465 (SD) *levynt* leave, omit   473 *sel* time   478 *claryfyed* revealed
483 *partbyl a* able to share   485 *xad* shed

451

(176)

>Takyth these chalys of the newe testament,
>And kepyth this evyr in your mende.
>As oftyn as ye do this with trewe intent,
>It xal defende yow fro the fende.
>>*Than xal the Dysciplys com and take the blod, Jhesus seyng*

(177)

>This is my blood that for mannys synne 490
>Outh of myn herte it xal renne.
>>*And the Dyscipulys xul sett them agen ther thei wore and Jhesus xal seyn*

(178)

>Takyth hed now, bretheryn, what I have do.
>With my flesch and blood I have yow fed;
>For mannys love I may do no mo
>Than for love of man to be ded.

(179)

>Werfore, Petyr, and ye every-chon,
>Gyf ye love me, fede my schep,
>That for fawth of techyng thei go not wrong,
>But evyr to hem takyth good kep.

(180)

>Gevyth hem my body as I have to yow, 500
>Qweche xal be sacryd be my worde,
>And evyr I xal thus a-byde with yow
>In-to the ende of the werde.

(181)

>Ho-so etyth my body and drynkyth my blood,
>Hol God and man he xal me take.
>It xal hym defende from the devyl wood,
>And at his deth I xal hym nowth for-sake.

498 *fawth* lack   505 *Hol* united   506 *wood* mad

THE LAST SUPPER

(182)

And ho-so not ete my body nor drynke my blood,
Lyf in hym is nevyr a dele.
Kepe wel this in mende for your good 510
And every man save hym-self wele.
Here Jhesus takyth a basyn with watyr and towaly gyrt abowtyn hym and fallyth beforn Petyr on his o kne.

(183)

A-nother exawmpyl I xal yow showe
How ye xal leve in charyte;
Syt here down at wordys fewe
And qwat I do ye sofre me.
Here he takyth the basyn and the towaly and doth as the roberych seyth beforn.

(184)

PETRUS: Lord, what wylt thou with me do?
This servyce of the I wyl for-sake;
To wassche my feet thou xal not so:
I am not worthy it of the to take.

(185)

JHESU: Petyr, and thou for-sake my servyce all 520
The weche to yow that I xal do,
No part with me have thou xal
And nevyr com my blysse on-to.
PETRUS: That part, Lord, we wyl not for-go.
We xal a-bey his comawndement,
Wassche hed and hond we pray the so;
We wyl don after thin entent.
Here Jhesus wasshyth his Dyscipulys feet by and by and whypyth hem and kyssyth hem mekely and sythy[n] settyth hym down thus seyng

515 (SD) *roberych* rubric

453

(186)

JHESU: Frendys, this wasshyng xal now prevayll.
Youre lord and mayster ye do me calle,
And so I am with-owtyn fayl, 530
Yet I have wasschyd yow alle;
A memory of this have ye xall,
That eche of yow xal do to othyr;
With umbyl hert submyt egal,
As eche of yow were otherys brother.

(187)

No thyng, serys, so wele plesyth me,
Nor no lyf that man may lede,
As thei that levyn in charyte;
In efne I xal reward here mede.
The day is come I must procede 540
For to fulfylle the prophecy.
This nyth for me ye xal han drede,
Whan noumbyr of pepyl xal on me cry.

(188)

For the Prophetys spoke of me,
And seydyn of deth that I xuld take;
Fro whech deth I wole not fle,
But for mannys synne a-mendys make.

(189)

This nyth fro yow be led I xal,
And ye for fer fro me xal fle,
Not onys dur speke whan I yow call, 550
And some of yow for-sake me.

(190)

For yow xal I dey and ryse ageyn;
Un the thrydde day ye xal me se
Be-forn yow, all walkyng playn
In the lond of Galyle.

534 *egal* equal   539 *efne* heaven   550 *dur* dare   553 *Un* on

THE LAST SUPPER

(191)

PETRUS: Lord, I wyl the nevyr for-sake,
    Nor for no perellys fro the fle,
    I wyl rather my deth take
    Than onys, Lord, for-sake the.

(192)

JHESU: Petyr – yn ferthere than thu doyst knowe[27] –
    As for that, promese loke thou not make,
    For or the cok hath twyes crowe,
    Thryes thou xal me for-sake.

(193)

    But all my frendys that arn me dere,
    Late us go: the tyme drawyth ny.
    We may no lengere a-bydyn here,
    For I must walke to Betany.

(194)

    The tyme is come; the day drawyth nere;
    On-to my deth I must in hast.
    Now, Petyr, make hall thi felawys chere.
    My flesch for fere is qwakyng fast[28].

560 *doyst* do   570 *hall* all

26. The Betrayal

Here Jhesus goth to Betany-ward, and his Dyscipulys folwyng with sad contenawns[1], Jhesus seyng

(195)

[JHESUS:] Now, my dere frendys and bretheryn echon,
    Remembyr the wordys that I xal sey;
    The tyme is come that I must gon
    For to fulfylle the prophesey
    That is seyd of me, that I xal dey
    The fendys power fro yow to flem,
    Weche deth I wole not deney
    Mannys sowle, my spouse, for to redem.

(196)

    The oyle of mercy is grawntyd playn
    Be this jorne that I xal take;
    Be my fadyr I am sent sertayn
    Be-twyx God and man an ende to make.
    Man for my brother may I not for-sake,
    Nor shewe hym un-kendenesse be no wey.
    In peynys for hym my body schal schake,
    And for love of man, man xal dey.

Here Jhesus and his Discipulys go toward the Mount of Olyvet and whan he comyth a lytyl ther be-syde in a place lych to a park he byddyt his Dyscipulys a-byde hym ther and seyth to Petyr or he goth

(197)

    Petyr, with thi felawys here xalt thou a-byde,
    And weche tyl I come a-geyn.

6 *flem* drive away   10 *jorne* journey   18 *weche* watch

THE BETRAYAL

I must make my prayere here you be-syde;
My flesch qwakyth sore for fere and peyn. 20
PETRUS: Lord, thi request doth me constreyn.
In this place I xal abide stylle,
Not remeve tyl that thou comyst ageyn,
In confermyng, Lord, of thi wylle.
Here Jhesu goth to Olyvet and settyth hym down one his knes and prayth to his Fadyr, thus seyng

(198)

JHESU: O, Fadyr, Fadyr, for my sake,
This gret passyon thou take fro me,
Wech arn ordeyned that I xal take
Gyf mannys sowle savyd may be.
And gyf it be-hove, Fadyr, for me
To save mannys sowle that xuld spylle, 30
I am redy in eche degre
The vyl of the for to fulfylle[2].
Here Jhesus goth to his Dyscipulis and fyndyth hem sclepyng, Jhesus thus seyng to Petyr

(199)

Petyr, Petyr, thou slepyst fast;
A-wake thi felawys and sclepe no more.
Of my deth ye are not agast;
Ye take your rest, and I peyn sore.
Here Cryst goth ageyn the second tyme to Olyvet and seyth knelyng

(200)

Fadyr in hevyn, I be-seche the,
Remeve my peynes be thi gret grace,
And lete me fro this deth fle,
As I dede nevyr no trespace. 40
The watyr and blood[3] owth of my face
Dystyllyth for peynes that I xal take;

32 *vyl* will   35 *agast* afraid   41 *owth* out

My flesche qwakyth in ferful case
As thow the joyntys a-sondre xuld schake.
> *Here Jhesus goth a-geyn to his Discipulis and fyndyth hem asclepe, Jhesus thus seyng, latyng hem lyne*

(201)

Fadyr, the thrydde tyme I come ageyn
Fulleche myn erdon for to spede[4].
Delyvere me, Fadyr, fro this peyn
Weche is reducyd with ful gret dred;
On to thi sone, Fadyr, take hede.
Thou wotyst I dede nevyr dede but good;   50
It is not for me this peyn I lede,
But for man I swete bothe watyr and blode.
> *Here an Aungel descendyth to Jhesus and bryngyth to hym a chalys with an host ther in.*

(202)

ANGELUS: Heyl, bothe God and man in-dede!
The Fadyr hath sent the this present.
He bad that thou xuldyst not drede
But fulfylle his intent.
As the parlement of hefne hath ment,
That mannys sowle xal now redemyd be,
From hefne to herd, Lord, thou wore sent;
That dede appendyth on-to the.   60

(203)

This chalys ys thi blood, this bred is thi body[5],
For mannys synne evyr offeryd xal be.
To the Fadyr of hefne that is al-mythty,
Thi dyscipulis and all presthood xal offere fore the.
> *Here the Aungel ascendyth sodeynly.*

JHESU: Fadyr, thi wyl fulfyllyd xal be;
It is nowth to say agens the case[6].

---

44 (SD) *lyne* lie   46 *erdon* errand   48 *reducyd* brought back   59 *herd* earth   60 *appendyth* belongs

THE BETRAYAL

I xal fulfylle the prophesye
And sofre deth for mannys trespace.
Here goth Cryst a-geyn to his Dyscipulys and fyndyth hem sclepyng stylle.

(204)

A-wake, Petyr, thi rest is ful long;
Of sclep thu wylt make no delay.   70
Judas is redy with pepyl strong
And doth his part me to be-tray.
Ryse up, serys, I you pray,
On-close your eyne for my sake.
We xal walke into the way
And sen hem com that xul me take.

(205)

Petyr, whan thou seyst I am for-sake
Amonge myn frendys and stond alone,
All the cher that thou kanst make
Geve to thi bretheryn every-chone.   80
Here Jhesus with his Dyscipulis goth in-to the place and ther xal come in a X personys weyl be-seen in white arneys and breganderys and some dysgysed in odyr garmentys with swerdys, gleyvys, and other straunge wepone as cressettys with feyr, and lanternys and torchis lyth, and Judas formest of al conveyng hem to Jhesu be contenawns, Jhesus thus seyng[7]

(206)

Serys, in your way ye have gret hast
To seke hym that wyl not fle.
Of yow I am ryth nowth a-gast;
Telle me, serys, whom seke ye?

76 *sen* see   80 (SD) *arneys* armour   *breganderys* body armour   *be contenawns* by gestures

(207)

LEYON: Whom we seke here I telle the now:
　A tretour is worthy to suffer deth.
　We knowe he is here a-mong yow.
　His name is Jhesus of Nazareth.

(208)

JHESU: Serys, I am here that wyl not fle,
　Do to me all that ye kan.　　　　　　　　　　　　　　　　90
　For sothe I telle yow I am he,
　Jhesus of Nazareth, that same man.
　　*Here alle the Jewys falle sodeynly to the erde whan thei here
　　Cryst speke and qwan [he] byddyth hem rysyn thei rysyn
　　agen, Cryst thus seyng*

(209)

A-ryse, serys! Whom seke ye? Fast have ye gon.
Is howth your comyng hedyr for me?[8]
I stond be-forn yow here echon,
That ye may me bothe knowe and se.

(210)

RUFYNE: Jhesus of Nazareth we seke,
　And we myth hym here a-spye.
JHESU: I told you now with wordys meke
　Be-forn you all that it was I.　　　　　　　　　　　　　　100

(211)

JUDAS: Welcome, Jhesu, my mayster dere,
　I have the sowth in many a place.
　I am ful glad I fynd the here
　For I wyst nevyr wher thou wace.
　　*Here Judas kyssyth Jhesus and a-noon alle the Jewys
　　come a-bowth hym and ley handys on hym and pullyn hym
　　as thei were wode and makyn on hym a gret cry all at-onys,
　　and aftyr this Petyr seyth*

THE BETRAYAL

(212)

[PETER:] I drawe my swerd now this sel.
    Xal I smyte, mayster? Fayn wolde I wete.
        And forth-with he smytyth of Malcheus here, and he
        cryeth 'Help, myn here! Myn here!' And Cryst blyssyth it
        and tys hol.
JHESUS: Put thi swerd in the shede fayr and wel,
    For he that smyth with swerd, with swerd xal be smete.

(213)

    A, Judas, this treson cowntyrfetyd hast thou,
    And that thou xalt ful sore repent;   110
    Thou haddyst be bettyr a ben un-born now;
    Thi body and sowle thou hast shent.

(214)

GAMALYEL: Lo, Jhesus, thou mayst not the cace refuse;
    Bothe treson and eresye in the is fownde.
    Stody now fast on thin excuse
    Whylys that thou gost in cordys bownde.
    Thou kallyst the kyng of this werd rownde;
    Now lete me se thi gret powere,
    And save thi-self here hool and sownde
    And brynge the out of this dawngere.   120

(215)

LEYON: Bryng forth this tretoure! Spare hym nowth!
    On-to Cayphas thi jewge we xal the ledde.
    In many a place we have the sowth,
    And to thi werkys take good hede.

(216)

RUFYNE: Come on, Jhesus, and folwe me.
    I am ful glad that I the have;
    Thou xalt ben hangyn up-on a tre:
    A melyon of gold xal the not save.

---

105 *sel* time   106 *wete* know   106 (SD) *here* ear   *tys* it is   *hol* whole
107 *shede* sheath   114 *eresye* heresy   128 *melyon* million

(217)

LEYON: Lete me leyn hand on hym in heye;
    On to his deth I xal hym bryng.   130
    Shewe forth thi wyche-crafte and nygramansye.
    What helpyth the now al thi fals werkyng?

(218)

JHESU: Frendys, take hede! Ye don un-ryth
    So un-kendely with cordys to bynd me here,
    And thus to falle on me be nyth
    And thow I were a thevys fere.
    Many tyme be-forn yow I dede a-pere;
    With-inne the temple sen me ye have,
    The lawys of God to teche and lere
    To hem that wele here sowlys save.   140

(219)

Why dede ye not me dysprave,
And herd me preche both lowd and lowe,
But now as woodmen ye gynne to rave,
And do thyng that ye notwth knowe.

(220)

GAMALYEL: Serys, I charge yow not o word more this nyth,
But on-to Cayphas in hast loke ye hym lede.
Have hym forth with gret dyspyte
And to his wordys take ye non hede.
    Here the Jewys lede Cryst outh of the place with gret cry and noyse, some drawyng Cryst forward and some bakwarde and so ledyng forth with here weponys a-lofte and lytys brennyng, and in the mene tyme Marye Magdalene xal rennyn to oure Lady and telle here of oure Lordys takyng⁹, thus seyng

---

129 *leyn* lay   *heye* ?haste   131 *nygramansye* magic   135 *nyth* night
139 *lere* learn   141 *dysprave* disprove

THE BETRAYAL

(221)

MARIA MAGDALENE: O in-maculate modyr, of all women most meke,
   O devowtest in holy medytacion evyr a-bydyng,   150
   The cawse, lady, that I to your person seke
   Is to wetyn yf ye heryn ony tydyng

(222)

   Of your swete sone and my reverent lord Jhesu,
   That was your dayly solas, your gostly consolacyon.
MARYA [VIRGO]: I wold ye xuld telle me, Mawdelyn, and ye knew,
   For to here of hym it is all myn affeccyon.

(223)

MARIA MAGD[ALENE]: I wold fayn telle, lady, and I myth for wepyng.
   For sothe, lady, to the Jewys he is solde;
   With cordys thei have hym bownde and have hym in kepyng;
   Thei hym bety spetously and have hym fast in holde.   160
MARIA VIRGO: A! A! A! How myn hert is colde!
   A hert hard as ston, how mayst thou lest
   Whan these sorweful tydyngys are the told?
   So wold to God, hert, that thou mytyst brest.

(224)

   A, Jhesu! Jhesu! Jhesu! Jhesu!
   Why xuld ye sofere this trybulacyon and advercyte?
   How may thei fynd in here hertys yow to pursewe
   That nevyr trespacyd in no maner degre?
   For nevyr thyng but that was good thowth ye.
   Where-fore than xuld ye sofer this gret peyn?   170
   I suppoce veryly it is for the tresspace of me;
   And I wyst that myn hert xuld cleve on tweyn.

---

152 *wetyn* find out   160 *bety* beat   *spetously* spitefully   162 *lest* listen
169 *thowth* thought

(225)

> For these langowrys may I susteyn,
> The swerd of sorwe hath so thyrlyd my meende.
> Alas, what may I do? Alas, what may I seyn?
> These prongys myn herte a-sondyr thei do rende.

(226)

> O Fadyr of hefne, wher ben al thi be-hestys
> That thou promysyst me whan a modyr thou me made?
> Thi blyssyd Sone I bare be-twyx tweyn bestys,
> And now the bryth colour of his face doth fade.

180

(227)

> A, good Fadyr, why woldyst that thin owyn dere Sone xal sofre al this?
> And dede he nevyr agens thi precept, but evyr was obedyent,
> And to every creature most petyful, most jentyl and benyng i-wys,
> And now for all these kendnessys is now most shameful schent.

(228)

> Why wolt thou, gracyous Fadyr, that it xal be so?
> May man not ellys be savyd be non other kende?
> Yet, Lord Fadyr, than that xal comforte myn wo,
> Whan man is savyd be my Chylde and browth to a good ende.

(229)

> Now, dere Sone, syn thou hast evyr be so ful of mercy,
> That wylt not spare thi-self for the love thou hast to man,
> On all man-kend now have thou pety,
> And also thynk on thi modyr, that hevy woman.

190

173 *langowrys* afflictions   174 *thyrlyd* pierced   *meende* mind   180 *bryth* bright   183 *benyng* benign

27. The Buffeting

Coliphizacio

TOWNELEY 21

The play is undoubtedly the work of the Wakefield Master, who contributed his revisions to the cycle in the first half of the fifteenth century. It is written throughout in his characteristic nine-line stanza. Besides this there are a number of literary and dramatic characteristics which point to him.

The language is vigorous and racy, with many examples of contemporary idiom, jokes, ambiguities, oaths and proverbs. The verse form is handled with great flexibility in the dialogue and with varied styles for the different speakers. The characterization is powerful. Christ himself, outwardly mocked and ridiculed, remains silent except for one brief speech, but the play is so constructed that his presence is felt throughout. The most voluble speaker is Caiaphas, who floods the scene with violent threats and hypocritical pretensions. His open purpose is to be as cruel as he can. He is opposed and controlled by Annas, who sees another, legal way of achieving their objectives. The result is a very fine piece of writing in which these two struggle for superiority. The Torturers are brutal, willing to carry out the threats of Caiaphas. Froward, their boy, adds his own touch of corruption in his insolent cheek and his enjoyment of the suffering.

Dramatically the buffeting is very powerful; it excites pity and terror. It is made more grim because the Torturers regard it as a new game for Yule. There is some justification for this in the Gospels. Matthew (26 67, 68), Mark (14 65), and Luke (22 63-5) all relate how the people beat him and then challenge him to use his prophetic powers to reveal who struck the blows. Mark and Luke mention that he is blindfolded during the episode. The dramatist works this into a horrifying sequence, and the silence of Christ, already established in the scene with Annas and Caiaphas, is an important part of the dramatic tension which is generated.

ಐಐ

[*The Torturers drive Christ to Caiaphas and Annas.*]

(1)

I TORTOR: Do io furth, io,   and trott on apase![1]
    To Anna will we go   and sir Cayphas;
    Witt thou well of thaym two   gettys thou no grace,
    Bot everlastyng wo   for trespas thou has
    So mekill.
    Thi mys is more
    Then ever gettys thou grace fore;
    Thou has beyn ay-whore
    Full fals and full fekyll.

(2)

II TORTOR: It is wonder to dre,   thus to be gangyng.   10
    We have had for the   mekill hart stangyng;
    Bot at last shall we be   out of hart langyng,
    Be thou have had two or thre   hetys worth a hangyng[2].
    No wonder!
    Sich wyles can thou make,
    Gar the people farsake
    Oure lawes, and thyne take;
    Thus art thou broght in blonder[3].

(3)

I TORTOR: Thou can not say agaynt,   if thou be trew;
    Some men holdys the sant,   and that shall thou rew;   20
    Fare wordys can thou paynt,   and lege lawes new.

---

8 *ay-whore* everywhere 9 *fekyll* fickle 10 *dre* endure 11 *hart stangyng* agony 13 *hetys* promises 20 *sant* saint 21 *lege* bring forward

THE BUFFETING

II TORTOR: Now be ye ataynt   for we will persew
On this mater.
Many wordys has thou saide
Of which we ar not well payde;
As good that thou had
Halden still thi clater.

(4)

I TORTOR: It is better syt still   then rise up and fall;
Thou has long had thi will   and made many brall;
At the last wold thou spill   and for-do us all,   30
If we dyd never yll.
II TORTOR: I trow not, he shall
Indure it;
For if other men ruse hym
We shall accuse hym;
His self shall not excuse hym;
To you I insure it,

(5)

With no legeance.
I TORTOR: Fayn wold he wynk,
Els falys his countenance[4];   I say as I thynk.
II TORTOR: He has done us grevance;   therfor shall he drynk;
Have he mekill myschaunsce   that has gart us swynke   40
In walkyng[5],
That unneth may I more.
I TORTOR: Peas, man, we are thore!
I shall walk in before,
And tell of his talkyng.

(6)

[*They speak to Caiaphas and Annas.*]
Haill, syrs, as ye sytt,   so worthi in wonys!
Whi spyrd ye not yit   how we have farne this onys?[6]

---

25 *payde* pleased   33 *ruse* praise   37 *legeance* mitigation   42 *unneth* hardly   43 *thore* there   47 *spyrd* asked   *farne* got on

467

II TORTOR: Sir, we wold fayn witt;   all wery ar oure bonys;
   We have had a fytt   right yll for the nonys,
   So tarid.   50
CAYPHAS: Say, were ye oght adred?
   Were ye oght wrang led?
   Or in any strate sted?
   Syrs, who was myscaryd?

(7)
ANNA: Say, were ye oght in dowte   for fawte of light
   As ye wached ther-owte?
I TORTOR: Sir, as I am true knyght,
   Of my dame sen I sowked   had I never sich a nyght[7];
   My een were not lowked   to-geder right
   Sen morowe;
   Bot yit I thynk it well sett,   60
   Sen we with this tratoure met;
   Sir, this is he that forfett
   And done so mekill sorow.

(8)
CAYPHAS: Can ye hym oght apeche?   Had he any ferys?
II TORTOR: He has bene for to preche   full many long yeris;
   And the people he teche   a new law.
I TORTOR: Syrs, heris!
   As far as his witt reche   many oone he lerys.
   When we toke hym,
   We faunde hym in a yerde;
   Bot when I drew out my swerde   70
   His dyscypyls wex ferde,
   And soyn thay forsoke hym.

(9)
II TORTOR: Sir, I hard hym say he cowthe dystroew   oure
      tempyll so gay,
   And sithen beld a new   on the thrid day.

49 *fytt* time   53 *sted* placed   57 *sowked* sucked   58 *lowked* closed
59 *morowe* daybreak   64 *ferys* companions   67 *lerys* teaches   71 *ferde*
afraid   74 *beld* build

468

THE BUFFETING

CAYPHAS: How myght that be trew? It toke more aray;
    The masons I knewe that hewed it, I say,
    So wyse,
    That hewed ilka stone.
I TORTOR: A, good sir, lett hym oone;
    He lyes, for the quetstone[8];   80
    I gyf hym the pryce.

(10)

II TORTOR: The halt rynes, the blynd sees thrugh his fals lyes[9];
    Thus he gettis many fees of thym he begyles.
I TORTOR: He rases men that dees; thay seke hym be myles;
    And ever thrugh his soceres oure sabate day defyles
    Evermore, sir.
II TORTOR: This is his use and his custom,
    To heyll the defe and the dom,
    Where so ever he com;
    I tell you before, sir.   90

(11)

I TORTOR: Men call hym a prophete, and Godis son of heven;
    He wold fayn downe bryng oure lawes bi his steven.
II TORTOR: Yit is ther anothere thyng that I hard hym neven:
    He settys not a fle wyng bi sir Cesar full even;
    He says thus;
    Sir, this same is he
    That excusyd with his sotelte
    A woman in avowtre[10];
    Full well may ye trust us.

(12)

I TORTOR: Sir Lazare[11] can he rase, that men may persave,   100
    When he had lyne iiij dayes ded in his grave;

82 *halt* lame   *rynes* runs   84 *dees* die   85 *soceres* ?sorceries   92 *steven* speech   93 *neven* say   98 *avowtre* adultery

ENGLISH MYSTERY PLAYS

All men hym prase,   both master and knave,
Such wychcraft he mase.
II TORTOR: If he abowte wave
Any langere,
His warkys may we ban;
For he has turned many man
Sen the tyme he began,
And done us great hangere.

(13)

I TORTOR: He will not leyfe yit,   thof he be culpabyll;
Men call hym a prophete,   a lord full renabyll.   110
Sir Cayphas, bi my wytt,   he shuld be dampnabill,
Bot wold ye two, as ye sytt,   make it ferme and stabyll
To geder;
For ye two, as I traw,
May defende all oure law;
That mayde us to you draw,
And bryng this losell heder.

(14)

II TORTOR: Sir, I can tell you before,   as myght I be maryd,
If he reyne any more,   oure lawes ar myscaryd.
I TORTOR: Sir, opposed if he wore,   he shuld be fon waryd;   120
That is well seyn thore   where he has long tarid
And walkyd.
He is sowre lottyn:
Ther is somwhat forgottyn;
I shall thryng out the rottyn,
Be we have all talkyd[12].

(15)

CAYPHAS: Now fare myght you fall   for youre talkyng!
For, certys, I my self shall   make examynyng.

---

104 *langere* longer   105 *ban* curse   108 *hangere* trouble   109 *thof* though   110 *renabyll* eloquent   118 *maryd* destroyed   120 *fon* found *waryd* accursed   123 *sowre* sour   *lottyn* looking

THE BUFFETING

Harstow, harlott, of all?   Of care may thou syng!
How durst thou the call   aythere emperoure or kyng?   130
I do fy the![13]
What the dwill doyst thou here?
Thi dedys will do the dere;
Com nar and rowne in myn eeyr,
Or I shall ascry the.

(16)

Illa-hayll was thou borne!   Harke! Says he oght agane?
Thou shall onys or to-morne   to speke be full fayne.
This is a great skorne   and a fals trane;
Now wols-hede and out-horne   on the be tane![14]
Vile fature!   140
Oone worde myght thou speke ethe,
Yit myght it do the som letht,
Et omnis qui tacet
Hic consentire videtur[15].

(17)

Speke on oone word   right in the dwyllys name!
Where was thi syre at bord   when he met with thi dame?
What, nawder bowted ne spurd   and a lord of name![16]
Speke on in a torde,   the dwill gif the shame,
Sir Sybre![17]
Perde, if thou were a kyng   150
Yit myght thou be ridyng;
Fy on the, fundlyng!
Thou lyfys bot bi brybre.

(18)

Lad, I am a prelate,   a lord in degre,
Syttys in myn astate   as thou may se,

129 *Harstow* do you hear?   134 *rowne* whisper   136 *Illa-hayll* evil fortune   138 *trane* trick   139 *wols-hede* wolf's head   *out-horne* horn blast (for outlaws)   140 *fature* deceiver   141 *ethe* easily   142 *letht* relief   145 *dwyllys* devil's   147 *nawder* neither   *bowted* booted   148 *torde* turd   153 *brybre* theft

Knyghtys on me to wate   in dyverse degre;
I myght thole the abate,   and knele on thi kne
In my present;
As ever syng I mes,
Whoso kepis the lawe, I gess,
He gettis more by purches
Then bi his fre rent[18].

(19)

The dwill gif the shame   that ever I knew the!
Nather blynde ne lame   will none persew the;
Therfor I shall the name   that ever shall rew the,
Kyng Copyn[19] in oure game,   thus shall I indew the,
For a fatur.
Say, dar thou not speke for ferde?
I shrew hym the lerd,
Weme![20] The dwillys durt in thi berd,
Vyle fals tratur!

(20)

Though thi lyppis be stokyn,   yit myght thou say, mom;
Great wordis has thou spokyn;   then was thou not dom.
Be it hole worde or brokyn,   com, owt with som,
Els on the I shall be wrokyn   or thi ded com
All outt.
Aythere has thou no wytt,
Or els ar thyn eres dytt;
Why bot herd thou not yit?
So, I cry and I showte.

(21)

ANNA[21]: A, sir, be not yll payde,   though he not answere;
He is inwardly flayde,   not right in his gere.
CAYPHAS: No, bot the wordis he has saide   doth my hart great dere.

---

157 *thole* allow   *abate* be humble   169 *lerd* taught   172 *stokyn* stuck
178 *dytt* stopped   182 *flayde* routed

THE BUFFETING

ANNA: Sir, yit may ye be dayde.
CAYPHAS: Nay, whils I lif nere.
ANNA: Sir, amese you.
CAYPHAS: Now fowll myght hym befall!
ANNA: Sir, ye ar vexed at all,
And peraventur he shall
Here after pleas you;

(22)

    We may bi oure law   examyn hym fyrst.   190
CAYPHAS: Bot I gif hym a blaw,   my hart will brist.
ANNA: Abyde to ye his purpose knaw.
CAYPHAS: Nay, bot I shall out thrist
Both his een on a raw.
ANNA: Sir, ye will not, I tryst,
Be so vengeabyll;
Bot let me oppose hym.
CAYPHAS: I pray you, and sloes hym.
ANNA: Sir, we may not lose hym
Bot we were dampnabill.

(23)

CAYPHAS: He has adyld his ded,   a kyng he hym calde;
War! Let me gyrd of his hede!
ANNA: I hope not ye wold;   200
Bot, sir, do my red   youre worship to hald.
CAYPHAS: Shall I never ete bred   to that he be stald
In the stokys.
ANNA: Sir, speke soft and styll;
Let us do as the law will.
CAYPHAS: Nay, I myself shall hym kyll
And murder with knokys.

---

184 *dayde* ?summoned   185 *amese* calm   191 *brist* burst   192 *thrist* thrust   193 *raw* row   196 *sloes* slay   199 *adyld* earned   *ded* death   200 *gyrd* strike   201 *worship* honour   202 *stald* set

ENGLISH MYSTERY PLAYS

(24)

ANNA: Sir, thynk ye that ye ar   a man of holy kyrk:
Ye shuld be oure techer,   mekenes to wyrk.
CAYPHAS: Yei, bot all is out of har   and that shall he yrk.   210
ANNA: All soft may men go far;   oure lawes ar not myrk,
I weyn;
Youre wordys ar bustus,
Et hoc nos volumus,
Quod de iure possumus[22]*;*
Ye wote what I meyn;

(25)

It is best that we trete hym   with farenes.
CAYPHAS: We, nay!
ANNA: And so myght we gett hym   som word for to say.
CAYPHAS: War! Let me bett hym.
ANNA: Syr, do away!
For if ye thus thrett hym   he spekys not this day.   220
Bot herys;
Wold ye sesse and abyde,
I shuld take hym on syde
And inquere of his pryde
How he oure folke lerys.

(26)

CAYPHAS: He has renyd over lang   with his fals lyys,
And done mekyll wrang.   Sir Cesar he defyes;
Therfor shall I hym hang   or I up ryse.
ANNA: Sir, the law will not he gang   on nokyn wyse
Undemyd;   230
Bot fyrst wold I here
What he wold answere;
Bot he dyd any dere
Why shuld he be flemyd?

210 *har* joint   *yrk* loathe   211 *myrk* dark   213 *bustus* violent
221 *herys* hear   226 *renyd* reigned   229 *nokyn* no kind (of)
230 *Undemyd* unjudged   233 *Bot* unless   *dere* harm   234 *flemyd* banished

THE BUFFETING

(27)

And therfor examynyng fyrst will I make,
Sen that he callys hym a kyng.
CAYPHAS: Bot he that forsake
I shall gyf hym a wryng that his nek shall crak.
ANNA: Syr, ye may not hym dyng: no word yit he spake
That I wyst.
Hark, felow, com nar!   240
Wyll thou never be war?
I have mervell thou dar
Thus do thyn awne lyst.

(28)

Bot I shall do as the law wyll, if the people ruse the;
Say, dyd thou oght this yll? Can thou oght excuse the?
Why standys thou so styll when men thus accuse the?
For to hyng on a hyll hark how thay ruse the
To dam[23].
Say, art thou Godys son of heven,
As thou art wonte for to neven?   250
IHESUS: So thou says by thy steven,
And right so I am;

(29)

For after this shall thou se when that [I[24]] do com downe
In brightnes on he in clowdys from abone.
CAYPHAS: A, ill myght the feete be that broght the to towne!
Thou art worthy to de! Say, thefe, where is thi crowne?
ANNA: Abyde, sir;
Let us lawfully redres.
CAYPHAS: We nede no wytnes:
Hys self says expres;   260
Whi shuld I not chyde, sir?

243 *lyst* will   244 *ruse* praise   247 *ruse* boast   248 *dam* condemn
250 *neven* claim   251 *steven* speech   256 *de* die

475

(30)

ANNA: Was ther never man so wyk　bot he myght amende
　When it com to the pryk,　right as youre self kend.
CAYPHAS: Nay, sir, bot I shall hym styk　even with myn awne
　　　　hend;
　For if he rene and be whyk　we ar at an end,
　All sam!
　Therfore, whils I am in this brethe,
　Let me put hym to deth.
ANNA: *Sed nobis non licet*
　Interficere quemquam[25]. 270

(31)

　Sir, ye wote better than I　we shuld slo no man.
CAYPHAS: His dedys I defy;　his warkys may we ban;
　Therfor shall he by[26].
ANNA:　　　　　　Nay, on oder wyse than,
　And do it lawfully.
CAYPHAS:　　　　As how?
ANNA:　　　　　　　Tel you I can.
CAYPHAS: Let se.
ANNA: Sir, take tent to my sawes;
　Men of temporall lawes
　Thay may deme sich cause,
　And so may not we.

(32)

CAYPHAS: My hart is full cold,　nerehand that I swelt; 280
　For talys that ar told　I bolne at my belt,
　Unethes may it hold,　my body, an ye it felt;
　Yit wold I gif of my gold　yond tratoure to pelt
　For ever.
ANNA: Good sir, do as ye hett me.
CAYPHAS: Whi shall he over-sett me?
　Sir Anna, if ye lett me
　Ye do not youre dever.

262 *wyk* wicked　265 *rene* reign　*whyk* living　266 *sam* together
272 *ban* curse　280 *swelt* faint　281 *bolne* swell　282 *Unethes* hardly
283 *pelt* strike　288 *dever* duty

THE BUFFETING

(33)

ANNA: Sir, ye ar a prelate.
CAYPHAS: So may I well seme,
My self if I say it.
ANNA: Be not to breme; 290
Sich men of astate shuld no men deme,
Bot send them to Pilate: the temporall law to yeme
Has he;
He may best threte hym,
And all to rehete hym;
It is shame you to bete hym;
Therfor, sir, let be.

(34)

CAYPHAS: Fy on hym and war![27] I am oute of my gate;
Say why standys he so far.
ANNA: Sir, he cam bot late.
CAYPHAS: No, bot I have knyghtys that dar rap hym on the pate. 300
ANNA: Ye ar bot to skar; good sir, abate,
And here;
What nedys you to chyte?
What nedys you to flyte?
If ye yond man smyte,
Ye ar irregulere.

(35)

CAYPHAS: He that fyrst made me clerk and taght me my lare
On bookys for to barke, the dwill gyf hym care!
ANNA: A, good sir, hark! Sich wordys myght ye spare.
CAYPHAS: Els myght I have made up wark of yond harlot and mare, 310
Perde!
Bot certys, or he hens yode,

290 *breme* fierce 292 *yeme* have charge of 294 *threte* threaten
295 *rehete* rebuke 301 *skar* scare 303 *chyte* chide 304 *flyte* quarrel
308 *barke* ?recite 310 *mare* nightmare 312 *yode* went

ENGLISH MYSTERY PLAYS

    It wold do me som good
    To se knyghtys knok his hoode
    With knokys two or thre.

(36)

    For sen he has trespast   and broken oure law,
    Let us make hym agast,   and set hym in awe.
ANNA: Sir, as ye have hast   it shalbe, I traw.
    Com and make redy fast,   ye knyghtys on a raw,
    Youre arament;   320
    And that kyng to you take,
    And with knokys make hym wake.
CAYPHAS: Yei, syrs, and for my sake
    Gyf hym good payment.

(37)

    For if I myght go with you,   as I wold that I myght,
    I shuld make myn avowe   that ons or mydnyght
    I shuld make his heede sow   wher that I hyt right.
I TORTOR: Sir, drede you not now   of this cursed wight
    To-day,
    For we shall so rok hym,   330
    And with buffettys knok hym,
CAYPHAS: And I red that ye lok hym,
    That he ryn not away.

(38)

    For I red not we mete   if that lad skap.
II TORTOR: Sir, on us be it,   bot we clowt well his kap.
CAYPHAS: Wold ye do as ye heytt,   it were a fayr hap.
I TORTOR: Sir, see ye and sytt   how that we hym knap,
    Oone feste[28];
    Bot or we go to this thyng,
    Sayn us, lord, with thy ryng.   340
CAYPHAS: Now he shall have my blyssyng
    That knokys hym the best.

---

317 *agast* afraid   320 *arament* accoutrement   327 *sow* sore   333 *ryn* run
334 *skap* escape   335 *kap* head   336 *heytt* promised   337 *knap* knock
338 *feste* feast   340 *Sayn* bless

THE BUFFETING

(39)

II TORTOR: Go we now to oure noyte   with this fond foyll.
I TORTOR: We shall teche hym, I wote,   a new play of Yoyll[29],
And hold hym full hote.   Fraward, a stoyll
Go fetch us!
FROWARD: We, dote!   Now els were it doyll
And unneth;
For the wo that he shall dre
Let hym knele on his kne.
II TORTOR: And so shall he for me;   350
Go fetche us a light buffit[30].

(40)

FROWARD: Why must he sytt soft – with a mekill myschaunce –
That has tenyd us thus oft?
I TORTOR: Sir, we do it for a skawnce;
If he stode up on loft   we must hop and dawnse
As cokys in a croft.
FROWARD: Now a veniance
Com on hym!
Good skill can ye show,
As fell I the dew[31];
Have this – bere it, shrew!
[*Hands stool to Jesus.*]
For soyn shall we fon hym.   360

(41)

II TORTOR: Com, sir, and syt downe.   Must ye be prayde?
Lyke a lord of renowne   youre sete is arayde.
I TORTOR: We shall preve on his crowne   the wordys he has sayde.
II TORTOR: Ther is none in this towne,   I trow, be ill payde
Of his sorow,
Bot the fader that hym gate[32].

<small>343 *noyte* business   345 *stoyll* stool   346 *doyll* pain   348 *dre* suffer
353 *tenyd* harmed   *skawnce* joke   360 *fon* befool</small>

ENGLISH MYSTERY PLAYS

I TORTOR: Now, for oght that I wate,
All his kyn commys to late
His body to borow.

(42)

II TORTOR: I wold we were onwarde.
I TORTOR: Bot his een must be hyd.
II TORTOR: Yei, bot thay be well spard   we lost that we dyd[33];
Step furth thou, Froward.
FROWARD: What is now betyd?
I TORTOR: Thou art ever away ward.
FROWARD: Have ye non to byd
Bot me?
I may syng ylla-hayll.
II TORTOR: Thou must get us a vayll.
FROWARD: Ye ar ever in oone tayll.
I TORTOR: Now ill myght thou the!

(43)

Well had thou thi name,   for thou was ever curst.
FROWARD: Sir, I myght say the same   to you if I durst;
Yit my hyer may I clame,   no penny I purst;
I have had mekyll shame,   hunger and thurst
In youre servyce.
I TORTOR: Not oone word so bold!
FROWARD: Why, it is trew that I told.
Fayn preve it I wold.
II TORTOR: Thou shalbe cald to pervyce.

(44)

FROWARD: Here a vayll have I fon –   I trow it will last.
I TORTOR: Bryng it hyder, good son.   That is it that I ast.
FROWARD: How shuld it be bon?
II TORTOR: Abowt his heade cast.
I TORTOR: Yei, and when it is well won   knyt a knot fast,
I red.

367 *wate* know   377 *tayll* story   381 *purst* put in my purse   387 *pervyce* legal argument   390 *bon* bound

THE BUFFETING

FROWARD: Is it weyll?
II TORTOR: Yei, knave.
FROWARD: What, weyn ye that I rafe?
Cryst curs myght he have
That last bond his head![34]

(45)

I TORTOR: Now sen he is blynfold, I fall to begyn,
And thus was I counseld the mastry to wyn.
[*Strikes him.*]
II TORTOR: Nay, wrang has thou told: thus shuld thou com in!
[*Strikes him.*]
FROWARD: I stode and beheld – thou towchid not the skyn 400
Bot fowll[35].
I TORTOR: How will thou do?
II TORTOR: On this manere, lo!
[*Strikes him.*]
FROWARD: Yei, that was well gone to;
Ther start up a cowll.

(46)

I TORTOR: Thus shall we hym refe` all his fonde talys.
II TORTOR: Ther is noght in thi nefe, or els thi hart falys.
FROWARD: I can my hand uphefe and knop out the skalys.
I TORTOR: Godys forbot ye lefe, bot set in youre nalys
On raw. 410
Sit up and prophecy[36] –
[*They strike in turn.*]
FROWARD: Bot make us no ly –
II TORTOR: Who smote the last –
I TORTOR: Was it I?
FROWARD: He wote not, I traw.

(47)

I TORTOR: Fast to sir Cayphas go we togeder.

394 *rafe* talk wildly 405 *cowll* lump 407 *nefe* fist 408 *knop* knock
skalys skittles 409 *forbot* forbid *lefe* stop

II TORTOR: Ryse up with ill grace;   so com thou hyder.
FROWARD: It semys by his pase   he groches to go thyder.
I TORTOR: We have gyfen hym a glase,   ye may consyder,
  To kepe.
II TORTOR: Sir, for his great boost 420
  With knokys he is indoost.
FROWARD: In fayth, sir, we had almost
  Knokyd hym on slepe.

(48)

CAYPHAS: Now sen he is well bett,   weynd on youre gate,
  And tell ye the forfett   unto sir Pylate;
  For he is a iuge sett   emang men of state,
  And looke that ye not let.
I TORTOR: Com furth, old crate[37],
  Be-lyfe.
  We shall lede the a trott.
II TORTOR: Lyft thy feete may thou not. 430
FROWARD: Then nedys me do nott
  Bot com after and dryfe[38].

(49)

CAYPHAS: Alas, now take I hede!
ANNA: Why mowrne ye so?
CAY: For I am ever in drede,   wandreth, and wo,
  Lest Pylate for mede   let Ihesus go;
  Bot had I slayn hym indede   with thise handys two,
  At onys,
  All had been qwytt than;
  Bot gyftys marres many man.
  Bot he deme the sothe than, 440
  The dwill have his bonys!

417 *groches* is unwilling   418 *glase* blow   421 *indoost* beaten
428 *Be-lyfe* quickly   434 *wandreth* misery

(50)
   Sir Anna, all I wyte you this blame,   for had ye not beyn,
   I had mayde hym full tame –   yei, stykyd hym, I weyn,
   To the hart full wan   with this dagger so keyn.
ANNA: Sir, you must shame   sich wordys for to meyn
   Emang men.
CAY: I will not dwell in this stede,
   Bot spy how thay hym lede,
   And persew on his dede.
   Fare-well! We gang, men.   450

   Explicit Coliphizacio.

28. The Dream of Pilate's Wife

YORK 30: TAPITERES AND COUCHERS

The play was performed by the makers of tapestry and couch covers; for a time they were assisted by the Linen-weavers. The entry in Burton's list appears to be earlier than the version here: Percula, the son, the maid, the Devil, and the Beadle are all omitted. The work is undoubtedly by the York Realist, who re-wrote the play in an alliterative style after 1415.

The main sources are the Gospel of Nicodemus *and* Matthew 27 11–19. *In Continental versions, and in* Ludus Coventriae, *Satan plays a larger part. The dramatist here confines him to the dream episode. The characterization of Pilate shows him to be boastful, lecherous and drunken. He is treated with showy deference by the Jews, but he acts with justice as in the Bible, and his coolness contrasts with the Jews. The scene between Pilate and Percula is probably original: it is a clever piece of dramatic writing, for though Pilate is not callous, he is shown to be detached from the issue, and self-interested. The Beadle also appears to be original, particularly as he is sympathetic to Christ and worships him. Thus the play has a number of convincing characters who are made to react to one another.*

The staging shows a flexible approach to locations. There is no simultaneous action, but several places are called for: Pilate's court, Percula's room, the palace of Caiaphas, and the gate and court of Pilate.

THE DREAM OF PILATE'S WIFE

[*Scene: Pilate's court.*]

(1)

PILATUS: Yhe cursed creatures that cruelly are cryand,
  Restreyne you for stryvyng for strengh of my strakis,
  Youre pleyntes in my presence use plately applyand,
  Or ellis this brande in youre braynes schalle brestis and brekis.
  This brande in his bones brekis,
  What brawle that with brawlyng me brewis[1];
  That wrecche may not wrye fro my werkis,
  Nor his sleyghtis noght slely hym slakis;
  Latte that traytour noght triste in my trewys.

(2)

For sir Sesar[2] was my sier, and I sothely his sonne,   10
  That excelent Emperoure exaltid in hight,
  Whylk all this wilde worlde with wytes had wone:
  And my modir hight Pila, that proude was o pight,
  O Pila that prowde, and Atus hir fadir he hight.
  This Pila was hadde in to Atus,
  Nowe, renkis, rede yhe it right?
  For thus schortely I have schewid you in sight
  Howe I am prowdely preved Pilatus.

(3)

Loo, Pilate I am proved, a prince of grete pride.
  I was putte in to Pounce[3] the pepill to presse,   20
  And sithen Sesar hym-selffe, with exynatores be his side,
  Remytte me to the remys, the renkes to redresse,
  And yitte am I graunted on grounde, as I gesse,
  To justifie and juge all the Iewes.

2 *strakis* strokes 3 *plately* perfectly, plainly *applyand* appealing
4 *brande* sword *brestis* burst *brekis* break 6 *brewis* stirs up 7 *wrye* turn 8 *slely* slily *slakis* abate 9 *triste* trust *trewys* faith
12 *Whylk* which 13 *o* always 16 *renkis* men 21 *exynatores* senators
22 *Remytte* gave back *remys* kingdoms

485

[*Enter Pilate's wife, Percula*[4].]
A, luffe! here, lady, no lesse!
Lo, sirs, my worthely wiffe, that sche is!
So semely, loo, certayne scho schewys.

(4)
UXOR PILATI: Was nevir juge in this Jurie of so jocounde generacion,
Nor of so joifull genologie to gentrys enioyned,
As yhe, my duke doughty, demar of dampnacion 30
To princes and prelatis that youre preceptis perloyned.
Who that youre perceptis pertely perloyned,
With drede in to dede schall ye dryffe hym;
By my trouthe, he untrewly is stonyed
That agaynste youre behestis hase honed:
All to ragges schall ye rente hym and ryve hym.

(5)
I am dame precious Percula, of pryncen the prise,
Wiffe to sir Pilate here, prince with-outen pere.
All welle of all womanhede I am, wittie and wise:
Consayve nowe my countenaunce so comly and clere. 40
The coloure of my corse is full clere,
And in richesse of robis I am rayed.
There is no lorde in this londe as I lere
In faith that hath a frendlyar feere
Than yhe, my lorde, myselffe yof I saye itt.

(6)
PILATUS: Nowe saye itt save may ye saffely, for I will certefie the same.
UXOR: Gracious lorde, gramercye, your gode worde is gayne.
PILATUS: Yhitt for to comforte my corse, me must kisse you, madame!
UXOR: To fulfille youre forward, my fayre lorde, in faith I am fayne.

29 *gentrys* nobility 30 *demar* judge 31 *perloyned* removed, set aside
33 *dryffe* drive 34 *stonyed* astonished 35 *honed* delayed 41 *corse* body 45 *yof* though

THE DREAM OF PILATE'S WIFE

PILATUS: Howe, howe, felawys! nowe in faith I am fayne 50
 Of theis lippis, so loffely are lappid;
 In bedde is full buxhome and bayne.
UXOR: Yha, sir, it nedith not to layne;
 All ladise we coveyte than bothe to be kyssed and clappid.

(7)

BEDELLUS: My liberall lorde, O leder of lawis,
 O schynyng schawe that all schames escheues,
 I beseke you, my soverayne, assente to my sawes,
 As ye are gentill juger and justice of Jewes.
UXOR: Do herke, howe thou javell, jangill of Jewes!
 Why, go bette, horosonne boy, when I bidde the. 60
BED: Madame, I do but that diewe is.
UXOR: But yf thou reste of thy resoune, thou rewis,
 For all is a-cursed carle, hase in, kydde the[5].

(8)

PILATUS: Do mende you, madame, and youre mode be amendand,
 For me semys it wer sittand to se what he sais.
UXOR: Mi lorde, he tolde nevir tale that to me was tendand,
 But with wrynkis and with wiles to wend me my weys[6].
BED: Gwisse of youre wayes to be wendand
 Itt langis to oure lawes.
UXOR: Loo, lorde, this ladde with his lawes,
 Howe thynke ye it prophitis wele 70
 His prechyng to prayse?
PILATUS: Yha, luffe, he knawis all oure custome, I knawe wele.

(9)

BED: My seniour, will ye see nowe the sonne in youre sight
 For his stately strengh he stemmys in his stremys;

---

51 *lappid* to touch 52 *buxhome* submissive 53 *layne* conceal 54 *clappid* embraced 56 *schawe* appearance 59 *javell* argue *jangill* prate 60 *horosonne* whoreson 65 *sittand* suitable 66 *to me ... tendand* about me 67 *wrynkis* twists 68 *Gwisse* certainly 69 *langis* belongs 73 *sonne* sun 74 *stremys* beams

487

Behalde ovir youre hede how he holdis fro hight
And glydis to the grounde with his glitterand glemys.
To the grounde he gois with his bemys,
And the nyght is neghand anone;
Yhe may dome aftir no dremys,
But late my lady here with all her light lemys 80
Wightely go wende till her wone.

(10)

For ye muste sitte, sir, this same nyght of lyfe and of lyme;
Itt is noght leeffull for my lady by the lawe of this lande
In dome for to dwelle fro the day waxe ought dymme;
For scho may stakir in the strete but scho stalworthely stande[7].
. . . .
Late hir take hir leve whill that light is.
PILATUS: Nowe, wiffe, than ye blythely be buskand.
UXOR: I am here, sir, hendely at hande.
PILATUS: Loo, this is renke has us redde als right is.

(11)

UXOR: Youre comaundement to kepe to kare forthe y caste me; 90
My lorde, with youre leve, no lenger y lette yowe.
PILATUS: Itt were appreve to my persone that prevely ye paste me,
Or ye wente fro this wones or with wynne ye had wette yowe[8].
Ye schall wende forthe with wynne whenne that ye have wette yowe.
[*To Servant*] Gete drinke! what dose thou? have done!
Come semely beside me, and sette yowe
Loke, nowe it is even here, that I are behete you;
Ya, saie it nowe sadly and sone.

78 *neghand* approaching 80 *lemys* appearance 81 *wone* dwelling-place 82 *lyme* limb 85 *stakir* stagger 87 *buskand* making ready 89 *redde* advised 90 *y* I 92 *paste* left 93 *wynne* wine 94 *wynne* joy 97 *are* before

THE DREAM OF PILATE'S WIFE

(12)

UXOR: Itt wolde glad me, my lorde, if ye gudly begynne.
PILATUS: Nowe I assente to youre counsaille, so comely and
    clere;
  Nowe drynke, madame: to deth all this dynne!
UXOR: Iff it like yowe, myne awne lorde, I am not to lere:
  This lare I am not to lere.
PILATUS: Yitt efte to youre damysell, madame.
UXOR: In thy hande, holde nowe, and have here.
ANCILLA: Gramarcy, my lady so dere.
PILATUS: Nowe fares-wele, and walke on youre way.

(13)

UXOR: Now fare wele, ye frendlyest, youre fomen to fende.
PILATUS: Nowe fare wele, ye fayrest figure that ever did fode
    fede,
  And fare wele, ye damysell, in dede.
ANCILLA: My lorde, I comande me to youre ryalte.
PILATUS: Fayre lady, he this schall you lede.
  [*To Son*] Sir, go with this worthy in dede,
  And what scho biddis you doo, loke that buxsome you be.

(14)

FILIUS: I am prowde and preste to passe on a-passe,
  To go with this gracious, hir gudly to gyde.
PILATUS: Take tente to my tale, thou turne on no trayse.
  Come tyte and telle me yf any tythyngis be-tyde.
FILIUS: If any tythyngis my lady be-tyde,
  I schall full sone, sir, witte you to say.
  This semely schall I schewe by hir side,
  Be-lyffe, sir, no lenger we byde.
    [*Exeunt Uxor, Filius and Ancilla.*]

(15)

PILATUS: Nowe fares-wele, and walkes on youre way.
  Nowe wente is my wiffe, yf it wer not hir will,

102, 103 *lere* learn, be taught   115 *a-passe* apace   117 *trayse* way

And scho rakis tille hir reste as of no thyng scho rought[9].
Tyme is, I telle the, thou tente me untill,
And buske the belyve, belamy, to bedde that y wer broght.
And loke I be rychely arrayed.
BED: Als youre servaunte I have sadly it sought,
And this nyght, sir, newe schall ye noght[10], 130
I dare laye, fro ye luffely be layde.
  [*Pilatus lies on his bed.*]

(16)

PILATUS: I comaunde the to come nere, for I will kare to my couche.
Have in thy handes hendely and heve me fro hyne,
But loke that thou tene me not with thi tastyng, but tendirly me touche.
BED: A! sir, yhe whe wele![11]
PILATUS: Yha, I have wette with me wyne.
Yhit helde doune and lappe me[12] even [here],
For I will slelye slepe unto synne.
Loke that no man nor no myron[13] of myne
With no noyse be neghand me nere.

(17)

BED: Sir, what warlowe yow wakens with wordis full wilde, 140
That boy for his brawlyng were bettir be un-borne.
PILATUS: Yha, who chatteres, hym chastise, be he churle or childe,
For and he skape skatheles itt were to us a grete skorne.
Yf skatheles he skape, it wer a skorne;
What rebalde that redely will rore,
I schall mete with that myron to-morne,
And for his ledir lewdenes hym lerne to be lorne.
BED: Whe! so, sir, slepe ye, and saies nomore.

---

125 *rakis* goes 127 *buske* hurry *belamy* my good friend 133 *hyne* hence 134 *tene* trouble 143 *and* if *skatheles* unscathed 147 *ledir* bad *lorne* lost

THE DREAM OF PILATE'S WIFE

(18)

[*Percula's room.*]

UXOR: Nowe are we at home, do helpe yf ye may,
For I will make me redye and rayke to my reste. 150
ANCILLA: Yhe are werie, madame, for-wente of youre way:
Do boune you to bedde, for that holde I beste.
FILIUS: Here is a bedde arayed of the beste.
UXOR: Do happe me, and faste hense ye hye.
ANCILLA: Madame, anone all dewly is dressid.
FILIUS: With no stalkyng nor no striffe be ye stressed.
UXOR: Nowe be yhe in pese, both youre carpyng and crye.

(19)

[*Enter Diabolus.*]

DIABOLUS: Owte! owte! harrowe! in-to bale am I brought,
this bargayne may I banne,
But yf y wirke some wile, in wo mon I wonne, 160
This gentilman Jesu of cursednesse he can
Be any syngne that I see, this same is Goddis sonne.
And he be slone, oure solace will sese[14],
He will save man saule fro oure sonde,
And refe us the remys that are rounde.
I will on stiffely in this stounde,
Unto sir Pilate wiffe, pertely, and putte me in prese.

(20)

[*Whispers.*]

O woman, be wise and ware, and wonne in thi witte.
Ther schall a gentilman Jesu un-justely be juged
Byfore thy husband in haste, and with harlottis be hytte. 170
And that doughty to-day to deth thus be dyghted,
Sir Pilate, for his prechyng, and thou
With nede schalle ye namely be noyed,
Youre striffe and youre strenghe schal be stroyed,

---

150 *rayke* go   151 *for-wente* exhausted   156 *stalkyng* creeping   164 *sonde* charge   165 *remys* kingdoms   166 *stounde* time, hour

Youre richesse schal be refte you that is rude,
With vengeaunce, and that dare I avowe.
   [*She awakes.*]

(21)

UXOR: A! I am drecchid with a dreme full dredfully to dowte.
Say, childe, rise uppe radly, and reste for no roo;
Thou muste launce to my lorde and lowly hym lowte,
Comaunde me to his reverence, as right will y doo.   180
FILIUS: O, what schall I travayle thus tymely this tyde?
Madame, for the drecchyng of heven[15],
Slyke note is newsome to neven,
And it neghes unto mydnyght full even.
UXOR: Go bette, boy, I bidde no lenger thou byde,

(22)

And saie to my sovereyne, this same is soth that I send hym.
All naked this nyght as I napped,
With tene and with trayne was I trapped
With a swevene, that swiftely me swapped,
Of one Jesu, the juste man the Jewes will undoo.   190
She prayes tente to that trewe man, with tyne be noght trapped[16],
But als a domes man dewly to be dressand,
And lelye delyvere that lede.
FILIUS: Madame, I am dressid to that dede.
But firste will I nappe in this nede,
For he hase mystir of a morne slepe that mydnyght is myssand.

(23)

[*The palace of Caiaphas.*]
ANNA[S]: Sir Cayphas, ye kenne wele this caytiffe we have cached,
That ofte tymes in oure tempill hase teched untrewly.

177 *drecchid* tormented   178 *roo* rest, peace   179 *launce* hurry   *lowte* bow
183 *newsome* annoying   185 *bette* quickly   189 *swevene* dream   *swapped* struck   196 *mystir* need

THE DREAM OF PILATE'S WIFE

Oure meyne with myght at mydnyght hym mached,
And hase drevyn hym till his demyng for his dedis undewly[17].   200
Wherfore I counsaile that kyndely we care
Unto sir Pilate, oure prince, and pray hym
That he for oure right will arraye hym
This faitour for his falsed to flay hym,
For fro we saie hym the soth I schall sitte hym full sore.

(24)

CAYPHAS: Sir Anna, this sporte have ye spedely aspied,
  As I am pontificall prince of all prestis.
  We will prese to sir Pilate, and presente hym with pride,
  With this harlott that has hewed owre hartis fro oure brestis,
  Thurgh talkyng of tales untrewe.   210
  And therfor, sir knyghtis!
I MILES: Lorde.
CAY: Sir knyghtis that are curtayse and kynde,
  We charge you that chorle be wele chyned,
  Do buske you and grathely hym bynde,
  And rugge hym in ropes, his rase till he rewe.

(25)

I MIL: Sir, youre sawes schall be served schortely and sone.
  Yha, do, felawe, be thy feith, late us feste this faitour full fast
II MIL: I am douty to this dede; delyver, have done;
  Latte us pulle on with pride till his poure be paste.
I MIL: Do have faste and halde at his handes.   220
II MIL: For this same is he that lightly avaunted
  And God son he grathely hym graunted.
I MIL: He bese hurled for the highnes he haunted.
  Loo, he stonyes for us, he stares where he standis.

---

204 *faitour* deceiver   *falsed* falsehood   213 *chyned* chained   214 *grathely* properly, readily   215 *rugge* pull   *rase* course   222 *God* God's   223 *hurled* dragged   224 *stonyes* is astonished

493

(26)

II MIL: Nowe is the brothell boune for all the boste that he blowne,
And the laste day he lete no lordynges myght lawne hym.
AN: Ya, he wende this worlde had bene haly his awne[18].
Als ye are dowtiest today tille his demyng ye drawe hym
And than schall we kenne how that he canne excuse hym.
I MIL: Here, ye gomes, gose a rome, giffe us gate, 230
We muste steppe to yone sterne of a-state.
II MIL: We muste yappely wende in at this yate,
For he that comes to courte, to curtesye muste use hym.
[*They take Christ to Pilate's gate.*]

(27)

I MIL: Do rappe on the renkis, that we may rayse with oure rolyng;
Come forthe, sir coward: why cowre ye behynde? [*Knocks.*]
BED: O, what javellis are ye that jappis with gollyng?
I MIL: A, goode sir, be noght wroth, for wordis are as the wynde.
BED: I saye, gedlynges, gose bakke with youre gawdes.
II MIL: Be sufferand, I beseke you,
And more of this matere yhe meke yow. 240
BED: Why, unconand knaves, an I cleke yowe,
I schall felle yow, be my faith, for all youre false frawdes.

(28)

PILATUS: Say, childe, ill cheffe you! What churlles are so claterand?
BED: My lorde, un-conand knaves thei crye and thei call.
PILATUS: Gose baldely beliffe, and thos brethellis be battand
And putte tham in prisoune uppon peyne that may fall.

---

225 *brothell* wretch   226 *lawne* ?humble   227 *awne* own   230 *gomes* men   *gose a rome* make room   *gate* way   231 *sterne* star   232 *yappely* eagerly   *yate* gate   234 *rappe* strike   *rolyng* noise   236 *gollyng* violence   238 *gose* go   241 *cleke* lay hold of   242 *felle* strike down, kill   243 *cheffe* befall

THE DREAM OF PILATE'S WIFE

Yha, spedely spir tham yf any sporte can thei spell,
Yha, and loke what lordingis thei be.
BED: My lorde, that is luffull in lee;
I am boxsom and blithe to your blee. 250
PILATUS: And if they talke any tythyngis, come tyte and me tell.

(29)

BED: My felawes, by youre faith, can ye talke any tythandis?
I MIL: Yha, sir Cayphas and Anna ar come both to-gedir
To sir Pilate o Pounce and prince of oure lawe;
And thei have laughte a lorell that is lawles and liddir.
BED: My lorde! my lorde!
PILATUS: Howe!
BED: My lorde, unlappe yow belyve wher ye lye.
Sir Cayphas to youre courte is caried,
And sir Anna, but a traytour hem taried:
Many a wight of that warlowe has waried. 260
They have brought hym in a bande, his balis to bye.

(30)

PILATUS: But are thes sawes certayne in soth that thou saies?
BED: Yha, lorde, the states yondir standis, for striffe are they stonden.
PILATUS: Now than am I light as a roo, and ethe for to rayse.
Go bidde tham come in both, and the boye they have boune.
BED: Siris, my lorde geves leve inne for to come.
[*They enter Pilate's court.*]
CAY: Hayle, prince that is pereles in price.
Ye are leder of lawes in this lande;
Youre helpe is full hendely at hande.
AN: Hayle, stronge in youre state for to stande. 270
Alle this dome must be dressed at youre dulye devyse.

---

249 *luffull* praiseworthy   *lee* delight   250 *blee* radiance   255 *laughte* caught   *lorell* wretch   *liddir* evil   261 *balis* sorrows   263 *states* estates, nobility   264 *roo* roe-buck   *ethe* easy   269 *hendely* graciously

495

ENGLISH MYSTERY PLAYS

(31)

PILATUS: Who is there? My prelates?
CAY: Yha, lorde.
PILATUS: Nowe be ye welcome, i-wisse.
CAY: Gramercy, my soverayne, but we beseke you all-same,
By-cause of wakand you unwarly be noght wroth with this,
For we have brought here a lorell, he lokis like a lambe.
PILATUS: Come byn, you bothe, and to the benke brayde yow.
CAY Nay, gud sir, laugher is leffull for us.
PILATUS: A, sir Cayphas, be curtayse yhe bus.
AN: Nay, goode lorde, it may not be thus.
PILATUS: Sais no more, but come sitte you beside me, in sorowe as I said youe. 280

(32)

FILIUS: Hayle, the semelieste seeg undir sonne sought,
Hayle, the derrest duke and doughtiest in dede.
PILATUS: Now bene-veneuew, beuscher, what boodworde haste thou brought?
Hase any langour my lady newe laught in this hede?
FILIUS: Sir, that comely comaundes hir youe too,
And sais, al nakid this nyght as sche napped,
With tene and with traye was sche trapped,
With a swevene that swiftely hir swapped,
Of one Jesu, the juste man the Jewes will undo.

(33)

She beseches you as hir soverayne that symple to save[19]. 290
Deme hym noght to deth, for drede of vengeaunce.
PILATUS: What! I hope this be he that hyder harlid ye have.
CAY: Ya, sir, the same and the selffe: but this is but a skaunce.
He with wicchecrafte this wile has he wrought:
Some feende of his sand has he sente,
And warned youre wiffe or he wente.

276 *byn* in *benke* bench *brayde* move 277 *laugher* lower *leffull* right, fitting 278 *bus* must 281 *seeg* man 283 *bene-veneuew* welcome *beuscher* good sir *boodworde* message 284 *langour* discomfort *laught* caught *hede* matter 290 *symple* fool 293 *skaunce* chance 295 *sand* message

THE DREAM OF PILATE'S WIFE

    Yowe! that schalke shuld not shamely be shente.
    This is sikir in certayne, and soth schulde be sought.

(34)

AN: Yha, thurgh his fantome and falshed and fendes-craft[20]
    He has wroght many wondir, where he walked full wyde.   300
    Wherfore, my lorde, it wer leeffull his liffe were hym rafte.
PILATUS: Be ye nevere so bryme, ye bothe bus abyde
    But if the traytoure be taught for untrewe,
    And therfore sermones you no more;
    I will sekirly sende hym selffe fore,
    And se what he sais to the sore.
    Bedell, go brynge hyme, for of that renke have I rewthe.

(35)

BED: This forward to fulfille am I fayne moved in myn herte;
    Say, Jesu, the juges and the Jewes hase me enioyned
    To bringe the before tham, even bounden as thou arte.   310
    Yone lordyngis to lose the full longe have thei heyned.
    But firste schall I wirschippe the with witte and with will.
    This reverence I do the for-thy;
    For wytes that wer wiser than I,
    They worshipped the full holy on hy,
    And with solempnite sange Osanna till[21].

(36)

I MIL: My lorde that is leder of lawes in this lande,
    All bedilis to your biding schulde be boxsome and bayne,
    And yitt this boy here before yowe full boldely was bowand
    To worschippe this warlowe – methynke we wirke all in vayne.   320
II MIL: Yha, and in youre presence he prayed hym of pees;
    In knelyng on knes to this knave,
    He be-soughte hym his servaunte to save.
CAY: Loo, lord, such arrore amange them thei have,
    It is grete sorowe to see, no seeg may it sese.

---

297 *schalke* man   299 *fantome* spirit, imagination   302 *bryme* fierce
311 *heyned* waited   324 *arrore* error

(37)

    It is no menske to youre manhed, that mekill is of myght,
    To for-bere such forfettis that falsely are feyned;
    Such spites in especiall wolde be eshewed in your sight.
PILATUS: Sirs, moves you noght in this matere, but bese myldely demeaned,
    For yone curtasie I kenne had som cause.   330
AN: In youre sight, sir, the soth schall I saye,
    As ye are prince, take hede, I you praye;
    Such a lourdayne unlele, dare I laye,
    Many lordis of oure landis might lede fro oure lawes.

(38)

PILATUS [*to Beadle*]: Saye, losell, who gave the leve so for to lowte to yone ladde,
    And solace hym in my sight so semely, that I sawe?
BED: A, gracious lorde, greve you noght, for gude case I hadde.
    Yhe comaunded me to care, als ye kende wele and knawe,
    To Jerusalem on a journay, with seele;
    And than this semely on an asse was sette,   340
    And many men myldely hym mette;
    Als a god in that grounde thai hym grette,
    Wele semand hym in waye with worschippe lele.

(39)

    'Osanna,' thei sange, 'the sone of David!'
    Riche men with thare robes thei ranne to his fete,
    And poure folke fecched floures of the frith,
    And made myrthe and melody this man for to mete.
PILATUS: Nowe, gode sir, be thi feith, what is 'Osanna' to saie?
BED: Sir, constrew it we may be langage of this lande as I leve,
    It is als moche to me for to meve –   350
    Youre prelatis in this place can it preve –
    Als 'oure saviour and soverayne, thou save us, we praye.'

---

326 *menske* honour   333 *unlele* untrue   339 *seele* happiness

THE DREAM OF PILATE'S WIFE

(40)

PILATUS: Loo, senioures, how semes yow the sothe I you saide?
CAY: Yha, lorde, this ladde is full liddir, be this light!
　Yf his sawes wer serchid and sadly assaied,
　Save youre reverence, his resoune thei rekenne noght with right.
　This caytiffe thus cursedly can construe us.
BED: Sirs, trulye the trouthe I have tolde
　Of this wighte ye have wrapped in wolde.
AN: I saie, harlott, thy tonge schulde thou holde, 360
　And noght agaynste thi maistirs to meve thus.

(41)

PILATUS: Do sese of youre seggyng, and I schall examyne full sore.
AN: Sir, demes hym to deth, or dose hym away.
PILATUS: Sir, have ye saide?
AN: 　　　　　Yha, lorde.
PILATUS: 　　　　　　　　Nowe go sette you with sorowe and care[22],
　For I will lose no lede that is lele to oure law.
　But steppe furth and stonde uppe on hight,
　And buske to my bidding, thou boy,
　And for the nones, that thou neven us anoy.
BED: I am here at youre hande to halow a hoy[23],
　Do move of youre maister, for I shall melle it with myght. 370

(42)

PILATUS: Cry 'Oyas!'
BED: 　　　Oyas!
PILATUS: 　　　　　Yit efte, be thi feithe.
BED: 　　　　　　　　Oyas! *A-lowde*[24].
PILATUS: Yit lower, that ilke lede may light,
　Crye pece in this prese, uppon payne ther-uppon,
　Bidde them swage of ther sweying bothe swiftely and swithe,

---

359 *wolde* power　362 *seggyng* talking　368 *neven* proclaim　*anoy* harm
370 *melle* meddle　374 *swage* stop　*sweying* noise　*swithe* immediately

And stynte of ther stryvyng and stande still as a stone.,
Calle 'Jesu, the gentill of Jacob, the Jewe,
Come preste and appere,
To the barre drawe the nere,
To thi jugement here,'
To be demed for his dedis undewe. 380

(43)

I MIL: Whe! harke how this harlott he heldis oute of harre[25];
This lotterelle liste noght my lorde to lowte.
II MIL: Say, beggar, why brawlest thou? Go boune the to the barre.
I MIL: Steppe on thy standyng so sterne and so stoute.
II MIL: Steppe on thy standyng so still.
I MIL: Sir cowarde, to courte muste yhe care —
II MIL: A lessoune to lerne of oure lare.
I MIL: Flitte fourthe, foule myght thou fare!
II MIL: Say, warlowe, thou wantist of thi will.

(44)

FILIUS: O Jesu ungentill, thi joie is in japes. 390
Thou can not be curtayse, thou caytiffe I call the.
No ruthe were it to rug the and ryve the in ropes.
Why falles thou noght flatte here, foule falle the,
For ferde of my fadir so free?
Thou wotte noght his wisdome i-wys,
All thyne helpe in his hande that it is,
Howe sone he myght save the fro this:
Obeye hym, brothell, I bidde the.

(45)

PILATUS: Now, Jesu, thou art welcome, ewys, as I wene;
Be noght abasshed, but boldely boune the to the barre. 400
What seyniour will sewe for the sore I have sene,
To wirke on this warlowe his witte is in waste.
Come preste, of a payne, and appere.

382 *lotterelle* scoundrel   401 *sewe* follow, pursue

THE DREAM OF PILATE'S WIFE

    And, sir prelatis, youre pontes bes prevyng:
    What cause can ye caste of accusyng?
    This mater ye marke to be mevyng
    And hendly in haste late us here.

(46)

CAY: Sir Pilate o Pounce, and prince of grete price,
    We triste ye will trowe oure tales thei be trewe,
    To deth for to deme hym with dewly device,   410
    For cursidnesse yone knave hase in case if ye knew,
    In harte wolde ye hate hym in hye.
    For if it wer so
    We mente not to misdo;
    Triste, sir, schall ye therto,
    We hadde not hym taken to the.

(47)

PILATUS: Sir, youre tales wolde I trowe, but thei touche none
        entente:
    What cause can ye fynde nowe this freke for to felle?
AN: Oure sabbotte he saves not, but sadly assente
    To wirke full unwisely, this wote I right wele;   420
    ....[26]
    He werkis whane he will, wele I wote,
    And therfore in herte we hym hate;
    Itt sittis you to strenghe youre estate
    Yone losell to louse for his lay.

(48)

PILATUS: Ilke a lede for to louse for his lay is not lele
    Youre lawes is leffull, but to youre lawis longis it
    This faitoure to feese wele with flappes full fele,
    And woo may ye wirke hym be lawe, for he wranges it.
    Therfore takes un-to you full tyte,

---

404 *pontes* points   418 *freke* bold man   424 *louse* destroy   *lay* words
425 *lede* man   427 *feese* punish   *flappes* ?blows   *fele* many

And like as youre lawes will you lede, 430
Ye deme hym to deth for his dede.
CAY: Nay, nay, sir, that dome muste us drede.

(49)

It longes noght till us no lede for to lose.
PILATUS: What wolde ye I did thanne? The devyll motte you drawe!
Full fewe are his frendis, but fele are his fooes.
His liff for to lose thare longes no lawe;
Nor no cause can I kyndely contryve
That why he schulde lose thus his liffe.
AN: A, gude sir, it raykes full ryffe
In steedis wher he has stirrid mekill striffe 440
Of ledis that is lele to youre liffe.

(50)

CAY: Sir, halte men and hurte he helid in haste,
The deffe and the dome he delyvered fro doole
By wicchecrafte[27], I warande, his wittis schall waste,
For the farles that he farith with, loo, how thei folowe yone fole;
Oure folke so thus he frayes in fere.
AN: The dethe he rayses anone.
This lazare that lowe lay allone,
He graunte hym his gates for to gone,
And pertely thus proved he his poure. 450

(51)

PILATUS: Now, goode siris, I saie, what wolde yhe?
CAY: Sir, to dede for to do hym or dose hym a-dawe.
PILATUS: Yha, for he dose wele his deth for to deme?
Go, layke you, sir, lightly; wher lerned ye such lawe?
This touches no tresoune, I telle you.
Yhe prelatis that proved are for price,

439 *raykes* moves *ryffe* plenty   443 *doole* suffering   445 *farles* wonders   446 *frayes* puts   448 *lazare* leper   452 *dose hym a-dawe* put him to death   454 *layke* (v) jest

THE DREAM OF PILATE'S WIFE

Yhe schulde be bothe witty and wise,
And legge oure lawe wher it lyse[28],
Oure materes ye meve thus emel you.

(52)

AN: Misplese noght youre persone, yhe prince with-outen pere! 460
It touches to tresoune, this tale I schall tell;
Yone briboure, full baynly he bed to for-bere
The tribute to the Emperoure: thus wolde he compell
Oure pepill thus his poyntis to applye.
CAY: The pepull he saies he schall save,
And Criste garres he calle hym, yone knave,
And sais he will the high kyngdome have.
Loke whethir he deserve to dye!

(53)

PILATUS: To dye he deserves yf he do thus in-dede,
But y will se my-selffe what he sais. 470
Speke, Jesu, and spende nowe thi space for to spede;
Thes lordyngis thei legge the thou liste noght leve on oure lawes.
They accuse the cruelly and kene;
And therfore, as a chiftene y charge the,
Iff thou be Criste that thou telle me,
And God sone thou grughe not to graunte ye,
For this is the matere that y mene.

(54)

JESUS: Thou saiste so thi-selve; I am sothly the same,
Here wonnyng in worlde to wirke al thi will;
My fadir is faithfull to felle all thi fame; 480
With-outen trespas or tene am I taken the till.
PILATUS: Loo! Busshoppis, why blame ye this boye?
Me semys that it is soth that he saies;
Ye meve all the malice ye may,

---

458 *legge* allege, use 459 *emel* amongst 466 *garres* (v) causes 476 *grughe* begrudge

With youre wrenchis and wiles to wrythe hym away,
Un-justely to juge hym fro joie.

(55)

CAY: Nought so, sir, his seggyng is full sothly soth;
   It bryngis oure bernes in bale for to bynde.
AN: Sir, douteles we deme als dewe of the deth,
   This foole that ye favour, grete fautes can we fynde   490
   This daye, for to deme hym to dye.
PILATUS: Saie, losell, thou lies be this light!
   Saie, thou rebalde! thou rekens unright.
CAY: Avise you, sir, with mayne and with myght,
   And wreke not youre wrethe nowe for-thy.

(56)

PILATUS: Me likes noght his langage so largely for to lye.
CAY: A, mercy, lorde! Mekely no malice we mente.
PILATUS: Noo done is it douteles, balde and be blithe,
   Talke on that traytoure and telle youre entente.
   Yone segge is sotell, ye saie;   500
   Gud sirs, wher lerned he such lare?
CAY: In faith we cannot fynde whare.
PILATUS: Yhis, his fadir with some farlis gan fare,
   And has lered this ladde of his laie.

(57)

AN: Nay, nay, sir, we wiste that he was but a write;
   No sotelte he schewed that any segge saw.
PILATUS: Thanne mene yhe of malice to marre hym of myght;
   Of cursidnesse convik no cause can yhe knawe.
   Me mervellis ye malyngne o mys.
CAY: Sir, fro Galely hidir and hoo   510
   The gretteste agayne hym ganne goo,
   Yone warlowe to waken of woo,
   And of this werke beres witnesse y-wis.

488 *bernes* knights   498 *Noo* now   504 *laie* lore   505 *write* carpenter
508 *convik* convicted   509 *o mys* at fault, amiss   512 *waken* watch

THE DREAM OF PILATE'S WIFE

(58)

PILATUS: Why, and hase he gone in Galely[29], yone gedlyng ongayne?
AN: Yha, lorde, ther was he borne, yone brethelle, [and brede.]
PILATUS: Nowe with-outen fagyng, my frendis, in faith I am fayne,
    For now schall oure striffe full sternely be stede.
    Sir Herowde is kyng ther, ye kenne;
    His poure is preved full preste,
    To ridde hym, or reve hym of rest;   520
    And therfore, to go with yone gest,
    Yhe marke us oute of the manliest men.

(59)

CAY: Als witte and wisdome youre will schalbe wroght,
    Here is kempis full kene to the kyng for to care.
AN: Nowe, seniours, I saie yow sen soth schall be soght,
    But if he schortely be sente it may sitte us full sare.
PILATUS: Sir knyghtis that are cruell and kene,
    That warlowe ye warrok and wraste,
    And loke that he brymly be braste;
    And therfore, sir knyghtis, [in haste]   530
    Do take on that traytoure you be-twene.

(60)

    Tille Herowde in haste with that harlott ye hye.
    Comaunde me full mekely unto his moste myght;
    Saie the dome of this boy, to deme hym to dye,
    Is done upponne hym dewly, to dresse or to dight,
    Or liffe for to leve at his liste.
    Say ought I may do hym in dede,
    His awne am I worthely in wede.
I MIL: My lorde, we schall springe on a-spede;
    Come thens to me this traitoure full tyte.   540

514 *ongayne* ungainly 515 *brede* bred 516 *fagyng* deceiving 526 *sare* sore 528 *warrok* bind *wraste* tug 529 *braste* braced 538 *wede* pledge

(61)

PILATUS: Bewe sirs, I bidde you ye be not to bolde,
 But takes tente for oure tribute full trulye to trete.
II MIL: Mi lorde, we schall hye this be-heste for to halde,
 And wirke it full wisely, in wille and in witte.
PILATUS: So, sirs, me semys itt is sittand.
I MIL: Mahounde, sirs, he menske you with myght –
II MIL: And save you, sir, semely in sight.
PILATUS: Now in the wilde vengeaunce ye walke with that wight,
 And fresshely ye founde to be flittand.

541 *Bewe* good 546 *menske* (v) honour 548 *wilde* dominant, powerful

29. The Scourging
Incipit Flagellacio

TOWNELEY 22

The sequence of events here follows the Scriptural narrative, and combines the incidents of the Condemnation and the Carrying of the Cross. In York and Chester they are shown in separate plays. The combination of the two incidents here appears to be the work of at least two dramatists. Stanzas 5 to 27 are written in the nine-line stanza characteristic of the Wakefield Master, and deal with the Scourging, whilst the Torturers maliciously recount the miracles. The Carrying of the Cross contains the lamentation of the Virgin and the Marys on the way to Calvary, and appears to be the work of another writer. Some of the elaboration of the Scriptural story derives from the work of commentators, particularly that giving the words of the Marys.

[Scene: Pilate's court.]

(1)

PILATUS: Peasse at my bydyng, ye wyghtys in wold!
    Looke none be so hardy to speke a word bot I,
    Or by Mahowne most myghty, maker on mold,
    With this brande that I bere ye shall bytterly aby.
    Say, wote ye not that I am Pylate, perles to behold?
    Most doughty in dedys of dukys of the Iury;
    In bradyng of batels I am the most bold;
    Therfor my name to you will I dyscry,
    No mys.

3 *mold* earth   4 *aby* pay for   5 *perles* unequalled   7 *bradyng* starting
8 *dyscry* describe

I am full of sotelty, 10
Falshed, gyll, and trechery;
Therfor am I namyd by clergy
As *mali actoris*[1].

(2)

For like as on both sydys the iren the hamer makith playn,
So do I, that the law has here in my kepyng;
The right side to socoure, certys, I am full bayn,
If I may get therby a vantege or wynyng[2];
Then to the fals parte I turne me agayn,
For I se more vayll will to me be risyng;
Thus every man to drede me shalbe full fayn, 20
And all faynt of thare fayth to me be obeyng,
Truly.
All fals endytars,
Quest-gangars and iurars,
And thise out-rydars
Ar welcome to me.

(3)

Bot this prophete, that has prechyd and puplyshed so playn
Cristen law, Crist thay call hym in oure cuntre;
Bot oure pryncys full prowdly this nyght have hym tayn:
Full tytt to be dampned he shall be hurlyd byfore me; 30
I shall fownde to be his freynd utward, in certayn,
And shew hym fare cowntenance and wordys of vanyte;
Bot or this day at nyght on crosse shall he be slayn,
Thus agayns hym in my hart I bere grete enmyte
Full sore.
Ye men that use bak-bytyngys,
And rasars of slanderyngys,
Ye ar my dere darlyngys,
And Mahowns for evermore.

11 *gyll* guile 19 *vayll* avail, advantage 21 *faynt* feeble 23 *endytars* writers 24 *Quest-gangars* those who seek law *iurars* jurors 25 *out-rydars* outriders (monastic officers who were permitted to leave the monastery) 31 *utward* outward 37 *rasars* raisers

THE SCOURGING

(4)

 For no thyng in this warld dos me more grefe   40
 Then for to here of Crist and of his new lawes;
 To trow that he is Godys son my hart wold all to-clefe,
 Though he be never so trew both in dedys and in sawes.
 Therfor shall he suffre mekill myschefe,
 And all the dyscypyls that unto hym drawes;
 For over all solace to me it is most lefe
 The shedyng of Cristen bloode, and that all Iury knawes,
 I say you.
 My knyghtys full swythe
 Thare strengthes will thay kyth,   50
 And bryng hym be-lyfe;
 Lo, where thay com now!

(5³)

1 TORTOR: I have ron that I swett   from sir Herode oure kyng
 With this man that will not lett   oure lawes to downe bryng;
 He has done so mych forfett,   of care may he syng;
 Thrugh dom of sir Pylate he gettys   an yll endyng
 And sore;
 The great warkys he has wroght
 Shall serve hym of noght;
 And bot thay be dere boght,   60
 Lefe me no more.

(6)

 Bot make rowme in this rese,   I byd you, belyfe,
 And of youre noys that ye sesse,   both man and wyfe;
 To sir Pylate on dese   this man will we dryfe,
 His dede for to dres,   and refe hym his lyfe
 This day;

---

42 *to-clefe* shatter   49 *swythe* quickly   50 *kyth* try   61 *Lefe* believe
62 *rese* crowd   64 *dese* dais   65 *dede* death   *dres* prepare

Do draw hym forward!
Whi stand ye so bakward?
Com on, sir, hyderward,
As fast as ye may!   70

(7)

II TORTOR: Do pull hym a-rase,   whyls we be gangyng;
I shall spytt in his face   though it be fare shynyng;
Of us thre gettys thou no grace,   thi dedys ar so noyng,
Bot more sorow thou hase   oure myrth is incresyng,
No lak.
Felows, all in hast,
With this band that will last
Let us bynde fast
Both his handys on his bak.

(8)

III TORTOR: I shall lede the a dawnce   unto sir Pilate hall;   80
Thou betyd an yll chawnce   to com emangys us all⁴.
Sir Pilate, with youre cheftance,   to you we cry and call
That ye make som ordynance   with this brodell thrall,
By skyll;
This man that we led
On crosse ye put to ded.
PILATUS: What! With-outten any red?⁵
That is not my wyll;

(9)

Bot ye, wysest of law,   to me ye be tendand:
This man withoutten awe   which ye led in a band,   90
Nather in dede ne in saw   can I fynd with no wrang
Wherfor ye shuld hym draw   or bere falsly on hand
With ill.
Ye say he turnes oure pepyll,
Ye call hym fals and fekyll;
Warldys shame is on you mekyll
This man if ye spyll.

71 *a-rase* quickly   81 *betyd* received   82 *cheftance* chieftains   83 *brodell* wretch

THE SCOURGING

(10)

    Of all thise causes ilkon   which ye put on hym,
Herode, truly as stone,   coud fynd with nokyns gyn
Nothyng herapon   that pent to any syn;   100
Why shuld I then so soyn   to ded here deme hym?
Therfor
This is my counsell:
I will not with hym mell;
Let hym go where he wyll
For now and evermore.

(11)

1 CONSULTUS: Sir, I say the oone thyng   without any mys,
He callys his self a kyng   ther he none is;
Thus he wold downe bryng   oure lawes, i-wys,
With his fals lesyng   and his quantys,   110
This tyde.
PILATUS: Herk, felow, com nere!
Thou knowes I have powere
To excuse or to dampne here,
In bayll to abyde.

(12)

IHESUS: Sich powere has thou noght   to wyrk thi will thus with me,
Bot from my Fader that is broght   oone-fold God in persons thre.
PILATUS: Certys, it is fallen well in my thoght   at this tyme, as well wote ye,
A thefe that any felony has wroght   to lett hym skap or go fre
Away;   120
Therfor ye lett hym pas.
1 TORTOR: Nay, nay, bot Barabas!
And Ihesus in this case
To deth ye dam this day.

99 *nokyns* no kind (of)   *gyn* trickery   100 *pent* belonged   101 *soyn* soon   110 *quantys* cunning

ENGLISH MYSTERY PLAYS

(13)

PILATUS: Syrs, looke ye take good hede: his cloyss eye spoyll hym fro,
Ye gar his body blede and bett hym blak and bloo.
II TORTOR: This man, as myght I spede, that has wroght us this wo,
How *Iudicare* comys in crede shall we teche, or we go,
All soyne.
Have bynd to this pyllar.   130
III TORTOR: Why standys thou so far?
I TORTOR: To bett his body bar
I haste, withoutten hoyne⁶.

(14)

II TORTOR: Now fall I the fyrst to flap on hys hyde.
III TORTOR: My hartt wold all to-bryst, bot I myght tyll hym glyde.
I TORTOR: A swap fayn, if I durst, wold I lene the this tyde.
II TORTOR: War! Lett me rub on the rust⁷ that the bloode downe glyde
As swythe.
III TORTOR: Have att!
I TORTOR: Take thou that!   140
II TORTOR: I shall lene the a flap,
My strengthe for to kythe.

(15)

III TORTOR: Where-on servys thi prophecy thou tell us in this case,
And all thi warkys of greatt mastry thou shewed in dyvers place?
I TORTOR: Thyn apostels full radly ar run from the a-rase;
Thou art here in oure baly withoutten any grace
Of skap.
II TORTOR: Do, rug him.

---

125 *cloysse* clothes 126 *bloo* blue 133 *hoyne* delay 136 *swap* stroke
142 *kythe* test 148 *rug* shake

512

THE SCOURGING

III TORTOR: Do, dyng hym.
I TORTOR: Nay, I myself shuld kyll hym
  Bot for sir Pilate.

(16)

  Syrs, at the Feste of Architreclyn[8]   this prophete he was;
  Ther turnyd he water into wyn,   that day he had sich grace;
  His apostles to hym can enclyn   and other that ther was;
  The see he past bot few yeres syn;   it lete hym walk theron apase[9]
  At wyll;
  The elementys all bydeyn,
  And wyndes that ar so keyn,
  The firmamente, as I weyn,
  Ar hym obeyng tyll[10].

(17)

II TORTOR: A lepir[11] cam full fast   to this man that here standys,
  And prayed hym, in all hast,   of bayll to lowse his bandys;
  His travell was not wast   though he cam from far landys;
  This prophete tyll hym past   and helyd hym with his handys,
  Full blythe.
  The son of centuryon[12],
  For whom his fader made greatt mone,
  Of the palsy he helyd anone;
  Thay lowfyd hym oft sythe.

(18)

III TORTOR: Sirs, as he came from Iherico   a blynde man[13] satt by the way;
  To hym walkand with many mo   cryand to hym thus can he say,
  'Thou son of David, or thou go   of blyndnes hele thou me this day.'

164 *helyd* healed   169 *lowfyd* loved

Ther was he helyd of all his wo;   sich wonders can he wyrk
   all way
At wyll.
He rasys men from deth to lyfe;
And castys out devyls from thame oft sythe,
Seke men cam to hym full ryfe;
He helys thaym of all yll.

(19)

1 TORTOR: For all thise dedys of great lovyng[14]   [iij] thyngys
   I have fond certanly,
   For which he is worthy to hyng: oone is oure kyng that he
      wold be;
   Oure sabbot day in his wyrkyng   he lettys not to hele the
      seke truly;
   He says oure temple he shall downe bryng   and in iij daies
      byg it in hy
All hole agane;
Syr Pilate, as ye sytt,
Looke wysely in youre wytt;
Dam Ihesu or ye flytt
On crosse to suffre his payne.

(20)

PILATUS: Thou man that suffurs all this yll,   why wyll thou
   us no mercy cry?
   Slake thy hart and thi greatt wyll   whyls on the we have
      mastry;
   Of thy greatt warkes shew us som skyll;   men call the kyng,
      thou tell us why;
   Wherfor the Iues seke the to spyll   the cause I wold knowe
      wytterly,
Perdee;
Say what is thy name,
Thou lett for no shame;
Thay putt on the greatt blame,
Els myght [thou] skap for me.

182 *byg* build

THE SCOURGING

(21)

II CONSULTUS: Syr Pilate, prynce peerles,   this is my red,
That he skap not harmeles   bot do hym to ded:
He cals hym a kyng in every place,   thus wold he over led
Oure people in his trace   and oure lawes downe tred   200
By skyll;
Syr, youre knyghtes of good lose,
And the pepyll, with oone voce,
To hyng hym hy on a crosse
Thay cry and call you untyll.

(22)

PILATUS: Now certys, this is a wonder thyng;   that ye wold bryng to noght
Hym that is youre lege lordyng,   in faith this was far soght;
Bot say, why make ye none obeyng   to hym that all has wroght?
III TORTOR: Sir, he is oure chefe lordyng   sir Cesar so worthyly wroght
On mold.   210
Pylate, do after us,
And dam to deth Ihesus,
Or to sir Cesar we trus,
And make thy frenship cold.

(23)

PILATUS: Now that I am sakles   of this bloode shall ye see;
Both my handes in expres   weshen[15] sall be;
This bloode bees dere boght, I ges,   that ye spill so frele.
I TORTOR: We pray it fall endles   on us and oure meneye,
With wrake.
PILATUS: Now youre desyre fulfyll I shall;   220
Take hym emangs you all;
On crosse ye put that thrall,
His endyng ther to take.

200 *trace* track   202 *lose* repute   207 *lege* lawful   215 *sakles* innocent
217 *frele* freely

(24)

I TORTOR: Com on! Tryp on thi tose   without any fenyng;
Thou has made many glose   with thy fals talkyng.
II TORTOR: We ar worthy greatte lose   that thus has broght a kyng
From sir Pilate and othere fose   thus into oure ryng.
Withoutt any hoyne.
Sirs, a kyng he hym cals,
Therfor a crowne hym befals.   230
III TORTOR: I swere by all myn elder sauls,
I shall it ordan soyne.

(25)

I TORTOR: Lo, here a crowne of thorne   to perch his brane within,
Putt on his hede with skorne   and gar thyrll the skyn.
II TORTOR: Hayll, kyng! Where was thou borne,   sich worship for to wyn?
We knele all the beforne   and the to grefe will we not blyn,
That be thou bold;
Now by Mahownes bloode
Ther will no mete do me goode
To he be hanged on a roode,   240
And his bones be cold.

(26)

I TORTOR: Syrs, we may be fayn   for I have fon a tree,
I tell you in certan   it is of greatt bewtee,
On the which he shall suffre payn,   be feste with nales thre
Ther shall nothyng hym gayn   ther on to he dede be,
I insure it;
Do bryng hym hence.
II TORTOR: Take up oure gere and defence.
III TORTOR: I wold spende all my spence
To se hym ones skelpt.   250

225 *glose* falsehoods 227 *fose* foes 234 *thyrll* pierce 248 *defence* ?weapons 249 *spence* money 250 *skelpt* beaten

THE SCOURGING

(27)

1 TORTOR: This cros up thou take   and make the redy bowne;
   Withoutt gruchyng thou rake   and bere it thrugh the towne;
   Mary, thi moder, I wote, will make   great mowrnyng and mone,
   But for thy fals dedys sake   shortly thou salbe slone,
   No nay;
   The pepyll of Bedlem,
   And gentyls of Ierusalem,
   All the comoners of this reme,
   Shall wonder on the this day.

(28)

[*John and the three Marys on another part of the stage*[16].]
IOHANNES APOSTOLUS: Alas for my master moste of myght,   260
   That yester even with lanterne bright
   Before Caiphas was broght;
   Both Peter and I sagh that sight,
   And sithen we fled away full wight,
   When Iues so wonderly wroght;
   At morne thay toke to red,   and fals witnes furth soght,
   And demyd hym to be dede,   that to thaym trespaste noght.

(29)

   Alas, for his modere and othere moo,
   My moder and hir syster also,
   Sat sam with syghyng sore;   270
   Thay wote nothyng of all this wo,
   Therfor to tell thaym will I go,
   Sen I may mend no more.
   If he shuld dy thus tyte   and thay unwarned wore,
   I were worthy to wyte;   I will go fast therfor.

252 *rake* go

(30)

    God save you, systers all in fere!
    Dere lady, if thi will were,
    I must tell tythyngys playn.

MARIA: Welcom, Iohn, my cosyn dere!
    How farys my son sen thou was here?   280
    That wold I wyt full fayn.

IOHANNES: A, dere lady, with your leyff,   the trouth shuld no man layn,
    Ne with Godys will thaym grefe.

MARIA: Whi, Iohn, is my son slayn?

(31)

IOHANNES: Nay lady, I saide not so,
    Bot ye me myn he told us two
    And thaym that with us wore,
    How he with pyne shuld pas us fro,
    And efte shuld com us to,
    To amende oure syghyng sore;
    It may not stand in stede   to sheynd youre self therfore.   290

MARIA MAGDALENE: Alas, this day for drede!   Good Iohn, neven this no more!

(32)

    Speke prevaly, I the pray,
    For I am ferde, if we hir flay,
    That she will ryn and rafe[17].

IOHANNES: The sothe behowys me nede to say,
    He is damyd to dede this day;
    Ther may no sorow hym safe.

MARIA IACOBI: Good Iohn, tell unto us two   what thou of hir will crafe,
    And we will gladly go   and help that thou it have.

(33)

IOHANNES: Systers, youre mowrnyng may not amende;   300
    And ye will ever, or he take ende,

---

282 *layn* conceal   285 *myn* remember   293 *flay* frighten   298 *crafe* ask

THE SCOURGING

Speke with my master free,
Then must ye ryse and with me weynd,
And kepe hym as he shall be kend
Withoutt yond same cyte;
If ye will nygh me nere,   com fast and felowe me.
MARIA: A, help me, systers dere,   that I my son may see!

(34)

MARIA MAGDALENE: Lady, we wold weynd full fayn,
Hertely with all oure myght and mayn,
Youre comforth to encrese. 310
MARIA: Good Iohn, go before and frayn.
IOHANNES: Lo, where he commes us even agayn
With all yond mekyll prese!
All youre mowrnyng in feyr   may not his sorow sese.
MARIA: Alas for my son dere,   that me to moder chese!
[*They meet Jesus carrying the cross.*]

(35)

Alas, dere son for care   I se thi body blede;
My self I will for-fare   for the in this great drede,
This cros on thi shulder bare,   to help the in this nede,
I will it bere with greatt hart sare   wheder thay will the lede.
IHESUS: This cros is large in lengthe   and also bustus with all; 320
If thou put to thi strengthe   to the erthe thou mon downe fall.

(36)

MARIA: A, dere son, thou let me   help the in this case!
  Et inclinabit crucem ad matrem suam[18].
IHESUS: Lo, moder, I tell it the,   to bere no mygt thou hase.
MARIA: I pray the, dere son, it may so be   to man thou gif thi grace:
  On thi self thou have pyte   and kepe the from thi foyse.

304 *kend* known   311 *frayn* ask   314 *in feyr* together   320 *bustus* rough

(37)

IHESUS: For sothe, moder, this is no nay: on cros I must dede dre,
And from deth ryse on the thryd day, thus prophecy says by me;
Mans saull that I luffyd ay I shall redeme securly;
Into blis of heven for ay I shall it bryng to me.

(38)

MARIA MAGDALENE: It is greatt sorow to any wyght, Ihesus to se with Iues keyn, 330
How he in dyverse payns is dight; for sorow I water both myn eeyn.
MARIA IACOBI: This lord that is of myght dyd never yll truly;
Thise Iues thay do not right if thay deme hym to dy.

(39)

MARIA MAGDALENE: Alas, what shall we say! Ihesus, that is so leyfe,
To deth thise Iues this day thay lede with paynes full grefe.
MARIA IACOBI: He was full true, I say though thay dam hym as thefe;
Mankynde he lufed all way; for sorow my hart will clefe.

(40)

IHESUS[19]: Ye doghters of Ierusalem, I byd you wepe nothyng for me,
Bot for youre self and youre barn-teme. Behald, I tell you securle,
Sore paynes ar ordand for this reme in days herafter for to be; 340
Youre myrth to bayll it shall downe streme in every place of this cyte.

326 *dre* endure   334 *leyfe* dear   337 *clefe* cleave   339 *barn-teme* spring   340 *reme* kingdom

THE SCOURGING

(41)

> Childer, certys, thay shal blys   women baren that never child bare
> And pappes that never gaf sowke, iwys,   thus shall thare hartys for sorow be sare;
> The montayns hy and thise greatt hyllys   thay shall byd fall apon them thare,
> For my bloode that sakles is   to shede and spyll thay will not spare.

II TORTOR: Walk on, and lefe thi vayn carpyng: it shall not save the fro thy dede,
> Wheder thise women cry or syng   for any red that thay can red[20].

(42)

III TORTOR: Say wherto abyde we here abowte
> Thise qwenes with scremyng and with showte?
> May no man thare wordys stere?   350

I TORTOR: Go home, thou casbald, with that clowte!
> Or, by that Lord I leyfe and lowte[21],
> Thou shall by it full dere!

MARIA MAGDALENE: This thyng shall venyance call on you holly in fere.

II TORTOR: Go, hy the hens with all   or yll hayll cam thou here!

III TORTOR: Let all this bargan be,   syn all oure toyles ar before;
> This tratoure and this tre   I wold full fayn were thore.

I TORTOR: It nedys not hym to harll,   this cros dos hym greatt dere;
> Bot yonder commys a carll   shall help hym for to bere.

[*Enter Simon of Cyrene*[22].]

---

350 *stere* control   351 *casbald* ?baldhead   355 *hayll* fortune   358 *h͏*͏ drag

521

ENGLISH MYSTERY PLAYS

(43)

II TORTOR: That shall we soyn se on assay. 360
Herk, good man, wheder art thou on away?
Thou walkes as thou were wrath.
SYMON: Syrs, I have a greatt iornay
That must be done this same day,
Or els it will me skathe.
III TORTOR: Thou may with lytyll payn   easse hym and thi self both.
SYMON: Good syrs, that wold I fayn,   bot for to tary were full loth.

(44)

I TORTOR: Nay, nay, thou shall full soyn be sped;
Lo here a lad that must be led
For his yll dedys to dy, 370
And he is bressed and all for bled,
That makys us here thus stratly sted;
We pray the, sir, for-thi,
That thou will take this tre,   bere it to Calvary.
SYMON: Good sirs, that may not be,   for full greatt hast have I,

(45)

No longere may I hoyn.
II TORTOR: In fayth thou shall not go so soyn,
For noght that thou can say.
This dede must nedys be done,
And this carll be dede or noyn[23], 380
And now is nere myd day;
And therfor help us at this nede   and make us here no more delay.
SYMON: I pray you do youre dede   and let me go my way;

(46)

And I shall com full soyn agane,
To help this man with all my mayn,
t youre awne wyll.

36... *athe* harm   371 *bressed* bruised   380 *or* before

522

THE SCOURGING

III TORTOR: What and wold thou trus with sich a trane?
Nay, fatur, thou shall be full fayn,
This forward to fulfyll;
Or, by the myght of Mahowne,   thou shall lyke it full yll.   390
I TORTOR: Tytt, let dyng this dastard downe   bot he lay hand ther tyll.

(47)

SYMON: Certys, that were unwysely wroght,
To beytt me bot if I trespast oght[24],
Aythere in worde or dede.
II TORTOR: Apon thi bak it shall be broght;
Thou berys it wheder thou will or noght!
Dewyll! Whom shuld we drede?
And therfor take it here belyfe   and bere it furth, good spede.
SYMON: It helpys not here to strife;   bere it behoves me nede;

(48)

And therfor, syrs, as ye have sayde   400
To help this man I am well payde,
As ye wold that it were.
III TORTOR: A, ha, now ar we right arayde,
Bot loke oure gere be redy grade,
To wyrk when we com there.
I TORTOR: I warand all redy   oure toyles both moore and les,
And sir Symon truly   gose on before with cros.

(49)

III TORTOR: Now by Mahowne, oure heven kyng,
I wold that we were in that stede
Where we myght hym on cros bryng.   410
Step on before, and furth hym lede
A trace.
I TORTOR: Com on thou!

387 *trus* go   *trane* trick   404 *grade* prepared

523

II TORTOR: Put on thou!
III TORTOR: I com fast after you,
 And folowse on the chace.

Explicit Flagellacio.

30. The Crucifixion
Crucifixio Christi

YORK 35: PYNNERES AND PAYNTERS

The Pinners were makers of wire articles, pins and nails. Their craft is thus grimly suitable to nailing Christ to the cross. The Painters and the Latoners (workers in the mixed metal, laten) are added in Burton's list. For all this, it is notable that the play has only five actors.

The detailed presentation of the cruelty of the Soldiers is very striking here. Each step in the process of nailing Christ to the cross is carefully enacted. This is made more terrifying because the Soldiers consult and compete to make their work more efficient. The comments on how much pain is caused by each action are matched by their occasional doubts as to whether they can achieve their objective. There is undoubted cruelty in the intentions of the Soldiers, but they show no real sense that Christ is a human being. It is notable that their speeches are short and colloquial, concentrated upon the technical problems of their task. They are concerned with their tools, and with estimating their physical effort. Nevertheless the dramatist takes opportunities of indicating the real truth which lies behind the actions, that this is the sacrifice which redeemed.

There is, as one would expect, considerable emphasis upon the Biblical narratives, but the author also draws upon contemporary traditions about the Crucifixion, especially the tendency to see it as a heartless game in which mockery and contempt played an important part.

The particular achievements of this play have led some critics to call the author 'the York Realist'.

[Scene: Calvary.]

(1)

I MILES: Sir knyghtis, take heede hydir in hye;
This dede on-dergh we may noght drawe;
Yee wootte youre selffe als wele as I
Howe lordis and leders of owre lawe
Has geven dome that this doote schall dye.

II MIL: Sir, alle thare counsaile wele we knawe.
Sen we are comen to Calvarie,
Latte ilke man helpe nowe as hym awe.

III MIL: We are all redy, loo,
That forward to fullfille.

IV MIL: Late here howe we schall doo,
And go we tyte ther tille.

(2)

I MIL: It may noght helpe her for to hone,
If we schall any worshippe wynne.

II MIL: He muste be dede nedelyngis by none.

III MIL: Thanne is goode tyme that we begynne.

IV MIL: Late dynge hym doune, than is he done,
He schall nought dere us with his dynne.

I MIL: He schall be sette and lerned sone,
With care to hym and all his kynne.

II MIL: The foulest dede of all
Shalle he dye for his dedis.

III MIL: That menes crosse hym we schall.

IV MIL: Behalde so right he redis.

(3)

I MIL: Thanne to this werke us muste take heede,
So that oure wirkyng be noght wronge.

II MIL: None othir noote to neven is nede,
But latte us haste hym for to hange.

2 *on-dergh* without trouble 5 *doote* fool 8 *awe* ought 13 *hone* delay
15 *nedelyngis* necessarily 18 *dere* trouble 19 *sette* placed 23 *crosse*
crucify 24 *redis* says 27 *noote* matter *neven* mention

THE CRUCIFIXION

III MIL: And I have gone for gere, goode speede,
    Bothe hammeres and nayles large and lange.   30
IV MIL: Thanne may we boldely do this dede;
    Commes on, late kille this traitoure strange.
I MIL: Faire myght ye falle in feere,
    That has wrought on this wise.
II MIL: Us nedis nought for to lere
    Suche faitoures to chastise.

(4)
III MIL: Sen ilke a thyng es right arrayed,
    The wiselier nowe wirke may we.
IV MIL: The crosse on grounde is goodely graied,
    And boorede even as it awith to be[1].   40
I MIL: Lokis that the ladde on lengthe be layde,
    And made me thane unto this tree.
II MIL: For alle his fare he schalle be flaied,
    That one assaie sone schalle ye see.
III MIL: Come forthe, thou cursed knave,
    Thy comforte sone schall kele.
IV MIL: Thyne hyre here schall thou have.
I MIL: Walkes oon, now wirke we wele.

(5)
JESUS: Almyghty God, my fadir free,
    Late this materes be made in mynde,   50
    Thou badde that I schulde buxsome be,
    For Adam plyght for to be pyned.
    Here to dede I obblisshe me,
    Fro that synne for to save mankynde,
    And soveraynely be-seke I the,
    That thai for me may favoure fynde;
    And fro the fende thame fende,
    So that ther saules be saffe,
    In welthe withouten ende;
    I kepe nought ellis to crave.   60

---

33 *in feere* together   35 *lere* teach   39 *graied* prepared   40 *boorede* bored   *awith* ought   42 *thane* then   43 *flaied* terrified   46 *kele* cool   47 *hyre* reward   52 *Adam* Adam's   *pyned* tormented   53 *obblisshe* compel

ENGLISH MYSTERY PLAYS

(6)

I MIL: We! herke, sir knyghtis, for Mahoundis bloode!
  Of Adam-kynde is all his thoght.
II MIL: The warlowe waxis werre than woode;
  This doulfull dede ne dredith he noght.
III MIL: Thou schulde have mynde, with mayne and moode,
  Of wikkid werkis that thou haste wrought.
IV MIL: I hope that he had bene as goode
  Have sesed of sawes that he uppe sought.
I MIL: Thoo sawes schall rewe hym sore
  For all his saunteryng sone.   70
II MIL: Ille spede thame that hym spare
  Tille he to dede be done!

(7)

III MIL: Have done belyve, boy, and make the boune,
  And bende thi bakke un-to this tree.
  [*Jesus lies on the cross.*]
IV MIL: Byhalde, hym-selffe has laide hym doune²,
  In lenghe and breede as he schulde bee.
I MIL: This traitoure here teynted of treasoune,
  Gose faste and fette hym than, ye thre.
  And sen he claymeth kyngdome with croune,
  Even as a kyng here have schall hee.   80
II MIL: Nowe, certis, I schall noght feyne
  Or his right hande be feste³.
III MIL: The lefte hande thanne is myne,
  Late see who beres hym beste.

(8)

IV MIL: Hys lymmys on lenghe than schalle I lede,
  And even unto the bore thame bringe.
I MIL: Unto his heede I schall take hede,
  And with myne hande helpe hym to hyng.

---

63 *werre* worse   *woode* mad   68 *sesed* stopped   *sawes* sayings   *uppe sought* made used of   73 *belyve* quickly   76 *lenghe* length   *breede* breadth   78 *fette* fetch, pull   81 *feyne* hold back   82 *feste* fixed   88 *hyng* hang

528

THE CRUCIFIXION

II MIL: Nowe sen we foure schall do this dede,
    And medill with this unthrifty thyng,   90
    Late no man spare for speciall speede,
    Tille that we have made endyng.
III MIL: This forward may not faile,
    Nowe are we right arraiede.
IV MIL: This boy here in oure baile
    Shall bide full bittir brayde.

(9)

I MIL: Sir knyghtis, saie, howe wirke we nowe?
II MIL: Yis, certis, I hope I holde this hande.
III MIL: And to the boore I have it brought
    Full boxumly with-outen bande.   100
[IV] MIL[4]: Strike on than harde, for hym the boght[5].
[I] MIL: Yis, here is a stubbe will stiffely stande;
    Thurgh bones and senous it schall be soght.
    This werke is well, I will warande.
[II] MIL: Saie, sir, howe do we thore?
    This bargayne may not blynne.
III MIL: It failis a foote and more,
    The senous are so gone ynne[6].

(10)

IV MIL: I hope that marke a-misse be bored.
II MIL: Than muste he bide in bittir bale.   110
III MIL: In faith, it was overe skantely scored;
    That makis it fouly for to faile.
I MIL: Why carpe ye so? Faste on a corde
    And tugge hym to, by toppe and taile.
III MIL: Ya, thou comaundis lightly as a lorde.
    Come helpe to haale, with ille haile.
I MIL: Nowe certis that schall I doo,
    Full suerly as a snayle.

---

96 *brayde* blows   100 *bande* rope   102 *stubbe* peg   103 *senous* sinews   106 *blynne* be held up   109 *hope* think   110 *bale* pain   111 *overe skantely* too short

ENGLISH MYSTERY PLAYS

III MIL: And I schall tacche hym too,
    Full nemely with a nayle.   120

(11)

    This werke will holde, that dar I heete,
    For nowe are feste faste both his handis.
IV MIL: Go we all foure thanne to his feete[7];
    So schall oure space be spedely spende.
II MIL: Latte see, what bourde his bale myght beete;
    Tharto my bakke nowe wolde I bende.
IV MIL: Owe! This werke is all unmeete;
    This boring muste all be amende.
I MIL: A! Pees, man, for Mahounde,
    Latte noman wotte that wondir.   130
    A roope schall rugge hym doune,
    Yf all his synnous go a-soundre.

(12)

II MIL: That corde full kyndely can I knytte,
    The comforte of this karle to kele.
I MIL: Feste on thanne faste, that all be fytte;
    It is no force howe felle he feele.
II MIL: Lugge on ye both a litill yitt.
III MIL: I schalle nought sese, as I have seele.
IV MIL: And I schall fonde hym for to hitte.
II MIL: Owe, haylle!
IV MIL: Hoo nowe, I halde it wele.   140
I MIL: Have done, dryve in that nayle,
    So that no faute be foune.
IV MIL: This wirkyng wolde noght faile
    Yf foure bullis here were boune.

(13)

I MIL: Ther cordis have evill encressed his paynes,
    Or he wer tille the booryngis brought.

---

119 *tacche* fasten   120 *nemely* quickly   121 *heete* promise   125 *bourde* jest   *beete* remedy   138 *seele* joy   139 *fonde* try   144 *bullis* bulls

THE CRUCIFIXION

II MIL: Yaa, assoundir are both synnous and veynis,
    On ilke a side, so have we soughte.
III MIL: Nowe all his gaudis no thyng hym gaynes;
    His sauntering schall with bale be bought. 150
IV MIL: I wille goo saie to oure soveraynes
    Of all this werkis howe we have wrought.
I MIL: Nay, sirs, a-nothir thyng
    Fallis firste to youe [and] me:
    I badde we schulde hym hyng
    On heghte that men myght see.

(14)

II MIL: We woote wele so ther wordes wore,
    But, sir, that dede will do us dere.
I MIL: It may not mende for to moote more,
    This harlotte muste be hanged here. 160
II MIL: The mortaise is made fitte therfore.
III MIL: Feste on youre fyngeres than in feere.
IV MIL: I wene it wolle nevere come thore.
    We foure rayse it noght right, to yere.
I MIL: Say, man, whi carpis thou soo?
    Thy liftyng was but light.
II MIL: He menes ther muste be moo
    To heve hym uppe on hight.

(15)

III MIL: Now certis, I hope it schall noght nede
    To calle to us more companye. 170
    Me thynke we foure schulde do this dede,
    And bere hym to yone hille on high.
I MIL: It muste be done, with-outen drede.
    Nomore, but loke ye be redy;
    And this parte schall I lifte and leede.
    On lenghe he schall no lenger lie.
    Therfore nowe makis you boune:
    Late bere hym to yone hill[8].

159 *moote* argue   164 *to yere* now   165 *carpis* talks   175 *leede* (v) lead

531

ENGLISH MYSTERY PLAYS

IV MIL: Thanne will I bere here doune:
    And tente his tase untill.

(16)

II MIL: We twoo schall see tille aythir side,
    For ellis this werke will wrie all wrang.
III MIL: We are redy, in Gode, sirs, abide,
    And late me first his fete up fang.
II MIL: Why tente ye so to tales this tyde?
I MIL: Lifte uppe!
    [*They attempt to raise the cross.*]
IV MIL: Latte see!
II MIL: Owe! Lifte a-lang.
III MIL: Fro all this harme he schulde hym hyde,
    And he war God.
IV MIL: The deuill hym hang!
I MIL: For grete harme have I hente;
    My schuldir is in soundre.
II MIL: And sertis I am nere schente;
    So lange have I borne undir.

(17)

III MIL: This crosse and I in twoo muste twynne,
    Ellis brekis my bakke in sondre sone.
IV MIL: Laye doune agayne and leve youre dynne,
    This dede for us will nevere be done.
    [*They lay down the cross.*]
I MIL: Assaie, sirs, latte se yf any gynne
    May helpe hym uppe, with-outen hone;
    For here schulde wight men worschippe wynne,
    And noght with gaudis al day to gone.
II MIL: More wighter men than we
    Full fewe I hope ye fynde.
III MIL: This bargayne will noght bee,
    For certis me wantis wynde.

180 *tente* attend   *tase* toes   182 *wrie* turn   184 *fang* take hold of
193 *twynne* separate   197 *gynne* machine, device   198 *hone* delay
199 *wight* strong

THE CRUCIFIXION

(18)

IV MIL: So wille of werke nevere we wore;
  I hope this carle some cautellis caste.
II MIL: My bourdeyne satte me wondir soore;
  Unto the hill I myght noght laste.
I MIL: Lifte uppe, and sone he schall be thore,
  Therfore feste on youre fyngeres faste. 210
III MIL: Owe, lifte!
  [*They raise the cross again.*]
I MIL: We, loo!
IV MIL: A litill more.
II MIL: Holde thanne!
I MIL: Howe nowe!
II MIL: The werste is paste.
III MIL: He weyes a wikkid weght.
II MIL: So may we all foure saie,
  Or he was heved on heght,
  And raysed in this array.

(19)

IV MIL: He made us stande as any stones,
  So boustous was he for to bere.
I MIL: Nowe raise hym nemely for the nonys,
  And sette hym be this mortas heere. 220
  And latte hym falle in alle at ones,
  For certis that payne schall have no pere.
III MIL: Heve uppe!
IV MIL: Latte doune, so all his bones
  Are a-soundre nowe on sides seere.
I MIL: This fallyng[10] was more felle
  Than all the harmes he hadde,
  Nowe may a man wele telle
  The leste lith of this ladde.

---

205 *wille* bewildered 206 *cautellis* tricks 207 *bourdeyne* burden
218 *boustous* huge 220 *mortas* mortice 224 *seere* several 228 *leste* least
lith joint

533

ENGLISH MYSTERY PLAYS

(20)

III MIL: Me thynkith this crosse will noght abide
Ne stande stille in this mo[r]teyse yitt.   230
IV MIL: Att the firste tyme was it made overe wyde:
That makis it wave, thou may wele witte.
I MIL: Itt schall be sette on ilke a side,
So that it schall no forther flitte;
Goode wegges schall we take this tyde,
And feste the foote, thanne is all fitte[11],
II MIL: Here are wegges arraied
For that, bothe grete and smale.
III MIL: Where are oure hameres laide
That we schulde wirke with all?   240

(21)

IV MIL: We have them here even atte oure hande.
II MIL: Gyffe me this wegge; I schall it in dryve.
IV MIL: Here is anodir yitt ordande.
III MIL: Do take it me hidir belyve.
I MIL: Laye on thanne faste.
III MIL: Yis, I warrande.
I thryng thame same, so motte I thryve.
Nowe will this crosse full stabely stande;
All yf he rave thei will noght ryve.
I MIL: Say, sir, howe likis thou nowe
This werke that we have wrought?   250
IV MIL: We praye youe sais us howe
Ye fele, or faynte ye ought?

(22)

JESUS: Al men that walkis by waye or strete,
Takes tente ye schalle no travayle tyne,
By-holdes myn heede, myn handis, and my feete,
And fully feele nowe, or ye fyne,
Yf any mournyng may be meete
Or myscheve mesůred unto myne.

243 *ordande* needed   246 *thryng* strike   254 *tyne* lose   256 *fyne* finish

534

THE CRUCIFIXION

My Fadir, that alle bales may bete,
For-giffis thes men that dois me pyne.   260
What thai wirke wotte thai noght;
Therfore, my Fadir, I crave,
Latte nevere ther synnys be sought,
But see ther saules to save.

(23)

I MIL: We! Harke! He jangelis like a jay.
II MIL: My thynke he patris like a py.
III MIL: He has ben doand all this day,
And made grete mevyng of mercy.
IV MIL: Es this the same that gune us say
That he was Goddis sone almyghty?   270
I MIL: Therfore he felis full felle affraye,
And demyd this day for to dye.
II MIL: Vah! *Qui destruis templum*[12].
III MIL: His sawes wer so, certayne.
IV MIL: And, sirs, he saide to some
He myght rayse it agayne.

(24)

I MIL: To mustir that he hadde no myght,
For all the kautelles that he couthe kaste;
All yf he wer in worde so wight,
For all his force nowe he is feste.   280
Als Pilate demed is done and dight,
Therfore I rede that we go reste.
II MIL: This race mon be rehersed right,
Thurgh the worlde both este and weste.
III MIL: Yaa, late hym hynge here stille,
And make mowes on the mone.
IV MIL: Thanne may we wende at wille.
I MIL: Nay, goode sirs, noght so sone,

---

266 *patris* patters   *py* magpie   277 *mustir* show   278 *kautelles* tricks
279 *wight* strong   286 *mowes* faces

535

(25)
    For certis us nedis anodir note:
    This kirtill wolde I of you crave.   290
II MIL: Nay, nay, sir, we will loke be lotte
    Whilke of us foure fallis to have.
III MIL: I rede we drawe cutte for this coote,
    Loo, se howe sone all sidis to save.
IV MIL: The schorte cutte schall wynne, that wele ye woote,
    Whedir itt falle to knyght or knave.
I MIL: Felowes, ye thar noght flyte
    For this mantell is myne.
II MIL: Goo we thanne hense tyte,
    This travayle here we tyne.   300

  290 *kirtill* tunic   291 *lotte* lot   293 *cutte* lot   297 *flyte* scold

31. The Death and Burial
Mortificacio Cristi

YORK 36: BOCHERES (AND PULTERS)

The manuscript attributes this play to the Butchers, and Burton's list adds the Poulterers.

The dramatic material is mainly Scriptural, and consists of a substantial number of events. Pilate is badgered by Annas and Caiaphas, who further show their hatred of Jesus by mocking him. The mockery is used by the dramatist to indicate the true state of affairs (like the mockery of the Soldiers in the Crucifixion). *Pilate is anxious – as in the Bible – to shift the blame on to the Jews. Jesus, speaking from the cross, commits Mary to the care of John. The final events of the Death are enacted – the thirsting, and Christ's last words to the Thieves, and his prayers. Longeus pierces Christ's side and is miraculously given his sight. Joseph of Arimathea and Nicodemus take down the body and bury it. Thus it is a play full of incident, with a variety of characters and moods. The staging would be complex, for it appears that Christ is seen on the cross, taken down, carried to the grave and buried.*

The play is thought to be the work of an alliterative poet writing after 1415 and relying upon the Gospel of Nicodemus. *This would suggest that the* Crucifixion *and the* Death and Burial *were revisions by different writers of the earlier single play on the Crucifixion which had passed into the* Towneley *cycle. The poet shows himself well able to create the emotional climax demanded by the Death, and to conclude the play in a mood of dignified sorrow.*

[*Scene: Calvary.*]

(1)

PILATUS: Sees, seniours, and see what I saie,
    Takis tente to my talkyng enteere,
    Devoyde all this dynne here this day,
    And fallis to my frenschippe in feere.
    Sir Pilate, a prince with-owten pere,
    My name is full nevenly to neven,
    And domisman full derworth in dere
    Of gentillest Jewry full even
        Am I.
    Who makis oppressioun,   10
    Or dose transgressioun,
    Be my discressioun
        Shall be demed dewly to dye.

(2)

    To dye schall I deme thame to dede,
    The rebelles that rewles thame un-right;
    Who that to yone hill wille take heede
    May se ther the soth in his sight,
    Howe doulful to dede thei are dight
    That liste noght owre lawes for to lere.
    Lo thus be my mayne and my myght   20
    Tho churles schalle I chasteise and cheere
        Be lawe.
    Ilke feloune false
    Shall hynge be the halse;
    Transgressours als
        On the crosse schalle be knytte for to knawe.

(3)

    To knawe schall I knytte thame on crosse,
    To schende thame with schame schall I shappe;

---

6 *nevenly* namely *neven* (v) name 7 *derworth* honourable 24 *halse* neck 25 *als* also 26 *knytte* tied

THE DEATH AND BURIAL

Ther liffis for to leese is no losse,
Suche tirrauntis with teene for to trappe. 30
Thus leelly the lawe I unlappe,
And punyssh thame pitously.
Of Jesu I holde it unhappe[1]
That he on yone hill hyng so hye
   For gilte.
His bloode to spille
Toke ye you till,
Thus was youre wille
   Full spitously to spede he were spilte.

(4)
CAIPHAS: To spille hym we spake in a speede, 40
For falsed he folowde in faie;
With fraudes oure folke gan he feede
And laboured to lere thame his laye.
ANNAS: Sir Pilate, of pees we youe praye.
Oure lawe was full lyke to be lorne;
He saved noght oure dere sabott daye,
And that for to scape it were a scorne,
   By lawe.
PILATUS: Sirs, be-fore youre sight,
With all my myght 50
I examynde hym right,
   And cause non in hym cowthe I knawe.

(5)
CAY: Ye knawe wele the cause, sir, in cace.
It touched treasoune untrewe;
The tribute to take or to trace
For-badde he, oure bale for to brewe.
AN: Of japes yitt jangelid yone Jewe,
And cursedly he called hym a kyng;
To deme hym to dede it is diewe,
For treasoune it touches that thyng 60
   In dede.

31 *leelly* rightly *unlappe* reveal 37 *till* to 52 *cowthe* could 56 *brewe* stir up

539

CAY: Yitt principall
   And worste of all
   He garte hym call
      Goddes sonne, that foulle motte hyme speede!

(6)

PILATUS: He spedis for to spille in space
   So wondirly wrought is youre will;
   His bloode schall youre bodis enbrace,
   For that have yet taken you till.
AN: That forwarde fulfayne to fulfille   70
   In dede schall we dresse us be-dene.
   Yone losell hym likis full ille
   For turned is his trantis all to teene,
      I trowe.
CAY: He called hym kyng,
   Ille joie hym wring!
   Ya, late hym hyng,
      Full madly on the mone for to mowe.

(7)

AN: To mowe on the moone has he mente,
   We! fye on the, faitour in faye,   80
   Who trowes thou to thi tales toke tente?
   Thou saggard, thi selffe gan thou saie
   The tempill distroie the to-daye,
   Be the thirde day ware done ilk-a-dele
   To rayse it thou schulde the arraye.
   Loo! howe was thi falsed to feele,
      Foule falle the!
   For thy presumpcyoune
   Thou haste thy warisoune;
   Do faste, come doune,   90
      And a comely kyng schalle I calle thee.

70 *fulfayne* very gladly   73 *trantis* tricks   82 *saggard* sagging body
84 *ilk-a-dele* every bit   89 *warisoune* reward

THE DEATH AND BURIAL

(8)

CAY: I calle the a coward to kenne,
  That mervaylles and mirakills made;
  Thou mustered emange many menne,
  But, brothell, thou bourded to brede.
  Thou saved thame fro sorowes, thai saide;
  To save nowe thi selffe late us see;
  God sonne if thou grathely be grayde,
  Delyvere the doune of that tree
    Anone: 100
  If thou be funne
  Thou be Goddis sonne,
  We schalle be bonne
    To trowe on the trewlye, ilkone.

(9)

AN: Sir Pilate, youre pleasaun[c]e we praye,
  Takis tente to oure talkyng this tide,
  And wipe ye yone writyng away;
  It is not beste it abide.
  It sittis youe to sette it aside,
  And sette that he saide in his sawe,   110
  As he that was prente full of pride:
  'Jewes kyng am I,' comely to knawe,
    Full playne.
PILATUS: *Quod scripci, scripci*[2].
  Yone same wrotte I;
  I bide ther-by,
    What gedlyng will grucche there agayne.

(10)

JESUS: Thou man that of mys here has mente,
  To me tente enteerly thou take.
  On roode am I ragged and rente,   120

---

95 *bourded* jested   *brede* broadly   98 *grathely* properly   *grayde* prepared
101 *funne* found   103 *bonne* bound   111 *prente* imprinted   117 *gedlyng* vagabond

Thou synfull sawle, for thy sake;
For thy misse amendis wille I make.
My bakke for to bende here I bide;
This teene for thi trespase I take;
Who couthe the more kyndynes have kydde
   Than I?
Thus for thy goode
I schedde my bloode;
Manne, mende thy moode,
   For full bittir thi blisse mon I by.   130

(11)

MARIA: Allas for my swete sonne, I saie,
That doulfully to dede thus is dight.
Allas! For full lovely thou laye
In my wombe, this worthely wight.
Allas! That I schulde see this sight
Of my sone so semely to see.
Allas! That this blossome so bright
Untrewly is tugged to this tree!
   Allas!
My lorde, my leyffe,   140
With full grete greffe,
Hyngis as a theffe,
   Allas! He did never trespasse.

(12)

JESUS: Thou woman, do way of thy wepyng,
For me may thou no thyng amende;
My Fadirs wille to be wirkyng,
For mankynde my body I bende.
MARIA: Allas! That thou likes noght to lende;
Howe schulde I but wepe for thy woo?
To care nowe my comforte is kende.   150
Allas! Why schulde we twynne thus in twoo
   For evere?

125 *kydde* shown 138 *tugged* tied 144 *do way of* stop 148 *lende* stay

THE DEATH AND BURIAL

JESUS: Womanne, in stede of me,
   Loo, John thi sone schall bee.
   John, see to thi modir free;
     For my sake do thou thi devere.

(13)

MARIA: Allas, sone, sorowe and sighte,
   That me were closed in clay!
   A swerde of sorowe me smyte!
   To dede I were done this day!   160
JOHANNES: A, modir, so schall ye noght saie.
   I praye youe be pees in this presse,
   For with all the myght that I maye,
   Youre comforte I caste to encresse
     In dede.
   Youre sone am I,
   Loo, here redy,
   And nowe for-thy
     I praye yowe hense for to speede.

(14)

MARIA: My steven for to stede or to steere   170
   Howe schulde I, such sorowe to see:
   My sone that is dereworthy and dere
   Thus doulfull a dede for to dye.
JOH: A, dere modir, blynne of this blee;
   Youre mournyng it may not amende.
MARIA CLEOPHE[3]: A, Marie, take triste un-to the,
   For socoure to the will he sende
     This tyde.
JOH: Fayre modir, faste
   Hense latte us caste.   180
MARIA: To he be paste
   Wille I buske here baynly to bide.

---

156 *devere* duty   170 *steven* voice   *stede* stay   *steere* control   174 *blee* sorrow   181 *To* until   *paste* dead   182 *buske* settle   *baynly* closely

(15)

JESUS: With bittirfull bale have I bought,
  Thus, man, all thi misse for to mende.
  On me for to looke lette thou noght,
  Howe baynly my body I bende.
  No wighte in this worlde wolde have wende
  What sorowe I suffre for thy sake.
  Manne, kaste the thy kyndynesse be kende,
  Trewe tente un-to me that thou take,   190
    And treste.
  For foxis ther dennys have thei,
  Birdis hase their nestis to paye,
  But the sone of man this daye
    Hase noght on his heed for to reste.

(16)

LATRO A SINISTRIS[4]: If thou be Goddis sone so free,
  Why hyng thou thus on this hille?
  To saffe nowe thi selffe late us see,
  And us now, that spedis for to spille.
LATRO A DEXTRIS: Manne, stynte of thy steven and be stille,   200
  For douteles thy God dredis thou noght;
  Full wele are we worthy ther-till:
  Unwisely wrange have we wrought
    I-wisse.
  Noon ille did hee,
  Thus for to dye;
  Lord, have mynde of me
    What thou art come to thi blisse.

(17)

JESUS: For sothe, sonne, to the schall I saie,   210
  Sen thou fro thy foly will falle,
  With me schall dwelle nowe this daye,
  In paradise place principall.

---

185 *baynly* obediently 187 *wende* thought 191 *treste* trust 198 *saffe* save

THE DEATH AND BURIAL

Heloy! Heloy!
My God, my God, full free,
Lamasabatanye?[5]
Whar-to for-soke thou me
  In care?
And I did nevere ille
This dede for to go tille,
But be it at thi wille. 220
  A, me thristis sare![6]

(18)

GARCIO: A drinke schalle I dresse the in dede:
  A draughte that is full dayntely dight.
  Full faste schall I springe for to spede;
  I hope I schall holde that I have hight.
CAY: Sir Pilate, that moste is of myght,
  Harke! *Heely!* now harde I hym crye.
  He wenys that that worthely wight
  In haste for to helpe hym in hye
    In his nede. 230
PILATUS: If he do soo,
  He schall have woo.
AN: He wer oure foo,
  If he dresse hym to do us that dede.

(19)

GARCIO: That dede for to dresse yf he doo,
  In sertis he schall rewe it full sore;
  Nevere the lees if he like it noght, loo,
  Full sone may he covere that care.
  Nowe, swete sir, youre wille yf it ware,
  A draughte here of drinke have I dreste, 240
  To spede for no spence that ye s[p]are,
  But baldely ye bib it for the beste
    For-why;
  Aysell and galle

219 *tille* to 225 *holde* carry out 241 *spence* expense 242 *bib* drink
244 *Aysell* vinegar

Is menged with alle:
Drynke it ye schalle;
   Youre lippis, I halde thame full drye.

(20)

JESUS: Thi drinke it schalle do me no deere;
Wete thou wele ther-of will I none.
Nowe, Fadir, that formed alle in fere,   250
To thy moste myght make I my mone.
Thi wille have I wrought in this wone,
Thus ragged and rente on this roode;
Thus doulffully to dede have thei done.
For-giffe thame be grace that is goode;
   Thai ne wote noght what it was.
My Fadir, here my bone,
For nowe all thyng is done;
My spirite to thee right sone
   Comende I *in manus tuas*[7].   260
[*Dies.*]

(21)

MARIA: Now, dere sone, Jesus so iente,
Sen my harte is hevy as leede,
O worde wolde I witte or thou wente;
Allas, nowe my dere sone is dede.
Full rewfully refte is my rede.
Allas for my darlyng so dere!
JOH: A, modir, ye halde uppe youre heede,
And sigh noght with sorowes so seere,
   I praye.
MA. CLEO: It does hir pyne   270
To see hym tyne.
Lede we her heyne,
   This mornyng helpe hir ne maye.
   [*Mary Cleophas and John lead Mary away.*]

245 *menged* mixed   248 *deere* harm   252 *wone* place   257 *bone* request
261 *iente* noble   265 *refte* taken   *rede* counsel   272 *heyne* hence

THE DEATH AND BURIAL

(22)

CAY: Sir Pilate, parceyve, I you praye,
Oure costemes to kepe wele ye canne;
To-morne is our dere sabott daye:
Of mirthe muste us meve ilke a mane.
Yone warlous nowe waxis full wane,
And nedis muste thei beried be.
Delyver ther dede, sir, and thane 280
Shall we sewe to oure saide solempnite
In dede.
PILATUS: It schalle be done
In wordis fone;
Sir knyghtis, go sone,
To yone harlottis you hendely take heede.

(23)

Tho caytiffis thou kille with thi knyffe;
Delyvere, have done, thei were dede.
MILES: Mi lorde, I schall lenghe so ther liffe
That tho brothelles schall nevere bite brede. 290
PILATUS: Ser Longeus[8], steppe forthe in this steede.
This spere, loo, have halde in thy hande.
To Jesus thou rake fourthe I rede,
And sted nought, but stiffely thou stande
A stounde.
In Jesu side
Schoffe it this tyde;
No lenger bide,
But grathely thou go to the grounde.
[*Longeus pierces Jesus' side.*]

(24)

LONGEUS *latus*[9]: O, maker unmade, full of myght, 300
O, Jesu so jentill and jente,

275 *costemes* customs 277 *mane* man 278 *warlous* wizard *wane* wan
280 *Delyver* hasten 281 *sewe* proceed 284 *fone* few 297 *Schoffe* shove

547

That sodenly has lente me my sight,
Lorde, lovyng to the be it lente.
On rode arte thou ragged and rente,
Mankynde for to mende of his mys;
Full spitously spilte is and spente
Thi bloode, Lorde, to bringe us to blis
    Full free.
A, mercy, my socoure,
Mercy, my treasoure,   310
Mercy, my savioure,
    Thi mercy be markid in me.

(25)

CENTURIO: O, wondirfull werkar i-wis,
This weedir is waxen full wan;
Trewe token I trowe that it is
That mercy is mente unto man.
Full clerly consayve thus I can;
No cause in this corse couthe thei knowe,
Yitt doulfull thei demyd hym than
To lose thus his liffe be ther lawe,   320
    No righte.
Trewly I saie,
Goddis sone verraye
Was he this daye
    That doulfully to dede thus is dight.
[Enter Joseph of Arimathea.]

(26)

JOSEPH: That Lorde lele ay lastyng in lande,
Sir Pilate, full preste in this presse,
He save the be see and be sande,
And all that is derworth on deesse.
PILATUS: Joseph, this is lely no lesse;   330
To me arte thou welcome i-wisse;
Do saie me the soth or thou sesse,
Thy worthyly wille what it is
    Anone.

329 *deesse* dais

THE DEATH AND BURIAL

JOS: To the I praye,
  Giffe me in hye
  Jesu bodye,
    In gree it for to grave al alone.

(27)

PILATUS: Joseph sir, I graunte the that geste;
  I grucche noght to grath hym in grave: 340
  Delyver, have done he were dreste,
  And sewe, sir, oure sabott to saffe.
JOS: With handis and harte that I have,
  I thanke the in faith for my frende.
  God kepe the thi comforte to crave,
  For wightely my way will I wende
    In hye.
  To do that dede
  He be my speede,
  That armys gun sprede, 350
    Manne kynde be his bloode for to bye.
  [*Enter Nicodemus.*]

(28)

NICHODEMUS: Weill mette, sir, in mynde gune [I] meffe[10]
  For Jesu, that juged was un-jente;
  Ye laboured for license and leve
  To berye his body on bente.
JOS: Full myldely that matere I mente,
  And that for to do will I dresse.
NICHO: Both same I wolde that wente
  And lette not for more ne for lesse,
    For-why 360
  Oure frende was he,
  Faithfull and free.
JOS: Therfore go we
  To berie that body in hye.

---

338 *gree* favour   339 *geste* deed   346 *wightely* quickly   355 *bente* field

549

ENGLISH MYSTERY PLAYS

(29)

    All mankynde may marke in his mynde
    To see here this sorowfull sight;
    No falsenesse in hym couthe thei fynde,
    That doulfully to dede thus is dight.
NICHO: He was a full worthy wight,
    Nowe blemysght and bolned with bloode.   370
JOS: Ya, for that he maistered his myght,
    Full falsely thei fellid that foode,
      I wene,
    Bothe bakke and side,
    His woundes wide;
    For-thi this tyde
      Take we hym doune us be-twene.

(30)

NICHO: Be-twene us take we hym doune
    And laie hym on lenthe on this lande.
    [*They take down the body and lay it in a new grave.*]
JOS: This reverent and riche of rennoune,   380
    Late us halde hym and halṣe hym with hande.
    A grave have I garte here be ordande,
    That never was in noote; it is newe.
NICHO: To this corse it is comely accordande,
    To dresse hym with dedis full dewe
      This stounde.
JOS: A sudarye
    Loo here have I;
    Wynde hym for-thy,
    And sone schalle we grave hym in grounde.   390

(31)

NICHO: In grounde late us grave hym and goo;
    Do liffely, latte us laie hym allone;
    Nowe, saviour of me and of moo,
    Thou kepe us in clennesse ilkone.

---

370 *blemysght* bruised   *bolned* swollen   372 *foode* creature, man
380 *riche* man   383 *noote* occupation   387 *sudarye* winding-sheet

THE DEATH AND BURIAL

JOS: [T]o thy mercy nowe make I my moone
    As saviour be see and be sande;
    Thou gyde me that my griffe be al gone,
    With lele liffe to lenge in this lande
        And esse.
NICHO: Seere oynementis here have I   400
    Brought for this faire body;
    I anoynte the for-thy
        With myrre and aloes[11].

(32)

JOS: This dede it is done ilke a dele,
    And wroughte is this werke wele i-wis.
    To the kyng on knes here I knele,
    That baynly thou belde me in blisse.
NICHO: He highte me full hendely to be his,
    A nyght when I neghed hym full nere;
    Have mynde, Lorde, and [m]ende me of mys,   410
    For done is oure dedis full dere
        This tyde.
JOS: This Lorde so goode,
    That schedde his bloode,
    He mende youre moode,
        And buske on this blis for to bide.

---

395 *moone* moan   397 *griffe* grief   399 *esse* ease   400 *Seere* many
407 *belde* protect

32. The Harrowing of Hell

YORK 37: SADILLERES

*The play was performed by the Saddlers. Burton's list refers to
Verrours (glaziers) and Fuystours (makers of saddle-trees).*

*The subject was a very popular one, appearing in all four cycles and
the Cornish cycle. There is a Middle English poem of the early thirteenth century, and the incident is given attention in* Piers Plowman.
The Descent into Hell, which is an article of the Creed, has no Scriptural basis. The Gospel of Nicodemus *almost certainly provides the
main source. It had appeared in the liturgy as part of the Easter ritual
in the* Sarum Breviary. *The subject is also treated in the earliest
French passion play,* La Passion du Palatinus *(early fourteenth
century).*

*Theologically the play represents the triumph of Christ. This is
achieved through a physical conflict – the Gates are burst – and by a
verbal dispute between Christ and Satan, which Christ wins. It is also
the culmination of the story of Adam, who is finally restored by Christ's
sacrifice.*

The Towneley *play is closely parallel, though there are some
passages in* York *which seem to have been written after the cycles were
divided. In the* Towneley *version the Devils are more unruly: the*
York *is notable for its dignity and restraint, and its close attention to
symbolic effect.*

※

[Scene: the Gates of Hell[1].]

(1)

JESUS: Manne on molde, be meke to me,
    And have thy maker in thi mynde,

  1 *molde* earth

THE HARROWING OF HELL

And thynke howe I have tholid for the,
With pereles paynes for to be pyned.
The forward of my Fadir free
Have I fulfillid, as folke may fynde;
Ther-fore a-boute nowe woll I bee,
That I have bought² for to unbynde.
The feende thame wanne with trayne
Thurgh frewte of erthely foode;   10
I have thame getyn agayne
Thurgh bying with my bloode.

(2)

And so I schall that steede restore
[Fro] whilke the feende fell for synne;
Thare schalle mankynde wonne evermore,
In blisse that schall nevere blynne.
All that in werke my werkemen were
Owte of thare woo I wol thame wynne,
And some signe schall I sende be-fore
Of grace to garre ther gamys be-gynne.   20
A light³ I woll thei have
To schewe thame I schall come sone;
My bodie bidis in grave
Tille alle thes dedis be done.

(3)

My Fadir ordand on this wise
Aftir his will that I schulde wende
For to fulfille the prophicye,
And als I spake my solace to spende.
My frendis that in me faith affies,
Nowe fro ther fois I schall thame fende,   30
And on the thirde day ryght uprise,
And so tille heven I schall assende.
Sithen schall I come agayne,

3 *tholid* suffered   13 *steede* place   16 *blynne* cease   23 *bidis* remains
25 *ordand* ordained   26 *wende* go   29 *affies* trusts   30 *fende* defend

To deme bothe goode and ill
Tille endless joie or peyne;
Thus is my Fadris will[4].

(4)

ADAME: Mi bretheren, harkens to me here;
Swilke hope of heele nevere are we hadde,
Foure thousande and sex hundereth yere
Have we bene heere in this stedde.   40
Nowe see I signe of solace seere,
A glorious gleme to make us gladde,
Wher-fore I hope oure helpe is nere,
And sone schall sesse oure sorowes sadde.
EVA: Adame, my husband hende,
This menys solas certayne;
Such light gune on us lende
In paradise full playne.

(5)

ISAIAH: Adame, we schall wele undirstande,
I, Ysaias, as God me kende,   50
I prechid in Neptalym[5], that lande,
And Zabulon even un-till ende.
I spake of folke in mirke walkand,
And saide a light sculde on thame lende;
This lered I whils I was levand;
Nowe se I God this same hath sende.
This light comes all of Christe,
That seede to save us nowe;
Thus is my poynte puplisshid.
But, Symeon[6], what sais thou?   60

(6)

SYMEON: Yhis, my tale of farleis feele,
For in this temple his frendis me fande;
I hadde delite with hym to dele,

38 *heele* cure   41 *seere* distinct, separate   50 *kende* taught   53 *mirke* dark
55 *levand* living   59 *puplisshid* revealed

THE HARROWING OF HELL

And halsed homely with my hande.
I saide, 'Lorde, late thy servaunt lele
Passe nowe in pesse to liffe lastand,
For nowe my selfe has sene thy hele,
Me liste no lengar to liffe in lande.'
This light thou hast purveyed
To folkes that liffis in leede;   70
The same that I thame saide,
I see fulfillid in dede[7].

(7)

JOHANNES BAPTISTA: Als voyce criand to folke I kende
 The weyes of Christe als I wele kanne,
I baptiste hym with bothe my hande
 Even in the floode of flume Jordanne.
The Holy Goste fro hevene discende,
 Als a white dowve[8] doune on hym thanne;
The Fadir voice, my mirthe to mende,
 Was made to me even als manne[9], 80
'This is my sone,' he saide,
'In whome me paies full wele.'
His light is on us laide,
He comes oure cares to kele.

(8)

MOYSES: Of that same light lernyng have I;
 To me, Moyses, he mustered his myght,
And also unto anodir, Hely[10],
 Wher we were on an hille on hight.
Whyte as snowe was his body,
 And his face like to the sonne to sight; 90
No man on molde was so myghty
 Grathely to loke agaynste that light.
That same light se I nowe
Shynyng on us sarteyne,

---

64 *halsed* embraced 70 *leede* land, earth 76 *flume* river 78 *dowve* dove

Wherfore trewly I trowe
We schalle sone passe fro payne.

(9)

I DIABOLUS: Helpe, Belsabub, to bynde thes boyes!
Such harrowe was never are herde in helle.
II DIAB: Why rooris thou soo, Rebalde[11]? Thou royis.
What is be-tidde, canne thou ought telle?
I DIAB: What! Heris thou noght this uggely noyse?
These lurdans that in Lymbo[12] dwelle,
Thei make menyng of many joies,
And musteres grete mirthe thame emell.
II DIAB: Mirthe? Nay, nay, that poynte is paste;
More hele schall thei nevere have.
I DIAB: Thei crie on Criste full faste,
And sais he schal thame save.

(10)

BELSABUB: Ya, if he save thame noght, we schall,
For they are sperde in speciall space.
Whils I am prince and principall
Schall thei never passe oute of this place.
Calle uppe Astrotte[13] and Anaball
To giffe ther counsaille in this case,
Bele-Berit[14] and Belial,
To marre thame that swilke maistries mase[15].
Say to Satan oure sire,
And bidde thame bringe also
Lucifer, lovely of lyre.
I DIAB: Al redy, lorde, I goo.

(11)

JESUS [*outside the gates*]: *Attollite portas, principes,*
Oppen uppe, ye princes of paynes sere,
Et elevamini eternales[16],
Youre yendles gatis that ye have here.

98 *harrowe* uproar   99 *royis* ?talkest folly   106 *hele* health   110 *sperde*
shut   116 *mase* makes   119 *lyre* face

556

THE HARROWING OF HELL

SATTAN: What page is there that makes prees,
   And callis hym kyng of us in fere?
DAVID: I lered levand, with-outen lees[17],
   He is a kyng of vertues clere,
   A lorde mekill of myght,
   And stronge in ilke a stoure[18],   130
   In batailes ferse to fight,
   And worthy to wynne honnoure.

(12)
SATTAN: Honnoure! In the develway, for what dede?
   All erthely men to me are thrall,
   The lady that calles hym lorde in leede
   Hadde never yit herberowe, house, ne halle.
I DIAB: Harke, Belsabub! I have grete drede,
   For hydously I herde hym calle.
BELLIALL: We! spere oure gates, all ill mot thou spede,
   And sette furthe watches on the wall.   140
   And if he call or crie
   To make us more debate,
   Lay on hym than hardely,
   And garre hym gang his gate.

(13)
SATTAN: Telle me what boyes dare be so bolde
   For drede to make so mekill draye.
I DIAB: Itt is the Jewe that Judas solde
   For to be dede, this othir daye.
SATTAN: Owe! This tale in tyme is tolde;
   This traytoure traves us alway.   150
   He schall be here full harde in holde.
   Loke that he passe noght, I the praye.
II DIAB: Nay, nay, he will noght wende
   A-way or I be ware;
   He shappis hym for to schende
   Alle helle or he go ferre.

---

125 *prees* uproar   130 *stoure* struggle   135 *leede* country   136 *herberowe* harbour   139 *spere* shut   144 *garre* make   *gate* way   146 *draye* disturbance   150 *traves* (v) crosses

557

(14)

SATTAN: Nay, faitour, ther-of schall he faile,
  For alle his fare I hym deffie,
  I knowe his trantis fro toppe to taile,
  He levys with gaudis and with gilery.   160
  Ther-by he brought oute of oure bale,
  Nowe late, Lazar[19] of Betannye,
  Ther-fore I gaffe to the Jewes counsaille
  That thei schulde alway garre hym dye.
  I entered in Judas[20]
  That forwarde to fulfille;
  Ther-fore his hire he has,
  All-way to wonne here stille.

(15)

BELSABUB: Sir Sattanne, sen we here the saie
  That thou and the Jewes wer same assente,   170
  And wotte he wanne Lazar awaye,
  That tille us was tane for to tente,
  Trowe thou that thou marre hym maye
  To mustir myghtis what he has mente?[21]
  If he nowe deprive us of oure praye,
  We will ye witte whanne thei are wente.
SATTAN: I bidde you be noght abasshed
  But boldely make youe boune
  With toles that ye on traste
  And dynge that dastard doune.   180

(16)

JESUS [*outside the gates*]: *Principes, portas tollite,*
  Undo youre gatis, ye princis of pryde,
  Et introibit rex glorie,
  The kyng of blisse comes in this tyde.
    [*Jesus enters the gates.*]
SATTAN: Owte! harrowe! [What harlot] is hee?
  That sais his kyngdome schall be cryed.

159 *trantis* tricks   160 *gilery* deceit   168 *wonne* stay   179 *toles* tools

THE HARROWING OF HELL

DAVID: That may thou in my sawter see
  For that poynte of prophicie.
  I saide that he schuld breke
  Youre barres[22] and bandis by name,   190
  And on youre werkis take wreke;
  Nowe schalle ye see the same.

(17)

JESUS: This steede schall stonde no lenger stoken.
  Opynne uppe, and latte my pepul passe.
DIABOLUS: Oute! Beholdes, oure baill is brokynne,
  And brosten are alle oure bandis of bras.
  Telle Lucifer alle is unlokynne.
BELSABUB: What thanne, is Lymbus lorne? Allas!
  Garre, Satan, helpe that we were wroken;
  This werke is werse thanne evere it was.   200
SATTAN: I badde ye schulde be boune
  If he made maistries more.
  Do dynge that dastard doune,
  And sette hym sadde and sore.

(18)

BELSABUB: Ya, sette hym sore, that is sone saide,
  But come thi selffe and serve hym soo.
  We may not bide his bittir braide;
  He wille us marre, and we wer moo.
SATTAN: What, faitours, wherfore are ye ferde?
  Have ye no force to flitte hym froo?   210
  Belyve loke that my gere[23] be grathed;
  Mi selffe schall to that gedlyng goo.
  Howe, belamy, abide,
  With al thy booste and bere,
  And telle to me this tyde
  What maistries makes thou here?

---

187 *sawter* psalter   191 *wreke* revenge   193 *steede* place   *stoken* stuck   196 *brosten* burst   197 *unlokynne* unlocked   198 *lorne* lost   214 *bere* outcry

(19)

JESUS: I make no maistries but for myne.
　　Thame wolle I save, I telle the nowe;
　　Thou hadde no poure thame to pyne,
　　But as my prisonne for ther prowe 220
　　Here have thei soiorned, noght as thyne[24],
　　But in thy warde, thou wote wele howe.
SATTAN: And what devel haste thou done ay syne
　　That never wolde negh thame nere or nowe?
JESUS: Nowe is the tyme certayne
　　Mi Fadir ordand be-fore,
　　That they schulde passe fro payne,
　　And wonne in mirthe ever more.

(20)

SATTAN: Thy fadir knewe I wele be sight.
　　He was a write his mette to wynne, 230
　　And Marie, me menys[25], thi modir hight,
　　The uttiremeste ende of all thi kynne.
　　Who made the be so mekill of myght?
JESUS: Thou wikid feende, latte be thy dynne!
　　Mi Fadir wonnys in heven on hight,
　　With blisse that schall nevere blynne.
　　I am his awne sone,
　　His forward to fulfille,
　　And same ay schall we wonne
　　And sundir when we wolle. 240

(21)

SATTAN: God sonne, thanne schulde thou be ful gladde;
　　Aftir no catel neyd thowe crave.
　　But thou has leved ay like a ladde,
　　And in sorowe as a symple knave.
JESUS: That was for hartely love I hadde
　　Unto mannis soule it for to save;

220 *prowe* profit, honour　　223 *syne* since　　230 *write* carpenter　　*mette* meat, food　　239 *wonne* abide　　242 *catel* property

THE HARROWING OF HELL

And for to make the mased and madde,
And by that resoune thus dewly to have,
Mi godhede here I hidde
In Marie modir myne, 250
For it schulde noght be kidde
To the nor to none of thyne.

(22)

SATTAN: A, this wolde I were tolde in ilke a toune.
So sen thou sais God is thy sire,
I schall the prove be right resoune
Thou motes his men in to the myre[26].
To breke his bidding were thei boune,
And, for they did at my desire,
Fro paradise he putte thame doune
In helle here to have ther hyre. 260
And thy selfe, day and nyght,
Has taught al men emang
To do resoune and right,
And here werkis thou all wrang.

(23)

JESUS: I wirke noght wrang, that schal thow witte,
If I my men fro woo will wynne;
Mi prophetis playnly prechid it,
All this note that nowe be-gynne.
Thai saide that I schulde be obitte,
To hell that I schulde entre in, 270
And save my servauntis fro that pitte,
Wher dampned saulis schall sitte for synne.
And ilke trewe prophettis tale
Muste be fulfillid in mee.
I have thame broughte with bale,
And in blisse schal thei be.

251 *kidde* known   269 *obitte* dead

(24)

SATTAN: Nowe sen the liste allegge the lawes[27],
    Thou schalte be atteynted, or we twynne,
    For tho that thou to wittenesse drawes,
    Full even agaynste the will be-gynne.   280
    Salamon[28] saide in his sawes
    That whoso enteres helle withynne
    Shall never come oute, thus clerkis knawes –
    And therfore, felowe, leve thi dynne.
    Job[29], thi servaunte also,
    Thus in his tyme gune telle
    That nowthir frende nor foo
    Shulde fynde reles in helle.

(25)

JESUS: He saide full soth, that schall thou see,
    That in helle may be no reles,   290
    But of that place than preched he,
    Where synffull care schall evere encrees.
    And in that bale ay schall thou be,
    Whare sorowes sere schall never sesse,
    And for my folke ther fro wer free,
    Nowe schall thei passe to the place of pees.
    Thai were here with my wille,
    And so schall thei fourthe wende,
    And thi selve schall fulfille
    Ther wooe with-outen ende.   300

(26)

SATTAN: Owe! Thanne se I howe thou movys emang[30]
    Some mesure with malice to melle,
    Sen thou sais all schall noght gang,
    But some schalle alway with us dwelle.
JESUS: Yaa, witte thou wele, ellis were it wrang,
    Als cursed Cayme that slewe Abell,
    And all that hastis hem-selve to hange
    Als Judas and Archedefell[31],
    Datan and Abiron[32]

THE HARROWING OF HELL

And alle of thare assente, 310
Als tyrantis everilkone
That me and myne turmente,

(27)
And all that liste noght to lere my lawe[33],
That I have lefte in lande nowe newe,
That is my comyng for to knawe,
And to my sacramente pursewe,
Mi dede, my rysing, rede be rawe,
Who will noght trowe thei are noght trewe,
Unto my dome I schall thame drawe,
And juge thame worse thanne any Jewe. 320
And all that likis to leere
My lawe and leve ther bye
Shall nevere have harmes heere,
But welthe as is worthy.

(28)
SATTAN: Nowe here my hande, I halde me paied,
This poynte is playnly for oure prowe.
If this be soth that thou hast saide,
We schall have moo thanne we have nowe.
This lawe that thou nowe late has laide
I schall lere men noght to allowe, 330
Iff thei it take thei be be-traied,
For I schall turne thame tyte, I trowe.
I schall walke este and weste,
And garre thame werke welle werre.
JESUS: Naye, feende, thou schall be feste,
That thou schalte flitte not ferre.

(29)
SATTAN: Feste! That were a foule reasoune,
Nay, bellamy, thou bus be smytte[34].
JESUS: Mighill![35] Myne aungell, make the boune,
And feste yone fende, that he not flitte. 340

317 *rede* learnt *be rawe* in turn

And, devyll, I comaunde the go doune
In-to thy selle, where thou schalte sitte.
SATTAN: Owt! Ay! Herrowe! Helpe, Mahounde!
Nowe wex I woode oute of my witte.
BELSABUB: Sattan, this saide we are,
Nowe schall thou fele thi fitte.
SATTAN: Allas, for dole and care,
I synke in to helle pitte.

(30)

ADAME: A! Jesu, Lorde, mekill is thi myght, 350
That mekis thi-selffe in this manere,
Us for to helpe as thou has hight,
Whanne both forfette I and my feere.
Here have we levyd with-outen light
Foure thousand and vi c yere;
Now se I be this solempne sight
Howe thy mercy hath made us clere.
EVE: A, Lorde, we were worthy
Mo turmentis for to taste,
But mende us with mercye
Als thou of myght is moste. 360

(31)

BAPTISTA: A! Lorde, I love the inwardly,
That me wolde make thi messengere,
Thy comyng in erth for to crye,
And teche thi faith to folke in feere,
And sithen be-fore the for to dye
And bringe boodworde to thame here,
How thai schulde have thyne helpe in hye.
Nowe se I all thi poyntis appere
Als David prophete trewe
Ofte tymes tolde untill us; 370
Of this comyng he knewe,
And saide it schulde be thus.

345 *are* before   346 *fitte* turn   350 *mekis* humblest

THE HARROWING OF HELL

(32)

DAVID: Als I have saide, yitt saie I soo,
   Ne derelinquas, domine,
   Animam meam in inferno[36];
   Leffe noght my saule, Lorde, aftir the,
   In depe helle where dampned schall goo,
   Ne suffre nevere saules fro the be,
   The sorowe of thame that wonnes in woo,
   Ay full of filthe, that may repleye[37].   380
ADAME: We thanke his grete goodnesse
   He fette us fro this place,
   Makes joie nowe more and lesse.
OMNIS: We laude God of his grace.

(33)

JESUS: Adame and my frendis in feere,
   Fro all youre fooes come fourth with me.
   Ye schalle be sette in solas seere,
   Wher ye schall nevere of sorowes see.
   And Mighill, myn aungell clere,
   Ressayve thes saules all unto the,   390
   And lede thame als I schall the lere
   To Paradise with playe and plente.
   [*Michael leads the Souls from Hell.*]
   Mi grave I woll go till[38],
   Redy to rise uppe-right,
   And so I schall fulfille
   That I be-fore have highte.

(34)

MICHILL: Lorde, wende we schall aftir thi sawe,
   To solace sere thai schall be sende;
   But that ther develis no draught us drawe[39],
   Lorde, blisse us with thi holy hende.   400
JESUS: Mi blissing have ye all on rawe,
   I schall be with youe wher ye wende,

382 *fette* fetched   400 *hende* hand

And all that lelly luffes my lawe,
Thai schall be blissid with-owten ende.
ADAME: To the, Lorde, be lovyng[40],
That us has wonne fro waa;
For solas will we syng
Laus tibi cum gloria[41].

33. The Resurrection
Resurreccio Domini

TOWNELEY 26

The episode of the Resurrection is perhaps the earliest manifestation of Christian drama. It occurs in the Mass for Easter Day when the Angel in the tomb sings a brief dialogue with the Marys. As a play, however, the episode proved difficult in the absence of Scriptural detail. The Towneley version here is closely dependent upon York 38 for long stretches. However the dramatist inserted several passages, especially Christ's monologue, which suggest that a new treatment of the dramatic potentialities of the story was being tried. Moreover the dramatist includes Christ's Appearance to Mary Magdalene in the Garden. Comparison with the York play makes it clear that the Towneley version is very much an accretion of dissimilar elements. The characters of the Soldiers are particularly vigorous in their craftiness. Probably this is ultimately derived from Continental sources.

ಜ಼

[*Scene: Pilate's court.*]

(1)

PILATUS: Peasse, I warne you, woldys in wytt!
    And standys on syde or else go sytt,
    For here ar men that go not yitt,
        And lordys of me[kill] myght;
    We thynk to abyde, and not to flytt,
        I tell you every wyght.

1 *woldys* rulers

ENGLISH MYSTERY PLAYS

(2)

Spare youre spech, ye brodels bold,
And sesse youre cry till I have told
What that my worship wold,
Here in thise wonys;
Whoso that wyghtly nold
Full hy bese hanged his bonys[1].

(3)

Wote ye not that I am Pilate,
That satt apon the iustyce late,
At Calvarie where I was att
This day at morne?
I am he, that great state,
That lad has all to-torne.

(4)

Now sen that lothly losell is thus ded,
I have great ioy in my manhede;
Therfor wold I in ilk sted
It were tayn hede
If any felowse felow his red,
Or more his law wold lede.

(5)

For and I knew it, cruelly
His lyfe bees lost, and that shortly,
That he were better hyng ful hy
On galow tre;
Therfor ye prelatys shuld aspy
If any sich be.

(6)

As I am man of myghtys most,
If ther be any that blow sich bost,

7 *brodels* wretches 10 *wonys* places 11 *wyghtly* quickly *nold* will not (do) 23 *felow* follow *red* advice

THE RESURRECTION

With tormentys keyn bese he indost
For evermore;
The devill to hell shall harry hys goost.
Bot I say nomore.

(7)

CAIPHAS: Sir, ye thar nothyng be dredand,
For Centurio, I understand,
Youre knyght is left abydand
Right ther behynde;
We left hym ther, for man most wyse,
If any rybaldys wold oght ryse,
To sesse theym to the next assyse,
And then forto make ende.
　　Tunc veniet Centurio velut miles equitans[2].

(8)

CENTURIO: A, blyssyd Lord Adonay[3],
What may this mervell sygnyfy
That here was shewyd so openly
Unto oure sight,
When the rightwys man can dy
That Ihesus hight?

(9)

Heven it shoke abone,
Of shynyng blan both son and moyne[4],
And dede men also rose up sone
Outt of thare grafe;
And stones in wall anone
In sonder brast and clafe.

(10)

Ther was seen many a full sodan sight.
Oure prynces, for sothe, dyd nothyng right,

---

33 *indost* overwhelmed　43 *assyse* assize　51 *abone* above　52 *blan* ceased　54 *grafe* grave　56 *clafe* split

And so I saide to theym on hight —
As it is trew —
That he was most of myght,
The son of God, Ihesu.

(11)

Fowlys in the ayer and fish in floode
That day changid thare mode,
When that he was rent on rode,
That Lord veray;
Full well thay understode
That he was slayn that day.
Therfor right as I meyn,   to theym fast will I ryde,
To wyt withoutten weyn,   what they will say this tyde
Of this enfray;
I will no longer abyde
Bot fast ride⁵ on my way.

(12)

God save you, syrs, on every syde!
Worship and welth in warld so wyde!
PILATUS: Centurio, welcom this tyde,
Oure comly knyght!
CENT: God graunt you grace well forto gyde,
And rewll you right.

(13)

PILATUS: Centurio, welcom, draw nere hand!
Tell us som tythyngys here emang,
For ye have gone thrughoutt oure land,
Ye know ilk dele.
CENT: Sir, I drede me ye have done wrang
And wonder yll.

(14)

CAY: Wonder yll? I pray the why?
Declare that to this company.

70 *weyn* doubt   71 *enfray* affray   83 *dele* part

THE RESURRECTION

CENT: So shall I, sir, full securly,
   With all my mayn;
   The rightwys man, I meyn, hym by   90
   That ye have slayn.

(15)

PILATUS: Centurio, sese of sich saw;
   Ye ar a greatt man of oure law,
   And if we shuld any wytnes draw,
   To us excuse,
   To maynteyne us evermore ye aw,
   And noght refuse.

(16)

CENT: To mayntene trowth is well worthy;
   I saide when I sagh hym dy
   That it was Godys son almyghty   100
   That hang there;
   So say I yit and abydys therby
   For evermore.

(17)

ANNA: Yee, sir, sich resons may ye rew,
   Thou shuld not neven sich notes new
   Bot thou couth any tokyns trew,
   Untill us tell.
CENT: Sich wonderfull case never ere ye knew
   As then befell.

(18)

CAY: We pray the tell us of what thyng?   110
CENT: Of elymentys, both old and ying,
   In thare manere maide greatt mowrnyng,
   In ilka stede;
   Thay knew by contenaunce that thare kyng
   Was done to dede.

96 *aw* ought   111 *ying* young

(19)

> The son for wo it waxed all wan,
> The moyn and starnes of shynyng blan,
> And erth it tremlyd as a man
> Began to speke;
> The stone, that never was styrryd or than,   120
> In sonder brast and breke;

(20)

> And dede men rose up bodely, both greatt and small.

PILATUS: Centurio, bewar with all!
> Ye wote the clerkys the clyppys it call
> Sich sodan sight;
> That son and moyn a seson shall
> Lak of thare light.

(21)

CAY: Sir, and if that dede men ryse up bodely,
> That may be done thrugh socery;
> Therfor nothyng we sett therby,   130
> That be thou bast.
CENT: Sir, that I saw truly,
> That shall I evermore trast.

(22)

> Not for that ilk warke that ye dyd wyrke,
> Not oonly for the son wex myrke,
> Bot how the vayll rofe in the kyrke,
> Fayn wyt I wold[6].

PILATUS: A, sich tayles full sone wold make us yrke
> If thay were told.

(23)

> Harlot! Wherto commys thou us emang   140
> With sich lesyngys us to fang?

120 *or* before 124 *clyppys* eclipse 128 *bodely* bodily 131 *bast* cast down 136 *rofe* split 138 *make us yrke* harm us 141 *lesyngys* lies *fang* fetch

THE RESURRECTION

Weynd furth! Hy myght thou hang,
Vyle fatur!
CAY: Weynd furth in the wenyande,
And hold styll thy clattur⁷.

(24)

CENT: Sirs, sen ye set not by my saw,   haves now good day!
God lene you grace to knaw   the sothe all way.

(25)

ANNA: With-draw the fast, sen thou the dredys,
For we shall well mayntene oure dedys.
PILATUS: Sich wonderfull resons as now redys   150
Were never beforne.
CAY: To neven this note nomore us nedys,
Nawder even nor morne,

(26)

Bot forto be war of more were
That afterward myght do us dere,
Therfor, sir, whils ye are here
Us all emang,
Avyse you of thise sawes sere
How thay will stand.

(27)

For Ihesus saide full openly,   160
Unto the men that yode hym by,
A thyng that grevys all Iury
And right so may,
That he shuld ryse up bodely
Within the thryde day.

(28)

If it be so, as myght I spede,
The latter dede is more to drede

144 *wenyande* time of ill fortune   147 *lene* give   154 *were* doubt   155 *dere* harm   158 *sere* many

Then was the fyrst, if we take hede
And tend therto;
Avyse you, sir, for it is nede,
The best to do.

(29)

ANNA: Sir, never the les if he saide so,
He hase no myght to ryse and go
Bot his dyscypyls steyll his cors us fro
And bere away;
That were till us, and othere mo,
A fowll enfray.

(30)

Then wold the pepyll say everilkon
That he were rysen hym-self alon,
Therfor ordan to kepe that stone
With knyghtys heynd
To thise iij dayes be commen and gone
And broght till ende.

(31)

PILATUS: Now certys, sir, full well ye say,
And for this ilk poynt to purvay
I shall, if that I may;
He shall not ryse,
Nor none shall wyn hym thens away
Of nokyns wyse.

(32)

Sir knyghtys, that are of dedys dughty,
And chosen for chefe of chevalry,
As I may me in you affy,
By day and nyght,
Ye go and kepe Ihesu body
With all youre myght;

174 *steyll* steal   181 *heynd* gracious   192 *affy* trust

THE RESURRECTION

(33)

    And for thyng that be may,
    Kepe hym well unto the thryd day,
    That no tratur steyll his cors you fray,
    Out of that sted;
    For if ther do, truly I say,   200
    Ye shall be dede.

(34)

I MILES: Yis, sir Pilate, in certan,
    We shall hym kepe with all oure mayn;
    Ther shall no tratur with no trayn
    Steyll hym us fro;
    Sir knyghtys, take gere that best may gayn,
    And let us go.

(35)

II MILES: Yis, certys, we are all redy bowne,
    We shall hym kepe till youre renowne;
    On every syde lett us sytt downe,   210
    We all in fere;
    And I shall fownde to crak his crowne
    Whoso commys here.

(36)

I MILES: Who shuld be where, fayn wold I wytt.
II MILES: Even on this syde wyll I sytt.
III MILES: And I shall fownde his feete to flytt.
IV MILES: We ther shrew ther![8]
    Now by Mahowne, fayn wold I wytt
    Who durst com here

(37)

    This cors with treson forto take,   220
    For if it were the burnand drake
    Of me styfly he gatt a strake,

198 *fray* from   212 *fownde* try   221 *drake* dragon

Have here my hand;
To thise iij dayes be past,
This cors I dar warand.
>   *Tunc cantabunt angeli 'Christus resurgens', et postea dicet Ihesus*[9]

(38)

IHESUS: Erthly man that I have wroght,
Wightly wake, and slepe thou noght!
With bytter bayll I have the boght
To make the fre;
Into this dongeon depe I soght   230
And all for luf of the.

(39)

Behold how dere I wold the by!
My woundys ar weytt and all blody;
The, synfull man, full dere boght I
With tray and teyn;
Thou fyle the noght eft for-thy,
Now art thou cleyn.

(40)

Clene have I mayde the, synfull man;
With wo and wandreth I the wan;
From harte and syde the blood out ran,   240
Sich was my pyne;
Thou must me luf that thus gaf than
My lyfe for thyne.

(41)

Thou synfull man that by me gase[10],
Tytt unto me thou turne thi face;
Behold my body, in ilka place
How it was dight;

235 *tray* grief   *teyn* injury   236 *fyle* defile   *eft* again   239 *wandreth* misfortune   244 *gase* goest

THE RESURRECTION

All to-rent and all to-shentt,
Man, for thy plight.

(42)

With cordes enewe and ropys toghe
The Iues fell my lymmes out-drogh,
For that I was not mete enoghe
Unto the bore;
With hard stowndys thise depe woundys
Tholyd I therfore.

(43)

A crowne of thorne, that is so kene,
Thay set apon my hede for tene;
Two thefys hang thai me betwene,
All for dyspyte;
This payn ilk dele thou shall wyt wele
May I the wyte.

(44)

Behald my shankes and my knees,
Myn armes and my thees;
Behold me well, looke what thou sees,
Bot sorow and pyne;
Thus was I spylt, man, for thi gylt,
And not for myne.

(45)

And yit more understand thou shall;
In stede of drynk thay gaf me gall;
Asell they menged it withall,
The Iues fell;
The payn I have, tholyd I to save
Mans saull from Hell.

248 *to-rent* torn to pieces *to-shentt* completely ruined 251 *fell* cruel
out-drogh drew out 263 *thees* thighs 270 *Asell* vinegar *menged* mixed

(46)

> Behold my body, how Iues it dang
> With knottys of whyppys and scorges strang;
> As stremes of well the bloode out sprang
> On every syde;
> Knottes where thay hyt, well may thou wytt,
> Maide woundys wyde.

(47)

> And therfor shall thou understand
> In body, heed, feete, and hand,
> Four hundreth woundys and v. thowsand
> Here may thou se;
> And therto ix were delt full even
> For luf of the.

(48)

> Behold on me noght els is lefte,
> And or that thou were fro me refte,
> All thise paynes wold I thole efte
> And for the dy;
> Here may thou se that I luf the,
> Man, faythfully.

(49)

> Sen I for luf, man, boght the dere,
> As thou thi self the sothe sees here,
> I pray the hartely, with good chere,
> Luf me agane;
> That it lyked me that I for the
> Tholyd all this payn.

(50)

> If thou thy lyfe in syn have led,
> Mercy to ask be not adred;
> The leste drop I for the bled

274 *dang* beat   288 *efte* again

THE RESURRECTION

Myght clens the soyn,
All the syn the warld with in
If thou had done.

(51)

I was well wrother with Iudas,
For that he wold not ask me no grace,
Then I was for his trespas
That he me sold.
I was redy to shew mercy;
Aske none he wold.

(52)

Lo, how I hold myn armes on brede,   310
The to save ay redy mayde;
That I great luf ay to the had
Well may thou knaw!
Som luf agane I wold full fayn
Thou wold me shew.

(53)

Bot luf noght els aske I of the,
And that thou fownde fast syn to fle[11];
Pyne the to lyf in charyte
Both nyght and day;
Then in my blys that never shall mys   320
Thou shall dwell ay.

(54)

For I am veray prynce of peasse,
And synnes seyr I may releasse,
And whoso will of synnes seasse
And mercy cry,
I grauntt theym here a measse
In brede, myn awne body.

304 *wrother* more angry   310 *on brede* wide   323 *seyr* many   326 *measse* dish   327 *brede* bread

579

(55¹²)
>That ilk veray brede of lyfe
>Becommys my fleshe in wordys fyfe;
>Who so it resaves in syn or stryfe   330
>Bese dede for ever;
>And whoso it takys in rightwys lyfe
>Dy shall he never.

(56)
>[*The Marys approach the tomb.*]
>MARIA MAGDALENE: Alas, to dy with doyll am I dyght!
>In warld was never a wofuller wight;
>I drope, I dare, for seyng of sight
>That I can se;
>My Lord, that mekill was of myght,
>Is ded fro me.

(57)
>Alas, that I shuld se hys pyne,   340
>Or that I shuld his lyfe tyne,
>For to ich sore he was medecyne
>And boytte of all;
>Help and hold to ever ilk hyne
>To hym wold call.

(58)
>MARIA IACOBI: Alas, how stand I on my feete
>When I thynk on his woundys wete!
>Ihesus, that was on[13] luf so swete,
>And never dyd yll,
>Is dede and grafen under the grete,   350
>Withoutten skyll.

(59)
>MARIA SALOMEE: Withoutten skyll thise Iues ilkon
>That lufly Lord thay have hym slone,
>And trespas dyd he never none,

334 *doyll* grief   336 *dare* tremble, shudder   343 *boytte* cure   344 *hyne* servant   347 *wete* wet   350 *grafen* buried   *grete* stone

THE RESURRECTION

In nokyn sted;
To whom shall we now make oure mone?
Oure Lord is ded.

(60)

MARIA MAGDALENE: Sen he is ded, my systers dere,
Weynd we will with full good chere,
With oure anoyntmentys fare and clere 360
That we have broght,
For to anoyntt his woundys sere,
That Iues hym wroght.

(61)

MARIA IACOBI: Go we then, my systers fre,
For sore me longis his cors to see.
Bot I wote never how best may be;
Help have we none,
And which shall of us systers thre
Remefe the stone?

(62)

MARIA SALOMEE: That do we not bot we were mo, 370
For it is hogh and hevy also.
MARIA MAGDALENE: Systers, we thar no farther go
Ne make mowrnyng;
I se two syt where we weynd to,
In whyte clothyng.

(63)

MARIA IACOBI: Certys, the sothe is not to hyde,
The grave stone is put besyde.
MARIA SALOMEE: Certys, for thyng that may betyde,
Now will we weynde
To late the luf, and with hym byde, 380
That was oure freynde.

355 *nokyn* no kind   360 *fare* fair   369 *Remefe* remove   371 *hogh* huge

(64)

I ANGELUS: Ye mowrnyng women in youre thoght,
  Here in this place whome have ye soght?[14]
MARIA MAGDALENE: Ihesu that unto ded was broght,
  Oure Lord so fre.
II ANGELUS: Certys, women, here is he noght;
  Com nere and se.

(65)

I ANGELUS: He is not here, the sothe to say,
  The place is voyde ther in he lay;
  The sudary here se ye may   390
  Was on hym layde;
  He is rysen and gone his way,
  As he you sayde.

(66)

II ANGELUS: Even as he saide so done has he,
  He is reysn thrugh his pauste;
  He shalbe fon in Galale,
  In fleshe and fell;
  To his dyscypyls now weynd ye,
  And thus thaym tell.

(67)

MARIA MAGDALENE: My systers fre, sen it is so,   400
  That he is resyn the deth thus fro,
  As saide till us thise angels two,
  Oure Lord and leche,
  As ye have hard, where that ye go,
  Loke that ye preche.

(68)

MARIA IACOBI: As we have hard so shall we say;
  Mare, oure syster, have good day!

390 *sudary* cloth   395 *pauste* power   404 *hard* heard

THE RESURRECTION

MARIA MAGDALENE: Now veray God, as he well may,
Man most of myght,
He wysh you, systers, well in youre way, 410
And rewle you right.
[*Exeunt Mary Jacobi and Mary Salome.*]

(69)

Alas, what shall now worth on me? 415
My catyf hart wyll breke in thre
When that I thynk on that ilk bodye,
How it was spylt;
Thrugh feete and handys nalyd was he
Withoutten gylt.

(70)

Withoutten gylt then was he tayn;
That lufly Lord, thay have hym slayn,
And tryspas dyd he never nane, 420
Ne yit no mys.
It was my gylt he was fortayn,
And nothing his.

(71)

How myght I, bot I lufyd that swete
That for me suffred woundys wete,
Sythen to be grafen under the grete,
Sich kyndnes kythe;
Ther is nothyng till that we mete
May make me blythe.
[*Exit Mary Magdalene. The Soldiers awake.*]

(72)

I MILES: Outt, alas! What shall I say? 430
Where is the cors that here-in lay?
II MILES: What alys the, man? He is away
That we shuld tent!

413 *catyf* wretched   422 *fortayn* punished   427 *kythe* show

583

I MILES: Ryse up and se.
II MILES: Harrow! Thefe! For ay
   I cownte us shent!

(73)

III MILES: What devyl alys you two
   Sich nose and cry thus forto may?
II MILES: For he is gone.
III MILES: Alas, wha?
II MILES: He that here lay.   440
III MILES: Harrow! Devill! How swa gat he away?

(74)

IV MILES: What, is he thus-gatys from us went,
   The fals tratur that here was lentt,
   That we truly to tent
   Had undertane?
   Certanly I tell us shent
   Holly ilkane.

(75)

I MILES: Alas, what shall I do this day
   Sen this tratur is won away?
   And safely, syrs, I dar well say   450
   He rose alon.
II MILES: Wytt sir Pilate of this enfray,
   We mon be slone[16].

(76)

IV MILES: Wote ye well he rose in dede?
II MILES: I sagh myself when that he yede.
I MILES: When that he styrryd out of the steed
   None couth it ken.
IV MILES: Alas, hard hap was on my hede
   Emang all men.

437 *nose* noise   441 *swa* so   442 *thus-gatys* in this way   447 *Holly* wholly   *ilkane* each one   452 *enfray* affray, matter   455 *yede* went

THE RESURRECTION

(77)

III MILES: Ye, bot wyt sir Pilate of this dede,   460
   That we were slepand when he yede,
   We mon forfett, withoutten drede,
   All that we have.
IV MILES: We must make lees, for that is nede,
   Oure self to save.

(78)

I MILES: That red I well, so myght I go.
II MILES: And I assent therto also.
III MILES: A thowsand, shall I assay, and mo,
   Well armed ilkon,
   Com and toke his cors us fro,   470
   Had us nere slone[17].

(79)

IV MILES: Nay, certys, I hold ther none so good
   As say the sothe right as it stude,
   How that he rose with mayn and mode,
   And went his way;
   To sir Pilate, if he be wode,
   Thus dar I say.

(80)

I MILES: Why, and dar thou to sir Pilate go
   With thise tythyngys, and tell hym so?
II MILES: So red I that we do also;   480
   We dy bot oones.
III MILES ET OMNES: Now he that wroght us all this wo,
   Wo worth his bones!

(81)

IV MILES: Go we sam, sir knyghtys heynd;
   Sen we shall to sir Pilate weynd,

464 *lees* (n) lies

I trow that we shall parte no freynd,
Or that we pas.
I MILES: Now and I shall tell ilka word till ende,
Right as it was.
   [*They go to Pilate.*]

(82)

Sir Pilate, prynce withoutten peyr,   490
Sir Cayphas and Anna both in fere,
And all the lordys aboute you there,
To neven by name;
Mahowne you save on sydys sere
Fro syn and shame.

(83)

PILATUS: Ye ar welcom, oure knyghtys so keyn;
A mekill myrth now may we meyn;
Bot tell us som talkyng us betwene,
How ye have wroght.
I MILES: Oure walkyng[18], lord, withoutten wene,   500
Is worth to noght.

(84)

CAY: To noght? Alas, seasse of sich saw.
II MILES: The prophete Ihesu[19], that ye well knaw,
Is rysen, and went fro us on raw,
With mayn and myght.
PILATUS: Therfor the devill the all to-draw,
Vyle recrayd knyght!

(85)

What, combred cowardys I you call!
Lett ye hym pas fro you all?
III MILES: Sir, ther was none that durst do bot small   510
When that he yede.
IV MILES: We were so ferde we can[20] downe fall,
And qwoke for drede.

507 *recrayd* recreant, coward   508 *combred* clumsy

THE RESURRECTION

(86)

I MILES: We were so rad, everilkon,
    When that he put besyde the stone,
    We quoke for ferd, and durst styr none,
    And sore we were abast.
PILATUS: Whi, bot rose he bi hym self alone?
II MILES: Ye, lord, that be ye trast,

(87)

    We hard never on evyn ne morne,   520
    Nor yit oure faders us beforne,
    Sich melody, mid-day ne morne,
    As was maide thore.
PILATUS: Alas, then ar oure lawes forlorne
    For ever more!

(88)

    A, devill! What shall now worth of this?
    This warld farys with quantys;
    I pray you, Cayphas, ye us wys
    Of this enfray.
CAY: Sir, and I couth oght by my clergys,   530
    Fayn wold I say.

(89)

ANNA: To say the best for sothe I shall;
    It shalbe profett for us all.
    Yond knyghtys behovys thare wordys agane call,
    How he is myst;
    We wold not, for thyng that myght befall,
    That no man wyst:

(90)

    And therfor of youre curtessie
    Gyf theym a rewarde for-thy.

---

514 *rad* afraid   519 *trast* believing   523 *thore* there   527 *quantys* cunning   530 *and if*   *clergys* learning

ENGLISH MYSTERY PLAYS

PILATUS: Of this counsell well paide am I; 540
  It shalbe thus.
  Sir knyghtys, that are of dedys doghty,
  Take tent till us;

(91)

  Herkyns now how ye shall say,
  Where so ye go by nyght or day;
  [Ten thowsand] men of good aray
  Cam you untill,
  And thefyshly toke his cors you fray
  Agans youre will.

(92)

  Loke ye say thus in every land, 550
  And therto on this covande
  [Ten thowsand pounds[21]] have in youre hande
  To youre rewarde;
  And my frenship, I understande,
  Shall not be sparde;

(93)

  Bot loke ye say as we have kende.
I MILES: Yis, sir, as Mahowne me mende,
  In ilk contree where so we lende
  By nyght or day,
  Where so we go, where so we weynd, 560
  Thus shall we say[22].

(94)

PILATUS: The blyssyng of Mahowne be with you nyght and day!
  [*At the tomb.*]
MARIA MAGDALENE: Say me, garthynere, I the pray,
  If thou bare oght my Lord away;
  Tell me the sothe, say me not nay,
  Where that he lyys,

551 *covande* agreement   563 *garthynere* gardener

588

THE RESURRECTION

    And I shall remeve hym if I may,
    On any kyn wyse.

(95)

IHESUS: Woman, why wepys thou? Be styll!
    Whome sekys thou? Say me thy wyll,   570
    And nyk me not with nay.
MARIA MAGDALENE: For my Lord I lyke full yll;
    The stede thou bare his body tyll
    Tell me I the pray;
    And I shall if I may   his body bere with me,
    Unto myn endyng day   the better shuld I be.

(96)

IHESUS: Woman, woman, turn thi thoght!
    Wyt thou well I hyd hym noght,
    Then bare hym nawre with me;
    Go seke, loke if thou fynde hym oght.   580
MARIA MAGDALENE: In fayth I have hym soght,
    Bot nawre he will fond be.

(97)

IHESUS: Why, what was he to the
    In sothfastnes to say?
MARIA MAGDALENE: A, he was to me –
    No longer dwell I may.
IHESUS: Mary, thou sekys thy God, and that am I.

(98)

MARIA MAGDALENE: Rabony, my Lord so dere!
    Now am I hole that thou art here.
    Suffer me to negh the nere,   590
    And kys thi feete;
    Myght I do so, so well me were,
    For thou art swete.

571 *nyk* deny   579 *nawre* nowhere   590 *negh* approach

(99)

IHESUS: Nay, Mary, neghe thou not me,
For to my Fader, tell I the,
Yit stevynd I noght;
Tell my brethere I shall be
Before theym all in Trynyte,
Whose will that I have wroght.
To peasse now ar thay boght   that prysond were in pyne;   600
Wherfor thou thank in thoght   God, thi Lord and myne.

(100)

Mary, thou shall weynde me fro;
Myn erand shall thou grathly go;
In no fowndyng thou fall;
To my dyscypyls say thou so,
That wilsom ar and lappyd in wo,
That I thaym socoure shall.
By name Peter thou call   and say that I shall be
Before hym and theym all   my self in Galyle.

(101)

MARIA MAGDALENE: Lord, I shall make my vyage   610
To tell theym hastely;
Fro thay here that message
Thay will be all mery.
This Lord was slayn, alas for-thy,
Falsly spylt, noman wyst why,
Whore he dyd mys;
Bot with hym spake I bodely;
For-thi commen is my blys.

(102)

Mi blys is commen, my care is gone,
That lufly have I mett alone;   620
I am as blyth in bloode and bone

596 *stevynd* ascended 603 *grathly* readily 606 *wilsom* bewildered *lappyd* wrapped

As ever was wight;
Now is he resyn that ere was slone,
Mi hart is light.

(103)

I am as light as leyfe on tre,
For ioyfull sight that I can se,
For well I wote that it was he,
My Lord Ihesu;
He that betrayde that fre,
Sore may he rew.

(104)

To Galyle now will I fare,
And his dyscyples cach from care;
I wote that thay will mowrne no mare:
Commyn is thare blys.
That worthi childe that Mary bare
He amende youre mys.

Explicit Resurreccio Domini.

633 *mare* more

34. Christ's Appearances to the Disciples

LUDUS COVENTRIAE 38

The first part of this play, to l.268, deals with the journey to Emmaus, a subject common in the liturgical drama and known as the Peregrini. *It is first recorded at Lichfield in 1188–98.*

The dramatic structure is rather simple, and this, together with the verse form in quatrains, has been held as evidence that this part of the cycle is one of the oldest. The Peregrini *and the* Incredulity of Thomas, *which is added here, appear as separate plays in* York *and* Towneley, *and it is notable that the Proclamation of Ludus Coventriae lists them as separate (nos. 36 and 37). The text does not make it very clear how the transition is made (see note 10) but one may suppose that this is another example of the simultaneous staging characteristic of this cycle. One part of the stage serves for the journey to Emmaus, and another for the room in Jerusalem where Christ appears to Thomas. The two episodes are made to relate closely in terms of the theme of disbelief overcome, and the speech by Thomas (ll.353–92) acts as a climax to this. The whole play follows Luke 24 13–49 very closely.*

ಚಿಲ

[*Scene: on the road to Emmaus.*]

    Hic incipit aparicio Cleophe et Luce.

(1)

CLEOPHAS: My brothir Lucas, I yow pray,
    Plesynge to yow if that it be,
    To the castel of Emawus[1] a lytyl way
    That ye vowche-saf to go with me.

CHRIST'S APPEARANCES TO THE DISCIPLES

LUCAS: All redy, brother, I walke with the
    To yone castell with ryght good chere.
    Evyn to-gedyr anon go we,
    Brother Cleophas, we to in fere.

(2)
CLEOPHAS: A, brother Lucas, I am sore mevyd
    Whan Cryst oure mayster comyth in my mynde.   10
    Whan that I thynke how he was grevyd
    Joye in myn herte kan I non fynde.
    He was so lowlye, so good, so kynde,
    Holy of lyf and meke of mood.
    Alas, the Jewys thei were to blynde,
    Hym for to kylle that was so good.

(3)
LUCAS: Brothyr Cleophas, ye sey ful soth:
    They were to cursyd and to cruell,
    And Judas that traytour, he was to loth,
    For gold and sylvyr his mayster to selle.   20
    The Jewys were redy hym for to qwelle,
    With skorgys bete out all his blood.
    Alas, thei were to fers and felle;
    Shamfully thei henge hym on a rood.

(4)
CLEOPHAS: Ya, be-twen to thevys, alas for shame!
    They henge hym up with body rent.
    Alas, alas, they were to blame;
    To cursyd and cruel was ther intent.
    Whan for thurste he was nere shent
    Eysil and galle thei govyn hym to drynke.   30
    Alas for ruthe! His deth thei bent
    In a fowle place of horryble stynke.

(5)
LUCAS: Ya, and cawse in hym cowde they non fynde.
    Alas for sorwe, what was here thought?

19 *loth* evil   21 *qwelle* kill

And he dede helpe bothe lame and blynde,
And all seke men that were hym browght.
A-gens vice alwey he wrought,
Synfull dede wold he nevyr do,
Yit hym to kylle thei sparyd nought:
Alas, alas, why dede they so? 40

(6)

[Christ joins them unrecognized.]
CHRISTUS: Well ovyr-take ye, serys, in same.
 To walke in felaschep with yow I pray.
LUCAS: Welcom, serys, in Goddys name.
 Of good felaschep we sey not nay.
CHRISTUS: Qwat is your langage, to me ye say,
 That ye have to-gedyr ye to?
 Sory and evysum ye ben alway;
 Your myrthe is gon². Why is it so?

(7)

CLEOPHAS: Sere, me thynkyth thou art a pore pylgrym
 Here walkynge be thi selfe a-lone, 50
 And in the cete of Jerusalem
 Thou knowyst ryght lytyl what ther is done.
 For pylgrymys comyn and gon ryth sone,
 Ryght lytyl whyle pylgrymes do dwelle.
 In all Jerusalem as thou hast gone
 I trowe no tydyngys that thou canst telle.

(8)

CHRISTUS: Why, in Jerusalem what thynge is wrought?
 What tydyngys fro thens brynge ye?
LUCAS: A, ther have they slayn a man for nought;
 Gyltles he was as we telle the. 60
 An holy prophete with God was he,
 Myghtyly in wurde and eke in dede;

36 *seke* sick   41 *in same* together   47 *evysum* heavy   53 *ryth* right

594

CHRIST'S APPEARANCES TO THE DISCIPLES

Of God he had ryght grett pooste.
Amonge the pepyl his name gan sprede.

(9)

He hyght Jhesu of Nazareth;
A man he was of ryght grett fame.
The Jewys hym kylde with cruel deth,
With-out trespas or any blame.
Hym to scorne they had grett game
And naylid hym streyte on tyll a tre.   70
Alas, alas, me thynkyth grett shame
With-out cawse that this xulde be.

(10)

CLEOPHAS: Ya, sere, and ryght grett trost in hym we had,
All Israel countre that he xulde save.
The thrydde day is this that he was clad
In coold cley and leyd in grave,
Yitt woundyrful tydyngys of hym we have,
Of women that sought hym be-forn day lyth.
Wethyr they sey truthe or ellys do rave
We can not telle the trew verdyth.   80

(11)

Whan Cryst in grave thei cowde not se
They comyn to us and evyn thus tolde,
How that an aungell seyd to them thre
That he xuld leve with brest ful bolde.
Yitt Petyr and Johan preve this wolde;
To Crystys grave they ran thei tweyne;
And whan they come to the grave so coolde
They fownde the women ful trewe sertayne.

(12)

CHRISTUS: A ye fonnys and slought of herte
For to be-leve in holy scrypture!   90

63 *pooste* power   78 *lyth* light   80 *verdyth* verdict   85 *wolde* would
89 *fonnys* fools   *slought* slothful

Have not the prophetys[3] with wurdys smerte
Spoke be tokyns in signifure
That Cryste xuld deye for your valure,
And syth entre his joye and blys?
Why be ye of herte so dure,
And trust not in God that myghtful is?

(13)

Bothe Moyses and Aaron and othyr mo —
In holy scrypture ye may rede it —
Of Crystis deth thei spak also,
And how he xuld ryse out of his pitt.   100
Owt of feyth than why do ye flitte
Whan holy prophetys yow teche so pleyne?
Turne youre thought and chaunge your witte
And truste wele that Cryst doth leve a-geyne.

(14)

LUCAS: Leve ageyn? Man, be in pes!
How xulde a ded man evyr a-ryse?
I cowncell the such wurdys to ses
For dowte of Pylat, that hygh justyce.
He was slayn at the gre a-syse
Be cowncell of lordys many on.   110
Of suche langage take bettyr a-vise
In evry company ther thou dost gon.

(15)

CHRISTUS: Trewth dyd nevyr his maystyr shame;
Why xulde I ses than trewth to say?
Be Jonas[4] the prophete I preve the same,
That was in a whallys body iij nyghtis and iij day;
So longe Cryst in his grave lay
As Jonas was with-inne the se.
His grave is brokyn that was of clay;
To lyff resyn agen now is he.   120

92 *signifure* meaning   93 *valure* health   107 *ses* cease   109 *gre* great
116 *whallys* whale's   120 *resyn* risen

CHRIST'S APPEARANCES TO THE DISCIPLES

(16)

CLEOPHAS: Sey nott so, man, it may not be,
  Thow thyn exaunple be sumdele good;
  For Jonas on lyve evyr more was he
  And Cryst was slayn upon a rood.
  The Jewys on hym they were so wood
  That to his herte a spere they pyght;
  He bled owt all his herte blood.
  How xulde he thanne ryse with myght?

(17)

CHRISTUS: Take hede at Aaron[5] and his dede styk,
  Which was ded of his nature,   130
  And yit he floryschyd with flowrys full thyk
  And bare almaundys of grett valure.
  The ded styk was signifure
  How Cryst that shamfully was deed and slayn,
  As that dede styk bare frute ful pure,
  So Cryst xuld ryse to lyve a-geyn.

(18)

LUCAS: That a deed styk frute xulde bere
  I merveyle sore ther of i-wys.
  But yitt hym self fro deth to rere
  And leve a-geyn more woundyr it is.   140
  That he doth leve I trost not this,
  For he hath bled his blood so red;
  But yitt of myrthe evyr moor I mys,
  Whan I have mende that he is ded.

(19)

CHRISTUS: Why be ye so hard of truste?
  Dede not Cryst reyse thorwe his owyn myght
  Lazare[6] that deed lay undyr the duste,
  And stynkyd ryght foule as I yow plyght?

---

122 *sumdele* somewhat   126 *pyght* fixed   132 *almaundys* almonds
144 *mende* remembrance   146 *thorwe* through

To lyff Cryst reysid hym a-gen ful ryght
Out of his grave, this is serteyn.   150
Why may nat Cryste hym self thus qwyght
And ryse from deth to lyve ageyn?

(20)

CLEOPHAS: Now trewly, sere, your wurdys ben good.
  I have in yow ryght grett delyght.
  I pray yow, sere, with mylde mood,
  To dwelle with us all this nyght.
CHRISTUS: I must gon hens a-non ful ryght,
  For grett massagys I have to do.
  I wolde abyde yf that I myght,
  But at this tyme I must hens go.   160

(21)

LUCAS: Ye xal not gon fro us this nyght.
  It waxit all derke; gon is the day;
  The sonne is downe; lorne is the lyght;
  Ye xal not gon from us a-way.
CHRISTUS: I may not dwelle, as I yow say.
  I must this nyght go to my frende.
  Therfore, good bretheryn, I yow pray,
  Lett me not my wey to wende.

(22)

CLEOPHAS: Trewly from us ye xall not go;
  Ye xal abyde with us here stylle.   170
  Your goodly dalyaunce plesyth us so
  We may nevyr have of yow oure fylle.
  We pray yow, sere, with herty wylle,
  All nyght with us abyde and dwelle,
  More goodly langage to talkyn us tylle,
  And of your good dalyaunce more for to telle.

151 *qwyght* release   163 *lorne* lost   168 *Lett* hinder   171 *dalyaunce* conversation   175 *tylle* to

CHRIST'S APPEARANCES TO THE DISCIPLES

(23)

LUCAS: Ya, brothyr Cleophas, be myn assent
　Lete us hym kepe with strenth and myght.
　Sett on youre hand with good entent
　And pulle hym with us the wey well ryght.　　　　180
　The day is done, sere, and now it is nyght;
　Why wole ye hens now from us go?
　Ye xal abyde, as I yow plyght;
　Ye xal not walke this nyght us fro.

(24)

CLEOPHAS: This nyght fro us ye go not away,
　We xal yow kepe be-twen us tweyne.
　To us therfore ye sey not nay
　But walke with us, the wey is pleyne.
CHRISTUS: Sythyn ye kepe me myght and mayn,
　With herty wyll I xal abyde.　　　　190
LUCAS: Of your abydyng we be fulfayn,
　No man more wel-kom in this werd wyde.

(25)

CLEOPHAS: Of oure maystyr Cryst Jhesu
　For ye do speke so mech good
　I love yow hertyly, trust me trew.
　He was bothe meke and mylde of mood;
　Of hym to speke is to me food.
　If ye had knowe hym, I dare wel say,
　And in what plyght with hym it stood,
　Ye wold have thought on hym many a day.　　　　200

(26)

LUCAS: Many a day! Ya, ya, i-wys,
　He was a man of holy levynge;
　Thow he had be the childe of God in blys
　Bothe wyse and woundyrfull was his werkynge.

181 *sere* sir　　183 *plyght* entreat　　194 *mech* much

599

But aftere your labour and ferre walkynge
Takyth this loff and etyth sum bred;
And than wyl we have more talkynge
Of Cryst oure maystyr that is now ded.

(27)

CHRISTUS: Beth mery and glad with hert ful fre,
For of Cryst Jhesu that was your frende   210
Ye xal have tydyngys of game and gle
With-inne a whyle or ye hens wende.
With myn hand this bred[7] I blys,
And breke it here as ye do se.
I geve yow parte also of this,
This bred to ete and blythe to be.
   Hic subito discedat Christus ab oculis eorum[8].

(28)

[CLEOPHAS:]   A, mercy, God! What was oure happe?
Was not oure hert with love brennynge
Whan Cryst oure mayster so nere oure lappe[9]
Dede sitte and speke such suete talkynge?   220
He is now quyk and man lyvenge
That fyrst was slayn and put in grave.
Now may we chaunge all oure mornynge,
For oure Lord is resyn his servauntys to save.

(29)

LUCAS: Alas, for sorwe! What hap was this
Whan he dyd walke with us in way?
He prevyd by scripture ryght wel i-wys
That he was resyn from undyr clay.
We trustyd hym not but evyr seyd nay.
Alas for shame! Why seyd we so?   230
He is resyn to lyve this day;
Out of his grave oure Lord is go.

206 *loff* loaf   *etyth* eat   211 *gle* joy   218 *brennynge* burning   220 *suete* sweet

(30)

CLEOPHAS: Latt us here no lengere dwelle,
    But to oure bretheryn the wey we wende;
    With talys trewe to them we telle
    That Cryst doth leve, oure mayster and frende.
LUCAS: I graunt ther-to with hert ful hende.
    Lete us go walke forthe in oure way.
    I am ful joyfull in hert and mende
    That oure Lord levyth that fyrst ded lay.   240

(31)

CLEOPHAS: Now was it not goodly don
    Of Cryst Jhesu oure mayster dere?
    He hath with us a large wey gon
    And of his uprysyng he dede us lere.
    Whan he walkyd with us in fere,
    And we supposyd hym both dede and colde,
    That he was a-resyn from undyr bere,
    Be holy scripture the trewth he tolde.

(32)

LUCAS: Ryght lovyngely don for-sothe this was.
    What myght oure mayster tyl us do more   250
    Than us to chere that forth dede pas
    And for his deth we murnyd ful sore?
    For love of hym oure myrth was lore;
    We were for hym ryght hevy in herte;
    But now oure myrth he doth restore,
    For he is resyn bothe heyl and qwert.

(33)

CLEOPHAS: That he is thus resyn I have grett woundyr;
    An hevy ston ovyr hym ther lay.
    How shulde he breke the ston a-soundyr
    That was deed and colde in clay?   260
    Every man this mervayle may

---

252 *murnyd* mourned   256 *qwert* ?hearty   261 *mervayle* (v) wonder at

And drede that Lord of mekyl myght.
But yit of this no man sey nay
For we have seyn hym with opyn syght.

(34)
LUCAS: That he doth leve I woot wel this;
He is a-resyn with flesch and blood.
A levynge man for-sothe he is
That rewly was rent upon a rood.
  [*They meet Peter*[10].]
All heyl, dere brothyr, and chaunge your mood,
For Cryst doth levyn and hath his hele.   270
We walkyd in wey with Cryst so good,
And spak with hym wurdys fele.

(35)
CLEOPHAS: Evyn tyll Emawus the grett castell
From Jerusalem with hym we went;
Syxti furlonge as we yow telle
We went with hym evyn passent.
He spak with us with good entent:
That Cryst xuld leve he tolde tyll us,
And previd it be scripture verament –
Trust me trewe, it is ryght thus.   280

(36)
Ya, and whan he had longe spokyn us tylle,
He wold from us agon his way.
With strenght and myght we keptyn hym stylle,
And bred we tokyn hym to etyn in fay.
He brak the loff as evyn on tway
As ony sharpe knyff xuld kytt breed;
Ther-by we knew the trewth that day,
That Cryst dede leve, and was not deed.

(37)
PETRUS: Now trewly, serys, I have grett woundyr
Of these grete merveylis that ye us telle.   290

268 *rewly* piteously   270 *hele* health

CHRIST'S APPEARANCES TO THE DISCIPLES

In brekynge of bred full evyn a-soundyr
Oure mayster ye knew and Lord ryght well.
Ye sey Cryst levith that Jewys dyd qwelle;
Tyll us glad tydyngys this is serteyn;
And that oure mayster with yow so longe dede dwelle,
It doth well preve that he levith a-geyn.
[*Enter Thomas.*]

(38)

A, brother Thomas, we may be ryght glad
Of these gode novell that we now have.
The grace of oure Lorde God is over us all sprad;
Oure Lord is resyn his se[r]vauntys to save.   300
THOMAS: Be in pes, Petyr, thou gynnyst to rave,
Thy wurdys be wantowne and ryght unwyse.
How xulde a deed man, that deed lay in grave,
With qwyk flesche and blood to lyve ageyn ryse?[11]

(39)

PETRUS: Yis, Thomas, dowte the not oure maystyr is on lyve;
Record of Mawdelyn and of here systerys too;
Cleophas and Lucas the trewthe for to contryve,
Fro Jerusalem to Emaws with hym dede they go.
THOMAS: I may nevyr in hert trust that it is so.
He was ded on cros and colde put in pitt,   310
Kept with knyhtys iiij, his grave sealyd also.
How xulde he levyn ageyn that so streyte was shitt?

(40)

PETRUS: Whan Mawdelyn dede tell us that Cryst was a-resyn
I ran to his grave and Johan ran with me.
In trewth ther we fownde he lay not in presyn;
Gon out of his grave and on lyve than he was.
Therfore, dere brother Thomas, I wole rede the
Stedfastly thou trust that Cryst is not deed;
Feythfully be-leve a qwyk man that he be,
A-resyn from his deth by myght of his godhed.   320

---

293 *qwelle* kill   294 *Tyll* to   312 *streyte* tight   *shitt* shut   317 *rede* advise

(41)

THOMAS: I may nevyr be-leve these woundyr merveles
    Tyl that I have syght of every grett wounde,
    And putt in my fyngyr in place of the nayles –
    I xal nevyr be-leve it ellys for no man on growunde.
    And tyll that myn hand the sperys pytt hath fowunde,
    Which dede cleve his hert and made hym sprede his blood,
    I xal nevyr be-leve that he is qwyk and sownde
    In trewth whyl I knowe that he was dede on rood.

(42)

PETRUS: Cryst be thi comforte and chawnge thi bad witt,
    For feyth but thou have thi sowle is but lorn[12].   330
    With stedfast beleve God enforme the yitt,
    Of a meke mayde as he was for us born.
    [*Christ re-appears.*]
CHRISTUS: Pees be amonge yow! Be-holde how I am torn;
    Take hede of myn handys, my dere brothyr Thomas.
THOMAS: My God and my Lorde! Nyght and every morn
    I aske mercy, Lorde, for my grett trespas.

(43)

CHRISTUS: Be-holde wele, Thomas, my woundys so wyde,
    Which I have sufferyd for all mankynde.
    Put thin hool hand in to my ryght syd,
    And in myn hert blood thin hand that thou wynde.   340
    So feythfull a frend were mayst thou fynde?
    Be stedfast in feyth, be-leve wel in me,
    Be thou not dowtefful of me in thi mynde,
    But trust that I leve that deed was on a tre.

(44)

THOMAS: My Lord and my God, with syght do I se
    That thou art now quyk which henge deed on rode.
    More feythful than I ther may no man be,
    For myn hand have I wasch in thi precyous blode.

---

325 *pytt* hole   330 *lorn* lost   339 *hool* whole   341 *were* where
346 *henge* hung

CHRIST'S APPEARANCES TO THE DISCIPLES

CHRISTUS: For thou hast me seyn, therfore thi feyth is good;
But blyssyd be tho of this that have no syght   350
And be-leve in me; they, for here meke mood,
Shall com in to hefne, my blysse that is so bryght.

(45)
THOMAS: As a ravaschyd man whos witt is all gon,
Grett mornynge I make for my dredfful dowte.
Alas, I was dowteful that Cryst from undyr ston
Be his owyn grett myght no wyse myght gon owte.
Alas, what mevyd me thus in my thought?
My dowtefful be-leve ryght sore me avexit;
The trewthe do I knowe that God so hath wrought,
Quod mortuus et sepultus nunc resurrexit[13].   360

(46)
He that was bothe deed and colde put in grave
To lyve is a-resyn by his owyn myght.
In his dere herte blood myn hand wasch I have
Where that the spere poynt was peyn-fully pyght.
I take me to feyth, for-sakynge all un-ryght.
The dowte that I had ful sore me avexit,
For now I have seyn with ful opyn syght,
Quod mortuus et sepultus nunc resurrexit.

(47)
I trustyd no talys that were me tolde
Tyll that myn hand dede in his hert blood wade.   370
My dowte doth aprevyn Cryst in levynge ful bolde
And is a grett argument in feyth us to glade.
Thou man that seyst this, from feyth nevyr thou fade;
My dowte xal evyr chere the that sore me avexit;
Truste wele in Cryst that such meracle hath made,
Quod mortuus et sepultus nunc resurrexit.

(48)
The prechynge of Petir myght not converte me
Tyll I felyd the wounde that the spere dyde cleve.

358 *avexit* vexes   378 *felyd* felt

I trustyd nevyr he levyd that deed was on a tre
Tyll that his herte blood dede renne in my sleve.　　　　380
Thus be my grett dowte oure feyth may we preve.
Be-hold my blody hand to feyth that me avexit;
Be syght of this myrroure from feyth not remeve,
Quod mortuus et sepultus nunc resurrexit.

(49)

Thow that Mary Magdalyn in Cryst dede sone be-leve
And I was longe dowteful, yitt putt me in no blame,
For be my grett dowte oure feyth we may preve
Agens all the eretykys that speke of Cryst shame.
Truste wel Jhesu Cryst: the Jewys kyllyd the same.
The fende hath he feryd oure feyth that evyr a-vexit.　　　　390
To hevyn yow brynge, and save yow all in same
That *mortuus et sepultus iterum resurrexit*[14].

388 *eretykys* heretics

35. The Ascension
The Ascention of Christe

CHESTER 20: TAILORS

This Chester play draws upon the Stanzaic Life of Christ which is thought to have originated locally in the fourteenth century. The Tailors were performing the play by 1439, and it is attributed to them in the 1467 Banns.

The subject of the Ascension was difficult in that it offered little but the spectacle of the ascending Christ. This must have been difficult to manage in the streets. It is clearly intended in the stage directions that Christ should be lifted up, and we may suppose that some stage machinery was devised to give the impression that he speaks as if above the clouds. Perhaps gauze was used, and a covered cart in which a lift could be set up.

This version is notable for the emphasis upon liturgical elements. The subject has a considerable history in the liturgical drama, at Canterbury and on the Continent. The dramatist clearly settled for the combined effects of elevation and the angel choir. It appears that the Chester play went somewhat further in its use of the liturgy than those in the other cycles, where the indications are rather brief.

ಐಣ

[*Christ appears to the Disciples*[1].]

(1)

IESUS: *Pax vobis! Ego sum, nolite timere!*[2]
    My brethren that sit in company,
    With peace I greet you hartfully:
    I am he that standes you by,

Ne dreed you nothing!
Well I know and witterly
That you be in greate extasy,
Whether I be rysen verely,
That makes you sore in longing.

(2)

Ther is no need to be anoyed so,
Neither through thought to be so in woe;
Your handes putt you now froe
And feele my wondes weet;
And leeves this, both all and one,
That ghost hath neither flesh ne bone,
As you may feele me upon,
On handes and on feet.

(3)

PETRUS: A! What is this that standes us bye?
A ghost me him semeth witterly;
Me thinks lightned much am I
This spirit for to see.
ANDREAS: Peter, I tell thee prively,
I dread me yet full greatly,
That Iesu should do such maystry,
And whether that this be hee.

(4)

IHON: Brethren, good is it to thinke on ever more
What wordes he sayd the day before
He dyed on rood, gone is not yore[3],
And we be stidfast aye.
IACOBUS MAIER: A! Iohon, that makes us in were,
That alway when he will apeare,
And when us best list to have him here,
Anon he is away.

---

7 *extasy* anxiety   9 *sore* afflicted   10 *anoyed* troubled   13 *weet* wet
14 *leeves* believe   22 *prively* secretly

THE ASCENSION

(5)

IHESUS: I see well, brethren, sooth to say,
For any signe I shew may,
You be not stidfast in the fay,
But flechinge I you finde.
More signes therfore ye shall see:
Have you ought may eaten bee?
SYMON: Yea, Lord, meat inough for thee, 40
Or ells we wear unkynd.

(6)

IHESUS: Now eate we then for charity,
My leife brethren, fayr and free,
For all thinge shall fulfilled bee
Written in Moses law.
Prophetts in Psalmes sayd of me
That death behoved me on the roode tree,
And ryse within dayes three,
To ioy mankynd to draw,

(7)

And preach to folke this world within 50
Penance, remission of ther synne;
In Ierusalem I should beginne,
As I have done for love.
Therfore, brethren, beleevs stidfastly,
And comes with me to Bethany!
In Ierusalem you shall all lye,
To abyde the grace above.
 Tunc comedet Iesus cum Discipulis suis et postea dicat[4]

(8)

PHILIPPUS: Lord, from us do not concele;
What tyme thou art in thy wayle,
Shalt thou restore Israell 60
Agayn her realm that day?

37 *flechinge* bending, wavering   54 *beleevs* believe   59 *wayle* prosperity

609

ENGLISH MYSTERY PLAYS

IESUS: Brother, that is not to thee
　　To know my Fathers privity;
　　That towcheth his owne posty,
　　Wyt that thou ne[ver] may.

(9)

　　But take you shall, through my behest,
　　Vertue of the Holy Ghost,
　　That send shall be to help you most,
　　In world wher you shall wend.
　　My witnes all you shalbe　　　　　　　　70
　　In Ierusalem and Iudye,
　　Samaria also, and ech contray
　　Unto the worldes ende.

(10)

　　Goe in all the world, through my grace;
　　Preach my word in eche place:
　　All that stidfast beleef hase,
　　And fully, shall saved be.
　　And who so leeves not in your lore,
　　The wordes that you preach them before,
　　Damned shall be for evermore,　　　　　80
　　That payne they may not flee.

(11)

　　By this thing they shall well know,
　　Who so leves stidfastly on you,
　　Such sygnes apertly they shall show,
　　Wher so ever the tyde to goe[5].
　　In my name well shall they,
　　Devills powers to doe away;
　　New tongs[6] shall have to preach the fay
　　And other misteries moe.

66 *behest* promise　　84 *sygnes* signs

THE ASCENSION

(12)

    And though the[y] poyson eate or drink,   90
    It shall nye them no-thinge;
    Sick men with ther helpinge
    Shall healed redely bee;
    Such grace shall be in their doinge.
    Now to my Father I am goinge;
    You shall have here my blessinge,
    For to heaven I must stye.

    Tunc abducet Discipulos in Bethaniam, et cum pervenerit ad locum Ihesus, stans in loco ubi ascenderit, dicat 'Data est mihi omnis potestas in caelo et in terra'[7].

(13)

IHESUS: My swet brethren, leife and deer,
    To me is graunted full power,
    In heaven and earth, farr and neere,   100
    For my godhead is most.
    To teach all men now goe yee,
    That in world will followed be,
    In the name of my Father and me,
    And of the Holy Ghost.

    Tunc Ihesus ascendet et in ascendendo cantabit Ihesus ut sequitur

IESUS: Ascendo ad Patrem meum et Patrem vestrum, Deum meum et Deum vestrum. Alleluia! Alleluya!

    Et cantico finito, stabit Ihesus in medio quasi supra nubes.

I ANGELUS: Quis est iste qui venit de Edom, tinctis vestibus de Bosra?

II ANGELUS: Iste formosus in stola sua, gradiens in multitudine fortitudinis suae?

IESUS: Ego qui loquor Iusticiam et propugnator sum ad salvandum.

III ANGELUS: Et vestimenta tua sicut calcantium in torculari.   110

91 *nye* harm   97 *stye* ascend   98 *swet* sweet

IHESUS: Torculor calcavi solus, et de gentibus non est vir mecum.[8]

(14)

I ANGELUS: Who is this that commeth within,
The blisse of heaven that never shall blyn?
Blody[9] out of the world of synne
And harrowed hell hath he.
II ANGELUS: Comely he is in his clothinge,
And with full power goeinge:
A number of Sayntes with him leadinge;
He semes great of posty.

(15)

Tunc Ihesus stans paulisper in loco eodem dicat[10]
IESUS: I that speake righteousnes,   120
And have brought man out of distres;
For Byar I am called and was
Of all mankynd through grace.
My people that were from me rafte
Through synne and through the Devills crafte,
To heaven I bringe, and never one lefte,
All that in hell was.

(16)

III ANGELUS: Why is thy clothing now so redd?
Thy body blody and also heade?
Thy clothes also all that bene lead,   130
Lyke to pressors of wyne?
IHESUS: For the Devill and his power,
That mankynd brought in great dangere,
Through death on crosse and bloud so clear,
I have made them all myne.

122 *Byar* Redeemer   124 *rafte* torn   130 *lead* ugly

THE ASCENSION

(17)

>These bloudy dropps that you may see,
>All they [freshe] shall resarved be
>Till I come in maiesty
>To deme the last day.
>This bloud shall witnes bear to me, 140
>I dyed for man on the rood tree,
>And rose with-in days three;
>Such love I loved them aye.

(18)

>These dropps now, with good intent,
>To my Father I will present,
>That good men that on earth be lent
>Shall know apertly
>How graciously that I them bought,
>And for good workes that they wrought,
>Everlasting blisse that they sought, 150
>To prove the good worthy;

(19)

>And that the wicked men, echone,
>May know and se, all and one,
>How worthely they forgone
>That blis that lasteth aye.
>For thes causes, leeve you me,
>The dropps I shedd on rood tree
>All fresh shall resarved be
>Ever till the last day.
>>*Tunc ascendet et in ascendendo cantant Angeli canticum subsequentem*
>
>Exaltare, Domine, in virtute tua, cantabimus, et psallemus virtutes tuas. Alleluya! 160
>>*Tunc descendent Angeli et cantabunt 'Viri Galilei quid aspicitis in coelum?'*[11]

146 *lent* placed

(20)

IV ANGELUS: You men that be of Galelye,
　Wher upon now wonder ye?
　Wayting him that through posty
　Is now[e] gone you froe?
I ANGELUS: Iesu Christ, leeve you me,
　That stayed to heaven, as you might se,
　Right so come agayn shall he,
　As you saw him goe.

(21)

PETRUS: Loe! Brethren, what these Angells sayen!
　That Iesu, which through his great mayne　　　　170
　To heaven is gone, will come agayne
　Right as he forth went.
ANDREAS: Many days sith so height he
　To send his Ghost with hart so free;
　And in Ierusalem we should be,
　Till it were to us sent.

(22)

SYMON: Brethren, I redd us in good fay
　That we thither take the way;
　And with devotion night and day
　Lenge in our prayer.　　　　180
PHILIPPUS: For now we know by signes veray
　That he is Gods Sonne, sooth to say;
　Therfore it is good we goe and pray,
　As he commanded here.

(23)

IOHANNES: For now must we leeve it no leasinge;
　For bothe by sight and handlinge,
　Speaking, eatinge and drinking[12],
　He proved his Deitie.

　166 *stayed* ascended　180 *Lenge* linger　185 *leasinge* lies

THE ASCENSION

IACOBUS MAIOR: Yea, also by his upstayinge
   He seemes fully heaven kinge.   190
   Who hath ther-in full leevinge,
   Saved lyfe and soule is he.

(24)

PETRUS: Goe we, brethren, with one assent,
   And fulfill his commandement;
   But looke that none through dreed be blent,
   But leevs all stidfastly.
   Pray we all, with full intent,
   That he to us his Ghost will sent.
   Iesu, that from us is went,
   Save all this company! Amen.   200

189 *upstayinge* ascension   191 *leevinge* faith   195 *blent* deceived
196 *leevs* believe   199 *went* gone

36. Pentecost

YORK 44: POTTERES

This play is attributed to the Potters in Burton's list and in the manuscript. The subject of the coming of the Holy Ghost had an important part in the liturgy, but there is no evidence that the dove was used in the plays, and the action itself is shown very simply. The main source of the York play is Acts 1 and 2. The election of a new Apostle to replace Judas is mentioned briefly but not developed as in the Bible.

There is some discrepancy between Burton's list of characters and those actually appearing in our text. Burton mentions eleven Apostles: only six speak (assuming that Peter and John are I and II). He records four Jews instead of two Doctors, and he gives two angels. The discrepancies may be accounted for by mutes, but the possibility that the play was modified after 1415 remains.

The play was written for simultaneous staging, with the Doctors outside the chamber in which the Apostles meet. This arrangement gives greater point to the mockery by the Doctors, and the Apostles are able to open the doors in a dramatic gesture (ll. 175–6).

༜

[*Scene: a house in Jerusalem: Mary and the Apostles inside, the Jews outside.*]

(1)

PETRUS: Brethir, takes tente unto my steven;
 Thanne schall ye stabily undirstande,
 Oure maistir hende is hence to hevyn,
 To reste there on his Fadirs right hande.

1 *steven* speech

And we are leved a-lyve, ellevyn,
To lere his lawes lely in lande.
Or we begynne us muste be even,
Ellis are owre werkis noght to warande.
For parfite noumbre it is none,
Off elleven for to lere;   10
Twelve may be a-soundir tone,
And settis in parties seere.
*Nobis precepit Dominus predicare populo et
testificare quia prope est iudex vivorum et mortuorum*[1].

(2)

Oure Lord comaunded us, more and lesse,
To rewle us right aftir his rede.
He badde us preche and bere wittenesse
That he schulde deme bothe quike and dede.
To hym all prophettis prevys expresse;
All tho that trowis in his godhede,   20
Off synnes thei schall have forgiffenesse,
So schall we say mekill rede.
And senne we on this wise
Schall his counsaile discrie,
Itt nedis we us avise
That we saye noght serely.

(3)

JOHANNES: Serely he saide that we schulde wende
In all this worlde his will to wirke,
And be his counsaile to be kende
He saide he schulde sette haly kirke.   30
But firste he saide he schulde doune sende
His sande, that we schuld noght be irke,
His Haly Gaste on us to lende,
And make us to melle of materes mirke.
Us menis he saide us thus[2]

---

6 *lere* teach 11 *tone* taken 12 *seere* even 18 *quike* living 24 *discrie* reveal 26 *serely* separately, differently 27 *Serely* surely 32 *sande* messenger *irke* oppressed 34 *melle of* be concerned with *mirke* dark, evil

ENGLISH MYSTERY PLAYS

    Whan that he fared us froo.
III APOS: *Cum venerit paraclitus*
    Docebit vos omnia[3].

(4)

JACOBUS: Ya, certaynely he saide us soo,
    And mekill more thanne we of mene[4].   40
    Nisi ego abiero[5],
    Thus tolde he ofte tymes us be-twene,
    He saide forsoth, but if I goo,
    The Holy Goste schall not be sene;
    Et dum assumptus fuero[6],
    Thanne schall I sende you comforte clene.
    Thus tolde he holy howe
    That oure dedis schulde be dight;
    So schall we trewly trowe,
    He will holde that he us highte.   50

(5)

IV APOS: He highte us fro harme for to hyde,
    And holde in hele both hede and hende;
    Whanne we take that he talde that tyde,
    Fro all oure foois it schall us fende.
    But thus in bayle behoves us bide,
    To tyme that sande till us be sende;
    The Jewis besettis us in ilke a side
    That we may nowdir walke nor wende.
V APOS: We dare noght walke for drede
    Or comforte come us till;   60
    Itt is moste for oure spede
    Here to be stokyn still.

(6)

MARIA: Brethir, what mene ye you emelle,
    To make mournyng at ilk a mele?
    My sone, that of all welthe is well,

47 *holy* wholly   50 *highte* promised   52 *hende* hand   63 *emelle* amongst
64 *mele* time

He will you wisse to wirke ful wele.
For the tente day is this to telle
Sen he saide we schull favoure fele.
Levys wele that lange schall it not dwell,
And therfore drede you nevere a dele, 70
But prayes with harte and hende
That we his helpe may have.
Thanne schall it sone be sende,
The sande that schall us save.

(7)

I DOCTOR: Harke, maistir, for Mahoundes peyne,
Howe that thes mobbardis maddis nowe.
Ther maistir that oure men have slayne
Hase garte thame on his trifullis trowe.
II DOCTOR: The lurdayne sais he leffis agayne;
That mater may thei nevere avowe, 80
For as thei herde his prechyng pleyne,
He was away, thai wiste noght howe.
I DOCT: They wiste noght whenne he wente,
Therfore fully thei faile,
And sais tham schall be sente
Grete helpe thurgh his counsaille.

(8)

II DOCT: He myghte nowdir sende clothe nor clowte;
He was nevere but a wrecche alway.
But samme oure men and make a schowte;
So schall we beste yone foolis flaye. 90
I DOCT: Nay, nay, than will thei dye for doute.
I rede we make noght mekill dray,
But warly wayte when thai come oute
And marre thame thanne, if that we may.
II DOCT: Now, certis, I assente ther-tille.
Yitt wolde I noght thei wiste.

76 *mobbardis* clowns   *maddis* rave   78 *garte* made   87 *clowte* kerchief
89 *samme* gather   90 *flaye* frighten   92 *dray* disturbance   93 *warly* cautiously

Yone carles than schall we kill
But thei liffe als us liste.
  [*The Holy Ghost descends.*]
  Angelus tunc cantare 'Veni creator spiritus'[7].

(9)

MARIA: Honnoure and blisse be ever nowe
  With worschippe in this worlde alwaye 100
  To my soverayne sone, Jesu,
  Oure Lord allone that laste schall ay.
  Nowe may we triste his talis ar trewe,
  Be dedis that here is done this day.
  Als lange as ye his pase pursue,
  The fende ne fendis yow for to flay[8].
  For his high Hali Gaste
  He lattis here on you lende,
  Mirthis and trewthe to taste,
  And all misse to amende. 110

(10)

PET: All mys to mende nowe have we myght;
  This is the mirthe oure maistir of mente.
  I myght noght loke, so was it light.
  A! loved be that Lorde that itt us lente.
  Now hase he holden that he us highte;
  His Holy Goste here have we hente.
  Like to the sonne itt semed in sight
  And sodenly thanne was itt sente.
II APOS: Hitt was sente for oure sele,
  Hitt giffis us happe and hele; 120
  Me thynke slike forse I fele
  I myght felle folke full feele.

(11)

III APOS: We have force for to fighte in felde
  And favour of all folke in feere,

105 *pase* steps 108 *lende* stay 109 *taste* enjoy 119 *sele* happiness
120 *happe* fortune 121 *slike* such 122 *felle* destroy *feele* many

PENTECOST

    With wisdome in this worlde to welde,
    Be knowing of all clergye clere.
IV APOS: We have bewteis to be oure belde,
    And langage nedis us none to lere.
    That Lorde us awe yappely to yelde
    That us has yemed unto this yere.   130
V APOS: This is the yere of grace
    That musteris us emang,
    As aungellis in this place
    That sais thus in ther sange.

(12)

I APOS: In thare sigging saide thei thus,
    And tolde ther talis be-twene them two:
    Veni, creator spiritus,
    Mentes tuorum visita[9].
    They praied the spirite come till us,
    And mende oure myndis with mirthis ma;   140
    That lered thei of oure Lorde Jesus,
    For he saide that itt schulde be swa.
II APOS: He saide he schulde us sende
    His Holy Goste fro hevyn
    Oure myndis with mirthe to mende;
    Nowe is all ordand evyn.

(13)

III APOS: Even als he saide schulde to us come,
    So has bene schewid un-to oure sight:
    Tristicia implevit cor vestrum,
    Firste sorowe in herte he us hight;   150
    Sed convertetur in gaudium[10],
    Sen saide he that [we] schulde be light.
    Nowe that he saide us, all and summe,
    Is mefid emange us thurgh his myght.
IV APOS: His myght with mayne and mode
    May comforte all man-kynde.

---

125 *welde* use   126 *clergye* learning   127 *bewteis* beauties   *belde* protection   129 *awe* ought   *yappely* eagerly   *yelde* give   130 *yemed* guarded   *yere* year   140 *ma* many   142 *swa* so   154 *mefid* moved

ENGLISH MYSTERY PLAYS

I DOCTOR [*outside*[11]]: Harke, man, for Mahoundes bloode,
    Ther men maddis oute of mynde.

(14)

    Thei make carpyng of ilke contre
    And leris langage of ilk a lande.
II DOCT: They speke oure speche als wele as we,
    And in ilke a steede it undirstande.
I DOCT: And all are noght of Galilee
    That takis this hardinesse on hande;
    Butt thei are drounken, all thes menye,
    Of muste or wyne, I wolle warande.
II DOCT: Nowe certis this was wele saide,
    That makis ther mynde to marre;
    Yone faitours schall be flaied,
    Or that thei flitte aught ferre.

(15)

IV APOS [*inside*]: Harke, brethir, waites wele aboute,
    For in oure fayre we fynde no frende;
    The Jewes with strengh are sterne and stoute,
    And scharpely schapes them us to schende.
I APOS: Oure maistir has putte alle perellis oute,
    And fellid the falsed of the fende;
    Undo youre dores, and haves no doute,
    For to yone warlowes will we wende,
II APOS: To wende have we no drede,
    Noght for to do oure dette,
    For to nevyn that is nede
    Shall none on-lyve us lette[12].
    [*They open the doors.*]

(16)

PETRUS: Ye Jewez that in Jerusalem dwelle,
    Youre tales are false, that schall ye fynde;

158 *maddis* rave   159 *carpyng* talk   160 *ilk a* every   165 *menye* company
166 *muste* new wine   172 *fayre* affair

PENTECOST

That we are dronken we here you telle,
Be-cause ye hope we have bene pynnyd.
A prophette preved, his name is Johell,
A gentill Jewe of youre awne kynde,
He spekis thus in his speciall spell,
And of this matere makis he mynde. 190
Be poyntis of prophicie
He tolde full ferre be-fore,
This may ye noght denye,
For thus his wordis wore,
Et erit in novissimus diebus, dicit Dominus:
effundam de spiritu meo super omnem carnem[13].

(17)

III APOS: Loo, losellis, loo, thus may ye lere
Howe youre elders wrotte alway;
The Holy Goste have we tane here,
As youre awne prophettis prechid ay. 200
IV APOS: Hitt is the myght of oure maistir dere,
All dedis that here are done this daye;
He giffis us myght and playne power
To conclude all that ye can saie.
I DOCT: There men hase mekill myght
Thurgh happe thei here have tone[14].
II DOCT: Wende we oute of ther sight,
And latte them even allone.
    [*Exeunt Jews.*]

(18)

I APOS: Nowe, brethir myne, sen we all meffe,
To teche the feithe to foo and frende, 210
Oure tarying may turne us to mischeffe;
Wherfore I counsaille that we wende
Untille oure lady, and take oure leve.
II APOS: Sertis so woll we with wordis hende.
Mi lady, takis it noght to greve,
I may no lenger with you lende.

186 *pynnyd* tormented   190 *mynde* mention

623

(19)

MARIA: Nowe Petir, sen itt schall be soo,
    That ye have diverse gatis to gang,
    Ther schall none dere you for to doo,
    Whils my sone musteris you emang.   220
    Butt, John and Jamys, my cosyns twoo,
    Loke that ye lenge not fro me lange.
JOH: Lady, youre wille in wele and woo
    Itt schall be wroght, ellis wirke we wrang.
JACOB: Lady, we bothe are boune
    Atte youre biddyng to be.
MARIA: The blissing of my sone
    Be boith with you and me.

219 *dere* (n) hurt   220 *musteris* reveals himself

37. The Assumption and Coronation of the Virgin

YORK 47: OSTELERES

The story of the death of Mary and her reception in heaven is not Scriptural, but the cult of the Virgin in late medieval times led to considerable elaboration. The source for this play is the Transitus Mariae. *The York writers extended this into four plays: the* Death, *the* Burial (*lost, but known as the play of Fergus*), *the* Appearance to Thomas, *and the* Assumption and Coronation. *Perhaps the subject matter was of such interest that the play was detached for separate performance. The text in the manuscript is written in a different hand from the rest, and there is another fragment at the end of the manuscript in yet another (later) hand. In 1483 four Innholders agreed to perform a separate version. At Chester the corresponding play was performed by the 'wives', though the text is now lost. The Towneley version may well have been torn out of the manuscript as an act of Reformation zeal in the sixteenth century when sentiment turned against the Virgin. Later references at York indicate that the play was given until 1542, but that by 1548 it was specifically prohibited. It was revived under Queen Mary in 1554, but the prohibition was re-imposed when the cycle was performed in 1561.*

The York play is written for a pageant cart, and carefully avoids the difficulties of ascension. It is notable for its gentle and restrained tone; more of a poem than a play.

༝

[*Scene 1: Heaven.*]

JESUS: Myne aungellis that are bright and schene,
   On my message take ye the waye
   Unto Marie, my modir clene,

  1 *schene* shining

625

> That berde is brighter than the daye.
> Grete hir wele haly be-dene,
> An to that semely schall ye saye,
> Off hevene I have hir chosen quene
> In joie and blisse that laste schall aye.
> I wille you saie what I have thoughte
> And why that ye schall tille hir wende,
> I will hir body to me be brought
> To beilde in blisse with-outen ende.
> Mi flesshe of hir in erthe was tone;
> Unkindely thing it were, i-wis,
> That scho schulde bide be hire allone¹,
> And I beilde here so high in blis.
> For-thy tille hir than schall ye fare,
> Full frendlye for to fecche hir hedir;
> There is no thyng that I love more
> In blisse thanne schall we belde to-gedir.

I ANGELUS: O, blissfull Lorde, nowe moste of myght,
> We are redye with all oure myght
> Thy bidding to fulfille
> To thi modir, that maiden free,
> Chosen cheffe of chastite,
> As it is thy wille.

II ANGELUS: Off this message we are ful fayne,
> We are redy with myght and mayne,
> Bothe be day and be nyght;
> Hevene and erthe nowe gladde may be,
> That frely foode nowe for to see,
> In whome that thou did light.

III ANGELUS: Lorde Jesu Criste, oure governoure,
> We are all boune att thi bidding;
> With joie and blisse and grete honnoure
> We schall thi modir to the bringe.

---

4 *berde* lady   5 *be-dene* at once   6 *semely* beautiful (woman)   12 *beilde* live   13 *tone* taken   24 *free* noble   31 *frely* noble   *foode* person, woman

THE ASSUMPTION AND CORONATION OF THE VIRGIN

[*Scene 2: Mary's grave.*]

IV ANGELUS: Hayle, the doughtir of blissid Anne,
The whiche consayved thurgh the Holy Goste
And thou brought forthe both God and manne,
The whiche felled doune the fendis boste.

V ANGELUS: Haile, roote of risse that fourthe brought
That blissid floure oure saveoure,
The whiche that made mankynde of noght
And brought hym uppe in to his toure.

VI ANGELUS: Of the allone he wolde be borne
In-to this worlde of wrecchidnesse,
To save mankynde that was for-lorne
And bringe tham oute of grete distresse.

I ANGELUS: Thou may be gladde, bothe day and nyght
To se thy sone, oure saveoure;
He will the croune nowe, lady bright,
Thou blissid modir and faire floure.

II ANGELUS: Marie, modir and mayden clene,
Chosen cheffe un-to thi childe,
Of hevene and erthe thou arte quene;
Come uppe now, lady, meke and mylde.

III ANGELUS: Thi sone has sente us aftir the
To bringe the nowe unto his blisse.
Ther schall thou belde and blithe be;
Of joie and mirthe schall thou noght misse.

IV ANGELUS: For in his blisse with-outen ende,
There schall thou alkynne solas see,
Thi liffe in likyng for to lende
With thi dere sone in Trinite.

MARIA: A, blissid be God, Fadir all weldand;
Hym selffe wottith best what is to doo.
I thanke hym with harte and hande
That thus his blisse wolde take me too:
And you also, his aungellis bright
That fro my sone to me is sente.

40

50

60

70

41 *risse* branch   59 *belde* live   62 *alkynne* all kinds of

I am redy with all my myght
For to fulfille his comaundement.

V ANGELUS: Go we nowe, thou worthi wight,
Unto thi sone that is so gente.
We schall the bringe in-to his sight;
To croune the quene thus hase he mente.

VI ANGELUS: Alle hevene and erthe schall worschippe the
And baynnely be at thi biddinge;
Thy joie schall evere incressid be;
Of solas sere than schall thou synge.

*Cantando*².

[*Scene 3: Heaven.*]

I ANGELUS: Jesu, lorde and hevene-is kyng,
Here is thi modir thou aftir sente;
We have her brought at thi biddynge.
Take hir to the as thou haste mente.

MARIA: Jesu, my sone, loved motte thou be;
I thanke the hartely in my thought,
That this wise ordandis for me,
And to this blisse thou haste me broght

JESUS: Haile be thou, Marie, maiden bright!
Thou arte my modir, and I thy sone;
With grace and goodnesse arte thou dight;
With me in blisse ay schall thou wonne.
Nowe schall thou have that I the hight;
Thy tyme is paste of all thi care;
Wirschippe schall the aungellis bright;
Of newe schall thou witte nevere more³.

MARIA: Jesu, my sone, loved motte thou be;
I thanke the hartely in my thoght,
That on this wise ordandis for me,
And to this blisse thou has me broght.

JESUS: Come forth with me, my modir bright,
In-to my blisse we schall assende,
To wonne in welthe, thou worthi wight,

81 *hevene-is* heaven's   87 *ordandis* arrangest

THE ASSUMPTION AND CORONATION OF THE VIRGIN

That nevere more schall it have ende.
Thi newis, modir, to neven thame nowe,
Are turned to joie, and soth it is,
All aungellis bright thei schall the bowe,
And worschippe the worthely i-wis.
For mekill joie, modir, had thou,
Whan Gabriell grette the wele be this, 110
And tolde the tristely for to trowe
Thou schulde consayve the kyng of blisse.

I ANGELUS: Nowe maiden meke and modir myne⁴,
Itt was full mekill myrthe to the
That I schulde ligge in wombe of thine,
Thurgh gretyng of an aungell free.

II ANGELUS: The secounde joie, modir, was syne
With-outen payne whan thou bare me.

III ANGELUS: The thirde aftir my bittir peyne
Fro dede on lyve thou sawe me be. 120

IV ANGELUS: The fourthe was when I stied uppe right,
To hevene unto my fadir dere;
My modir, when thou saugh that sight,
To the it was a solas seere.

V ANGELUS: This is the fifte, thou worthy wight:
Of the jois this has no pere;
Nowe schall thou belde in blisse so bright,
For ever and ay, I highte the here.

VI ANGELUS: For thou arte cheffe of chastite,
Off all women thou beris the floure, 130
Nowe schalle thou, lady, belde with me,
In blisse that schall evere in-dowre.

I ANGELUS: Full high on highte in mageste,
With all worschippe and all honnoures,
Wher we schall evere samen be,
Beldand in oure bigly boures.

II ANGELUS: Alle kynnys swetnesse is ther-in
That manne uppon may thynke, or wiffe;

---

105 *newis* sorrows   111 *tristely* steadfastly   115 *ligge* lie   121 *stied* rose
135 *samen* together   136 *Beldand* dwelling   *bigly* great, immense

With joie and blisse that nevere schall blynne,
Ther schall thou, lady, lede thy liffe. 140
III ANGELUS: Thou schalte be worshipped with honnoure
In hevene blisse that is so bright,
With martiris and with confessouris[5],
With all virginis, that worthy wight.
[JESUS:] Be-fore all othere creatours
I schall the giffe both grace and might
In hevene and erthe to sende socoure
To all that servis the day and nyght.
I graunte thame grace with all my myght
Thurgh askyng of thi praier 150
That to the call be day or nyght,
In what disease so that thei are.
Thou arte my liffe and my lekyng,
Mi modir and my mayden schene;
Ressayve this croune, my dere darlyng;
Ther I am kyng, thou schalte be quene.
Myne aungellis bright, a songe ye singe,
In the honnoure of my modir dere,
And here I giffe you my blissing,
Haly nowe, all in fere. 160

160 *Haly* wholly

38. Judgement Day

YORK 48: MERCERES

The Judgement Day *was performed by the Mercers. Burton's list confirms this, and gives Mary, who does not appear in the text, as one of the characters. If we discount doubling, his list demands thirty-eight players. This may be an indication of the prosperity of the Mercers' Guild. One may suppose that the last play in the cycle would be given to a Guild rich enough to provide for a notable spectacle.*

The text is partly paralleled by the Towneley Juditium, *but the beginning of the latter is lost, up to l.145 in York. The Towneley version has a more elaborate treatment of the Devils, who satirize the evils of man.*

The York *play is an emphatic and dignified ending to the cycle. Based upon many Scriptural references, but particularly Matthew 25 31–46, it echoes many themes and subjects which precede it. The notion of completed time is present here, and so are the Creation, the Fall, and Noah, the one good man in a world of sinners. Christ appears as the Judge, and his speeches refer to the Crucifixion, the Resurrection, and the Redemption. The raising of the bodies of the dead is an echo of his own Resurrection. He presents himself as an example of the perfection of man, and gives a grim portrayal of human corruption.*

One of the chief features of the Judgement Day *was its spectacle. It was frequently portrayed in other art forms (as in the East Window of York Minster, 1405–8). Burton's list mentions that the Angels carry trumpets, as well as crowns, lances, and whips, which are the traditional emblems of the Passion.*

Attempts to divide the play into scenes seem artificial. However, the staging is very carefully handled. The play begins with God the Father in Heaven. The Souls are raised by the First Angel at l.86. God the Son appears at l.176, and subsequently takes his seat of judgement (stage direction, l.216). The Devils are located in another place, and the main action of the play, the Judgement, begins at l.229. The final stage direction shows Christ returning to Heaven.

ENGLISH MYSTERY PLAYS

The tone is solemn and powerful throughout. The Devils are muted, and there appears to be no opportunity for comic or undignified by-play as the damned are carried off to Hell. A similar restraint is shown in the writing of Christ's part, which is carefully designed to give the maximum effect to the theological significance of the Judgement, and to complete many themes of the earlier plays. There is a very strict economy of action, and the writer seems to strive – with no little success – to achieve a formal, ceremonial balance.

※

[*Scene: The Place of Judgement.*]

(1)

DEUS *incipit*: Firste when I this worlde hadde wroght,
   Woode and wynde and wateris wan,
   And all-kynne thyng that nowe is oght[1],
   Fulle wele me thoght that I did thanne.
   Whenne thei were made, goode me thame thoght;
   Sethen to my liknes made I man.
   And man to greve me gaffe he noght;
   Therfore me rewis that I the worlde began.

(2)

   Whanne I had made man at my will,
   I gaffe hym wittis hym selve to wisse,
   And paradise I putte hym till,
   And bad hym halde it all as his.
   But of the tree of goode and ill
   I saide, 'What tyme thou etis of this,
   Manne, thou spedes thi selve to spill,
   Thou arte broght oute of all blisse'[2].

---

2 *wan* pale   3 *oght* anything   6 *Sethen* then   7 *gaffe* cared

JUDGEMENT DAY

(3)

    Belyve brak manne my bidding;
He wende have bene a god therby,
He wende have wittyne of all-kynne thyng,
In worlde to have bene als wise as I.   20
He ete the appill I badde schulde hyng,
Thus was he begilid thurgh glotony.
Sithen both hym and his ospring,
To pyne I putte thame all for-thy.

(4)

    To lange and late me thoghte it goode
To catche thois caitiffis oute of care;
I sente my Sone with full blithe moode
Till erthe, to salve thame of thare sare.
For rewthe of thame he reste on roode,
And boughte thame with his body bare;   30
For thame he shedde his harte and bloode;
What kyndinesse myght I do thame mare?

(5)

    Sethen aftirwarde he heryed hell,
And toke oute thois wrechis that ware thare-inne.
Ther faughte that free with feendis feele
For thame that ware sounkyn for synne.
Sethen in erthe than gonne he dwelle;
Ensaumpill he gave thame hevene to wynne,
In tempill hym-selffe to teche and tell,
To by thame blisse that nevere may blynne.   40

(6)

    Sethen have thei founde me full of mercye,
Full of grace and for-giffenesse,
And thei als wrecchis, wittirly,
Has ledde ther liffe in lithirnesse.

---

17 *Belyve* quickly   19 *wittyne* known   23 *ospring* progeny   28 *sare* suffering   36 *sounkyn* sunken   44 *lithirnesse* idleness

Ofte have thei greved me grevously,
Thus have thei quitte me my kyndinesse;
Ther-fore no lenger, sekirlye,
Thole will I thare wikkidnesse.

(7)

Men seis the worlde but vanite,
Yitt will no manne be ware ther-by;
Ilke a day ther mirroure may thei se,
Yitt thynke thei noght that thei schall dye.
All that evere I saide schulde be
Is nowe fulfillid thurgh prophicie;
Ther-fore nowe is it tyme to me
To make endyng of mannes folie.

(8)

I have tholed mankynde many a yere
In luste and likyng for to lende,
And unethis fynde I ferre or nere
A man that will his misse amende.
In erthe I see butte synnes seere,
Therfore myne aungellis will I sende
To blawe ther bemys, that all may here
The tyme is comen I will make ende.

(9)

Aungellis, blawes youre bemys belyve,
Ilke a creatoure for to call;
Leerid and lewde, both man and wiffe,
Ressayve ther dome this day thei schall;
Ilke a leede that evere hadde liffe,
Bese none for-getyn, grete ne small.
Ther schall thei see the woundes fyve
That my sone suffered for them all.

48 *Thole* suffer   59 *unethis* with difficulty   63 *bemys* trumpets
67 *lewde* ignorant   69 *leede* person

JUDGEMENT DAY

(10)

And sounderes thame be-fore my sight;
All same in blisse schall thei not be.
Mi blissid childre, as I have hight,
On my right hande I schall thame see:
Sethen schall ilke a weried wight
On my lifte side for ferdnesse flee.
This day ther domys thus have I dight,
To ilke a man as he hath served me.   80

(11)

I ANGELUS: Loved be thou, Lorde of myghtis moste,
That aungell made to messengere!
Thy will schall be fulfillid in haste,
That hevene and erthe and helle schalle here.
Goode and ill, every ilke agaste[3],
Rise and fecche youre flessh[4] that was youre feere,
For all this worlde is broght to waste;
Drawes to youre dome, it neghes nere.

(12)

II ANG: Ilke a creature, bothe olde and yhing,
Be-lyve I bidde you that ye ryse,   90
Body and sawle with you ye bring
And comes be-fore the high justise.
For I am sente fro hevene kyng
To calle you to this grette assise.
Therfore rise uppe and geve rekenyng
How ye hym served uppon sere wise.
   [*The dead souls arise.*]

(13)

I ANIMA BONA[5]: Loved be thou, Lorde, that is so schene,
That on this manere made us to rise
Body and sawle to-gedir, clene,

---

73 *sounderes* separate   77 *weried* cursed   89 *yhing* young   96 *sere* many *wise* ways

ENGLISH MYSTERY PLAYS

    To come before the high justise.
    Of oure ill dedis, Lorde, thou not mene,
    That we have wroght uppon sere wise,
    But graunte us for thy grace be-dene
    That we may wonne in paradise.

(14)

II ANIMA BONA: A! loved be thou, Lorde of all!
    That hevene and erthe and all has wroght,
    That with thyne aungellis wolde us call,
    Oute of oure graves hidir to be broght.
    Ofte have we greved the, grette and small;
    Ther aftir, Lorde, thou deme us noght[6].
    Ne suffir us nevere to fendis to be thrall,
    That ofte in erthe with synne us soght.

(15)

I ANIMA MALA[7]: Allas! allas! that we were borne,
    So may we synfull kaytiffis say.
    I here wele be this hydous horne
    Itt drawes full nere to domesday.
    Allas, we wrecchis that ar for-lorne,
    That never yitt served God to paye,
    But ofte we have his flessh for-sworne,
    Allas! allas! and welaway!

(16)

    What schall we wrecchis do for drede,
    Or whedir for ferdnes may we flee,
    When we may bringe forthe no goode dede
    Before hym that oure juge schall be?
    To aske mercy us is no nede[8]
    For wele I wotte dampned be we.
    Allas! that we swilke liffe schulde lede,
    That dighte us has this destonye.

---

103 *be-dene* at once   111 *thrall* enslaved   118 *paye* please   122 *ferdnes* fear

JUDGEMENT DAY

(17)

 Oure wikkid werkis thei will us wreye,
 That we wende never schuld have bene weten,   130
 That we did ofte full prively,
 Appertely may we se them wreten.
 Allas! wrecchis, dere mon we by;
 Full smerte with helle fyre be we smetyn.
 Nowe mon nevere saule ne body dye,
 But with wikkid peynes evermore be betyne.

(18)

 Allas! for drede sore may we quake,
 Oure dedis beis oure dampnacioune,
 For oure mys-mevyng mon we make;
 Helpe may none excusacioune[9].   140
 We mon be sette for our synnes sake;
 For evere fro oure salvacioune,
 In helle to dwelle with feendes blake,
 Wher never schall be redempcioune.

(19)

II ANIMA MALA: Als carefull caitiffis may we ryse;
 Sore may we wringe oure handis and wepe;
 For cursidnesse and for covetise,
 Dampned be we to helle full depe.
 Rought we nevere of Goddis servise;
 His comaundementis wolde we noght kepe,   150
 But ofte than made we sacrafise
 To Satanas, when othir slepe.

(20)

 Allas, now wakens all oure were!
 Oure wikkid werkis may we not hide,
 But on oure bakkis us muste them bere;
 Thei will us wreye on ilke a side.

---

129 *wreye* destroy   130 *weten* known   139 *mys-mevyng* evil-doing
149 *Rought* cared   153 *were* confusion

I see foule feendis that wille us feere,
And all for pompe of wikkid pride;
Wepe we may with many a teere.
Allas, that we this day schulde bide!   160

(21)
Before us playnly bese fourth brought
The dedis that us schall dame be-dene;
That eres has herde, or harte has thoght,
Sen any tyme that we may mene[10],
That fote has gone or hande has wroght,
That mouthe has spoken or ey has sene,
This day full dere thanne bese it boght.
Allas, unborne and we hadde bene.

(22)
III ANG: Standis noght to-gedir; parte you in two:
All sam schall ye noght be in blisse;   170
Mi fadir of hevene woll it be soo,
For many of yowe has wroght amys.
The goode, on his right hande ye goe,
The way till hevene he will you wisse;
Ye weryed wightis, ye flee hym froo,
On his lefte hande, as none of his.

(23)
DEUS[11]: This woffull worlde is brought till ende,
Mi fadir of hevene he woll it be;
Therfore till erthe nowe will I wende,
Mi-selve to sitte in mageste.   180
To deme my domes I woll descende;
This body will I bere with me,
Howe it was dight, mannes mys to mende,
All mankynde there schall it see.

(24)
Mi postelis and my darlyngis dere,
The dredfull dome this day is dight.

175 *weryed* cursed   185 *postelis* apostles

JUDGEMENT DAY

Both heven and erthe and hell schall here
Howe I schall holde that I have hight;
That ye schall sitte on seetis sere[12],
Be-side my selffe to se that sight, 190
And for to deme folke ferre and nere,
Aftir ther werkyng, wronge or right.

(25)

I saide also whan I you sente
To suffre sorowe for my sake,
All tho that wolde thame right repente
Schulde with you wende and wynly wake;
And to youre tales who toke no tente
Shulde fare to fyre with fendis blake,
Of mercy nowe may noght be mente,
Butt aftir wirkyng, welth or wrake. 200

(26)

My hetyng haly schall I fullfille.
Therfore comes furth and sittis me by
To here the dome of goode and ill.
1 APOST: I love the, Lord God all myghty;
Late and herely, lowde and still,
To do thy bidding bayne am I:
I obblissh me to do thi will,
With all my myght, als is worthy.

(27)

11 APOST: A, myghtfull God, here is it sene
Thou will fulfille thi forward right, 210
And all thi sawes thou will maynteyne.
I love the, Lorde, with all my myght,
Ther-fore us that has erthely bene,
Swilke dingnitees has dressed and dight[13].

---

189 *sere* many, various   196 *wynly* joyfully   *wake* watch   200 *wrake* wreck, ruin   205 *herely* early

DEUS: Comes fourthe, I schalle sitte you betwene,
And all fullfille that I have hight.
Hic ad sedem iudicij cum cantu angelorum[14].

(28)

I DIABOLUS: Felas, arraye us for to fight;
And go we faste oure fee to fange;
The dredefull dome this day is dight;
I drede me that we dwelle full longe. 220
II DIAB: We schall be sene evere in ther sight,
And warly waite, ellis wirke we wrange[15].
For if the domisman do us right,
Full grete partie with us schall gang.

(29)

III DIAB: He schall do right to foo and frende,
For nowe schall all the soth be sought;
All weried wightis with us schall wende;
To payne endles thei schall be broght[16].

(30)

DEUS: Ilke a creature, takes entent,
What bodworde I to you bringe. 230
This wofull worlde away is wente,
And I am come as crouned kynge.
Mi fadir of hevene, he has me sente
To deme youre dedis and make ending.
Comen is the day of jugement;
Of sorowe may ilke a synfull synge[17].

(31)

The day is comen of kaydyfnes,
All tham to care that are unclene,
The day of bale and bittirnes,
Full longe abedyn has it bene, 240
The day of drede to more and lesse,

217 *Felas* companions 218 *fee* property *fange* take 222 *warly* warily
237 *kaydyfnes* wretchedness 240 *abedyn* awaited

640

JUDGEMENT DAY

Of care, of trymbelyng and of tene.
That ilke a wight that weried is
May say, 'Allas this daye is sene!'

(32)
Here may ye see my woundes wide,
The whilke I tholed for youre mysdede,
Thurgh harte and heed, foote, hande, and hide[18],
Nought for my gilte, butt for youre nede.
Beholdis both body, bak, and side,
How dere I bought youre brotherhede.   250
Thes bittir peynes I wolde abide
To bye you blisse, thus wolde I bleede.

(33)
Mi body was scourged with-outen skill;
As theffe full thraly was [I] thretto;
On crosse thei hanged me, on a hill,
Blody and bloo, as I was bette.
With croune of thorne throsten full ill;
This spere unto my side was sette;
Myne harte bloode spared noght thei for to spill;
Manne, for thy love wolde I not lette.   260

(34)
The Jewes spitte on me spitously;
Thei spared me nomore than a theffe;
Whan thei me strake I stode full stilly;
Agaynste tham did I no thyng greve.
Behalde mankynde, this ilke is I,
That for the suffered swilke mischeve;
Thus was I dight for thy folye:
Man, loke thy liffe was to me full leffe.

(35)
Thus was I dight thi sorowe to slake;
Manne, thus behoved the to borowed be[19].   270

253 *skill* reason   254 *thraly* like a slave   *thrette* threatened   268 *leffe* dear

In all my woo toke I no wrake;
Mi will itt was for the love of the.
Man, sore aught the for to quake,
This dredfull day this sight to see.
All this I suffered for thi sake;
Say, man, what suffered thou for me?

(36)

Mi blissid childre on my right hande,
Youre dome this day ye thar not drede,
For all youre comforte is command;
Youre liffe in likyng schall ye lede.   280
Commes to the kyngdome ay lastand,
That you is dight for youre goode dede;
Full blithe may ye be where ye stande,
For mekill in hevene schall be youre mede.

(37)

Whenne I was hungery[20] ye me fedde;
To slake my thirste youre harte was free;
Whanne I was clothles ye me cledde;
Ye wolde no sorowe uppon me see.
In harde presse whan I was stedde,
Of my paynes ye hadde pitee;   290
Full seke whan I was brought in bedde,
Kyndely ye come to coumforte me.

(38)

Whanne I was wikke and werieste
Ye herbered me full hartefully;
Full gladde thann were ye of youre geste,
And pleyned my poverte piteuously.
Be-lyve ye brought me of the beste,
And made my bedde full esyly;
Therfore in hevene schall be youre reste,
In joie and blisse to be me by.   300

278 *thar* need   279 *command* coming   287 *cledde* clothed   295 *geste* guest   296 *pleyned* pitied

JUDGEMENT DAY

(39)

I ANIMA BONA: Whanne hadde we, Lorde that all has wroght,
    Meete and drinke the with to feede,
    Sen we in erthe hadde nevere noght
    But thurgh the grace of thy godhede?
II ANIMA BONA: Whanne waste that we the clothes brought,
    Or visite the in any nede,
    Or in thi sikenes we the sought?
    Lorde, when did we the this dede?

(40)

DEUS: Mi blissid childir, I schall you saye
    What tyme this dede was to me done: 310
    When any that nede hadde, nyght or day,
    Askid you helpe and hadde it sone.
    Youre fre hartis saide them nevere nay,
    Erely ne late, mydday ne none,
    But als ofte sithis as thei wolde praye,
    Thame thurte but bide, and have ther bone[21].

(41)

    Ye cursid caytiffis of Kaymes kynne,
    That nevere me comforte in my care,
    I and ye for ever will twynne,
    In dole to dwelle for evermare;   320
    Youre bittir bales schall nevere blynne,
    That ye schall have whan ye come thare.
    Thus have ye served for youre synne,
    For derffe dedis ye have done are.

(42)

    Whanne I had mistir of mete and drynke,
    Caytiffis, ye cacched me fro youre gate;
    Whanne ye wer sette as sirs on benke,
    I stode ther-oute, werie and wette,
    Was none of yowe wolde on me thynke,

315 *sithis* times   324 *derffe* wicked   325 *mistir* need   327 *benke* bench

Pyte to have of my poure state; 330
Ther-fore till hell I schall you synke,
Weele are ye worthy to go that gate.

(43)
Whanne I was seke and soriest,
Ye visitte me noght, for I was poure;
In prisoune faste whan I was feste,
Was none of you loked howe I fore.
Whenne I wiste nevere where for to reste,
With dyntes ye draffe me fro your dore;
Butte ever to pride thanne were ye preste;
Mi flessh, my bloode ofte ye for-swore. 340

(44)
Clothles whanne I was ofte and colde,
At nede of you yede I full naked;
House ne herborow, helpe ne holde,
Hadde I none of you, thof I quaked[22].
Mi mischeffe sawe ye many-folde,
Was none of you my sorowe slaked,
Butt evere for-soke me, yonge and alde;
Therfore schall ye nowe be for-saked.

(45)
I ANIMA MALA: Whan had thou, Lorde that all thyng has,
Hungir or thirste, sen thou God is? 350
Whan was thou in prisonne was,
Whan was thou naked or herberles?
II ANIMA MALA: Whan was it we sawe the seke, allas?
Whan kid we the this unkyndinesse,
Werie or wette to late the passe,
When did we the this wikkidnesse?

(46)
DEUS: Caistiffis, als ofte als it be-tidde
That nedfull aught askid in my name,

333 *seke* sick   336 *fore* lived, fared   338 *dyntes* blows   343 *herborow* shelter   354 *kid* showed

JUDGEMENT DAY

Ye herde them noght, youre eris ye hidde,
Youre helpe to thame was noght at hame,
To me was that unkyndines kyd[23].
Ther-fore bere this bittir blame,
To leste or moste whan ye it did,
To me ye did the selve and the same.

(47)

Mi chosen childir, comes unto me;
With me to wonne nowe schall ye wende;
There joie and blisse schall ever be;
Youre liffe in lyking schall ye lende.
Ye cursed kaitiffis, fro me ye flee,
In helle to dwelle with-outen ende.
Ther ye schall nevere butt sorowe see,
And sitte be Satanas the fende.

(48)

Nowe is fulfillid all my for-thoght,
For endid is all erthely thyng[24],
All worldly wightis that I have wroght,
Aftir ther werkis have nowe wonnyng;
Thei that wolde synne and sessid noght,
Of sorowes sere now schall thei syng,
And thei that mendid thame whils thei moght,
Schall belde and bide in my blissing.
   Et sic facit finem cum melodia angelorum
   transiens a loco ad locum[25].

Notes

Notes

THE BANNS

1. *Bannes*. They are addressed to the audience, but they were themselves something of a performance, since the speaker also gives instructions to the actors from time to time.
2. *pagens*. Of obscure origin, this word had two meanings:

   1. A *scene* or *episode* in the cycles, equivalent to modern 'play' or 'scene'. This seems to be the sense in the Banns of *Ludus Coventriae*, where each play is called a pageant. Many stage directions in that cycle demanded fixed performance, which rules out the second meaning as follows.
   2. The *movable cart* which was pulled from station to station round the streets of Chester, York, and Norwich, and many other places. David Rogers' *Breviary* (Harl. MS 1944) mentions six wheels for the Chester cart. At York in 1500 and at Norwich in 1565 the carts had four wheels.

   In 1534 the Norwich Grocers set aside 1d for 'sope to grese the wheles'. A stage direction in their second play (1565 text) gives evidence of two levels –

   Then Man and Woman departyth to the nether parte of the pageant.

   The carts became the centre of dramatic action, but it is clear that on many occasions the actors would spread out over a wider area.
3. *a while abyde*. Abyde a while, MS.
4. *Mappa Mundi*. 'the map of the world': this expression was used for a chart representing the world, but here it indicates the world itself in contrast to Paradise.
5. *cariage*. This supports the evidence that these Banns were written for a performance on wheels. The Norwich records refer to a 'cart'.
6. *wyll*. No rhyme for this: formerly the Painters had been associated with the Barbers, but see below, n. 8.
7. *Colyn*. Cologne. The corresponding play at Coventry, Newcastle, Norwich and Reading was also called 'The Kings of Cologne'. The relics of the Three Kings were taken to Cologne Cathedral in 1164.
8. *Presentation*. i.e. The Offering of the Kings. Salter supposes that the original of the Kings–Herod–Innocents play was performed by

NOTES

the Merchants, Vintners and Goldsmiths. After they re-grouped, the Merchants retained the Presentation. *Skyle* (l. 64) might be the lost rhyme for *wyll* (l. 52).

9. *Taffyta sersnett of poppyngee grene*. 'Shining silk, bright green in colour like a parrot.' A noteworthy indication of the cheerful and costly appearance of the carts.

10. Line missing in MS.

11. *Maunday*. Christ washing the feet of his Disciples at the Last Supper: *John* 13 34 (from *Mandatum novum do vobis*).

12. *Skynners*. Earlier the Resurrection was performed by the Tanners and Shoemakers as well as the Skinners. The Emmaus play was included about 1467, and this may account for the dislocation in rhyme between stanzas 16 and 17. Possibly read *see you shall* (l. 120) to rime with *befall* (l. 116).

13. *doe thair slayth*. 'exercise their cunning.'

14. *Wyffys*. Though in *York* and *Ludus Coventriae* the Assumption Play survives, it has been lost from Chester. The inclusion of a play not performed by the members of a guild is unique. Note that although *might* (l. 132) rimes with ll. 124 and 128, stanza 19 is defective.

15. *Antycryst*. The Chester Antichrist is the only survival of its type in the cycles. It tells how Antichrist, an impostor in the power of the devils, misleads the kings of the earth by a false resurrection. The text is particularly interesting as it survives in a separate manuscript written out in 1475: the copy is folded and bears signs of use which may indicate that it was an actor's script.

16. *day of Corpus Christi*. The Feast of Corpus Christi, celebrated on the Thursday after Trinity Sunday, was established by Pope Clement V at the Council of Vienne in 1311. It was quickly adopted in Western Europe, and reached England by 1318. The Beverley and York plays were performed at this time at least from 1377 and 1378, and subsequently cycles or groups of Corpus Christi plays are recorded at Coventry, Newcastle upon Tyne, Ipswich, Dublin, and Hereford. Whilst the Chester plays were performed at Whitsun, these lines indicate that the clergy continued a separate play at Corpus Christi. Such a play would not accord with post-Reformation sentiment, and the erasure here is probably a step in the process by which attempts were repeatedly made to preserve the plays by compromising with Protestant criticism.

17. *Sur Iohn Aneway*. Probably refers to Sir John Arnway who died in 1278. Though he was a famous citizen, it is likely that the attribution to him is spurious, there being no evidence that the plays existed during his lifetime.

NOTES

18. *erazed.* This cut was no doubt made out of Protestant sentiment against the Virgin.

I. THE FALL OF LUCIFER

1. For the most part the text here and for all the *Chester* plays is that of MS Harley 2124, but in the case of lines 1–12 I have based my text on the reconstruction in the Early English Text Society edition. As will be seen from the following lines, which correspond to the lines in question, the MS Harley 2124 version shows considerable dislocation.

> DEUS PATER: *Ego sum Alpha et Omega, primus et Nobilissimus,*
> It is my will yt sholde be soe:
> Yt was, it is, yt shall be thus;
> I am God, greate and glorious,
> Without beginninge.
>
> The holy food of parentes
> Is sett in my licentia;
> I am the tryall of the Trinitie,
> That never shall be twynninge.
>
> Peareles Patron Imperial,
> And *Patris Sapientia,*
> My beames be all beatytude,
> All blisse is in my buyldinge,
>
> All myrthe is in my mansuetude,
> *Cum Dei Potentia;*
> Bothe visible and eke invisible,
> All is in my weldinge;
> As God so greate and glorious all lyeth in my . . .

2. *Ego . . . nobilissimus.* 'I am the Alpha and Omega, the first and the most famous.' One MS of the *Chester* plays and the *York* MS read *novissimus* – 'the last', cf. *Revelations* 21 6. Both *Ludus Coventriae* and *Towneley* begin 'Ego sum Alpha et O'.
3. *The holy . . . essentia.* MSS have *essencion*, but, as Diemling suggests, the rime requires *essentia.* The sense seems to be 'The holy food of parenthood is to be found in my spiritual being', a reference to God as the father of mankind.
4. *tryall.* usually an adjective, 'threefold': here 'threefold form'.
5. *patris sapientia.* 'wisdom of the father.'

NOTES

6. *cum dei potentia.* 'with the power of God.'

7. *in mea licentia.* 'in my control.' The use of impressive words, Latin and vernacular, is no doubt dictated by the need to give solemnity and theological weight to the character of God.

8. *Sett ... sothenes.* The 'substance' of God was thought to be his divine essence: the phrase means 'established in divine reality'.

9. *Dissolved ... experyence.* Probably 'United by my divine knowledge under one crown', but the passage may be corrupt.

10. *Neene orders of angells.* The theological tradition of the nine orders, or choirs, of angels goes back at least to the writings of Pseudo-Dionysius (fifth century). Some of the orders are mentioned in the Old Testament, but the hierarchy is Christian, being arranged (highest first) – Seraphim, Cherubim, Thrones, Dominations, Virtues, Powers, Principalities, Archangels, Angels.

11. *For ... lawdation.* 'For all the pleasure found under this rule is added praise to me.'

12. *Lucifer* does not appear in the Bible, but cf. *Isaiah* 14 12, and *Revelations* 12 7–9. In neither case is the name used; indeed in the last case the dragon is called Satan. *Lightborne* is a medieval invention; possibly it was another name for Lucifer, but the *Chester* dramatist treats them as two characters. Lightborne does not appear in *Le Mistère du Viel Testament* (where the chief Devils are Lucifer and Satan), nor in the other English cycles.

13. *lookes ... attendinge.* 'be sure to attend upon me in lowly fashion.'

14. *cast ... comprehendinge.* 'never try to understand.' God warns them not to presume to seek knowledge of His achievements.

15. *Tunc cantabunt.* 'Then they shall sing.'

16. *I have ... stature.* 'I have commanded you that you do nothing but what is written in this statute.'

17. God's face was a gilded mask.

18. *Tunc ... Deus.* 'Then they shall sing, and God shall go away.'

19. *Wherfore ... chayre.* i.e. 'Do not sit in that throne.'

20. *wall of lewtye.* *Wall* probably means 'well, spring': this makes *lewtye* a suspect reading (two MSS have *bewtye*). The context implies that pride is the source of disloyalty.

21. *Et sedet.* 'And he sits down.'

22. *Tunc ... tremescunt.* 'Then they shake and tremble.'

23. *Tunc ... Lightburne.* 'Then Lucifer and Lightborne shall fall.'

24. In contrast to God's face, Lucifer's now shows signs of decay, perhaps by the mask cracking. In *Le Mistère du Viel Testament* Lucifer, before his treachery, has a great sun shining behind him.

25. *Ruffian.* A name for a devil.

NOTES

26. The dramatist attributes the fall to pride – a traditional view, and one that fits well with the fall of Adam.
27. *to my pay.* 'to my pleasure.'
28. This is the first act of the Creation. The subject matter thus overlaps with the beginning of the second pageant (stanza 2).
29. *for more or myn.* 'neither more nor less.'
30. *Finis primae paginae.* 'End of the first pageant'.

2. THE CREATION, AND ADAM AND EVE

1. In the first sequence (ll. 1–104) God describes the Creation (*Genesis* 1 1 to 2 4).
2. *Tunc ... ipsum.* 'Then he shall go from his former place to the place where he created Adam, and he shall make a sign as though he were making him.' This stage direction is partly a narrative – 'where Adam was created'. There are Latin notes to the text which relate it to Scripture. The Creation story as told in the Bible had an overlap: Adam is created in *Genesis* 1 27, and the incident is repeated with elaboration in *Genesis* 2. The structure of the play reflects this: the action really starts at l. 105.
3. *To ... might.* 'He shall have authority ...'
4. *Et ... eius.* 'And he breathed the spirit of life into his face.'
5. *Tunc ... lignum.* 'Then the Creator shall lead him to the tree in Paradise.'
6. *Death ... me.* 'You will deserve death, believe me.'
7. *Tunc ... costam.* 'Then the Creator, taking Adam's hand, shall make him lie down, and He shall take a rib from him.' *Genesis* 2 21–2.
8. *Helpe ... wee.* 'We shall now make a helpmate for him.'
9. *Dormit.* 'He sleeps.'
10. *Adam surgit.* 'Adam gets up.'
11. *Tunc ... dicat.* 'Then Adam and Eve shall stand naked and they will not be ashamed, and the Serpent shall come to Paradise in the appearance of the Devil, and walking about he shall say.' This stage direction appears to be confused. The intention was that the Devil should appear first in his own shape and as he prepared for the temptation assume the form of the Serpent, who was already in Paradise, at l. 206.
12. i.e. Lucifer: perhaps a clue that he still retained some of his former angelic appearance.
13. He swears by Beelzebub, a conventional sign of his depravity.
14. *Nay ... laye.* 'not by my way of doing things.'
15. *That ... shooe.* 'Woman will do what she is forbidden to do for

NOTES

any trivial excuse.' He reminds the audience of the traditional frailty of women (cf. l. 199). This pre-figures the cursedness of Noah's wife.

16. The creature with the wings of a bird, feet of a serpent and a girl's face is not Scriptural; it derives probably from classical sources. It represents the adder before God's curse.

17. The Devil's intention is thus to repeat his own damnation in the fall of man.

18. *as ... pane.* 'as I may endure my suffering.'

19. This marginal quotation refers to ll. 193–5 above.

20. *Eate ... amisse.* 'We do wrong if we eat from it.'

21. *Tunc ... dicat.* 'Then Adam eats and at once they are naked, and weeping he shall say.'

22. 'Eve' means 'life'. The implication of Adam's remark is that she was the mother of all who live and sin (cf. *Genesis* 3 20).

23. *For ... we.* 'For certainly when God comes to us we shall be sent out of this place.'

24. *Tunc ... voce.* 'Then Adam and Eve shall cover their genitals with leaves and hide beneath the tree, and God comes, calling with a loud voice.'

25. *I did att ... eate.* 'I acted in accordance with her request: I did eat of it.'

26. If the adder is seen as above (n.16), the curse that he must now creep on his belly is more intelligible.

27. *Tunc ... faciens.* 'Then the serpent shall go away hissing.'

28. *And ... to-daye.* 'And because of what you have done today.'

29. *Of ... wayved.* 'I have now lost happiness.'

30. Gluttony was generally given as the cause of Eve's deceit.

31. *deadlie.* i.e. mortal, subject to death.

32. *Tunc ... pelliciis.* 'Then God shall clothe Adam and Eve with garments of hide.'

33. *Tunc ... Paradiso.* 'Then God shall send them from Paradise.'

34. *To ... wyn.* 'To guard the place of happiness and plenty.'

3. THE KILLING OF ABEL

1. *He ... bore.* 'He must blow my black hollow arse.' The first of a series of obscenities (cf. ll. 59, 63–4, 88, 238, 287) which are grotesque and comic, and indicate corruption.

2. *Bot ... ten.* 'But let your lips cover your teeth,' i.e. be mum.

3. *Greynhorne ... Gryme.* Names of horses; seven more appear below.

4. *Pikeharnes.* The name indicates theft (stealer of armour).

5. He has been preventing them from eating.

NOTES

6. *Even . . . hay.* probably an obscenity.

7. *And . . . brend.* 'And then our produce should be burned in his honour.'

8. *Yis . . . lone.* 'Yes, all the benefits of God's grace which you have in plenty are simply his gifts.'

9. *To . . . gif.* 'To share or give my goods.'

10. *And . . . me.* 'And may it be against God's will that you showed thanks or courtesy to me.'

11. Cain appears to be examining the sheaves one by one, and he finds that he can part with only two (ll. 219, 253), whilst his own pile mounts up.

12. *Deyll . . . thrife.* 'I must share out in this unequal way or I shall never survive.'

13. He hides his eyes and finds that he still divides to his own advantage.

14. *For . . . take.* 'For if you take notice of my tithe.'

15. *Thar . . . chyde.* 'You need neither to quarrel nor grumble.'

16. *craw to pull.* 'To have a crow to pluck' is proverbial for having a quarrel to settle.

17. By tradition this was the jaw-bone of an ass (perhaps from the story of Samson).

18. *and . . . rede.* 'and cannot think what to do.'

19. *Yei . . . gone.* 'Yes, hand out your punishments, but I don't want any – enjoy them for yourself when I have gone.'

20. *Gudeboure . . . hede.* 'Goodybower, by the quarry,' an identifiable place in Wakefield.

21. *Harstow . . . pot.* 'Do you hear, boy? There is work to be done.'

22. *Oyes, oyes, oy.* 'Oyez' – 'listen', the traditional crier's call.

23. *Browes . . . boy.* 'Broth, broth, for the boy,' a mocking echo of the previous line. Garcio continues to mock Cain's proclamation line by line.

24. *ill . . . out.* from weaving – 'badly spun thread always breaks.'

25. There were two levels – God had appeared from above – and Garcio probably climbed up the pageant cart at this point to escape Cain.

26. Cain's blasphemies increase – he swears by Christ.

27. He accepts his condemnation here in spite of his earlier attempt to proclaim his own pardon.

28. *Explicit . . . Noe.* '*The Killing of Abel* is finished. *Noah* follows.'

4. NOAH (TOWNELEY)

1. Noah's first words are obviously meant to recall the Creation and the Fall. His speech is not essential to the plot, but it presents a number of themes, especially the corruption of mankind.

655

NOTES

2. *Yit ... expres.* 'Yet their unnaturalness was seven times more than I can properly describe.'

3. *Bot ... dyssever.* 'But they shall burn in torment for ever, and never get away.'

4. *in paynes ... knowe.* 'to endure the cruellest torments.'

5. *Bot ... trawe.* 'Unless he declare his mercy on those that will believe in him.'

6. *Oyle ... hight.* 'He promised us the oil of his mercy.' Cf. p. 456, l. 9.

7. *Most ... night.* 'For the majority of day and night.'

8. *that bargan ... done.* 'Those who have done evil will curse their bargain.'

9. *In erth ... unsoght.* 'I see nothing on earth but sin that has not been paid for.'

10. *Hym ... go.* 'I will quickly go to bring him great advantage.'

11. *ichon other fo.* 'each man an enemy to the rest.'

12. *The water ... spar.* 'to keep out the water.'

13. *chese*, Sisam *et alii*: *chefe*, MS. 'in three tiers' – cf. *Genesis* 6 16.

14. The conflict between Noah and his wife is anticipated here: it was a well-known topic in medieval times, cf. Chaucer, *Miller's Tale*, l. 352ff.

15. *Tunc ... uxorem.* 'Then he shall go to his wife.' This implies two separate locations.

16. *To dede ... want.* 'As far as you are concerned we may live, or die from penury.'

17. i.e. 'black and blue' from being beaten.

18. i.e. the bonds of child-birth.

19. *With ... sory.* 'With sad expression.'

20. *for ... do.* 'for I have affairs to see to.'

21. *as ... ro.* 'as I may hope to have peace.'

22. *I may ... ken.* 'I may sit down and be taken for a fool.'

23. *In nomine ... sancti.* 'In the name of the Father, of the Son, and of the Holy Ghost.'

24. He begins to build the Ark in full view of the audience. Probably some of the parts would be carried on in large sections.

25. *Thoro ... myn.* 'through large and small.'

26. *Ther ... dame.* 'There is something more to be done, my lady.'

27. *ich a deyll.* 'every bit.'

28. *Therfor ... bayll.* 'Therefore with all our strength let us thank that noble one who heals our misery.'

29. *I wote ... tayll.* 'I do not know whither – I am bewildered and confused for fear of your story.'

30. Her changes of mood are so violent as to be unrealistic. The

NOTES

dramatist is probably following a number of interpretations which cannot be reconciled with strict psychological realism. Thus she must protest here, but be afraid at ll. 312–14.

31. *hertely full hoylle.* 'sound in heart.'
32. *shuld . . . doyll.* 'I should give a mass penny.' i.e. she would like to have to pay for the mass at Noah's funeral, and eat widow's food.
33. *wedmen emong.* 'among those who are wed.'
34. Cf. l. 345. Perhaps her entry into the Ark is the beginning of peace. Hereafter they work the ship together, and she gives Noah good advice.
35. *This . . . tyne.* 'I should describe this labour had I time to waste.'
36. for *Armenia*, where Mt Ararat is situated.

5. NOAH (CHESTER)

1. *Et primo . . . sua.* 'And first, situated in some high place or in the clouds if possible, God shall speak to Noah who is outside the Ark with the whole of his family.'
2. *My ghost . . . blynne.* 'My spirit shall only remain in mankind, who is my foe because of his fleshly desires, until six-score years are gone, to see whether men will cease their sins.' cf. ll. 149–50.
3. Cf. *Genesis* 6 15: but there, and in *Towneley* l. 125, the height is thirty cubits.
4. *the mete . . . about.* 'take the measurements yourself; make the dimensions as I have indicated.'
5. *And . . . spill.* 'And refrainest from destroying me and my family.'
6. *Tunc . . . instrumentis.* 'Then they make signs as if they were working with various tools.' The building of the Ark was enacted, or perhaps mimed (cf. l. 85).
7. *topcastle.* Platform at the mast-head – the Ark is a medieval sailing vessel.
8. *Tunc . . . instrumentis.* 'Then Noah with all his family again make signs of working with various tools.'
9. *For . . . master.* 'For they (the audience) all think you are the boss.'
10. Cf. *Genesis* 7 1–3; but elsewhere in *Genesis* it appears that only two of each species were taken.
11. *Hee . . . bringe.* 'Male and female, mate to mate, be sure to bring in quickly.'
12. *And that I have.* 'And all that which I have . . .'
13. *Tunc . . . Filius.* 'Then Noah shall go into the Ark, and his family shall give to him and call out all the animals painted on cards; and after each has spoken his part he shall enter the Ark, with the exception

NOTES

of Noah's wife; and the animals as painted must coincide with the words, the First Son beginning thus.'

This suggests cards with pictures held up as each actor recites the names of the animals.

14. *Here ... crowse.* 'Here cats are enjoying themselves.'
15. *on Gods half.* 'for God's sake.'
16. *But ... wife.* 'Either you will let them into your Ark, or else you can row forth, Noah, wherever you like and find a new wife.'
17. *full ... fast.* 'flooding very fast.'
18. *pottell of malmesy.* 'quart bottle of malmsey wine.'
19. ll. 233–6 are missing in MS Harley 2124.
20. *For ... boughte.* 'For the love of Christ who redeemed you.'
21. *Tunc ibit.* 'Then she shall go.' She is carried in by her sons.
22. *Et dat alapam vita* (for *victa?*). 'And having been overcome, she strikes him a blow on the ear.'
23. *Tunc ... respiciens.* 'Then Noah shall shut the window of the Ark, and for a short time under the roof they shall sing the psalm "Save me, O God"; then he shall open the window and look about.'
24. *Tunc. ... dicat.* 'Then he shall send forth the raven, and taking the dove in his hands he shall say.'
25. *Tunc ... Noe.* 'Then he shall send forth the dove, and there will be in the ship another dove bearing an olive branch in its beak. This Noah will send by a rope attached to the mast into his hands, and afterwards Noah shall say.'
26. *Therfore ... wise.* 'Therefore let them all come out.'
27. *Tunc ... mactabit.* 'Then coming out of the Ark with his whole family he shall receive his animals and birds, and he shall offer them, and make sacrifice.'
28. *For of youth ... syne.* 'For man, from his youth, has always been inclined to sin.'
29. *To eate ... knowe.* 'Do not hesitate to eat of those which you know to be clean.'
30. *in feare.* 'together.'
31. *That shedes bloode ... be.* 'He or she who sheds blood anywhere amongst mankind – who sheds blood, his blood shall be shed.'
32. Cf. *Genęsis* 9 13–14. The appearance of the rainbow at times of storm means that God has remembered his promise that there will never be another Flood: cf. *York*, Play IX, stanza 21, and *De Noé*, ll. 6292–5, in *Le Mistère du Viel Testament*. The texts give no hint of how the rainbow was portrayed; but for Benjamin Britten's musical version, *Noye's Fludde*, a large fan with the extremities appropriately painted is customarily used today.

NOTES

6. ABRAHAM AND ISAAC (CHESTER)

1. *Gobet-on-the-Grene.* Perhaps a hint of a folk-play Presenter.
2. *Lothe.* Lot, *Genesis* 14 16.
3. Melchisadech, *Genesis* 14 18–20. He was a king and a priest.
4. *Tunc ... Melchisadech.* 'Then the knight comes to Melchisadech.'
5. *Melchisedech ... Caelum.* 'Melchisadech raising his hands towards heaven.'
6. A figure of the Communion, and the justification for including the incident in the cycle. It does not appear in the other English mystery plays.
7. *without danger.* 'without limit.'
8. *Tunc ... patinam.* 'Then Melchisadech shall ride to Abraham, giving (him) a chalice with wine, and bread on a paten.'
9. *Tunc ... sibi.* 'Then he shall give (him) a horse laden (with spoils)'.
10. *Tunc ... Decimae.* 'Then Abraham shall accept the bread and wine, and Melchisadech the laden horse and the tithe of Lot.'
11. *Tunc ... Melchisadech.* 'Then Lot shall offer the cup with wine and bread, and Melchisadech shall accept them.'
12. *maundye.* From *John* 13 24, '*Mandatum novum ...*', the command to wash the feet of the poor.
13. The conception of Abraham as a representation of God the Father is continued in the play. His name means 'Father of a Multitude'.
14. This appears to be Ishmael, Abraham's son by the slave-girl, Hagar, *Genesis* 16 15, 16.
15. *Genesis* 17 9–14.
16. The correspondence with the *Brome* version begins here, and continues to l. 420.
17. *Tunc ... ibunt.* 'Then Isaac shall take the wood upon his back, and together they shall go to the mountain.'
18. Isaac, ironically, sees his fate, but Abraham is not yet ready to face the truth. This dramatic device is not present in the *Brome*.
19. *Tunc ... ligabit.* 'Then he shall gather him up and bind him.'
20. *Upon ... you.* 'In truth, father, I will not hinder you in the purpose on which you have determined.'
21. *For ... blood.* 'for fear of shedding blood.'
22. *Harte ... me.* 'O heart, even if you break in three, you shall never over-rule me' – he will not give way to his love.
23. *Tunc ... Angelus.* 'Then he shall take his sword, making a sign as though to kill him, and the Angel coming shall seize the point of his sword, and then the Angel shall say.' The correspondence with the *Brome* version ends here.

NOTES

24. *lambe*. It is a ram in the next stage direction and in *Genesis* 22 13. The lamb anticipates Christ.
25. *Tunc . . . arietem*. 'Then Abraham shall sacrifice the ram.'
26. *Of . . . feare*. 'You and your descendants with you shall have power over your enemies.'
27. *this significacion . . . good*. 'The meaning of this deed of devotion – if you wish, you may learn it – will bring you to much good.'
28. The Expositor is used to indicate the parallels and implications of the plays; here the importance is that Abraham, like God, is ready to sacrifice his son. It is thought that for these processional performances the Expositor may have been on horseback – though it is clear that on the day of performance many of the plays would need their own Expositor riding with them.

7. ABRAHAM AND ISAAC (BROME)

1. *I . . . all*. 'I thank thee greatly evermore for this.'
2. *Genesis* 21 2.
3. *glad*, MS: *prest*, Manly. The latter would fit the rime-scheme, but here and elsewhere I have tended to follow the manuscript rather than editorial conjecture, however plausible. It will be evident from a close study of this text that there are many places where the manuscript reveals uncertainty on the part of the scribe.
4. Abraham is meant to exemplify the virtue of obedience to God's will.
5. *Vysyon*. ?'the land of Moriah'; *Genesis* 22 2.
6. *I had . . . I have*. 'I would rather, if God had wished it, have lost all the goods I own.'
7. The correspondence with the *Chester* version begins here.
8. *all . . . packe*. 'I will carry all this in a bundle.'
9. ll. 141–2 are reversed in MS.
10. *thy . . . synke*. 'Let your grace descend (upon us).'
11. At this point Abraham must tell the truth, however reluctantly. It is notable that in *Chester* his unwillingness is made more of.
12. *but . . . kyll*. 'unless I kill thee.'
13. *I . . . styll*. 'I will never complain, loudly or continuously.'
14. *owt of yowre mynd*. This is very close to *Chester*, l. 319.
15. *Let . . . I*. 'Consider it as lightly as I do.'
16. *Thy meke . . . songe*. cf. *Chester*, ll. 349–50.
17. *Excepe . . . wyll*. 'Unless (I follow) God's will alone.'
18. *Do on . . . hardly*. 'Go on boldly, and do with me as you will.'
19. *my hart . . . therageyn*. 'my heart rebels against this.'
20. The *Chester* version diverges here.

660

NOTES

21. *an C sythe.* 'a hundred times.'
22. *ram. Chester* has *lamb* at l. 434.
23. *in hy*, Manly: *of hevyn* MS.
24. *But . . . trowe.* 'But, father, if I bend down low, you will not kill me with your sword, I trust?' It appears that the dramatist could not leave the idea of death.
25. *the by.* 'with you.'
26. *yowrys botherys sede.* 'the seed of you both.'
27. *gret.* Manly adds *won*, 'quantity'.
28. *have*, Manly: *hath*, MS.
29. *Thys . . . a-voee.* Davis places this line after l. 432.
30. *I pray . . . to.* 'I pray God to give grace evermore to us and to all those who are close to us.'
31. After *story* MS adds *hath schowyd*.
32. *yowre chyld to slayn*, Holthausen: *to smygth of yowr chyldes hed*, MS.
33. *Whan . . . kynd.* 'When their children die and go from them as nature wishes.'

8. MOSES

1. *as . . . asse.* 'as elders will agree.'
2. *Now . . . layse.* 'now are they likely to destroy our laws.'
3. *And . . . fee.* 'and herdsmen who keep their flocks.'
4. *qwantile*, MS: *qwantyce*, Towneley.
5. *Exodus* 1 16.
6. *That . . . fynde.* 'that we find no weakness.'
7. Perhaps a reference to the finding of Moses in the bullrushes.
8. *Jetro.* Jethro, *Exodus* 3 1.
9. *So . . . bide.* 'So as to await a better destiny.'
10. *If . . . wrayste.* 'If they, wrongfully, take anything from you.'
11. *Exodus* 4 2–7.
12. *ego sum qui sum.* 'I am that I am', *Exodus* 3 14.
13. *meke*, MS: *meve*, Smith, 'speak'.
14. *we . . . myne.* 'we may mourn and remember.' *we may mowrn, both more and myn*, Towneley.
15. *Beeths . . . blyne.* 'Cease your mourning.'
16. R. Woolf points out similarities between the dialogue of Moses and Pharaoh and that of Christ and Satan in the Harrowing of Hell (*The English Mystery Plays*, pp. 153–4).
17. *Wenes . . . laye?* 'Do you think you can destroy our law with tricks?'
18. *Hopp illa hayle.* Exclamation of surprise: perhaps 'an ill chance occurs'.

NOTES

19. *tadys*. Glossed as 'toads' by Smith, but 'taddies' is still used for 'tadpoles' in Yorkshire. There are no toads in *Exodus* 8.
20. *myses*. 'maggots'; *Exodus* 8 16.
21. *And ... done*. 'and we fear all this is done ...'
22. *loppis*. 'flies'; *Exodus* 8 21: 'fleas', Smith.
23. *They ... last*. 'They appear to be able to survive.'
24. *poudre*. 'powdre': 'soot'; *Exodus* 9 8.
25. *this ... lese*. 'I am not lying.'
26. *wormes*. 'locusts'; *Exodus* 10 12.
27. *lande of lykyng*. 'the Promised Land.'
28. *Ther ... thrall*. 'There must we halt until we are enslaved once more.'
29. *Horse ... tyte*. 'Harness the horses quickly.'
30. It seems likely that this difficult action was accomplished by the use of a large sheet or cloth. The Coventry accounts mention a purchase of cloth for the Red Sea. The Flood in the Noah plays might have been represented in the same way.

9. BALAAM, BALAK AND THE PROPHETS

1. This begins the Ten Commandments, *Exodus* 20 1–17.
2. *Tunc ... Moysen*. 'Then the Chief of the Synagogue shall take his position on the stage and shall speak to God and to Moses as if on behalf of the people.'
3. *Tunc ... populum*. 'Then Moses standing on the mountain shall speak to the people.' Note that an upper level or high place is called for.
4. *To prove ... synne*. 'To show that he is with you, God has done this to make you so afraid as always to avoid sin in deed and thought.'
5. The rays of light were represented as horns, but the appearance was also taken to be threatening (cf. l. 48).
6. *Wherfore ... sene*. 'And so we take the most valuable parts from it, as you shall see.' Perhaps the reference to brevity is a hint that the play has been shortened.
7. *Tunc ... equitando*. 'Then Moses shall come down from the mountain, and King Balak shall ride from another part of the mountain saying.'
8. These stanzas, (a) to (e), are not in MS Harley 2124.
9. *mediaters*. ?the Jews.
10. *Who ... good*. 'Whoever tries to fight with them gets little good by it.'
11. *Seon and Ogg*. Sihon and Og, *Numbers* 21 23–4, 33–5.
12. *For sicker ... be*. 'For certainly we may not be revenged on them in any way.'

NOTES

13. *Tunc ... Balaam.* 'Then (the Knight) shall go to Balaam.'
14. *in ... loco.* 'From above.'
15. *Tunc equitabunt ... Balaam.* 'Then they shall ride towards the king, and as he goes Balaam shall say.'
16. *Now ... maye.* 'Now by the law in which I believe, since I have permission to go, they shall all be cursed if I can gain anything by it.'
17. *Tunc Angelus ... asina.* 'Then the Angel, with a drawn sword in his hand, shall meet Balaam, and the ass shall halt.'
18. *Or ... crowne.* 'Or as I can use my head.'
19. *Tunc percutiet ... asina.* 'Then he shall beat the ass, and someone from inside the ass shall speak.' The device of hiding someone – probably a small boy – was used in the liturgical drama.
20. *Tunc ... dicat.* 'Then Balaam, seeing the Angel carrying the drawn sword, shall say in worship.'
21. *Tunc ... obviam.* 'Then Balaam and the Knight shall go on their way, and Balak comes to meet them.'
22. *Nought ... kin.* 'As I hope for bliss, I can say nothing but what God allows if I am to save all my property and kindred.'
23. *To ... to-day.* 'If you curse the men – and cursed they should be – whom you shall see today.'
24. *Tunc ... sequitur.* 'Then leading Balaam with him on to the mountain and looking to the south side, he shall say as follows.'
25. (f) is not in MS Harley 2124.
26. *Tunc ... dicat.* 'Then Balaam facing the south shall say.'
27. *Eyles the, poplart?* 'What is the matter with you, hypocrite?'
28. *Tunc ... partem.* 'Then he shall lead him to the north side.'
29. *Is ... mawmentry.* 'There are no idols worshipped.'
30. *lyon.* Numbers 23 24.
31. *Ad ... partem.* 'To the west.'
32. *That ... is.* 'Whoever curses them is accursed.'
33. *Tunc ... prophetando.* 'Then Balaam, looking up to heaven, makes a prophecy.'
34. *As ... deale.* 'ruling and holding power as king.'
35. *Esayas.* Isaiah 7 14, 15. The prophets appear in a procession, giving their prophecies: this sequence is the oldest part of the play in type, originally in the liturgical drama. Each of the prophetic speeches is headed by the Latin text from the Bible.
36. *Cleane ... wayle.* 'Pure without any evil deeds, who shall win blessing for mankind.'
37. *Ezechiell.* Ezekiel 44 2, 3.
38. *Iheremia.* Jeremiah 14 17.
39. *Ionas.* Jonah 2 2–10.

NOTES

40. *in . . . any.* 'in great distress.'
41. *David.* Psalm 18 7–16.
42. *May . . . apeare.* 'No man may imagine them, nor judge what is prepared for man; but all must then be revealed.'
43. *Ioell.* Joel 2 28–9.
44. *On . . . mynd.* 'Have him profoundly in our thoughts.'
45. *Micheas.* Micah 5 2.
46. The Expositor, mentioning the Incarnation, Passion, and Resurrection, acts as a bridge between the Old Testament and the New.
47. *heavenlye. ?* 'region of heaven.'
48. *Thus . . . before.* 'Thus is prophesied here that belief – which we hold – in the deeds of God who in freeing man had pity on him.'
49. The prophecies being over, Balak – in a somewhat awkward manner – brings his story to an end. Possibly the prophets' procession is an interpolation.
50. A hint that the prophets' procession has been curtailed to fit it into this play.

10. THE PARLIAMENT OF HEAVEN, THE SALUTATION AND CONCEPTION

1. *Ysaie.* Isaiah 30 18.
2. *captyvyte.* This refers to the souls captive in Hell – who are released at the Harrowing – and also to the bondage of Israel.
3. *Jeremye.* Lamentations 2 18, 3 48–9.
4. *Of Locyfere . . . place.* 'To be a substitute for Lucifer.'
5. *Propter . . . exurgam.* 'On account of the misery of the needy and of the groaning of the poor now shall I arise.'
6. The debate between the four daughters of God, Truth, Mercy, Justice, and Peace, appears widely in Christian literature, and derives from *Psalm* 85 10–11. It was used in the drama a number of times (*Respublica, Castle of Perseverance*; and see *The Macro Plays*, ed. M. Eccles, p. 200, note to l. 312). Since it does not appear in the other English cycles, its appearance here may be a reflection of the more didactic strain in *Ludus Coventriae*, and perhaps an indication of the influence of morality plays.
7. *Veritas . . . ipso.* 'My truth and my mercy are with me.'
8. *Thi love . . . kepe.* 'Let him no longer control man whom you love.'
9. *As wyse . . . be.* 'He wanted to be as wise as God.'
10. *a seyth.* Obscure. The general sense is 'Therefore let this be our conclusion: let him who sinned grievously remain in sorrow; he may never act by reason (?) who might save him from there.'

NOTES

11. *Endles ... restore.* 'God, who is everlasting, can put right sin which has lasted for ever.'
12. *tweyn dethis.* i.e. the deaths of Adam and Christ. This doctrine operating in later drama is sometimes known as 'the fortunate Fall': the deaths were held to be fortunate for man, not tragic.
13. *Qwere ... se.* 'Look and see how such (a death) were his.'
14. *Misericordia ... sunt.* 'Mercy and Truth have met, Justice and Peace have kissed.' *Psalm* 85 10–11.
15. *Et hic ... omnes.* 'And here they shall kiss one another.'
16. *Sey here.* 'Tell her.'
17. *Ave Maria ... tecum.* 'Hail, Mary, full of grace, the Lord is with thee.'
18. *His name ... be.* 'His name shall be called Jesus by you.'
19. ll. 262–285: R. Woolf, *The English Mystery Plays*, pp. 167–8, suggests a possible source for these lines in St Bernard's homilies.
20. *persevere.* Probably an error for 'preserver'.
21. *be mene passage.* 'during my pregnancy.'
22. *Thorwe ... renew.* 'Through your body is born the babe who will renew our joy.'
23. *Angeli ... serena.* 'With the Angel singing this sequence: Hail, Mary, full of grace, the Lord is with thee, serene Virgin.' In MS there is a cancelled stage direction, '*and than Mary seyth*'. This suggests that there has been an alteration in the order of the plays.

II. JOSEPH

1. *his wyl were wrought.* 'As he wishes.'
2. This is a reference to the glory which now shines in her face, but Joseph fails to appreciate its significance.
3. *Hens ... went.* 'Since I went away.'
4. Joseph here begins the comedy of the deceived husband: it is noticeable that he addresses other husbands also deceived.
5. Probably an obscene reference to the impotence of old age.
6. Mary's friend or attendant: the Proclamation (l. 160), describing the Annunciation, spoke of 'iij maydenys that with here dwelle.'
7. The proverb is from bird-catching – all those who beat the boughs do not necessarily catch a bird. The proverb fits the folk-humour of Joseph's predicament.
8. The punishment for adultery was stoning (cf. *John* 8 5).
9. *But if ... qwy.* 'Unless I knew a very good reason for it.'
10. *abyde respyt.* 'endure spite.'
11. *To wyte ... synne.* 'to lay the blame for any sin upon you.'

NOTES

12. THE NATIVITY

1. *blomyght.* 'blooms.' The Cherry Tree miracle is apocryphal, though widely known; cf. W. Hone, *Ancient Mysteries Described*, 1823, pp. 90–93.

2. i.e. 'let your lover get them.' Dramatic probability makes it likely that he knows that the 'lover' is God, but the passage is really a relic from the comedy about his doubts.

3. *hous of haras.* A stable for breeding horses.

4. *Hic ... unigenitum.* 'Here, while Joseph is away, Mary gives birth to her only-begotten Son.'

5. *Zelomy.* Zelumi. The midwives are named in the *Pseudo-Matthew Gospel*, ch. 13. They appeared early in the liturgical drama, being priests dressed up (Chambers, *The Mediaeval Stage*, II, pp. 41–2). They were used to point out the reality of the birth, and to vouch for Mary's virginity (see Grace Frank, *The Mediaeval French Drama*, pp. 32–3).

6. *Hic ... dicat.* 'Here, with a smile, Mary shall say.'

7. Joseph's mistake is an echo of his much bigger misunderstanding about paternity.

8. *Hic ... dicens.* 'Here Zelumi touches the blessed Virgin saying.'

9. *As other ... arayd.* 'Not foul in appearance as others are.'

10. Like the incredulity of Thomas, Salome's disbelief can only be dispelled by physically touching Mary.

11. *Hic ... dicit.* 'Here Salome touches Mary, and when her hand dries up, she shrieks, and as though in tears she says.'

12. *Hic ... dicens.* 'Here Salome touches the garment of Christ saying.'

13. FIRST SHEPHERDS' PLAY

1. *what thay ar weyll.* 'How happy are they.'

2. *Now in hart ... blast.* 'Now cheerful, now in good health; now in rain, now in gale.'

3. *Hors-man ... weyn.* Cawley identifies this as 'Jack Plenty', a figure of prosperity. 'Jack Plenty, who normally rides a horse, must then walk, I think.'

4. *Bot ... forsake.* 'Unless some good occurs, the land is ruined.'

5. i.e. to risk everything at dice.

6. The playwright's account of the wretched state of the First Shepherd is circumstantial and specific in that he has lost all his sheep through the plague ('rott'), and is ready to risk anything. Thematically the distress is important as a prologue to the Nativity: the Second Shepherd's prayer to Christ (ll. 50–54), although strictly an anachronism, reinforces this.

NOTES

7. The wasters described in stanzas 7 and 8 live off the poor, and depress their living standards by force. They boast ('crak', l. 59) and adopt superior manners like those of their masters (ll. 70–71).

8. At this point the Second Shepherd notices the First. It is clear from the following dialogue that the First Shepherd is called Gyb (Gilbert), the Second John Horne, and the Third Slawpase (Slowpace).

9. *I am ... wars.* 'I am always the same, I don't know what causes it: there is no one in this kingdom but a shepherd is, in comparison, worse off.' The Second Shepherd recognizes the First by the state of his clothes.

10. The First Shepherd imagines he has a flock of sheep: the Second tries to stop him from driving them into his pasture. The disagreement – about non-existent sheep – gets out of hand and they come to blows.

11. *Longys thou oght whedir?* 'Do you wish to go to some place or other?'

12. *a letter of youre grace.* 'give a little good will.'

13. *bett*, MS (? beat, place): *flett*, Cawley.

14. *It is ... go.* 'It is difficult to tell an egg to move before it is hatched.'

15. *Tytter ... pray.* 'May you sooner be without sauce than sorrow.' A comment upon their incompetence.

16. *Mowll.* Moll. This is a folk-tale. By day-dreaming about many sheep she does not have, Moll loses her pitcher, and is worse off.

17. He asks them to throw the sack upon his back while he holds the neck. He then calls them to stand by him and tips the meal from the sack on the ground between them. This demonstrates their stupidity in arguing over the non-existent sheep because the meal cannot be picked up again (ll. 174–5).

18. The folk-tale in note 17 was known as the Fools of Gotham: but Jack Garcio, the servant, has to point out that the Third Shepherd is as foolish as the rest because he has lost his meal – he cannot pick it up any more than the other two can.

19. It appears that they do have some sheep, but Jack Garcio is watching over them.

20. No doubt Jack Garcio is very small in stature – a lad.

21. They are still disposed to quarrel, perhaps to emphasize that the coming of Christ was to bring peace on earth.

22. *cryb.* i.e. 'feast'.

23. They produce a vast meal from various pockets and parcels. It is thought that this is a reflection of Christmas feasting. It is notable that many of the items are scraps which might be plentiful at Christmas when the winter slaughtering of stock took place.

24. *Hely.* Cawley suggests that this is Healey, a village near Wakefield.

NOTES

25. The quarrelling is continuing.
26. *Be my dam saull, Alyce.* 'By the soul of my mother, Alice.'
27. *Then ... kest.* 'Then I think we should settle who shall put this food into a pannier.' They intend to give the remnants to the poor.
28. *Ye ... frerys.* An irreverent allusion to the supposed gluttony of mendicant friars.
29. He makes the sign of the Cross and recites a scrap of Latin which is distantly related to the Latin for 'Jesus of Nazareth, crucified, Mark, Andrew'.
30. *with ... emang.* 'with small notes in it', i.e. decorative musical phrases.
31. *That betokyns ... owte.* 'The star which stands up there in the sky signifies this.'
32. *Exiet virga De radice Iesse.* cf. *Isaiah* 11 1, 'A shoot shall grow from the stock of Jesse.' *Virga* is mistranslated as '*vyrgyn*' (*virgo*) in l. 342. In spite of this, the Shepherds show considerable learning in the following sequence, possibly an identification of shepherds and priests.
33. *Sybyll.* This is the Erythraean Sibyl. Chambers (*The Mediaeval Stage*, II, pp. 52–3) describes an eleventh-century Prophets' Play from Limoges which contains most of the authorities cited in this passage. The probability is that our author derived his list from some similar source in liturgical drama.
34. Nebuchadnezzar threw Shadrach, Meshack, and Abednego into the furnace, and he saw four men walk about in the fire, the fourth looking like a god, *Daniel* 3 19–25.
35. *Jeremiah* 23 5; *Exodus* 3 2–4.
36. *So soyne.* 'very soon.'
37. Habakkuk and Elijah were prophets; Elizabeth and Zechariah were the parents of John the Baptist who prophesied Christ (*Luke* 1).
38. *Iam nova ... regna.* From Virgil's *Eclogue IV*, ll. 6–7, but the Latin is slightly distorted and the lines are reversed. 'Now a Virgin returns, and the kingdoms of Saturn are renewed; now a new race is sent down from the height of Heaven.' These lines were widely taken as a pagan prophecy of the Nativity. The First Shepherd gives his translation in stanza 45: clearly the reign of Saturn would be an age of plenty.
39. *Caton. Disticha Catonis* – the Poems of Cato – used as a school book for centuries.
40. *foure ... long.* 'Twenty-four short notes to a long note.'
41. *This ... lose.* 'Don't forget this song.' V. Kolve, *The Play Called Corpus Christi*, pp. 171–2, suggests that they must make an effort to remember the important words so that they can spread the news.
42. The Shepherds do not make gifts in the Gospel: this is perhaps an

NOTES

imitation of the Kings. The gifts here, as in other Shepherds' plays, are touchingly simple.

43. *as he ... seven.* 'as He made everything in the space of seven days.'

14. SECOND SHEPHERDS' PLAY

1. *shepardes*, MS: *husbandys* suggested by Manly.
2. The theme of the oppression of the Shepherds by extortion is found in the First Shepherds' Play. The oppressors seem to be the servants of the gentry who ape their masters (cf. ll. 28–36) and were maintained by them.
3. *what mastry he mays.* 'whatever abuse of power he employs.'
4. *wane ... ploghe.* cf. First Shepherds' Play, ll. 62–3.
5. Violence is also mentioned, *ibid*, ll. 56–61.
6. *wyndys*, Cawley: *weders*, MS.
7. Copyle is the name of the hen.
8. *Had I wyst.* 'If only I had known.'
9. The subject of marriage plays an important part here. The attitudes to women are similar to those in *Noah*, that women talk too much, and are a curse – widespread subjects of medieval comedy.

As an extension of this the fertility of Mak's wife is a contrast to the Nativity.

10. *I wald ... hir.* 'I wish I had run until I had lost her.'
11. *God ... raw.* 'Let God see to the audience!' – i.e. 'Attend to me.'
12. The Third Shepherd.
13. *Noe ... stormes.* The bad weather is a sign that a divine intervention is imminent.
14. He does not recognize the other two at first.
15. *all-wyghtys.* ?monsters (Cawley).
16. *Abyde ... it.* 'Wait until later on – we have already eaten.'
17. *to ... wowyng.* 'to accompany a wooer' – not trustworthy because selfish.
18. *Tunc ... vestitus.* 'Then Mak comes in wearing a cloak over his garment.'
19. *Et ... ipso.* 'And he takes the cloak from him.'
20. *sothren tothe.* 'southern dialect' – Mak uses some southern forms in his speeches at ll. 201–7 and 211–13 (e.g. *ich*, *sich*).
21. *pepe.* 'look around' – it is obvious, the Second Shepherd suggests, that if he is wandering around at night Mak must be up to no good.
22. *Seldom ... gate.* 'The devil doesn't often lie dead by the wayside.' Proverbial. He means that the Devil is never innocent, and neither is Mak.

NOTES

23. *sho. she* MS.

24. *Then . . . rowne.* 'If I do, I could immediately prevent you whispering together.'

25. *Manus . . . Pilato.* Corruption of 'Into thy hands I commend my spirit', but addressed to Pilate.

26. *Tunc . . . dicit.* 'Then when the Shepherds are asleep, he gets up and says.'

27. He draws a circle round them, and casts a spell on them to keep them asleep.

28. Though he has never been a shepherd, he will now learn to be one and drive off the sheep.

29. *Eft-whyte . . . may.* 'I will pay it back when I can.'

30. *I hope . . . hight.* 'I fear I cannot gain a penny by getting up (from spinning), curse them!'

31. Proverbial.

32. *Then . . . pak.* 'Then might I have a bad time, they being so many.'

33. *Bot . . . blast.* 'If I don't get back to my place before they rise, the wind will blow cold.'

34. *Resurrex . . . dominus.* The first is a corruption of 'He rose again from the dead', but the second is inexplicable.

35. *My . . . skyn.* 'My heart is out of my body.'

36. Wearing a wolf skin would suggest deception and thieving.

37. Manly attributes ll. 370–71 to Third Shepherd, and ll. 372–4 to Second.

38. Indicates that his costume has large sleeves useful for hiding stolen articles.

39. *Then . . . Gyle.* 'Then here we are like the devil, Sir Cunning, with his companions.' The sense is doubtful, but Manly's emendation *se* for *be* is not justified.

40. *I hope . . . lak.* 'I expect they won't be pleased when they find the sheep missing.'

41. *Coll.* The First Shepherd (cf. l. 449).

42. i.e. lie down by the wall and cry out for help from Mary and John.

43. Horbury, south of Wakefield.

44. Apparently Mak is singing (?a lullaby), somewhat out of tune.

45. *qwytt is my hyre.* 'I have received my wages.' He refers to his dream (ll. 386–8).

46. *And . . . forthynkys.* 'and that troubles us.'

47. *tymely.* 'early'; the line is proverbial.

48. She does intend to eat the 'child'. But one may also take this as an indirect reference to the bread and wine of the Mass.

49. *Gybon Waller* and *Iohn Horne* may be the First and Second Shep-

NOTES

herds in the *First Shepherds' Play*. If the plays are alternatives one may conclude that their names may be those of real people.

50. *lytyll day-starne*. This phrase is used again of the Christ-Child (l. 727), an indication of the parallel between Mak's baby and Mary's.

51. *Gyb*. The Second Shepherd.

52. *I trow . . . go.* 'I am sure Nature will creep even if it cannot walk.' i.e. The evil will show itself somehow.

53. *It was . . . wast.* 'It was a grave deceit. Yea, sirs, so it was.'

54. *hornyd lad*. 'horned lad', perhaps an allusion to the devil. Some critics see here a relic of pagan worship.

55. Manly suggests that these speakers' names should be reversed.

56. Tossing in a canvas is perhaps a symbolic death.

57. *of vii skore*. 'of seven score pounds' (measurement of weight still used for farm animals).

58. *Angelus . . . dicat*. 'The Angel sings "Gloria in the highest", and afterwards shall say.'

59. *let . . . dyn.* 'be quiet' – an aside, perhaps addressed to the First Shepherd who is still singing.

60. *Ecce . . . Concipiet*. 'Behold, a virgin shall conceive.' *Isaiah* 7 14.

61. *gyler of teyn*. 'evil deceiver', i.e. the Devil.

62. As in the *First Shepherds' Play*, the gifts are simple, but the following symbolism has been suggested –

    cherries indicate blood and death (cf. The Cherry Tree Carol), parallel to myrrh;

    the bird represents divinity (many visual representations show the Christ Child holding a dove), parallel to frankincense;

    the tennis ball stands for kingship, parallel to gold.

(Joseph A. Longo, 'Symmetry and Symbolism in the *Secunda Pastorum*', *Nottingham Mediaeval Studies*, 13, 1969, pp. 65–85.)

63. *That . . . seven.* 'Who made everything in seven days' (cf. *First Shepherds' Play*, l. 489).

15. INTRODUCTION TO THE THREE KINGS

1. Herod's boast is notable for its divine pretensions, which are blasphemous, and perhaps for his ignorance – Jupiter and Jove being the same, and Venus being feminine.

2. Herod had a mask at Chester (F. M. Salter, *Mediaeval Drama in Chester*, p. 79), and it is likely that it was so at York. God's mask was gold, and the boast here that the red is superior is blasphemous. See also his self-display in the *Coventry Shearmen and Tailors' Play*, ll. 507–10.

NOTES

3. At this point the manuscript continues with the same text as the following play, starting at l. 73 and continuing to l. 216.

16. THE ADORATION

1. By tradition the Kings were descendants of others who had long awaited Christ.
2. ll. 73–216 are also given in the previous play.
3. *Lorde ... wyte.* 'My lord, no one should blame messengers.' The punishing of messengers who bring bad news is a very old stage tradition, being found in Greek tragedy and in Shakespeare.
4. *A sterne ... by-forne.* 'A star stood before us.'
5. *Be ... knave?* 'How should you know by any celestial event who is a king and who is a commoner?'
6. *And ... pay.* 'And if your business be to my advantage.'
7. *Sir ... newes.* 'Sir, there is no need to wonder at this affair which is now coming about in this way.'
8. *Balaham.* Balaam's prophecy, *Numbers* 24 17. There is no Prophets' Play in the *York* cycle, but the prophecies are proclaimed by a Doctor at the beginning of the Annunciation (*York* 12).
9. *Osee.* 'He may flower like the lily,' *Hosea* 14 5.
10. The rest of the play does not appear in the Masons' play.
11. In one liturgical version of the Kings they are met by midwives who admit them to the stable. Possibly this Maid here is a relic of them; see Chambers, *The Mediaeval Stage*, II, p. 46, and R. Woolf, op. cit., p. 195.
12. The text makes it clear that gold stands for kingship, frankincense for judging, and myrrh for death.

17. THE FLIGHT INTO EGYPT

1. *dos to dy.* 'puts to death.'
2. Joseph's complaints make him a partially comic figure.

18. THE PURIFICATION, AND CHRIST WITH THE DOCTORS

1. *But heaven-blisse ... we.* 'But as for heaven's bliss after life – until God's son come, to say truth, to ransom his people, we shall never reach bliss.'
2. *Esay. Isaiah* 7 14.
3. *Tunc ... filium.* 'Then looking at his book, he shall read the prophecy, "Behold, a virgin shall conceive and bring forth a son."'

NOTES

4. *Tunc ... vidua.* 'Then he shall rub the book as if to remove this word 'Virgin'; and afterwards he shall place the book on the altar, and an Angel shall come, and having taken the book, shall give the appearance of writing; and when he has closed the book, he shall go away, and Anna, the widow, shall say.'

For Anna the widow, see *Luke* 2 36–8.

Lines 41–211 are missing in H2124.

5. A line missing.

6. *Tunc ... dicat.* 'Then he shall take the book, and, astonished, he shall say.'

7. *Tunc iterum ... dicat.* 'He does again as before, and he shall say.'

8. *Tunc ... antea.* 'Then he puts the book on the altar, and the Angel shall do as before.'

9. *For ... man.* 'For God will take on natural life as a man.'

10. *Nowe ... bliss.* 'Now I do believe that a maiden, on this occasion, shall bear a child of bliss.'

11. *Tunc ... Maria.* 'Then Simeon shall sit down looking for consolation from another place far from the temple, and Mary shall say.'

12. Cf. ll. 133–4; there are two doves in the Coventry *Weavers' Pageant* and in *Luke* 2 24.

13. *Tunc ... ulnas.* 'Then Simeon shall receive the boy in his arms.'

14. *Tunc ... pace.* 'Then he shall sing "Lord, now lettest thou thy servant depart in peace".' *Luke* 2 29.

15. *For ... pittie.* 'For there you have set up your power, to protect people on whom you have pity.'

16. *For sword ... woo.* 'For the sword of sorrow shall pierce your heart – and so people will know many of the secret thoughts of those who will oppose you and seek to harm you.' Cf. *Luke* 2 35.

17. A new scene opens here although there is no break or stage direction in the manuscript. In the remaining part of the play Christ is twelve years old.

18. *Greatly ... day.* 'Happy, for many a day.' Obscure, but *York* 20, ll. 1–8, shows that Mary and Joseph were very pleased with Jesus while they were in Jerusalem.

19. *In all ... hye.* 'I therefore think that we should go homeward with all our strength for fear of wicked company which may meet us on the way.'

20. *He wenes ... knowes.* 'He thinks he knows more than he really understands.' *York* 20, l. 90: 'He wenes he kens more than we knawes.'

For a full account of the text see W. W. Greg, 'Bibliographical and Textual Problems of the English Miracle Cycles', *The Library* 5, 1914, pp. 280–319, and *Chester Play Studies* (Malone Society), 1935, pp. 101–20.

NOTES

21. *That . . . be.* 'Which God commanded should be observed on earth.'
22. *all . . . teene.* 'lose all my labour.' The phrase appears in *York* 20 (ll. 229–32); the Chester dramatist clumsily re-arranged the lines of the stanza.
23. This line may possibly be a reference to Christ's recital of the Ten Commandments, though it appears that the dramatist forgot to adapt this final speech to the inserted Doctors' play in which the Angel has no part.

19. THE DEATH OF HEROD

1. *Tunc . . . dicens.* 'Then looking behind him, the Steward rushes up to Herod saying.'
2. *so moty the.* 'as I hope to thrive.'
3. *Thei . . . unkende.* 'They shall have bloody faces because of one whom I call unnatural', i.e. Christ.
4. *selcouthys.* 'wonders': *schel chownys*, MS, which is incomprehensible.
5. *Doth . . . ray.* 'Make your horses run, with stabbing spears (in your hands), till in that red dance ribs are torn.'
6. *Lete . . . may.* 'Let no child remain with his back unbeaten until a beggar in the stall of beasts shall bleed – Mahound will do the best.'
7. *ryd be-lyff.* 'ride quickly.'
8. *Tunc . . . femina.* 'Then the Soldiers shall go to kill the boys, and the First Woman shall say.'
9. He has one of the victims impaled on his spear.
10. Herod's pride invites disaster (cf. ll. 164–7).
11. *Goddys masangere.* A regular conception of death, found in *Everyman*: Herod's pride, humbled by death, is also reminiscent of *The Pride of Life*, c. 1350.
12. *Hic . . . eos.* 'Here, while the trumpets blow, Death shall kill Herod and the two Soldiers suddenly, and the Devil shall receive them.'
13. *feynt felachep.* 'poor company.'
14. He probably wore a costume which represented a skeleton with worms painted on it.

20. THE SHEARMEN AND TAILORS' PLAY

1. *The Sofferent . . . seycrette.* 'The Sovereign that sees every secret.'
2. *uncion. Daniel* 9 24–7.
3. *Ecce virgo consepeet.* 'Behold, a virgin shall conceive.' *Isaiah* 7 14. (The Latin in this play has been subject to scribal distortion.) The

NOTES

Coventry Plays appear to have had no separate Prophets' play, the prophecies being incorporated as link passages in the two extant plays.

4. *In secula seculorum.* 'For ever and ever.'
5. *He ... forlorne.* 'He shall save what was lost.'
6. Joseph assumes Mary's infidelity, and sees himself as a fool. There is little Scriptural justification for this except *Matthew* 1 18, 19, but the idea is much developed in medieval times, especially in *Ludus Coventriae*.
7. *and that acold.* 'and that a cold one!' i.e. sad.
8. *truse.* Obscure. Perhaps *truste*: 'Now may I stand like a trusting fool'.
9. *scho.* 'show' – for the census.
10. *The were tyme.* 'The very time.'
11. *schortist dey.* This does not appear to be Scriptural.
12. *Et in tarra pax omynibus.* 'And in earth peace to all men.'
13. *Ase I owt rodde.* Song I, p. 379.
14. *of pore reypaste.* ?'humble in state.'
15. Song III, p. 380.
16. The Prophets cannot be identified in detail, though their function is to link the episodes of the play by recalling anticipations of the Nativity in the Old Testament. The method used is characteristic of the episodic style of the *Coventry Plays*.
17. *And lyve ... brothur.* 'And live equally with man as a brother.'
18. *Aronis rod.* Aaron's rod, *Numbers* 17 6–11.
19. *pallays* Sharp 1817: *pyle*, Sharp 1825.
20. This stanza is in mock French, chosen to give an outlandish and superior quality to Herod's reputation. French was still closely associated with the Court in the fifteenth century. Some of the reconstruction is conjectural; see Manly, *Specimens*, pp. 136–7.

Peace, lords, barons of great renown; peace, lords, knights of noble power; peace, gentlemen, companions small and great – I command you to preserve complete silence! Peace while your noble king is here present! Let no one lack due deference, nor be bold to applaud; but keep all patience – but keep for your lord reverence in your heart; for he is your all-powerful king. In his name, silence all! I command you; and (here is) King Herod the Great ... may the devil take you!

21. *Qui statis ...* 'Who stands ...' His Latin does not last very long.
22. He blasphemously claims divine creative powers.
23. *Magog and Madroke.* Magog *Genesis* 10 2, *Ezekiel* 38. Madroke has not been identified.
24. *In-to ... tyde.* 'To what place do you wish to go at this time?'

NOTES

25. *be-semyng all afar.* 'seeming to come from afar.'
26. *Skant twellve deyis old fulle.* 'Only twelve days old.' The Epiphany which celebrates the Coming of the Kings traditionally takes place on the twelfth day after Christmas Day.
27. *For there ... crafte weylde.* 'There you must be careful and use cunning.'
28. *And cum ... wey.* 'And return home the same way, visiting me.'
29. *Tawrus ... Arraby ... Aginare.* Tarshish ... Arabia ... ?Egriseula (Craig).
30. Herod's rage is proverbial (cf. *Hamlet* III ii 14). Much interest has been aroused by the stage direction, which indicates that he puts on a special performance, taking him from the pageant cart to the street.
31. Unusually the Angel speaks to both.
32. *to sum cun off*, Kittredge ('to some kind of'): *sum tocun off*, Sharp.
33. Song II, p. 379.
34. *A stroke ... here.* 'You shall have a blow from me here.'
35. *Fynes ... scharmen.* 'End of the Play of Shearmen and Tailors.'

21. JOHN THE BAPTIST

1. *John* 1 8.
2. *but ... aperte.* 'but soon I appeared quite openly.'
3. *For ... be.* 'For God will not stay with those in whom sin is rife.'
4. The rest of the stanza is missing.
5. *more or myne.* 'more or less.'
6. *But ... twa.* 'But I will show you two reasons.'
7. i.e. heaven.
8. *Fyrst ... leche.* 'First I shall receive (baptism), then I shall preach like a true physician: for mankind must act righteously.'
9. *Tunc ... spiritus.* 'Then two Angels shall sing "Come, creating Spirit".'
10. *The dragons ... I.* 'I have destroyed every part of the dragon's (Satan's) power through my baptism.'
11. *And lere ... thrall.* 'And teach that lore to every man who was formerly in bondage.'

22. THE TEMPTATION OF CHRIST, AND THE WOMAN TAKEN IN ADULTERY

1. *Doseberd.* ?'Dosey-beard' – muddlehead.
2. Satan describes the perfection of Christ.

NOTES

3. i.e. he seems to be mortal.

4. *For ... amisse.* 'For I am sure that he is more than human or else he would have committed some sin or other ...'

5. Because Christ is hungry, Satan thinks he cannot be a God.

6. Christ refers to the common belief that Adam sinned through gluttony.

7. *Adam ... can.* 'I brought Adam, whom God himself made, into torment by my deception; but as for this man whom I have looked for, being born of woman – because he has no personal needs, I have no chance of harming him by any advice I give – my cunning is of no use.'

8. *Tunc ... templi.* 'Then he shall place Jesus on a pinnacle of the temple.'

9. *Descendet de pinnaclo.* 'He shall come down from the pinnacle.'

10. *Tunc ... Diabolus.* 'Then Satan shall lead Jesus to the top of a mountain, and the Devil says.'

11. Satan realizes that he has lost the battle and makes his will.

12. St Gregory's sermon appears in the *Stanzaic Life of Christ* which the *Chester* dramatists used frequently. Christ has overcome the temptations by which Adam fell: Gluttony, Vainglory, Ambitious Pride (or Covetousness).

13. *Tunc ... Primus.* 'Then two Jews shall come with the woman taken in adultery in order to tempt Jesus: so the First shall say.'

14. The temptation is to try whether Christ follows the law and condemns her, or follows his own teaching and pardons her. Either way, the Jews expect that he will do wrong: see the Expositor, ll. 281–8.

15. *Tunc ... Iesum.* 'Then they shall come to Jesus.'

16. *Tunc ... terram.* 'Then Jesus writes on the ground.'

17. *Tunc ... scripsionem.* 'Then they read his writing' – and see their own guilt.

18. *Et fugiett ... dicat.* 'And he shall run off, and afterwards the First Pharisee shall say.'

19. *Alas ... Fraunce.* 'Alas! I wish I were the other side of France!'

20. *Et fugiet ... Mulierem.* 'And he shall run off, and Jesus shall say to the Woman.'

21. *Yet ... knew.* 'None of them knew anything about the sins of others, but saw only his own.' In the Gospel the Jews do not read what was written (though the writing clearly has some importance and relevance), but the Expositor presses the point that each man miraculously saw only his own guilt.

NOTES

23. LAZARUS

1. *untill Iude.* 'into Judaea.'
2. ll. 3 and 4 are transposed in MS but corrected by means of letters *a* and *b* in the margin.
3. The Disciples feared he would again be stoned, *John* 11 7, 8.
4. *John* 11 13.
5. *rysyng.* resurrection: *John* 11 25. This is the main theme of the first part of the play. Its connection with Christ's own Resurrection was no doubt the main reason for the choice of the Lazarus episode.
6. *Et ... dicens.* 'And Jesus wept saying.'
7. In popular legend Lazarus related many horrifying details of what he had seen in hell.
8. *eke his dayse.* 'lengthen his days.'
9. The rest of the play is taken up by the warning about the grave and the inevitability of death. The effect is more lyrical than homiletic.
10. That all ranks of society would become food for worms was the theme of the *Dance of Death*.
11. *The royfe ... towche.* 'Your bare nose shall touch the roof of your hall (i.e. your coffin).'
12. Toads were thought to be evil and poisonous in popular lore.
13. *For you ... goode.* 'The person who has the largest part of your possessions weeps for you least when you are dead.'
14. The idea that possessions, family, and friends are no use in death is the main theme of the play *Everyman*.
15. *Agane ... gate.* 'Against the time when you will follow another way.'

The Passion Play I

24. THE COUNCIL OF THE JEWS

1. The Demon's speech is typical of the mystery plays in that it recounts the events of the Christian story, particularly the temptation of Christ: but the technique of soliloquy by a villain was much developed in the morality plays, especially the self-revelation and the description of devices used to catch victims.
2. *Revelations* 12 7-9, but the story was much elaborated in the plays dealing with the Fall of Lucifer.
3. *where ... ensuryd.* 'where I set about tempting he at once attacks me – he has also confirmed Magdalene's full forgiveness.'
4. *Quia ... redempcio.* 'Because in Hell there is no redemption.' Derives

NOTES

from *Job* 7 9; see *The Macro Plays*, ed. M. Eccles, p. 200, note to ll. 3096–7.

5. *And I wyl ... alyauns.* 'And I will give in return the power of love's bond.' The whole stanza is hypocritical, but it is a valuable reflection of the importance of love in the play.

6. *the dyvercyte ... varyauns.* 'the variety of clothes I am wearing as a disguise.' He is stagily dressed in the new fashions – a device common to devils in morality plays – e.g. Newguise in *Mankind*, Lucifer in *Wisdom*.

7. *cordewan.* Leather from goat-skins, made at Cordova, Spain.

8. *With two doseyn ... feyn.* 'With two dozen cords of kid leather, tagged with fine silver.' The *points* held up the hose.

9. *holond.* Linen from Holland.

10. *stomachere of clere reynes.* 'waistcoat' of cloth from Rennes.

11. *And ... nowth.* 'and value as nothing those who condemn pride.'

12. *Cadace wolle.* 'Cotton wool.'

13. *And there ... debat.* 'and where sin is condemned, make sure to protest.'

14. *And gadere ... entent.* 'And collect a following after your own heart.'

15. *Both sevyle ... nowth.* 'care nothing for civil and canon (church) law.'

16. *ermyn calabere or satan.* 'ermine fur or satin.'

17. Another device from the morality plays, in which the names of vices are turned into virtues (cf. Skelton's *Magnyfycence*).

18. *Seyse ... chef.* 'At assizes or sessions let Perjury reign.'

19. *Matthew* 3 11; *Luke* 3 16; *John* 1 27.

20. The preaching of John in the Bible is more symbolic and prophetic than the words given him here. The style here is closer to the pulpit and the morality plays with the elaboration of the simple figure of the narrow path.

21. Annas appears on his own stage, evidence that the play was being performed with a number of fixed locations in the acting area. Clearly there was a means by which the actor could conceal himself until his cue, perhaps a curtain.

22. *Saraʒyn.* The exotic eastern clothing is used to suggest evil.

23. *pellys.* fur.

24. *To severe ... termynable.* 'It lies in my power to separate right from wrong.'

25. *We must ... reprevable.* 'We must seek a means of bringing blame to him.'

26. i.e. Rewfyn and Leon.

NOTES

27. We should note that this summoning of the Council is very long-winded. Perhaps the speeches had to be long to allow for due ceremony in the Messenger's errand.

28. *sythe present.* 'says in this place.'

29. The scene apparently ends here. There follows a cancelled stage direction and eight lines of speech by Peter which end the sheet (fol. 142 verso). The new scene shows Jesus speaking to the Apostles.

30. Presumably Philip.

31. *Burgeys.* 'Citizen.'

32. *blynde.* The incident below (ll. 470–77) bears this out. He also applies blindness, deafness, lameness and dumbness in a spiritual sense.

33. *On to the cety-ward.* 'towards the city.'

34. *prophetys prophese.* Matthew 21 4, 5.

35. These lines on the theme of mercy are repeated from ll. 343–6 above.

36. *perfyth of corde.* 'perfect accord.'

25. THE LAST SUPPER

1. *wepyng.* Luke 19 41–4.

2. *Maunde.* Holy Thursday. The writer has moved rapidly from Palm Sunday.

3. *paschall lomb.* The lamb is slain and eaten at the Passover. Christ becomes the lamb – Agnus Dei. See ll. 381–448.

4. Attention suddenly switches to the Conspiracy. Christ and the Disciples presumably continue their meal whilst the Jews talk.

5. *But do ... fast.* 'But cause Jesus to be arrested.'

6. *constreyn,* Block: *conseyve,* MS.

7. *Be ... instawns.* 'by what means you can arrest him, for he has many followers at command.'

8. A cancelled stage direction indicates that an entry for Judas stood here. The following speech by Mary Magdalene begins a new quire containing the scene with Jesus up to the soliloquy by Judas (l. 269).

9. *I xal ... to.* 'I shall be destroyed because of the great sins I have committed, unless my Lord God spares me somewhat and receives me to his great mercy.'

10. *To fede ... ken.* 'to feed our poor kindred.'

11. *Pore men xul abyde.* 'The poor will always be.'

12. *In ... be-gynne.* 'He who shall begin this treason eats from my dish.'

13. *of grett age.* 'at the age of discretion.' Judas is held to be responsible for his actions.

14. Judas leaves the Disciples and speaks two stanzas on his way to the

NOTES

Jews. E. Prosser, *Drama and Religion in the English Mystery Plays*, pp. 131–6, suggests that the writer has Judas leave at this point as a result of his scorn for Mary Magdalene's love and faith. This variation from the Scriptural version gives Judas an additional motive for betrayal besides the mercenary one.

15. *and we a-corde.* 'if we agree.'
16. Irony: cf. the love of Magdalene which Judas rejected, and his kiss.
17. *Smyth up.* lit. 'smite up' – clap hands on a bargain.
18. The conspirators descend from their chamber and prepare themselves to make the arrest. The attention is switched back to the Last Supper as the curtain is opened. Judas has resumed his place.
19. *mystery.* In M.E. 'A religious truth known only by divine revelation' (N.E.D.). This meaning is probably the one preserved in '*Mystery* Plays' (not that derived from *mysterium* – 'craft').
20. *oble.* i.e. the Host.
21. *to your apparens.* 'as it appears to you.'
22. Besides the general theological relationships between love and the bread, there is a dramatic point here in regard to the want of love shown to Jesus.
23. *Of this lombe . . . levyth.* 'If anything of this lamb be left uneaten.'
24. Christ's words, recalling l. 259, point the treachery of Judas, who has condemned himself by eating. Shortly afterwards he leaves the gathering to the praises of the Demon (l. 465ff.).
25. *Is it owth I, Lord?* 'Is it I, in any way, Lord?'
26. Foreshadows the Harrowing of Hell.
27. *Petyr . . . knowe –.* 'yn' is doubtful in MS. Perhaps the sense is 'Peter – (you rush) in further than you realize –'.
28. There is no real break in the action here. Christ's speech is broken by the stage direction, and the number of the play in the margin (28) is arbitrarily placed.

26. THE BETRAYAL

1. Christ comes from the upper room and sets out for Bethany, the first part of the scene taking place on the way.
2. *The vyl . . . fulfylle.* 'to carry out your will.'
3. *Luke* 22 44, but elaborated to anticipate the water and blood of the Crucifixion: see also l. 52.
4. *Fulleche . . . spede.* 'to urge my request to the fullest degree.'
5. Significantly the Angel offers Christ his own body and blood.
6. *It is nowth . . . case.* 'It is no use to plead against the cause.'
7. The waiting groups of soldiers and priests at last come forward to

NOTES

make the arrest. It is clearly meant to be a spectacular moment, particularly the appearance of the ten persons in armour.

8. *Is howth ... me?* 'Is your coming here in any way for me?'

9. Prosser, *op. cit.*, cogently suggests that Mary Magdalene must have remained with Jesus throughout the Last Supper and the Agony.

27. THE BUFFETING

1. *Do io ... apase.* 'Gee up! Trot on quickly.'

2. *Be thou ... hangyng.* 'when two or three promises of hanging have been given to you.'

3. *Gar ... blonder.* 'making the people forsake our laws and follow yours; this is why you are now in trouble.'

4. *Fayn ... countenance.* 'He would like to sleep; if not, he looks sad.'

5. *that has ... walkyng.* 'who has made us work hard in walking here.' They resent having to drive Jesus, who will not walk as fast as they want.

6. *Whi ... onys?* 'Why have you not yet asked how we have been getting on?'

7. They have guarded Christ overnight, and make it appear that they have had a hard time of it.

8. *quetstone.* 'whetstone', a sign for lying (Cawley).

9. *lyes*, MS: *wyles*, England.

10. *avowtre. John* 8 3-11. There is no *Towneley* play.

11. *Lazare. John* 11 1-44. See Play 23 (*Towneley* 31).

12. *I shall ... talkyd.* 'I shall drive out what is rotten by the time we have all had a talk.'

13. *I do fy the.* 'I scorn you.'

14. *wols-hede ... tane.* 'Let the calls for catching outlaws be given against you.'

15. *Et ... videtur.* 'And anyone who says nothing is thus seen to consent.'

16. *Where ... name.* Jokes about Christ's alleged noble birth – 'Where was your father dining when he met your mother? You, a man of position, without boots or spurs!'

17. *Sir Sybre.* Term of abuse. Cawley suggests that it is a reference to the offspring of an illegal marriage.

18. *As ... rent.* 'As I hope to sing Mass, I think that whoever keeps the law gets more by graft than by his due income.'

19. *King Copyn.* Not explained. Caiaphas gives him this title for being a trickster.

20. *Weme.* An expression of impatience.

NOTES

21. Annas and Caiaphas are distinguished carefully by the author. Annas is much more cunning and seeks a legal way of condemning Christ. Caiaphas is a bully and is anxious to ensure that Christ is beaten. The argument between them is very vigorous, both threatening and amusing. In the end, Annas apparently wins his point that Christ be handed over to Pilate, but he does agree to the buffeting (l. 318).

22. *Et ... possumus.* 'And we want this thing which we are legally entitled to do.' The saying supports his attempt to proceed legally.

23. *For ... dam.* 'See how the boasting of the people (about your alleged kingship) will condemn you to be hanged.'

24. *I*, England: MS omits.

25. *Sed ... quemquam.* 'But it is not lawful for us to put any man to death.' *John* 18 31.

26. *Therfor ... by.* 'Therefore he shall pay for it.'

27. *war.* 'worse.' In the next sentence Caiaphas complains that he is out of his usual way – he wants to strike Christ, and wonders why he is so far off.

28. *Oone feste.* Obscure – 'one feast', perhaps an anticipation of the pleasure to come. Cawley suggests 'a fair treat'.

29. *play of Yoyll.* 'A new Yule game.' Cawley identifies this as 'Hot Cockles', in which a blindfolded player has to guess which of the other players strikes him.

30. *buffit.* ?a stool (cf. l. 345).

31. *Good ... dew.* Froward is now convinced that there is good reason for fetching the stool – as sure as he is alive (feels the dew).

32. *Ther ... gate.* 'No one in this town, I believe, will be sad about his sorrow except the father that begot him.'

33. *Yei ... dyd.* 'Yes, unless they are closed tight, we shall lose our labour.' Christ must be properly blindfolded or he will guess.

34. One of the Torturers binds the cloth and Froward curses him.

35. *thou ... fowll.* 'You hardly touched the skin – a poor effort.'

36. For Gospel references see Introductory Note.

37. *crate.* ?'decrepit man' (England). Cawley reads *trate*, 'hag'.

38. *Then ... dryfe.* 'Then what I must do is to drive him from behind.'

28. THE DREAM OF PILATE'S WIFE

1. *What ... brewis.* 'Any brawler who stirs me with his brawling.'
2. He presents his family tree: Caesar was his father, Pila, daughter of Atus, his mother.
3. *Pounce.* Pontius, cf. ll. 254, 408.
4. *Percula.* i.e. Procula.

NOTES

5. *But ... the.* Percula resents the Beadle's criticism of their amorousness, but the passage is obscure; perhaps 'unless you stop your arguing you will be sorry; for the slave is accursed, as you can see.'
6. *But ... weys.* 'But with twists and tricks he sends me away.'
7. *For scho ... stande.* 'For she may stagger in the street unless she walks firmly' – obscure, perhaps because the following line is missing.
8. Pilate, to appease his wife on her being sent home, suggests a drink.
9. *as ... rought.* 'as if she had no cares.'
10. *newe ... noght.* 'you shall not be uncomfortable.'
11. *yhe whe wele.* 'you are a heavy weight' – he is drunk.
12. *lappe me.* 'tuck me up.'
13. *myron.* ?'servant'.
14. *And ... sese.* 'If he is slain our comfort will end.' The Devil reasons that the death of Christ will bring salvation, and therefore he must induce Percula to persuade Pilate not to condemn him. This theme is treated more extensively in Continental plays. Here the Devil warns Percula that her property will be lost.
15. *for ... heven.* 'by the passion of heaven.'
16. *with ... trapped.* 'that he does not receive pain.'
17. *Oure ... undewly.* 'Our followers at midnight met him with force, and have driven him to judgement for his evil deeds.'
18. *he ... awne.* 'he thought this world was entirely his own.' Annas does not perceive the irony of what he says.
19. *Matthew* 27 19.
20. *fendes-craft.* 'devil's craft.' Caiaphas attributes the dream to Christ's witchcraft; Annas adds that devil's craft accounts for the miracles.
21. The Beadle worships Christ. Later (ll. 337–47) he recalls Palm Sunday.
22. *Sir ... care.* 'Have you said your piece? Yes, lord. Now go and sit down, with sorrow and care.' Pilate's sharp rebuke is as pithy as modern Yorkshire ('Have done!').
23. *halow a hoy.* 'give a shout.'
24. *Oyas.* 'Oyez' – 'listen'. The ancient call for silence used by ushers and criers. Pilate is determined to assert his authority with due ceremony. The word *A-lowde* is not clearly a stage direction in MS.
25. *heldis ... harre.* 'acts out of order' (lit. 'moves off the hinge').
26. One line missing.
27. The miracles, allegedly witchcraft, are cause for condemnation.
28. *Yhe prelatis ... lyse.* 'You prelates who are known to be so worthy, you should be clever and wise, and refer to our law where it is relevant.'
29. Because Jesus was born in Galilee he must be tried by Herod. *Luke* 23 6–7.

NOTES

29. THE SCOURGING

1. *mali actoris.* 'of a doer of evil'; though *mali auctor* ('author of evil') or *mali a(u)ctor is* ('that author of evil') might make better sense.
2. This self-revelation is characteristic of Devils and Vices in the morality plays. This is one of the evil Pilates, unlike the corresponding Pilate in *York*.
3. Stanzas 5 to 27 are written in the nine-line stanza, and attributed to the Wakefield Master.
4. *Thou betyd . . . all.* 'It was bad luck for you to come among us all.'
5. Here Pilate shows some of the reluctance of a good Pilate – which is Scriptural. It may be that this turn in the characterization results from the revision.
6. Asked why he stands back so far, the First Torturer says it is to give himself room to strike.
7. *rust.* 'red'; perhaps he means to strike (*rub*) where the skin is already reddened to make the blood flow quickly.
8. *Architreclyn.* The Torturers begin to recount the miracles – a dramatic device which heightens Christ's present submission. This is the wedding at Cana-in-Galilee (*John* 2 1–11): Architricinus (Lat.), ruler of the feast (vv. 8–9).
9. *Matthew* 14 24–7; *Mark* 6 48.
10. *Matthew* 8 26–7.
11. *Matthew* 8 1–4; *Luke* 5 12–13.
12. *Matthew* 8 5–10.
13. *Luke* 18 35–43; *Mark* 10 46–52.
14. Again the Torturer is condemned by his own words.
15. *weshen.* Pilate washes his hands; *Matthew* 27 24–6.
16. The play now turns to the journey to Calvary, which has little Scriptural basis, but derives from the *Meditationes Vitae Christi*. It introduces the theme of lamentation which plays an important part in the drama of the Passion. The three Marys are Mary the Virgin, Mary mother of James (Maria Jacobi), and Mary Magdalene.
17. *For I am ferde . . . rafe.* 'For I fear that if we frighten her she will run wild and rave.'
18. *Et inclinabit . . . suam.* 'And he shall bend the cross towards his mother.' This incident appears to be of fifteenth-century origin.
19. The warning appears in *Luke* 23 27–30, though it is not there addressed to the Marys, but to the weeping women of Jerusalem.
20. *for red . . . red.* 'for any counsel that they can take.'
21. *by that Lord . . . lowte.* 'by the Lord whom I believe in and worship.'

NOTES

This oath would refer to Christ if spoken in medieval times: used by the Torturer it is ironic.

22. *Matthew* 27 32.

23. *noyn*. The ninth hour (Lat. *nona hora*) of the day, reckoned from sunrise by the Roman method: i.e. Christ must be dead by about 3 p.m.

24. *To beytt . . . oght.* 'To beat me unless I did any wrong.'

30. THE CRUCIFIXION

1. The cross, with the holes already bored, is laid on the ground.
2. Christ's willing submission here shows the sacrificial nature of the Crucifixion, cf. ll. 49–60.
3. The Soldiers take up their stations: the First holds the head, the Second pulls the right hand, the Third the left, and the Fourth the legs.
4. [*IV*] *Mil*. This and the following speech are given to the Second Soldier in the manuscript: see J. P. R. Wallis, 'The Miracle Play of *Crucifixio Christi* in the York Cycle', *Modern Language Review* 12 (1917), pp. 494–5.
5. *for hym the boght*. 'for the sake of him who redeemed thee.' An anachronism since the Redemption has not yet occurred, but the expression contains cruel irony.
6. The right hand being pinned, the Third Soldier finds the left will not reach, and so he and the First Soldier stretch it to the hole.
7. All four now pull the legs with a rope to reach the hole.
8. The cross, with Christ fixed upon it, must now be carried up the hill.
9. *Why tente . . . tyde?* 'Why are you talking so much at this moment?'
10. The cross is dropped into the hole in the ground with a jolt.
11. The foot of the cross must be supported by wedges to keep it erect.
12. *Qui destruis templum*. From *Matthew* 27 40 – 'You would pull the temple down, would you, and build it in three days?'

31. THE DEATH AND BURIAL

1. In this play, Pilate is presented as the reluctant judge of Christ. He is concerned to shift the blame for Christ's death on to the Jews.
2. *Quod scripci, scripci*. 'What I have written, I have written', *John* 19 22. Note that the details of Christ are drawn from all four Gospels, suggesting that the direct source was not the New Testament, but probably the *Gospel of Nicodemus*.
3. Sister of the Virgin, wife of Clopas, *John* 19 25.
4. *Latro a Sinistris . . . Dextris*. 'Thief on the left . . . right.'

686

NOTES

5. *Matthew* 27 46; *Mark* 15 34. Both Gospels recount the mistake of bystanders who think Christ calls upon Elijah (l. 227).
6. *me thristis sare.* 'I am very thirsty.'
7. *in manus tuas.* 'into thy hands', *Luke* 23 46.
8. *Longeus.* Also known as Longinus, this character is not Scriptural. In medieval lore, he was supposed to have received his sight (l. 302) when he pierced the body of Christ, and this was a sign of his salvation (also in *Towneley*, *Chester*, *Ludus Coventriae* and the Cornish cycle).
9. *Longeus latus.* In the non-dramatic versions of this episode (*The Northern Passion*, ll. 1869–74, *St Bernard's Lamentation on Christ's Passion*, l. 616, *The Southern Passion*, ll. 1635–6, *Cursor Mundi*, ll. 16835–40) it is clear that Longeus is brought forward to stand under the cross, unable to see where he is. He is then made to thrust the spear into Christ's side. Possibly '*latus*' is a stage direction indicating that he has been led forward.
10. *in mynde gune I meffe.* 'I began to be moved in my mind' (with sorrow).
11. *John* 19 38–42.

32. THE HARROWING OF HELL

1. The stage setting was probably a castle gate, with heavy doors.
2. Refers to the Redemption; cf. l. 12.
3. The symbolism of the story demands that the souls in Hell sit in darkness. Christ's coming to release them is heralded by his light (cf. *Isaiah* 9 2). Since the play was performed in daylight, some means of representing light would be necessary, perhaps a representation of the sun.
4. At this point a later scribe has written *Tunc cantent* – 'Then they shall sing' – marking the shift of dramatic interest from outside the Gates of Hell to the interior. At l. 41 Adam perceives the light.
5. 'The land of Zebulun, and the land of Naphtali,' *Isaiah* 9 1.
6. Simeon, see *Luke* 2 25–35.
7. *This light . . . dede.* 'Thou hast sent this light to those living on earth: what I foretold I see is now fulfilled in reality.' Again emphasis upon light, l. 69.
8. For the Baptism see *Matthew* 3 13–17; *Mark* 1 9–11.
9. *Was . . . manne.* 'Was made to sound to me like that of a man.'
10. Refers to the Transfiguration, in the presence of Moses and Elijah; *Matthew* 17 1–8; *Mark* 9 2–8.
11. The name of the First Devil. This character is given a somewhat larger and more unruly role in *Towneley*.

NOTES

12. *Lymbo.* Limbo, the edge of hell, where those who died before Christ were kept. Its special feature was the absence of God.
13. *Astrotte.* 'Ashtoreth, the loathsome goddess of the Sidonians ...' 2 *Kings* 23 13. Anaball has not been identified.
14. *Bele-Berit.* Written as though two persons in MS, but see *Judges* 8 33, 'The Israelites again went wantonly to the worship of the Baalim, and made Baal-berith their god.'
15. *To marre ... mase.* 'To destroy them who make such rebellions.'
16. *Attollite ... eternales.* Version of *Psalm* 24 7, 'Lift up your heads, you gates, lift yourselves up, you everlasting doors.'
17. *I lered ... lees.* 'I taught when I was alive, without deceit ...'
18. Here begins the symbolism of the military battle between Christ and Satan.
19. *Laʒar.* Lazarus, *John* 11 1–44.
20. Satan's part has some Scriptural basis, *John* 13 27.
21. *And wotte ... mente?* 'And know that he won Lazarus away, who was given to us to guard, do you believe that you can prevent him from using his powers – as he intends to do?'
22. David, *Psalm* 107 16, refers to the Lord: 'He has shattered the doors of bronze; bars of iron He has snapped in two.'
23. *gere.* Satan calls for his armour.
24. *But as ... thyne.* 'But they have stayed here as in my prison for their good, not as your property.'
25. *me menys.* 'as I remember.'
26. *Thou motes ... myre.?* 'You argue his men into the mud.' *Towneley* reads *moyttys*, 'slip'.
27. Satan now enters a theological argument with Christ.
28. *Salamon.* Solomon, *Proverbs* 2 19 and 21.
29. *Job* 10 21.
30. *movys emang.* 'goest about.' Sisam suggests the *Towneley menys*, 'thinks'.
31. These are suicides: Judas, *Matthew* 27 5; Ahithophel, 2 *Samuel* 17 23.
32. Dathan and Abiram were killed by divine intervention for challenging Moses, *Numbers* 16 27–32.
33. *lawe.* Refers to the Creed and items in it – the Coming, the Sacrament, the Death and Resurrection.
34. *Nay ... smytte.* 'No, my fine friend, you must be destroyed.'
35. *Mighill.* Michael does not appear in the *Towneley* version, and he is not mentioned in Burton's list: his inclusion here is probably the result of a later revision.
36. *Als ... inferno.* 'As I have said, so I still say, "Thou wilt not leave my soul in Hell, O Lord".' Cf. *Psalm* 16 10.

NOTES

37. *Ne suffre ... repleye.* Probably corrupt, differing from *Towneley*. The passage here may be read 'nor ever allow (thy) souls to be separated from thee, nor permit those who may repent to share the sorrow of those who dwell in woe, always full of corruption.'
38. The Harrowing is carried out by the soul of Christ, while his body lies in the tomb.
39. *no draught us drawe.* 'make no move against us', as in chess or draughts.
40. *lovyng.* 'praise.'
41. *Laus tibi cum gloria.* 'Praise be to thee with glory.'

33. THE RESURRECTION

1. *Whoso ... bonys.* 'Whoever will not do so quickly, may his bones hang high!'
2. *Tunc ... equitans.* 'Then the Centurion shall come in like a cavalryman', i.e. on horseback. From this point the *Towneley* text is dependent upon *York* 38.
3. *Adonay.* Hebrew name for God.
4. *Of ... moyne.* 'The sun and the moon ceased to shine.'
5. *Bot fast ride.* The Centurion is now on the way from Calvary to Pilate's house.
6. *Not for that ... wold.* 'Not only why you did that deed, or why the sun went dark, but also how the veil in the church split asunder, I should like to know.'
7. ll. 140–45 not in *York*.
8. *Who shuld ... ther!* 'I wish to know where each should sit.' 'I will sit on this side.' 'And I shall try to avoid his feet.' 'We must curse there!' As they prepare to guard the body they jest about the possibility of being kicked.
9. *Tunc ... Ihesus.* 'Then the Angels shall sing "Christ Rising", and afterwards Jesus shall say.' *Christus resurgens* is the Easter antiphon.
10. *Thou synfull man that by me gase ...* An independent lyric; see R. Woolf, *The English Mystery Plays*, p. 275. The passage which leads up to this long monologue, and the speech itself (ll. 214–333) are not in *York*. This invention may have been arrived at because the liturgical drama offered very little material for the Resurrection itself.
11. *And that ... fle.* 'And that you try hard to keep from sin.'
12. This stanza is clumsily crossed out in MS. 'Becommys my fleshe' would be taken as a reference to the doctrine of Transubstantiation not acceptable to Protestant feeling in the sixteenth century.
13. *on.* 'of', *York*.

NOTES

14. *whome have ye soght?* This is the *Quem quaeritis* episode of the liturgical drama. It is perhaps the oldest episode in Christian drama, and many scholars see it as the germ around which the cyclic plays grew.
15. *Alas ... me?* 'Alas, what shall now become of me?'
16. *Wytt ... slone.* 'If Sir Pilate gets to know of this matter, we shall certainly be slain.'
17. *A thowsand ... slone.* 'I shall claim a thousand men and more, each one well-armed, came and took his corpse from us, and almost killed us.'
18. *walkyng.* 'wakyng', *York*, which seems more appropriate.
19. The Soldiers' account of the Resurrection is inconsistent with what the audience has seen happening. This may possibly be attributed to their duplicity, but it seems more likely that the discrepancy is due to difficulties arising from two different traditions in the liturgical drama. One makes them fall asleep (as they do in *Ludus Coventriae*), but the other shows them transfixed by the power of what they see. There is no doubt (from l. 461) that they do sleep, but the account here describes the miraculous trance. (See Woolf, op. cit., p. 407, n. 20.)
20. *can* for *gan*, 'did'.
21. *Matthew* 28 11–15 substantiates the bribe, but the corruption of the Soldiers was well established in liturgical drama on the Continent (Woolf, op. cit., pp. 276–7).
22. The dependence upon *York* 38 ends here. *York* has a separate play for the Appearance to Mary Magdalene, No. 39.

34. CHRIST'S APPEARANCES TO THE DISCIPLES

1. *Emawus.* Emmaus, seven miles from Jerusalem (*Luke* 24 13).
2. *Qwat ... gon.* 'Tell me what you are talking about between yourselves: you are utterly sad and heavy, your mirth has gone.'
3. *prophetys.* *Luke* 24 25.
4. Christ sets out to prove his point by the figure of Jonas, who represented or foreshadowed the resurrection.
5. *Aaron.* A second figure for the return of life.
6. *Laȝare.* This clinches the argument, cf.

The grettest meracle that evyr Jhesus
In erthe wrouth be-forn his passyon
....
That pagent xal be of Lazarus. (*Ludus Coventriae*, Proclamation, ll. 295–9)

7. As in *Luke* 24 30, the breaking of the bread reveals Christ to the Disciples, and he leaves at once.

NOTES

8. *Hic ... eorum.* 'Here Christ shall suddenly disappear from their eyes.'
9. *so nere oure lappe.* 'so near to us physically.'
10. This is the point at which the two incidents are joined. In *Towneley* there is a decision to go back to Jerusalem, and l. 273 below suggests that they are no longer at Emmaus (cf. *Luke* 24 33).
11. The doubts expressed by Thomas recall the disbelief of Luke and Cleophas.
12. *For ... lorn.* 'For unless you have faith, your soul is lost.'
13. *Quod ... resurrexit.* 'Because he who was dead and buried has now arisen.' This speech is a formal poem addressed to the audience, showing how the incredulity of Thomas has turned to faith.
14. *The fende ... resurrexit.* Elliptic: 'He (Christ) has frightened the fiend that always vexes our faith, (and may he) who was dead and buried and has now arisen bring you to heaven and save you all.'

35. THE ASCENSION

1. There should be eleven Disciples present, but only six have speaking parts – Peter, Andrew, John, James the Greater, Simon, Philip.
2. *Pax ... timere!* 'Peace be with you! It is I, do not be afraid!'
3. *gone is not yore.* 'not long ago.'
4. *Tunc ... dicat.* 'Then Jesus shall eat with his Disciples, and afterwards (Philip) shall say.'
5. *Wher ... goe.* 'Wherever they happen to go.'
6. *tongs.* 'languages', *Acts* 2 4–11.
7. *Tunc ... terra.* 'Then he shall lead the Disciples to Bethany, and when he has come to the place, Jesus, standing in the place where he shall ascend, shall say "All power in heaven and earth is given to me."' This may be a reference to performing in two acting areas; the second area being that prepared for lifting the actor playing Christ during the Ascension.
8. *Tunc ... mecum.* This passage, used in the liturgy of Holy Week, is derived from *Isaiah* 63 1–3, but here it is re-arranged as a sung dialogue.

> Then Jesus shall ascend, and in ascending Jesus shall sing as follows
>
> JESUS: I ascend to my Father and to your Father, my God and your God. Alleluia! Alleluia!
>
> And when the song is over, Jesus shall stand in the middle as though above the clouds.
>
> 1 ANGEL: Who is this who comes from Edom, coming from Bozrah in (red) stained garments?

NOTES

II ANGEL: Who is this magnificent in his clothing, striding in the greatness of his strength?
JESUS: I who speak justice, and who am defender unto salvation.
III ANGEL: And your clothes are (red) as of those treading in the wine press.
JESUS: I have trodden the wine press alone, and no man from the nations was with me.

As with the passage at ll. 160 ff. below, an English paraphrase follows.
9. *Blody*. Though the syntax of this line may be distorted, it is clear from l. 128 that Christ is blood-stained.
10. *Tunc ... eodem dicat*. 'Then Jesus standing for a short while in the same place shall say.'
11. *Tunc ... coelum*.

> *Then he shall ascend, and as he does so the Angels sing the following song*

We shall sing to rejoice in your excellence, O Lord, and we shall sing psalms of your virtues. Alleluia!

> *Then the Angels shall descend and sing 'Ye men of Galilee, why do you look up to Heaven?'*

12. *Speaking, eatinge and drinking*. These were the signs that Christ was not a ghost, but a risen body (cf. l. 42).

36. PENTECOST

1. *Nobis ... mortuorum*. 'The Lord commanded us to proclaim (him) to the people, and to bear witness that the judge of the living and the dead is near.' Cf. *Acts* 10 42.
2. *Us menis ... thus*. 'We remember that this is what he said to us.'
3. *Cum ... omnia*. 'When the Advocate shall come, he will teach you all things.' *John* 14 26.
4. *And ... mene*. 'And much more than we have in mind.'
5. *Nisi ego abiero*. 'Unless I go from you.' *John* 16 7.
6. *Et dum assumptus fuero*. 'And when I have ascended.'
7. *Angelus ... spiritus*. 'An Angel shall then sing the hymn "Come, creating Spirit".' The name of the hymn is written in a later hand, but ll. 137–8 and the other cycles justify it here.
8. *Als lange ... flay*. 'As long as you follow his steps, the fiend shall not put you to flight.'
9. *Veni ... visita*. 'Come, creating Spirit, visit the minds of your people.'
10. *Tristicia ... gaudium*. 'Grief has filled your heart ... But it shall be changed to joy.' *John* 16 20.

NOTES

11. Simultaneous staging here.
12. *For to ... lette.* 'No one alive shall prevent us saying what must be said.'
13. *Et erit ... carnem.* 'The Lord says, "And this will be in the last days: I shall pour out from my spirit on all flesh."' *Acts* 2 17, from *Joel* 2 28. The accusation of drunkenness is also found in *Acts* 2 13.
14. *There ... tone.* 'These men have great power through the fortune they have received here.'

37. THE ASSUMPTION AND CORONATION OF THE VIRGIN

1. *That ... allone.* 'That she should remain by herself, alone.'
2. *Cantando.* 'Singing', during which Mary is carried up to Heaven.
3. *Of newe ... more.* 'Nevermore shalt thou know harm.' Probably a reference to the sufferings of Mary at the Crucifixion.
4. *modir myne.* At this point the Rubricator assigns the recital of the five joys of Mary to five Angels, but the words 'modir myne' suggest that Christ should speak them. If this were so, Christ would have a very long speech, from l. 101 to l. 160, and it seems likely that in a performance Angels might very well have been used simply to provide variety.
5. *confessouris.* A Confessor endures suffering and torture for his faith, but does not undergo martyrdom.

38. JUDGEMENT DAY

1. *And all-kynne ... oght.* 'And everything that now exists.'
2. A verbal echo of *York* 4, ll. 57–9, the first of many instances in which earlier events of the cycle are recalled.
3. *every ilke agaste.* Perhaps *every ilka gaste*, 'every single soul'.
4. *fecche your flessh.* Refers to the belief in the physical resurrection of the dead.
5. First Good Soul.
6. *Ther aftir ... noght.* 'Do not judge us, Lord, in accordance with these deeds.'
7. First Bad Soul.
8. *To aske ... nede.* 'It is no use for us to ask for mercy.'
9. *Helpe ... excusacioune.* 'No excuse can help us.'
10. *That eres ... mene.* 'Whatever ears have heard, or heart has thought since any time that we can remember ...'
11. *Deus.* i.e. Jesus, who is to judge mankind.
12. The Apostles assisted at the Judgement by a Scriptural tradition.

NOTES

13. *Ther-fore ... dight.* Read *That fore*, 'Because (thou) hast prepared and made ready such recompense for us who have been mortal.'

14. *Hic ... angelorum.* 'Here (he goes) to the seat of Judgement, with song from the Angels.'

15. *We schall ... wrange.* 'We must keep them always in sight, and warily wait, or else we shall do badly.' He is preparing for the arrival of many souls of the damned.

16. Half a stanza is missing here. A marginal note indicates that another version was written.

17. *Of ... synge.* 'Every sinful person must sing of sorrow.'

18. This appears to be a reference to the Five Wounds of Christ, though usually they are one in each foot, one in each hand, and one in the side (or heart).

19. *Manne ... be.* 'It was necessary thus, man, for you to be saved.'

20. The works of mercy are enumerated in *Matthew* 25 35–6. R. Woolf, op. cit., p. 414, n. 104, reads *prison* (from *Towneley*) for *presse* at l. 289.

21. *Thame thurte ... bone.* 'They had only to ask to receive their request.'

22. *House ... quaked.* 'Though I shivered, I had no house or shelter, help or aid from you.'

23. *To me ... kyd.* 'That unkindness was shown to me.'

24. Time has passed away. The cycle ends with a specific reference to the belief in eternity, cf. the opening speeches of Deus in Play 1.

25. *Et ... locum.* 'And thus crossing from the place to the place, he makes an end with the melody of angels.' A reference to Christ's final return to Heaven, presumably an upper stage.

Glossary

Glossary

A

a have
abast cast down
abate be humble
abite pay for
able empowered
abone above
aby buy
adred afraid
adyld earned
affy trust
agaste afraid
aght eight
aght owe
aght possessions
aleond alien
algatys always
almes-deedes charities
alonly alone
alowed praised
als as
alys ails
amese calm
an on
a, and if
anoye grief
apayre spoil
aperte, apertlie open(ly)
appech delay
appendyth belongs
arament accoutrement
aray arrangement
arere raise
armone harmony
arneys armour
arow reluctant
aspey perceive

assent act of will
assyse assize
aught anything
avowtre adultery
aw fear
awe ought
awith ought
awne own
awre anywhere
aye ever
ayer air
ayles troubles
aysell vinegar

B

bachler knight
bad commanded
baftys behind
bale sorrow, torment
ball head
ban curse
barme bosom
barne(s) children
barn-teme offspring
baron child
bayle power
bayles bailiffs
baylie castle
bayll sorrow
bayn bone
bayn(e) obedient
be(a)mes, bemys trumpets
bedellys messengers
bedene, bedeyn at once, indeed
bedyng bidding
begownne begun

GLOSSARY

beheighte command
behet command, promise
behetes promises
behoves, behufys is fitting, must, requires
belde, beilde comfort, protection
belife, belyve quickly
bene been
benignitie meekness
benke bench
bent field
berde woman
bere bier
bere, beere tumult
berre carry
berryng exception
bese is, be
beseke beseech
besele busily
best beast
betaght devoted
betake give
betydde happened
betyme in good time
beuscher good sir
bewe good
bewsprytt bowsprit
bib drink
biglie firm
blaw blow
blayne sore
ble complexion
blent deceived
blithes cheers
blyn(ne) stop
bofettys blows
bolne swell
bone request
boneers willing
boodword message, command
boorede bored
borow guarantee

borwe save
bot unless
bourded jested
bourgh town
boustous huge
bowne ready, prepared, bound
bowrde game, trick
boyne prayer
boyte, beete cure
boyte use
brast break
brayde moment
brede bread
brede breadth
brede broad(ly)
breganderys body armour
breme fierce
brend burned
bren(e) burn
brerys, breeres briars
brest, brist burst
brodell wretch
bronde sword
browes broth
browke use, enjoy
brybour scoundrel, thief
brybre theft
brydde bird
brygge strife
bryme fierce
bryst burst
bryth bright
bus must
busk bush
buske prepare, hurry
bustus violent
but (if) unless
buxum obedient
byar redeemer
bydene at once, indeed
bye near
byke hive

GLOSSARY

bylde protect
byr rush
byttour bitterns

C

cache drive
canker rust
carlis slaves
carp(e) speak, complain
carpyng criticizing
cast set up
cast trick
castel cabin
casten tried
catel goods, property
cattis cats
cautellis tricks
caytife wretch
cele, ceyll happiness, luck
cest ceased
ceteceyn citizen
chaffare bargain
charys chores
chawmere chamber
cheare gladness
cheare state
cheffe achieve, befall
chepe cost
ches tiers
chese chose
chevelures knights
chevesaunce trick
chist ark
chyned chained
clarkes learned men
claryfyed revealed
cledde clothed
clepyd called
clerge learning
cloute mend
clowte kerchief
clowtt clothes

clyppys eclipse
cod pillow
comber become entangled
combrance harassment
comely, comlye beautiful
comen come
command coming
compass boundary
conande cunning
coning (n) learning
conseons conscience
cors corpse, body
coryous fine
cost place
costage experience
coth illness
couthe could, can
coveytande desiring
cowle turnip
cowll lump
cowth can, could
coyle cabbage
coynt clever
coyntice cunning
crabbed bad-tempered
crafe crave
crenseyn crimson
cressetys lanterns
crokyd lame
cutte lot
cullors colours
cyttie city

D

dare tremble
daynty pleasure
day-starne day-star
daw fool
dawngere power, pride
deadlich mortal
dear damage
deceave deceive

GLOSSARY

ded deed
ded did
dede dead
deere suffer
deese dais
defawth fault
degth death
deill scrap
dele, dell part
delice delight
delt shared
delyver hurry
demand judging
demar judge
dem(e) (v) judge
departe relieve
dere harm
dere-wordy beloved
derffe wicked
des seat
dessece harm
desysed unhappy
dever(e), devyr duty
devyne divine
dey day
dey die
deyll give
diggs ducks
dight(e) prepare
dighte ordained
distance disagreement
dit stopped
dith, dight ready
divident dividing
dold old
dold stupid
dool, dule grief
dose do
dote dotard
doubte fear
doufe, dowfe dove
doute fear

dowm dumb
dowtere daughter
doy do
doyllys grief
drake dragon
draw turn
dray pull
dre suffer
drife drive
drive go
drofe drove
dughty brave
dule grief
dur dare
dwere grief, fear
dwill, dwyll(ys) devil('s)
dyn noise
dyng strike
dyntes blows
dyrthe shortage
dyspyth cruelty
dysses discomfort
dyssever depart
dystempurst sadden

E

eals ails
eck, ek, eke also
edefie establish
eerly earthly
ees eyes
efne heaven
eft again
emang among
emyde amidst
encheson reason
endeavour duty
enderes just past
endlang along
endytars writers
eneryth inherit
enewe enough

GLOSSARY

enfray affray, matter
envie malice
eretykys heretics
ethe easy
ether each
etyht eats
evyn evening
experence knowledge
expresse complete
extasy anxiety

F

fagyng deceiving
fand try
fang(e) take, fetch
fare behaviour
farly, ferly wonder
faver appearance
fawcun sword
fawth fault, lack
faye faith
fayn pleased
fayntyse cowardice
faytour, fa(y)ture deceiver
fee cattle, property
feele many times
felde field
fell cruel
fell feel
felle destroy, strike down
felle many
felle skin
fend prohibit
fer far
fer(e), feere, feare company, companions
ferde fear, afraid
fermes rents
fervent glowing
ferys companions
fett(e) fetch, fetched
feyll feel

fitt hardship
flaied terrified
flay scare
flayn skinned
flechinge bending
flem drive away
flitte escape
flowyng flood
flume river
flyt go
flyt moved
flyte quarrel
foder feed
fold times
folde land
fole fool
folys fools
fon doubt
fon (v) jest
fone few
fone foes
fone fool
fonge catch, seize
food(e) offspring, person
foore, fowre fared
forby(e) redeem
fordo destroy
fore-reyner fore-runner
forewyll farewell
forfayt forfeit
forfet(t)e sin, wrong
forgang go without
forgone lost
forlorn lost
formation act of creation
forshapyn changed
forspokyn bewitched
forthye therefore
forthynkys displeases
fortyfye ensure
forwakyd tired
forward(e) promise, bargain

701

GLOSSARY

forwhi because
foryeten forgotten
fott get
foun found
founde try
foyde child
foyne few
foytt food
fraie strife
frankish fancy
frast(e) ask, attempt
fray fear
fre(a)ke man
fre(e) noble
frerys friars
frese doubt
frete wear, waste
freynchepe friendship
freyne ask
froward perverse
fry children
fryth wood
fulgence brightness
fulmart polecat
fyer fire
fylde defiled
fyn noble
fyrmament sky
fytt time

G

gables ropes
gad go
gaffe cared
gam delight
gammon jest
garn yarn
garray noise
gars noises
garthynere gardener
gate way
gawdes tricks

geates goats
geder gather
gedlungis fellows
gere equipment, tools
gerles children
ges guess
Ges Jesus
geste guess
gesyne childbed
geve(n) give(n)
geyse geese
ghost(e) spirit
ghostelie spiritual
gif, gyf give
gif if
gilery deceit
glad sheath
glade enliven
gle mirth
gle song
glede fire
gleyvis weapons
glose falsehood
goffe given
gollyng violence
gomys men
gone go, move
gossyppys friends, godparents
goys goose
grame anger, sorrow, harm
gramery learning
grath speed
grathe(ly) direct(ly), proper(ly)
gravell stones
grayth readiness
gren grass
gret(e) weep
grete greet
gretyng weeping
greved harmed
greyn grass
gright forfeited

GLOSSARY

grill complain
grill vex
grith peace
groch complain of
groved grew
grownde(d) ground(ed), founded
grucched complained
grufe grow
grughe grumble
grw Greek
gryll anger
gyf if
gyle, gyll guile
gyn plan
gyrd cut
gys(s)e way of life, manner, custom

H

hackstock chopping block
haide had
hakt sang
hale whole
halse neck
haly holy
haly wholly
hame them
hand-lang little
hap(pyd) cover(ed)
happys fortune
har joint
hard heard
hardely, harly certainly
harie distress
harrode herald
harrowe uproar
harstow do you hear?
hartyng encouragement
hasse has
hat is called
haunsed exalted
hayfe have

haytt hot
he(e), hey high
heale health
hearbes plants
hearnes herons
hee loudly
heght height
hek inner door
hekys rack
hem them
hend, hynd gentle
hend hand
hende end
hent take
her here
her(e) their
herborw(e) shelter
heris hear(s)
herys listen(s)
hestes commands
het praise, promise
heth heath
heyll health
heyly greatly
hidus frightful
hight(e) is called
hight(e) promise
hilled covered
hillinge covering
hise his
hit it
ho stop
ho who
holgh hollow
hone, hoyne delay
hope think, except
hore hair
hote hot
hover delay
hower hour
hoyse hose
hufe wait

GLOSSARY

hurled dragged
hy I
hy(e) go
hyde hurried
hydygth hide
hyghe high
hynde near
hyne servant
hyrdes shepherds
hyte go

I, J

ianglis, jangill chatters, prates
javell argue
ich (a) every, each
jebet gibbet
jesen childbed
ilke same
illa-hayll evil fortune
incheson cause
indoost beaten
induyr last
intent will
intisement enticement
jorne journey
ioy joy
i-wisse indeed
i-wrought completed

K

katyffis wretches
kaydyfnes wretchedness
kayssaris emperors
keill, keyle cool
ken(n) know, teach
kend nature
kend taught
kent advised, instructed
kerch(er) kerchief
kest thrown
kever gain
kinde nature, race

kindenes likeness
kine cattle
knafe man
knaveschild boy
knawe know
knen knees
knowledge (v) acknowledge
knoyng knowledge
knyth tied
konne give
kyndly natural
kynnys, kyndis kind of
kyppys snatches
kythes show

L

la(y)ke (v) play
langett thong
langowrys affliction, disease
langyd longed
lap wrap
lare lore
late seek
latyng hindrance
laugher lower
laughte caught
launce hurry
lawe low
lawse untie, loosen
laye bet
laye law
layne conceal, hide
leasing(e) lie, lying
leche (n) healer
ledden song
lede kingdom
leder, lidder lazy, evil
ledys people
lee brightness
lee delight
lee shelter, protection
leede person

GLOSSARY

leefe rather
lees (n) lies
lefe believe
lefe, leffe, life, leif dear, beloved
leif stay
leke leek
leke likely
lele loyal
lele truly
lemyd shone
lene give
lenge linger, stay
lent placed
lenys gives
lere teach
lese loss
lest listen
let(t) prevent, refrain, forbid
leve believe
leve, leeve leave
lever rather
levyn lightning
levyr liver
lewdnes ignorance
lewed, lewyd ignorant
lewtye loyalty, faith
leyde man
leyfe leaf
leym, leeme beam
leyn give
leyn lazy
leyn lean
libardes leopards
liccorris eager for dainties
lief live
lifyng living
lig lie
ligys lies
lik lick
list pleasure
liste will
lith(t) joint

lithirnesse idleness
lodesterne guiding star
lofyng praise
lone gift
long lung
looe hill
lordeyn, lordan, lurdeyn oaf, fool
lore advice
lorell wretch
lorne destroyed, lost
losellis wretches
losyngere flatterer
lote noise
lowsyd loosened
lowt(e) bow down, revere
loyse destroy
lufe palm
luffull praiseworthy
lufly beautiful person
lurk stumble
lyckenes likeness
lygen lain
lygth lies
lykes pleases
lyre face
lyvelod living
lyys lies

M

ma many
maddis rave
maistry power
make mate
males malice
malison curse
manas threat
mangyng eating
mansuetude gentleness, mildness
maryd destroyed
mawmentrye idols
maye maid
mayll pack

GLOSSARY

mayne power, strength
maystry(e) power
meanye, meneye company, followers
measse dish
mech much, great
mede reward
medyll-erth, middle-yorde world, earth
meede desert
meet, mete (v) dream
meke (v) humble, soften
mekill great
melle be concerned with
membre limb
mende spoken
mending improving
mene speak
menge mix
menske honour
mercyabyl merciful
mervayles wonders
mes mass
meschevyd harmed
mesel measly
mete meat
mete meet
mett measure(d)
meve move
mevid moved, shifted
meyn small
meyne middle
mickle great
midwayes midwives
mo(e) more
mod mood
mode temper
mold(e) ground, earth
mone moan
mone moon
monys complaints
moren plague

mor(e)we morning
mornyng grieving
morwyn morning
mow may
mowes faces
moyne moon
muck earth
muste new wine
myddes midst
myd(d)yng midden, dunghill
myln mill
myn less, loss
myn remember
mynder mention
mynnyng remembrance
myrke dark
myry merry
mysprase blame
myster need, show
myster, muster reveal
mystery revelation
myth (v) might
myth (n) power

N

nar near
naroo hard
nateley thoroughly
naye denying
neene nine
nefe fist
negh(and) approach(ing)
neld needle
nere never
nere nor
nere hande near
nese nose
nesh soft
neven say, mention, name, proclaim
nevis news
newsome annoying

GLOSSARY

nokyns no kind (of)
none own
noote, nott affair, occupation
nores nurse
nose noise
novellis news
nowche jewel
nowgth not
noye harm
nyce foolish
nye (v) annoy, harm
nye near
nygramansye magic
nyk deny
nynee eye

O

o one
oder other
off of
on one
on-dergh without trouble
one on
onely alone
on-ethys with difficulty
onone at once, soon
onys once
oo always
oone one
oostre inn
operacion labour
or before
other-gatys otherwise
ought-were anywhere
overgoe pass by
overtwhart across
owre hour
owt out

P

pace passes
padde, paddokys frog, toad(s)

pallays palace
parayl apparel
parde by God
parellis dangers
parfyte perfect
parloures rooms
parlous perilous
parson person
pasch Passover
paulle royal robe
payde pleased
paye advantage
paye please
pearles without equal
peasse silence
perels perils
perye jewellery
pik pitch
pikis chooses
playe game, risk
plecer pleasure
plete plead
pleyned pitied
ploghe plough
plom plumb
ployde ploughed
plyght bend, bent
po peacock
poll head
popelard hypocrite
poste, postye, powste power
prese crowd
preste ready
prose story, words
provand food
provaylys benefit
prow profit, advantage
pryce high esteem
purveyed provided
pyght placed, set
pyn wooden bolt
pyn(e) pain, suffering

707

GLOSSARY

Q

quan when
quantis, quaintyce cunning
quarte good health, alive
quetstone whetstone
quod said
quyte, qwite give back, repay
qwantt crafty
qweasse breathe
qwedyr (v) quiver
qwelle kill
qweme unite
qwenys women
qwere where
qwy why
qwyke, qweke alive

R

rad afraid
rad quickly
rade ready
rakis goes
rakke clouds
rape force
rappely quickly
rappis blows
rase rush, current
raw row
ray striped
raykand wandering
recrayd coward
recure obtain
red advice
redd command
re(e)de advise
rede red
redrure harshness
reepe handful
refe take away
rehete rebuke
rek care
reme realm
renabyll eloquent
renke man
rente income
repleat full
reprefe reprove
rerd roar
resave receive
reves takes
revisible seen again
reyde advise
reyles release
reyll reel, stagger
reynand ruling
reynes loins
risse branch
rok distaff
rose praise
rost roast
rote root
rotten rats
rought cared
roune run
rowel spur
rowes groups
rowncys horses
rowne whisper
rowte audience, crowd
rowthe, rewthe pity
royfe roof
rug(ge) pull
ruse praise
ryfe (v) tear
ryfe often
ryffe plenty
ryffen torn
ryfys splits
ryke kingdom
rykis breaks
ryn run
ryth right

GLOSSARY

S

saf(f)e except, unless
sagh saw
sakles innocent
sam together
samme gather
santis saints
sare sore
sate sat
saul(is) soul('s)
savers stinks, smells
saw saying, command
sawe save
sawes words
scape-thryft spendthrift
schapman merchant
schene brightly
schep plenty
schepe sheep
schereys cheers
schonge change
schoyt shows
scloo slay
se see
se(e) seat
sea seat
sectures executors
sede seat
see sea
seeg man
seele, seyll happiness
sees cease
sek sack
seke sick
sekyr secure, sure
selcouth wonderful
sely wretched
semelye beautiful
sen see
sen then, since
sending request
senous sinews
sere many, various
sere sir
serkyll circle
seryattly in succession
sesyd placed
sew beg
seyde seed
seyn say
seyr various, many
shamfastness shyness
shank(ys) leg(s)
shede sheath
sheene bright
shefys sheaves
shende destroy
shente destroyed, disgraced
Sherthursday Maundy Thursday
sheynd destroy
sho she
shone shoes
shrew (v) curse
shrewys villains
shrife shrive
shrogys bushes
shyne brightly
shyrle shrill
shytt shut
sicker certain(ly)
sickerlie certainly
side shore
sithen, sithe, sythen then, since
sithis times
skabbid scabby
skant shortage
skaunce, skawnce joke
skelp(e) blow
skill reason, good sense, right
skryke shriek
slake neglect, stop, cease
slawthe sloth
sleelie slily, carefully

709

GLOSSARY

slefe sleeve
slich mud
slo slay
sloghe skin
slought slothful
slowe slay
sloys slays
slyght craft, trick
slyke similar, such
smeke smoke
smyth smite
snek latch
snelle quick
sofferent sovereign
sogh saw
sokelyng clover
solace comfort
solemne ceremonial
solemplye with ceremony
solom serious
somp with ceremony
sond messenger
sone, soyn soon
sonne sun
sopere supper
sor harm
sorys sirs
sote sweet
sotell clever
sothelie certainly
sothenes reality
sothfast true
sottys fools
souther more true
soverayntlie in the manner of a king
sowked sucked
sownde message
sowre sour
sowth, sowte sought
soyn soon
spar, spere fasten, shut

spell(e) words, speech
spelle (v) relate
spence money, expense
spere sphere
speres ask
spill destroy, spoil
spir ask
spitus spiteful
spon spun
sprote shoot
spurne kick, blow
spyndill spindle
stakir stagger
stalk stride
stanys stones
stark stiff
stature law
stayed ascended
sted pressed
sted placed
stede horse
steed, sted, stydd place
stere-man steersman
stere-tre tiller
sterne star
sterring stirring
sterrys stars
steryed stirred
steven, stevyn voice
stevynd ascended
stid, styd place
still, styll constantly, persistently
stold stuck
stonyd astonished
storred stirred
stounde time, hour
stower hour
stremys beams
strykeand striking
stubbe peg
stuf gorge

GLOSSARY

sty path
stye ascend
styrte go
subsequence consequence
sudary winding sheet, linen
sumdele somewhat
suthly truly
swage stop
swane serving-man
swap blow
swedyll wrap
swelt faint
swemyth grieves
swet sweet
swette sweat
sweven dream
swithe immediately
swogh faint
swounde faint
swych such
swyme swoon
swynke, swynkys toil(s), labour(s)
syth sight

T

taken token
talent pleasure
tall, tayll tale, words
tane taken
tase toes
tast(e) feel, test
te(e)ne pain, suffering
tend pay tithe
tende behave
tene anger, injury
tent tenth
tent(e) notice
tery delay
tethee bad-tempered
teyed tied
teyn rage
teyn suffering

tharmys is lacking
the they
the thee
the(e) thrive
thegh those
theider thither
then than
ther there
therlys serfs
thertyll to that
thesternes darkness
thew courtesy
thoe then
thole allow, suffer
thondour, thoners thunder
thore there
thorwe through
thowt thought
thrafe measure
thrall slavery, servant
thrang gathering
thraw(e), throw time, while
threpe wrangle, dispute
thro eager
thrye thrice
thus-gate in this way
thwang be beaten
thyrlyd pierced
till to, towards
to till
to two
to-clefe shatter
todys toads
toose toes
to-rent, to-torn torn to pieces
toute backside
to-wond wound deeply
towre tower
trace way
trane trick
travell labour
trawe trust

711

GLOSSARY

traye grief, misery
trist trust
trone throne
trott hurry
trowde believed
truage tribute
trussell bundle
turtill, turtyl turtle-dove, beloved
twey two
tweyn twain
twyn divide
twynninge dividing
twyys twice
tyde time
tyde (v) lead
tydely quickly
tymbre-wryth carpenter
tynde lost
tyte quickly, soon
tyter sooner
tyth tithe
tythande tidings
tythyngis news

U

umthinke meditate
unbeyne unkind
unceyll misery
uncouth unknown
underfoe undergo
unfylyd pure
ungayn awkwardly
unhappely unfortunately
un-hende churlish
unkende unnatural
unknit untied
unlosne untie
unnes scarcely
unrightes wrongs
unryde harm
unshent unharmed

untrost mistrust
unyth with difficulty
upstayinge ascension

V

valure health
variance inconsistency
vengeabyl revengeful
verament truly
verey true, truly
vetaylys food
viallis viols
vyset visit

W

wafe wander
wake weak
wan won
wandreth misfortune, misery
wane waggon
wanyand vengeance
wanyd waned
war care
ward world
warisoune reward
warldlys worldly
warlow wizard
warrok bind
wars worse
wary curse
waryed cursed
wat chap
wate know
wathe prey
wawghes waves
wayle grief
wayll prosperity
wayved overcome
weare guard
wedder weather
wede pledge
wede clothing

712

GLOSSARY

wedyr whither
wedys weed
weere doubt
weete rainstorm
weldand, weldinge making
welkin sky
wemay hurry
weme stop
wemlesse without blemish
wend(e) go
wende thought
wendinge going
wene think
wene belief
wenyand waning, time of ill-luck
wenys thinks
werd(l) world
were weary
were doubt
were protect, defend
werkys actions, business
weryed cursed
weryt wore
wete know
wether whichever
weylde use
weyll happy
weyn think
weynd go, went
weytt wet
whall(es) whale ('s)
whie why
whight, wight man
whilke which
whilom formerly
wholle holy
whonde hesitate
whyk living
wilsom wild
win happiness
wisse guide, lead

wissyng knowing
wiste known
wite blame
with-owte outside
witlie knowingly
witte find out
witterly(e) surely, certainly
wogh harm, woe
wold hill
wole will
won place
won live
wond omit
wone dwelling-place
wonnande dwelling
wonnes live
wonnyng-stede dwelling-place
wood(e) mad
worch make
worethe worthy
worm(e) serpent
worthchup worship
wot(tes) know(s)
woth(is) danger(s)
wowyng wooing
wrake revenge, ruin
wraw angry
wreke revenge
wrest trick
wreth anger
wreye destroy
wright, write carpenter
wrightry carpentry
wrogth done
wrott wrote
wrowth wrought
wrye turn, twist
wyde-where everywhere
wyghtly quickly
wyll well
wyn escape
wynne pleasure, joy

713

GLOSSARY

wynne wine
wyrk act
wyt know
wythe man

X

xad shed
xal shall
xulde should

Y

yappely eagerly
yare prepared
yarning desire
yelde give
yelp boast
yelpe sing loudly

yeme(d) guard(ed)
yenge young
yere year
yerthe earth
yethed eased
yhing, ying young
yoode went
yore for a long time
yorth earth
yrk loathe
yrke weary
yt it
yyn yon
yynd end
yynder yonder
yyt yet

MORE ABOUT PENGUINS, PELICANS AND PUFFINS

For further information about books available from Penguins please write to Dept EP, Penguin Books Ltd, Harmondsworth, Middlesex UB7 0DA.

In the U.S.A.: For a complete list of books available from Penguins in the United States write to Dept DG, Penguin Books, 299 Murray Hill Parkway, East Rutherford, New Jersey 07073.

In Canada: For a complete list of books available from Penguins in Canada write to Penguin Books Canada Ltd, 2801 John Street, Markham, Ontario L3R 1B4.

In Australia: For a complete list of books available from Penguins in Australia write to the Marketing Department, Penguin Books Australia Ltd, P.O. Box 257, Ringwood, Victoria 3134.

In New Zealand: For a complete list of books available from Penguins in New Zealand write to the Marketing Department, Penguin Books (N.Z.) Ltd, P.O. Box 4019, Auckland 10.

In India: For a complete list of books available from Penguins in India write to Penguin Overseas Ltd. 706 Eros Apartments, 56 Nehru Place, New Delhi 110019.

THE PENGUIN ENGLISH LIBRARY

FOUR MORALITY PLAYS
The Castle of Perseverance/Magnyfycence/King Johan
Ane Satire of the Thrie Estaitis

Edited by Peter Happé

These four major morality plays, written between 1400 and 1562, are in the mainstream of the development of English drama. In a period of increasing professionalism they combine moral ideas with a subtle awareness of the nature of drama and stage technique. The earliest, *The Castle of Perseverance*, gives a general account of the struggle for salvation. Skelton's *Magnyfycence*, Bale's *King Johan* and Lindsay's panoramic *Ane Satire of the Thrie Estaitis* have a more political purpose, and use allegory and satire as polemic weapons.

THOMAS NASHE
THE UNFORTUNATE TRAVELLER AND OTHER WORKS

Edited by J. B. Steane

Thomas Nashe, a contemporary of Shakespeare, was a pamphleteer, poet, story-teller, satirist, scholar, moralist and jester. His work epitomizes everything that comes to mind when we think of the character of the Elizabethans. Nashe himself wrote: 'I have written in all sorts of humours ... more than any young man of my age in England.'

BEN JONSON
THREE COMEDIES
Volpone, The Alchemist *and* Bartholomew Fair

Edited by Michael Jamieson

This volume contains Jonson's best-known comedies. *Volpone*, which is perhaps his greatest, and *The Alchemist* are both *tours de force* of brilliant knavery, unflagging in wit and comic invention. *Bartholomew Fair*, an earlier work, portrays Jonson's fellow Londoners in festive mood – bawdy, energetic, and never at a loss for words.

THE PENGUIN ENGLISH LIBRARY

SIR THOMAS MALORY
LE MORTE D'ARTHUR
In Two Volumes With an Introduction by John Lawlor

Writing in the uncertain times of the Wars of the Roses Sir Thomas Malory looked wistfully back to the days of a great king, to a dead age of chivalry, and to a national disaster wreaked by treachery. The various parts of this most famous of medieval legends – the love of Launcelot and Guenever, the quest for the Holy Grail, the fellowship of the Round Table, the treason of Mordred – are handled by him as separate episodes: yet they are given a unity by the magic of his prose style.

RICHARD HAKLUYT
VOYAGES AND DISCOVERIES
Edited by Jack Beeching

One of the epics of the period of English expansion, this was the life-work of Richard Hakluyt, Renaissance diplomat, scholar and spy. The narratives of voyages and discoveries included in this volume have been selected from its total of a million and a half words.

AUBREY'S BRIEF LIVES
Edited by Oliver Lawson Dick

Many English personalities, great and small, of the sixteenth and seventeenth centuries owe their third dimensions to the antiquarian John Aubrey, that assiduous compiler of gossip and hearsay. His disjointed jottings, however inaccurate and ribald, are delightfully phrased and invariably entertaining. This edition contains about a third of the 'Brief Lives' and incorporates much of the remainder in an introduction entitled 'The Life and Times of John Aubrey'.